SAP® R/3® Handbook, Third Edition

José Antonio Hernandez
Jim Keogh
Franklin Martinez

McGraw-Hill/Osborne
New York Chicago San Francisco
Lisbon London Madrid Mexico City
Milan New Delhi San Juan
Seoul Singapore Sydney Toronto

The McGraw·Hill Companies

McGraw-Hill/Osborne
2100 Powell Street, 10th Floor
Emeryville, California 94608
U.S.A.

To arrange bulk purchase discounts for sales promotions, premiums, or fund-raisers, please contact **McGraw-Hill**/Osborne at the above address.

SAP® R/3® Handbook, Third Edition

Copyright © 2006 by The McGraw-Hill Companies. All rights reserved. Printed in the United States of America. Except as permitted under the Copyright Act of 1976, no part of this publication may be reproduced or distributed in any form or by any means, or stored in a database or retrieval system, without the prior written permission of the publisher, with the exception that the program listings may be entered, stored, and executed in a computer system, but they may not be reproduced for publication.

1234567890 DOC DOC 0198765

ISBN 0-07-225716-4

Acquisitions Editor
Wendy Rinaldi

Production Coordinator
Azadeh Poursepanj

Project Manager
Jody McKenzie

Acquisitions Coordinator
Alexander McDonald

Technical Editor
German Mesa

Copy Editor
Rose Kernan

Proofreader
Shelly Gerger

Indexer
Marilyn Rowland

Composition
G&S Book Services

Illustration
G&S Book Services

Series Design
Peter F. Hancik and Lyssa Wald

Cover Design
Pattie Lee

This book was composed with Adobe® InDesign®.

Information has been obtained by **McGraw-Hill**/Osborne from sources believed to be reliable. However, because of the possibility of human or mechanical error by our sources, **McGraw-Hill**/Osborne, or others, **McGraw-Hill**/Osborne does not guarantee the accuracy, adequacy, or completeness of any information and is not responsible for any errors or omissions or the results obtained from use of such information.

"SAP," mySAP.com, mySAP Business Suite, and SAP NetWeaver are trademarks of SAPAktiengesellschaft, Systems, Applications and Products in Data Processing, Neurottstrasse 16, 69190 Walldorf, Germany. The publisher gratefully acknowledges SAP's kind permission to use its trademark in this publication. SAP AG is not the publisher of this book and is not responsible for it under any aspect of press law.

This book is dedicated to
Anne, Sandy, Joanne, Amber-Leigh Christine, and Graff,
without whose help and support
this book couldn't have been written.
—Jim Keogh

I would like to dedicate this book to
my wife Jenelle and son Maxwell
whose patience, compassion, and love
afforded me the ability to participate in this creation.
I love you both, you are my life.
—Franklin F. Martinez

Contents

Acknowledgments xvii

Chapter 1 SAP: From SAP R/3 to SAP NetWeaver 1

SAP Strategic Evolution 1
- The ERP Basics 2
- SAP Transformation into a Global Business Solutions Company 4
- SAP for Industries 5
- The Emergence of the New Dimension Products 6
- Solution Maps and Business Scenario Maps 7
- mySAP.com 8
- SAP Product Portfolio in the SAP NetWeaver Age 10

SAP R/3 Releases and Fundamentals 13
- R/3 Release 3.0 13
- R/3 Release 3.1 14
- R/3 Release 4.0 15
- R/3 Release 4.5 16
- EnjoySAP Release: R/3 4.6 17
- Enterprise Release: SAP R/3 4.7 17

Description of Our Good Old and Still Great R/3 21
- Multitier Client/Server Solutions 22
- Open Technology 24
- User Interface 27
- ABAP Development Workbench 27
- Application Integration 28
- Customizing Tools 28

SAP Enterprise Core (R/3) Applications Overview 30
- Financial Applications 30
- Human Resources Applications 32
- Logistics Applications 33
- Cross-Application Components 37

SAP Services Overview 38
- Online Services: The SAP Service Marketplace 39
- SAPnet-R/3 Front End (OSS) 40
- EarlyWatch and EarlyWatch Alert 41

Chapter 2 The Architecture of the SAP Web Application Server 43

The SAP Web Application Server 44

SAP R/3 up to 4.6C: The Basis Software 45

Basic Architectural Concepts 46
 Transaction 46
 Dialog Step 46
 Logical Units of Work (LUWs) 47
 Clients 48
The System Central Interfaces 48
 Operating System Interface 49
 The Dispatcher Process 50
 Work Process Architecture 51
Services: Work Processes Types 53
 Dialog Work Processes 54
 Background Work Processes 55
 Spool Work Process 57
 Enqueue Work Process 58
 Update Work Process 59
 Message Server 61
 Gateway Server 61
 Presentation Interface 62
 Database Interface 63
SAP Web AS Communication Protocols and Interfaces 64
Memory Management 66
The Concept of SAP Instance 67
Building the Client/Server SAP Web AS System 68
 SAP Business Framework 68
 Client/Server Foundation 69
 RFC: A Key Communication Middleware 71
 BAPI 71
 IDOCs 72
 ALE 72
The Internet Transaction Server (ITS) 74
Internet Business Framework 76
 XML 77
The Architecture of the SAP Web Application Server 78
 The Internet Communication Manager 78
 ICM Plug-Ins 79
 A Closer Look at the HTTP Plug-In 79
 A Look at the Internet Server 80
 An Inside Look at the Web Dispatcher 81
 Memory and the Web Dispatcher 81
 Running and Stopping the Web Dispatcher 82
Dual Role for the Web Application Server 83
The Web Dispatcher and the SAP J2EE Engine 83
Distributing SAP Systems and Services 83
 Instance Profiles 84

User Distribution: Logon Load Balancing and the SAP Logon Utility 89
Logon Groups Configuration 89
The SAP Logon Application 92
Starting and Stopping SAP Systems 96
Starting and Stopping SAP WAS for ABAP under Windows 99
Further Guidelines for Productive Environments 100

Chapter 3 SAP NetWeaver: An Overview 101
Enterprise Service Architecture 101
What's SAP NetWeaver? 102
SAP NetWeaver Application Platform 105
SAP Enterprise Portal 107
iViews 109
The Portal Platform 110
The Knowledge Management Platform 110
Collaboration 110
Predefined Content and Content Tools 111
SAP Mobile Infrastructure 111
SAP Business Information Warehouse 112
Architecture of the Business Warehouse 113
BW within SAP NetWeaver and New Features 115
SAP Master Data Management 117
SAP Exchange Infrastructure 3.0 117
SAP XI Communication Options 119
SAP NetWeaver Developer Studio 119
Developing Web Dynpros 122
Steps for the Creation Process of a Web Dynpro Application 123
Basic Web Dynpro 123
Planning SAP NetWeaver Installations 139
Installation and Planning Concepts 140
Installation Elements 141
Documentation Required for Planning and Installation 142
Variants of SAP Web AS 142
Platforms 143
System Landscape Directory 143
SAP NetWeaver Rapid Installer 144
The Sizing Process 145
Installation Notes 147

Chapter 4 Using SAP Systems 149
Logging On and Off the System 149
Passwords 151

Logging Off 154
The User Interface: Main Screen Elements of the SAP GUI 155
The Standard Toolbar 158
The Screen Layout Menu 159
Personalizing the Favorites 164
Role-Based Scenarios 164
Shortcuts 166
System Status Information 166
Working with SAP User Sessions 168
Moving Around the SAP Systems 169
Moving Around with Transaction Codes 171
Working with Information 172
Possible Entries for an Input Field 172
Facilities for Entering the Same Data Repeatedly 174
Input Field Default Values with User Parameters 175
Getting Help in SAP Systems 176
Working with Reports 178
Looking for Reports 179
Executing Reports 180
Using Selection Criteria 180
Working with Reports Variants 181
Working with Background Jobs 183
Scheduling Background Jobs 184
User Printing 186
Print Attributes 187
Monitoring the Status of Your Print Requests 189
Additional User Utilities 189
Sending Short Messages 189
Downloading Files to Your Desktop Workstation 190

Chapter 5 Upgrading to SAP R/3 Enterprise: The First Step into SAP NetWeaver 191
Considerations for an Upgrade Project 192
Upgrading to SAP R/3 Enterprise: What Is New? 193
SAP Upgrade Projects 195
Key Success Factors in an Upgrade Project 196
Methodology: The Upgrade Roadmap 196
Upgrade Project Plan 197
The Upgrade Script 199
Gap Analysis 200
Upgrading to SAP R/3 Enterprise: An Organizational View 200
Key Users and the Functional Team 201
Upgrading to SAP R/3 Enterprise: Technical Point of View 201
Factors Influencing the Technical Upgrade 202

The Upgrade Process ... 202
Upgrade Preparation: PREPARE Program ... 205
Additional Upgrade Tools ... 208
The Software Upgrade: R3UP ... 209
After R3UP ... 210
Modification Adjustment ... 210
Troubleshooting the Upgrade ... 214
Unicode Conversion ... 214

Chapter 6 The Change and Transport System ... 215
What's New in the Transport System with the Web Application Server? ... 217
Overview of the Complete Process of Transporting Objects from a Source System to a Target System ... 217
Transport System Concepts ... 220
Repository and Development Objects ... 220
Customizing ... 220
The Two Main Types of Change Requests ... 220
Clients and Type of Data in SAP Systems ... 221
Roles Involved in the Transport Process ... 222
SAP System Group ... 224
Transport Layer ... 224
Transport Routes ... 224
Extended Transport Control ... 225
Change Requests ... 225
Tasks ... 227
Development Teams ... 228
Packages (Formerly Development Classes) ... 228
Version Management ... 228
Requests Documentation ... 229
Repairs and Original Objects ... 229
System Types ... 231
System Change Options ... 231
Functions of the Systems ... 232
Managing Packages ... 235
Configuration of the Transport System ... 236
Step 1. Initializing the Change and Transport Organizer ... 237
Step 2. Setting Up the Transport Directory and the tp Program (TPPARAM) ... 238
Step 3. Configuring the Transport Management System (TMS) ... 238
Step 4. Setting the System Change Option and the Client Settings ... 239

The Transport Management System (TMS) 239
Configuring Systems and Domains 240
Configuring Transport Routes 243
Distributing and Verifying TMS Configuration 245
Working with the Transport Organizer 246
Creating Change Requests 246
Releasing Tasks and Requests 248
Monitoring Transports and Repairs 249
Transport Rules 250
Checking Transport Results 252
Object Attributes 253
Transport Organizer Tools 255
Performing Transports with the TMS 255
Using tp, the Transport Control Program 258
Setting Up the tp Program 259
Overview of Options for the tp Program 263
Working with Imports Using tp 265
Managing Special Transports 267
The Interface between tp and ABAP 268
Overview of the R3trans Program 269

Chapter 7 Development Options with SAP Solutions: ABAP Engine 271
The ABAP Workbench 271
Basic Concepts of the Development Environment 272
The ABAP Dictionary 274
The ABAP Dictionary in SAP Systems 275
ABAP Dictionary Objects 278
Introduction to the ABAP Programming Language 303
Basics of the Syntax of the ABAP Programming Language 305
My First ABAP Program, Hello SAP World!!! 314
Testing and Debugging ABAP 315
ABAP Debugger 317
Extended Program Check 319
ABAP Units 320
Connectors 321
SAP Business Connector 322
SAP Marketplace Connector 322
SAP Java Connector 323
SAP .Net Connector 323
SAP DCOM Connector 323
RFC Library 324
SOAP Processor 324
What Is New in the ABAP Development Environment with the SAP WAS 324

What Is New in the ABAP Development Environment 324
New Elements of the ABAP Programming Language 333
Web Development with ABAP: Business Server Page (BSP) 340
Developing a BSP 340
Your First BSP: Hello World!!! 341
Overview of BSP Concepts 345

Chapter 8 User Management and Security in SAP Environments 351
Overview of Security Concepts 352
Security Policy Basics 353
Risks and Vulnerabilities 354
Basic Security Processes 354
Cryptography 356
Single Sign-On (SSO) 359
LDAP 360
Secure Socket Layer Protocol (SSL) 360
SAP Security Infrastructure 361
What Type of Security Is Standard on SAP Systems? 362
How Can SAP Security Be Improved? 363
The Multilayer SAP Security Infrastructure 363
Security at the Presentation Level 363
Application-Level Security 364
Security at the Database Level 364
Operating System–Level Security 365
Network-Level Security 365
Transport System–Level Security 366
Secure Network Communications (SNC) 366
Remote Communications–Level Security 367
Document Transfer–Level Security 367
Introduction to SSF (Secure Store and Forward) 367
Internet-Level Security 369
Logging and Auditing 369
SAP Trust Center Services 370
Management of Users, Authorizations, and Roles 370
Overview of User Administration 371
Managing User Master Records 371
Creating Users 373
User Master Records Fields 376
Available Defaults and Options for User Master Records 377
Managing User Groups 379
Modifying User Master Records 379
User Information System 380
Password Management 380
Managing SAP System Superusers 383

The Authorization System in SAP WAS 385
Authorization Profiles 386
Roles 389
Working with the Role Maintenance Tool 391
How the Role Maintenance Works 392
Configuring the Profile Generator 392
Basic Concepts for Working with Roles 393
Creating Roles 394
Tracing Authorizations 397
Organizing the Maintenance of the Authorization System 398
Creating New Authorization Checks 399

Chapter 9 Web Application Server System Management 401
General SAP System Management 401
Checking the Installation 402
Displaying and Monitoring the SAP Instances and Application Servers 402
Monitoring the System Work Processes 404
Monitoring and Managing User Sessions 408
Posting System Messages 409
Displaying and Managing Update Records 410
Update Process Concepts 411
Distribution of Update Work Processes 412
Monitoring Update Records 412
Displaying and Managing Lock Entries 415
Client Copies 416
Client Copy Tools 417
Creating a New Client 418
Requirements for Creating Clients and for the Copy Process 421
Client Copy Logs 425
Transporting Clients between Two SAP Systems 425
Managing the Background System 427
Introduction to Background Processing 428
Background Jobs 429
Starting Background Processing 430
Defining Background Jobs 431
Management Operations on Background Jobs 442
The Graphical Monitoring Tool 445
SAP Printing System 447
Concepts of the SAP Spool System Architecture 448
The Spool Work Process 450
Spool Servers, Hierarchies, and Loan Balancing 451
Defining Spool Server 452
Managing Spool Requests 453

Printing and Displaying Spool Requests ... 455
Connecting Printers to the Operating Systems Spool ... 457
Defining SAP Printer Devices ... 458
Logical Output Devices and Device Pools ... 462
Troubleshooting Printing Problems ... 466
SAP Printing System Administration Tasks ... 466
The Web Components of the SAP Web Application Server ... 468
The SAP Web Dispatcher ... 468
Monitoring the Internet Communication Manager ... 468
The SAP J2EE Engine ... 470
Monitoring the SAP J2EE ... 471

Chapter 10 Performance and Troubleshooting with SAP Solutions ... 473
Performance Analysis ... 473
The Work Process Monitor ... 474
Analyzing Possible Performance Issues ... 476
The Workload Analysis Monitor ... 478
Troubleshooting RFC Communications ... 484
Troubleshooting the Presentation Server Response Time ... 486
Analyzing Specific Business Transactions ... 487
Troubleshooting Specific Performance Problems with the SQL Trace ... 488
Troubleshooting Specific Performance Problems with an ABAP Trace ... 490
Memory Management ... 490
The Memory Areas in a SAP System ... 491
The Buffers in a SAP Instance ... 495
Monitoring SAP Buffers ... 498
Hardware Capacity Analysis ... 499
The Operating System Monitor ... 499
Troubleshooting CPU Bottlenecks ... 500
Troubleshooting Physical Memory ... 501
Database Analysis ... 501
Workload Distribution ... 506
The SAP Instance ... 506
The SAP Profiles for Parameter Settings ... 508
Working with Workload Distribution ... 510
Troubleshooting in System Administration ... 513
Troubleshooting the Update Process ... 513
Troubleshooting Lock Entries ... 515
The System Log ... 516
Displaying and Troubleshooting ABAP Short Dumps ... 518
The System Tracing Utilities ... 520
Troubleshooting the Background Processing System ... 522

Database Space Management ... 528
The Tables and Indexes Monitor ... 529
The Alert Monitors ... 530
Architecture of the Alert Monitors ... 531
The Alert Monitors ... 532

Chapter 11 SAP for IT Managers: Implementation, Planning, Operation, and Support of SAP Systems ... 535
SAP Projects ... 535
SAP Implementation Tools ... 537
SAP Customizing ... 540
Introduction to AcceleratedSAP (ASAP) ... 540
Phase 1: Project Preparation ... 542
Phase 2: Business Blueprint ... 543
Phase 3: Realization ... 544
Phase 4: Final Preparation ... 545
Phase 5: Go Live and Support ... 545
SAP Solution Manager ... 546
SAP Solution Manager for Functional Implementation ... 547
Solution Manager Roadmaps ... 551
Solution Manager Implementation Tools ... 554
Business Blueprint ... 558
Realization ... 559
Challenges of SAP Solution Projects: Technology Issues ... 560
SAP Technical Implementation ... 560
Systems Landscape ... 561
Sizing ... 562
Security ... 563
SAP System Management ... 563
Skill Sets for Systems Managers ... 565
Planning Systems Management ... 567
Organizing Change Management and Transport Requests ... 568
Installations and Upgrades ... 569
Information Integrity Issues ... 570
High Availability and Cluster Systems ... 570
Backup and Recovery ... 571
Operating System Backup Utilities ... 574
SAP Procedures Guide ... 575
The Administration and Operation Manual ... 577
Roles When Implementing and Supporting SAP Solutions ... 580
Introduction to the Help Desk ... 583

Index ... 587

About the Authors

José Antonio Hernandez is the Managing Director of Offilog in Spain, a subsidiary of CIBER Novasoft. He is responsible for the SAP Technology Business Unit, concentrating on SAP NetWeaver–related projects, and in one year built a highly qualified team of nearly 40 technical consultants to complement the company's successful SAP application consulting, both in Spain and in the other countries where CIBER is present. Besides his management and sales duties, Hernandez has been a senior SAP technical consultant, expert in SAP implementation issues and project management with a solid background and experience in multiple international SAP projects since 1994. He is a well-known author of the books *The SAP R/3 Handbook*, *Así es SAP R/3*, *SAP R/3 Implementation Guide*, and *Roadmap to mySAP.com*. The first of those books, now ready for the third edition and translated into several languages, is one of the best-selling SAP books in the world.

Jim Keogh is on the faculty of Columbia University and Saint Peter's College in Jersey City, New Jersey. He developed the e-commerce track at Columbia University. Keogh has spent decades developing applications for major Wall Street corporations and is the author of more than 65 books, including *J2EE: The Complete Reference*, *Java Demystified*, *JavaScript Demystified*, *Data Structures Demystified*, *XML Demystified*, and others in the Demystified series.

Franklin Martinez is a partner in Effective Internet Solutions LLC, a nationally recognized firm that provides custom solutions to enterprises that are re-engineering mission-critical systems. Martinez has spent over a decade developing and implementing Enterprise Resource Planning (ERP) systems for major corporate clients and has been a technical project manager responsible for hands-on integration of SAP and PeopleSoft products

About the Contributing Writer

Rafael Perez has been a SAP employee for over eight years, acquiring experience in a wide variety of areas, including education, consulting, support, marketing, and account management. He developed his technical skills delivering SAP system administration services and is considered an expert in performance tuning and optimization of SAP systems. He has a great deal of experience in large implementations of SAP installations worldwide, utilizing both his technical and project management expertise. Because of his knowledge and leadership skills, he is considered a key advisor within SAP, and has been an acclaimed speaker at SAP's TechEd forum.

About the Technical Editor

German Mesa is a NetWeaver technology consultant with SAP Spain. German received his master's degree in science from the University of Madrid in 1994. From 1994 to 1997, he was a researcher at the Department of Metallurgy and Materials Engineering in Leuven, where his main research topics concerned new composite materials and advanced numerical modeling. Back in Madrid he joined Telecinco Television where he specialized in integration between SAP and non-SAP components and applications. Prior to joining SAP in 2004, he worked with SAP-related technologies for seven years at the Fortune 500 companies Telefonica and REPSOL. In 2004, German joined SAP as a member of the Consulting Group in Spain, where he is currently working in the area of system integration and master data management.

Acknowledgments

I want to take this opportunity to give my sincere thanks to the many people who helped me and supported me through the sometimes painful process of making this book project a reality.

In the first place I want to thank my two main contributors and collaborators, Rafael Perez of SAP America and José Luis Herreros of CIBER Offilog in Spain, two extremely talented people who demonstrated not only their impressive technical knowledge but also their friendship and support. Rafael was the author of most part of Chapter 10 and also helped with several sections of Chapters 5 and 9. José Luis was the soul of Chapter 8 and contributed to some of the most complex topics in Chapter 4.

I want to thank my friend Patrick Osterhaus for his contribution to Chapter 6, and some of my colleagues at CIBER Offilog and SAP for providing me with insights, documentation, suggestions, and material: Fernando López, Laura Hernandez, Gari Basabe, and Jordi Marti. Thank you also to my good friend Fabrizio Grisoni, one of the most impressive SAP consultants in Italy and the best friend a person can have.

I also want to thank one of my customers, the IT director of Miele in Spain, Roberto Calvo, who provided me with some "cooking" ideas for the book.

Finally to my family and friends for all the time I stole from them, again and again: Juan Carlos Moya, Africa, Pedro Ruiz, Ester, José Ramón Bustamante, Sergio, José Miguel, María, and so many other friends. Thank you very much for your caring support.

José A. Hernandez
Madrid,
November 2005

1

CHAPTER

SAP: From SAP R/3 to SAP NetWeaver

This first chapter provides a broad overview of the current SAP solutions, how they have evolved, and the basics of the new architecture or technology foundations that are found in the new set of products or components of the SAP NetWeaver integration platform.

Because of the evolution of the SAP solutions, and although the third edition of this book is still called *SAP R/3 Handbook,* you must notice that most topics apply the same way to either R/3 Enterprise (mySAP ERP) or any other SAP solution that is based on the SAP Web Application Server, including several of the SAP NetWeaver components.

At the same time, and since SAP R/3 is still and will be for the coming years, and whatever the name it might have in the near future, the basic application platform for the huge SAP customer base, in this chapter and in this book in general, SAP R/3 Enterprise (release 4.7) and more specifically the SAP Web Application Server is the main topic. An organizational and technical overview of the SAP NetWeaver components is presented in Chapter 11.

Right now, one of the biggest concerns of SAP customers and prospects is to understand the SAP solution sets, what business processes they are meant to solve, what benefits they provide, and, most of all, what options are available to solve or improve their business processes or business requirements.

Some of the common questions usually found in customers are as follows: What was mySAP.com? What's the buzz about SAP NetWeaver? How do I evolve my SAP systems? What are the options? How will the different solutions and components integrate?

This chapter includes an overview of the current state of the SAP solutions, focusing on the main features of SAP R/3 Enterprise release and providing background information about the evolution of the SAP solutions so that SAP solution can be better understood. It also provides useful information for the thousands of customers still running on previous R/3 releases.

SAP Strategic Evolution

SAP AG started operations in 1972 and became successful in the 1980s with their SAP R/2 solution. The company name, SAP, stands for Systems, Applications and Products in Data Processing. After the introduction of SAP R/3 in 1992, SAP AG became the world's leading vendor of standard application software.

SAP R/3 was the business solution that placed SAP in its leadership position and led to the company becoming extremely successful in the 1990s. The introduction of release 3.1 of R/3 in 1996 provided the first SAP Internet-enabled solutions. In 1998 SAP transformed from a single-product company to a global business solutions company. The "first draft" of the mySAP.com strategy was introduced in 1999. The first years of the new millennium (2001–2003) were the ones in which mySAP.com was adapting and reinventing itself; the solid technological foundation was improved by the introduction of the SAP Web Application Server, which enables running programs either on an ABAP or on top of a Java engine (J2EE). During these years mySAP.com was also getting ready for the massive deployment and benefits offered by a new Web services–based architecture, which is now represented by a reality integration platform known as SAP NetWeaver.

SAP NetWeaver is defined by SAP as the Web-based integration and application platform that is used across all SAP solutions. In a general way, SAP NetWeaver is the realization of what it was meant to be with the 1999 mySAP.com strategy.

SAP history is of an evolution from a traditional, integrated, and solid ERP software company to one company that can offer a full set of business, integration, and collaboration solutions and services in the open and global business world.

The ERP Basics

Enterprise Resource Planner (commonly known as ERP) software is a concept that started in the 1970s and was meant to provide computerized solutions for integrating and automating business processes across companies' back offices, such as the financial, logistics, or human resources departments. The idea behind ERP was that companies could see a cost reduction and better efficiency in the way they operated with their business partners (customers, providers, banks, authorities, etc.) and also in the way their users could access and process the information. From that concept, there were already several solutions in the market during the 1980s and beginning of the 1990s. The adoption of ERP software revolutionized the way companies conduct their traditional business.

Since the introduction of SAP R/3 in the first part of the 1990s, SAP R/3 became a clear market leader in ERP solutions.

SAP invests approximately 20 percent of its annual sales revenue in research and development in order to remain at the edge of technological innovation. With more than 25 percent of its employees working in the research area, SAP wants to make sure that it can maintain a constant dialogue with customers and users and exchange with them experiences and ideas to enhance its systems and service offerings. This information exchange is vital in order for SAP to maintain a long-term relationship with its customers and to attract new ones not just to SAP R/3 but also to the SAP NetWeaver wave.

In the mid-1990s SAP had two main products in the business software market: mainframe system R/2 and client/server R/3. Both were targeted to business application solutions and feature a great level of complexity, business and organizational experience, strength, and integration. SAP software systems can be used on different hardware platforms, offering customers flexibility, openness, and independence from specific computer technologies. Currently, the SAP offering is comprehensive and it's meant not only for the ERP back office business processes but also for the Web-enabled collaboration, integration, the full supply chain. In significant scenarios, it can also run front office processes, such as CRM, or provide vertical solutions, such as SAP for Healthcare. SAP R/3 and any of the solutions within mySAP Business Suite are all business solutions providing a high degree of integration of business processes.

For SAP a *business process* is the complete functional chain involved in business practices, whatever module, application, system, or Web Service that has to deal with it. This means, specifically for the SAP R/3 systems, that the process chain might run across different modules. SAP sometimes referred to this kind of feature as an "internal data highway." For instance, travel expenses, sales orders, inventory, materials management, and almost all types of functions have in common that most of them finally link with the finance modules. SAP understands that business practices and organization change often and quickly, so it left the systems flexible enough to adapt efficiently.

Currently, in the age of global business and collaboration, those business processes and the integration chain can run across different services, which can be provided by SAP and non-SAP solutions. The capacity of an integration platform and the concept of an Enterprise Service Architecture is what best defined the need for the SAP NetWeaver concept.

SAP R/3, which provides the core functionality for many SAP standards, mySAP Business Suite, and SAP for Industries (formerly known as SAP Industy Solutions), includes a large amount of predefined business processes across all functional modules that customers can freely select and use for their own way of doing business.

With releases 4.5, 4.6, and 4.7 (Enterprise) of R/3, SAP has incorporated a library of more than 1000 predefined business processes across all functional modules that customers can freely select and use for their own way of doing business. SAP makes new business functions available regularly.

Other main features that SAP R/3 included from the start were the internationalization of the product and integration capability.

International applicability was a very important part of the strategy to meet today's complex and global business needs. For SAP, this means not only having the software available in different languages but also having the capacity to cover the differentiating aspects of each country: currency, taxes, legal practices concerning human resources, import/export regulations, and so on. Users from a multinational company in different countries can work simultaneously in the same system using their own language, currency, and taxes. With Enterprise release (4.7) and SAP NetWeaver, most SAP solutions are now able to run natively in Unicode format.

An additional aspect of the software integration capability is *real time.* In fact, the *R* from R/3 originally is meant for real time. When new input is made into the system, the logical application links will concurrently update related modules so that the business can react to immediate information and changes. This type of updating reduces the overhead of manual processing and communication and enables companies to react quickly in the nonstop and complex business world, which makes SAP R/3 software and the SAP Business Intelligence solutions very valuable tools for executive planning and decision making.

ERP systems such as R/3 were often implemented as a result of a business process reengineering, which was based on analysis of current business processes and how to improve them. Many companies could improve radically their efficiency, but this change process could not (can never) stop in a global and vast marketplace where the competition is on every corner ("one click away").

From internal integrated ERP systems, companies look further to improve their supply chain and therefore to extend the reach of their processes to other partner companies. This step forward is known as interenterprise collaboration, and the goal was to integrate and make more efficient the supply chain. This concept, together with the emergence of eCommerce using the Web as the comprehensive communication platform, was key in the emergence of mySAP.com strategy in 1999.

Let's review in the next section the motivations and strategic vision of SAP to transform itself from a single-product company into a global business solutions company.

SAP Transformation into a Global Business Solutions Company

The evolution of information technology systems from the beginning was quite similar in all industries and activity areas. In the 1960s and 1970s companies chose a hardware provider, and from there some basic software development products (programming languages), and started to develop their business applications. Most companies started with critical areas, like accounting and financial applications, that were somehow easier. Later, these companies advanced and introduced applications in other, more complex areas like distribution and production.

In any case, they always made their own development using the previously chosen hardware and software. Already in the 1970s there were some companies that realized the possibility of developing business software that could be used by different companies; the opportunity existed to develop the applications only once and then sell the software to other companies. Among these companies was SAP AG, created in 1972.

Obviously the development of "standard" software was more viable in those business areas that were more "standard," like accounting and financial services. There were also more "standard" processes common to companies from the same or similar industry sectors (like manufacturing or financial industries).

At the beginning, there were many problems with this standard software and many technical obstacles that would make it difficult to sell these systems in large quantities. One of these problems was the dependency of the hardware and software platforms in which the systems were developed. At the time, it was not possible to use the same software in different hardware platforms. Another problem was that companies did not behave as standard as initially thought. For instance, payroll calculation was quite different between companies, and even more different between countries, since each country has its own laws and legal rules, agreements, contract types, and so on.

In the late 1970s and during the 1980s, these problems led to companies developing standard applications that were flexible enough to provide functional features to different types of companies and in different countries. During the 1980s, with the emergence of PCs and the massive deployment of computing and computer networks in companies, it was time to make applications independent of hardware platforms and to make those applications portable among platforms. This was the open systems wave, when different hardware vendors were designing computers that could work with (nearly) the same operating systems (UNIX flavors, Windows NT) and with the same database engines (Oracle, Informix, and others). This technological advance also enabled the development of standard applications that could be independent of hardware and software platforms.

At the beginning of the 1990s, SAP AG had a product, SAP R/2, that covered reasonably well the needs of different types of businesses in different countries and in different areas, like financial services (accounting, accounts payable and receivable, controlling, and so on), logistics (materials management, warehousing, distribution, sales, and production), and human resources (payroll, time management, personnel development). This system was installed in approximately 3000 companies around the world.

The logical and natural evolution from R/2 to an open systems environment led to the birth of R/3 in 1992. SAP R/3 was developed through SAP AG's 20 years of accumulated experience in solving the business problems of its customers, along with experience in computing and managing complex networks. The company had experience and enough technological background for R/3 to succeed.

In a few years, the growth in the number of customer installations of the R/3 system was exponential: 900 installations at the end of 1993, 2400 in 1994, 5200 at the end of 1995, 20,000 by the middle of 1999, and more than 60,000 at the end of 2004, reaching the amazing number of over 20,000 customers in more than 120 countries.

In the mid-1990s it was clear that the standard business software (commonly known as ERPs or Enterprise Resource Planner applications) was mature enough so that many companies chose standard software and could abandon the traditional strategy of local and custom development, which was often more costly in the middle term. At the same time, SAP AG started to gain enough critical mass to take a new step in the development of standard software. This was to start developing software for those company areas that were less standard and more dependent on the business or industry area. These were, for instance, the upstream and downstream systems of oil companies, the call center and customer care systems for telecom or utilities companies, the selling of advertisement in the media sector, and so on. It was necessary to make a move from the back office applications (financial, logistics, human resources) to the front office in the different industry areas. It was also necessary to transform a company selling a product (SAP R/3) independently of the target customer to a company offering specific solutions for the needs of its customers.

SAP AG had enough customers in many different industries to think that the development and selling of specific industry solutions could be profitable.

SAP for Industries

Until 1996 SAP R/3 was traditionally presented in the classical diamond figure as shown in Figure 1-1. There was an area representing financial applications, an area for logistics, and one for human resources; the central area represented the basis and development system.

In 1996 SAP's industry solutions started to appear. As a base for many of them, SAP used solutions from R/2 or R/3, which had been previously developed by partners or customers in different business areas, like RIVA in the utilities sector for customer billing. The development of these industry solutions was first coordinated through the industry centers of expertise (ICOEs), where SAP's experience in the development of standard software is joined by the business knowledge and requirements of its customers, as well as the experience of big consulting firms for the inclusion of best business practices for each industry sector.

The initial step in developing industry solutions has been steadily consolidated and required SAP to specialize its teams into different industries, called industry business units (IBUs), which included and supplanted the previous ICOEs. These business units are responsible for gathering the market and industry knowledge and developing specific solutions and applications for each of the industry sectors in which SAP is committed to provide. Currently (end of 2005), there are 23 different industry solutions.

Refer to http://www.sap.com/solutions/industry/ for updated information about SAP-specific industry solutions.

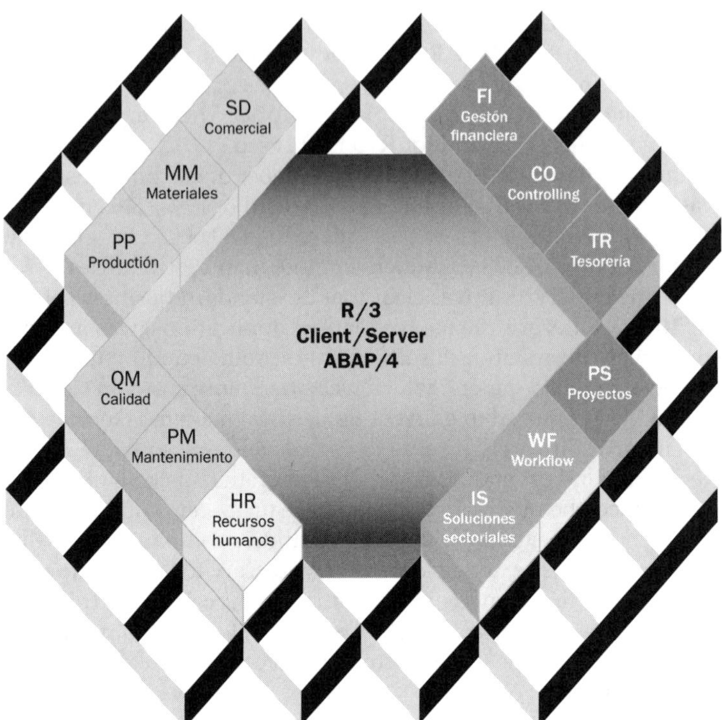

FIGURE 1-1 SAP R/3 classical representation

From a technical point of view, the SAP Industry Solutions were a SAP R/3 system with a special and industry-specific add-on that modified some of the standard R/3 transactions and applications to adapt them to that particular industry and that included new functionality relevant to that industry sector.

The Emergence of the New Dimension Products

Around the end of the 1990s, SAP was developing additional modules that initially were included within an IBU, but when looking more closely at these new developments, SAP was aware that some of the requested functionalities for these modules were common to different industry sectors. Examples of such common applications were the Customer Interaction Center or Call Center (CIC) or the Sales Force Automation (SFA), which later became Mobile Sales within the mySAP CRM and which matched those systems that have the objective of automating sales and that can be deployed in industries as different as consumer products, media, pharmaceuticals, and others.

Since these modules could not be grouped under a specific industry solution, they were positioned by SAP as an equivalent to IBUs called Strategic Business Units (SBUs). Initially SAP created three SBUs:

- *SAP Supply Chain Management (SCM),* which included products such as SAP Advanced Planner and Optimizer (APO), SAP Business to Business (B2B), and SAP Product Data Management (PDM)

- *SAP Customer Relationship Management (CRM),* which included SAP Sales, SAP Marketing, and SAP Service
- *SAP Business Intelligence (BI),* which included the SAP Business Information Warehouse and the SAP Knowledge Warehouse (formerly InfoDB)

The New Dimension products evolved to become an integral part of the mySAP Business Suite and SAP NetWeaver integration platform, as we will see in the following sections.

From these SAP products and solutions initiatives and the initial R/3 application modules, SAP has significantly increased the number of solutions that can be sold separately from R/3, some of which can also be deployed together with non-R/3 applications.

Solution Maps and Business Scenarios Maps

In 1998 SAP was ready to complete its strategic move from being a single-product (R/3) company to being a company offering complete business solutions to its customers.

In 2004, after the adjustment and fine tuning and right placement of the products within the initial mySAP.com offering, what started as complementary solutions became components of the mySAP Business Suite.

SAP offered solutions for different industry sectors when it introduced New Dimension and launched the SAP solution maps.

The solution maps gather not only the R/3 product vision but a full and structured view of the customer business as well. This is achieved with a firm decision to complete the company's catalog of products and services so that it can offer its customers a complete solution, either directly with SAP products and services or with third-party products developed by complementary software partners.

In the SAP solution maps, the customer business processes are collected in the horizontal colored boxes. Different colors signify different processes within the company. To build a complete solution for the customer business it will be necessary to deploy different products. As an example, Figure 1-2 shows the SAP solution map for the media industry.

In this case, the SAP solution for the media industry would include several modules of SAP R/3 Enterprise, such as FI for financial accounting and asset management, CO for the economic and strategic management of business, TR for treasury, MM for procurement, HR for human resources, and so on. It would then also include mySAP Business Suite applications and SAP NetWeaver components like the SAP Business Warehouse or the mySAP CRM. Finally would come IS-Media with its two modules: Media Advertising Management (MAM) and Media Sales and Distribution (MSD), which include the management of selling advertising for papers, journals, magazines, television, radio, the Internet, and other venues, as well as the management of subscriptions, paper and magazine sales, and distribution.

SAP considers it a must to provide its customers with a complete solution by developing required connections with those systems that must coexist with SAP. In SAP for Media this is the case with production systems that must interface with content servers or with systems for the design and pagination of publications. This was achieved initially by the Business Framework architecture based on open interfaces that could be used by products of complementary software partners. Currently this is enabled by the SAP integration technology represented by SAP NetWeaver.

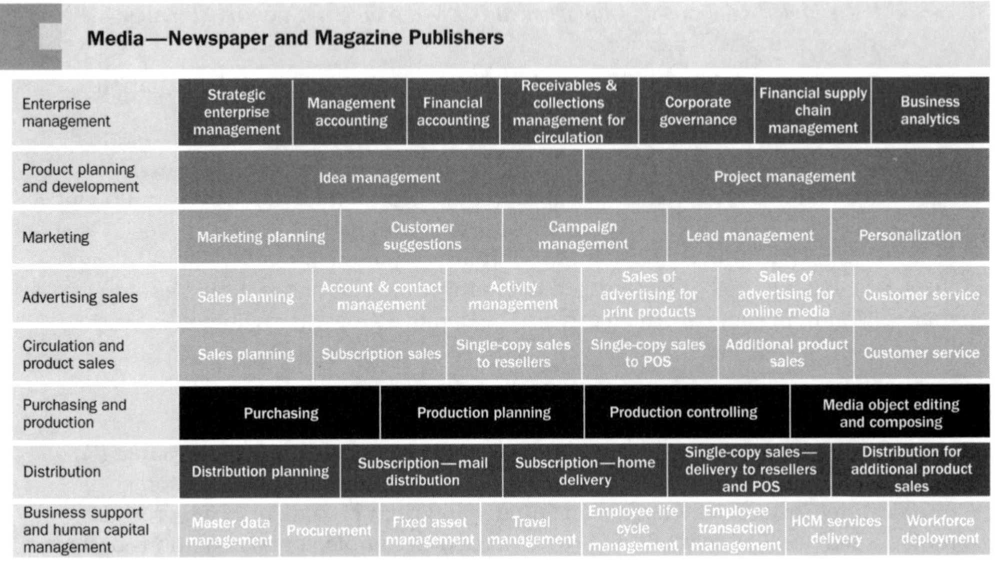

Media—Newspaper and Magazine Publishers
Enterprise management
Strategic enterprise management
Management accounting
Financial accounting
Receivables & collections management for circulation
Corporate governance
Financial supply chain management
Business analytics
Product planning and development
Idea management
Project management
Marketing
Marketing planning
Customer suggestions
Campaign management
Lead management
Personalization
Advertising sales
Sales planning
Account & contact management
Activity management
Sales of advertising for print products
Sales of advertising for online media
Customer service
Circulation and product sales
Sales planning
Subscription sales
Single-copy sales to resellers
Single-copy sales to POS
Additional product sales
Customer service
Purchasing and production
Purchasing
Production planning
Production controlling
Media object editing and composing
Distribution
Distribution planning
Subscription—mail distribution
Subscription—home delivery
Single-copy sales—delivery to resellers and POS
Distribution for additional product sales
Business support and human capital management
Master data management
Procurement
Fixed asset management
Travel management
Employee life cycle management
Employee transaction management
HCM services delivery
Workforce deployment

FIGURE 1-2 SAP solution map for the media industry

This structure guarantees SAP customers a complete integration of products, providing a full solution map for the integrated management of their businesses.

mySAP.com

Making a debut in 1999, mySAP.com was the initial SAP strategy for providing electronic commerce solutions in the age of the Net economy. With mySAP.com, SAP aimed to help its customers in their e-business strategies, providing a full set of software and service solutions that completely embraced the Internet strategy with a standard-based technological foundation known as the Internet Business Framework.

At the time of its introduction, mySAP.com was defined as the collaborative e-business platform that included *all* of the SAP solutions, technologies, and services. Figure 1-3 represents the mySAP.com strategy.

The mySAP concept, and specifically the Enterprise Portal component (initially the mySAP Workplace), was designed by supporting itself in the broad knowledge and experience of the different industries.

The mySAP components included solutions that could cover the specific requirements of companies and their users, such as the following:

- Access to business solution applications
- Access to internal corporate information, reports, and press releases
- Access to services available on the Internet
- Access to any user applications
- Access to marketplaces

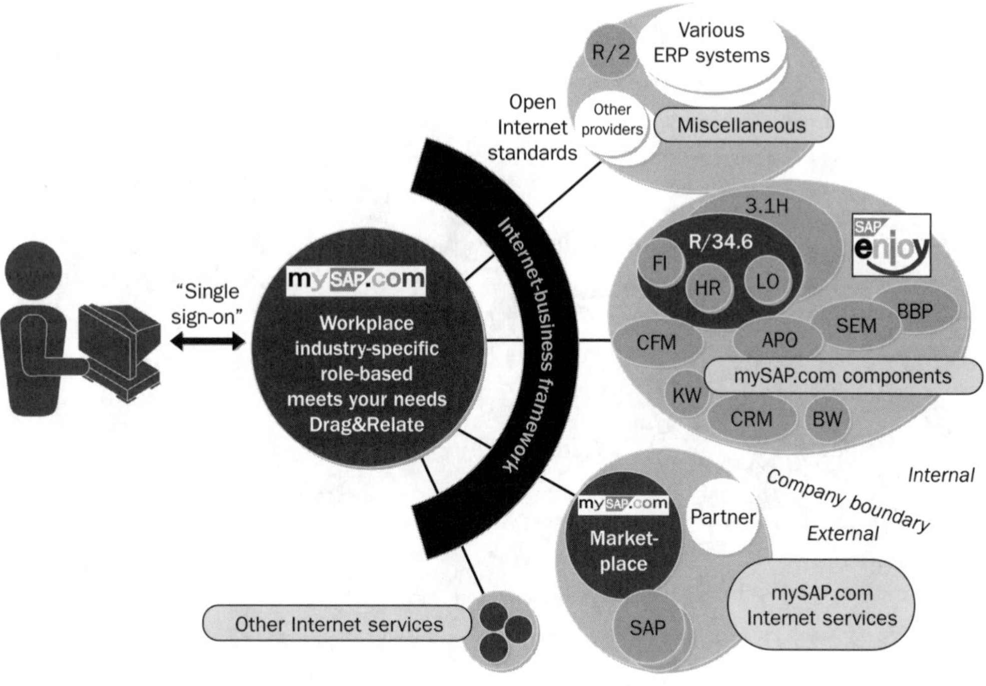

FIGURE 1-3 mySAP.com strategy

In order to support those requirements, the initial mySAP.com offering comprised the following components:

- mySAP.com Workplace
- mySAP.com Business Scenarios
- mySAP.com Application Hosting
- mySAP.com Marketplace

All that came with the underlying technology represented by the solid foundation of the SAP Basis Technology, whose name evolved to mySAP.com Technology.

mySAP.com could also be considered as an open, flexible, and comprehensive e-business solution environment, and, as such, it can integrate all the SAP software solutions but also other non-SAP applications. Clearly, it was the antecessor concept of what it is now the SAP NetWeaver integration platform.

Within mySAP.com companies can design their corporate portal and integrate specific Internet- and Web-based applications.

One of the main design principles of mySAP was to facilitate the integration of business processes not only internally but also among different companies (collaboration), which can be grouped by communities, with the purpose of increasing the effectiveness and productivity by potentially reducing the cost of collaboration within a vast marketplace.

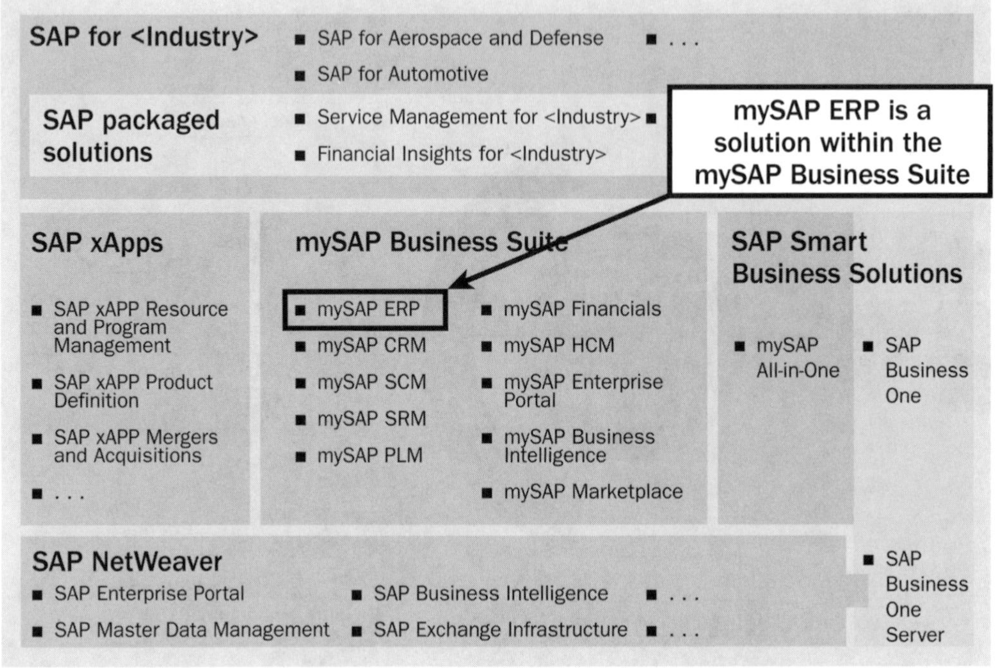

FIGURE 1-4 SAP product portfolio (2004)

This complex and ambitious goal of mySAP.com was supported by the technological foundation of the Internet Business Framework, so that there was an easy exchange of data and communication among Internet applications using XML; security systems based on standard certificates by certification authorities; content standards; and so on.

SAP Product Portfolio in the SAP NetWeaver Age

As of the end of 2004, SAP had repositioned its product strategy and solutions and the NetWeaver platform brought new elements or components (Figure 1-4).

This is a brief introduction, and major elements of this redefined solutions and product portfolio are as follows:

- SAP for <Industry>, based on previous SAP Industry Solutions and for the most part still based on SAP R/3 Basis (4.6C), is being migrated first to Enterprise R/3 and to the SAP Web Application Server and therefore will also have elements of SAP NetWeaver.
- mySAP Business Suite represents the bundle of all cross-industry SAP products, and it's based on the SAP NetWeaver integration platform. Some of the solutions within the Business Suite are mySAP CRM, mySAP SCM, and mySAP ERP. A key

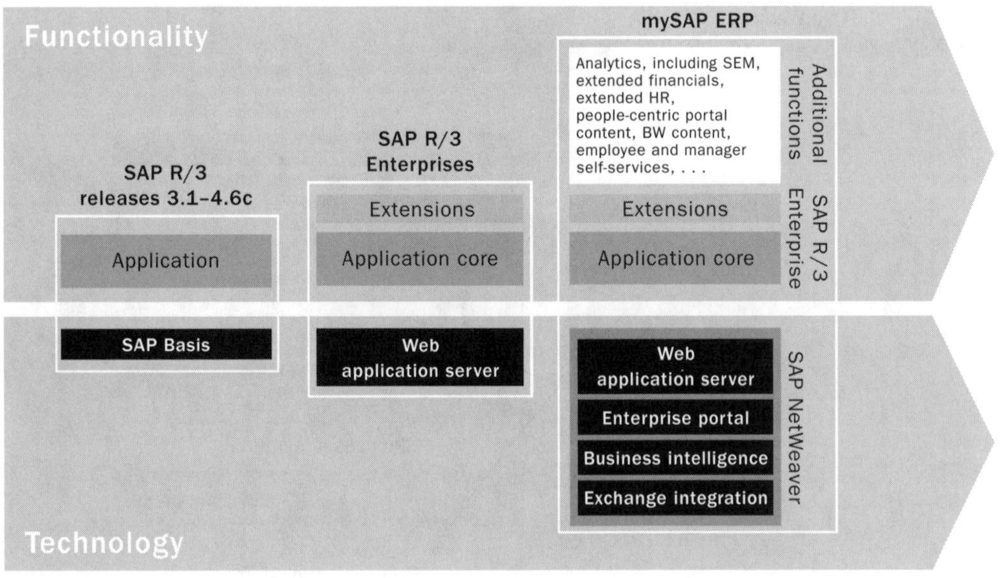

FIGURE 1-5 mySAP ERP

player here is mySAP ERP, or, in other words, a broader way of looking at SAP R/3 Enterprise, with the inclusion of additional functions and solutions such as Analytics and mySAP Human Resources. Figure 1-5 shows the role of mySAP ERP, and Figure 1-6 shows how SAP R/3 has evolved into the current product portfolio.

- SAP xApps, derived from SAP Cross Applications, is also a special development based on Java that allows for the so-called Composite Applications, based on SAP NetWeaver, that allow the integration of specific functions from several of the SAP Solutions.

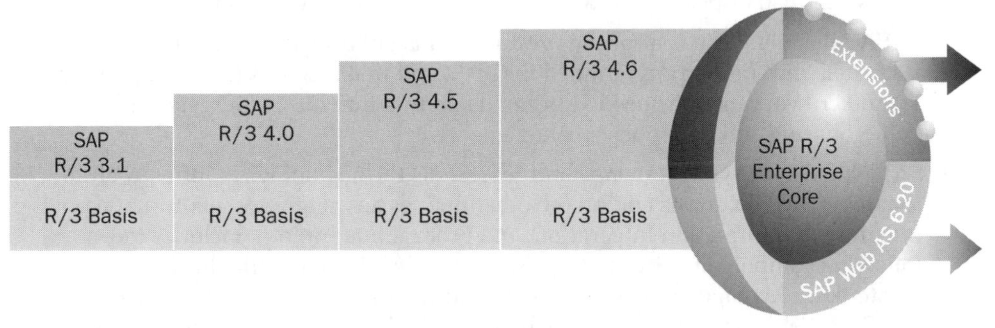

FIGURE 1-6 Evolution of SAP R/3

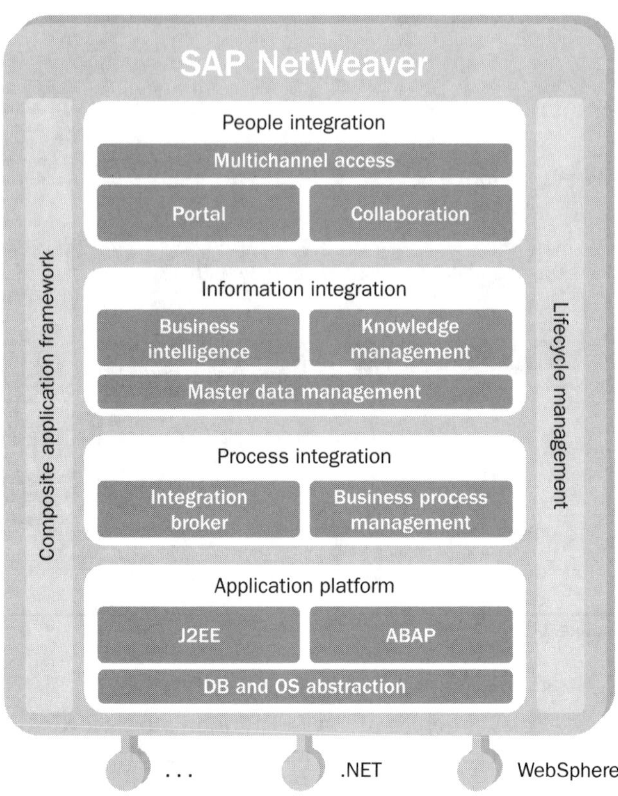

FIGURE 1-7 SAP NetWeaver integration layers

- SAP Smart Business Solutions, targeted to the market segment of the small and medium business. The products within these solutions include the following:
  - mySAP All-in-One is a special package based on a SAP R/3 system that has been enhanced with functions and applications from other SAP Solutions. This special solution is typically provided by SAP Business Partners that create their own industry-specific solutions (packages) for micro vertical markets.
  - SAP Business One is a special product that is not directly based on the SAP R/3 system, but rather programmed in C++, and that includes the most important and critical functions needed in small and medium businesses, such as accounting and warehouse management.
- SAP NetWeaver, which on one hand represents the technological infrastructure for all the SAP Solutions and on the other defines an integration platform (People Integration, Information Integration, and Process Integration), includes the following components: SAP Enterprise Portal, SAP Business Intelligence, SAP Master Data Management, SAP Exchange Infrastructure, SAP Mobile Business, and SAP Web Application Server. Chapter 11 includes an introduction of SAP NetWeaver architecture and components. Figure 1-7 shows the SAP NetWeaver concept and integration layers.

SAP R/3 Releases and Fundamentals

SAP R/3 technology was the natural evolution of the SAP R/2 system, and it is the product that has really fueled the expansion of SAP since its introduction in 1992, establishing itself as the leader and de facto standard in the industry. SAP R/3 was the first solid ERP standard client/server system, with a high degree of technological complexity and application functionality.

SAP explains the implicit complexity of R/3 systems by reasoning that the business world is complex, and for a standard system to cover it, it had to include a large number of functions. SAP not only includes business functionality, it also includes efficient implementation tools, a comprehensive development environment, and a full-featured set of tools to monitor and manage the system efficiently.

In the 1990s, SAP R/3 became the system of choice for those companies anchored in character-cell legacy applications wishing to downsize their centralized mainframe class computer system to newer and cheaper client/server technology.

The following sections introduce some of the features of the main R/3 releases, since release 3.0, showing some of the areas where SAP concentrated its strategic efforts and directions.

R/3 Release 3.0

R/3 release 3.0, introduced early in 1996, was a major step forward for SAP, both in starting to build the Business Framework architecture and in making customization tools easier. Some of the most important features introduced in 3.0 were as follows:

- Application Link Enabled (ALE) technology. With these interfaces to link different SAP systems and external application systems, SAP overcomes the problem of having a unique centralized database server and allows big companies to distribute their business processes without losing integration. ALE is still a major component and technology within the Internet Business Framework architecture and even SAP NetWeaver.
- Integration with standard PC applications, mainly the Microsoft Office suite. With this release, SAP included standard links to interact with MS-Excel, MS-Word, MS-Access, and others, using OLE technology.
- Enhanced graphical user interface (GUI) with lots of new options, buttons, captions, and images. There was also a set of utilities for interacting with SAP, such as the SAP Automation, RFC interfaces, and so on, included in standard Desktop SDK.
- Technological enhancements in the architecture of the system, such as new memory management features and easier installation and upgrade procedures.
- New APIs and standard calls for software developers, further opening the system and broadening the spectrum of functionality, with add-ons like Archiving, EDI, forms management, external workflow, plant data collection devices, mail and fax solutions, and so on.
- First steps to a more business-object-oriented system with an enhanced SAP Business Workflow and the introduction of the business objects, which are components of a business workflow.

- The introduction of the Business Framework architecture with the goal of making it faster and easier for customers to introduce new functionalities into the system, as well as making the system even more flexible and open.

R/3 Release 3.1

By year end 1996, SAP announced the availability of release 3.1. This version was known as the Internet release because the main new features and capabilities related to the possibility of expanding the capacity of the R/3 systems, using the Internet for doing business while preserving the functionality and support of the core R/3 applications. Users would be able to make transactions with the system directly using their Internet browsers. Release 3.1 allows for efficient communication in the business world among companies, customers, and providers.

SAP R/3 release 3.1 was the first to broaden the typical three-tier client/server architecture to a multitier one by introducing a new layer, known as the Internet layer, located between the presentation and application layers. With this approach SAP increased the potential access to the system of thousands of users (better known as *business partners*). To support this new architecture, SAP introduced several modifications to the application level, based on the *thin client* concept, which is in turn based on making a very reduced data transfer between the presentation and the application levels. This is a very important concept considering the limited bandwidth that was often found on Internet connections. And it made available the Internet Transaction Server (ITS).

R/3 release 3.1 offered the same functionality as the previous 3.0 release but enabled the ability of business processes using both intranets and the Internet. Some of its features were as follows:

- *Java enabling,* with the possibility of avoiding the code for the presentation server in clients and making presentation software distribution easier.
- *Introduction of Business Application Program Interfaces* (BAPIs), which can be used as a mechanism to communicate R/3 with external applications using the Internet. BAPIs are object-oriented definitions of business entities. The concept behind BAPIs was the key in the Business Framework architecture as well as in the overall SAP R/3 Internet and electronic commerce strategy, as the object-oriented interface to integrate external applications. Based on business objects, such as company, vendor, employee, material, and so on, a BAPI defines the methods that can be used to interact and communicate with those objects. Release 3.1 included more than 100 predefined BAPIs ready to integrate R/3 with third-party solutions and applications.
- *Internet Application Components* (IACs) were the new components on R/3 application servers that allow the use of software modules to support business transactions through an Internet layer. Initially SAP provided a small number of IACs (around 40), including components for human resources applications. IACs were based on ITS.
- *Initial support for Web browsers,* including Java-enabled components that became a new user interface (a new presentation). Most typical browsers, such as Netscape and Microsoft Internet Explorer, were fully supported.

- *Internet Transaction Server* (ITS) is the component located at the Internet level in the architecture and connects the Web server with the SAP Application Server and enabled running the SAP Internet Application Components.
- *SAP Automation* was the programming interface that allowed Internet components and other applications to interact with R/3.

Besides total support for the Internet layer, within the business engineering tools, release 3.1 incorporated a new process configuration based on models. This feature allowed for a quicker and more dynamic configuration of the business processes, oriented to the processes, and the system included several "industry" models that could be used directly by customers, thus reducing the time needed for configuring and customizing the system.

With the introduction of the R/3 solutions for supporting business processes through the Internet, it was possible for companies to widen their businesses by providing a new communication channel between companies and between customers and companies.

Standard with release 3.1 of SAP R/3 was the possibility of using three different types of Internet and intranet scenarios for supporting electronic commerce:

- Intranet corporate applications
- Intercompany applications, extending the possibilities of the supply management chain
- Applications from consumer to companies, enabling final customers with a simple Internet browser to communicate and trigger transactions with an R/3 system

R/3 Release 4.0

With the introduction of release 4.0 in 1997, and in the context of the Business Framework, SAP's strategy for enterprise computing was to develop R/3 into a family of integrated components that could be upgraded independently.

Following a well-known study by the Gartner Group, SAP closely watched the strategy depicted for the survival of the Enterprise Software Vendors and put the corresponding actions in place well before 1997. The four actions indicated were as follows:

- *Move toward componentization, both in products and sales force.* This move can be clearly seen with the emergence of R/3 release 4.0.
- *Add consulting content.* This is another step that SAP has added to its overall business, although in a more silent way, in order not to provoke the legion of consulting partners. SAP figures showed that 1997 and 1998 have seen a percentage growth both in revenue and people from services and consulting.
- *Develop industry-specific components or templates.* This was not a new strategic direction for SAP. With release 4.0, some industries, such as retail and the public sector, can find some additional and specific business processes; however, some other industries were not yet ready to go the SAP way.
- *Focus on fast implementation: methodologies and solutions.* ASAP and TeamSAP were excellent examples of SAP's reaction to the continuous criticism of implementation times and overbudgeted projects.

In addition to the logical evolution of technological aspects and the increase in functionality on release 4.0, there are two features that should be highlighted: componentization and inclusion of industry solutions. To these features, from a strategic and pragmatic point of view, we should also add the increased accent on the use of solution sets for rapid implementation, such as AcceleratedSAP or ASAP.

Componentization is a practical consequence of possibility enabled by the Business Framework architecture. When SAP introduced release 4.0, it explained that R/3 had evolved into a family of distributed business components.

Among the new components and functional add-ons to the kernel R/3 application modules are the following:

- *Introduction of new distributed scenarios* using ALE and its integration using BAPIs.
- *Enhancements for the management of the global supply chain* (from the provider of the provider to the customer of the customer) together with the New Dimension products within the Supply Chain Optimization Planning and Execution (SCOPE) and SAP Advanced Planner and Optimizer (APO) initiatives.
- *Introduction of new specific functionality* for particular industry solutions, starting with retail and the public sector.
- *New Business Framework architecture components.* With these new components customers could add new enhancements to the system independently of other R/3 functionalities. For instance, there was a large group of new Internet scenarios that could be used to fulfill some business processes.
- *Some of the new business components* within New Dimension were introduced at the time of the release of R/3 4.0; for example, Product Data Management (PDM), ATP Server (Available-to-Promise), the Business Information Warehouse, and the system of catalog and purchase requisitions using the Internet. These products were installed separately and were release independent.

It was SAP's goal to include substantial improvement for implementing R/3 more quickly, making it a business solution that is easy to use and easy to upgrade. With new R/3 Business Engineer components, the system includes an advanced mechanism for model-based configuration (business blueprints) and for continuous change management.

Technologically, the programming language ABAP/4 also evolved toward a completely object-oriented language based on the so-called ABAP objects, and from release 4.0 on it is called simply ABAP. These new objects allow interoperability with other types of external and standard object architectures.

There were also enhancements in security and data integrity by means of using authentication and electronic signature techniques.

There was also the extension of the SAP Business Workflow via the addition of new wizards for rapid workflow scenario configuration and deployment as well as the possibility of launching Workflows from the Internet using HTML forms.

R/3 Release 4.5

Release 4.5 was announced in 1998; with it SAP continues its process of introducing new functional components for logistics, financial, and human resources modules, many of which are based on a new open standard provided by the Business Framework architecture.

Strategically, release 4.5 is the strongest SAP bet to introduce and enhance industry solutions. In this version solutions for automotive, distribution, and consumer products are especially strong.

Among the new and enhanced technological features of this release, special mention must be made of the new extensions for centralized systems management; new GUI components for integration with PC applications, including new ActiveX controls; more BAPIs; more enhancement and ease of use and configuration of the Business Workflow; enhanced features for object-oriented ABAP; and the capability of accessing archived documents from the Internet using an enhanced Web ArchiveLink Interface.

There are also some major changes in the programs and utilities used for systems installations as well as for upgrading.

By using the architecture provided by the Business Framework, release 4.5 introduced new possibilities of extending the system using third-party solutions via BAPIs in many R/3 areas: enhanced system administration and control with CCMS, human resources management, enhanced global supply chain, report generation, and so on.

EnjoySAP Release: R/3 4.6

EnjoySAP was an initiative announced by SAP at SAPPHIRE'98 in Madrid, targeted to receive as much feedback as possible, mainly on R/3's usability—that is, on enhancing the system from an end user point of view. Customer and user feedback, together with new strategic and marketing campaigns such as the New Dimension Solutions and the Next Generation, established the cornerstone for release 4.6, initially known as EnjoySAP release.

Previous R/3 releases included many new components, functionalities, add-ons, industry solutions, and technology advances, as well as new but not revolutionary user features. EnjoySAP dramatically changed the user interface, going beyond just designing appealing and colorful features to fundamentally distinguishing between different types of users by delivering a role-based user interface. One of the features included in EnjoySAP more demanded by users was the ability to tailor the interface, so that now users can add their own icons for their most-used functions to the application toolbar.

The enjoySAP interface has been used ever since and it's still used in most SAP Solutions, except in those ones not based on the SAP Web Application Server.

Besides the completely new graphical interface, release 4.6 brought the actual foundation of the Internet Business Framework, with support for most standards meant for the integration with the Web applications such as HTTP, XML, Directory Integration with LDAP, and so on, thus creating the technological foundation of mySAP.com, and just one step ahead and currently, SAP NetWeaver.

The last functional release SAP R/3 4.6C brought additional performance and functionality to many of the application modules of R/3.

Figures 1-8 and 1-9 show the difference between the classical SAP graphical user interface and the new SAP GUI that came with release 4.6.

Enterprise Release: SAP R/3 4.7

SAP R/3 Enterprise is the next version of SAP R/3 after functional release 4.6C, which was codenamed Mercury as the internal project name. Although the mySAP.com strategy provided the collaborative e-business platform for intracompany and intercompany processes, it is equally important that SAP R/3 evolves and integrates tightly into the

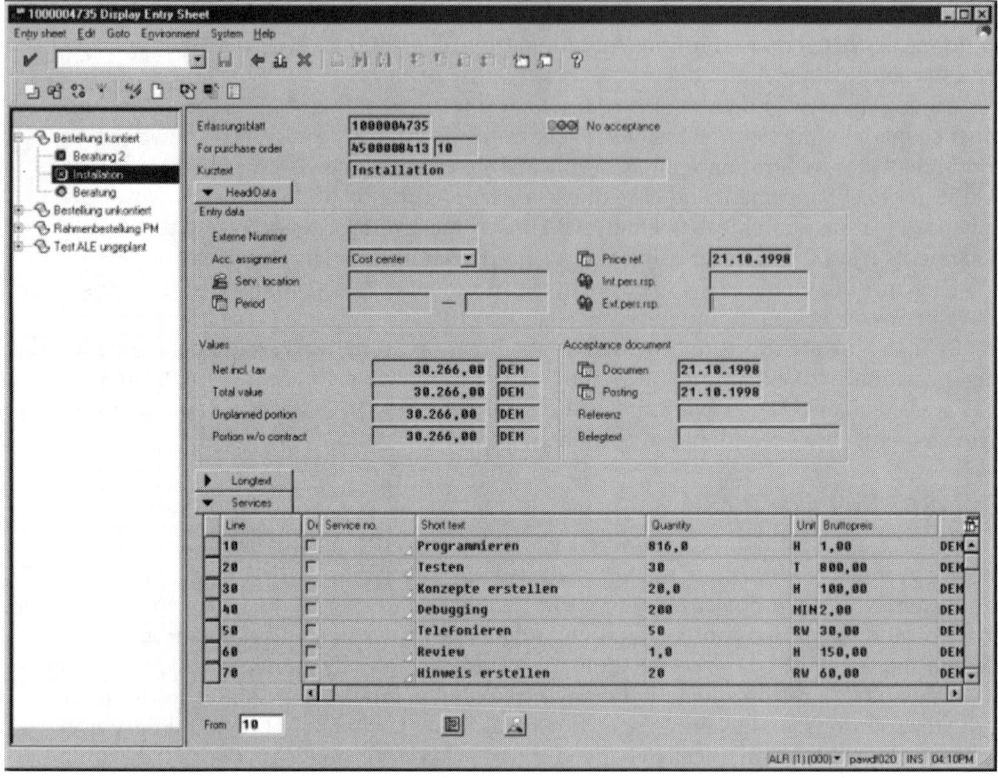

FIGURE 1-8 Classical SAP GUI (Copyright by SAP AG)

whole strategy. For this reason, SAP R/3 Enterprise, the new release of SAP R/3, was designed and intended as the platform for providing the optimal integration into the complete mySAP.com picture, and now into SAP NetWeaver.

SAP R/3 Enterprise initially was a part of the mySAP.com solutions and, as such, should be considered an extension of mySAP.com. For instance, if a SAP customer is using the SAP R/3 logistics applications and would like to take advantage of the advanced functions provided by mySAP SCM, the customer can still use those back end functions while integrating them with the Business Warehouse, APO, or the Enterprise Portal. Exactly the same happens now with mySAP ERP or mySAP Business Suite.

One of the main changes with SAP R/3 Enterprise is the delivery strategy for new functionality by implementing new methods of application upgrades. Therefore, besides the enhancement to business functions and applications, SAP R/3 Enterprise provides a new core technology for supporting these new delivery methods.

SAP R/3 Enterprise consists of two main components: the *SAP R/3 Enterprise Core* and *SAP R/3 Enterprise Extensions* (or Add-Ons). Both components interface with each other in the so-called nonmodifying fashion.

The SAP R/3 Enterprise Core contains new enhancements in the areas of legal requirements, performance, infrastructure, and continuous improvement. The SAP R/3 Enterprise Add-Ons contain primarily all new functional enhancements.

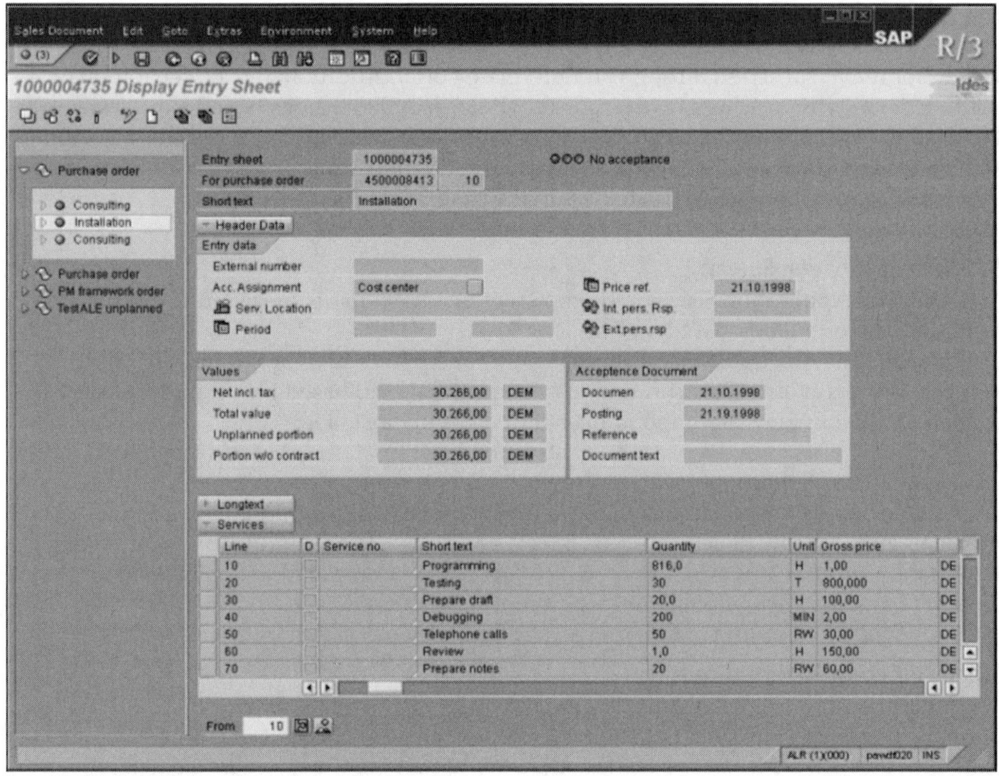

FIGURE 1-9 enjoySAP GUI (Copyright by SAP AG)

These components are built in the SAP R/3 Enterprise system around the concept of separating developments in technology and in functionality. Therefore, for instance, new developments in application functionality will no longer be mandatory, so the customer can choose which ones to use and install.

The SAP R/3 Enterprise Core is necessary to operate the SAP R/3 Enterprise Extensions (Add-Ons). The functionality of the SAP R/3 Enterprise Core is very similar to that found in release 4.6C of R/3, but customers can upgrade to Enterprise from releases 3.1I and above.

SAP R/3 Enterprise Core

The Core component of SAP R/3 Enterprise focuses on enhancing areas such as performance, quality, legal changes, and requirements, as well as specific infrastructure.

This is particularly possible and improved with the new Basis release, now called the SAP Web Application Server. Refer to Chapter 2.

The SAP R/3 Enterprise Core has integrated the Internet and Web technologies into all areas of the system, which previously required additional systems or components, such as ITS. The SAP R/3 Enterprise Core will be maintained separately from the Add-Ons, and the upgrades will be performed with specific service packages.

Regarding the benefits and improvements of the SAP R/3 Enterprise compared to release 4.6 of SAP R/3, the fundamental change in the Basis system must be noted. This change provides Web enablement to all the areas of the system and makes it easier for integration with other mySAP Business Suite components on top of SAP NetWeaver, as well as for universal access through an Enterprise Portal. Additionally, the separation of the functionality represented by the SAP R/3 Enterprise Extensions benefits the system especially when considering upgrade strategies and thus will influence systems availability, stability, and performance. This is particularly important because it was one of the main concerns voiced by many SAP customers in the past.

SAP Web Application Server

The SAP Web Application Server, also known as SAP Web AS, is the evolution of the SAP technological foundation based on SAP R/3 Basis.

In addition to the traditional runtime environment for ABAP programs, SAP Web Application Server also has a runtime environment for J2EE-based Java programs, known as the SAP J2EE Engine, although it must be specifically installed.

The SAP Web AS and its platform abstraction layer, with the OS and Databases, form the Application Platform of SAP NetWeaver.

As a further development of SAP Basis, the SAP Web AS support all the Internet-based protocols and standards such as HTTP, SMTP, XML, SOAP, SSO, and WebDAV and very importantly support Unicode format, which facilitates technically the deployment of different languages, traditionally with different code pages.

SAP R/3 Enterprise Extensions

The Enterprise Extensions or Add-Ons are the components that will provide functionality, normally in a nonmodifying fashion. In case of the same functionality in more than one Add-On, SAP will incorporate such functionality within the Core. According to SAP, normally an Add-On, does not depend in any way on other Add-Ons, which allows for an easier and more flexible upgrade strategy.

In the case that two or more Add-Ons would interface with each other, they would do so in such a way that they do not become dependent on each other; rather they are dependent on the release of the SAP R/3 Enterprise Core.

The SAP R/3 Enterprise Extensions application packages will have their own release schedules. Functional changes will be made in the Add-On components.

Integration Technology

The SAP R/3 Enterprise is based on a new technical architecture, the SAP Web Application Server, which will enable developments specific to an application area to be encapsulated. There is a clear goal in Application Integration Technology for improving heterogeneous applications and landscapes, specifically in collaborative Web-based processes.

The SAP R/3 Enterprise Core incorporates an Application Integration Technology, based on what SAP calls a Collaborative Service Architecture, with the goal of supporting new types of interfaces and integration with other systems or applications.

The Core will have a special component, known as the Interface Layer, which will be responsible for the management of interfaces that might be required for the connection between application components or with other systems. These can be, for example, the case of BAPIs, BADIS, RFC, or others.

Description of Our Good Old and Still Great R/3

Previous sections have discussed the use of this software system and who decides to implement it: SAP R/3 or mySAP ERP controls business processes and manages essential company information. Enterprises needing those services implement this standard software.

To manage the complex business needs of companies, the SAP product family offers leading technology solutions:

- *Multitier client/server architecture.* Based on middleware for supporting open systems technology. Initially based on the Business Framework architecture, then the Internet Business Framework, and now with the Integration platform of SAP NetWeaver, SAP is open to a total integration with other components, applications, systems, or services.
- Homogeneous user interface among applications.
- Comprehensive development environment.
- Total application integration.
- Solution Sets for configuring the system.
- Wide range of services, including hotline support, training, consulting, quality checks, and so on.

Figure 1-10 shows the classical SAP R/3 components from a functional point of view, before the SAP Web AS. The overall SAP R/3 system is represented by everything included inside the ellipse.

The lower layer is made of the operating system, the physical database (whose software is normally included in the SAP kit, although licenses can sometimes be negotiated with the DB software vendor), and the network. The *middleware layer,* which is above it, interfaces with the lower one and integrates the SAP R/3 applications on top of it. This middle layer was known as the *basis system* and includes components such as the ABAP development workbench, the system administration tools, batch job handling, authorization and security management, and all *cross-application* modules.

ABAP/4 is a fourth-generation programming language that was used to develop all R/3 application modules. When releases 4.0 and 4.5 were introduced and SAP's strategy began to focus on object orientation, it was decided to rename the programming language to simply ABAP, abandoning the 4 in reference to fourth generation. Chapter 7 gives an overview of the SAP Solutions development components and options, including ABAP.

Middleware are the layered software components that facilitate the development of client/server applications that can be deployed in heterogeneous vendor platforms. The basis system, also known as the kernel, is the SAP R/3 middleware. The SAP Web Application Server uses exactly the same concept and components, with the inclusion of an additional and native Internet layer, known as Internet Communication Manager or ICM.

The upper layer, the *functional layer,* contains the different business applications: financial, human resources, sales and distribution, materials management, and so on. The integration of all applications relies on the basis system.

SAP defines *client/server* also from a business solution point of view: a technology concept that leverages computing power to link core business processes with software, tying together various functions, such as financial services, human resources, sales and distribution, logistics, and manufacturing.

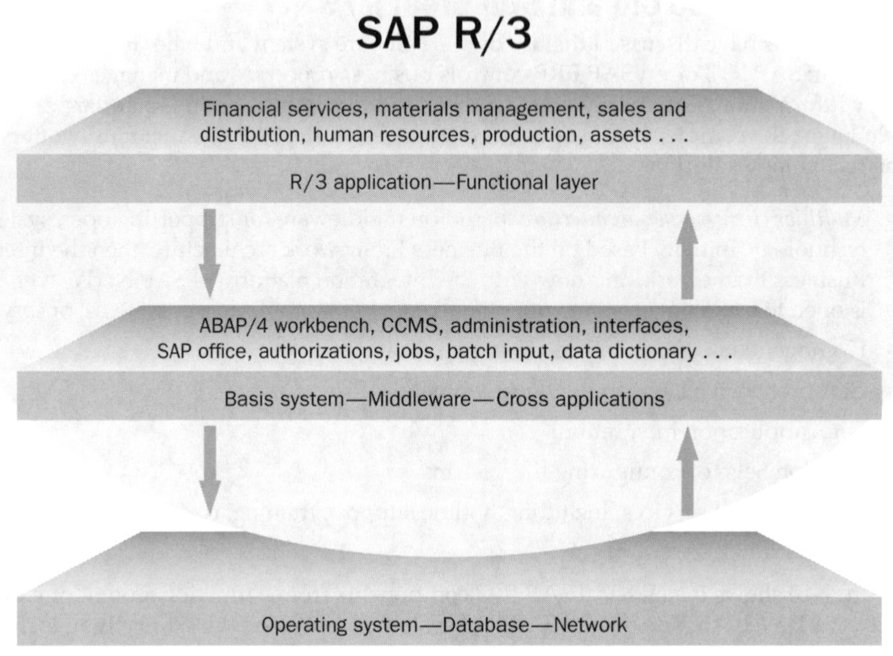

Figure 1-10 Classical SAP R/3 components

A common way for SAP to illustrate the R/3 system was the one shown earlier in Figure 1-1, with the R/3 kernel system providing the necessary integration and infrastructure for the R/3 applications.

The R/3 kernel makes use of standard communications and application program interfaces to access the operating system, the database, and the network. This kernel layer is located below the application logic and data layers of the system and operates independently from the applications.

This architecture allows users to change system configuration and install new systems without interrupting or altering the applications themselves.

Multitier Client/Server Solutions

In general, *client/server* is a style of computing that distributes the workload of a computer application across several cooperating computer programs.

This type of computing separates user-oriented, application, and data management tasks. Client/server is mainly a software concept that includes a set of service providers and service requesters. In client/server computing, individual software components act as service providers, service requesters, or both. These software services communicate with each other via predefined interfaces.

With the emergence of the Web and Web standards and the ability to have an Internet browser as user interface, together with the development of the ITS, the classic three-tiered client/server architecture became a multitier system.

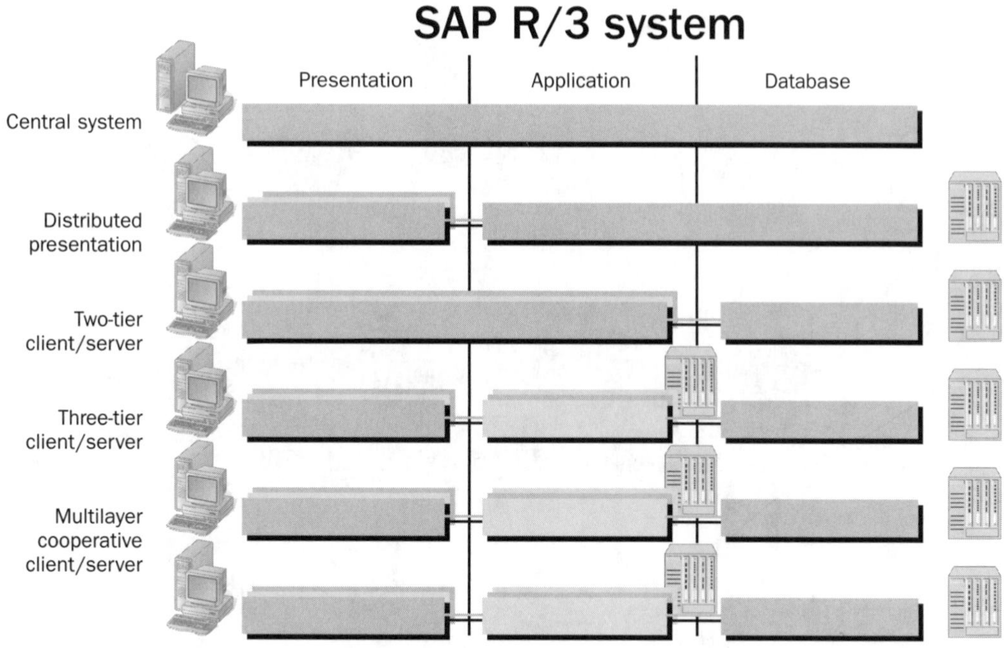

FIGURE 1-11 SAP client/server configurations

Major advantages of the client/server approach are as follows:

- *Flexible configuration.* With the deployment of standard communication interfaces, there are many possibilities for distributing and planning a client/server installation: from a centralized configuration to a highly distributed system. See Figure 1-11.
- *Workload distribution.* Because application servers work in parallel and communicate with the database, users can be evenly distributed based on their job tasks. Also, there is the possibility of deploying dedicated application servers to specific business areas.
- *High scalability.* Client/server permits users to adapt the capacity of their hardware according to the performance needs of their businesses, such as adding additional application servers when there is an increase in number of users, when additional modules start production, and when the database becomes larger. This enables companies to protect software and hardware investments.

One of the widely used client/server configurations with SAP systems is the three-tiered architecture (see Figure 1-12), which separates a system's computers into three function groups: presentation, application, and database. Since client/server is a software concept, it must be clear that an application server includes the software components that make up the provider services for the presentation, acting as a server, but also acting as service requester of the database services.

The Internet layer became a new special layer, as can be seen in Figure 1-13.

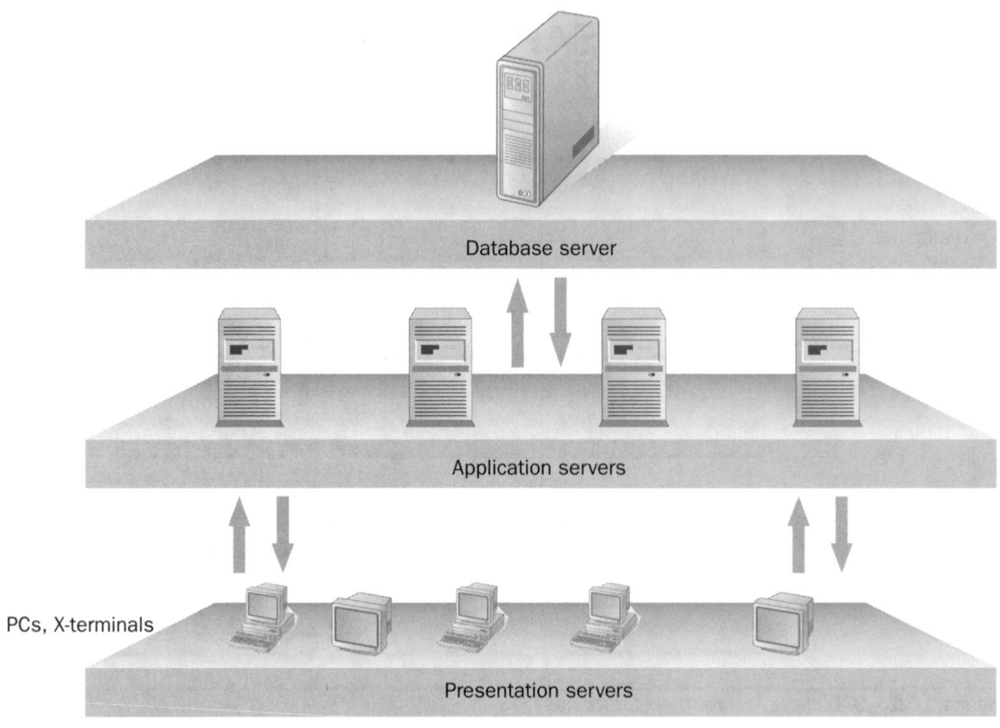

FIGURE 1-12 Classical SAP three-tier architecture

With the three-tiered architecture, each group is set up to support the demands of its functions. The central server contains the database, widely known as the *database server. Application servers* include the processing logic of the system, including services such as spooling, dispatching user requests, and formatting data. The tasks related to presentation of the data are handled by the *presentation servers,* which typically are personal computers or workstations, enabling easy access to the system.

Communication among the three tiers or server types is accomplished with the use of standard protocol services, such as the ones provided by TCP/IP or CPIC.

CPIC stands for Common Programming Interface Communication and includes standard functions and services for program-to-program communication with the ABAP programming language.

Chapter 2 shows in greater detail the services, processes, and components of the client/server architecture of SAP Systems, and in particular how all this evolved into the SAP Web Application Server technology.

Open Technology

The key to SAP R/3 success was the strategy of making *open solutions,* in which the applications can run on multiple operating systems, databases, and communication technologies. This enables customers to remain independent of a single vendor if they wish.

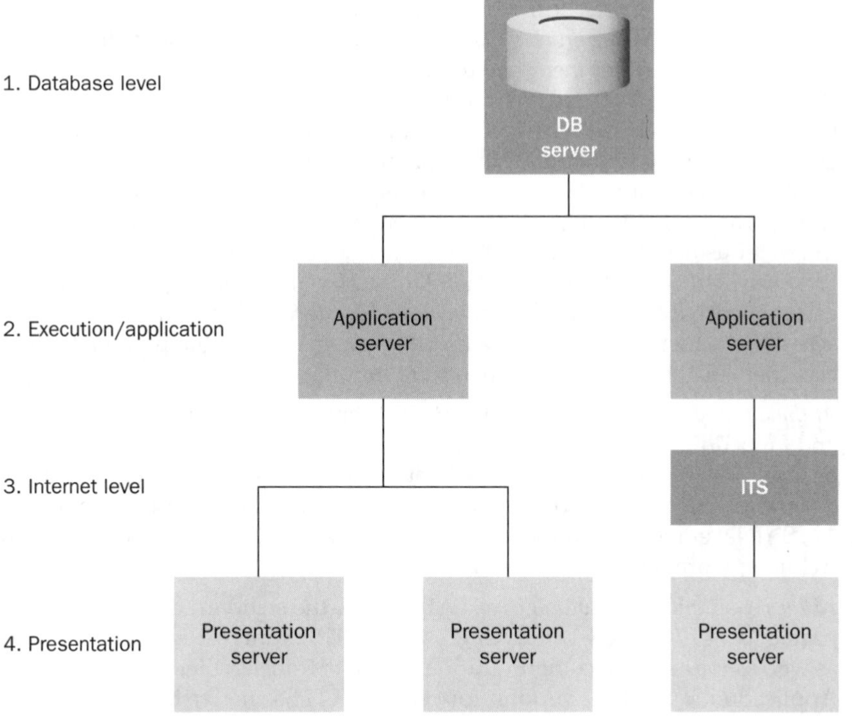

Figure 1-13 SAP client/server with the Internet layer

The list of current SAP-supported systems can be found also on the SAP Service Marketplace in their *Platform* link (currently in service.sap.com/platform, but watch for updates).

What basically makes systems open is the use of standard formats for data exchange, communication interfaces, and program-to-program communication. SAP extends the openness concept in several respects:

- *At the system level.* Support for multiple hardware platforms and operating systems, such as all types of UNIX from main system vendors, Microsoft Windows platforms, AS/400, OS/390, and Linux. Support for a large number of graphical user interfaces (GUIs), such as for all Windows flavors (currently only Windows 32 bits are supported), Macintosh, Internet Browsers, JavaGUI, and so on.
- *At the database level.* R/3 supports various relational database systems such as Oracle, Informix, SAP-DB or mySQL (MaxDB), DB2, and Microsoft SQL-Server.

  Access to the data managed by SAP R/3 is possible using standard R/3 reports as well as any other SQL standard tool: ODBC, SQL browsers, and so on. SAP has incorporated the standard ANSI-SQL as the database manipulation language, which allows users and programmers to store, view, and retrieve data to and from all different underlying database products.

- *At the application level.* The system is open to be enhanced and extended to meet specific business requirements. This can be accomplished either using the ABAP repository and development environment or currently all the facilities provided by the tools and development environment enabled by SAP NetWeaver components. On the foundations, SAP R/3 programming interface lets other SAP systems and external programs invoke SAP function modules via RFCs (remote function calls) or RPCs (remote procedure calls), using Business Application Program Interfaces (BAPIs), and all new types of interfaces enabled by the Business Framework and the Internet Business Framework (DCOM, Java Connector, Business Connector, etc.).

  At the URL http://ifr.sap.com (SAP Interface Repository), there is a comprehensive collection of all interface and interface types that can be used to access or exchange information with SAP systems, using different methods, and classified by application components and interface types.
- *At the desktop level.* With the initial deployment of Microsoft OLE (Object Linking and Embedding) technology, then with COM and now with .NET, SAP systems enables desktop users to access SAP data and functions from many Windows client programs. With the introduction of SAP R/3 release 4.0 and especially with 4.5 and 4.6, SAP leveraged the concept of integration with PC programs, mainly with the technology provided by ActiveX and Java.
- *At the communication protocol level.* SAP can use the standard communication protocols TCP/IP, SNA-LU6.2, CPIC, and HTTP for interprogram communications as well as for network communication and data transfer. Since SAP Web Application Server 6.10, support for HTTP/HTTPS is native in the system.
- *At the external communication level.*
  - Since release 3.0, SAP systems have included support for EDI (Electronic Data Interchange) interfaces to automate the exchange of data (invoices, orders, etc.) between SAP systems and other applications systems used by business partners.
  - It also uses MAPI (Messaging Application Program Interface) technology, supporting standard X.400 and SMTP protocols. These standards allow R/3 users to communicate with other mail systems and the Internet. With the SAP Web Application Server, SMTP is now native in the system without the need to install or set up e-mail gateways or additional connectors, and lets the SAP system act as an MTA (Message Transfer Agent).
  - Since release 3.1, with the incorporation of the BAPI technology, SAP has actively supported the new *electronic commerce technology* with the deployment of the Internet, which allows business transactions to happen between Internet users and SAP systems. Many of the new interface types and data exchange standards are still based on BAPIs.
  - With the ALE (Application Link Enabled) technology, SAP allows communication between distributed applications: between SAP systems and between SAP and external application systems.
  - Using development languages such as standard ANSI C, C++, Java, Delphi, Visual Basic, and the newer development environments, developers can

integrate external applications with SAP systems, exchanging information on the level of business objects.

User Interface

The SAP systems user interface is designed for ease of use and friendliness by all levels of staff. The SAP graphical user interface, known as SAP GUI, acts as the presentation server and is available in Windows and Macintosh platforms. They all look identical, whatever underlying system they are running on.

The SAP GUI includes all graphical capabilities of modern Windows interfaces, with push buttons, menu bars, toolbars, hypertext links, tabstrips, on-focus descriptions, and right-clicking options. The graphical design and functionality is homogeneous across the entire system, which makes training easier and more straightforward for all levels of SAP users.

Depending on which SAP application or processing tasks are to be run, screens may be very simple or may contain multiple fields and graphical elements. Customers can also customize and create new menus and screens with the help of the development workbench. Chapter 4 contains all the information needed to learn how to use the system and discusses the available icons, how to move around the system, and some very useful hints.

In SAP R/3 releases 4.x and up, the new GUI was designed to be able to show several types of information at the same time. There is also the possibility of transferring the presentation components on demand from SAP to the workstations. This is possible because of the enhancements in the architecture introduced using ActiveX under Windows or JavaBeans.

As of the introduction of the ITS, with SAP GUI for HTML, and currently with the possibilities enabled with Web Dynpro, the user interface is slowly switching to a complete Web-based environment, which would ultimately make SAP users able to deploy SAP systems through the SAP Enterprise Portal (the People collaboration layer of SAP NetWeaver).

ABAP Development Workbench

ABAP/4 was SAP's own fourth-generation programming language, and that was the name up to release 3.1. When release 4.0 was introduced, the name lost the 4 suffix and the language started to be known simply as ABAP. It is exactly the same language with several new technical improvements, mainly in the field of adding all the features that make a programming language object oriented. The name is taken from **A**dvanced **B**usiness **A**pplication **P**rogramming Language and is the programming language used by SAP for the development of all standard business applications included within the R/3 suite, as well as many other of the SAP Solutions included in the mySAP Business Suite.

On top of ABAP, SAP has designed a full-purpose development environment, known as the ABAP development workbench, which is integrated within the R/3 system and is available for customers to develop their own solutions and enhance or extend the capabilities of the existing applications.

The ABAP development workbench includes all tools necessary to develop and design programs, screens, menus, and so forth. It also contains performance and debugging facilities. Central to the workbench is the ABAP object repository and the data dictionary. The *object repository* stores all the development objects of the workbench: programs, dictionary data, *dynpros* (dynamic programs), and documentation.

The repository is the key to managing and testing ongoing development.

The *data dictionary* contains the descriptions of the data structures used within programs. This is the *metadata* repository that includes table definitions, allowed values, and relationships between tables. Administrators should be very familiar with this SAP component because it is widely and extensively used.

As of version 3.0, the development workbench included the workbench organizer, not the transport organizer. The organizer handles the transition of new developments and customizations into productive systems. Some of the available features are version management, programs modification control, and team project developments.

The transport system handles the movement of development work from one system to another. For instance, migrations to new SAP releases are, in reality, massive objects transported from the systems at SAP to customers' systems. This is a very important tool in all SAP Solutions that are based either in SAP Basis or SAP Web Application Server, and it is explained in Chapter 6.

Application Integration

The data from the different SAP functional applications are shared and integrated, building what is often known as an *internal information highway.*

This integration can be seen as an implicit applications workflow. One of the main benefits of the set of SAP applications is their capacity for creating a perfect integration between the different business processes of companies. It is that integration between applications that ensures that all business and management information is available to all areas of a company.

An accompanying feature that makes application integration stand out is the capacity of doing it in *real time.* This means that information is constantly updated, so when a manager requests a report about the current balance the system provides instant information about the status of the financial statements. This avoids the difficulty of running end-of-period reports and programs from a traditional legacy system, which has to search and incorporate needed data from other applications before the run.

From the point of view of the business processes, the integration of the R/3 application modules used to be represented using the tools available within the *R/3 Business Engineer,* which is no longer available in latest releases. At the level of data models, this integration can be accessed using the available functions included in the *Data Modeler.*

Customizing Tools

Customizing is the cornerstone of SAP systems implementation. Once you get your kit, you have all the application modules with all the business processes from the selected solution.

The next step is to *customize* the system to suit your business needs and practices. This is the method of implementing and enhancing the SAP R/3 systems or other SAP Solutions, as well as upgrading to new SAP releases.

Some of the customizing tasks are as easy to implement as electronically entering the countries where the company is located. That has an automatic effect on currencies, tax calculations, legal requirements, and so on. Other tasks are very industry specific and somewhat more complicated. Customizing the system is a long, time-consuming process because it can only be done by expert company users and with help from consultants that know the real business. Customizing must precisely match business organization,

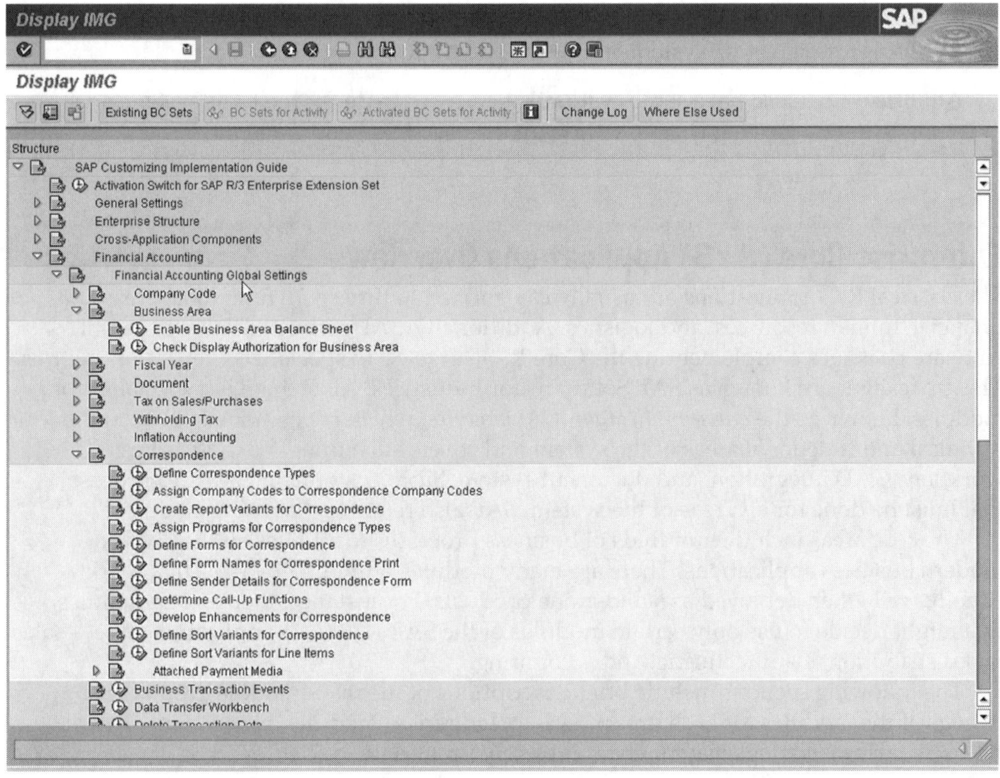

Figure 1-14 Example of customizing screen (Copyright by SAP AG)

processes, and functions with those of the SAP system. Figure 1-14 shows an example of one of the multiple screens used by SAP systems for help in customizing.

SAP includes some standard tools to help customers and consultants with this process and also provides many templates to be used for adapting the SAP functions to their corresponding business practices.

Some of the tools and documentation provided are as follows:

- *The IMG (Implementation Guide).* An interactive model to help users and consultants map company requirements for specific business needs. IMG can handle the automatic creation of recommendations for organizing and implementing the project. It acts like an electronic manual for consultants, linking hypertext documentation with real transactions.
- *The transport system.* Tools for transferring system configuration from test systems to production systems.
- *ASAP (Accelerated SAP),* which is an implementation roadmap, and now included within the SAP Solution Manager.

- *SAP Solution Manager,* a framework for monitoring and implementing SAP systems.
- Tools for managing system and release upgrades.

Administrators also have some customization work to do for the basis system, such as setting printers, copying clients, setting up the correction and transport system, and so on.

SAP Enterprise Core (R/3) Applications Overview

The classical R/3 applications are usually categorized in three core functional areas: financial, human resources, and logistics. Additionally, SAP actively develops special software packages complementing the Core R/3, targeted to specialized vertical industries. These packages are known as SAP Solutions for Industries. Also, there is a special set of modules, known as the *cross-application (CA) modules,* which is positioned between the technical and functional areas of the system and covers such things as the business workflow, CAD integration, and document system. Since customizing is also a process that must be done for all areas of the system, SAP also refers to it as a CA module.

The core areas include hundreds of business processes to address all the needs of modern business applications. There are many modules within these areas that work equally well when deployed as stand-alone products. For instance, there are companies that might decide to use only certain modules of the SAP R/3 Core application suite—sales and distribution, manufacturing, and accounting.

The following sections include brief descriptions of the main module groups and listings of the modules for each group. SAP includes new modules as new versions are released, so these listings may not be completely up-to-date.

Financial Applications

SAP financial modules give customers the whole picture of the accounting functions, with extensive report facilities to allow for fast decision-making support. They are also perfectly suited for international corporations with multiple subsidiaries, including support for foreign currencies and multilingual capabilities.

The financial area contains the following module groups:

- FI. Financial accounting
- CO. Controlling
- EC. Enterprise controlling
- IM. Capital investment management
- TR. Treasury

Latest additions within the financial application of the SAP Enterprise Core include *Corporate Finance Management (CFM), mySAP Banking, Real Estate Management, Public Sector,* and others. Please refer to the SAP Web site for the latest information. The following sections briefly describe the traditional and main components of SAP application modules.

FI: Financial Accounting

These modules constitute the operational aspects of the general accounting and financial information for the enterprise. They connect and integrate with other financial modules such as treasury and controlling, as well as parts of human resources, such as payroll and travel expenses. Also, the transactions of accounts receivable and accounts payable are directly related to the sales and distribution and purchasing modules. The following list contains the financial accounting modules. Each one includes multiple business processes and capabilities.

- FI-AA. Asset accounting
- FI-AP. Accounts payable
- FI-AR. Accounts receivable
- FI-GL. General ledger accounting
- FI-LC. Consolidation
- FI-SL. Special-purpose ledger

An important aspect of the financial accounting system is the real-time generation of the current balance and profit and loss sheets.

Latest additions include also bank accounting (FI-BL), travel management (FI-TV), and fund management (FI-FM).

CO: Controlling

This module is used to represent the company's cost structures and the factors that influence them. The module includes areas such as cost controlling, product and production cost controlling, and profitability analysis.

The CO module is intended to answer key management questions such as, "What does a product or service cost?" To answer that, the CO product costing system uses different valuation strategies and quantity structures, enabling the cost of manufactured goods to be planned as precisely as possible.

With the help of a planned/actual comparison, the CO module enables users to quickly recognize weak points in the production process. The following are the controlling modules and their descriptions.

- CO-OM-CEL. Cost element accounting
- CO-OM-CCA. Cost center accounting
- CO-OM-OPA. Internal orders
- CO-ABC. Activity-based costing
- CO-PA. Sales and profitability analysis
- CO-PC. Product cost controlling

EC: Enterprise Controlling.

The EC module is another very important decision-making tool that monitors the critical success factors and key figures of the company from a controller's point of view.

The executive information system (EIS) is basically a collection of tools that helps to quickly filter and analyze the enterprise's most important data and get critical and up-to-date business information into graphical form or customized reports.

With the management consolidation (EC-CS) system, subsidiary data, even from different countries and with different legal regulations, passes directly into the central MC system, automatically performing all the required consolidation work.

The EC module allows profit analysis for independent business areas of a company. The system takes care of automatically retrieving and grouping the necessary information for this process. The following list contains the areas included in the enterprise controlling module group.

- EC-EIS. Executive information system
- EC-CS. Consolidation
- EC-PCA. Profit center accounting

IM: Capital Investment Management

IM is an application module designed to plan and manage capital investment projects and budgets. It is also used for monitoring the bookkeeping functions associated with assets under construction on capital investment projects and orders. It consists of two parts:

- IM. Capital investment management (programs)
- IM-FA. Tangible fixed assets (measures)

TR: Treasury

The treasury module of SAP R/3 integrates cash management and forecasting with the financial and logistics-related applications. It provides tools to analyze budgeting, process electronic account statements, analyze foreign money markets, and so forth. The following list shows the components of the treasury module.

- TR. Cash budget management
- TR-CM. Cash management
- TR-TM. Treasury management
- TR-LO. Loans management
- TR-MRM. Market risk management

Human Resources Applications

The HR module includes all necessary business processes to manage efficiently all the needs of a company's human resource area—from applicant screening to payroll accounting or personnel development. As with the rest of the SAP applications, the aim of the HR module is to enter data just once and make it available to other related applications, such as accounting, plant maintenance, or business workflow.

The HR module includes full support for salary administration and payroll, work schedule models, planning, travel expenses, and so forth.

It must be noted that the HR module and its associated business process are very country specific, because the software must adhere to specific country laws concerning employment, tax, benefits, and so on. For this reason, SAP includes different procedures and transactions for different countries.

With the newer releases of the Enterprise Core (R/3), there are four module groups within the human resources applications:

- PA. Personnel management and personnel administration, which includes the following:
  - PA-RC. Recruitment
  - PA-BN. Benefits administration
  - PA-CM. Compensation management
  - PA-PM HR. Funds and position management
  - PA-MA. Managers desktop
  - Personnel development (former PD)
- PT. Personnel time management, which includes the following functions for Work Schedules, Time Evaluation, Incentive Wages, Shift Planning, Time Data recording, and so on
- PY. Payroll
- PE. Training and event management

Logistics Applications

Logistics is the most extensive area of the SAP applications and contains the largest number of modules. The logistics applications manage all processes involved in the supply chain of goods: from raw material procurement to final customer delivery and billing. These applications contain comprehensive business processes for flexible manufacturing systems and lots of tools for decision support. These applications integrate seamlessly with virtually every other SAP application, from the financial and controlling modules to the human resources processes.

The main logistics applications include the following modules:

- LO. General logistics
- MM. Materials management
- PM. Plant maintenance
- PP. Production planning
- PS. Project system
- QM. Quality management
- SD. Sales and distribution

Latest releases have incorporated additionally the following applications:

- LE. Logistics execution
- CS. Customer service
- PLM. Product lifecycle management

- EH&S. Environment, health, and safety
- Global trade

LO: General Logistics

These applications contain the basic intelligence engine of the SAP logistics system: tools and reports to analyze and manage the status and make forecasts about the supply chain. The following is a list of the general logistics modules.

- LO-MD. Logistics basic data
- LO-BM. Batch management
- LO-ECH. Engineering change management
- LO-LIS. Logistics information system
- LO-HU. Handling unit management
- LO-CM. Configuration management
- LO-VC. Variant configuration
- LO-SCI. Supply chain planning interface
- LO-ASM. Assembly to order
- LO-PLM. Product lifecycle management

MM: Materials Management

The materials management module comprises all activities related with material acquisitions (purchasing) and control (inventory, warehouse).

The purchasing module includes a complete range of operations: request for quotations, requisition limits, vendor price comparisons, agreements, order status, and so on.

Inventory management is a great tool for planning and enables users to compare materials ordered with those received. It has direct links with purchasing and quality management. Stock is always controlled since every material movement is immediately recorded.

The warehouse module can manage complex warehouse structures, storage areas, and transportation routes. It links with the sales and distribution modules and capital investment management.

The invoice verification module is the right tool to avoid paying more than necessary. It handles information directly with the accounting and controlling modules and allows users to define tolerance values and analyze the movement of goods.

The MM system is made up of the following components:

- MM-CBP. Consumption-based planning
- MM-PUR. Purchasing
- MM-SRV. External services management
- MM-IM. Inventory management
- MM-IV. Logistics invoice verification

Additionally, MM includes an evaluation module closely linked with CO, and allowing functions around price changes or a special material ledger to have an accurate view of product costing.

PM: Plant Maintenance

The PM modules take care of the complex maintenance of the plant systems. This includes support for having graphical plant representations, connecting to geographical information systems (GISs), and detailed diagrams. The modules support management of operational and maintenance problems, equipment, costs, and purchase requisitions. The modules' extensive information systems allow users to identify weak points quickly and plan preventive maintenance. It's also remarkable that all the workflow scenarios are available in PM/CS as Maintenance Notifications, Maintenance and Service Orders, or Service Notifications.

The PM system includes the following modules:

- PM-EQM. Equipment and technical objects
- PM-PRM. Preventive maintenance
- PM-WOC. Maintenance order management
- PM-WCM. Work clearance management

PP: Production Planning

This business area is a very complex and extensive part of the SAP logistics application system. It contains modules for the different phases, tasks, and methodologies used in the planning of production (product quantities, product types, materials procurement, time, etc.) and the process of production itself. Since release 3.0 of R/3, the PP-PI (production planning for process industries) module was included, providing an extensive planning tool for batch-oriented manufacturing. This module also enables the connection with external plant control systems and the management of different plants.

The PP modules are extensively integrated and connected to other R/3 applications, such as sales and distribution and materials management. The production planning application is made up of the following modules:

- PP-ATO. Assembly orders (now within General Logistics LO-ASM)
- PP-BD. Basic data
- PP-SOP. Sales and operations planning
- PP-MP. Master planning
- PP-CRP. Capacity requirement planning
- PP-MRP. Material requirements planning
- PP-SFC. Production orders
- PP-KAB. Kanban/just-in-time
- PP-REM. Repetitive manufacturing
- PP-PI. Production planning for process industries
- PP-PDC. Plant data collection

PS: Project System

The PS application is a complete project system that handles all aspects of activities, resource planning, and budgeting of complex tasks. It includes a complete information system to keep track of current project status. It connects with the accounting and logistics applications and has many graphical capabilities as well as the ability to interface with external applications such as Microsoft Project. The following are the modules included in the project system application.

- PS-APP. Project budgeting
- PS-BD. Basic data
- PS-EXE. Project execution/integration
- PS-IS. Information system
- PS-OPS. Operative structures
- PS-PLN. Project planning

QM: Quality Management

The SAP system as a whole, and the Core R/3 applications independently, take care of quality control of the managed business areas: human resources, financial controlling, and so on. As integral parts of the logistics application, the QM modules handle the tasks involved in quality planning, inspection and control, and complying with internationally defined standards on quality, as specified in ISO9000.

The main tasks of the QM modules have to do with the quality control of the sales and distribution processes, the materials management, and all production-related quality issues. The following is a list of the QM modules:

- QM-PT. Quality planning
- QM-IM. Quality inspection processing
- QM-QC-AQC. Quality control
- QM-CA. Quality certificates
- QM-QN. Quality notifications
- QM-IT. Test equipment management
- QM-PT-RP. Control in logistics
- QM-CR. General functions

SD: Sales and Distribution

The SD modules are the most intensive transactional applications and usually are used as a base for benchmarking different platform architectures because they virtually connect and integrate with every other SAP application: production, materials, accounting, quality, project, human resources, and so on.

This collection of modules enables the management of all aspects of sales activities: ordering, promotions, competition, sales leads, call tracking, planning, mail campaigns, and so forth. Other useful features include immediate product availability information and the ability to make early quotations. Customers benefit with better and faster service and can receive direct order confirmation by fax or mail.

These modules also allow the definition and control of the pricing structures and, with the connections to accounting and controlling, the receivables and revenues are immediately updated.

The SD system is made up of the following components:

- SD-BF. Basic functions and master data in SD processing
- SD-BF-PR. Pricing and conditions
- SD-BF-CM. Credit and risk management
- SD-BF-OC. Output determination
- SD-SLS. Sales
- SD-SLS-OA. Customer service processing
- SD-FT. Foreign trade
- SD-BIL. Billing
- SD-BIL-IV. Payment card processing
- SD-CAS. Sales support
- SD-EDI. Electronic data interchange
- LE-SHP. Shipping
- LE-TRA. Transportation

Cross-Application Components

The CA (cross-application) modules or components include all SAP functions and tools that are not directly related to a unique part of the system. These are general-purpose components, applications, or tools that can be used independently or in connection with any of the functional application modules. Some of the main CA components are as follows:

- *SAP Business Workflow.* A workflow automation system that allows the integration of transactions across different SAP applications. This is a very powerful tool that SAP is going to promote and enhance further, as we are currently seeing with the deployment of Web Workflow–based standards.
- *Data Archiving and SAP ArchiveLink.* Components that enable the archiving to other devices of historical data, as well as providing an interface to optical and physical systems archiving important input or output documents or print lists. SAP systems include the Archive Development Kit (ADK), which is a collection of specific function modules that allow customers to develop archiving objects and methods for archiving their own customer objects.
- *SAP Business Workplace (formerly SAPoffice).* Formerly an integrated mail and office system, and currently an environment for the communication processes within and beyond the enterprise. This system allows message exchanges within the SAP system and to and from outside mail systems. The folder system allows the integration of internal SAP and PC documents. The messaging features extend beyond the mail capabilities, allowing integration and processing with other business applications. For instance, a message might have a transaction associated with it, which can be triggered when a user processes a message.

Other cross-application tools or components that can be used in many different SAP modules are CAD integration, document management system (DMS), classification guide, characteristics guide, Application Link Enabled (ALE) technology, EDI, and external system communication interfaces.

The implementation tools including SAP customizing are also considered CA modules because they are overall activities of SAP R/3 projects.

SAP Services Overview

Since the start of the boom of SAP R/3, SAP put in place a comprehensive set of quality services to help customers during the process of implementing and supporting their SAP solutions, and they are in constant evolution and improvement.

These services include product information, education services, installation and upgrade services, consulting, and more. All this can be found in the *SAP Service Marketplace* (http://service.sap.com).

SAP bases its support services mainly on remote connections with customers through the international networks.

Administrators, support personnel, and consultants should be particularly familiar with the former SAP *Online Service System* (OSS), now known as SAPnet-R/3 front end, which is now accessible through the Web using the SAP Service Marketplace and which is the primary source of service and support.

SAP offers a certification process in the technical, functional, and developing areas of the system and an extensive number of training courses worldwide.

SAP provides many types of services:

- *Consulting services.* This type of individualized consulting can be given on-site or via a remote connection to SAP. With remote consulting, customers receive immediate and updated technical support and answers to their questions. SAP also gives weekend support when upgrades or installations are done outside regular working hours.

  Customers open the connection so SAP consultants may directly access their systems and evaluate the problems online. Once the consulting session is finished, the customer closes the connection.

- *Maintenance services.* This is the basic and most common type of support for customers in the preproduction and production phases of a SAP Solution implementation. This service deals with answering questions and helping to resolve the errors or problems with the system.

  For maintenance, SAP has set up a *helpdesk,* or *hotline,* which monitors the calls and resolves them or directs them to the appropriate SAP expert, and a *first-level customer service team,* which is in charge of resolving the problems, prioritizing the calls, and, if needed, referring questions to other experts. Customers obtain this service via phone, fax, the SAP Service Marketplace, or the SAPnet-R/3 front end. It is available 24 hours a day, 7 days a week. For example, if you have a severe problem at 5 A.M., log it in on the SAPnet-R/3 front end, give it a "very high" priority (meaning "my system does not work"), and you might expect a fast call back from Japan, Philadelphia, or Walldorf, Germany.

- *Preventive services.* The primary one was the EarlyWatch service, which ensured successful and efficient installation of the SAP solutions in all phases. This service makes regular (usually once a month) performance checks and analyzes the system to identify potential problems and help system managers and SAP administrators tune the system and realize its full potential. Soon after an EarlyWatch session, SAP sends the customer a report with the results of the analysis and recommendations for avoiding potential problems, such as database tablespaces becoming full, shortage of system parameters, and buffer tuning. In 1999, SAP launched the *EarlyWatch Alert* mechanism, which proactively monitors the core technical indicators in the systems and sends that information to the SAP network, as well as provides administrators with significant alerts in case of problem discovery. SAP has been constantly evolving its role in the preventive service area for customer self-service, and part of that strategy is the deployment of the SAP Solutions Manager. (Refer to Chapters 9 and 10.)

- SAP provides additional services, such as the development request service, which submits enhancement requests, and the first customer shipment (FCS), now *Ramp up programs,* which gives selected customers the opportunity to test new SAP solutions and releases functionality before the products are officially released.

In the search for total customer services solution, SAP has also designed a comprehensive Service Map that gathers the requirements for a full life cycle of services, including evaluation, implementation, and continuous improvement phases for each of the identified key customer processes:

- Management activities
- Business processes
- Technical management
- Development activities
- Knowledge transfer
- Hosting
- Help and care

For each of these processes and phases, SAP and its partners have an extensive portfolio of services. Updated information and service maps can be found at www.sap.com/service.

Online Services: The SAP Service Marketplace

As stated previously, SAP has made online services through remote connections its preferred and most convenient way to support customers. For this reason, obtaining a network connection to SAP became critical in any SAP project.

SAP has built a worldwide network of support servers for customers to use to obtain the support they need for successful implementation and operation of their SAP systems. Customers can also download patches and upgrades from those servers via *ftp* (a file transfer protocol very common in TCP/IP networks), and directly from their Web site at service.sap.com.

SAP also offers extensive information and correction services for customers and partners through the Internet by means of the SAP Service Marketplace, which gathers all and more of the facilities previously found on the Online Service Systems (OSS) but with much more content.

However, customers will still need a remote connection to SAP for certain services, like EarlyWatch, Telnet, remote upgrade, and others.

The only thing customers need in order to gain access to these servers is a remote connection to the nearest support server. Currently, SAP has support servers in Walldorf, Foster City, Tokyo, Sydney, and Singapore.

This is the connection that you use for the OSS, EarlyWatch, and remote consulting. It is the only way that you can permit the SAP experts to log on to your system and solve problems online. Imagine the costs saved in travel. Currently this connection can be easily established using the SNC (Secure Network Communication) protocol and digital certificates.

SAPnet-R/3 Front End (OSS)

The SAPnet-R/3 front end (formerly known as OSS or Online Service System) is nothing more (and nothing less) than an SAP system that customers with remote connections to SAP support servers can use free of cost.

NOTE *All this functionality can now be found and deployed directly from the SAP Service Marketplace (service.sap.com).*

This is a brief list of what is available at the SAPnet-R/3 front end system:

- Problem and information database (SAP notes), so that users can try to find the solution to their problems before they call SAP or send it a problem report. Looking and reading notes is a great way to learn tidbits about SAP solutions.
- Latest SAP news in the HotNews section.
- Up-to-date release, installation, and upgrade information. To have these very latest notes is a mandatory step in any installation or upgrade procedure of SAP systems.
- Online problem registry. Problems or questions are treated the same way (and sometimes better) and with the same priority as they are when registered by telephone.
- Training offerings and course descriptions. These have just recently been included.
- Access to the SSCR (SAP Software Change Registration), where customers can register developers and SAP repository objects and get the keys required to continue development.
- Downloadable Support Packages (formerly Hot Packages) for correcting system and program errors.
- Registration of Knowledge Products CDs.
- Downloadable installation or migration keys.
- Registration of customer systems and request SAP licenses.
- Definition and management of service connections.
- Display of EarlyWatch Alert reports.
- Manager user accounts for accessing the system.

SAPnet-R/3 front end has been for years the star service system provided by SAP and the most widely used by SAP customers and partners, especially consultants and administrators. The SAPnet-R/3 front end interface is intuitive and a very easy system to learn and use. SAP provides initial user accounts for accessing the SAP Service Markeplace or the SAPnet. Customers can create and maintain additional user accounts from within the SAPnet-R/3 front end.

EarlyWatch and EarlyWatch Alert

EarlyWatch is an SAP offering for preventive services, providing proactive diagnosis and analysis online. Through the connection, an SAP expert accesses the customer system and obtains all the information needed for preparing a report that is later sent to the customer.

SAP is used to provide a free session before customer systems go into a productive stage. Subsequent sessions must be separately contracted.

Overview: Alert Messages

The following table contains an overview of all alerts.

Rating	Performed Check
⚠	Software Configuration
⊗	Performance Overview
✔	License Audit Correction
✔	Update Errors
✔	Number of Jobs in the Spool
⚠	Program Errors (ABAP Dumps)
⚠	Table Reorganization
✔	DB Load Profile
✔	Hardware Capacity
⚠	Database server load from expensive SQL statements
⊗	Expensive SQL Statements
✔	Missing Indexes
✔	Database Growth

Priority	Description	New Alert
High	At least one ABAP dump of type 'SAPSQL_ARRAY_INSERT_DUPREC' was found.	New
High	Performance problems exist or are expected.	
Medium	Some expensive statements were found.	
Medium	Update your SAP R/3 Plug-In to the latest release available.	

FIGURE 1-15 Sample EarlyWatch Alert report page (Copyright by SAP AG)

The first thing revealed in the EarlyWatch report is a summary diagnosis indicating the problem's level of severity found in the system. This diagnosis might indicate that most parameters are well tuned and that systems are running fine, or it might say that there are some problems, which can be either normal or critical—in which case, customers should solve them as soon as possible.

The checkups done by the EarlyWatch service include detecting potential problems in the SAP applications, as well as in the database and operating system. The service provides information, for example, about tablespaces getting full, SAP system log error messages, buffer tuning, and database parameters.

SAP systems have hundreds of parameters, with many of them directly affecting other values. The EarlyWatch team analyzes the past week's evolution of the system, and if it detects bottlenecks or an increase in processing times, it usually recommends new values for the profile parameters.

With the EarlyWatch Alert system, the customer systems are automatically monitored and the data sent to SAP and collected locally or within the SAP Solution Manager. Refer to Chapter 10, which discusses troubleshooting, for more information about SAP Solution Manager and the EarlyWatch Alert. Figure 1-15 includes a sample of one of the initial pages of the EarlyWatch Alert report.

CHAPTER 2

The Architecture of the SAP Web Application Server

This chapter explains the SAP kernel and how it evolved and prepared for the Web: from the traditional SAP Basis and the client/server architecture to the Internet Business Framework and then up to the current SAP Web Application Servers.

The SAP kernel is a component of the SAP Web Application Server that executes applications and manages user processes by distributing tasks to work processes. The kernel also manages memory, manages database access, and manages communication with other applications in addition to being the interface between the operating system and SAP applications.

The SAP Basis system, up to release 4.6C, provided a runtime environment for running ABAP programs and applications, whereas with the SAP Web Application Server, the system includes also a J2EE environment, known as the SAP J2EE Engine, which allows one to run Java programs based on J2EE and thus supports Web services and Web applications that support the Java development environment.

It must be noted that with SAP R/34.7, also known as SAP R/3 Enterprise Release 4.7 (the successor to release SAP R/3 4.6C), and other SAP Solutions, which are mostly based on the SAP Web Application Server, the J2EE engine can be optionally installed and configured. For several of the SAP Solutions you can decide whether you want the ABAP runtime alone, the J2EE, or both. Of course, any SAP Solution based on ABAP based applications will always need the ABAP engine. SAP Web AS forms the Application Platform of SAP NetWeaver. SAP NetWeaver is the Web-based platform that is the foundation for Enterprise Services Architecture (ESA).

What was normally known as SAP Basis has been expanded so much in recent years to support multiple SAP solutions and components. After SAP Basis release 4.6C, the new name has become the SAP Web Application Server.

This second chapter is meant for explaining the technological foundation of the mySAP.com strategy. It first deals with SAP's Business Framework Architecture, present in previous SAP releases, like ALE, BAPIs, and ITS, and how from the "componentization" and "openness," SAP has built on to a new generation of openness and integration by means of Web technology and Web standards, including HTML/HTTP, LDAP, XML, and Web Services (WSDL), which is the real basis of ESA from SAP Web AS 6.40 onward. SAP's Internet Business Framework is the open architecture that enables arrangement of modularized components into an integrated functional package and provides the collaboration technology for building a solid Web application infrastructure at all levels (presentation, application, data).

The second part of this chapter is meant for describing and introducing some of the features that users and system managers will find within mySAP.com components. It briefly discusses the user interface and some of its options. For system managers, the chapter includes a basic explanation of classical technology and system admin topics such as the transport system, printing system, CCMS, administration topics in the mySAP.com age and others.

The SAP Web Application Server

SAP Web AS is the logical result of further development of the SAP Application Server Technology (formerly also known as SAP Basis), with particular attention being paid to Web-based applications.

SAP Web Application Server offers the following:

- A reliable and thoroughly tested runtime environment, evolved over more than 10 years.
- A framework for executing complex business processes that meets the highest security standards.
- A reliable and user-friendly development environment. Using the SAP Web AS allows for rapid development of Internet applications such as portals/online stores. The applications are displayed using Business Server Pages (BSPs).
- Support for open technical standards, such as HTTP, HTTPS, SMTP, WebDAV, SOAP, SSL, SSO, X.509, Unicode, HTML, XML, and WML and WSDL from SAP Web AS 6.40.
- High scalability, inherited from SAP Basis.
- Support for various operating systems and database and OS independent systems.

Several SAP Web Application Servers can run on one application server. Before we discuss various client/server configurations in the context of SAP systems, we first need to define the concepts client and server.

There are basically two ways of doing this:

- In the *hardware-oriented* view, the term *server* (service provider; back end) means the central server in a network that provides data, memory, and resources for the workstations (clients).
- In the *software-oriented* view, client and server are both defined at the process level (service). A service in this context is a service provided by a software component. This software component can consist of a process (such as a work process) or a group of processes (such as a SAP Web Application Server) and is then called a server for that service. In the SAP system the SAP GUI front ends are the clients, and the application servers are the servers. Software components that use this service are called clients. At the same time, clients can also be servers for other specific services. For the database the application servers behave as clients.

SAP R/3 up to 4.6C: The Basis Software

Up to SAP R/3 release 4.6C, that is, right before R/3 Enterprise, the R/3 *Basis software* is the set of programs and tools that interfaces with the computer operating system, the underlying database, the communication protocols, and the presentation interfaces. This software enables the R/3 applications (FI, CO, SD, etc.) to have the same functionality and work exactly the same way no matter what operating system or database the system is installed on. The R/3 basis software is an independent layer that guarantees the integration of all application modules.

When referring to the basis software in this sense, it was generally known as the R/3 *common kernel* or even the R/3 *middleware.* Kernel and middleware have become generic computing terms that are widely used: *kernel* usually refers to the core or nucleus of a system; *middleware* means a set of programs that allows an independent interface between an upper layer and a lower layer (it stands in the *middle*).

Often these terms are also referred to as the R/3 *basis system* or simply R/3 *basis,* both of which have a broader meaning. Besides the interfaces with the other system elements such as the operating system, database, network, and user interface, the tools and components of R/3 Basis provide the following:

- The environment for the applications that are built based on the ABAP development workbench and the ABAP repository, which includes the ABAP data dictionary (centralized logical repository with all the business and system data). This environment is closely linked to the transport system and transport organizer to facilitate the modification and enhancement of the system and the integration of new developments across SAP systems within a SAP system group.
- System administration and monitoring tools, including a common printing system and a complex and comprehensive set of management transactions within the CCMS (computer center management system), which is used to monitor, tune, and control the SAP R/3 systems.
- Architectural software client/server design, which permits system growth both vertically and horizontally and allows the distribution of available resources.
- Authorization and profile management tools, which take care of user management and internal access control to system and business objects.
- Database monitoring and administration utilities.
- Support for Internet protocols and server-side scripting in ABAP and JavaScript, enabling easy building of online stores and portals using Business Server Pages (BSPs).

These SAP R/3 basis topics are covered in greater detail in the following chapters. The following sections in this chapter discuss the central interfaces and the client/server architecture, which is still the technological foundation for the SAP Web Application Server.

The SAP R/3 middleware uses common APIs (application program interfaces) and has the function of interfacing with the underlying operating system, the database, the communication protocols, and the graphical user interfaces (GUIs). The features of the SAP R/3 basis system that enable these types of interfaces are as follows:

- The client/server architecture and configuration
- The use of relational database management systems
- Graphical user interface design for presentation

The Web AS system is based on standards: ANSI-C and C for the programming of the runtime environment, Open SQL for embedded SQL calls inside ABAP for interfacing with the database, communication standards such as TCP/IP, and standard graphical interfaces such as Microsoft Windows.

Basic Architectural Concepts

The SAP R/3 system uses some widely known terms to which SAP gives specific meanings. This section includes some of those terms, needed for a clear understanding of the architecture of SAP Basis, now the SAP Web Application Server.

Transaction

Generally, a *transaction* is an operation that lets a user make changes to a database. The overall SAP R/3 system must be seen as a business transaction processing system. This means that the whole data flow that runs across application modules is executed using transactions.

In the SAP systems, a transaction is a sequence of related steps. These logically related steps, known as *dialog steps,* are screens in which data are introduced, causing the generation of other events. There is a special transaction monitor, the *SAP dispatcher,* which takes care of handling the sequence of those steps.

The final task of a transaction is to modify the information that ultimately goes into the database. The database is not updated until a transaction has finished. For the sake of consistency, if the transaction has not finished, all changes are still reversible.

The transactions usually contain two phases: an interactive phase and an update phase. The interactive phase may be at least one step, but can have many. This phase is responsible for preparing the database records that can update the database. The update phase may have no steps or many. This phase processes the previously prepared records and updates the database.

Many users have the ability to access the same information, so, in order for the transactions to be consistent, there is a lock mechanism engaged during the time it takes to process the transaction.

All the transactions in the SAP R/3 systems have an associated *transaction code.* A fast and useful way to move around the SAP R/3 system is by typing the transaction code directly in the command field of a SAP R/3 window. The available transaction codes are held in table TSTC. To see this table, from the main screen menu, select the following options from the SAP standard menu: Tools | ABAP Workbench | _Development | Other Tools | Transactions. Or, type SE93 in the command field. Then press F4 or click on the possible list arrow (the small icon to the right of the field) and just click the enter icon in the dialog box, or input wildcards (for example, S*, Z*, etc.) in the Transaction code field. Note that by default the number of entries to be shown is limited to 200.

Chapter 4 deals with the basics of using and moving around the SAP R/3 system both with menu options and with transaction codes. A fast way to specify table entries is by using transaction *SE16* (Data Browser) and entering the table name in the input field.

Dialog Step

A *dialog step* is a SAP R/3 screen that is represented by a dynpro. A *dynpro,* or *dynamic program,* consists of a screen and all the associated processing logic. It contains field definitions, screen layout, validation and processing logic, and so forth. A dialog step is controlled exactly by a dynpro.

The processing logic means that the dynpro controls what has to be done before the screen is displayed (process before output or PBO) and what has to be done after the user finishes entering information (Process After Input or PAI).

When users are navigating in the SAP R/3 system from screen to screen, they are actually making dialog steps. A set of dialog steps makes up a transaction.

Logical Units of Work (LUWs)

Conceptually, a *logical unit of work* (LUW) is defined as an elementary processing step that works as a locking mechanism to protect the transaction's integrity. A LUW is a set of dialog steps within a transaction, and all of those steps must be correctly completed to go ahead with the transaction logic. If there are errors before the end of the transactions, the current LUW is canceled, but not the previous ones.

Within the SAP system, three conceptually different types of transactions may be distinguished:

- A database transaction, known as LUW or database LUW, is the period of time in which the operations requested must be performed as a unit. This is known in the database world as an *all or nothing* operation. At the end of the LUW, either the database changes are committed (performed) or they are rolled back (thrown away). As you can see in Figure 2-1, there are four database transactions (database LUWs) corresponding to the period of time from the beginning of a new database operation to the DB-commit operation.
- An update transaction or SAP LUW is the equivalent to the database concept for the SAP systems. It means that as a logical unit, these SAP LUWs are either executed completely or not at all. Generally, a SAP LUW can have several database LUWs. The special OpenSQL command, COMMIT WORK, marks the end of a SAP LUW and the beginning of a new one. In Figure 2-1, the SAP transaction or SAP LUW comprises all the database operations until the COMMIT WORK statement; in this case, it is made up of four database LUWs.

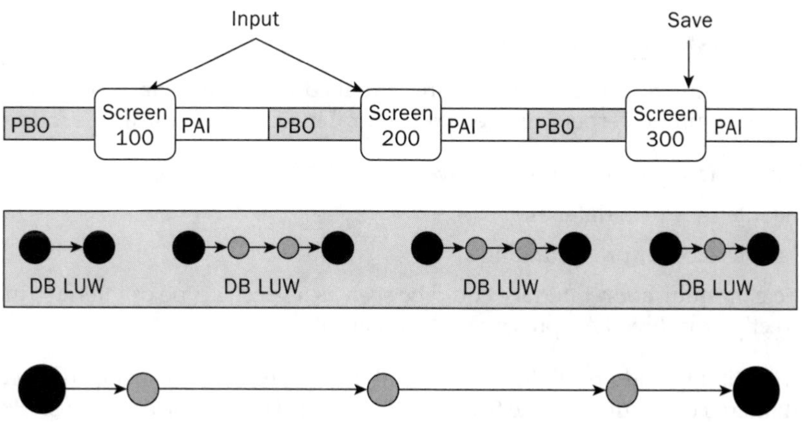

FIGURE 2-1 Example of SAP LUWs

- A SAP transaction or ABAP transaction is made up of a set of related tasks combined under one transaction code. This concept is related more to the programming environment, in which an ABAP or SAP transaction functions like a complex object containing screens, menus, programming logic, transaction code, and so forth.

Clients

A *client* is defined as a legally and organizationally independent unit within the SAP Web AS or SAP R/3 system, for example, a company group, a business unit, or a corporation. Client records are stored in common tables. The MAND T field distinguishes records for particular clients.

At the beginning of the SAP Web AS technical phase of the implementation, right after installation of the software, one of the first things that usually must be done is to copy one of the standard clients included in the package.

With the copied clients, customers can make tests, can use them for training, or can start real customization.

SAP comes with three standard clients: 000, 001, and 066. Client 000 contains a simple organizational structure of a test company and includes parameters for all applications, standard settings, configurations for the control of standard transactions, and examples to be used in many different profiles of the business applications. For these reasons, 000 is a special client for the R/3 system because it contains the client-independent settings.

Client 001 is a copy of the 000 client, including the test company; if this client is configured or customized, its settings are client dependent. It does not behave like 000. It is reserved for the activities of preparing a system for the production environment. SAP customers usually use this client as a source for copying other new clients. Client 066 is reserved for SAP access to its customers' systems to perform the EarlyWatch service that enables SAP to open a diagnostic service with clients.

The SAP systems include tools for creating, copying, transferring, resetting, deleting, and comparing clients. When the loads of individual clients differ, the buffer manager of the application service is able to respond and allocate resources appropriately. As shown in Figure 2-2, the client is the first field when logging on to the system.

The System Central Interfaces

In this section the main system interfaces are described in greater detail. The R/3 middleware or common kernel is made up of central interfaces. These are as follows:

- The interface with the operating system.
- The interface with database.
- The interface for presentation.
- The communication interface could be seen as a special type of interface that directly or indirectly is present in the other three types.

For compatibility and portability reasons, all these interfaces are grouped together in the central interface functions of the SAP system kernel. The interfaces in the SAP system are a group of software programs running as daemon processes in the UNIX operating system or as services on Windows NT, which is a background process.

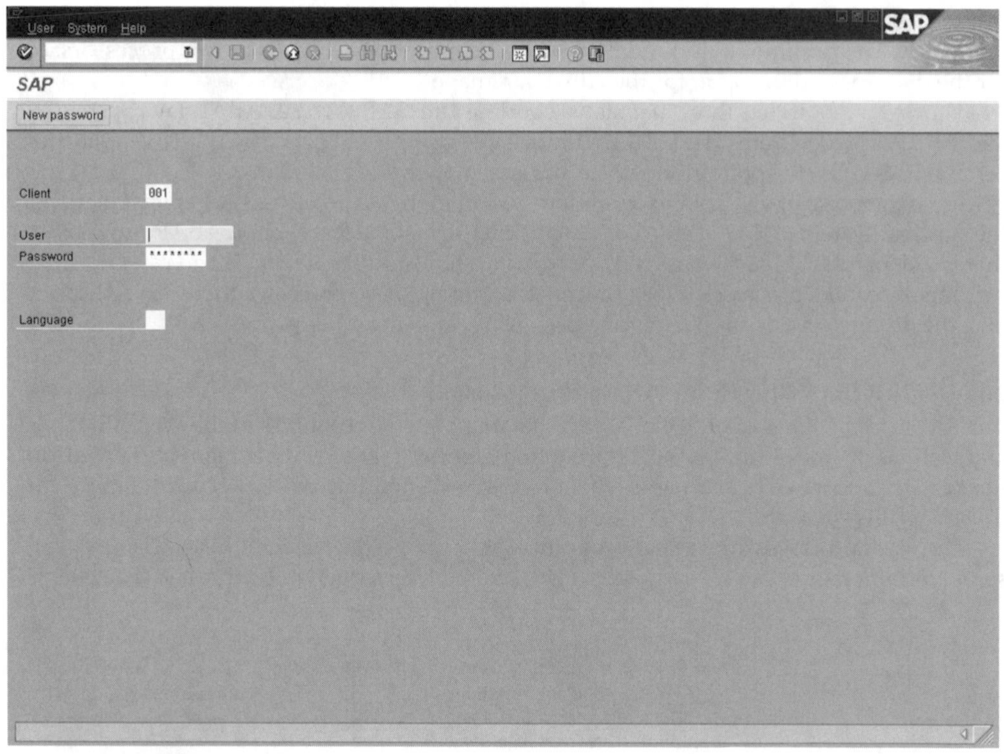

FIGURE 2-2 Logon screen with client field (Copyright by SAP AG)

Operating System Interface

One of the main tasks of the basis system is to guarantee the portability of the whole system. That is done using an internal SAP portability layer.

This layer offers to the applications the nearest services to the system, such as message handling and memory management, independently of the platform and optimized for performance. The inherent openness of R/3 makes it run over different operating systems, which have to be Portable Operating System Interface (POSIX) standard–compliant. For a list of supported technical and platform environments for a specific SAP release, refer to service.sap.com/pam (Product Availability Matrix section).

The mission of the system interfaces is to provide services such as scheduling, memory management, and similar tasks, which could be partially done by the operating system software, but SAP executes them internally for performance and portability reasons.

The SAP systems runtime environment, commonly known as the kernel, is written in ANSI-C or C++, but all application programs inside R/3 are written in the interpreted programming language ABAP developed by SAP. Currently, with the SAP Web Application Server, there are other options, such as Java, which will be covered later in this chapter.

In ABAP transactions (Java or BSPs), the components in charge of controlling the user dialogs are the dynpros (dynamic programs). The technology base for the R/3 applications is made up of the interrelation of the dynpro interpreters and the ABAP language. For their tasks, both use the global image of the data environment of R/3, which is held on the ABAP dictionary. The runtime environment of the R/3 applications consists of two processors: one for the dynpros and the other for the ABAP language.

The SAP Web AS has three installation options, the SAP Web AS ABAP, Java System, and ABAP + Java System. The J2EE engine is a key component of the SAP Web Application Sever. The SAP Web Application Server implements the J2EE Standards.

From the point of view of the operating system in the SAP Web AS ABAP installations, the runtime system of SAP Web AS is a platform (virtual machine) of an ABAP program that is independent of hardware, the operating system, and the database and can be seen as a group of parallel processes (work processes). Among these processes there is a special one, the dispatcher, which controls and assigns tasks to the other processes.

The Dispatcher Process

The SAP *dispatcher* is the control program that manages the resources of the Web AS applications. It works like a typical transaction monitor that receives screens and data from the presentation services and passes them to the corresponding work processes. Figure 2-3 illustrates this concept.

The work processes are special programs in charge of some specific tasks. Using client/server terminology, a *work process* is a service offered by a server and requested by a client.

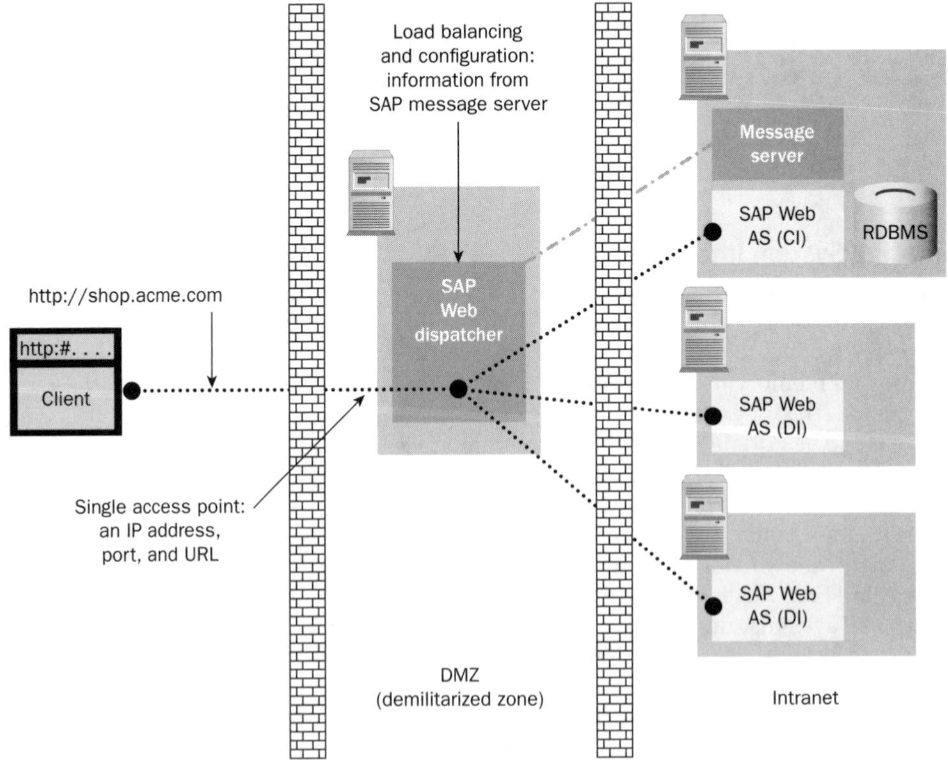

FIGURE 2-3 SAP dispatcher process

The dispatcher manages the information exchange between the SAP GUIs or other type of presentation interface and the work processes, enabling users to share the different work processes available.

The main tasks of the dispatcher are as follows:

- Balanced assignment of the transaction load to the work processes
- Connection with the presentation level
- Organization of the communication processes

The logical flow of execution of a user request follows:

1. Users enter data in their presentation server; the data are received by the SAP GUI, converted to a SAP format, and sent to the dispatcher using a special optimized protocol called DIAG. The DIAG protocol is also used for ITS-driven applications.
2. Initially, the dispatcher keeps the requests in queues, where the dispatcher later processes them one by one.
3. The dispatcher allocates the user requests using the free work processes. The real execution takes place inside the work processes themselves.
4. At the end of execution, the result of the work process task goes back to the SAP GUI through the dispatcher. SAP GUI interprets the received data and fills up the user screen.

SAP has optimized the data flow between the presentation and the application servers. Before release 4.6 and the enjoySAP GUI interface, typically the quantity of data that went in the network from the dispatcher to the SAP GUI did not exceed 2K (for dialog processes). However, this has been largely increased with later releases, although the communication technology has also decreased the impact. This network traffic does not include the print requests that are managed by spool or print managers on users' PCs or workstations.

The communication is established via standard TCP/IP sockets. The dispatcher has a special *advanced program-to-program communication* (APPC) server built into it that communicates and responds to requests submitted by the work processes. On each application server there is one dispatcher but multiple work processes.

NOTE *If an application server (hardware point of view) is running more than one SAP instance (application server, from a software point of view), there is one dispatcher for every instance.*

Work Process Architecture

A work process is a program in charge of executing the Web AS application tasks. Each work process acts as a specialized system service. From the point of view of the operating system, a group of parallel work processes makes up the SAP Web AS ABAP runtime system.

As shown in Figure 2-4, a work process consists of a task handler, a dialog or dynpro processor, an ABAP interpreter, and a database interface. The work processes execute dialog steps for the end users. These steps generally relate to the processing or display of a single screen, which means that right after one work process finishes the execution of a dialog step for a user session, it is immediately available for use by another user session.

For its processing, each dialog step needs code, dictionary objects, and data. These elements may come from the database server or from the memory buffers that reside on the

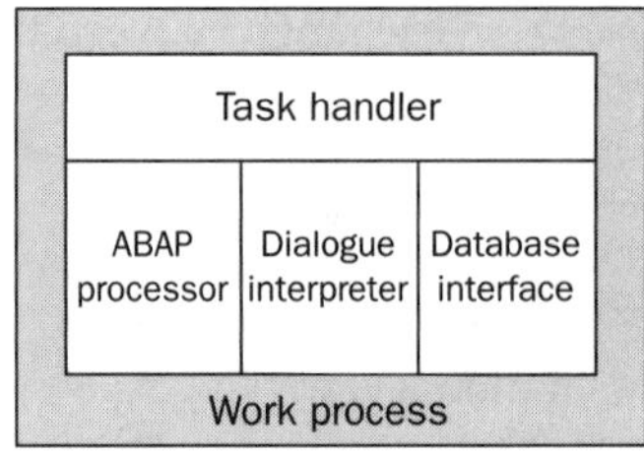

FIGURE 2-4 Work process architecture

application server. The dialog processes usually request read-only information from the database and rely on other types of work processes for read-write information. This is explained in the following sections.

The activities within a work process are coordinated by the task handler. It manages the loading and unloading of the user session context at the beginning and end of each dialog step. It also communicates with the dispatcher and activates the dynpro interpreter processor or the ABAP interpreter as required to perform its tasks. The ABAP processor is in charge of executing the ABAP programs, whereas the dialog interpreter (also known as the dynpro interpreter) is in charge of interpreting and executing the logic of SAP screens. The database interface allows the work processes to establish direct links with the database.

The work processes might need the same data for more than one dialog step, in which case the data are held in shared memory areas (buffers) and are available for other work processes. It must be noted that users of the same or similar Web AS business applications, such as FI (financial accounting) and CO (controlling), logging in to the same application servers will benefit from this feature because they often access the same tables. If these tables already reside in the buffer areas, the system doesn't have to go to the database to get them, and thus performance will be improved.

Work processes make use of two special memory attributes: paging and roll. The *paging area* holds application program data such as internal tables or report listings for the current session. The *roll area* holds the user context data entered in previous dialog steps and other control and user information such as authorizations.

Where there is main memory available, these areas are held in the main memory of application servers; otherwise they are *paged out* or *rolled out* to physical disk files. The size of these areas is configurable using SAP system profile parameters.

The system shared memory areas also contain read-only images of other parts of the Web AS system, such as the program or table buffers. The sizing and configuration of these buffers are very important for overall performance of the system. The configuration and refresh rate of these caches are critical to the overall performance of the system.

To make a more efficient use of available resources, work processes are run in parallel, which makes this architecture especially suitable for multiprocessor equipment and able to run the group of work processes distributed among different CPUs.

The number of available work processes per application server is configurable using the appropriate SAP system profile parameters. The following sections include examples of such parameters. For more information about profiles, refer to the section entitled "Instances Profiles" in Chapter 3.

There are several types of work processes: dialog, background, update, enqueue, and spool. Additionally, the Web AS runtime system includes three other special types of services: message service, gateway, and the system log collector.

Because the work processes are in charge of executing the ABAP programs and applications, a group made of a dispatcher and a set of work processes is known as the *application server.*

Services: Work Processes Types

Every work process is specialized in a particular task type: dialog, background, update, enqueue, spool, message, or gateway. The last two types are somewhat different than the rest. In client/server terms, a work process is a *service,* and the computing system that is running the particular services is known as a *server.* For example, if the system is just providing dialog services, this is a *dialog server,* although commonly called an *application server.*

The dispatcher assigns tasks to the free work processes, making optimal use of system resources and balancing the system load. The dispatcher knows and distributes accordingly the pending tasks according to the processing type of the defined processes. The work process definitions are instance specific. The difference among the various work processes only affects their mission or special services as assigned to the work processes through the dispatching strategy. Figure 2-5 shows the work processes from within R/3. To get to this screen, select Tools | Administration | Monitor | System Monitoring | _Process Overview, or type /NSM50 in the command field.

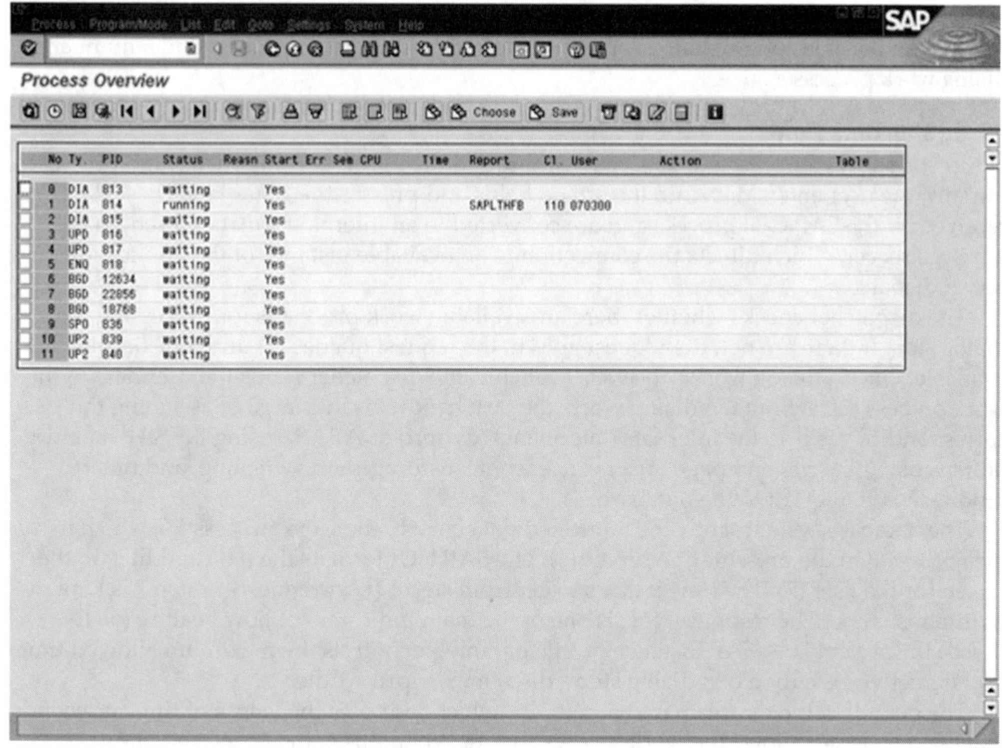

FIGURE 2-5 Displaying work process within Web AS (Copyright by SAP AG)

Dialog Work Processes

The dialog work processes are in charge of the interactive tasks of the R/3 system. A dialog work process performs the dialog steps corresponding to the interactive user sessions. The jobs held by the dispatcher in the request queues after user input are assigned to the next free work process. The dialog work processes execute just one single dialog step at a time and become immediately free for the next user request (dialog step), which is assigned by the dispatcher. This is called work process multiplexing. This means that the dialog work processes can be constantly switching between different user sessions. This type of processing allows a great deal of resource distribution; otherwise the system would need as many dialog work processes as the number of expected interactive users. It works exactly the same as multiuser operating systems.

The SAP profile parameter that controls the number of interactive dialog work processes per instance is rdisp/wp_no_dia. Chapter 3 explains with greater detail the profile parameters.

Depending on the type of business transactions the users are working on, a dialog work process can support from 5 to more than 10 simultaneous users each. This means that 10 dialog work processes could theoretically support approximately 100 users. However, this is just a rule of thumb. *Tuning* this parameter means that if users have to wait long to get a free work process, you should increase the parameter. This, however, has some limitations, such as the total number of processes running on the server and the availability of main memory.

When there are a large number of concurrent interactive users expected in a SAP Web AS system, there will certainly be a number of application servers. Some of these application servers can become special dialog servers, containing a dispatcher process and a number of dialog work processes.

Dialog Step Data Flow

Figure 2-6 shows the flow of a user request through the different components and processes. Initially, the user enters data into the screen fields and presses the Enter key. These data are received by the SAP GUI process and are converted to an internal format and sent to the Message server, which directs the connection to an available instance of the application server dispatcher (1).

The dispatcher checks whether there are available work processes for processing the dialog step. If there are not, the request goes to the request queues (2) until one becomes available. Once a dialog work process is available, the dispatcher sends the user data to the work process (3). Within the dialog work, the task handler is in charge of assigning the corresponding tasks to the internal components (dynpro or ABAP), using the SAP memory buffers, using the roll and page area for user context storage and switching, and finally sending a SQL request to the database (4).

The database system sends the requested data back to the work process (5), which in turn passes it to the presentation server (6). The SAP GUI formats the data and fills up the screen for the user (7). The time it takes to get from step 1 (user request) to step 7 is known as response time. The response time is one of the main indicators of how healthy (well-tuned) the system is. A SAP instance profile parameter controls the maximum allowed time for interactive execution of a dialog step: rdisp/max_wprun_time

The default value for this parameter is 300, which indicates the length of time in seconds that the dispatcher allows the work process to run. When this value is reached, the dispatcher stops the work process and the user gets a TIME_OUT error.

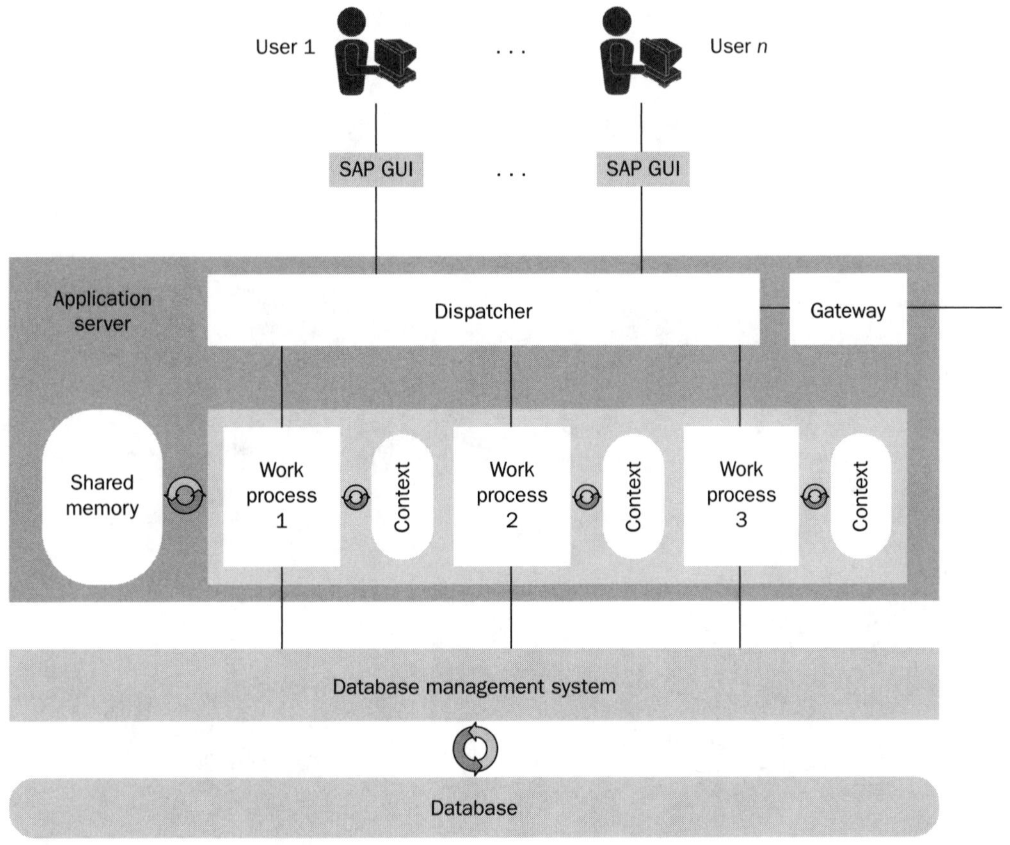

FIGURE 2-6 Data flow in dialog steps

Background Work Processes

The background work processes are in charge of executing ABAP programs submitted for background execution. Large background processes are best suited for periods when the system isn't used interactively such as in the evenings. Figure 2-7 shows a simple scheme of an application server which includes background work processes. From an administrative point of view, the background work processes correspond to the batch jobs queues. The ABAP programs submitted for background processing are executed in the planned time by the background work processes. The sequence of program execution is scheduled with *batch jobs.*

Every job can be made of one or several steps that are consecutively processed. A *step* is an ABAP program or an external program. There are many types of jobs and different ways to submit them for execution. Normally, these background jobs are not immediately processed but are processed when the system reaches the planned time for execution if there are available resources.

Background processing is very useful for submitting programs requiring long processing times, because interactive execution would exceed the allowed processing time

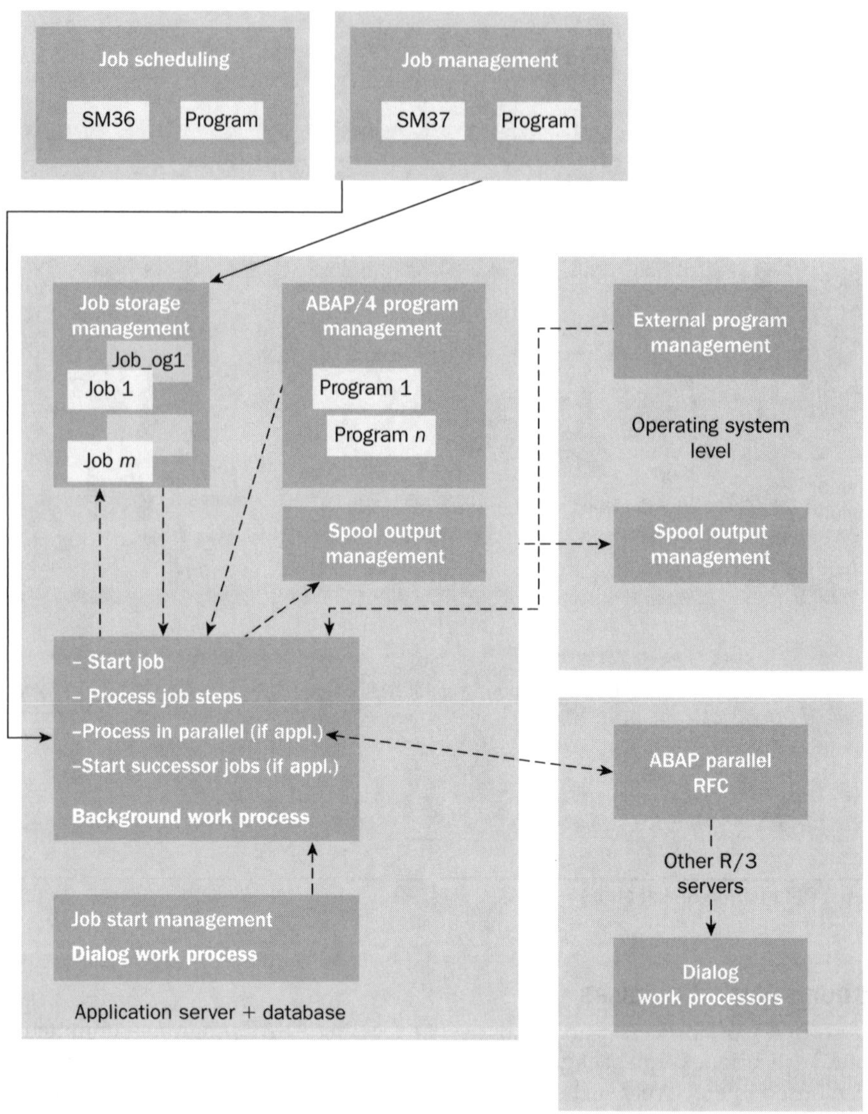

FIGURE 2-7 Application server with background work process

(rdisp/max_wprun_time) and thus abort with a TIME_OUT error, as indicated in the previous section.

There is a batch scheduler that takes care of initiating the jobs at the specified time. The system allows for periodic jobs' execution. This means that programs are submitted with a repetition interval, and when the jobs execute themselves, the first thing they do is plan a new execution time at the required interval. This feature is very useful for control or cleaning jobs within Web AS.

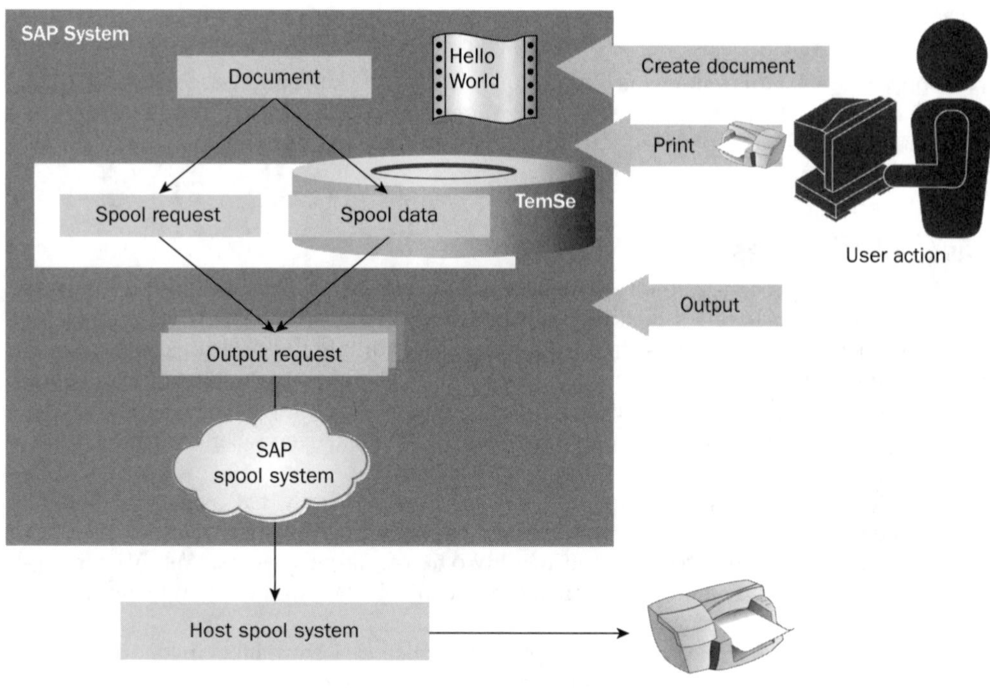

FIGURE 2-8 Spool work process

The SAP profile parameter that controls the number of background work processes per instance is rdisp/wp_no_btc.

The background process can be further organized into different types of job queues based on the priorities needed in the particular installation. Background jobs are very important in the daily management and operation of the system.

In Chapter 11 you will learn how the dialog and background work processes can be automatically switched with the use of operation modes.

Spool Work Process

The spool work process is in charge of formatting the data for printing and passing it to the host spool system. Figure 2-8 includes a simple scheme of a SAP instance with a spool work process. The spool requests, indicating the printer and the printing format of the spool request, are generated during dialog or background processing and are held on the spool database. The data themselves are kept in a special area, known as TemSe (temporal sequential objects), which is additional SAP Web data that is stored temporarily. There is a profile parameter *rspo/store_location* that controls where the *TemSe* stores the Web AS spool data. It can be either on the database or on a file. When the data are to be printed for the spool job, an output request is generated, which is executed by the spool work process. Once the spool work process has edited the data for printing, it sends a print request to the operating system host spool.

The SAP profile parameter that controls the number of spool work processes per instance is rdisp/wp_no_spo.

Before release 4.0 this value was limited to one spool work process per SAP instance, although there was the possibility of installing more than one instance per host and getting more than one spool work process. That restriction does not exist anymore with release 4.0 and newer releases.

Enqueue Work Process

The enqueue work process, also known as the lock work process because it has direct access to the lock table, is in charge of the lock management system. It allows multiple application servers to synchronize their access to the database and maintain the data consistency. In order for the system to run in a consistent manner, it must ensure that when a transaction's dialog steps are handled by different work processes, they retain the assigned locks until the end of the transaction or the intentional release of the lock, even when switching work processes.

Commonly there is only one enqueue work process for a single SAP system; however, there are circumstances where, for performance reasons, it might be useful to configure up to four enqueue work processes for a setting of two to four large systems. Web AS note 127773 contains details. The profile parameter that controls the number of enqueue work processes is rdisp/wp_no_enq.

The function of this work process is to protect applications from blocking among themselves during data access. For that reason, a locking/unlocking mechanism must be present. This is the function of the enqueue work process.

The locks (enqueues) are managed by the enqueue work process using a lock table that resides in the main memory. When the processes receive a locking request, the enqueue work process verifies whether the requested lock object interferes with other existing entries in the lock table.

The ABAP applications logic considers that data modifications are usually done when a previous reading has taken place. For that reason, the locking requests are made before the data reading requests.

SAP designed the locking mechanism so that each lock not only needs to be respected by the application server executing the transaction but also by all other servers within the SAP system.

The name of the SAP instance running the enqueue service is included in the common parameter profile, the DEFAULT.PFL file. The parameter is rdisp/enqname = <instance _name>, for example, rdisp/enqname = adminix_C12_00.

Lock Objects

The lock objects are special types of objects defined in the ABAP dictionary. The blocking type can be shared (type S), exclusive (type E), or exclusive but not cumulative (type X). The exclusive locks are used to avoid parallel modification of the data, which means that exclusively locked data can be displayed or modified by only one user. With the shared mode, several users can access the same data at the same time in display mode. As soon as any user processes the data, the remaining users do not have further access to them. An optimistic lock is established when a user accesses a record and a concurrent transaction has not updated the record. If the concurrent transaction updates the record, the current user's transaction is rejected.

Locks of type exclusive but not cumulative can only be called once. So a lock request will be rejected if an exclusive lock already exists. When the lock objects are defined in the dictionary, there are two ABAP function modules automatically generated for them: one to lock the object (enqueue) and another function to unlock it (dequeue). These functions are called at the beginning and at the end of a transaction, respectively. If for some reason there are problems between the locking and unlocking of an object, it remains locked until the administrator manually deletes the lock. Refer to Chapter 10 on how to proceed with the locking mechanism management.

The locking object mechanism is intimately related with the SAP logical units of work (SAP LUWs).

Update Work Process

The update work process is in charge of executing database changes when requested by the dialog or background work processes. Figure 2-9 shows a simple scheme of how the update process works.

The dialog work processes can generate database modifications with the corresponding instructions to the database server, independently of whether these work processes run on the same or different machines as the database.

However, when the ABAP language element CALL FUNCTION . . . IN UPDATE TASK is executed, it raises the order for the modification to occur in the update server. Specific update work processes then modify the database accordingly.

It is recommended to have the update service on the same server as the database for better performance. However, with fast network controllers, it does not make much difference having the update server on a different host than the database.

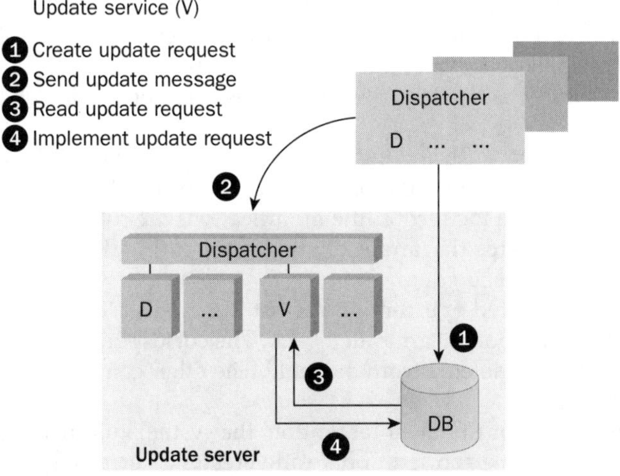

FIGURE 2-9 Update work process

The update is an asynchronous process, which means that the update requests are processed at the moment and in the order they arrive at the work process. This makes a more homogeneous response time. The drawback is that the transaction might not have finished when another update transaction is waiting.

If for any reason the update transaction cannot be completely accomplished, the user will get a system message and an express mail. Sometimes this is due to database problems, such as tablespaces becoming full and the like.

If the transaction could not finish correctly, the system rolls it back. The rollback of a transaction is possible by having a separate dialog part from the update part. The dialog program first generates log records in the VBLOG table, which are then processed by the update program (run within the update process) once the dialog is finished.

The log records, read by the update work process, contain all the necessary information to make the modifications. During the update phase, the database is modified. The update of a log record can have several parts, known as the *update components.* This division permits the system to structure the objects that make up the update transaction components according to their importance.

An update request can contain a primary update component (V1) and several secondary ones (V2). The time-critical processes are held inside the V1, the less critical within the V2. In order to be able to initiate the V2 components of the log record, the V1 component must have finished.

However, the V2 components can be executed in any order and even in parallel if there are enough update processes defined. The execution of primary components (V1) corresponding to different log records can be also done in parallel using several update work processes.

Before release 3.0 of R/3 , there was only one type of update work process taking care of both V1 and V2 components. With the release of version 3.0, a new profile parameter was established to indicate the number of update work processes for secondary components, also.

The important profile parameter is rdisp/vbname = <instance name>. This is a common parameter for the full SAP system and therefore is always in the DEFAULT.PFL file. The other parameters, rdisp/wp_no_vb and rdisp/wp_no_vb2, indicate the number of update work processes of types V1 and V2, respectively. These are defined inside the instance-specific profile parameter file.

If there are error situations during the update, these cannot be solved with user online actions. The active update process component is then stopped. If the errors occurred in the primary component (V1) of a log record, the modifications are rolled back. The log record receives a corresponding status flag and is not taken out of the VBLOG table. Subsequent V2 update actions are not executed.

However, if the interrupted or error component is a type V2, only the modifications done by this particular component are rolled back. The corresponding log record is marked with a status flag and is not deleted from the table. The other components can follow normal update processing.

After an error situation or update interruption, the system automatically notifies the user by express mail about the aborted update and creates an error log entry in the system log. Then it is possible to evaluate and treat the update according to the error message received. Refer to the section entitled "Monitoring Update Records" in Chapter 10 for how to proceed under such circumstances.

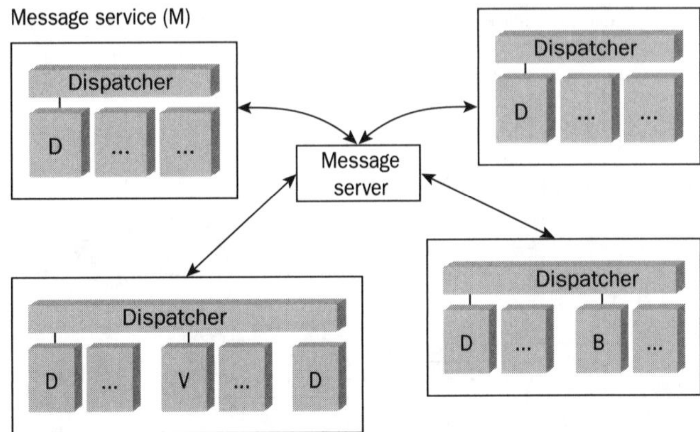

FIGURE 2-10 Message server

Message Server

The message server is a service used by the different application servers to exchange data and internal messages. This server does not have the structure of the typical work processes previously described. However, it acts like a service.

The message server routes the messages between application servers. Since the release of version 3.0, it is also used for license checking and workload balancing together with the SAP logon utility.

As depicted in Figure 2-10, there is only one message server per SAP Web AS system. The message server process is the one that makes the application servers exchange messages between them, such as brief internal messages: update start, enqueue, dequeue, and batch job start. The communication is established among the dispatchers using the TCP/IP network protocol and the sockets defined in the *services* file.

Every application server has a unique name for the message server. All application servers know which the update server, the enqueue server, and the batch and spool servers are and set those services active, indicating an address to the message server.

The location of the host running the message server is configured in the DEFAULT.PFL common profile. The parameter is rdisp/mshost = <hostname>. Notice the difference from previous parameters such as the update or enqueue services, in which the value of the parameter pointed out the instance name. In this case, the value is a hostname, as included in the standard TCP/IP hosts database. The message server host is not restricted to the database server. It can run on any of the hosts that make up the SAP client/server system.

The way this service is started is also different from other work processes. It has its own start execution line in the start profile. Chapter 4 includes more information on the start profiles.

Gateway Server

The gateway server allows the communication among Web AS R/3, R/2, and external applications. This service is a CPIC handler that implements the CPIC protocol for communication. This is commonly known as a *SAP gateway.*

The function of the SAP gateway is to exchange larger amounts of data between application servers, in contrast to the message server, which only exchanges brief internal

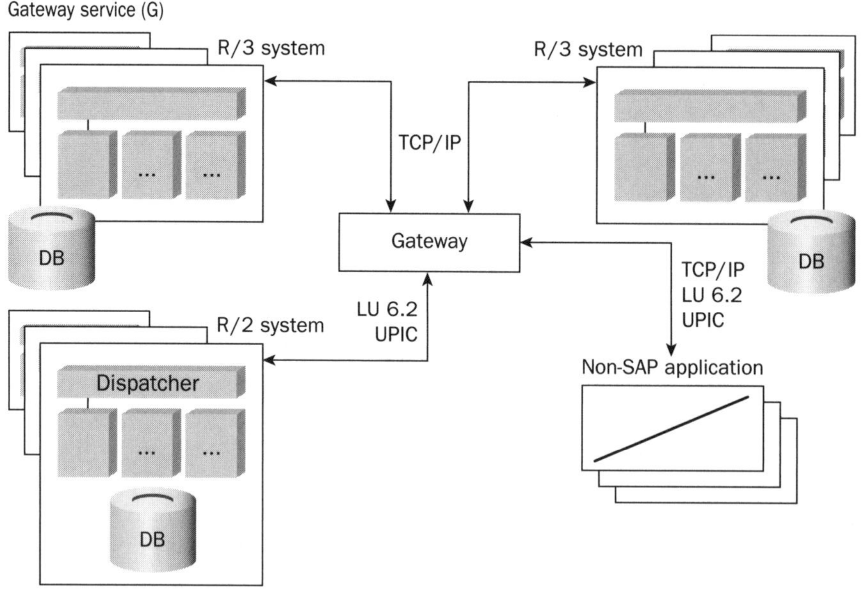

FIGURE 2-11 Gateway server

and control messages. The SAP gateway exchanges application data; thus the amount of information is larger. The communication agents can be located on the same system, in another Web AS system, in an R/2 system, and also in an external program. Figure 2-11 shows a simple architecture of the SAP gateway server. The SAP gateway processes communicate using the TCP/IP protocol in the Web AS side and the LU 6.2 when communicating with IBM mainframes running R/2. In the case of Siemens equipment running R/2, the protocol used is UPIC.

Presentation Interface

The presentation interface is the component in charge of making functionally equivalent the presentation and the handling of Web AS, no matter the type of front end used. For each user session there is a SAP process (SAP GUI) that enables the use of all available presentation possibilities of the corresponding window software. These processes (historically known as *terminal processes*) are in charge of, among other things, managing the graphical elements of the Web AS system.

The connection between the SAP GUIs and the SAP dispatcher is made with an optimized protocol, known as DIAG, in which small data packages are sent through the network.

In the SAP R/3 system, all the menus options, the buttons, and even most of the graphical elements are inside the database. This means that the real screens are not held in the PC software, but are sent on demand.

You may notice that the time it takes to go from one screen to another is longer when you are among the first users to log on to the system. As the buffers become filled with cached data, this time noticeably decreases.

The presentation interface allows for upload and download functions from the application server. It also includes possibilities for file transfers and communication with popular Windows applications, including MS-Excel, MS-Word, and MS-Access. This is possible, of course, when using a Windows-based front end. Both SAP GUI for HTML and SAP GUI for Windows have this capability.

Another feature available in the presentation interface is the SAP graphic utility, which establishes a dialog between the ABAP application and the graphic utility in the presentation server for extracting data to make up graphical representations of the information.

You should refer to the SAP online documentation or print document file called SAP Graphics: User's Guide for more information and instructions on the subject.

Database Interface

The underlying database of the SAP Web AS system acts as the main container for all the information managed by the system. The database includes almost everything the users can see on their screens: program source code, screens, texts, menu options, customer information, printer definitions, statistical information, transactional data, and so forth.

The database interface supports different relational databases from different vendors. The main task of the database interface is to convert the SQL requests (ABAP open SQL) from the SAP development environment to the database's own SQL requests. During the interpretation of the ABAP open SQL statements, the database interface makes a syntax check to verify that the statement is correct, and it also automatically tries to make an optimal use (reuse) of the SAP buffers in case a similar SQL statement was requested previously. These buffers are held locally in the main memory of each application server.

Besides using the portable SQL dialect from SAP (ABAP open SQL, previously known as SAP-SQL), it is also possible to access the database directly using ABAP native SQL (previously known as EXEC-SQL) statements. With ABAP native SQL calls, a developer can make specific database SQL calls, which are not supported using the standard ABAP open SQL statements. However, this method is not recommended because the code might not be completely portable or could cause problems during upgrading of the database engine or the Web AS applications. This method could also compromise sap's consistency/ authorization security. SAP tools assist in maintaining authorization integrity.

The database interface also has a cursor caching method. Database cursors are like portions of memory that are allocated by the system to process SQL statements. A *cursor caching method* means that the system tries to reuse, if possible, the access paths that were previously used to process SQL statements. However, this method is not recommended because the code might not be completely portable or could cause problems during upgrading of the database engine or the Web AS applications.

The database is the heart of the SAP Web AS system. It not only is the central source of information for companies' business data, but also the container of user information, software components, documentation, and administrative statistical data to be used when managing or monitoring the system.

One of the most important logical parts of the database is the ABAP object repository, which contains the following:

- *The ABAP dictionary (formerly known as the data dictionary).* This is the central source for the definition of objects, such as type and length of fields, indexes, table relationships, and so on. In database terms, these types of definitions are known as metadata. The dictionary is intimately connected to all parts of the business applications and is a core part of the ABAP development workbench.

- *The ABAP source and executable programs.* Because ABAP is an interpreted language, it can be dynamically regenerated by the application servers (remember the ABAP processor inside the work processes).

The database, of course, includes the data themselves. SAP distinguishes three different types of data: master, control, and transaction data. *Master* data contains information that does not change often, such as a user's name, printer's definition, or address of a supplier. This type of data is usually used the same way for similar objects. *Control* data is held in control tables and includes system and technical functions of the SAP system. *Transaction* data is the most volatile and frequently used information in day-to-day business operations, such as customer orders or accounting transactions including payments, debits, credits, and so on.

The SAP-declared dictionary tables have the corresponding structure in the physical underlying database. The Web AS system handles different types of tables. SAP *transparent tables* are structures that exactly match an underlying database table. With certain database knowledge, users can view or manage these tables directly from the database's own utilities—but this is not advised because it may introduce inconsistencies.

Other table types managed by SAP that may eventually disappear are *cluster tables,* made of several SAP tables related using foreign keys, and *pooled tables,* corresponding to a set of tables stored in a single table.

For more detailed information on these types of SAP tables, refer to the corresponding sections in Chapter 8.

The database interface sends the data read from the ABAP dictionary tables to the ABAP programs by placing them in special work areas (memory buffers known to the work processes). Conversely, the database interface gets the modified data from those areas and sends them to the database.

Software developers can easily declare and work with such areas because the dictionary is integrated with ABAP. Within an ABAP program, the developer can create additional tables that only exist as long as a program is running. These internal tables can be dynamically enlarged so that it is not necessary for developers to know in advance the amount of memory the internal tables will occupy.

SAP Web AS Communication Protocols and Interfaces

Inside R/3, communication is an overall process that involves most of the components of the systems both internally and to the exterior world (external systems). Communication among systems, modules, and components is based on protocols. The Web AS basis system supports most standard and de facto standard communication and networking protocols.

At the operating system level, the protocol used is TCP/IP. Communication with the database is accomplished using remote SQL calls. Between applications there are many different programming interfaces that use an underlying communication layer, such as CPIC, RFC, ALE, EDI, BAPIs, and HTTP and SOAP in SAP Web AS 6.40.

The communication interfaces are deployed to integrate all layers of the client/server architecture, from database server to application server to presentation servers. Additionally, they define the channels for the exchange of electronic information, such as the input of data from external systems and the exchange of standardized business information using ALE EDI. The communication interfaces are also deployed for sending and receiving mail from the exterior world (Internet, for example) using the standard X.400 mail protocol.

At the programming level, the Web AS system uses the CPIC protocol for program-to-program communication and also includes support for *remote function calls* (RFCs), Microsoft OLE interface, ActiveX, and many other standard interfaces based on objects, such as CORBA, COM/DCOM, and others. Extensive information about communication at the programming level can be found in the Web AS online documentation. SAP also provides support for connecting and exchanging data and information with traditional mainframes using SNA or other standard protocols.

The system has utilities that enable communication and data exchange with special peripheral devices such as presence card readers and production plant devices.

Common Programming Interface Communications

CPIC (Common Programming Interface Communications) is the interface deployed by the ABAP language for program-to-program communication. CPIC was defined and developed by IBM as a standardized communication interface and was later modified and enhanced by the X/Open organization.

The CPIC interface is useful when setting up communications and data conversion and exchange between programs. Because CPIC is based on a common interface, an additional advantage is the portability of the programs across different hardware platforms.

SAP divides the possibilities and the scope of the CPIC interface into two function groups: the CPIC starter set and the advanced function calls. This division is simply meant to guide the user and not to restrict the available functions. For instance, the CPIC starter set would just be used for the basic and minimum set of functions shared by two partner programs, such as establishing the connection and exchanging data. The advance calls cover more communication functionality, such as converting data, checking the communication, and applying security functions. For more information on these CPIC function groups, refer to the SAP documentation *BC SAP Communication: CPI-C Programmer's Guide.*

CPIC communication is always performed using the internal SAP gateway that takes care of converting the CPIC calls to external communication protocols such as TCP/IP.

Remote Function Calls

RFC (remote function calls) is a standard programming interface for making remote calls between programs located on different systems. Functions that are developed or exist in a system can be remotely called by another local program. This is particularly useful for data manipulation and processing load balancing between systems. Even when the same functions exist on both systems—called and caller—it is a way of making another system send or receive data, and the remote CPU assigns the needed resources.

RFC is a higher-level logical interface than CPIC, and it makes life easier for programmers because they do not have to worry about implementing communication routines. With the RFC interface, function calls can be accomplished between two SAP systems or between SAP systems and external ones (for instance, with Microsoft Windows applications). The library functions included with RFC support the Visual Basic and C programming languages on Windows platforms. The RFC interfaces come basically with two services:

- A calling interface for the ABAP programs. Any ABAP program can call a remote function using standard programming sentences, providing the remote system has allowed the module to be called remotely.
- An RFC API (application program interface) for programs other than ABAP (non-SAP). SAP even provides an RFC program generator to help implement RFC partner programs in external systems. With these API calls, external programs can call ABAP function modules in SAP Web AS systems (also in R/2). At the same time, with the RFC API, ABAP programs can use functions provided by external programs.

SAP online help and the documentation print files include extensive information about remote programming with RFC and the RFC API.

Memory Management

Starting with release 3.0 of R/3, SAP introduced a new concept in its use of main memory to improve the overall performance of the system, in respect to previous Web AS releases (2.2 and earlier). The main change was to make use of an extended memory management system to optimize the access to the user contexts and thus avoid the overhead caused by heavy roll-in/roll-out tasks of previous releases. User context is defined as the user data that are kept by the system between dialog steps to continue the processing of the transaction. The user context contains a user-specific area where user and authorization data are stored as well as a session context for each SAP session. These data contain such things as authorizations, field information, internal tables, runtime environment management information, and so on. Roll-in is the process of making the data available to the work processes when they need it.

With the extended memory management functions, all user contexts of an application server are held in main memory and are shared by all work processes. In previous releases, the user contexts were in the roll files and had to be copied from one place to another when user sessions were handled by different work processes. With the new memory management, those previous copy functions (copying user contexts to roll areas) are handled by just reassigning pointers in main memory.

With this technique there is a significant improvement in performance, because context switching is a very frequent task when attending to interactive users. In order to observe the real improvements, the system needs more memory and swap space than previous versions.

With SAP releases prior to 3.0, the user context area used by the dialog processes was limited to the size of the roll area. The new memory management allows the size of this area to be extended as the size of user contexts increases. All the data in the user context are directly accessible, as shown in Figure 2-12.

SAP, and not the operating system, takes care of page management for the user contexts held in shared memory because SAP's strategy is for openness and thus it is platform independent.

This shared memory is technically implemented using an *unnamed* mapped file. In UNIX systems, this means that the address space is mapped onto the operating swap space. For more information on memory mapping, refer to the operating system manuals or online help.

To tune and configure memory management, make sure that your system meets all requirements regarding memory and swap space. SAP automatically sets some default

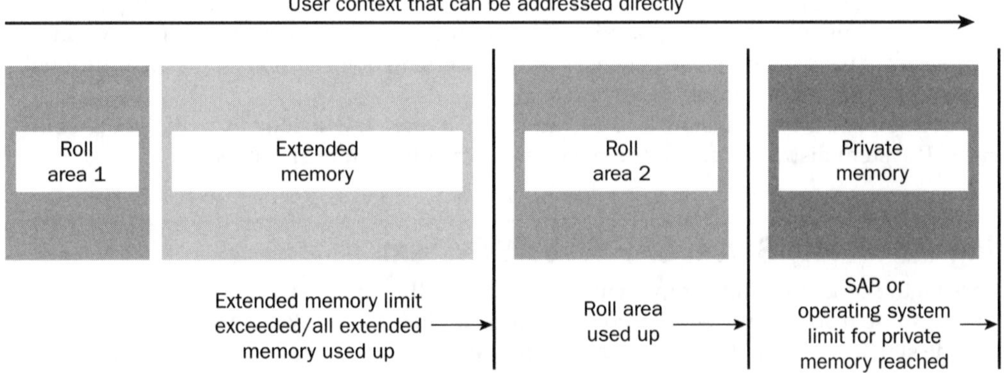

FIGURE 2-12 Work process memory allocation (Copyright by SAP AG)

parameters depending on your particular configuration. There are some utilities available for monitoring the operation of the memory management to later fine-tune it.

The configuration is accomplished setting parameter values in the system profile. SAP provides a comprehensive manual for administrators full of examples for setting different values for the required parameters that directly affect the mode of operation of the memory management system.

Refer to this manual, *BC—Memory Management,* for a detailed description of particular configurations and a deeper description regarding the mode of operation.

Setting the many profile parameters related to memory management can be a very complex job due to the many relationships of these parameters. Web AS notes 88416 (Zero administration memory management from 4.0A/NT) and 103747 (Performance 4.0/4.5: Parameter recommendations) are a good complement to the memory management online documentation.

The Concept of a SAP Instance

An *instance* is an administrative entity that groups together Web AS components that offer one or several services. These offered services are started or stopped together. All instance components are configured using a common instance profile. For more information on SAP profiles, please refer to the section entitled "Profiles" in Chapter 4.

A centralized SAP Web AS system would be made of a unique instance. Another feature that distinguishes the instances is that every SAP instance has its own buffer area, which means that it allocated its own main memory space.

SAP distinguishes between *central instances* and *dialog instances.* Every SAP system has just one central host, which contains all basic services such as the message server, gateway, update, enqueue, dialog, spool, and background right from installation. Dialog instances, as defined, only contain a set of basic services such as dialog and background work processes from the time of installation.

Administrators can later customize all the services and their server locations by using SAP instance profiles. A central system can be further configured to a distributed system, creating additional instances offering additional services. The usual way of configuring the system right out of the box is to have just one instance per computer; however, providing your systems have enough main memory and processing power, you can install additional instances, which have some advantages.

More information on instances is included in Chapter 4, which deals with the benefits of the SAP system distribution and the components involved in the process.

Building the Client/Server SAP Web AS System

Once all the processes and components that make up the SAP system are known, we can see how all these pieces come together to form a whole client/server Web AS system.

The starting point is a server system (hardware point of view) with the required memory, disks, network controller cards, and operating system.

On this first server, add the relational database management system with its corresponding database processes. At this moment, you have the *database server.* The database is, of course, installed on the disks connected to this computer server.

Now, add basic Web AS services (work processes).We have added a printer to this system to get a connection between the SAP spool work process and the host spool system.

Generically, we link the update and the enqueue work processes to the database. But, as stated in previous sections, there is a database interface component within the dialog and the background work processes that can directly access the database, too.

At this moment, you have the database server and the SAP central instance (because it has all the basic services). From a software client/server point of view, the services provided by the central instance make up an application server.

When the central instance and the database are running together on the same machine, which is usual, this is known as a *database server with central instance,* or simply a *database server.*

In the SAP naming convention, a *service* is a process (such as the message process) or a group of work processes. It is a software concept, and the component that offers those services is called a *server.*

The software components that request those services are known as the *clients.* The clients can be servers at the same time. Because there already is a dispatcher process and dialog work processes, it is possible for presentation servers (clients) to connect to this system (server). It is also possible to configure the directly attached printers or network printers to the SAP system. This would be a centralized system or a two-tier client/server configuration.

Include additional work processes (service types) on a different server, which make up an additional application server. Now it is a SAP Web AS three-tiered client/server configuration. A complete SAP system is the set of clients and server components that make use of or are assigned to the same database.

The connection between the presentation process and the dispatcher is the one that makes the transition between the presentation and application servers. The update process is the one that makes the separation between the application and database servers.

SAP Business Framework

As discussed in Chapter 1, the SAP Business Framework is the architecture that SAP put in place for supporting seamless integration of components, thus making SAP products a set of integrated products that can be installed, managed, and upgraded independently, without affecting other systems' components.

Business Framework was technically supported on integration technologies such as BAPIs and ALE as well as the underlying technology of the solid Web AS multitier client/server architecture, the standard communication protocol such as CPIC and RFC, the openness and independence of hardware platforms, or the portability of the applications based on the ABAP language.

Business Framework architecture was based on the technological concepts of *components, interfaces,* and *integration:*

- The *components* would provide the business functionality. So, for instance, the Logistic applications, the Business Information Warehouse, the Business to Business Procurement, and the many other applications could be considered components that would integrate among themselves by using standard *interfaces.*
- The *interfaces,* mainly based on BAPIs, provided the communication technology, based on business objects, that would be used for connection and data exchange among the business components.
- *Integration technologies* were provided by means of Application Link Enabled (ALE) (using IDocs to exchange data between logical systems) and others, like the SAP Business Workflow, and the goal of these technologies was to guarantee the integration of the business processes among different components.

The evolution of the Business Framework toward Web standards and Web-based applications introduced the Internet Business Framework, which can be considered the technological foundation of the mySAP.com platform. However, the client/server technology of the classical Web AS systems is still in place, and the dispatcher and work processes are still behaving with the same technical advantages and solid architecture that made Web AS such a good software system. Nonetheless, the client/server technology has been evolved and enhanced, with new process architecture, new memory management, and support for protocols such as HTTP and the ability to interpret directly JavaScript.

The following sections provide an overview of the classical features and technical characteristics of Web AS systems, many of which are present in the mySAP eBusiness platforms.

Client/Server Foundation

Client/server is a software concept that first appeared in the late 1980s but that was deployed seriously and with a solid technical foundation in the early and mid-1990s. As a software concept it included "service providers" (servers) and "service requesters" (clients). A specific program could act at the same time as provider and requester. So, for instance, the SAP Web AS typical application server was a service provider for the users (SAP GUI) but a service requester of the database server.

The main point of this type of computing was the separation of the user-oriented tasks, the execution or application tasks, and the data management tasks. These three types of tasks are normally matched with the terms presentation, application, and data levels.

With client/server computing, it was possible and easier to distribute the workload of computer applications among different and cooperating computer programs or processes.

From the very beginning SAP Web AS systems were designed this way so that there was a presentation level (user interface or presentation server), an application level (application server), and a database level (database server).

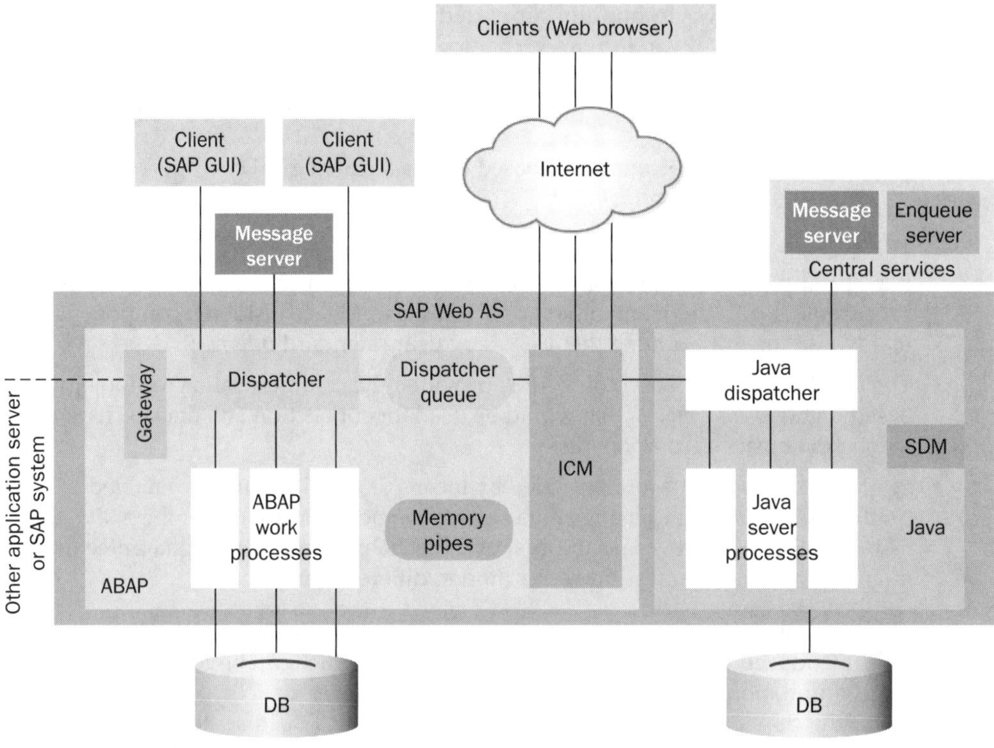

FIGURE 2-13 SAP Web AS multitier client/server architecture

The software services provided by client/server computing would communicate among them using predefined interfaces over standard communication protocols (for instance, remote SQL calls from the application server to the database server over TCP/IP).

With the emergence of the Web, the ability to have a simple Internet browser as the user interface, and the development of ITS back in 1996, the classical three-tiered client/server architecture became a multitier system, as shown in Figure 2-13.

The classical three-level or the multilevel client/server configurations offered a series of advantages that are still available in mySAP system environments:

- *Efficient distribution of workload.* Because application servers work in parallel and communicate with the database, application tasks could be easily distributed. With Web AS systems it was also common to find installations in which one or more application servers were dedicated to specific tasks, such as background or printing.
- *Flexible configurations.* Client/server architectures offered many different ways of installing, distributing, or upgrading a system landscape. In the mySAP.com age, this has been even increased with the ability of having several different mySAP components with several databases in a single server.

- *High scalability.* With client/server it was quite easy to increase or adapt the power capacity of the systems according to the changing needs of the business. So, for instance, when the number of users increases, or the load of the applications, it is simple to install additional application servers without stopping the systems.

RFC: A Key Communication Middleware

RFC stands for "remote function calls" and is the standard programming interface long used by SAP for making remote calls among programs located on the same or on different systems. This means that a function that is developed in one system could be remotely called by another program.

Web AS has a function library where programmers can find useful subroutines to reuse in their ABAP programs. This library has the function modules organized in groups like arithmetic functions, character string manipulation functions, controlling functions, and so on. You can access this function library from the function builder transaction SE37. These functions can be documented as well as each of the interface parameters helping the programmer to understand how to call these functions from ABAP.

From release 2 SAP Web AS supports RFCs to call a function module from another Web AS system, from an R/2 system, or from external systems. This was a key factor in the current Business Framework strategy. The first types of RFC were synchronous RFC, allowing a program to call a function in another Web AS system and get the results online.

SAP provided libraries for non-SAP environments in order to call these function modules, like C and C++ libraries in the supported SAP operating systems, including Windows, UNIX, Linux, OS/390, or OS/400. There has been also support for DLL and ActiveX in Windows or Java-RFC.

For transactional environments SAP developed the tRFC (transactional RFC) in release 3.0. In this case the program calls the remote function and the system guarantees the delivery of the call, recalls in the case the partner system is not available, and assures that the function is executed only once. tRFC is asynchronous but if the partner system is available is executed as soon as possible.

With release 4.6B a new extension of tRFC was made, and it was called queued RFC (qRFC) in order to define an order and queue the calls that are executed one after the other. The queue can be in the source or in the target system. This qRFC can be downloaded to versions 3.1I of R/3.

BAPI

With release 3.0 SAP started the object-oriented approach. From that release there is a Business Object Repository containing the SAP Business Objects like a purchase order or a customer. These business objects have attributes or properties and methods like *Create, Release,* and others depending on the object type. The methods of the Business Objects are implemented mainly as function modules, so they can be called in an object-oriented view or directly like function modules. Some of these methods were flagged by SAP as *stable methods.* This means that SAP guarantees that the method interface (export–import–table parameters) will not change in two major SAP releases. These stable methods are called BAPIs (Business APIs). BAPIs were announced for general availability in release 3.1G.

There are more than 1100 BAPIs in release 4.6. SAP has published the BAPI catalog, allowing the developer community to develop external programs with a guarantee in the developing investment, because the program will work even if customers change their SAP release. These BAPIs were used also by SAP internally to develop initial load programs faster than the old batch input method and to integrate the different SAP applications with these BAPI calls.

IDOCs

IDOC history is related to the EDI interface. EDI stands for Electronic Data Interchange and was one of the first efforts to define a flat text format for business documents, like invoices or sales orders so that they could be exchanged between systems and applications. SAP supported EDI from the very beginning, since release 2. The major problem to support EDI was that actually there are several substandards in EDI, like EDIFACT, ANSI X-12, ODETTE, and others (Europe, America, Automobile Industries) and there is the need for translating your internal documents to the substandard your partner speaks. In order to support this, SAP defined its own standard representation of the document, known as IDOCs or intermediate documents. Then the customer should choose certified software that understand the IDOC format and translate it to the EDI substandard chosen, which is also in charge of sending and receiving them. You can see a list of certified software third parties at www.sap.com/csp.

At the beginning SAP defined IDOCs mainly for the type of documents used in EDI. Then SAP realized that these IDOC could be used directly if the partner system was another SAP system, so it started to use it to send and receive documents between SAP systems as well. IDOCs from older releases can be interpreted by newer SAP releases and new releases can adapt the IDOC release depending on the target system. This was the foundation of ALE.

ALE

ALE stands for Application Link and Enabled, and the idea was to be able to integrate applications in different SAP or non-SAP systems in a loosely coupled way. Imagine the scenario shown in Figure 2-14.

We want to have a central Web AS system with all the financial and controlling in our headquarters and one Web AS system in our sales office in Houston, another Web AS system in our factory in New Jersey. So it is possible to have different Web AS systems, autonomous but integrated between them. When, for example, a relevant financial document is created in our sales office, this is sent to our central financial system automatically.

This could be useful for different reasons:

Some large organizations have subsidiaries in different continents and perhaps it makes little sense for support reasons to have the Web AS system for the plant in Singapore in the U.S. headquarters. This could be useful from the network point of view; the users are connected to their system in Singapore and not via expensive lines to the central system with the bandwidth required for an online user.

Other reasons are organizational in nature (in some cases they are nearly autonomous business units) or relate to performance: to distribute the load.

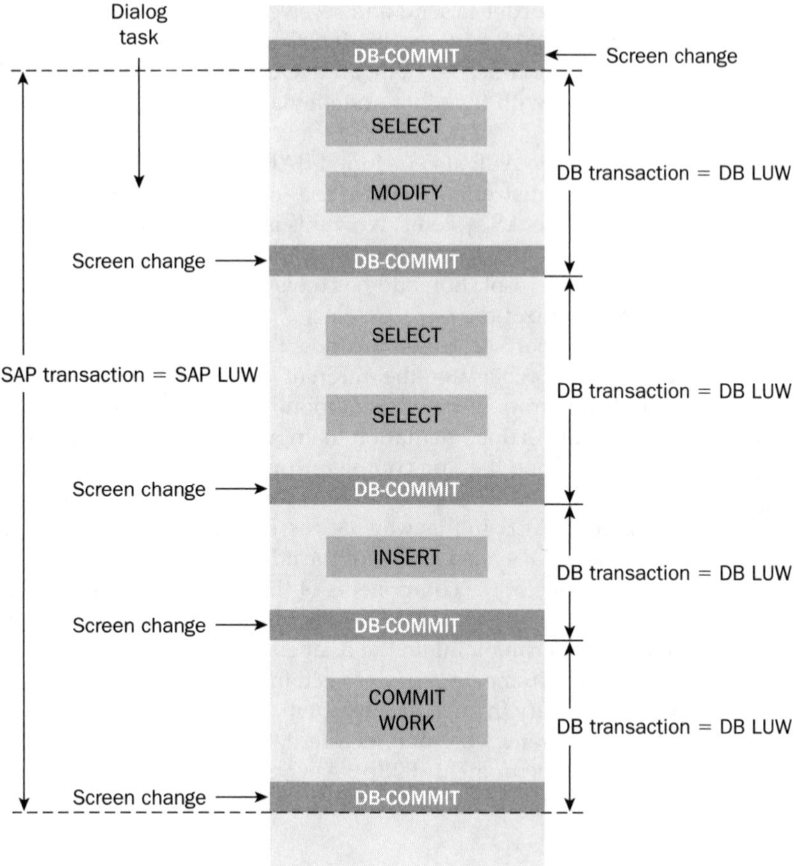

FIGURE 2-14 ALE scenario

This is why SAP developed the ALE inside R/3. With ALE you can define which systems participate in your ALE network (in the ALE world a system is an external system or a *client* of an Web AS system) and which data should be sent from one system to the others.

In ALE it is possible to distribute master data (customers, materials . . .), document data (purchase orders, financial documents, invoices . . .), and also customize data (entries in selected customizing tables).

In the case of distributing master data, you can define one system where you maintain centrally the materials and then distribute the creation or changes to the other systems. But the system can be defined also with ranges and filters (for example, to define centrally some materials but allow the plants to have their own range for internal use, or even define a bidirectional maintenance in which changes in any system are replicated to the other). This is defined in the ALE model.

ALE started using IDOCs in order to send and receive documents between systems (SAP or non SAP). In the case of SAP systems, the IDOCs are sent usually by tRFC to the other system. If the partner is a non-SAP system, an IDOC translator can be used that understands IDOCs and speaks with the other system via EDI messages, or uses file or CPIC interface.

When the BAPIs appeared the ALE also included BAPIs for the new scenarios. For example, the Central User Administration scenario uses only BAPIs to exchange the user definition and roles between Web AS systems. Now this is used between mySAP components.

ALE uses workflow for error resolution and has tools for supporting multiple restore situations and systems synchronization.

ALE is the foundation for what SAP called Business Framework. At the beginning the ALE scenarios allowed integration between the different logical systems in the ALE network, but not the whole integration if all the components were in one central system. You have to look at each scenario's documentation to know which restrictions apply compared to a central system. Then the first complete application that was decoupled was the HR module. With HR, all the possible interfaces between HR and the different applications were supported in ALE. In this way it's possible to have a system with the HR module integrated with other SAP systems. One of the advantages of this approach is that you can change the release of one of the components of the Business Framework without changing the release of the others. Perhaps the customer needs the new release for the HR module due to legal reasons but can maintain the financial system in the same release without involving the FI people in the upgrade project. In the case of HR this has other advantages, like improved security in an isolated system.

With mySAP, the Business Framework and its Internet evolution is even more used than before. With mySAP CRM, E-procurement (B2Bp), APO, SEM, and other systems integrated between them and the Web AS backends, it is possible to change the release of one of them without disturbing the others.

The Internet Transaction Server (ITS)

SAP joins its applications with the Internet world in release 3.1 (1996) by means of the Internet Transaction Server (ITS). This server combines Internet technology with R/3 technology, enabling reliable access to SAP transactions from the Internet and from intranets. ITS uses the following:

- SAP GUI for HTML (ITS 4.6DC4 or Higher), which dynamically converts R/3 transaction screens to HTML pages.
- Web Transactions, which enables HTML pages to call R/3 transactions.
- WebRFC, which enables HTML pages to call R/3 function modules.
- WebReporting, which links SAP reports and pregenerated lists from an HTML pages and links to the Web Reporting Browser that displays R/3 report trees. Web Reporting is a special-case WebRFC.

ITS middleware allows accessing SAP Web AS scenarios from a Web browser and call function modules via an URL. It also allows the SAP GUI for HTML access with the enjoySAP interface to nearly all standard SAP transactions from a browser. ITS is also the portal service for the Workplace portal. ITS is one of the key pieces in the SAP Internet strategy and it is present in almost every mySAP system landscape.

SAP transactions can run as Web transactions (IACs), Standard SAP transactions using the SAP GUI for HTML (or SAP GUI for JAVA), WebRFC, or WebReporting.

In a IACS, the transaction finds all of the information needed for the presentation layer in it's a IACS or Web Transaction service file and templates, which includes the transaction code to start in the SAP system (defined with the parameter ~transaction in the service file). The SAP GUI for HTML is accessed through the SAP GUI for HTML (ITS service webgui) or SAP GUI for JAVA (ITS service jvgui).

Access to WebRFC and WebReporting is also supported. Only WebRFC or WebReporting modules that have been specifically written to adhere to Internet scenarios can be accessed via this method. After release 4.5, all reports must be released in order to have access to them via the Web.

IACS Architecture

WGate Located on the same machine as the Web server, the WGate component connects the ITS to the Web server. The WGate supports standard Web server interfaces (e.g., Microsoft's Information Server API (ISAPI) on Windows NT, The Microsoft Information Server API , Netscape Server API (NSAPI) on Windows NT, Common Gateway Interface (CGI) on UNIX, and AS/400 (controlled availability as of Release 4.5A)).

On the UNIX and AS/400 platforms, the Common Gateway Interface starts the WGate as an external executable program.

The AGate program is implemented as a Windows NT service. Although the AGate can be located on the same machine as the WGate, we recommend that you keep the two components on two separate machines.

AGate The AGate is responsible for the following communication tasks:

- Enabling connectivity to the SAP system using DIAG (SAP GUI) or RFC protocols
- Generating the HTML documents for the SAP applications
- Managing user logon data
- Managing session context and time-outs
- Code page conversions and national language support

Process The process depends on the model you use. These can be EWT.Flow Logic or Web GUI. With the Web GUI process, the Web browser passes the request to the Web server, which loads the WGate (Web gateway) that links ITS to the Web server.

The WGate connects to the AGate and sends the AGate a request. TCP is used to establish the WGate connection. The WGate and AGate interact/share data through the SAP Network Interface. The AGate receives an HTTP request from the WGate using DIAG or RFC. The HTTP request is then processed, and the data and logon information is sent to the SAP system. The SAP system retrieves information, processes the information, and sends a response back to the WGate.

Security The ITS architecture allows for the WGate and AGate to run on separate hosts. The AGate keeps logon data, which is why it is good to keep components separated. SAP recommends that clients set up a network infrastructure that makes use of these features to control access from the Internet to internal networks. Other security components, such as firewalls, packet filters, and SAP routers, should be used to separate the individual parts of the network from one another. It is important to use various security mechanisms so that, in the event of a security breach, the consequences are limited to a subset of the system.

Users can be authenticated in multiple ways:

1. *Authenticating Internet users.* You'll need to make Web transactions available to anonymous Internet users because it is impractical to set up a separate account for each user since you don't know which users want to access the application data within SAP systems.

   Define these services as Web transactions.
   Set up the as service users with predefined passwords in the SAP system.
   Assign service users only the authorizations needed to access the application.
2. *Authenticating named users with user ID and password.* For users with SAP usernames and accounts, do not set up passwords in the ITS service file. This authentication method would take place internal to the SAP system.
3. *Authenticating named users using X.509 client certificates* (offered with release 4.5B and higher). Users can present a X.509 client certificate. This authentication would use the SSL and no password would be required. For this approach there are a series of prerequisites; for implementation please see http://service.sap.com/security.

Internet Business Framework

One of the success factors for SAP was the seamless integration between applications. In SAP you can see the whole business process, no matter if it has interaction with Finances (FI), Controlling (CO), Asset Management (AM), Sales and Distribution (SD), or Human Resource (HR) modules.

The ALE allows integration between applications in distributed systems. The Internet will increase the integration between processes not only inside one company but between companies, as the common media to exchange data and information. SAP evolution is the integration between systems via the Internet, and this is mainly what mySAP is for.

SAP supports all the Internet standards, as we will see, and participates actively in all Internet initiatives. mySAP allows Internet process integration with new scenarios that will revolutionize the way of doing business today.

As has been mentioned several times, the Internet Business Framework is the technological foundation of mySAP.com, based on the previous SAP Business Framework Architecture and adding Web technology and standards. The following are some of these Web technologies, the protocols used, and the business standards.

- *HTML and HTTP.* HTTP is the protocol used between a Web browser and a Web server to exchange documents. These documents are called HTML pages.

We will see that mySAP supports complete access via a Web browser with HTTP or HTTPS (secure HTTP) (see Chapter 5). You can find these and other Internet standards at the www.w3c.org Web site.

- *LDAP.* LDAP (Light Directory Access Protocol) is an open protocol to define directory services and how to access them. These directories can be user directories or file directories. These services are already included in operating systems like Windows 2000. SAP supports LDAP integration with the LDAP Connector in order to define the Web AS users or the HR employees centrally with LDAP support. More information about the LDAP integration will be explained in Chapter 8.

XML

The HTML language was so successful for exchanging information between users (browsers) and machines (Web Server) that a similar method was developed for exchanging information between machines (systems). XML is a tag (meta) language similar to HTML used to describe documents in a predefined way, understandable for machines. XML and HTML are based on SGML (Standard Generalized Markup Language), a formal definition on how to describe languages based on tags.

The following is an example of the data part of an XML document:

```
<order>
  <orderNo>4711</orderNo>
  <items>
    <item>
      <description>coca cola tins</description>
            <units>144</units>
      <price currency="USD">1.25</price>
    </item>
    <item> ...  </item>
    ...
  </items>
    <delDate format="mm/dd/yyyy">08/15/2005</delDate>
</order>
```

XML (eXtendable Markup Language) defines how you can define document standards based on tags but does not define the documents themselves. The door is open in order that third parties define their own substandards for specific industries. XML is not only used for ERP systems; there are XML specifications for patients at hospitals, for exchanging information between libraries, and so on. You can find a list of the XML initiatives in different sectors at www.xml.org.

Every XML document should have a DTD (Data Type Definition) at the beginning of the document. The DTD specifies which tags are allowed in the document data section and which parameters or values are allowed in the tags. The DTD could be in the document sent, or could be just an URL to a Web site where the DTD is stored, or in practice could be an agreement between both parties and is not sent.

DTD definition is based on the SGML definition and is not based on tags but on a formal language. In order to facilitate this, a new standard has arrived known as XML

Schema. XML Schema is like the DTD as the definition of the allowed tags and parameters, but looks like XML as well. In the next example you can see an example of a DTD and a XML schema.

DTD

```
<!DOCTYPE order [
  <!ELEMENT  order (orderNo,
                    items*,
                    delDate)>
  <!ELEMENT  orderNo     #PCDATA>
  <!ELEMENT  items       (item+)>
  <!ELEMENT  item        (description,
                          units,
                          price)>
  ...
  <!ATTLIST  price
             currency    (USD|DEM)  "USD">
]>
```

XML Schema

```
<elementType name="area">
    <sequence>
     <elementTypeRef name="city" minOccur="0" maxOccur="2"/>
     <elementTypeRef name="country" minOccur="1" maxOccur="1"/>
    </sequence>
```

SAP has participated in the XML world since the beginning. The SAP Business Connector allows SAP to send and receive documents via XML and standard communication protocols like HTTP, HTTPS, FTP, or e-mail. SAP has defined a SAP-XML for documents based on the IDOC definition and a XML-BAPI in order to define how to call BAPIs with XML and get the result in XML (a similar initiative was done by Microsoft in order to call a COM object method via internet with SOAP, Simple Object Access Protocol). SAP has participation in xml.org, RosettaNet XML definition initiative, BizTalk Microsoft initiative, and supports also EDI ports of type XML in release 4.6.

The Architecture of the SAP Web Application Server

SAP Web provides the greatest flexibility by separating technology infrastructure into solutions. SAP Web Application server is a natural progression of SAP Basis and supports all existing and future components of mySAP Business Suite and SAP R/3 Enterprise in addition to all J2EE-based applications. These applications can be customized or provided by a third party.

SAP Web Application Server also has the underlying technology for SAP Enterprise Portal, SAP Business Information Warehouse, and SAP Exchange Infrastructure.

The Internet Communication Manager

The Internet Communication Manager ensures communication between the SAP system (SAP Web Application Server) with the outside world using the HTTP, HTTPS, and SMTP protocols. In the server role, it can process requests from the Internet that have URLs with the server/port combination that the ICM responds to. Independently of the URL, the ICM then calls the corresponding local handlers.

You need the ICM if you want your SAP Web AS to communicate with the Internet using HTTP(S), SMTP, or NNTP.

The ICM is part of the SAP Web AS. The ICM is implemented as an independent process and is started and monitored by the dispatcher. You can use profile parameters to set whether the ICM should be started and how it should be configured

The ICM process uses a pool of worker threads to parallel process the load. Besides the pool of worker threads, which process incoming requests, the following ICM components are also implemented as threads:

Thread control. This thread accepts incoming TCP/IP requests and creates (or calls) a worker thread from the thread pool to process the request. From this point on, thread control initializes the connection info data.

Worker threads. These threads handle requests and responses for a connection. A worker thread contains an I/O handler for network input and output and various plug-ins for the different protocols supported by the system (HTTP, SMTP, and so on). The plug-ins decide when a sent packet is complete (this process is protocol dependent).

Watchdog. Usually, a worker thread waits for the response, regardless of whether the worker thread is a server or a client. If a time-out occurs, the watchdog takes on the task of waiting for the response. This makes the worker thread available for other requests. When the watchdog receives the response, it informs the thread control components, which then call a worker thread.

Signal handler. This thread processes signals sent from the operating system or from another process (for example, the dispatcher).

Connection info. This table contains information about the state of the connection, the memory pipes, and the plug-in data for every existing network connection.

Memory pipes. Memory pipes are memory-based communication objects that handle data transfer between the ICM and the work processes. There are four pipes for every connection: one data pipe per request and response and one out-of-band (OOP) pipe. The OOP pipe is used for control information.

ICM Plug-Ins

The ICM contains plug-ins for the protocol-dependent tasks. The Internet protocols HTTP and SMTP each have a plug-in. The plug-ins perform the following tasks:

- All protocol-specific tasks
- Input and output data handling, data manipulation
- Local handling in the ICM or forwarding to the work process

A Closer Look at the HTTP Plug-In

HTTP is the protocol used to make HTTP requests and HTTP responses over an IP network. The HTTP plug-in has all the built-in features to handle both an HTTP request and an HTTP response. A key element in the HTTP plug-in is that the URL and the port are used to access the local ICM handler. This eliminates the need to create a user context in the work process each time that an HTTP request is made from an application.

The HTTP plug-in uses a chain-forwarding approach to processing an HTTP request. Each handler is capable of processing a request; however, if the handler is unavailable, the HTTP request is forwarded to the next available handler for processing. This increases performance.

Local handlers are referred to as subhandlers and are called in series depending on the handler's profile parameter. A profile parameter associates a handler with a URL prefix. Therefore, a request for a particular URL prefix is sent to the next available handler in the series that corresponds to the URL prefix.

ICM has six handlers:

Logging handler. The logging handler records each HTTP request.

Server cache handler. The server cache handler is responsible for reading and writing information to and from the cache. First, the request is read. The requested object may or may not be already stored in the cache. If it is, then the server cache handler responds to the request by reading the requested object from the cache. If the object is not in the cache, then the server cache handler forwards the request to the next handler for processing.

File access handler. The file access handler responds to requests for a file from the file system such as pictures or static HTML pages. The ICM knows which URL prefix to use by reading the icm/HTTP/file_access_<xx> parameter.

Redirect handler. The redirect handler has the job of redirecting an HTTP request to another HTTP server. The target URL prefixes are identified in the icm/HTTP/redirect_<xx> parameter.

SAP R/3 handler. The SAP R/3 handler responds to a request to access the SAP system. This is the default handler and therefore handles requests that none of the other handlers processes. This is the only handler where a user context is created in the workplace.

J2EE handler. The J2EE handler responds to request for J2EE objects that are handled by the integrated J2EE server.

A Look at the Internet Server

The Internet server has a cache where HTTP objects are stored before those objects are forwarded to the client who requests the object. This is more efficient than retrieving the object from the disk each time a client requests it.

The Internet server requires one millisecond to process a request for an object that is already in cache. This means that 3000 requests can be processed every second if a 4 CPU computer is used as the server.

The first time a client requests an object, the object is retrieved from the disk (or from its original source) and is stored in the ICM server cache. Once in the cache, the object is then sent to the client.

Each object stored in the ICM server cache has an expiration time that is identified by the icm/HTTP/server_cache_<xx>/expiration parameter. The object remains in cache until it expires. A subsequent request for the object requires that the object be again retrieved from disk and placed into cache before it is sent to the client.

An Inside Look at the Web Dispatcher

The web dispatcher is a key component of integrating the Internet with SAP because the web dispatcher is the software switch between SAP and the Internet. As HTTP requests are received, the web dispatcher directs the request to one or multiple SAP Web application servers based on the capacity of the server. In this way, clients receive the fastest possible response.

The web dispatcher is a software switch that runs on the proxy server or whatever server is directly connected to the Internet. The icm/server_port_<xx> parameter tells the web dispatcher the port that will receive client requests. The rdisp/mshost parameter identifies the SAP message server and the ms/http_port identifies the port that the SAP message server uses to receive requests. Both of these are used by the web dispatcher to process incoming HTTP(S) requests.

The number of requests the dispatcher sends to a SAP Web AS will depend on the capacity of the server, and capacity is linked to the number of configured dialog work processes. If the request is the second or subsequent request from an existing session (a session cookie for HTTP requests, and the client IP address for HTTPS requests), then the web dispatcher makes sure that the request is sent to the application that is processing the client's requests for that session.

Memory and the Web Dispatcher

Memory Requirement

You'll need to make sure that there is sufficient memory to run the web dispatcher. The best way to estimate memory requirement is to first assign values for the various settings shown in Table 2-1 and then use those values in the following formula to arrive at your estimate.

$$\text{Memory Requirement} = (S \cdot N_S + G \cdot N_G + U \cdot N_U) \cdot 2 \text{ Bytes}$$

Web Dispatcher Requirements

In order to run the web dispatcher, you'll need the following:

- SAP Web AS 6.20 with a 6.20 kernel
- Configure the HTTP port using the ms/http_port profile parameter
- A link for the web dispatcher to contact the HTTP port on the SAP message server
- Activate /sap/public/icman and /sap/public/icf_info/* (Transaction SICF)

Table 2-1 Parameters Used to Estimate Memory Requirements for the Web Dispatcher

Variable	Parameter
S	wdisp/max_servers
N_S	wdisp/max_server_name_len
G	wdisp/max_server_groups
N_G	wdisp/max_server_group_name_len
U	wdisp/max_url_map_entries
N_U	wdisp/max_url_map_path_len

Command Line Option	Description
-f	Names the trace file other than the standard dev_webisp file.
-t	Sets the trace level.
-cleanup	Releases common resources such as shared memory. Use this if the web dispatcher crashed the last time it ran.
-shm_attch_mode <mode>	Tells the web dispatcher what you want to happen to the shared memory. The mode value is one or a combination of the following numbers: 1. Clean up by deleting the shared memory. 2. Attach to the shared memory. 3. Create a new shared memory. 4. Delete the existing shared memory and then create new shared memory. 5. Attach to existing shared memory, but create shared memory if shared memory doesn't exist.
-auto_restart	Makes the web dispatcher highly available because the web dispatcher automatically restarts if it crashes.
-version	Displays the version of the web dispatcher without starting the web dispatcher.

Table 2-2 Command Line Options for Starting the Web Dispatcher

Running and Stopping the Web Dispatcher

Start the web dispatcher by entering the following command:

```
sapwebdisp pf=<Prof<k0>ile name>
```

You'll notice there are several optional parameters that can be used to customize how the web dispatch functions. Table 2-2 describes each optional parameter. Here's how to use it on the command line.

```
sapwebdisp pf=<profile name> [-f <tracefile> -t <tracelevel> -cleanup
-shm_attch_mode <mode> -auto_restart -version]
```

You can stop the web dispatcher by issuing the Kill or Sapntkill command depending on the operating system used to run the web dispatcher. If you're running UNIX, then use the Kill command followed by the process ID for the web dispatcher as shown here:

```
Kill -2 <pid>
```

If you're running Windows NT, then use the Sapntkill command followed by the process ID for the web dispatcher as shown here:

```
Sapntkill - INT <pid>
```

You'll find the process ID for the web dispatcher in the dev_webdisp trace file located in the working directory.

Dual Role for the Web Application Server

Although we tend to think of the web application server as only a web server, it can also operate as a web client that creates HTTP requests in an ABAP program and then sends the request to the web server (the same server). The web server treats the HTTP request as if it came from a web client located on a different machine.

In the web client role, the request is written to an MPI, which sends the request to the ICM using TPC/IP over a network connection. The MPI processes the request and sends the response to the ICF process.

The Web Dispatcher and the SAP J2EE Engine

You can utilize features of J2EE in your application if you integrate the SAP J2EE Engine into your system. The integration is a fairly straightforward process. You'll need to configure the Web AS so that it can process both ABAP and J2EE requests or so that it can process only J2EE requests. Your choice depends on whether you have a dedicated system for J2EE.

In order to used the J2EE Engine, you'll need to activate /sap/public/icman and /sap/public/icf_info. Icman is the service ICM uses to forward requests to the J2EE server. Icf_info supplies the web dispatcher with various information needed to carry out load balancing.

When a request is received, the web dispatcher decides if it should be sent to the web application server or the J2EE server. The web application server can process both the ABAP request and a Java request. If the web application server receives a Java request from the web dispatcher, the web application server forwards that request to the SAP J2EE engine.

The J2EE Engine and the SAP Web AS must run together in order for the J2EE Engine to leverage the load balancing mechanism. In the event you want to use the J2EE Engine without ABAP and other SAP Web AS functions, an alternative is to run the stand-alone dispatcher dpj2ee. The stand-alone dispatcher doesn't require a database, work process, or a SAP gateway. It starts the ICM and the J2EE Engine itself and connects to the message server. You'll need to set the profile parameter icm/dpj2ee to TRUE in order to run the stand-alone dispatcher.

Before starting the SAP J2EE engine, you'll need to set the rdisp/j2ee_start parameter to 1. This can be done dynamically in the Transaction RZ11. Next, start the ICM monitor (Transaction SMICM). From the opening screen, select Administration J2EE Server to see a list of options for the J2EE Server.

Distributing SAP Systems and Services

SAP provides the tools needed to configure a distribution to achieve a consistent optimal performance. The system administrator uses these tools to tailor the distribution for the specific needs of clients. For example, the system administrator is able to create logon load balancing that enables the system to automatically select the most efficient instance server based on current operating performance and usage.

In this section, you'll learn how to use dynamic load balancing and other tools to make your SAP system and services custom perform for your distribution.

Instance Profiles

A *profile* in the SAP system is an operating system file containing parameters and configuration information of an instance. Because a SAP system might contain from one to several instances, many profiles may also exist.

Individual setup parameters can be customized to the requirements of each instance.

The profiles are an essential part of technical and basis settings of the system, and the values they contain play the most important role when tuning the system.

The profiles are used when starting and stopping the system because they are in charge of allocating or deallocating the necessary resources as specified in the profile parameters.

These individual parameters let you customize the following:

- The runtime environment of the instance (resources such as main memory size, shared memory, roll size)
- Which services are available for the instance (which work processes and how many)
- Where other services are located (database host, message server, etc.)

The profile files are located under the directory /usr/sap/<SID>/SYS/profile (logically should point to the directory /sapmnt/<SID>/profile), which is shared by all application servers belonging to the same SAP system (same SID). These profile files are text files that are structured in the following ways:

> The comment lines are preceded by a # sign, for example, # *Parameters corresponding to dispatcher functions.*
>
> There are lines with parameter value with the syntax *parameter = value.* For example, the number of background work processes running in this instance is *rdisp/wp_no_btc* = *4*. Usually, parameters belonging to a group of logically related functions are prefixed by a common root (in the preceding example, the *rdisp/* prefix controls the group of dispatcher parameters within an instance).

All host computers in an SAP R/3 system can access these profiles. It is possible for several Web AS instances to use a single profile simultaneously. Separate profiles are not required for each Web AS instance.

Profiles can be edited and maintained manually using the sappad editor, which can be very useful if the system cannot start because of some error in parameters. However, it is strongly recommended that all profile maintenance be performed from within SAP R/3 using the transaction RZ10 (*Edit Profiles*), which is part of the Computer Center Management System (CCMS).

An edited profile is not active (its values are not considered by the system) until the corresponding instance is restarted.

Profile Types

There are several types of profiles available on the SAP R/3 system for correct setup and configuration. These profiles are as follows:

- The *start profile,* which defines the SAP R/3 services to start. There might be as many start profiles as instances.
- The *default profile,* which acts as a common configuration of profile values for instances taking part of the SAP system. There is only one default profile in a SAP system.
- The *instance profile,* which contains specific instance parameter values. There might be as many as the number of instances.

All the SAP profiles are located under a common directory, /usr/sap/<SID>/SYS/profile, shared by all instances belonging to the same SID.

Before continuing with the profile types, there are a couple of interesting topics common to profiles: how the variables are handled in the profiles and what the actual value assigned to a SAP parameter is, considering that it can either be in the default profile, the instance profile, or no profile.

Variables Substitution in the Profiles

The SAP profiles include some syntax rules used when substituting parameter values using variables. These rules are very similar to the ones used in normal shell script commands.

The parameter values in the profiles can include the following variables:

- *$(parameter_name)* at runtime is substituted by the value of the parameter specified in parentheses. For example,

  ```
  global_dir_param = '/usr/sap/DD1/SYS/global'
  syslog_param = $(global_dir_param)/SLOGJ
  ```

  Therefore, syslog_param = /usr/sap/DD1/SYS/global/SLOGJ
- *$$* is replaced by the SAP system number. For example,

  ```
  rslg/collect_daemon/talk_port = 13$$ and the SAP system number is 00,
  ```

  then

  ```
  rslg/collect_daemon/talk_port = 1300
  ```

The profiles might also include some *local substitute variables.* These variables only have an effect within the profiles and are not used by the SAP programs. The names of the local variables always begin with an underscore (_) sign and are mainly used for setting other parameter values. For example, if

_EXEDIR = /usr/sap/DD1/SYS/exe/run

and

myparam = _EXEDIR

then

myparam = /usr/sap/DD1/SYS/exe/run

The Values of the Profile Parameters

The parameter values that influence the way the Web AS system allocates resources or services can be set either in the default profile, in the instances profiles, in both at the same time, or in none of them.

The SAP profile parameters are read by the startup program to assign the needed resources to the SAP processes. The parameter values are set by following these rules:

- If a specific parameter appears in the instance profile, this value is the preferred one used by the SAP processes.
- If the parameter is not included in the instance profile, then the system checks whether it is contained in the default profile. If it is there, then the system takes this value for the SAP processes.
- If the parameter is not in any of the profiles, then the default value from the source program code is assumed.

Administrators should ensure that the parameters do not appear in both profiles at the same time on occasions where that's not needed. There are, however, situations where it is convenient to have a particular parameter in the default profile and also in some instance profiles. For example, suppose you want to set the default login language to English in all instances but two, which belong to the Italian subsidiary. In this case, you can set the parameter for the language in the default profile as English and set the system login language parameter to Italian in the two instances to use Italian as the preferred language.

To see a list of all profile parameters in a SAP instance, you can run the standard SAP report, RSPARAM or RSPFPAR. To do so, select System | _Services | _Reporting from any Web AS window, enter RSPARAM or RSPFPAR in the program input field, and press the Execute button. You get a long report list, which should be sent to the printer to see it in full because it usually does not fit on the screen.

Start Profile

The start profile is an operating system file that defines which Web AS services are started. The start profile is a parameter file that is read by the startsap program. Among the services that the start profile can initiate are the message server, the gateway, dialog, enqueue, system log collector and log sender programs, or any other locally defined program.

The start profile is located under the /usr/sap/<SID>/profile directory. These profiles are generated automatically by SAP when the system is first installed. Depending on the release version, the names assigned are either START_<instance_name> or START_<instance_name>_<hostname>; for example, START_DVEBMGS00, START_D01_copi02, where *DVEBMGS00* and *D01* are instance names and *copi02* is the hostname of instance D01.

The start profile includes some general system variables, which are substituted by their real values at runtime, such as the following:

- SAPSYSTEMNAME, which is substituted by the name of the SAP R/3 system. For example, *DD1* as shown in the previous listing.
- INSTANCE_NAME is the variable for the name of the SAP R/3 instance. For example, *DVEBMGS00.*

Besides those general SAP system parameters, the start profile only allows for some specific parameter names and syntax. Those permitted parameters are as follows:

- Execute_xx, where *xx* can go from 00 to 99. These lines can be used to start operating system programs or commands to prepare the Web AS system for start.

For example, this parameter can be used to set up logical links to the executable programs on the UNIX platforms.

- Start_Program_xx, where *xx* can go from 00 to 99. This parameter is used to start the Web AS instances services in an application server.
- Stop_Program_xx, where *xx* can go from 00 to 99. Know the meaning of this parameter because the word *stop* can be confusing. This parameter is used to start an operating system program, command, or SAP program *after* the Web AS instance is stopped, for example, running the program that stops the saposcol, the saprouter, or the cleaning of shared memory areas that were being used by the Web AS system.

The number *xx* defines the sequence of execution. The programs specified in Execute lines are the first executed. Then the system starts the programs included in the Start_Program parameters. After the specific SAP instance is stopped, then the programs specified in the Stop_Program parameters are started.

To the right of the equal sign in the three preceding parameters, SAP allows for the execution of local programs (located in the same server) or remote programs (located in a remotely connected server).

Programs running on the local server are preceded by the word *local* in the parameter value. In the previous listing you can see that all the lines are preceded by the *local* keyword.

To run programs on a remote host instead of the local host, the parameter values must be preceded by the remote hostname. For example, Execute_00 = copi01 saposcol, where *copi01* is a remote hostname and *saposcol* the name of the program to execute.

Default Profile

The SAP default profile is an operating system file that contains parameter values used by all application servers from the same SAP system.

The name for this profile cannot be changed. It is always called DEFAULT.PFL. The default profile, like all other profiles, is located in the common profile directory of the SAP R/3 system: /usr/sap/<SID>/SYS/profile.

There is always one active default profile. Default profiles are also called *system profiles.*

The profile parameters included in the default profile are meant for those values that either are unique in the system, and therefore are the same for all instances, or to enter global parameters to be shared by all instances. Examples of such parameters are the hostname of the database server, the message server, and so forth.

Figure 2-15 shows the same parameter file as seen from CCMS. The default profile is generated automatically by the system when this is first installed. It includes the usual parameters.

Parameter Description

```
SAPDBHOST Hostname of the database server
rdisp/vbname Name of the update server
rdisp/btcname Name of the default background server
rdisp/mshost Name of the message server
rdisp/sna_gateway Name of the host running the SNA gateway service
rdisp/sna_gw_service Name of the TCP/IP service to connect to the SNA
gateway service
rdisp/enqname Name of the enqueue server
```

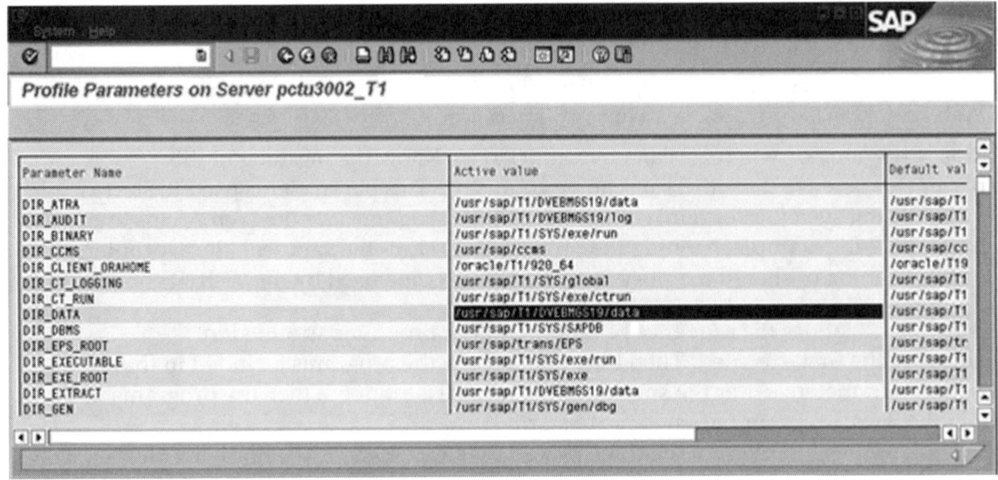

Parameter Name	Active value	Default val
DIR_ATRA	/usr/sap/T1/DVEBMGS19/data	/usr/sap/T1
DIR_AUDIT	/usr/sap/T1/DVEBMGS19/log	/usr/sap/T1
DIR_BINARY	/usr/sap/T1/SYS/exe/run	/usr/sap/T1
DIR_CCMS	/usr/sap/ccms	/usr/sap/cc
DIR_CLIENT_ORAHOME	/oracle/T1/920_64	/oracle/T19
DIR_CT_LOGGING	/usr/sap/T1/SYS/global	/usr/sap/T1
DIR_CT_RUN	/usr/sap/T1/SYS/exe/ctrun	/usr/sap/T1
DIR_DATA	/usr/sap/T1/DVEBMGS19/data	/usr/sap/T1
DIR_DBMS	/usr/sap/T1/SYS/SAPDB	/usr/sap/T1
DIR_EPS_ROOT	/usr/sap/trans/EPS	/usr/sap/tr
DIR_EXECUTABLE	/usr/sap/T1/SYS/exe/run	/usr/sap/T1
DIR_EXE_ROOT	/usr/sap/T1/SYS/exe	/usr/sap/T1
DIR_EXTRACT	/usr/sap/T1/DVEBMGS19/data	/usr/sap/T1
DIR_GEN	/usr/sap/T1/SYS/gen/dbg	/usr/sap/T1

FIGURE 2-15 Default profile as seen from the CCMS utility (Copyright by SAP AG)

System administrators can modify or add to the default profile and include any other SAP parameter from the CCMS tool. For new parameters to have effect, the profile has to be activated and all instances belonging to the same SAP system must be restarted.

Instance Profiles

The instance profiles are the third type of profiles and are very important for providing the SAP instances with lots of parameters that directly affect the configuration and resources for the application servers.

The instance parameters typically define how many and what type of work processes are to be started for an instance. They also define the amount of shared memory, the allocation of buffer space and related pools, the instance default login language, and so forth. Parameters set in the instance profiles have precedence over the same ones defined in the default profile.

Instance profiles are automatically generated by the R3 setup utility when an instance (dialog or central) is installed. By default, the name assigned to them has the format <SID>_<instancename> or <SID>_<instancename>_<hostname>, but you can choose any name for them. If you choose a different name than the standard, you should modify accordingly the start profiles to reflect the new names.

It is also possible to use the same instance profile to start SAP instances on different computers. In this case, make sure that the hardware resources available are the same or very similar. You cannot allocate more memory in an instance profile than the actual available memory in the server.

Profiles Maintenance

You should only edit the profiles from the SAP R/3 system using the CCMS profile maintenance tool. Figure 2-16 shows one screen of the maintenance tools in display mode.

Refer to the section entitled "Profile Maintenance Options" in Chapter 11 for extensive information on profile maintenance.

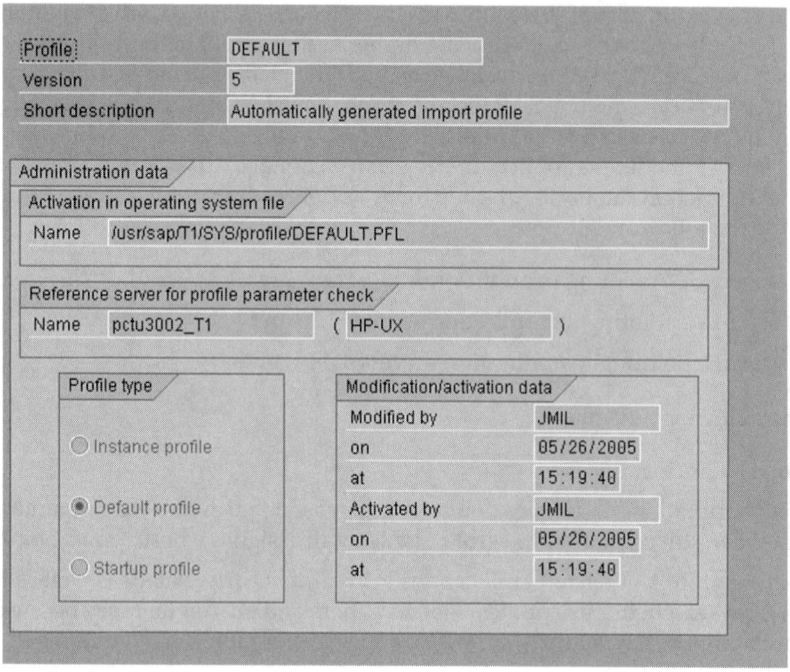

FIGURE 2-16 Only edit SAP R/3 system profiles using the CCMS profile maintenance tool (Copyright by SAP AG)

User Distribution: Logon Load Balancing and the SAP Logon Utility

SAP provides utilities to configure and efficiently divide the system load among the available servers. The load balancing is provided dynamically.

For example, you can define the number of total users allowed to log on in a particular instance and the response time threshold for that instance.

With those values the system will decide upon a user logon request which is the best application server for the user to log on.

The process of configuring logon balancing involves two tasks:

1. Configuring the logon groups, which is accomplished from the CCMS utilities within the Web AS system
2. Installing and configuring the SAP logon Windows application in every workstation that is going to log on to the Web AS system

Logon Groups Configuration

System administrators can centrally configure several logon groups containing one or more application instances. When users log on in a defined group, the system automatically selects the instance server, according to the best performance and the number of connected users.

Configuring logon groups is not only meant to balance the load; when enough instances are defined it is also a good way to provide higher system availability for users. For example, suppose you have a SAP installation with one database server and seven application servers running one SAP instance each. Your installation has 400 concurrent users from the SAP application modules: FI, MM, SD, and CO. Every module has 100 users.

However, SAP modules support different transactional loads. It's well known that an average SD transaction can be about three times as demanding as an average FI transaction. If you define the following groups:

- *Group FI/CO,* pointing to application servers 1, 2, and 3
- *Group MM,* pointing to application servers 4, 5, and 6
- *Group SD,* pointing to application servers 4, 5, 6, and 7

you get the following advantages:

- Load balancing.
- If an application server goes down for any reason (hardware error, maintenance, etc.) users can still connect to the group, which will assign the best application server.
- Setting groups of related applications (MM and SD are related, as well as FI and CO) makes a better use of the instance buffers and shared memory because the probability of having the same called programs or tables in the buffers is high.

In the preceding example, application server 7 is only assigned to SD users because it is the most demanding module among those applications and also because you can configure this server to allow a smaller number of users with the most time-critical work, for instance, printing invoices, getting orders, and so on. Other very demanding SAP application modules are PP (production planning) or PS (project system).

To log on to the SAP R/3 system, users only need to know the SID of the R/3 system and the name of the logon group. They don't need to specify the hostname or system numbers of the SAP instances.

To create a logon group, from the main menu, select Tools | _CCMS | Configuration | _Logon Groups. Or enter transaction code SMLG in the command field.

This procedure can be done while the SAP R/3 system is running normally; there is no need to stop it.

If there are no logon groups defined yet, the system displays a window with just the name of the current instance. If there are groups already set, then it displays a list with the group names, the SAP instances, and the status of the instances.

To create or edit a logon group, click the Create Entry button on the application toolbar. The system displays the Create Assignment window, like the one shown in Figure 2-17. If you only see the first two fields, press the right arrow button to see the remaining fields.

On this screen, you can enter

- *Logon group.* Enter a name for the logon group to be defined. Use a name that can be easily understood. For example, for SD users, set something like "SD group," "SD module," or "Sales." If there were previously created groups, you can click on the possible entries arrow to display or select a group.

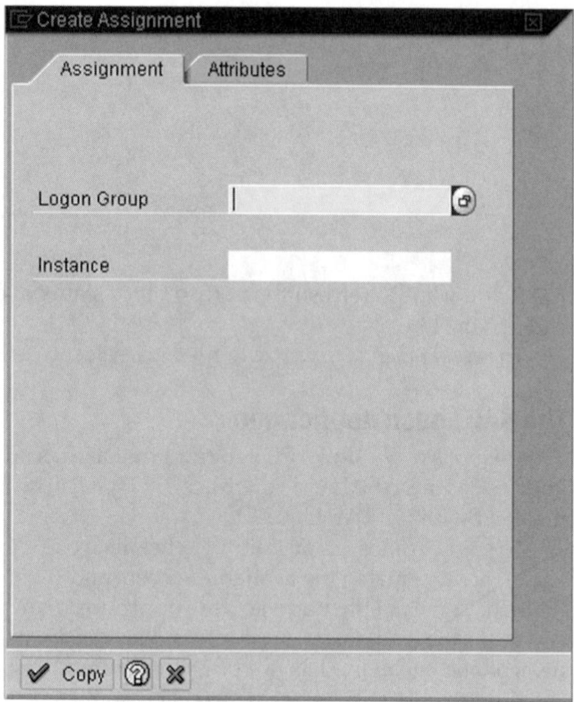

FIGURE 2-17 Creating entry dialog box for logon groups (Copyright by SAP AG)

- *Instance.* Enter at least one instance for a group. Clicking on the possible entries arrow displays the available SAP instances defined in the system.

To get information about a particular logon group, double-click on any line where the group appears. The > button is useful both for editing and displaying the load limit information about a logon group and instance.

The screen is extended showing the response time and number of users limit set for that instance in the logon group. These fields are not mandatory; you can leave them blank if you don't want to set any restriction on that group or instance. But if the response time has been defined for a group in a particular instance, then you have to define a response time limit for every group using the same instance.

When all the information is entered, press the Copy button to save your entries.

Define at least another instance for the same logon group. Having a single instance in a group does not make much sense from the point of view of load balancing. It would be the same as logging in with the normal SAP GUI pointing to the hostname and instance number.

From the main logon load balancing screen, administrators can monitor the load of the groups and the users connected. To do this, select Goto | Load Distribution from the menu.

The system displays a list with an overview of the current load, showing the performance status of the instances assigned to logon groups. Each application server writes its performance statistics to a memory resident table on the message server every five minutes.

FIGURE 2-18 SAP logon main menu (Copyright by SAP AG)

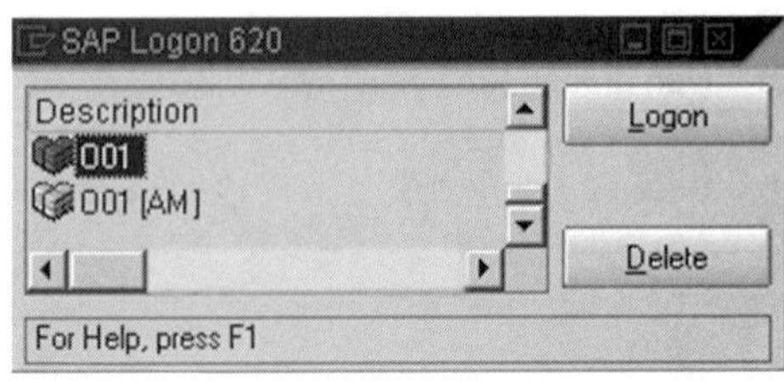

If you want to refresh the performance status of any application server, just double-click on the line.

To see the users currently logged on, select Goto | User List from the menu.

The SAP Logon Application

SAP logon is a Windows PC program that acts as an interface between the Web AS system and the common SAP user interface, SAP GUI. The SAP logon program is automatically installed with the SAP GUI.

To start SAP logon, just double-click its icon. Figure 2-18 shows an example. The SAP logon menu contains the available servers and logon groups that must be previously defined. You can either add servers or groups manually, or you can request a particular server for the available groups and make it add entries automatically. If it is the first time using it and the menu has not been configured by someone else, it might be empty.

To log on to a SAP system, just click on the entry and press the Logon button or simply double-click on the entry. When selecting a logon group, the system will select the application server with the best response time.

This procedure is accomplished by SAP by means of the message server, which logs the availability and response times of all application servers for a SAP system.

SAP Logon Configuration

To make good use of the features of the SAP logon application, users or the administrator must configure some settings on the logon menu, such as adding servers or groups.

To add a new server to the menu automatically, select the Server . . . button. A dialog window will show up requesting the data for the new server.

Now you have to specify the SAP system ID, the hostname where the message server is running, and the application server where the SAP router is running. SAP router is a special SAP program used for the connection with the message server. If SAP router is not running, you can leave this field blank (select <NONE>). You can add servers from different SAP systems to the same SAP logon menu or even configure a direct access to the SAP net system.

Upon pressing the Generate List button, if there are available application servers, they are displayed in the list box in the window. From this screen, you can decide either to log on to the server (Logon button), add it to the list of servers (Add button), or do both things at once (Add and Logon button). If there are none, then you have to add them manually.

Defining groups is a very similar process. From the main SAP logon window, select the Group Selection button. The system displays a new window that has exactly the same fields as the server selection windows.

Enter the SAP system ID, the message server, and SAP router information and press the OK button. The list box will display the active logon groups in the SAP system. From this screen, you can decide either to log on to the group (Logon button), add it to the list of groups (Add button), or do both things at once (Add and Logon button).

The SAP logon application also provides the possibility of manually entering new entries or editing existing ones. To add a new entry, click on the New button from the SAP Logon menu. In the New Entry window, enter the necessary information in the available input fields:

- *Description.* You can enter here any short description you want for the server. For example, you can enter the system name or something like *Development System.*
- *Application server.* Specify in this field the name of the host for the application server.
- *SAP router string.* If you are reaching your server via the SAP router program, then enter the routing entry here.
- *System number.* Enter the system or instance number of the SAP system to which you want to connect.

If you want to change an existing entry, click on the Edit button on the main SAP logon menu and change the data you want, except for the application server and system number when modifying logon group entries.

The SAP logon application also includes some configuration options that are not seen directly on the menu. To show those options, click on the top left corner of the SAP logon window and select Options.

Figure 2-19 shows the dialog box displayed on the screen. This dialog box is mainly used for troubleshooting the SAP logon application or looking for connection problems. The available fields are grouped in two boxes. The first one is the Sap Logon Options, which includes the following:

- *Language.* This is used for selecting the SAP logon language. It must have been previously installed, and not all languages are available.
- *Message server time-out.* The value, specified in seconds, is the time the SAP logon waits for a response from the message server of the SAP R/3 system. The default value is 10 seconds. If you experience time-out problems, then increase this value.
- *Confirmation of listbox entry delete.* When this check box is selected, the system displays a warning before an entry is deleted from the SAP logon menu.
- *Disable editing functionality.* This entry can be used to disable users from modifying logon entries. If the check box is selected, then the buttons in the SAP logon menu (Edit, New, Delete, and other options in the entry or group selection menu such as Add and Add and Logon) are grayed out and can't be used. However, the easiest way to protect the SAP logon configuration from editing is to force users to use the SAP logon-PAD program (SAPLGPAD.EXE), which behaves just like SAP logon but without editing and configuration options. This is automatically installed with the SAP GUI from R/3 release 4.5. Newer SAP logon versions include also a list of configuration files so that you can edit those files directly.

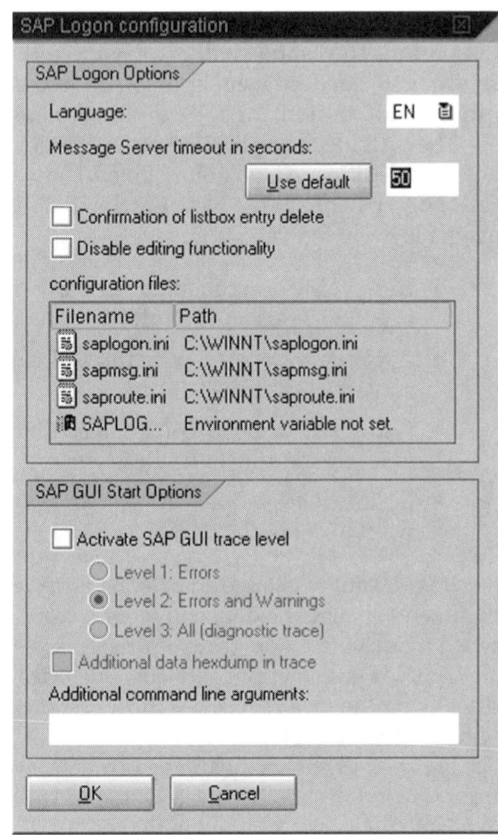

FIGURE 2-19 SAP logon configuration dialog box (Copyright by SAP AG)

The second box is the SAP GUI Start Options, which has the following fields:

- *Activate SAP GUI trace level.* When this option is set, you first can activate a trace. Then select the radio buttons to the right to choose the level of information that the trace file will record.
- *Additional data hexdump in trace.* This option can only be selected when the trace has been activated. When this option is selected, the trace will include additional memory areas. Please note that having both the trace file and the hexdump activated can result in loss of performance and the generation of very large trace files. When you finish a trace, deactivate those options and delete the trace files.
- *Additional command line arguments.* In this field, you can enter additional arguments to the command line when starting the SAP GUI. Use this field and commands as requested by the SAP hotline in case of problems.

Administering the SAP Logon Application

SAP system managers can configure the settings for the SAP logon application and then distribute those settings to the end users. In order to do that, they must know what the configuration files are that the SAP logon application uses.

The configuration files of the SAP logon are standard Windows system initialization files (INI files) located under the main Windows environment directory (normal locations for this directory are c:\win95, c:\winnt, depending on the Windows version and the users installation directory).

These INI files are as follows:

- *sapmsg.ini.* This is the initialization file that contains the list of hosts running the message servers. In the following example, the user can connect to SAP systems TT1 and DD1, which are running the message server in the node specified to the right of the equal sign.

  [Message Server]

  TT1 = copi01

  DD1 = copi02

  The first line of the file must contain the [Message Server] keyword. This file is updated automatically when users enter new SAP systems in the SAP logon menu.

- *saproute.ini.* This initialization file contains route strings for the entries included in the SAP logon menu. For example,

  [Router]

  DD1 Development = /H/copi02/S/sapdp00

  For every possible connection, there must be a line with the format

  <route_name> = <route_string>

  Route strings can concatenate multiple route entries when a connection uses multiple SAP routers. The format for this strings is

  /H/<host with saprouter>/S/<service where saprouter is running>/H/. . . .

- *saplogon.ini.* This is the initialization file that stores all the configuration settings, servers, groups, system, routes, and so forth that have been defined for the SAP logon menu.

Finally, there is a very important file for the SAP logon to communicate correctly with the SAP system message servers. This communication is established via standard TCP/IP sockets. These are defined in the services file \WINNT\system32\drivers\etc for W2000. This file can be located in the same Windows directory or in a different one depending on the TCP/IP software you are using. You must ensure that for each entry in the sapmsg.ini file, you have a corresponding TCP service entry in the services file. These entries have the form of sapms<SID> <socket number>/TCP. For example,

sapmsDD1 3600/tcp

sapmsTT1 3605/tcp

NOTE *A typical cause of problems with SAP logon configurations when editing the services file and including the entry for the message server in the last line is not placing a carriage return after the entry. A way to avoid the problem is not to insert the entry at the end.*

You also must ensure that the service names and numbers are exactly the same as those defined on the SAP servers in the corresponding services file.

If you as administrator want to present for end users the available options with SAP logon, you have to make a base configuration for them, which is recorded in the saplogon .ini file.

If you don't want users to define their own settings, you have to deactivate the selection options Groups and Server. In order to preset the settings and protect them against modifications, just copy them to the saplogon.ini file and make sure they have the right entries in the services file. Then make sure they don't have the sapmsg.ini and the saproute .ini files.

With the saplogon.ini file, when users start the SAP logon application, they have all the selections preset. This is the only one really needed. If you want even better protection against users modifying their entries, you can set the entry *Restricted Mode = 1* in the Configuration section of the saplogon.ini file and make this file write-protected.

You can use any of the programs for software distribution available in the market to send those files to all end users connected to the network.

Starting and Stopping SAP Systems

To start the SAP R/3 system, log on at the operating system level using the *<sid>adm* (lowercase) user account that was created during installation.

For example, if the SID was defined as DD1, then log in as UNIX user *dd1adm* and enter the password.

To start SAP R/3 on UNIX systems, just execute the *startsap* command. For example,

```
dd1adm> startsap
```

The *startsap* command is really a UNIX *alias* (a symbolic name pointing to something else) that calls the needed start programs. To stop the system, enter *stopsap* in the command line.

The startsap options are

- UNIX

  STARTSAP = startsap R3

  STOPSAP = stopsap R3

- Windows

  STARTSAP = \\$(SAPGLOBALHOST)\sapmnt\$(system)\sys\exe\run\startsap.exe

  name = <SID> nr 5 <SYSTEMNR> SAPDIAHOST 5 <HOST>

  STOPSAP 5 \\$(SAPGLOBALHOST)\sapmnt\$(system)\sys\exe\run\stopsap.exe

  name = <SID> nr = <SYSTEMNR> SAPDIAHOST = <HOST>

On Windows NT systems, you can start and stop Web AS from within the SAP Service Manager that is located on the NT Programs menu, within the SAP R/3 programs group.

Starting the SAP R/3 system involves starting the underlying database and all the SAP processes configured to run in all application servers. The type and number of processes are configurable with the start profile and the instance profile parameters. These processes might include the following:

- The operating system and/or network performance collectors
- The central system log collection process
- The CPIC gateway server
- The message server
- The dispatcher processes
- The spool processes
- The dialog and background processes

The SAP R/3 system can be started and stopped by using operating system commands or from within the CCMS utilities. However, for the latter, at least the database server and the central instance must have been started first using the operating system startup commands. In current releases, the database system is not stopped from within Web AS either.

In centralized installations, with just one single server, one start and one stop command are enough for starting or stopping the whole system.

However, in distributed configurations, some configuration is needed to start and stop the group of application servers of a SAP system.

Starting the SAP system first requires starting the database and then the instance processes. Stopping is the opposite process: first you have to stop the instance processes and then the database background processes. For example, you can write a shell script command file that can start the whole system from a single server. In these cases, many people use remote shell commands to execute the start programs in remote computers.

Stopping can be done the same way. Remember that using remote commands (for example, rsh, remsh, or similar) can be a security violation in some systems because a list of permitted hosts is necessary. For this, check with your security manager.

To start or stop the SAP system in a UNIX environment, you must log on as user <sid>adm, for example, for SAP system DD1, as user *dd1adm*. The following commands are available.

NOTE *The brackets indicate optional parameters where you can choose just one from the list or none at all.*

1. startsap [R3] [DB] [ALL]
   - Using the command, startsap R3, only the SAP instance is started. It is assumed that the database is already running. Otherwise, the instance will not start successfully.
   - With the command, startsap DB, only the database is started.

- Using startsap ALL, the system will first start the database and then the SAP instance. *ALL* is the default setting and can be omitted. If the database is running, it will just start the instance.

2. stopsap [DB] [R3] [ALL]
   - Using stopsap R3, all the instance processes are stopped.
   - With the command, stopsap DB, the system stops just the database. Make sure you first stop the instance processes; otherwise, the SAP processes will "hang" because no update is possible.
   - Issuing the command, stopsap [ALL], the system stops the SAP instance and then the database. *ALL* is the default parameter and can be omitted.

When in distributed SAP installations with several application servers, pay attention to stopping all the instances before stopping the database, which is only located in the database server.

To check if the system has been correctly started or stopped, you can use standard UNIX operating system utilities such as the ps command. From the UNIX system, the SAP processes are prefixed by dw, so, for example, issuing the command

```
dd1adm> ps -eaf | grep dw
```

will show the SAP running processes. If you see no lines from the command output, then no SAP processes are running on this system.

NOTE *In different UNIX implementations, the options for the ps command might differ.*

Another way to check whether the SAP processes in an application server are running correctly is by selecting Tools | Administration | Monitor | _System Monitoring | _Process Overview from the standard SAP monitoring tools. Or, use the CCMS, which permits a check of all the application servers in the system by choosing Tools | _CCMS | Control Monitoring | Global Process Overview.

In the Web AS startup process, the startsap script calls the sapstart program with the startup profile as the argument. The startup profile is specified in the variable START_FILES, which is contained in the script. The script can be found under the home directory of the SAP administration user account, <sid>adm. The actual name of the script is usually startsap_<hostname>_<sap_system_number>, for example, startsap_copi01_00; the script startsap is really a UNIX alias defined in the login environment variables for the <sid>adm user.

When stopping the SAP system, the stopsap script calls the kill.sap script, which is located under the instance work directory (/usr/sap/<SID>/SYS/<INSTANCE>/work). The kill.sap script activates the shutdown processing in the sapstart process.

As can be seen, both the start and the stop process of the SAP R/3 system are initiated from the sapstart program, which is located under the executables directory. The syntax of this program is sapstart pf = <start_profile>.

For example,

```
tt1adm>/usr/sapC11/SYS/exe/run/sapstart
pf=/usr/sap/C11/SYS/profile/START_DVEBMGS00
```

When the sapstart program is executed, it reads from the start profile to determine the preliminary commands it has to process. These commands are preceded by the Execute_xx keyword, and often they just establish logical links or clean the shared memory.

It then launches the SAP processes as described in the Start_program_xx statements. The *xx* indicates the processing order. However, you should know that sapstart processes the entries asynchronously, which means it will not check the status of one process before proceeding with the next one.

The sapstart process is the mother of all the processes running in a SAP R/3 system. For that reason, when this process is shut down, all the child processes are shut down as well.

When in shutdown processing, the sapstart program executes the commands in the start profile and it will wait until all of its child processes terminate or it receives a stop signal from the system. The stopsap script works by sending the stop message to the sapstart program by means of the kill.sap script. This script is very simple, and what it contains is simply the PID of the sapstart process running in the system.

The SAP processes are also shut down asynchronously and therefore in parallel. Both the startsap and stopsap procedures are logged into files that are left in the home directory of the SAP administrator user account, <sid>adm. The names of these files are startsap_<hostname>_<sap_system_number>.log and stop_<hostname>_<sap_system_number>.log.

The sapstart program itself logs its processing in a log file located under the instance work directory: sapstart.log. This log file can be seen either from the operating system or inside the Web AS system from the monitoring and tracing utilities.

Starting and Stopping SAP WAS for ABAP under Windows

The process for starting or stopping SAP R/3 systems on Windows NT systems is basically the same as under UNIX, except that some of the programs are different, and also Windows NT includes a graphical interface, known as the *SAP Service Manager.*

Additionally,Windows NT reads some of the required SAP R/3 variables directly from the Registry. Starting Web AS from the SAP Service Manager requires that the SAP R/3 Service SAP<SAPSID>_<Instance_number> (for example, *SAPK2P_00*) be started. This is usually done automatically because the SAP R/3 service is defined for automatic start at system boot by default. In any case, to check whether the SAP R/3 service is running, on the Windows NT server, select Control Panel | Services and make sure that the SAP R/3 service has the status Started. If this is not the case, you will need to start it manually.

If the SAP R/3 service is started, to start the SAP R/3 system, select Programs | SAP R/3 | SAP Service Manager <SID>_<Instancenumber>. This program can be located in different places according to the Web AS release. It is recommended that system managers or SAP administrators create shortcuts on their desktops. Press the Start button to start the SAP R/3 system. It will start the database first and then the central instance. If the database was already started, then only the central instance is started. The system is completely started when the stoplights turn green. Stopping Web AS is also done from the SAP Service Manager, by pressing the Stop button. However, this procedure will not stop the database. In the case of Oracle and Informix, SAP R/3 can be stopped using *sapdba,* or the database-specific tools that in Windows NT can be used graphically or from the command line. For Microsoft SQL Server, the database can be stopped from the taskbar.

When the SAP R/3 system includes several instances (application servers), the procedure for starting those instances can be done from the SAP Service Manager of each server, or from the CCMS, once the database and central instance have been started.

However, when stopping the full SAP R/3 system, the first things to stop are the application servers, then the central instance, and finally the database.

The process of starting and stopping a full SAP R/3 system with several instances has been simplified since release 4.5 of SAP R/3 because installation of SAP R/3 on Windows NT requires the installation of the Microsoft Management Console, which enables starting and stopping all the instances centrally.

Notice, however, that on SAP R/3 installations on Microsoft Server Cluster Services (MSCS), the procedure for starting and stopping the system is quite different on the cluster nodes. Starting and stopping SAP R/3 and the database is done from the Cluster Administration application by selecting the service and choosing the action (Start, Stop, Move, etc.)

Further Guidelines for Productive Environments

The purpose of this section is to make the people in charge of technically implementing the system aware that installing the system is not the same thing as having it ready for productive day-to-day business work.

There are certain aspects of the SAP R/3 system that, from a technical and management point of view, must be carefully considered. Many of them apply to all installations, and others might not be necessary. All these points are discussed in more detail in different sections of this book.

These points are as follows:

- A backup and recovery strategy for R/3.
- Well-defined technical, functional, and development support lines for the users and developers of the system. This includes hardware and database vendors as well as SAP.
- Cleaning background jobs.
- Definition of daily or periodic tasks for the operation and support teams.
- Database administration.
- Printing strategy.
- System management procedures.
- Definition and setup of the CCMS operation modes and alerts.
- SAP R/3 monitoring (CCMS) and administration, including performance and tuning.
- Network monitoring and administration.
- Users and authorizations management.
- Preventive maintenance and EarlyWatch.
- External systems interfaces and batch input strategy.
- Upgrading the system: SAP, database, operating system.
- Hardware maintenance policy.
- Connection to SAP support servers.
- Implementation quality control.
- Disaster recovery strategy.

CHAPTER 3

SAP NetWeaver: An Overview

Responding to the major industry shift to a services-based, enterprise-scale, integrated business architecture, SAP has introduced Enterprise Services Architecture (ESA) by means of its integration and service-based platform, SAP NetWeaver.

SAP NetWeaver is the integration platform and the technical foundation on which almost all SAP solutions are currently based. SAP NetWeaver provides core functions for the infrastructure of all the SAP business solutions organized in four layers: people integration, information integration, process integration, and the application platform.

From this point on, SAP will develop all its business solutions based on this foundation. For customers, that will mean that every piece of modularized functionality—provided as part of a SAP solution, third-party solution, or developed by a customer or partner—can be made available as a Web service.

Enterprise Service Architecture

The concept of Enterprise Service Architecture is based on providing business functionality using Web services, located on an independent layer of the user interfaces and based on an abstract layer between these UIs and the business applications providing the different services.

Web services are services made available from a business's Web server for Web users or other Web-connected programs and applications. These services typically include a combination of data and programming.

Web services are very varied and range from business intelligence reports to customer relationship management, news, and tracking services.

Users can access some Web services through a peer-to-peer arrangement rather than by going to a central server. Some services can communicate with other services, and this exchange of procedures and data is generally enabled by a class of software known as middleware.

Besides the standardization and wide availability to users and businesses of the Internet itself, Web services are also increasingly enabled by the use of XML (eXtensible Markup Language) as a means of standardizing data formats and exchanging data. XML is the foundation for the Web Services Description Language (WSDL).

A number of new products have emerged that enable software developers to create or modify existing applications that can be "published" (made known and potentially accessible) as Web services. Providers of Web services are generally known as application service providers.

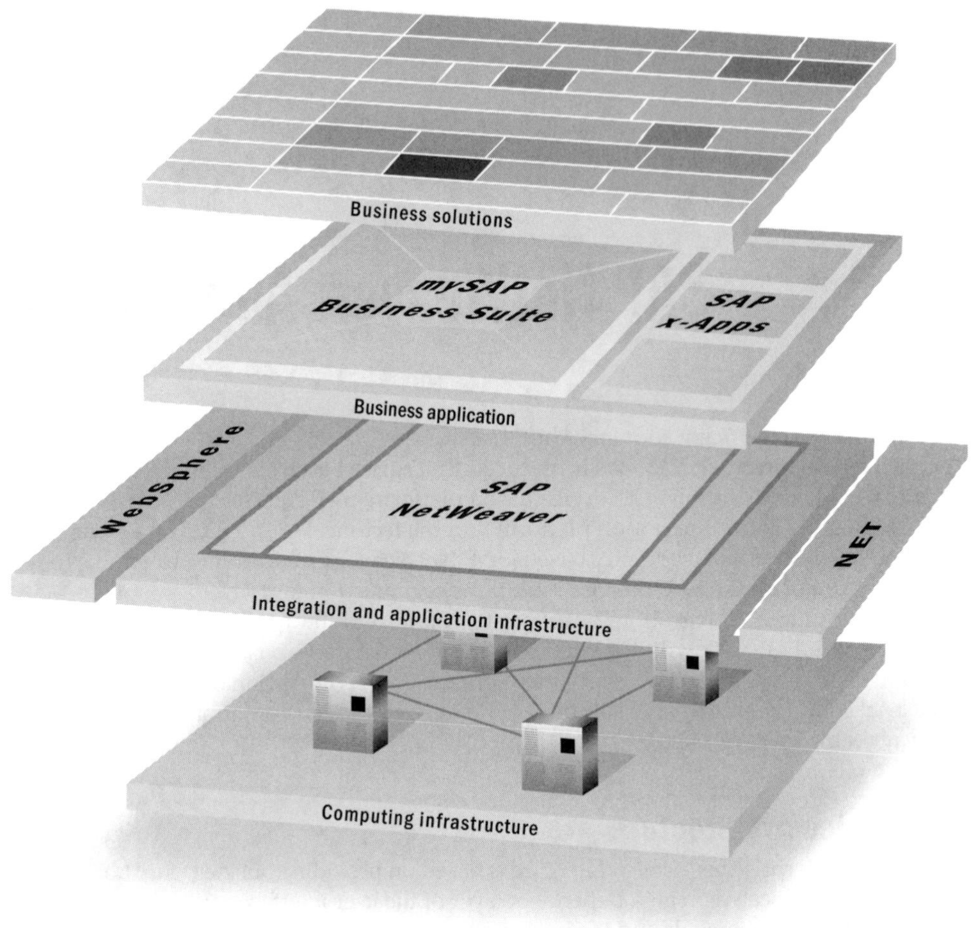

FIGURE 3-1 Evolution to Enterprise Service Architecture

Under this umbrella of ESA principles, SAP designed and built the NetWeaver platform. In other words, NetWeaver constitutes SAP's new services-oriented architecture. Figure 3-1 shows the evolution of the architectures supporting integrated business applications, ERP, and how NetWeaver now supports the SAP Business Solutions.

What's SAP NetWeaver?

As we have discussed, the SAP Enterprise Services Architecture (ESA) is implemented with the SAP NetWeaver, which is also the technological basis for the development of new solutions.

SAP NetWeaver it is the technical framework for all components of mySAP ERP, mySAP Business Suite, and the SAP composite applications, referred to as xAPPs.

FIGURE 3-2 SAP NetWeaver components

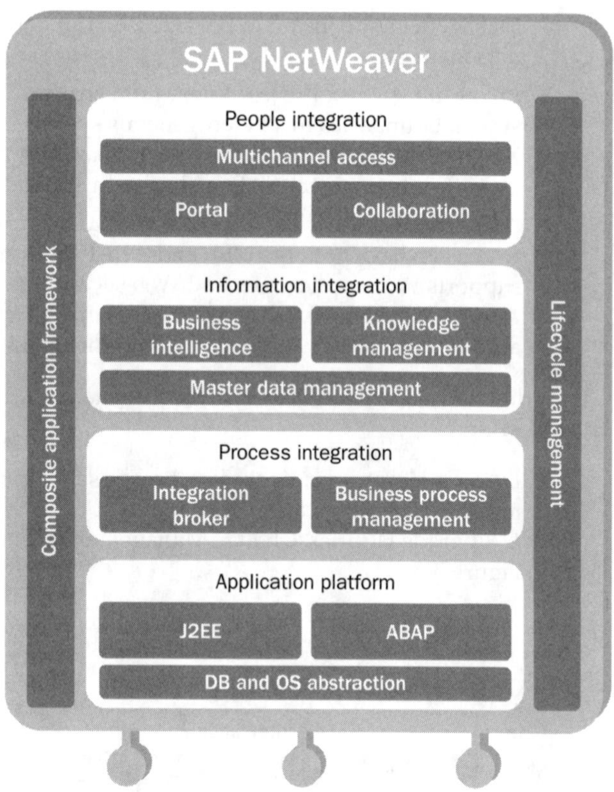

SAP NetWeaver is an application builder from SAP for integrating business processes, business applications, and databases from a number of sources while exploiting the leading Web services technologies.

NetWeaver is the first fully interoperable Web-based cross-application platform that can be used to develop not only SAP applications but others as well. NetWeaver allows a developer to integrate information and processes using diverse technologies, including Java technologies, IBM Websphere, and Microsoft's .NET.

Figure 3-2 shows the classical representation of the SAP NetWeaver platform.

The main elements of SAP NetWeaver include three integration layers and an application platform:

- *People Integration.* People Integration ensures that users have the information and functions that they require to perform their work as quickly and efficiently as possible. Solution at this level includes mainly the SAP Enterprise Portal, enhanced by multichannel access such as that enabled by the SAP Mobile Infrastructure.
- *Information Integration.* The Information Integration level provides access to all structured and unstructured information in the company. The core component here is the SAP Business Information Warehouse, which provides data from many different systems for evaluation and the decision-making process. Knowledge Management, a component of the SAP Enterprise Portal, and Master Data

Management are meant to provide functionality for consistent and central data management.

- *Process Integration.* Process Integration ensures that business processes run across system boundaries in a heterogeneous system landscape. This is achieved by using XML data packages and workflow scenarios, among other things. The main enabler component here is the SAP Exchange Infrastructure (XI).
- *Application platform.* The application platform is the SAP Web Application Server, which can have both the J2EE and ABAP runtime environments and therefore supports Web applications and Web services in an open development environment. Additionally, it includes the services required to provide connectivity and the abstraction layer for the database and the operating system.

Additionally, SAP NetWeaver includes some vertical or cross layer components, such as the following:

- *Lifecycle Management,* including a large set of applications and services available to other SAP NetWeaver components such as System Management, Installation & Upgrade Utilities, Change Management, Data Archiving, and so on. Refer to Figure 3-3.

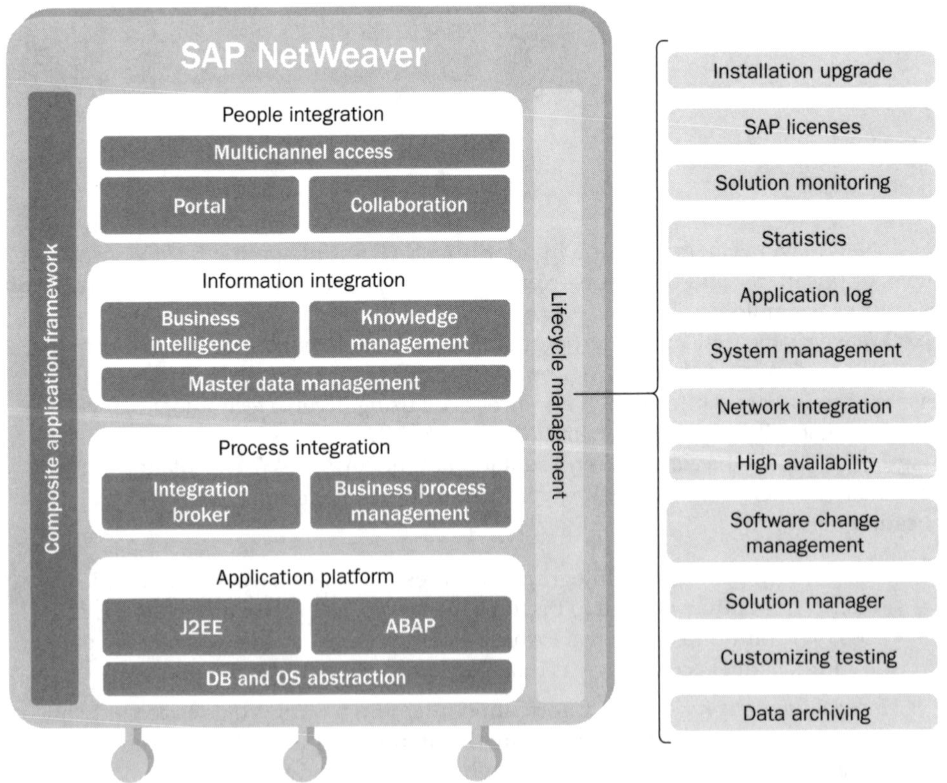

FIGURE 3-3 Utilities within the Lifecycle Management

- *Composite Application Framework (CAF),* which is basically a development environment based on business models, using Web services. From the model, the system can generate the code. With this framework, SAP NetWeaver is able to provide custom-built composite applications, composite applications within the mySAP Business Suite (for instance, to enhance a particular application), or the famous xApps, or cross applications.
- *Connectivity.* SAP NetWeaver and the supported solutions include a large number of connectors (Business Connector, Java Connector, .NET Connector, Marketplace Connector, SOAP Processor, etc.) and others that are supported from older SAP Basis releases, such as DCOM connector, and additionally support connectivity with environments based on IBM WebSphere or Microsoft .NET.

In summary, SAP NetWeaver is the SAP strategic integration and application platform that helps to organize people, information, and business processes across system and organization boundaries.

Different software interfaces, and the connectivity capabilities, ensure full interoperability of applications that are running on Java, Microsoft .NET, and IBM WebSphere, and for this reason, SAP NetWeaver can easily integrate information and applications from many sources.

Technologies for integrating business applications include the following:

- *SAP NetWeaver Developer Studio.* Development Environment based on the ECLIPSE standard and used to build Web Dynpro for Java.
- *Business Server Pages (BSP).* Web applications based on the ABAP engine.

These technologies interoperate with and can be extended using the primary market technologies—Microsoft .NET, Sun's J2EE, and IBM WebSphere.

Because all SAP solutions will be consolidated on the SAP Web Application Server, any dependencies between components will be resolved before customers install them. In addition, SAP's SQL-to-Java database capabilities will eliminate the need to create and maintain separate databases for various solutions. The following sections introduce in greater detail the different components of SAP NetWeaver.

SAP NetWeaver Application Platform

The SAP NetWeaver Application Platform is completely based on the SAP Web Application Server. The majority of SAP NetWeaver components and application modules are based on the SAP Web Application Server, typically known as SAP Web AS, as introduced in the previous chapter. Here we just summarize the main features of the SAP Web AS. For greater details please refer to Chapter 2. Figure 3-4 shows the SAP Web Application Server architecture. The second and most important difference now is that the SAP Web Application Server can both run either the traditional ABAP engine or the Java engine (J2EE) so that the SAP Web AS supports the development and operation of J2EE and ABAP-based applications and Web services.

The Web AS is divided into three layers:

- The presentation layer enables communication with clients, such as the SAP GUI or the Web browsers.

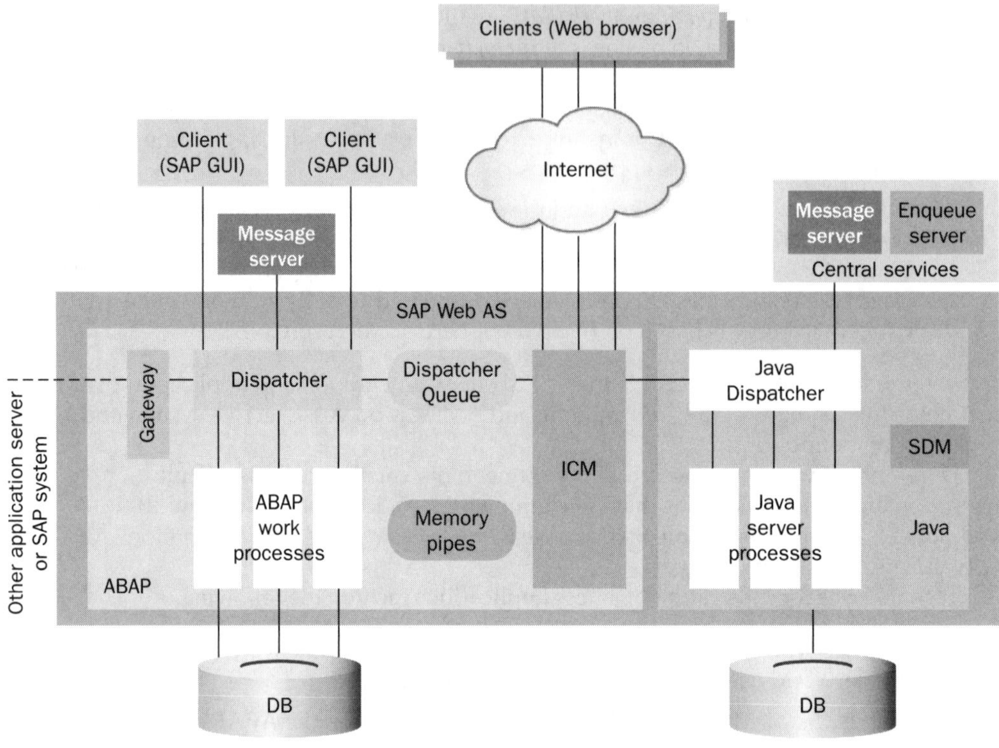

FIGURE 3-4 From the SAP Application Server to the SAP Web AS

- The business logic level defines business rules and processes.
- External connections are made via the integration layer.

The Java engine, Enterprise Edition (J2EE) is the basis for Java support via the SAP Web AS. For example, J2EE is one option for implementing Web services, Web front ends, or mobile clients. Mobile clients access the Web Dynpro application, which is built using the Web Dynpro development and runtime environment. J2EE also allows the rapid and simple integration of clients via standards such as Web services. Within any J2EE environment, a central role is played by the adapter engine. The engine generates the XML files required for data transfer and exchange.

With the release of the SAP Web Application Server 6.40, the following new and enhanced components were introduced:

ABAP

- Web services framework
- New ABAP debugger and memory inspector
- Shared objects

- Assertions and breakpoints
- Simple XSLT transformations
- Web Dynpro development for ABAP

Java

- Advanced Web Dynpro development tools for Java: Data Modeler, Dictionary Import, support for data types such as currency and conversion routines
- Integration of Adobe Document Services for Interactive PDF Forms in Web Dynpro
- Component-based development for J2EE and Web Dynpro
- Java Development Infrastructure that covers the whole life cycle of application development and offers a server side environment consisting of a design time repository (DTR), component build service (CBS), and change management service (CMS)

For more extensive information about the SAP Web Application Server, its layers, architecture, and features, refer to Chapter 2.

SAP Enterprise Portal

The SAP Enterprise Portal (SAP EP) is the core SAP NetWeaver component from the point of view of the role-based user access to a world of applications and Web services. At the time of the SAP NetWeaver '04 release, the SAP Portal solution is now being called SAP Enterprise Portal 6.0 on Web AS 6.40 (SAP EP 6.0 on Web AS 6.40).

Main and basic capabilities of the SAP Portal include the Portal Infrastructure, Knowledge Management, and Collaboration.

The SAP Enterprise Portal is designed to provide standardized, role-based access to all relevant information and functions throughout the enterprise. It is the user's central point of entry into the mySAP Business Suite solutions or other applications.

As it is usual with Web-based portals, the SAP Enterprise Portal is based on a conventional Web server, which can be provided by different vendor technologies, the most popular being the ones by Microsoft or Apache.

Before the SAP Web Application Server, Web connectivity for SAP solutions was achieved via SAP Internet Transaction Server (SAP ITS). As with Web AS 6.40, SAP ITS is integrated.

In order to reference data from diverse sources, such as applications or databases, the SAP Enterprise Portal features a unification server, which includes a collaboration component, supporting real-time collaboration among teams and communities via virtual rooms and different collaboration tools.

As one of the strategic and user centric components of SAP NetWeaver, the SAP Enterprise Portal provides key capabilities such as Portal Infrastructure, Knowledge Management, and Collaboration, all completely based on open technology and standards.

After the release of the SAP Enterprise Portal 6.0, after the SP3, SAP included many new technical features to improve the management, the construction, and the performance of the Portal, such as an improved load balancing and clustering architecture, extended platform support, new connectors, performance optimization, and enhanced portal development kits.

SAP Enterprise Portal consists of the following:

- The Portal Platform, which includes all the components and tools to build the portal:
  - iView technology
  - Unification technology
  - Users and roles management
- The Knowledge Management Platform, which provides the mechanism to access the information repositories of a company, and whose major functional areas are as follows:
  - Content management
  - Search and classification (TREX)
  - Collaboration
  - Predefined content and tools for creating content

The portal can be customized for different types of users by creating interfaces for the various roles. Dedicated interfaces help the users to complete both their general tasks, as well as those specific to their professional roles. To speed up the process of customizing the portal for each user, SAP provides predefined content that has been packaged, tested, and certified by SAP. This content is bundled in business packages.

In addition to the business packages, SAP provides a number of tools that customers can use to enhance and customize content, including tools for end users, for content administrators, for business users with no coding experience, and for professional programmers.

Figure 3-5 shows an overview of the SAP Enterprise Portal architecture in a typical example of connecting with different applications and sources of information.

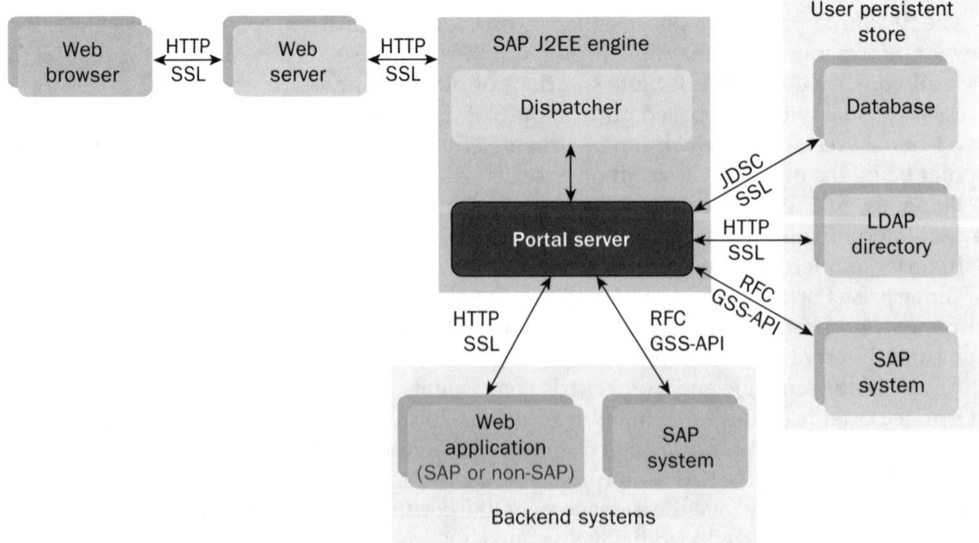

FIGURE 3-5 Architecture of SAP Enterprise Portal in one scenario

Let's briefly review in the next sections the main components and features of the elements of the SAP Enterprise Portal, but let's start with the iViews.

iViews

iViews (from Integrated Views) are the basic and most important components or building blocks for the portals. iViews are defined as the logical portal content building blocks representing an application or a part thereof.

There are many standard iViews, but users have the option to create new customized iViews using different technologies such as Java, .NET, XML, BSPs, and others.

iViews let you build and extend the portal to many available information and applications sources, regardless of where they may be stored. The sources for iViews can be

- ERP systems, such as SAP R/3 or mySAP ERP
- Legacy or custom developed applications
- Business Intelligence solutions, such as BW
- CRM systems
- E-mail
- Web sites
- File systems and intranets
- Collaboration tools

iViews are not static links that retrieve data, but they also allow special links or searching capabilities for displaying related information or running related transactions or applications.

iViews are generally based on portal components, which are the pieces of code (typically written in Java) that provide the iView its functionality and ability to display specific content.

Each iView comprises a set of properties, which are used at run time to parameterize the portal component on which the iView is based. The properties of an iView provide the iView with its unique personalized behavior. iViews can be based on other iViews, acting as templates, and therefore inheriting properties.

At design time, iViews are selectively distributed to end users through portal roles in the following manner:

- iView are assigned to portal pages. In turn, pages can be assigned to worksets or user roles (one or many). Users will have access to all iViews contained in the pages to which they have authorization (they have been granted access).
- iViews can also be directly assigned to a user role or workset, and not using pages. iViews assigned directly to roles are known as full-page application iViews.

SAP provides many standard and default iViews with the SAP Enterprise Portal, and there is also a large catalog of iViews provided with SAP Business Packages that can be downloaded from the iViewStudio at http://www.iviewstudio.com or from the SAP Developer Network at http://sdn.sap.com.

The Portal Platform

The Portal Platform includes those components and tools that are necessary to build a portal, including the following:

- *iView technology*, for creating and administering iViews. You can either use standard iViews delivered by SAP or create your own iViews, either by programming them or by using the portal content creation tools.
- *Unification technology* includes services for resolving relations between business objects of back-end systems.
- *User Role Management*, for creating user roles that provide access to portal pages for the users or user groups.

The Knowledge Management Platform

SAP Knowledge Warehouse (SAP KW) delivers the technical infrastructure you need to set up and manage your own enterprise-specific knowledge base in the areas of documentation, training, and manuals in SAP Enterprise Portal. For project teams and end users, SAP KW streamlines training and business processes. In addition, the possibility to reuse, supplement, and continually update SAP content offers great savings potential.

The Knowledge Management platform provides access to an organization's unstructured information (documents). The information may reside in various repositories that can be connected to the portal by means of components called repository managers.

Some repository managers are delivered by SAP; other repository managers can be developed based on open APIs. The functions of the KM platform can be exposed to the documents in all connected repositories, given that the respective repository manager allows it. The major functional areas of KM are as follows:

- *Content Management*, which supports the entire life cycle of documents, including the authoring, storage, management, and display of documents. It also manages the connection between document repositories and the portal and provides collaborative functions such as feedback, rating, and subscription. The content exchange service is also used to import documents to KM.
- *Search and Classification (TREX)*, which processes search queries on free-text or attributes and provides automatic classification in taxonomies and text mining. Search and Classification is also used in other building blocks of SAP NetWeaver such as SAP Business Intelligence.

Collaboration

Collaboration closes the communication gap between users, or teams of users, by providing real-time collaboration (such as application sharing, chat, instant messaging) and asynchronous collaboration capabilities (such as tasks, calendaring, discussions).

Collaboration Rooms offer a virtual work environment for teams or communities. These Collaboration Rooms can be populated with predefined content and services that may already be available within SAP Enterprise Portal. As a flexible integration framework for groupware (such as Microsoft Exchange, Lotus Notes) and synchronous collaboration applications, they let customers reuse and integrate existing assets.

Predefined Content and Content Tools

Predefined content and tools for creating and managing content complete the portal offering by helping to speed up the portal implementation and support its maintenance and continued improvement. The content is bundled in business packages, and tools for creation and support are as follows:

- Business packages based on SAP solutions that provide content for over 100 roles
- Business packages based on industry-specific queries for inclusion in customer content scenarios
- Business packages based on third-party vendor solutions, to leverage existing investments
- Personalization tools for end users
- A comprehensive environment for content managers for creating, managing, and deploying content
- A visual modeling tool for allowing business users to create content based on SAP R/3 transactions, without the need to write code
- A portal development kit to support professional Java and .NET programmers

SAP Mobile Infrastructure

SAP Mobile Infrastructure (SAP MI) is a technology solution within SAP NetWeaver on which all SAP Mobile Business applications are or can be based. It is positioned within the People Integration, since the Mobile Infrastructure provides the basis for the Multichannel access to SAP and non-SAP solutions, applications, and information. With SAP MI it is also possible to develop mobile applications that are not SAP based.

SAP MI is based on industry standards such as Java and XML, comes also with a Java virtual machine, and includes a development environment to design and develop mobile applications.

The SAP MI is installed locally on mobile devices and includes all the elements so that users can work remotely, that is, offline with the applications: a Web server, a database, and the application containing business logic. Additionally, the SAP MI includes the tools for synchronization and replication of the data, so that the mobile devices information is consistent with the back-end systems.

The architecture of the SAP Mobile Infrastructure makes the platform open and independent of the mobile devices and the network and therefore includes supports for a full range of devices such as PDAs, tabletops, latptops, and advanced mobile phones. Supported connection types include the following:

- Global System for Mobile Communications (GSM)
- General Packet Radio Service (GPRS)
- Universal Mobile Telecommunications Service (UMTS)
- Local area network (LAN)
- Wireless networks

Some of the SAP Mobile Solutions include the following:

- SAP Mobile Asset Management (FI-AA)
- SAP Mobile Service (as part SAP CRM)
- SAP Mobile Sales (as part of SAP CRM)
- SAP Mobile Procurement (for instance, vendor catalogs)
- SAP Mobile Time & Travels (HR—travel expenses, time sheets)

The two main elements or components of the SAP Mobile Infrastructure include the following:

- *Client*, represented by the SAP Mobile Infrastructure Client Component. The main elements of the client in a mobile device based on J2EE include
  - A local Web server to enable working with J2EE applications locally.
  - A browser as user interface.
  - Applications (JSPs, Servlets, . . .).
  - Data persistence represented by a database, or JDBC.
  - APIs for data compacting and encryption (HTTPs), connections with the mobile device, application distribution, and information replication and synchronization.
  - The mobile client also has capabilities for application configuration, logging, and tracing.
- *Server*, or *SAP Mobile Infrastructure Server*, includes a collection of components:
  - SAP MI J2EE Server Component
  - SAP MI ABAP Server Component
  - SAP Mobile Development Kit (MDK)

The server includes capabilities and tools for replication and data synchronization, guaranteeing that the information is not lost. It also guarantees the security and privacy of the information, error control, logical blocking of the information, and the consistency of the data against the back-end systems.

SAP Business Information Warehouse

SAP Business Intelligence captures, combines, and organizes data from a variety of internal and external sources and makes it available to decision-making processes.

The Business Information Warehouse (SAP BW) is the key component of the Information Integration layer of SAP NetWeaver, part of the SAP Business Intelligence together with the Knowledge Management.

SAP first introduced BW in 1997 as one of the major components of the Business Framework architecture and as one of the first New Dimension products. BW is the data warehousing solution of the mySAP Business Suite.

SAP BW allows you to analyze data from operative SAP applications as well as all other business applications and external data sources such as databases, online services, and the Internet.

SAP BW enables Online Analytical Processing (OLAP), which processes information from large amounts of operative and historical data. OLAP technology enables multidimensional analyses from various business perspectives. You can look for information within the entire enterprise by using the Business Information Warehouse Server when preconfigured with Business Content.

The importance and use of data warehouse and data mining techniques generally have been increasing during the last few years in the search for business intelligence, particularly in the collection of tools and applications that support company-wide knowledge.

Data warehouses and analytical tools used for unleashing the meaning of huge amounts of data are thought of as an integral component of getting business knowledge feedback. The analytical processes supported by the SAP BW are key to providing a broader business knowledge that can give feedback on the continuous change and improvement on companies by providing key figures and taking business decisions.

SAP strategy is to position the BW as a ready-to-go warehouse, including all the components required by a global data warehouse architecture and all the tools for designing, extracting, building, and managing the system. As part the SAP NetWeaver, it is also designed for a seamless integration with the rest of the SAP solutions, and to provide dynamic information through the portal or other GUIs, such as the Mobile devices.

Architecture of the Business Warehouse

Figure 3-6 shows an overview of the SAP BW conceptual architecture.

- *OLAP processor (server).* This includes the data and information models from SAP systems. SAP BW includes information models and report libraries for all the SAP business areas.
- *Metadata repository.* This manages and controls the full data warehouse environment.
- *Administrator Workbench.* This is the central data warehouse management tool, which can be used for maintaining and extending the BW. The Administrator Workbench is the tool for controlling, monitoring, and maintaining all of the processes connected with data staging and processing in the SAP BW system.
- *Business Explorer.* This is the component providing the reporting and analysis tools. This user interface is based on Web technology and MS Excel and contains a large standard report library, as well as the required analysis tools. The Business Explorer works as an information catalog, allowing users to browse the available information from the business applications. The analysis tools that can support complex and multidimensional analysis based on different data views are also a central component of the BW. The Business Explorer offers many possibilities for users to access the information in SAP BW using the Enterprise Portal, the intranet (Web application design), or mobile technologies.

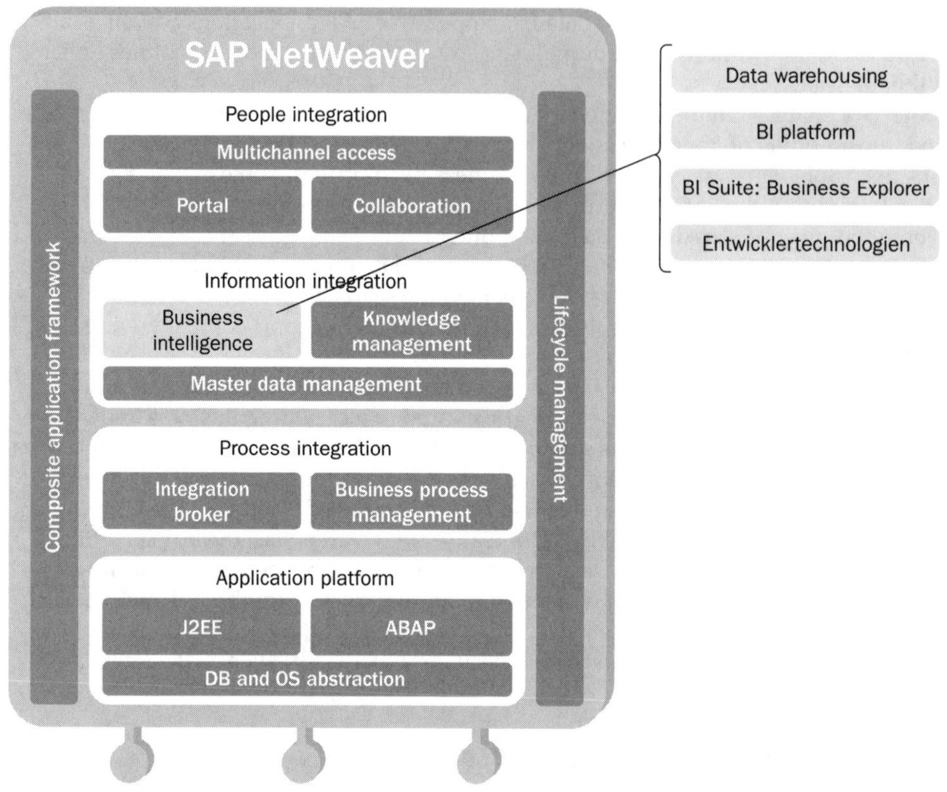

FIGURE 3-6 SAP BW architecture

- *Staging engine.* Additionally, the BW includes the processes that can automatically extract the data from the source SAP systems and from other external data sources. These are represented by a staging engine with integrated data staging routines that normally run in the background, supplying the BW with current data from data sources. These routines can run at predefined update intervals and are managed from the Administrator Workbench.

There are staging and reporting scenarios. For the staging scenario, you can use SAP systems or external databases as data source. The reporting scenarios are based on the staging scenario with SAP systems as data source.

All the communication processes between the SAP BW and data sources are based on BAPIs (Business Application Programming Interfaces), which provide a large degree of openness and extendibility so that the BW can be integrated with other applications, data sources, or tools.

The SAP BW systems can be used by all types of users. Besides their main purpose of providing business intelligence and historical performance and key figures to other SAP solution components such as SCM or SEM, SAP BW systems can also be an alternative or a complement to the standard SAP reporting options, and therefore it can help reduce the load and impact on performance of extensive online reporting.

The BW kernel, which is the same as the SAP R/3 Kernel, is on the SAP Web Application Server.

Additionally, there is a smooth integration between the BW metadata repository and the ABAP repository, so changes in objects and processes can be immediately transferred to the BW. Users can use the provided and predefined BW reports or can use them as models and create their own. The use of Web browsers and MS Excel spreadsheets makes analysis and reporting easy and simple. Just like many other SAP components, the BW also includes wizards for creating new reports, as well as much functionality for users to customize their own reporting and analysis environment.

Another key point of the SAP BW strategy is its very low implementation costs, because the kit includes all the needed models, configurations, and staging services for being able to work with data from other SAP systems right out of the box. This makes the need for data modeling only for special purposes or when loading the warehouse with external legacy systems.

BW within SAP NetWeaver and New Features

Within the SAP NetWeaver Integration platform, BW offers new features and capabilities that position it as one of the key components.

One of the new features of special importance is the Business Intelligence Information Broadcasting, which enables users to broadcast and schedule reports as needed. SAP Enterprise Portal serves as the single point of entry for the end user to access the complete business intelligence (BI) information portfolio.

A SAP Business Information Warehouse (SAP BW) is designed like a conventional R/3 system. However, a number of special characteristics need to be considered. For example, connections to source systems (for example, operated by suppliers) call for high performance and continuous availability. Extraction and loading processes must be stable and rapid. Data warehouses are associated with extremely large volumes of data, and this requires a database cost-based optimizer to guarantee the required level of performance.

Other specific new features of the integration of Business Intelligence processes and tools within SAP NetWeaver include the following:

- Based on the SAP Web Application Server
- Seamless integration of BI applications within the SAP Enterprise Portal
- Deployment of precalculated BI Web applications on mobile devices via SAP Mobile Infrastructure
- Integration with new Internet Graphics Server (IGS)
- Wizard-based information delivery
- Business Information Java Integration Kit
- BI platform enhancements

As part of the SAP NetWeaver architecture, SAP BW draws from and utilizes the capabilities of the other components for business intelligence usage. The sum of the functionality of SAP BW and the contribution of other components of SAP NetWeaver form a platform that represents the next major step in the evolution of business intelligence.

Depending on what extra components you use and how you configure your SAP BW system, you can use SAP BW for different business purposes.

BI Information Broadcasting

Information Broadcasting allows the user to precalculate BEx Web applications, BEx queries, and BEx Analyzer workbooks as required, or to distribute these in SAP Enterprise Portal, which means automatically distributing, sharing, and providing information to the enterprise in a dynamic way.

The BEx Portfolio represents the central point of entry for accessing Business Intelligence information in this respect. BI Information Broadcasting leverages Knowledge Management features such as subscription, feedback, discussion, collaboration, rating, and enterprise search.

Information broadcasting with SAP Business Information Warehouse (SAP BW) enables users to broadcast and schedule reports as needed.

BI Information Broadcasting includes the following features:

- BEx Broadcaster (including wizard) as a Web-based user interface
- BEx Broadcasting precalculation and distribution services as the infrastructure
- BEx Analyzer precalculation server for precalculating BEx Analyzer workbooks
- Business Intelligence services for integrating with SAP Enterprise Portal and presenting BEx Portfolios
- BEx Portfolio (as part of SAP Enterprise Portal) containing precalculated documents and current documents in one overview

You can call the BEx Broadcaster from the BEx Web Application Designer, the BEx Query Designer, and the BEx Analyzer. You can also call the Broadcasting wizard in the Context menu of Web applications.

The following existing scenarios are also replaced by BI Information Broadcasting:

- The precalculation of BEx Web applications for offline usage. It was previously possible to precalculate BEx Web applications with the Reporting Agent and download them with the BEx Download Scheduler. This function, which is still possible with SAP BW 3.5, supports the grouping of precalculated documents using scheduling packages in the Reporting Agent and the periodic scheduling of downloads in the Download Scheduler.

  As of SAP BW 3.5, this scenario can be performed with BI Information Broadcasting. Precalculated BEx Web applications can be sent by e-mail and documents or directories can be downloaded from the BEx Portfolio using Knowledge Management services. BI Information Broadcasting makes the following functions available:
- Grouping precalculated documents in directories
- Receiving notification when precalculated documents are changed
- Sending of documents when changed

As of SAP BW 3.5, BEx Web applications containing BI specific content can be created as iViews directly in SAP Enterprise Portal 6.0 on Web AS 6.40 by using the BEx Web Application Designer or the BEx Query Designer.

SAP Master Data Management

SAP Master Data Management (SAP MDM) is the SAP NetWeaver component that enables companies to store, improve the quality, and harmonize master data across the applications of a system landscape. SAP Master Data Management (MDM) consolidates master data throughout the enterprise irrespective of the system location or vendor.

This is a precondition for end-to-end business processes that transcend departmental and functional barriers. To this end, SAP MDM identifies identical or highly similar data records.

This information is made available to business processes via the Master Data Management component. SAP MDM employs the SAP Exchange Infrastructure (SAP XI) in order to gain access to the various source systems.

Heterogeneous IT landscapes consisting of SAP and third-party systems are quite common in today's business world. Businesses need to communicate with one another, be it within one company or beyond company boundaries. As a result, the challenge is to manage business-critical information that is often spread across many disparate systems.

Companies are looking for ways to integrate and consolidate their master data without giving up their investments in the existing infrastructure.

In this context, Master Data Management (MDM) enables you to store, change, and consolidate master data, and ensures that these data are consistently distributed to other systems within the IT landscape.

Everyone in the company gets up-to-date information on products, product catalog information, business partners, and documentation—be it in engineering, procurement, manufacturing, marketing, sales, or service.

SAP Exchange Infrastructure 3.0

The SAP Exchange Infrastructure (XI) is the component of the SAP NetWeaver in charge of communicating and exchanging data among systems. XI can be defined as the Information Broker acting as a central data hub within the SAP application and system landscape. It links SAP applications to one another and also allows the integration of external applications.

The key focus of the SAP Exchange Infrastructure is the integration of entire process chains. In other words, the SAP Exchange Infrastructure (SAP XI) is the technical solution for integrating heterogeneous software components of your system landscape or integrating the business systems of your business partners. Theoretically, you can integrate all kinds of business systems by using SAP XI. In addition, business partners can connect to your business systems by using the SAP Partner Connectivity Kit (PCK).

Business Process Management capabilities ensure seamless communication between application modules.

The SAP Exchange Infrastructure is an autonomous Java-based application that makes use of the SAP J2EE server. Via the integration broker, it is possible to incorporate heterogeneous components form a wide variety of vendors. SAP XI includes an adapter framework and a large selection of predefined adapters.

The solution exchanges data with file systems, message queuing systems, legacy software, and database systems. It provides the corresponding queuing, routing, and mapping services, and enhanced process control for functions such as synchronization, separation, and combination of messages.

SAP XI includes three major components: the Integration Server, Integration Builder, and Adapter Environment:

- The Integration Server is the main XI engine for the exchange and distribution of messages. Every business partner in collaborative integration scenarios have to use this server for the exchange of messages. Using the configuration defined in the Integration Directory, the Integration Server resolves to which receivers it must send the message and also whether mapping is required.
- The Integration Builder is the main tool for the configuration and design of the integration and collaboration processes. It includes the two major components of XI, namely the Integration Repository and the Integration Directory.
- Adapter Environment represents all the communication options of the SAP Exchange Infrastructure. Refer to the following section.

Figure 3-7 shows an overview diagram of the XI components.

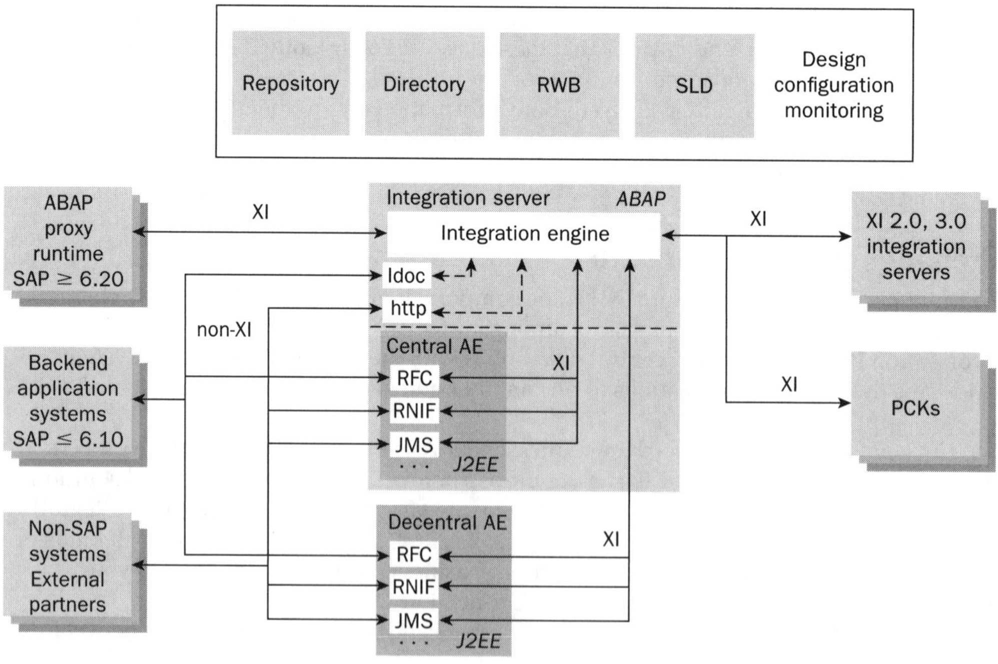

FIGURE 3-7 Overview of the XI components

SAP XI Communication Options

SAP Exchange Infrastructure provides multiple communication options that take into account the capability of involved business systems to exchange content among them. Business systems are determined by the existing system landscape that you want to integrate, taking into account both SAP business systems and non-SAP business systems.

The following parameters are defined to determine a communication option:

1. *Type of business system.* Since the communication occurs using the XML messaging service of the Integration Engine, the capability of sending or receiving XML messages is crucial for involved business systems.
2. *Type of messaging concept* (middleware technology) to be used for exchanging content.

Different messaging concepts are used, such as the following:

- Intermediate documents (IDocs)
- Remote function call (RFC)
- Text files
- Java Messaging Service (JMS)
- JDBC data access
- SOAP
- RNIF
- Plain HTTP
- Marketplace access
- Proxy-based messaging

SAP NetWeaver Developer Studio

The SAP NetWeaver Development Environment is used to develop both ABAP and Java applications. While the ABAP development is based on the SAP Web Application Server (SAP Web AS), the development environment for Java and Web Dynpro is based on Eclipse, which is implemented by SAP as the SAP NetWeaver Development Studio.

From SAP Web Application Server release 6.30 and upward, Eclipse is the IDE (Integrated Development Environment) selected by SAP for the development of Java applications that makes up the SAP NetWeaver Developer Studio.

Although you can use any IDE to develop Java applications for SAP, the version of Eclipse included with SAP NetWeaver Developer Studio includes an open plug-in architecture to accelerate the Java development for SAP environments.

You can use the release in the SAP NetWeaver software kits or, alternatively, download it from the SAP Developer Network Web site at www.sdn.sap.com. You need to be a registered user.

The Eclipse IDE is one of the industry standards for establishing a development workbench. The official Web site is www.eclipse.org. On top of the Eclipse IDE, users can build development environments for any language, by implementing the necessary plug-ins.

The Eclipse plug-in architecture allows users to integrate several programming languages on top of the same IDE, to introduce other complementary applications such as

- UML tools
- Visual user interface editors
- Online help

IDE Overview

The first time that the SAP version of Eclipse is run, you can see a similar screen to the one shown in Figure 3-8.

Let's briefly review the specific features of the developing environment, the way of organizing the work, and some of the additional tools included.

- *Editors.* The main screen is known as the Editor, which is used to do the code writing. You can have several editors opened at the same time piled on top of each other.

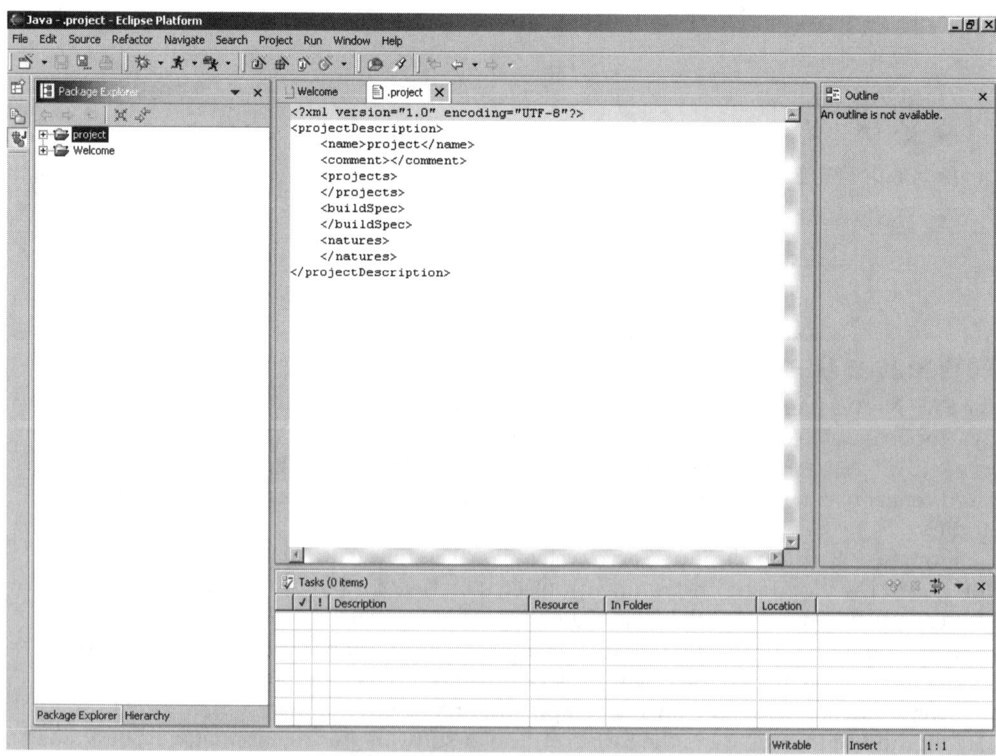

FIGURE 3-8 The SAP version of Eclipse (Copyright by SAP AG)

- *Views.* This is a type of "secondary" window. Views are used for many different tasks, such as to navigate within a hierarchy, show the content of a SQL statement, and others. Views can be considered as auxiliary windows to show information or request data.

With every plug-in you can define your editors and all the necessary views. In Figure 3-8 there are several views. The vertical view to the left will normally show the directory tree for project (if any). The horizontal view shows a small agenda of pending tasks which can be entered directly by the users or automatically by Eclipse, depending on different events such as the compilation of a program.

Toolbars

The third component of the IDE are the toolbars. There are two types of toolbars:

- *Main tool bar,* which contains shortcuts to the most common operation (Save, Open, and others) and buttons that allow users to launch external tools and tasks related with the active editor (run a program, debug, etc.).
- *Perspectives bar,* which contains shortcuts to the perspectives being used in the project. A perspective is a set of windows (editors and views) that are related. For instance, there is a perspective Java that facilitates the development of Java applications and includes, besides the editor, views for navigating classes, packages, and so on. Users can also defined personalized perspectives. Besides the main toolbar, each view can have its own toolbar.

Programming with Eclipse

As stated previously, Eclipse is an IDE that is not oriented to any specific programming language. The use of a programming language depends if there is a plug-in to support it. The standard version of the Eclipse environment provides the required plug-in for the Java programming language, which is known as JDT. From the official Eclipse Web site you can also download the CDT plug-in for the C/C++ languages.

Code Completion

Code completion is the feature of the environment that automatically completes programming sentences being coded by the developer. The code completion feature in Eclipse is very similar to those implemented by other IDEs: when the developer stops writing for a time interval, the system shows all the possible continuations: reserved words, function names, variables, fields, and so on, starting with the written characters. Some specific characters, such as the period, automatically trigger the code completion mechanism without waiting for the time interval.

Templates

Eclipse also provides for the possibility of defining and using templates: code templates that are used often and that can be written automatically. Templates have two parts: a code block (or comment) frequently used and written automatically, and a string that triggers the template. The JDT plug-in includes by default a significant number of templates, both for building code and for writing javadoc.

Code Formatting

Eclipse includes tools for performing automatically the formatting of the code according to some preestablished criteria. This function is the Source format included in the Context menu within the active editor. You can also manipulate code under the Source menu, including Comment and Uncomment, Add javadoc comment, Add import, Organize imports, and others.

Refactoring

Refactoring tools are used when the modifications or manipulations of code, or elements of the design, should involve several classes written in different files, belonging to the same project. These functions can be found under the menu Refactor.

Compilation

Compilation is a task automatically launched when saving the changes made to the code. If required, there are the Rebuild Project or Rebuild All options in the Project menu option.

Run

From the Run menu option in the toolbar, you can handle most execution options. The Run menu has two parts:

- Run As allows the direct execution of the class that is being showed in the active editor, using the default run configuration.
- Run . . . allows for defining new run configurations. A run configuration is a set of parameters that will be used when launching a program. Some of these parameters can be a classpath, the specific JRE release being used of the parameters that will be passed to the class that is going to be run.

Debugging Applications

The main difference between a code editor and a good development environment is that the last one integrates a good visual tool for debugging the code being developed. Eclipse includes an easy, powerful, and user-friendly debugger.

Launching the debugger is a task similar to running a program, but using the debugging pushbutton. The options are identical but when in debugging the program will make a step to step execution of the programs. When the debugger is launched, the system automatically opens the Debugging Perspective, in which users can see all the information regarding the program being debugged.

Developing Web Dynpros

The following are the basic concepts for developing Web Dynpro applications:

- *User Interface (UI) elements.* UI refers to all the graphic elements that can be displayed and used in a Web Dynpro application.
- *Contexts.* The context concept in Web Dynpro projects refers to a structured data repository that is used to save data. Each view has a corresponding context, which can save the local data of the view in a context, known as "view context."

Steps for the Creation Process of a Web Dynpro Application

Let's briefly describe the process of creating a basic Web Dynpro application, which includes three parts:

- Concept, modeling, and visual design
- Element declaration
- Programming

Web Dynpro Concept and Modeling

This is the first step when developing a Web Dynpro application. It will consist in analyzing the application requirements and translating those requirements into visual elements for the Web Dynpro. The following tasks are involved:

- Modeling: Creating a "view set" and inserting it in a window, creating views with visual content and empty view, defining a "view composition," creating the input and output of the view, and navigating among the views
- Design: Designing the view layout and inserting the elements of the user interface in the views, assigning static values to individual attributes

The visual elements that you can use when creating a Web Dynpro application are the following:

- Web Dynpro window
- View set
- View area
- View

The visual part of a Web Dynpro component is a Web Dynpro window, which is a group of views that can be organized in view sets. And these view sets can be divided in different view areas.

In the Web Dynpro applications, views are the structures containing the visual elements of the user interface.

View Composition

This is the process to include views (with elements UI or empty) in the view areas of a view container and in the definition of structures of navigation between these views. For it, we have the tool Navigator Modeler within the Web Dynpro perspective.

Views Layout

In this step you have to define the view layout, that is, the UI elements that you want to appear within the views. These actions can be performed directly within the Web Dynpro perspective.

Basic Web Dynpro

This section shows a simple Web Dynpro application using the SAP NetWeaver Developer Studio.

As we have already introduced, Web Dynpro is the SAP technology to develop Java applications using the same standards for all the SAP NetWeaver components and solutions.

The following section shows a practical example creating a Web Dynpro with SAP NetWeaver Developer Studio 6.40. The application is made up of two "dynpros." The first one enters the name of the user for the application and the second one shows a dynamic and personalized greeting.

Basic Web Dynpro Application

In order to perform this practical example, there are some requirements:

- Mandatory: You must have installed SAP NetWeaver Developer Studio in your workstation. This exercise assumes that the configuration options have the default values.
- Mandatory: You must have access to the SAP J2EE engine.
- Recommended: You need some good Java programming skills.

In this example we show all the steps required to develop, distribute, deploy, and run a basic Web Dynpro application. The user interface of our application will be composed by two views, which call each other. In the first view, the user is prompted to enter its name in an entry field. If the Go button is pressed within the view, the system will present a second view with a personalized greeting, using the name entered in the first view. When in the second view, pressing the Back button, the system will take us to the first view to interact again with the application.

The steps required for this example are the following:

- Creating a Web Dynpro project
- Creating a Web Dynpro component
- Creating the views
- Specifying the navigation options
- Creating the actions and implementation of the navigation options.
- Designing the views layout
- Defining the Data Binding for the User Interface (UI) elements
- Creating the Web Dynpro application
- Building the application
- Deploying the application
- Running the application

Creating a Web Dynpro Project

In order to work with development objects within SAP NetWeaver Developer Studio, it is necessary to place them within a project. For this reason, the first step will be creating a project. We will use a wizard to generate our project structure, in this example, of the type Web Dynpro. Once the project is created, we will be able to place under it all the required components to develop the application.

Launch the development environment, SAP NetWeaver Developer Studio, by double-clicking on its icon.

Select File | New | Project to launch the wizard for creating new projects. Once you make this selection, the system will show the wizard for project creation. In the left panel, select the category Web Dynpro and in the right panel select the only existing project type, Web Dynpro Project. Then, press the Next button.

Enter the project name, for example "Welcome" and leave the other entry fields with their default values. Next, press the Finish button.

The wizard will generate an initial structure for the new Web Dynpro project and will automatically open the Web Dynpro perspective. The difference with the J2EE projects is that this perspective only allows us to see the project structure with two views, Web Dynpro Explorer and Navigator.

If the system did not do it automatically, you should press the Web Dynpro Explorer tabstrip to see the project structure. This view will be the start point of all the actions that we must perform for completing this practical exercise.

Creating a Web Dynpro Component

The project structure was already created in the previous step but does not contain the elements that will be required to perform the application. These additional elements are encapsulated in what are known as Web Dynpro components. For that reason, before starting with the definition of layouts, navigation, or even handling, it is required to explicitly create a Web Dynpro component.

The steps to create a Web Dynpro component are the following:

- Expand the "Welcome" project structure until reaching the Web Dynpro Component node. To launch the creation wizard, open the Context menu and select the option Create Web Dynpro Component.
- As component name, we enter "WelcomeComponent," and as packet name "com.offilog.examples.welcome" to specify where we want the Java classes to be generated. We also enter StartView as the name of the view. Leave the other suggested or default values and press the Finish button.
- The wizard generates a Web Dynpro component in the project with a set of elements that we will be analyzing in the following steps in this example. We can see that the wizard has created the following:
  - A view with the name StartView. The view is the visual representations of our application.
  - A window with the same name as that of the created component, "WelcomeComponent." Windows include views.
- The system also opens the right panel of the Diagram view.
- Save the current work by clicking on the Save button.

Creating Views

As we have already introduced, the views are the elements that allow users to interact with the application. The Web Dynpro projects allow users to organize or divide the user interface in a set of views. We could consider each view as an independent entity, and together they make up all the elements of a graphical user interface.

In our example application, we have two views. The first one, StartView, was already created with the wizard for the Web Dynpro components. Now we have to create the second one. The steps are as follows:

- Expand the node Web Dynpro | Web Dynpro Components | WelcomeComponent | Windows.
- Double-click on the window node WelcomeComponent of the Window node, so that you can see the diagram view in the right panel (in case it was not already active).

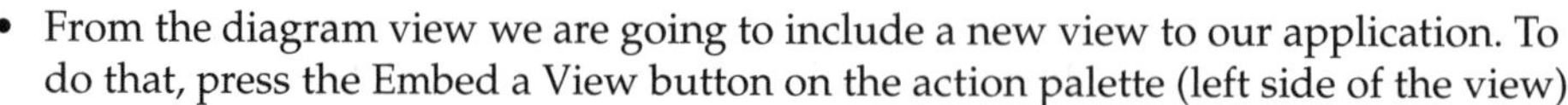

- From the diagram view we are going to include a new view to our application. To do that, press the Embed a View button on the action palette (left side of the view).
- Next, place the cursor on any position of the diagram and without releasing the mouse button, draw the rectangular area for the new view.
- In the wizard that the system shows, select the option Embed New View, which is the default options, and click on the Next button.
- Assign a name to the view, for example, ResultView, and leave the other fields with the default values. Click the Finish button.

Now, in the diagram view, you have two areas that represent the two views. The first view, StartView, appears as the active view, while the new view ResultView shows as inactive. The difference is the color of the view. This means that when the application is executed, the first view to be shown is the one defined as active.

We can also see that in the Web Dynpro Explorer a new view appears, ResultView, hanging from the WelcomeComponent window.

Save the current work by pressing the Save button.

Specifying the Navigation Options

In order to define the navigation among the views, we must first create the entry and exit points of each view. We can only define the navigation between the options using those points. The procedure is therefore divided in two steps:

- Defining the entry and exit points (inbound and outbound)
- Defining the navigation scheme

The next sections explain these topics.

Defining the Inbound and Outbound Points

The steps to be performed are the following:

- In the diagram view we have two rectangular areas that represent the two views of our application. Select the rectangle on the first view, StartView, open its Context menu, and select Create Outbound Plug (creating an exit point).
- The system will show a new dialog to request the name for the outbound plug. You will see in the diagram view that the first rectangle area includes now a new graphical element representing the outbound or exit point.
- Next, select the second view, ResultView, in the diagram view, open its Context menu, and select Create Inbound Plug (create entry point).
- Enter the name for the inbound plug in the Name field FromStartView, and leave the other fields with their default values. Press the Finish button.

With this simple procedure we have created the necessary plugs or points to navigate from the StartView to the ResultView. We are going to create additional navigation inbound and outbound plugs, proceeding as specified previously. The blue elements represent the inbound plugs, whereas the red ones represent the outbound ones.

Save the project by pressing the Save button.

Defining the Navigation Scheme

To create a navigation link from the first view to the second, select the Create a Navigation Link icon from the actions palette and draw a line in the diagram view, from the outbound plug from the StartView up to the inbound plug for the ResultView. Repeat the same procedure to link the outbound plug for the ResultView with the inbound plug of the StartView. The result is shown in Figure 3-9.

You can also see these modifications from the Web Dynpro Explorer.

With these actions we have defined the navigation scheme between the views of the application. The system also automatically created an event handler with the name onPlug<plugname> for each defined inbound plug.

In the next section we will show how to implement the event handler onPlugFromStartView from the ResultView to generate dynamic text from the information entered in the view StartView.

Save your work by pressing the Save button.

Creating Actions and Implementing Navigation

To navigate from view to view, we need an action to be generated within our view. This action can be activated by a graphical element such as a form button. Next we must implement the event handler that will react to this action and will implement the changes within the view. These actions are performed from the Designer View.

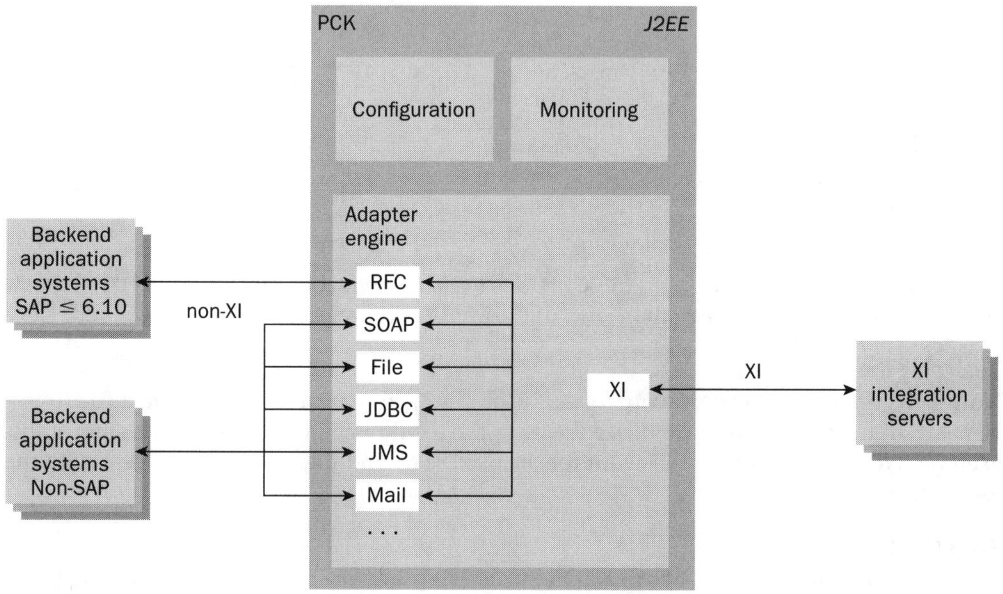

FIGURE 3-9 The outbound plug for ResultView is linked with the inbound plug for StartView

The steps are as follows:

- To open the design view, double-click on the node representing the view in the Web Dynpro Explorer. A new view will show up in the right panel of the screen.
- Select the Actions tabstrip and press the New button to create, with the help of a wizard, a new action.
- As an action name, enter Go, and leave the other fields of the Event Handler with the default values. Select the outbound plug ToResultView as Fire Plug. Finally, click on the Finish button.
- After pressing the Finish button, the Go action and its associated event handler onActionGo will show up in the actions list.

Repeat the previous steps to create the Back action for the ResultView view. In this case, the outbound plug ToStartView will be assigned as Fire Plug.

Save all the work performed, but on this occasion press the Save All Metadata button (save all metadata) of the application toolbar.

With the previous steps we have created the actions Go and Back. The necessary implementation for performing the navigation has been automatically inserted in the associated event handlers. For example, to verify the source code generated for the event handler onActionGo() we can press on the Implementation tabstrip in the designer view for the StartView view.

This method contains only one line. To activate the navigation from the StartView view to the ResultView, we use the associated method with the outbound plug, wdFirePlugTo ResultView(). The predefined private variable wdThis is used when invoking the method and it is always mandatory if we need to make calls to methods within the view controller.

The source code for the event handler onActionBack is the following:

```
public void
onActionBack(com.sap.tc.webdynpro.progmodel.api.IWDCustomEvent
wdEvent)
{
   //@@begin onActionBack(ServerEvent)
   wdThis.wdFirePlugToStartView();
   //@@end
}
```

In the next step we will assign these actions to the view layout buttons. With this last action, the navigation between the views of the application will be completely defined.

Designing the View Layout

Now is the time to define the layout for our user interfaces (UI). We are going to add UI elements in the two views created, according to the result we have defined at the start of this exercise. We will first define the layout for the StartView and then the same process with the ResultView.

StartView Layout

As the starting point, we must have active the design view for the StartView. Selecting the Layout tabstrip, we can see the output text that the system will generate by default with the name of the view.

Simultaneously, we can see in the Outline view (under the Web Dynpro Explorer view) the list of UI elements included, lined up under the root node and with a tree representation. If we select an element in this view, or in the Layout tabstrip of the design view, the system shows the element properties in a new view, known as the properties view.

We can see that all the active views within the screen have their role when developing Web Dynpro applications.

From the Outline view, we select the root element RootUIElementContainer and set the following properties:

Property	Value
Layout	GridLayout
cellPadding	5
colCount	3

NOTE *While we have not selected the layout type, some properties do not show on the property view.*

Some properties can only accept certain values. When this happens, in the column of values there is a button that will show up the list of possible values. We can select the value with keyboard arrow keys or with the mouse (Figure 3-10). The default value for the properties is shown with an asterisk to the right of the field.

Next, let's modify the element DefaultTextView, which was automatically generated, using the following values:

Property	Value
Design	header2
Text	Welcome to the WEB DYNPRO World . . .
ColSpan	3

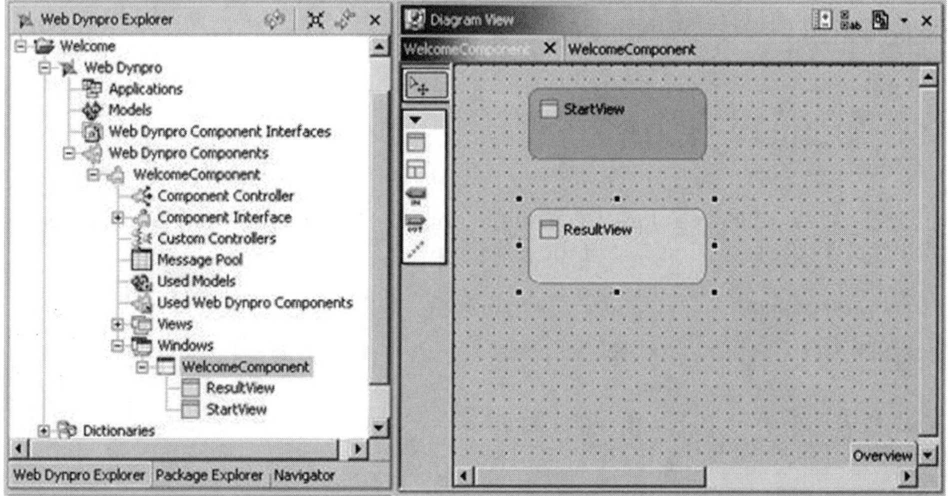

FIGURE 3-10 Selecting a value using keyboard arrow keys or using the mouse (Copyright by SAP AG)

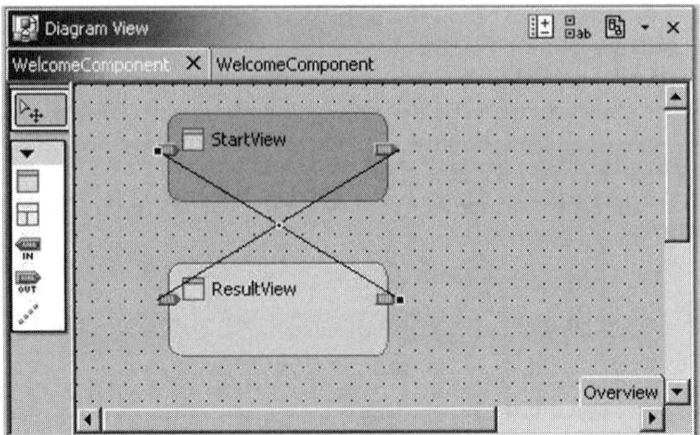

FIGURE 3-11 The root element is selected in the Outline view (Copyright by SAP AG)

In the Outline view, let's select the root element, RootUIElementContainer, open the Context menu, and select Insert Child (Figure 3-11).

As Element ID enter Label and select also Label in the Type field. Next, press the Finish button.

Update the properties as follows:

Property	Value
Text	Enter your name
labelFor	DefaultTextView
paddingTop	Large

Using the same procedure, let's create two new graphic elements using the following properties:

First element:	ID: "Name," Type: InputField
Property	Value
Tooltip	Your name
Value	

For the moment, we will leave blank (no value) within the "value" property. We will see a way to fill it up in the following step of the procedure.

Second Element:	ID: "go," Type: Button.
Property	Value
Text	Next
Tooltip	Go to the next view
event I onAction	Go

In the design view Layout tabstrip, we can see the result of these actions in Figure 3-12.

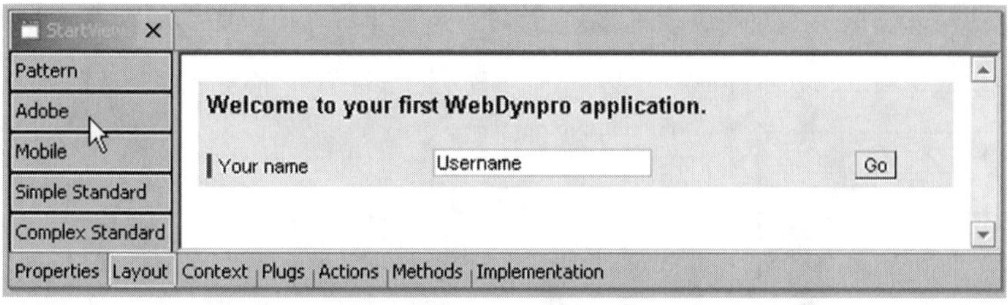

FIGURE 3-12 First Web Dynpro application (Copyright by SAP AG)

Save your work by clicking on the Save All Metadata button. We should not worry at this stage in case you see some information or warning messages in the task list.

ResultView Layout

Open the view ResultView from the design view.

In the Outline view, select the root element RootUIElementContainer and modify the following properties:

Property	Value
Layout	GridLayout
cellPadding	5
colCount	2

Select the element DefaultTextView that was automatically generated and update the following properties:

Property	Value
design	header2
text	
colSpan	2

Leave the "text" property with a blank value.

We will later see the way to fill out this field automatically.

In the Outline view, select the root element RootUIElementContainer, open its Context menu, and select Insert Child. Enter the name "message," of the type TextView, and click the Finish button.

Let's do the same procedure to create a new element of type Button with the ID "back." Let's assign the following properties to the fields we have just created:

First element:	ID: "message", Type: TextView
Property	Value
Text	The application works fine . . .
paddingTop	Large

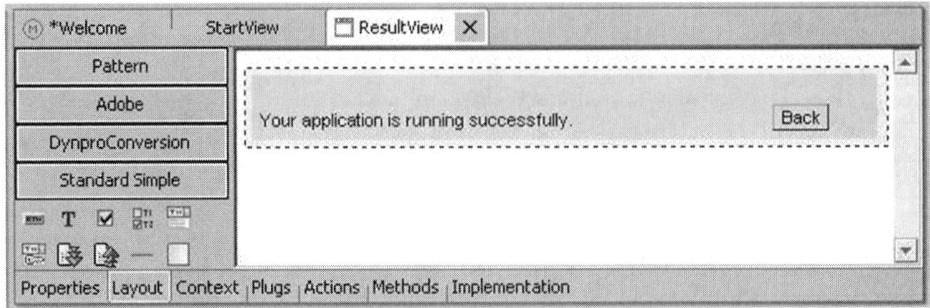

Figure 3-13 Output of procedure to create a new element (Copyright by SAP AG)

Second element:	ID: "back," Type: Button.
Property	Value
Text	Back
Tooltip	Back to the first screen
Event | onAction	Back

In the design view Layout tabstrip, you can see the output in Figure 3-13.

Save your work.

Although using wizards, we have already developed the basic parts of our application. Now, we only need that the value entered in the first view should be processed and displayed in the second view. To do that, it is not required to implement an explicit data transfer. The Web Dynpro applications allow us to implement this requirement in a very simple way, making a data link on a "context."

Data Binding Definition in UI Elements

For implementing data transfer between the views of a Web Dynpro application, the method to use is called data binding. This can only be done with UI elements that have properties that can accept this type of binding. If this is the case, as a value of the property there will be a reference to a corresponding context element. Refer to the definition of context given previously.

The following procedure has several parts:

- First, we will create a global storage space that will be used for the component context.
- Next, we will create the necessary view contexts.
- Then, we will map the elements of the view with the context elements created in the previous steps.
- Finally, we will bind the context elements of the view to the UI elements, using the properties of these elements.

Creating a Component Context

From the Web Dynpro Explorer, expand the node Web Dynpro | Web Dynpro Components | WelcomeComponent and double-click on the node Component Controller.

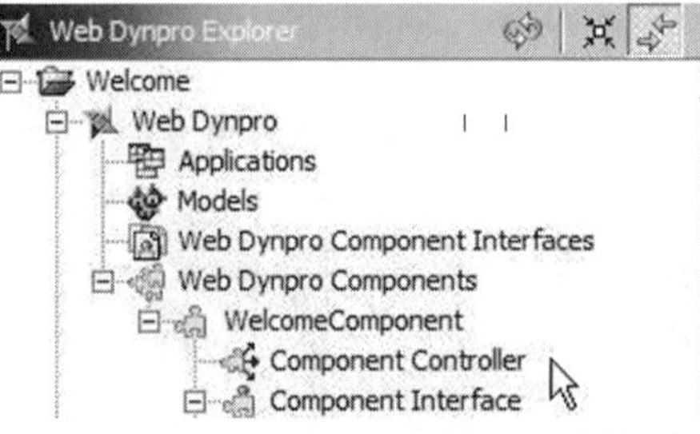

(Copyright by SAP AG)

In the displayed editor, select the Context tabstrip.

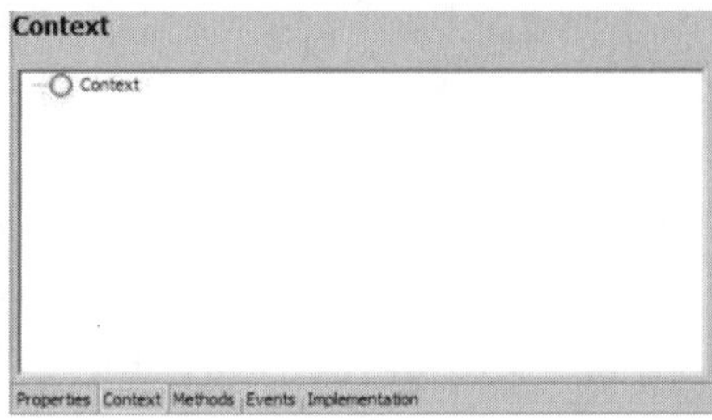

(Copyright by SAP AG)

Open the Context menu of the root node Context and select the option New | Value Attribute.

(Copyright by SAP AG)

Now we can create a new attribute from the wizard that is displayed. Enter the name "Username" and press the Finish button. An attribute node is added to the root node of the context.

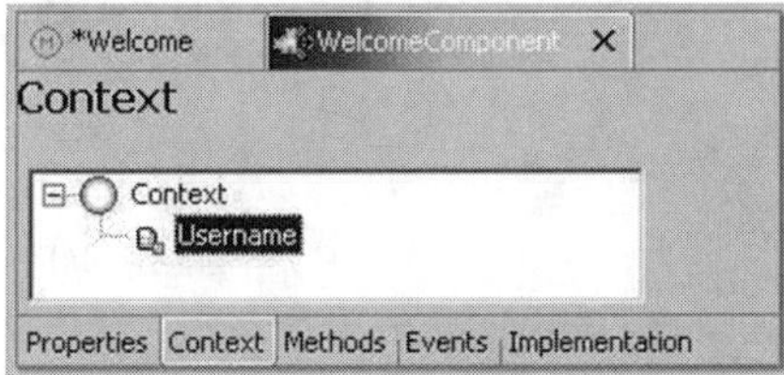

(Copyright by SAP AG)

We will use this context definition in the following points to implement the data binding in the local view contexts.

Auditing and Additing Dependencies to the Views

Open the design view of StartView, select the Property tabstrip, and under the label Required Controllers, press the Add button.

In the new screen, select WelcomeComponent - com.offilog.examples.welcome and confirm it by pressing the OK button.

(Copyright by SAP AG)

Repeat the last steps, but in this case with the view ResultView.

With these actions we have created the appropriate dependencies for each view in our project "Welcome."

Creating the View Contexts

Let's open again the StartView in design mode and select the Context tabstrip. In the Context menu of the root node, select the option New | Value Attribute.

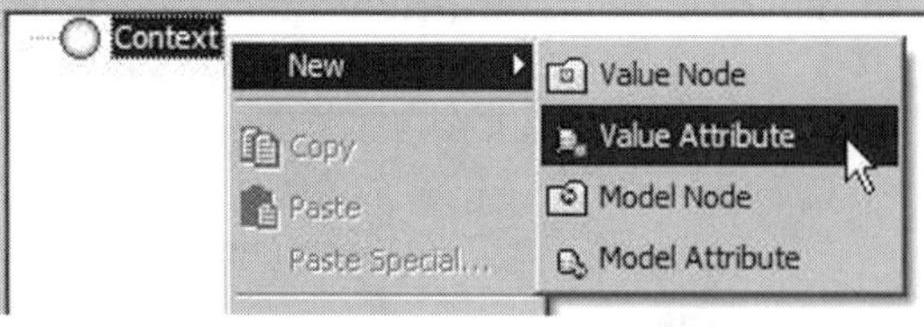

(Copyright by SAP AG)

Enter the value "Name" and press the Finish button.

From the Context menu of the Name attribute just created, select Edit Context Mapping.

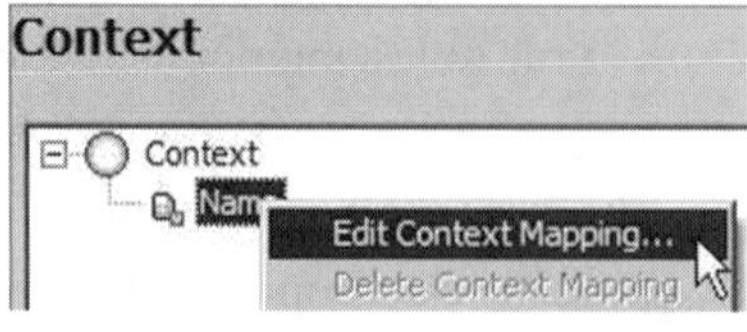

(Copyright by SAP AG)

From the component context, select the element Username and click the Finish button.

After this action, we can see that the icon that shows up next to the Context attribute has changed, so that we can easily see that the attribute has been mapped with an element of the component context.

(Copyright by SAP AG)

Now, we have to repeat the last steps to do the same procedure in the view ResultView. The attribute to create we can name it HeaderText and on this occasion we will not map the attribute with any element of the component context.

Assigning UI Elements to Contexts

Open again the StartView in design mode, and select the Layout tabstrip.

Select as input field "name." In the "value" property in the properties window, assign the appropriate context attribute by selecting the possible entries from a list box. In the dialog box that is displayed, select the context attribute "Name" and click the OK button.

Let's go know to the ResultView.

In the design view, select the view ResultView and click the Layout tabstrip. Select the text element DefaultTextView and, in the properties window, update the value of the "text" property with the corresponding context element HeaderText.

Now, in the design window, we can see the layout shown in Figure 3-22.

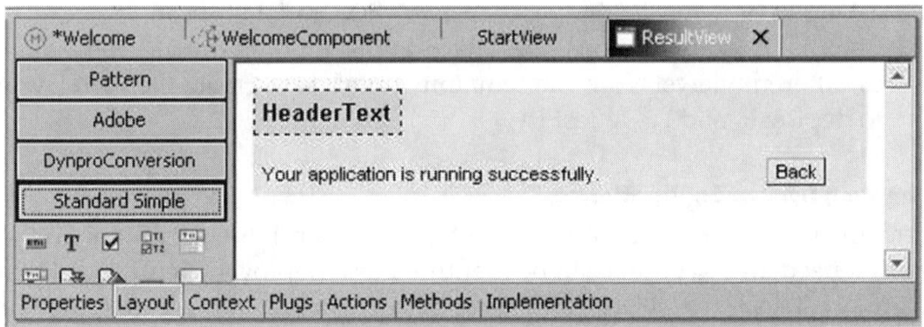

(Copyright by SAP AG)

With these last actions we have defined the "data binding" between the UI elements and their corresponding context attributes.

Dynamic Generation of a Text Line Using Data Binding

Select the view ResultView in design mode and click the Implementation tabstrip. Now, we enter some coding (the first one in the whole exercise) on the method of the event handler onPlugFromStartView().

```
public void
onPlugFromStartView(com.sap.tc.webdynpro.progmodel.api.IWDCustomEven
t wdEvent)
  {
    //@@begin onPlugFromStartView(ServerEvent)
    String headerText = "Congratulations ";
    headerText +=
```

```
wdThis.wdGetWelcomeComponentController().wdGetContext().currentConte
xtElement().getUsername();
    headerText += "!!!";
    wdContext.currentContextElement().setHeaderText(headerText);
    //@@end
  }
```

The event handler of the entry point onPlugFromStartView is launched when the view ResultView is processed. We can use this event, as in this case, to generate text dynamically. The dynamic value is saved in the contexts of the local views and it can be available for all the associated context elements.

Remember that to enter code we can use the code wizard, which is automatically activated when we enter a period sign (.) after the name of an object.

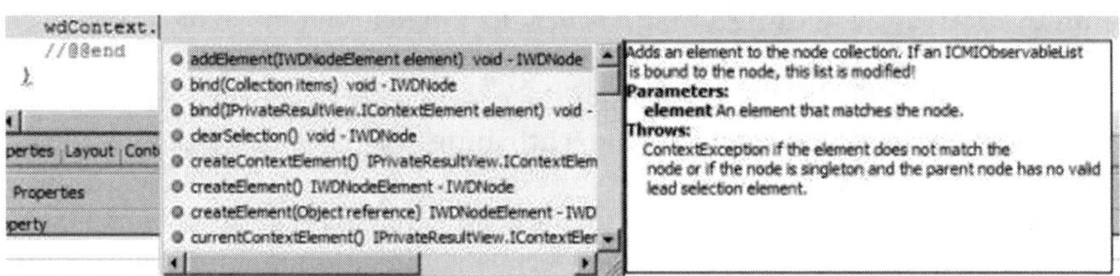

(Copyright by SAP AG)

Save your work up to now by clicking on the Save All Metadata button.

As a result of the previous actions, we have established data transfer between the UI elements of different views. Now, the remaining work is to create the Web Dynpro application, to deploy it, and . . . to test it!

Creating the Web Dynpro Application

Before launching the compilation of the complete project and its distribution to the J2EE engine, we first need an object that can be identified as a deployable entity and that includes the whole project. This is the object that we are going to create at this point, the Web Dynpro application.

To open the corresponding wizard, from the Web Dynpro Explorer node, select Applications, open its Context menu, and select the Create Application option.

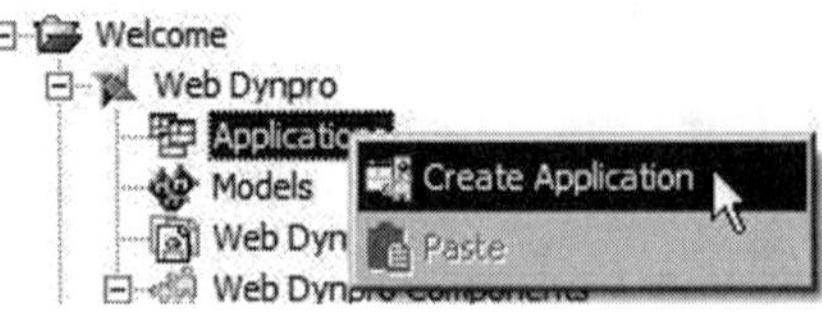

(Copyright by SAP AG)

Enter the name for the application, for example, "WelcomeApplication," and specify a package, for instance, "com.offilog.examples.welcome," for the Java class that will be generated. Then, continue by pressing the Next button.

In the following dialog screen, select the default value Use Existing Component and continue by clicking on the Next button.

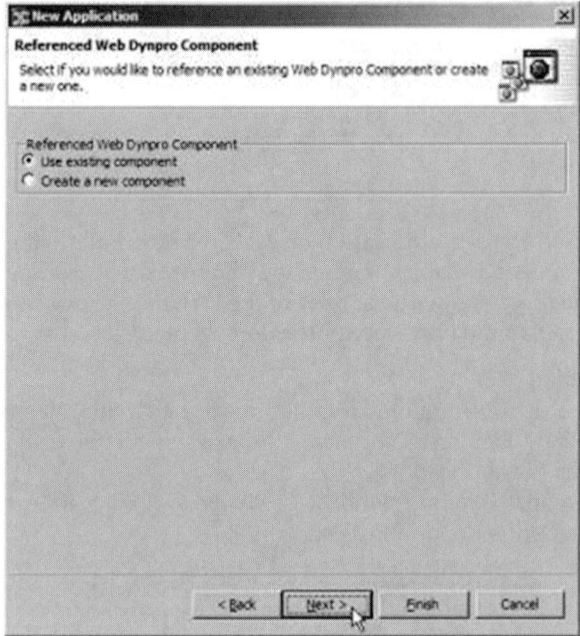

(Copyright by SAP AG)

In the following dialog box, leave the three values proposed by the system and click on the Finish button.

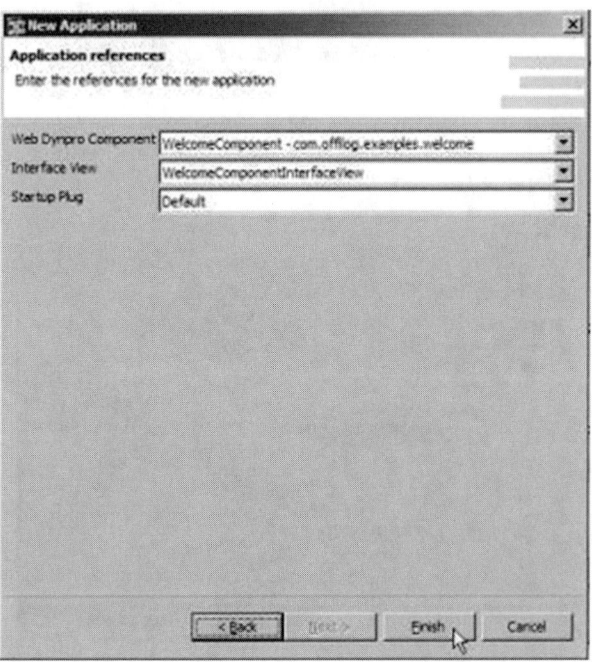

(Copyright by SAP AG)

In the Web Dynpro Explorer you can see the new created object.

(Copyright by SAP AG)

The generated Web Dynpro application object is what completes the structure of our project. Now, we are in good shape to launch the distribution of our application. The WelcomeApplication object allows us to refer to the Web application as a whole set, and therefore it will be used in the next step for the deployment.

Building the Application

Before deploying and distributing the application, we need a final step of building it. Save your work up to now by clicking on the Save button. This will make all the objects to be saved before building the application.

From the Web Dynpro Explorer window, select the Welcome node, open the Context menu, and select the option Rebuild Project.

(Copyright by SAP AG)

Make sure that there are no error or warning messages in the tasks window for the "Welcome" project. We are referencing the "Welcome" project because it is possible to have more than one project opened.

Deploying the Application

In the window Web Dynpro Explorer, select the object Welcome Application, activate its Context menu, and select Deploy New Archive and Run.

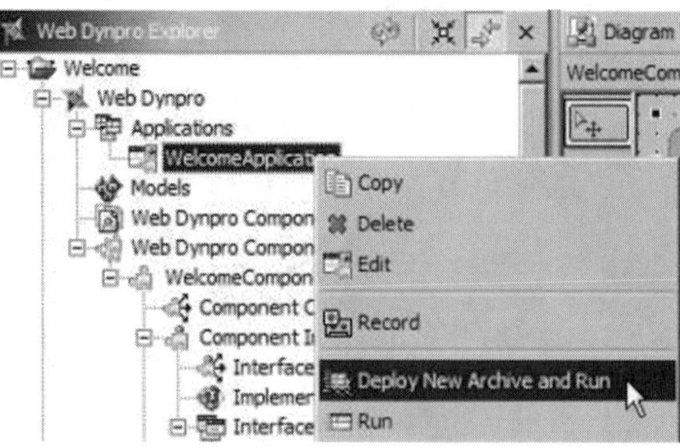

(Copyright by SAP AG)

After the deployment, which can take some time, the SAP NetWeaver Developer Studio will launch the associated browser and run the application.

Running the Application

In the browser we can interact with the application by pressing the appropriate buttons. Enter a name in the input field and click on the Next button.

(Copyright by SAP AG)

In the second page, press the Back button to return to the first screen.

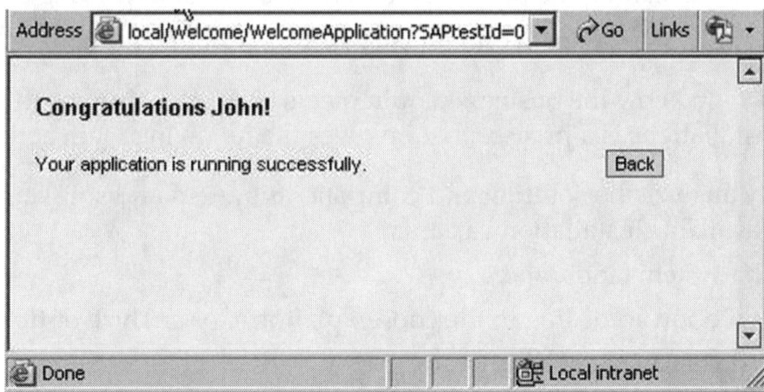

(Copyright by SAP AG)

With this simple example we have seen how to

- Create a project for a Web Dynpro application and its associated development objects
- Create views and navigation options for the application
- Create actions for the views and implementing simple event handlers
- Design layouts for simple views
- Define data binding for the UI elements using context attributes
- Deploy and run a Web Dynpro application

Planning SAP NetWeaver Installations

The purpose of this chapter is to introduce readers the installation planning process, landscape, and services distribution of SAP Solutions, mainly around the SAP Web Application Server, SAP R/3 Enterprise, and other related components of SAP NetWeaver.

It deals with the layout and design of system landscapes, the concepts involved in setting up SAP systems, as well as the platform considerations, including some hardware and software topics.

The goal is to make the installation planning process easier and more understandable. This chapter under no circumstances replaces the official SAP installation manuals, because every new SAP solutions or the SAP NetWeaver platform release might contain differences concerning system setup, installation, dependencies, or technical requirements.

Particularly important are the dependencies with the software and operating system requirements, where a wrong file or directory permission or incorrect system parameters might lead to installation errors or unexpected behaviors. It is also very important to browse and read carefully all the associated SAP notes with the specific installation.

Due to the open technology of SAP software solutions and thus the number of supported hardware platforms, operating systems, and databases, it is beyond the scope of this chapter to cover all installation variants.

Installation and Planning Concepts

With the many SAP solutions that have been available during the last few years, and especially since the global release of the SAP NetWeaver platform and the J2EE engine, the planning process for installing the proper system landscape for deploying and implementing SAP Solutions has become increasingly important and is critical for getting a correct installation.

Provided that you know the business requirements and SAP solutions to be implemented, planning SAP installations is a process that involves the following main activities:

- Carefully analyze the solution and components system and software requirements, and the available installation variants.
- Define the system landscape.
- Size the solution according to the chosen platform, or analyze options.
- Procure the hardware and software.
- Make sure to meet all the prerequisite requirements before installation, especially last-minute information included in SAP notes.
- Perform actual installations.
- Follow postinstallation activities according to the components installed.

Installing SAP software successfully, providing all requirements are met (for example, the SAP R/3 Enterprise with the SAP Web AS ABAP), is a process that may last from one to two days, depending on the landscape strategy, the solution to be installed, the multiple installation options, and the processing power of the hardware chosen. After installation, there are also some additional postinstallation steps, basis customization or security settings that most likely need to be done before any productive operation.

A good level of expertise with operating systems and management of database systems will ease your way into fast and successful installations.

These guidelines will not cover such topics as failover systems or storage RAID options because those issues are dependent on hardware vendor products and configuration utilities.

When a company decides to implement some of the SAP solutions to fulfill its business information needs, it is aware that to customize the functional aspects of the business is the critical and most time-consuming part of a SAP implementation project; however, all the technical elements involved must be seriously considered to overcome the availability issue: the systems and applications must be up and running. SAP defines availability as the fraction of time the system can be used to perform the functions for which it was designed. It does not define it as an isolated hardware or software element, but as a property of the whole information system.

Installation Elements

In any of the SAP solutions installation, you may encounter and require the following hardware elements:

- Several server computers with sufficient main memory and storage space
- An appropriate network infrastructure
- Many presentation servers, commonly personal computers, with network interface cards
- File and print servers
- One or several printers

The following software elements may also be present:

- Server computers operating system and base software kits.
- Graphical operating environment for the personal computers and a supported network operating system.
- SAP software kits.
- Either optional or required third-party software kits.
- A relational database management system as the SAP information container. This usually comes bundled with the SAP kit.

All previous plus other additional requirements you might need are to be found in several of the planning and installation manuals, which comes bundled in the installation kit, either in printed form, in a CD or DVD online help, or that you download from the SAP Service Marketplace.

Finally, a very important element, which is sometimes scarce, is experienced people. Although SAP systems and solutions can be quite complex, managing the SAP systems is not so difficult if the right support lines and procedures are in place.

These items are not a SAP requirements list but are the set of elements that should be taken into consideration when starting a SAP technical implementation project. Every element is important, and the right configuration of every one—people configuration used to be known as training—is what makes the planning, installation, and technical implementation a successful base for SAP implementation projects.

Let's review some of the core concepts for a successful planning and installation of SAP solutions, in particular, the base platform for the SAP NetWeaver, aka, the SAP Web Application Server.

Documentation Required for Planning and Installation

There is a comprehensive set of documentation for the planning and installation of SAP solutions, and specifically about the SAP NetWeaver platform and other mySAP Business Suite components. It might seem in fact, that there is so much documentation that sometimes the problem is where to start.

- *SAP Online Library.* The SAP Library is the set of documentation for each of the SAP components. This documentation can be installed locally on users' workstations, on file servers, or can be accessed directly in the SAP Help portal at http://help.sap.com.
- *Master Guides.* The SAP NetWeaver Master Guide is the initial reference point in order to implement and install SAP NetWeaver components. This guide includes a comprehensive list with all the requirements and cross dependencies between components or third-party software. From this guide you will find the appropriate reference to the installation and implementation of specific components or the required SAP Notes.
- *Planning Guides.* These guides are also extremely useful and often mandatory in order to plan the installation of a particular component of the SAP NetWeaver or an individual component, listing all the possible installation variants and the description of the parameters that will be required when perform the actual installations.
- *Component Installation Guides.* The Component Installation Guides describe the installation and technical implementation of a SAP component, taking into account the combinations of operating systems and databases.

Other important documentation you might want to look at is as follows:

- *Security Guide.* The Security Guide describes the available options and settings for raising the security level of SAP system landscapes. There is a collective security guide for the SAP NetWeaver platform that includes specific security settings for technologies such as the SAP Web Application Server (SAP Web AS). This document contains general guidelines and suggestions about system security. Other technologies and individual applications have a Security Guide of their own.

Variants of SAP Web AS

At the writing of this book, the SAP Web AS 6.40 was the main component of SAP NetWeaver. It can be installed in different basic system variants: as ABAP+Java system, as Java system, as ABAP system, or as a combination of an ABAP system with a Java system.

The installation documentation of SAP Web AS contains the information required to install each of the basic system variants of SAP Web AS:

- *SAP Web AS ABAP system.* This variant only consists of the ABAP Engine. There is no J2EE Engine.
- *SAP Web AS Java system.* This variant only consists of the J2EE Engine, with auxiliary services. There is no ABAP Engine.
- *SAP Web AS ABAP+Java system.* With this variant, you can operate both the ABAP Engine and the J2EE Engine in one system (that is, one SAP system with one <SAPSID>).

- *SAP Web AS ABAP system + SAP Web AS Java system.* With this variant, you can also operate both the ABAP Engine and the J2EE Engine. But in contrast to a SAP Web AS ABAP+Java system, the two engines run separated in two systems (that is, two SAP systems, each with a different <SAPSID>). Normally, the two SAP systems also use two separate databases.

It is important to choose correctly the variant required for the particular component being installed.

Platforms

Customer decisions about hardware platforms are quite variable and factor for decisions are many, from the price to scalability, performance, the confidence in your preferred vendor, and the current experience of the internal IT personnel.

Most SAP NetWeaver and SAP Business Suite components run in major flavors of UNIX, Microsoft Windows, Linux, and AS400. However, there are some restrictions in some of the components, and therefore you should check the product availability matrix in the SAP Service Marketplace.

Regarding databases, ORACLE and Microsoft SQL Server are the two major database management systems selected, but you can find others, such as Informix and DB2 for the IBM platforms. Recently we have seen the appearance of the MaxDB database, as a joint effort between the SAP DB and the mySQL databases.

To explain the decision making among different vendors or operating system architectures is beyond the scope of this book and depends on many factors, such as overall system size (number of users, estimated size of database, business solutions to be implemented and related SAP components, batch load, etc.), budget, expected response time threshold, former database know-how, and so on.

System Landscape Directory

System landscapes for SAP solutions, and in particular for SAP NetWeaver scenarios, are made up of several components with specific platform dependencies, connections, interfaces, and different requirements regarding installation and change management.

An overall concept is required that facilitates the implementation, upgrade, and maintenance of your system landscapes—including the SAP NetWeaver system landscape you want to install. This is where SAP System Landscape Directory (SLD) comes into play.

The SLD is the central information provider that stores information about all the components installed and that can be installed in your system landscape. The SLD is required for a SAP NetWeaver system landscape when using the SAP Web Application Server for Java, 6.40.

To bring the SLD server into operation, you only have to configure and activate it. For most SAP system landscapes, the recommended installation scenario of SLD is to use only one SLD server. The most common installation scenario is that all systems inside a system landscape including all subnetworks share a single SLD server.

The advantages of using a single SLD server for the entire system landscape are as follows:

- Consistent data
- Easier administration and lower operating expense

Unlike this single SLD server installation, the installation of multiple SLD servers may be a good idea for certain SAP system landscapes. For example, if you want to install multiple SLD servers that are distributed over different geographic locations or an additional SLD server dedicated for a particular group of systems (such as a production landscape), then we recommend that you build up a hierarchy of SLDs so that the SLDs of system groups propagate their information to one central SLD. For this propagation, you have to configure the bridge of every SLD so that it forwards any information also to the central SLD. This way, the central SLD hosts consistently the information of your overall system landscape.

We recommend that you run SLD on a host that is highly available, as the information stored in SLD could be essential for applications running in your production landscape. For example, Web Dynpro applications require the RFC destinations that are stored in SLD for their operation. Also, SAP Exchange Infrastructure relies on information stored in the SLD. In contrast to the Web Dynpro applications, this information gets cached persistently, so that a downtime of SLD would only be critical during the first startup of SAP Exchange Infrastructure when SAP XI retrieves this information from SLD.

For SAP NetWeaver, we recommend that you operate SLD on the Central SAP Administration and Monitoring System in a dedicated, nonproductive and highly available SAP Web AS ABAP+Java system.

SAP NetWeaver Rapid Installer

SAP NetWeaver Rapid Installer 2.0 is an installation and configuration wizard that reduces implementation of SAP Enterprise Portal along with other software components and designated SAP business packages from days to hours. SAP NetWeaver Rapid Installer enables you to lower the total cost of ownership (TCO) by reducing the time needed to install, deploy, and configure SAP Enterprise Portal and business packages to a minimum of time.

SAP NetWeaver Rapid Installer also provides back-end connectivity to systems for Enterprise Resource Planning (ERP), Business Warehouse (BW), Customer Relationship Management (CRM) and SAP Computing Center Management Systems (CCMS). It enables you to connect easily to these systems through a preconfigured portal with a minimum of interaction and configuration time.

SAP NetWeaver Rapid Installer 2.0 installs a clearly defined set of business scenarios for mySAP ERP 2004 and mySAP CRM 4.0. Thus the SAP NetWeaver Rapid Installer allows an easy and rapid step into the world of SAP NetWeaver and SAP Enterprise Portal for mySAP ERP and mySAP CRM customers and also for customers who prefer to install SAP Enterprise Portal stand-alone without additional business packages.

SAP NetWeaver Rapid Installer is available as of SAP NetWeaver '04 SR1. You cannot use SAP NetWeaver Rapid Installer to install components of earlier releases of SAP NetWeaver '04.

SAP NetWeaver Rapid Installer 2.0 installs the following NetWeaver components:

- Portal
- Knowledge Management (including Search and Classification [TREX])
- Collaboration
- SAP Web AS Java 6.40

It also installs the following software components:

- Business packages with Employee Self Service (ESS) and Manager Self Service (MSS) business scenarios (prerequisite: mySAP ERP 2004 is installed)
- SAP Self Service (XSS) 5.0 which is based on SAP NetWeaver '04 Java Stack and connects to the back-end functions in the ERP system. For more information on SAP XSS, see SAP Service Marketplace at http://service.sap.com.
- Business packages with business scenarios for mySAP CRM (prerequisite: mySAP CRM 4.0 and SAP BW 3.5 is installed)
- A SAP System Landscape Directory (SLD) if you want SAP NetWeaver Rapid Installer to install a new SLD
- CCMS agents to enable monitoring in the Portal

You can find detailed product information at http://service.sap.com. Read this information and check if SAP NetWeaver Rapid Installer 2.0 is a viable alternative for you to install SAP Enterprise Portal based on SAP NetWeaver '04.

Limitations: You can use the SAP NetWeaver Rapid Installer 2.0 as a viable alternative for installing SAP Enterprise Portal (plus other software components).

Note the following limitations:

1. *Platform availability.* One of the following combinations of operating systems and databases is required for installation:
   - Microsoft Windows Server 2000/2003 operating system with Microsoft SQL Server 2000 Enterprise Edition
   - Microsoft Windows Server 2000/2003 operating system with Oracle 9.2.0.4 64-bit database
   - Sun Solaris SPARC 8 or 9 operating system with Oracle 9.2.0.4 64-bit database
2. *Installation type.* SAP NetWeaver Rapid Installer supports a one-node installation on the same server. An additional J2EE cluster environment can be set up by using the standard SAP installation tool.
3. *Scalability and sizing.* SAP NetWeaver Rapid Installer installs a SAP Enterprise Portal that is optimized for a small number of business users (about 200 concurrent users). But you are not limited to this scenario: you can scale the system and add new hardware according to the standard portal sizing.

The Sizing Process

Sizing may have an impact on the overall installation process. But if you just want to perform a simple installation test, you can skip this section as long as you have a system with minimum hardware requirements.

Sizing is a complex and inaccurate procedure that involves a few different persons and organizations. A SAP customer usually requires the help of the chosen hardware vendor and of SAP itself. At the same time, these providers pass on to the customers lengthy questionnaires, with data that are fed into a sizing application to calculate the estimated size of the system. The goal of the sizing process is to define three very important figures: how much CPU power is needed (type and number of processors, memory, number of servers), how big the database will be (disk space necessary), and the minimum recommended network infrastructure to support the network traffic for the SAP Solutions. The quality of the sizing is just as good as the quality of the data supplied by the customer.

Sizing SAP systems is based on a unit known as the SAP Application Benchmark Performance Standard (SAPS). 100 SAPSs are equivalent to 2000 order line items processed in an hour (SD module) or 6000 dialog steps with 2000 postings in an hour (FI module).

Usually the CPU and memory requirements are calculated considering the estimated user population per application module and an approach of transaction volumes at peak times. Every SAP application module can have different processor power consumption depending on the depth of the transactions, and therefore they are assigned a load factor. Be aware that every SAP release or even the hardware partners could use different factors depending on their technology.

Additional information such as requested average CPU and memory utilization and scalability of the platforms further defines the needed hardware.

Database sizing requires more in-depth business knowledge to be able to fill out the lengthy questionnaires supplied by SAP. Often customers are unable to supply these data accurately. In these cases, the approach usually is to supply a moderate amount of disk space based on similar configurations and later monitor the system growth and add more disk space when needed. This, however, might have some drawbacks, including file system redesigns or time-consuming database reorganizations.

SAP has and supplies its partners with a sizing tool to help calculate the amount of disk space needed based on a business questionnaire.

This sizing tool also helps to calculate the estimated tablespace sizes and the biggest tables it will include.

An easy and first approach to sizing can be the QuickSizer tool provided by SAP through SAP Service Marketplace (service.sap.com/quicksizer). With the quick sizing service, SAP customers can make an initial and categorized calculation of CPU, memory, and disk resources, based either on users by application module or on a transaction load profile. The results in terms of SAPSs and average disk volume requirements are immediately available, and customers can decide to pass on this information to the hardware partner directly from the QuickSizer form.

This self-service tool can be used in the initial project phase to gain an approximate idea for planning the systems infrastructure. As the project progresses and more usage data is available, a double check should be done, either by using the Quicksizer tool again or by directing the information to the selected hardware partner.

A third and sometimes underestimated factor for a correct sizing is the expected network traffic. Usually there are two types of network connections that require appropriate bandwidths: from the application servers to the database server (server network) and from the presentation servers (usually PCs) to the application servers (access network).

The sizing of an overall SAP installation has a direct impact on the following elements of the process:

- The installation type (a factor of how many servers and their intended tasks)
- The hardware and network configuration
- The layout and size of the file system

- The installation of the database
- The load of a customer database
- The printing infrastructure and strategy
- The postinstallation steps
- The description of this first step is solely intended to make you aware of all the implications of a correct system sizing.

Installation Notes

SAP, as well as any other information technology provider, supplies last-minute information and problem corrections through the SAP Service Marketplace. Before proceeding with the installation, you must get the current installation notes. The actual note numbers depend on what release version you are installing, and they can be found in your SAP installation manual.

SAP notes are updated constantly. If you have the notes from previous installations or from someone else, you should still obtain the latest, unless the note modification date (which is referred to in the field Set by at the beginning of the note) is exactly the same.

At this stage before the actual installation has started, you might find it difficult to understand some of the concepts and requirements included in the notes, but try to follow them. They usually contain instructions for all supported operating systems, but you just have to pay attention to your particular one. Occasionally, you will find everything is OK by default and there are no additional corrections to do. (Do not count on it.)

CHAPTER 4

Using SAP Systems

The SAP presentation interface will be the main point of access for all types of users of SAP systems, their business applications, and administration and development functions. SAP provides different ways of accessing the systems or applications, such as using only an Internet browser, through the Enterprise Portal, the Business Explorer for the SAP Business Warehouse, or the most typical one, known as the SAP graphical user interface, or SAP GUI. The SAP GUI is the program that connects the user workstations with the SAP systems.

SAP GUI behaves very similarly to any other typical Windows application with a bit of "Web flavor" and with many options to personalize or adapt the interface to specific users' requirements.

The purpose of this chapter is to give an overview of the main functions and possibilities of the classical SAP R/3 windows presentation interface, also known as SAP GUI, because currently it is still the most widely used interface by millions of SAP users worldwide. It is very possible that we will soon see the SAP GUI completely Web based by means of the SAP Enterprise Portal. An overview about SAP EP is found in Chapter 11.

Basic topics such as logging in and out of the system, changing the passwords, the elements of the SAP GUI window, how to move around, getting help, filling up screen fields, launching and looking at background and printing jobs, personalizing the interface, and the basics of user sessions and transactions are covered.

Related topics concerning administration and technical tasks, such as roles and user management, passwords, authorizations, and security are covered in greater detail in Chapter 8.

Logging On and Off the System

Logging on to the system requires that the SAP GUI software be installed on your PC or workstation and a valid SAP user identification and password from the system administrator. Generally, there is a SAP utility installed in users' computers, known as SAP logon, which is the program that actually runs the SAP GUI. Refer to the section about SAP logon in Chapter 2 for more information about this utility.

The user identification and initial password are generally provided by the system managers or project leaders.

If you meet those basic requirements, having the SAP logon and username and password, then you are ready to *log on* to the SAP system. When you finish your working task, you must *log off*. The SAP system administrator can automatically log off users when their session is idle for a certain amount of time; this is achieved by means of an instance profile parameter.

To access the SAP systems, find the SAP logon utility and click on the group or server of your choice, provided you have a valid account and password.

As shown in Figure 4-1, a new window with the SAP R/3 logon screen appears. This screen has four fields: the Client, the User, the Password, and the Language.

In the Client field, enter the client number. This numbers defines a whole business entity within the company, or the whole company. Very possibly this field has a default client number in it, which is defined by the system administrator with the instance profile parameter *login/system_client*. In Figure 4-1, the client is automatically set to 100. You can accept this value or type over an existing client where you have user identification.

Once satisfied with the Client field, move to the next field by pointing and clicking with the mouse or pressing TAB.

The next field is the User field. Enter the name of the SAP user identification. Users of the SAP system are client specific, which means that having a user identification (user master record) on one client will only allow access to that particular client.

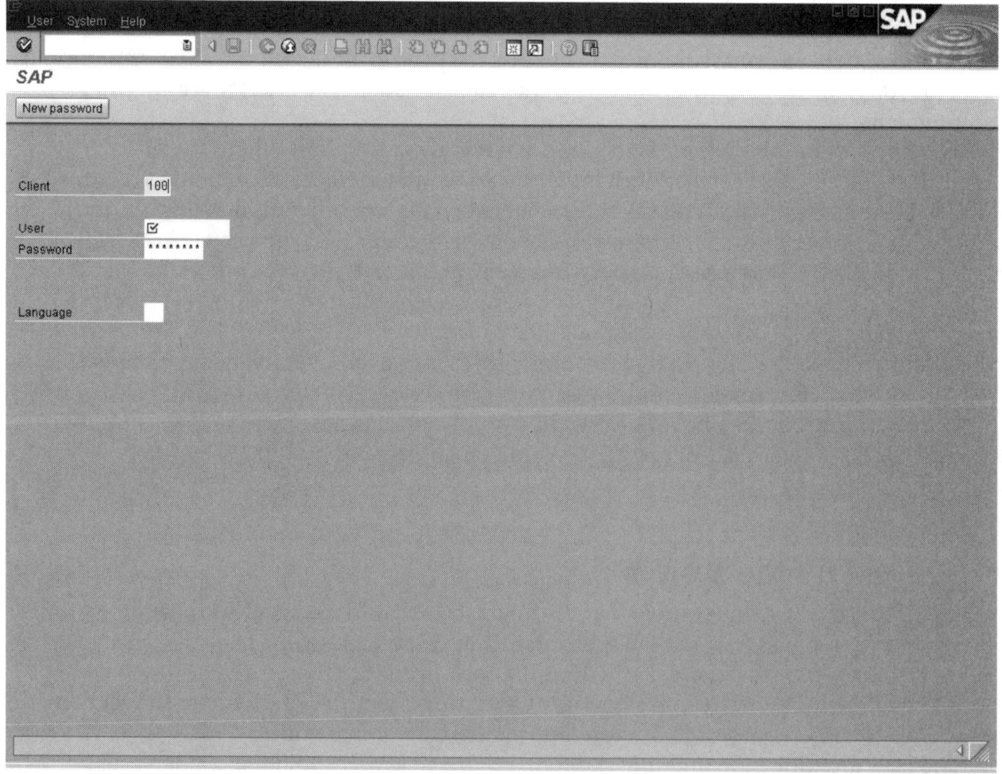

FIGURE 4-1 Initial SAP window for logon (Copyright by SAP AG)

In the Password field, enter the password that has been assigned by the system administrator or the user administrator. If this is the very first time a user accesses the system, pressing ENTER gets a screen requesting the user change the password.

Passwords in the SAP system must follow certain rules. These rules and how the user and the system administrator can change passwords are explained more fully in the next section. User passwords should be changed at regular intervals to enhance users' security and reduce the risk of intrusions.

The last field on the logon screen is the Language field. SAP systems support multinational character sets and languages on the same system at the same time, which is very useful for multinational companies with employees working in several countries and possibly using different languages.

SAP R/3 comes bundled with English (language code EN) and German (language code DE). The default language code is defined with the instance profile parameter *zcsa/system_language*. Additional languages have to be imported (installed) by the system administrator. On the same SAP system, different instances can be defaulted to different languages.

When the required fields are correctly completed, pressing ENTER takes you into the SAP system. If you made a typing mistake in any of the fields, you will see a message in the status bar (the bottom part of the SAP window).

When logging on for the very first time, the first thing you see is the copyright notice. Clicking on the Continue button removes the copyright notice. If the system administrator wrote a system message, this appears in your SAP window. In this case, pressing ENTER or clicking on the Continue button closes the System Message dialog box.

In the standard SAP system, the main menu screen, known as SAP Easy Access, is displayed. Figure 4-2 shows the initial screen of a SAP R/3 Enterprise 4.7, on an special Education and Demo system, known as IDES.

Users might get a different left side menu if the default settings of the user master records were modified to default them to other menus. A more detailed description on setting values for users is given later in this chapter.

Multiple logons to the system using the same username and passwords are allowed in SAP systems, but since release 4.6, the system keeps tracks of these logins both for security and licensing reasons. So if users are trying to log on with the same username while another session with that username is still active, the system will show a dialog box show three options:

- Continue with the current logon and end other logons in the system
- Continue with the current logon and not ending the other logons in the system
- Terminate the current logon process

Passwords

A *password* is a string of characters (letters and numbers) known to a single user that prevents other users from accessing the system using that user identification. As stated before, when logging on for the very first time, the New Password dialog box is displayed, as shown in Figure 4-3.

There are specific rules for setting passwords. The following section explains the most important ones.

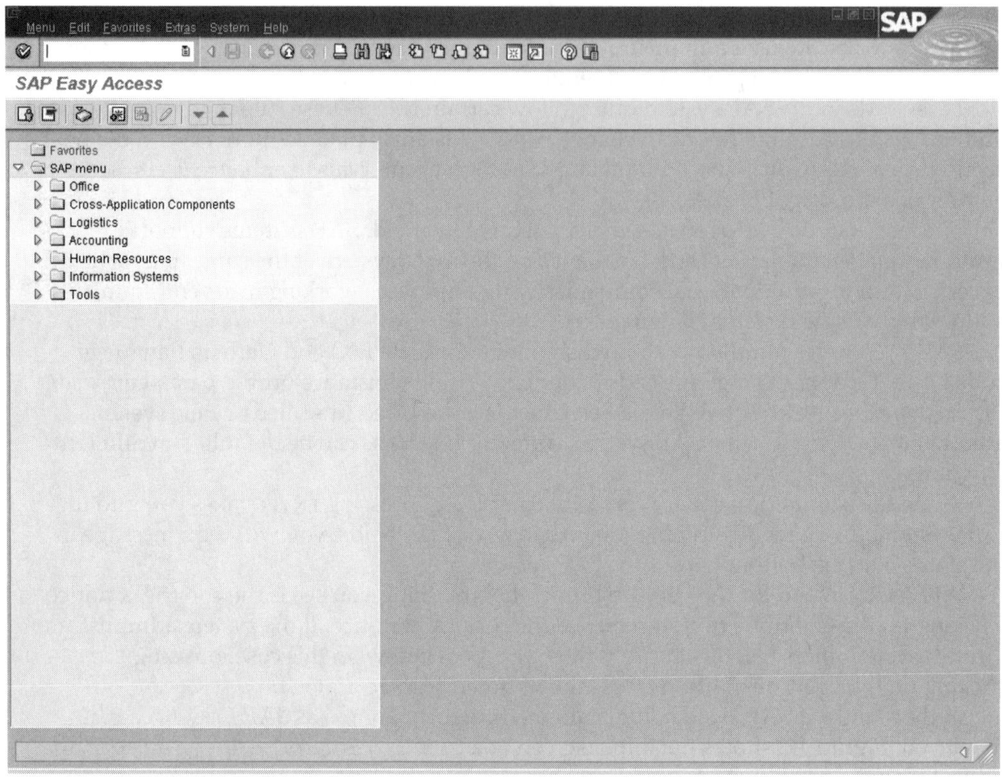

Figure 4-2 SAP Easy Access window (Copyright by SAP AG)

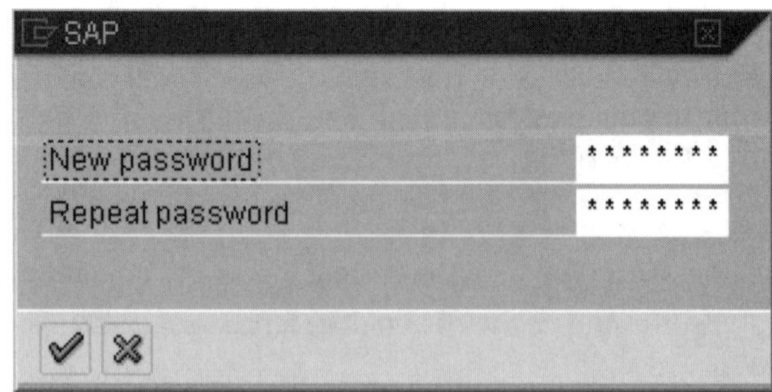

Figure 4-3 New Password dialog box (Copyright by SAP AG)

Password Rules

In the SAP system, users must follow certain rules when entering passwords. Some rules are fixed in the SAP code and others can be set by the system administrator using certain profile parameters or by forbidding entries by specifying values in tables. These administrative topics are dealt with in the section entitled "Password Management" in Chapter 8.

Providing the administrator made no changes, the standard password rules of the system are as follows:

- Password length must be at least three characters long and no more than eight.
- Passwords are not case sensitive, so, for example, if your password is *laura,* all strings *laura, LAuRa,* and *LAURA* behave just fine.
- Valid alphanumeric characters include all the letters (from *a* to *z*), the numbers, and even the punctuation marks, as long as the password does not begin with a question mark (?), a blank space, or an exclamation point (!).
- The first three characters of a password cannot be the same.
- You cannot use the string *pass* or *SAP** as your password. You cannot use any of the *forbidden* passwords, which are maintained by the system administrator in a special table.
- You cannot use any of the last five passwords.

The following list gives some examples of valid and invalid passwords.

Valid Passwords	Invalid Passwords	
13071985	pass	(it's a system nonpermitted password)
maria099	!jun97	(begins with an invalid character)
hello=98	sapr3	(just because the system manager decided to include it among forbidden passwords)
Uandme2	mmmycar	(begins with the three identical characters)

System administrators can impose additional password rules, such as forbidding some strings of characters as passwords, setting a minimum password length other than three, setting an expiration time, and so forth. Refer to the section entitled "Password Management" in Chapter 8 for additional information.

Changing the Password

Users can change their password during the logon process; passwords can also be changed by the system administrator or by any other user with the proper authorization for changing user master records.

Users must change their passwords when logging on for the very first time. The procedure that follows shows how:

When all the logon window fields have been filled up as described in the previous section (client, user ID, password—assigned by your system administrator—and language), pressing ENTER will display the Password Change dialog box, like the one shown in Figure 4-3.

In the New Password field, type in your new password, adhering to the previous rules, and click with the mouse or press TAB to move to the Repeat Password field; then repeat exactly the same password. This is a security measure to avoid typing mismatches. Next, press ENTER.

Users must follow exactly the same procedure of changing passwords in case the system administrator changes their passwords.

At any time, users can change their own passwords when logging in. To do so, they have to click on the New Password button located on the application toolbar. When the fields are complete, the system proceeds with the New Password dialog box and just follows the previous simple procedure.

It's important to know and make the users aware that they are not allowed to change their passwords more than once a day unless they are privileged users with certain authorizations.

System administrators might decide to enforce a rule requiring users to change their passwords at regular intervals, say every 45 days. In such cases, the system sends the users a message requesting they do so. When the password expiration interval arrives, the New Password logon windows automatically appear when the users log on requesting the password change. Users are forced to change the password; otherwise they cannot log in to the SAP system and will have to contact the system administrator to request a new password.

System Administrator Procedure to Change Passwords for Other Users

Changing passwords for end users is a frequent task for system managers of most computer systems and applications. SAP is no exception.

Sometimes users forget their original passwords and need to request new ones. In these cases, the SAP administrator must follow this procedure.

From the main tree hierarchy menu, select Tools | Administration | User Maintenance | Users, or, alternatively, go directly to the transaction by entering SU01 in the command field.

In the User field, type the user ID corresponding to the user whose password you want to change, and then select the options User Names | Change Password, or directly press the Change Password button on the application toolbar. Type in the new password and then repeat it in the second field and press ENTER (Copy button) to confirm the change.

Inform the user of the new password. When the system administrator performs this procedure, the system automatically requests that the user change the password when he or she logs on.

Since release 4.7 of R/3 and SAP other solutions using the SAP Web Application Server, there is a new wizard for automatic password generation. This wizard is a pushbutton located in the logon data tabstrip within the User Maintenance transaction.

Logging Off

Users can log off SAP systems from any screen. There are several procedures to log off:

1. From the menu bar, choose System Log Off. You get the Logoff dialog box as shown in Figure 4-4. The box informs the user that any data or transaction not saved will be lost if continuing with the logoff procedure. If you are not sure whether the data you were working on were saved, click on the No button in the dialog box, and you will be returned to the screen where you were working. Otherwise, press the Yes button to log off. This procedure will log you off from all your SAP sessions, meaning it will close off the SAP windows with the current user sessions. More information on sessions can be found in later sections of this chapter.

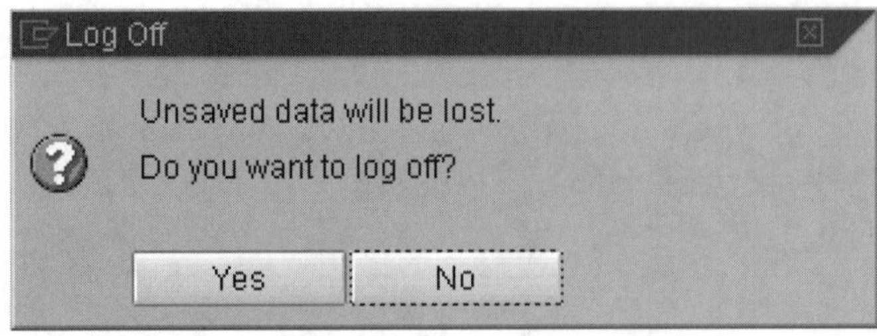

FIGURE 4-4 SAP Logoff screen (Copyright by SAP AG)

2. Another way to exit all your SAP sessions quickly is to use the transaction codes /NEND or /NEX in the command field. /NEND asks you to save data; /NEX does not. With both transaction codes you will be logged off of all your current SAP sessions.

CAUTION *Using the /NEX transaction will not ask you to save your data. So, if you are unsure whether you saved all your data, do not use this procedure.*

3. Clicking on the Exit button in the standard toolbar located on the SAP initial screen also displays the Logoff dialog box.

The User Interface: Main Screen Elements of SAP GUI

This section discusses the main features of the SAP GUI Windows interface and all the elements found in this user environment.

The windows environment of the SAP GUI includes most of the elements of popular Microsoft Windows applications, following the same style guides and ergonomic design methods. Depending on the nature and functionality of the particular SAP Solution application screen where the user is doing its tasks, the SAP GUI screens will contain popular check boxes, radio buttons, dialog boxes, icons, tabstrips, pushbuttons, menu items, and so forth. After the introduction of the EnjoySAP release and interface (R/3 4.6 and up), SAP has concentrated on improving the user interface, making it easier, more flexible, and more adaptable to job roles. SAP GUI includes a better-looking interface, additional drag-and-drop capabilities, Internet browser features, favorites, and integration with the Web and other applications from the SAP GUI. The standard menu became an easy-to-use hierarchical tree menu structure.

The SAP standard windows elements behave exactly the same as any other standard windows applications concerning scroll bars, minimizing a screen, moving windows, setting the active window, and so on. Therefore, reference to standard functions of the windows environment is not included in the following sections.

Figure 4-5 shows an example of a SAP R/3 window from the human resources module which includes most typical elements, including radio buttons, tabstrips, a navigation frame, possible entries input fields, and so on.

The menu bar contains the menu items corresponding to the particular SAP application you are working on. In Figure 4-5, the application belongs to the human resources modules

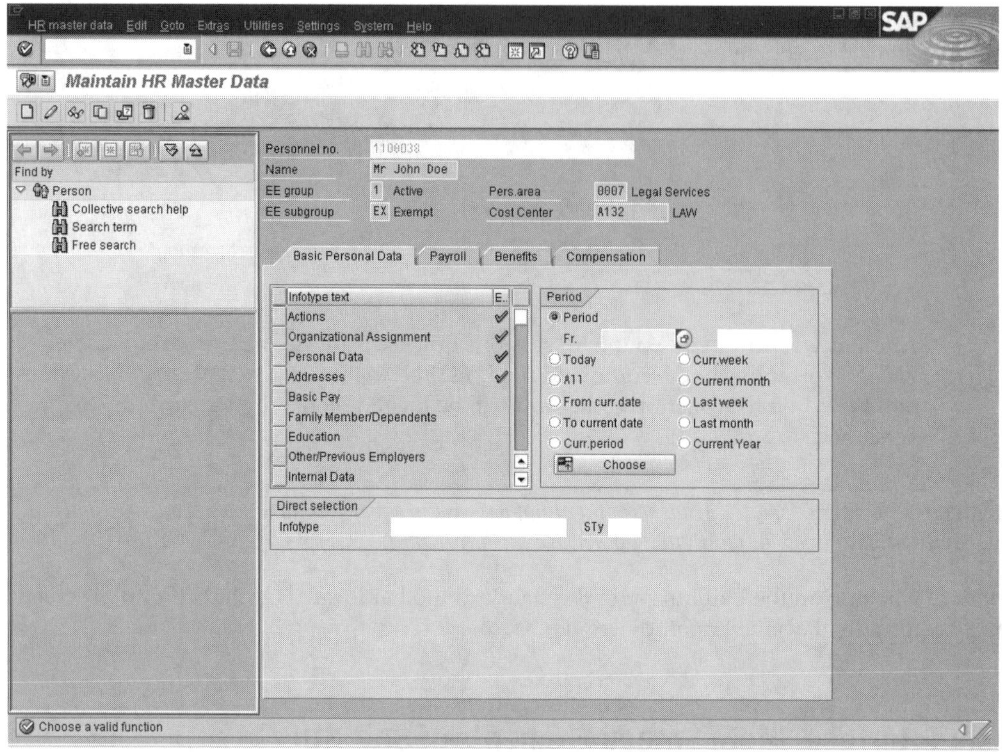

FIGURE 4-5 Typical SAP window from the HR module (Copyright by SAP AG)

FIGURE 4-6 SAP GUI standard toolbar (Copyright by SAP AG)

(Display HR Master Data). In this application, the menu bar contains eight options: HR Master Data, Edit, Goto, Extras, Utilities, Settings, System, and Help. The whole SAP R/3 system includes virtually hundreds of different menu items, depending on the task.

There are two menu options that are always present in every SAP window: the System and the Help menus. The System menu contains groups of functions and utilities that are available to users at all times, including working with session, looking at print requests, batch jobs, and so on. The Help menu contains all the available options for the different types and methods of obtaining online help in the system.

The following sections describe in detail all the available functions and utilities of these standard menus.

The next SAP GUI windows element is the *standard toolbar,* present in every application. It's a collection of icons that perform the most common functions available in the R/3 system. Figure 4-6 shows this toolbar. From left to right you find Enter, the command field, Save, Back, Exit, Cancel, Print, Find, Find Next, First Page, Previous Page, Next Page, Last Page, Create New Session, Generate Shortcut, Help, and Customizing of Local Layout.

FIGURE 4-7 Example of application toolbar (Copyright by SAP AG)

Make an entry in all required fields

FIGURE 4-8 Status bar (Copyright by SAP AG)

Within the standard toolbar, you normally find the command field, which is very important for moving around the system with transactions. The command field can be hidden or shown at will. The command field also behaves like a list box or history list, remembering the last commands (transactions) performed. The icons in the SAP GUI windows support the Focus property of many windows applications. This means that if you place the cursor over an icon and wait for a moment, the system will show the function or definition of the icon.

The next part of the screen (shown in Figure 4-7) is the *application toolbar,* which normally contains icons or buttons most frequently used in that task or transaction and from which options may be selected from the specific application menu bar. This design makes it more efficient for end users; however, some screens do not include application toolbars.

The *status bar* is the bottom line of the screen and usually shows informational or error messages to the users (see Figure 4-8). The status bar also shows other useful information, such as system data like the ID (E47), the session number (1), the client (800), the hostname of the application server (offsrv06), or the writing mode (INS, insert). This information is further extended using the down arrow on the system data, so that users can also see the transaction code, user name, program, and response time (see Figure 4-9).

Between the application toolbar and the status bar users find the normal working area for particular applications. This working area is the one intended for user input and output and can be made of frames, icons, tabstrips, fields, pushbuttons, radio buttons, and so forth.

Now let's have a closer look at the most common options.

FIGURE 4-9 Additional info from status bar (Copyright by SAP AG)

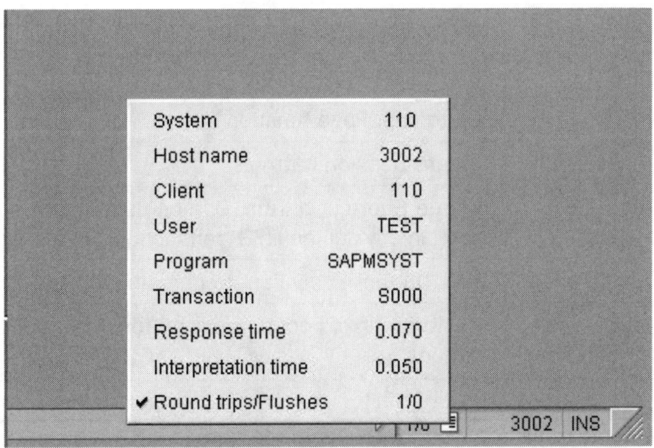

The Standard Toolbar

The standard toolbar is made of a collection of icons that perform the most common functions in every SAP application. Table 4-1 shows the available icons together with a description of the functions they perform.

These functions are also normally available from the menu bar or from the function keys. Some functions, such as those performed by the scrolling icons, can be achieved by using standard windows functions—moving the scroll bars or pressing the PageUp and PageDown keys on a standard PC keyboard.

Icon	Description
ok	OK button. Performs the same function as pressing ENTER. It's useful for continuing the transaction and going to the next screen. Also, when users get an error and are presented with a No Application screen, pressing the OK button takes them back to the previous transaction.
save	Save button. This function is available when there is something to save in the current transaction or application. Otherwise, this button is grayed out. It is sometimes available even if the data was already saved.
back	Back button. Takes the user to the previous screen in a transaction.
exit	Exit button. This function returns the user to the previous transaction.
cancel	Cancel button. The Cancel function stops the current transaction and goes back to the previous menu.
print	Print button. Performs the print function. This is equivalent to choosing System | List | Print. This function is only available when printing report lists or other printable formats such as program codes, traces, and the like.
find	Find button. Allows users to search for any particular screen in lists, reports, programs code, and so forth.
findnext	Find Next button. Searches for the next occurrence of a previously searched term.
gotofirstpage	Go to First Page function button. The R/3 scrolling functions can be faster than using standard windows functions.
gotoprevious	Go to Previous Page button.
gotonext	Go to Next Page button.
gotolast	Go to Last Page function button.
createsession	Create Session button.
createshortcut	Create Shortcut button. Can be used for creating an icon in the desktop that can directly call an R/3 transaction, report, or system command.
help	Help button. Equivalent to pressing F1.
customizelayout	Customizing of Local Layout button. Can be used to setup screen color and options.

TABLE 4-1 Available Icons on the Standard Toolbar

The standard toolbar also contains a very important field, the command field, where users can directly enter transaction codes to move directly to other applications or choose a transaction from a history list from the available list entries arrow in the field.

The Screen Layout Menu

The Layout menu is used for customizing the display options of the SAP GUI windows, and it has a group of utilities that mainly affect the appearance and behavior of these windows, such as colors, fonts, graphic appearance, as well as other utilities for working with local sessions such as cut and paste, graphics, and so on. Figure 4-10 shows the available options under the Layout menu.

If you are an experienced Windows user, you will find that most tasks are basically the same as those available with the standard functions of the Windows environment.

Options to configure the layout and behavior of the SAP windows elements allow you to

- Change the text fonts, SAP GUI theme, size, sounds, and the colors of the SAP windows.
- Use the clipboard to transfer information from the SAP GUI window to other windows applications.
- Set the default size of the SAP GUI window.
- Change the behavior of the cursor positioning in fields and set the automatic tabbing function when the input field is complete.
- Create SAP GUI shortcuts on the desktop.
- Configure history and internationalization settings.

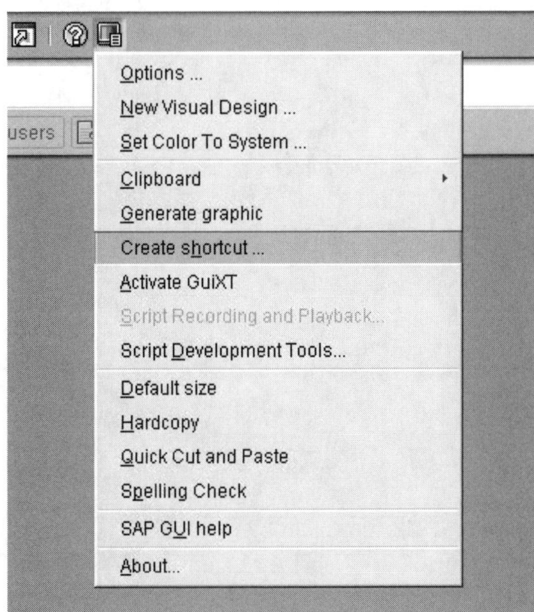

FIGURE 4-10 Customizing of Local Layout menu (Copyright by SAP AG)

- Run SAP GUI traces.
- Change the behavior of messages, for instance, toggling between messages in the status bar or dialog boxes.

Many of these tasks are performed with additional functions inside the Options or the New Visual Design menu. For the Options menu, the system displays an additional screen known as the Options folder, from which most of the tasks previously introduced are performed. Colors and fonts are now found within the New Visual Design screen. The Options folder looks like Figure 4-11. The New Visual Design screen is shown in Figure 4-12.

Changing the Fonts of the Text Elements

To change the font's appearance and size of the text elements within the SAP GUI, you can use the Fonts scrollbar within the SAP GUI settings screen, which is accessed by selecting the NewVisual Design option. See Figure 4-12.

The allowed range of font size goes from 80 to 120% of standard size, but it won't take effect until you open a new session.

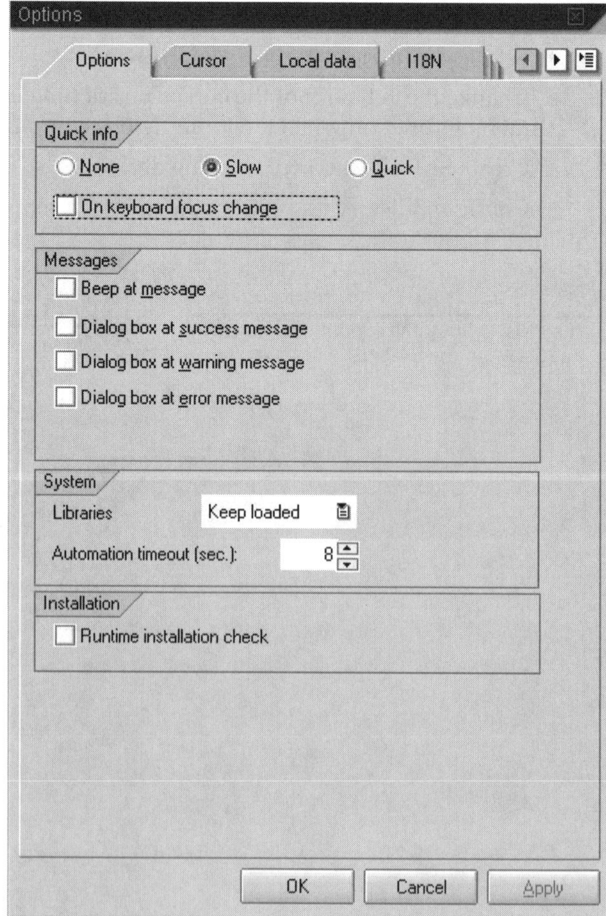

Figure 4-11 Options window within Customizing of Local Layout menu (Copyright by SAP AG)

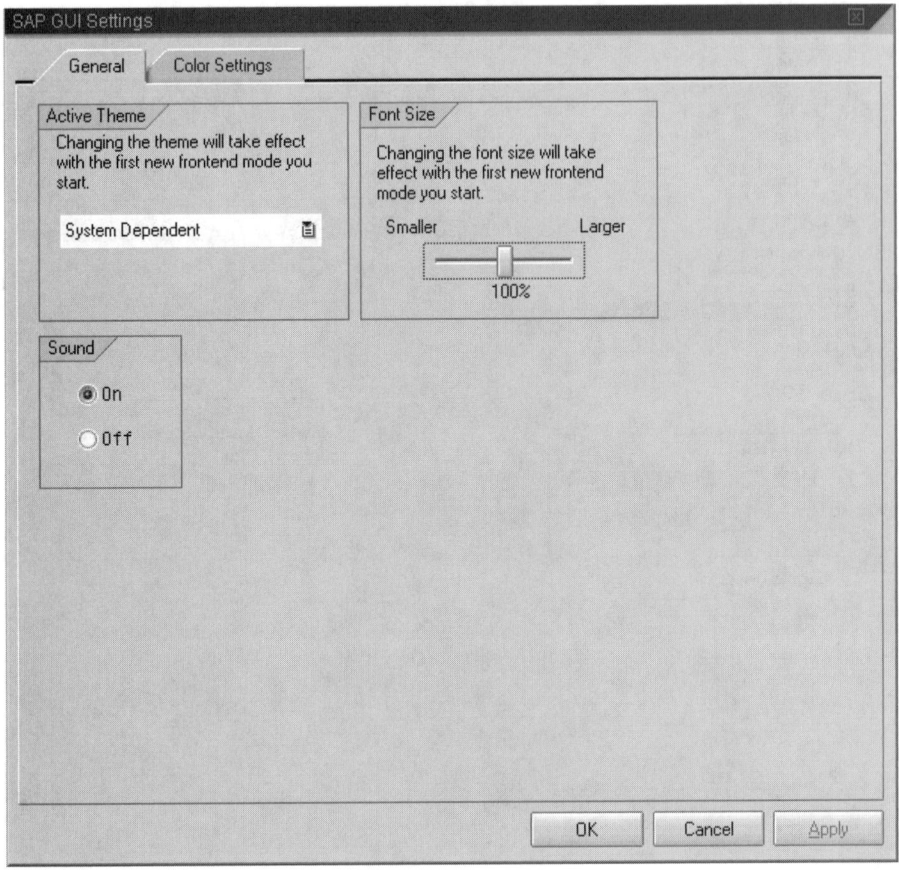

FIGURE 4-12 New Visual Design screen (Copyright by SAP AG)

Changing the Colors of the SAP GUI Windows

Since latest releases of SAP GUI, you can customize some of the colors of the SAP GUI window, basically by choosing among the predefined color schemes or by defining your own colors.

To access the color customizing options, select New Visual Design from the Customizing of Local Layout menu, and then click on the Color Settings tabstrips. Figure 4-13 shows an example.

From this window you have the following options:

- Select a standard color scheme; standard color schemes guarantee a correct readability of SAP GUI screens.
- Choose foreground or background luminosity using the provided bar. You can additionally double-click the shaded bar on the top right to select additional colors (the Color Picker window). Notice the Link option between foreground and background colors, which automatically ensures an optimal combination of both.

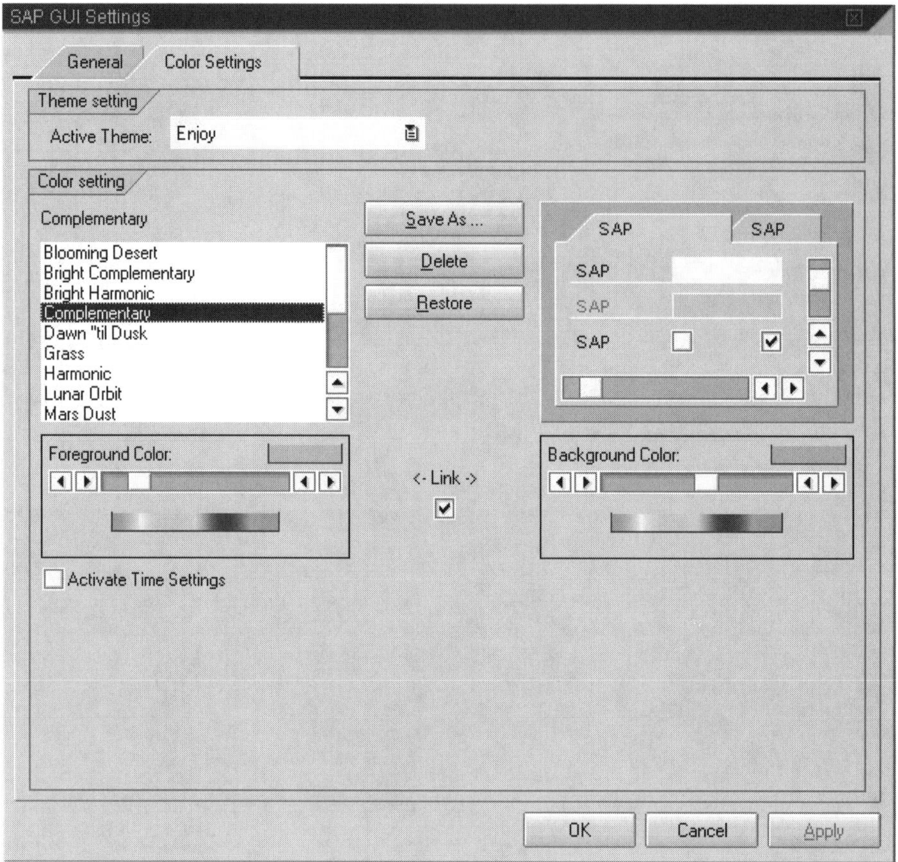

FIGURE 4-13 Customizing of color settings (Copyright by SAP AG)

- Additionally, there is a time setting option, which can be activated to make a gradual color shift during the day.

Configuring Automatic Tabbing between Fields

The SAP GUI includes an automatic tabbing feature, which can be very useful when users must enter information in many fields and don't want to press TAB to move from field to field. When the automatic tabbing feature is enabled, the cursor automatically moves to the next field when you reach the end of an actual input field.

Automatic TAB only works at the end of an input field. For example, if the a field can hold up to nine characters and you enter only four, you still have to press TAB to move to the next input field. To enable the automatic tabbing, select the Cursor tabstrip under the Options menu, and then select the check box next to Automatic TAB at Field End. The check box works like a toggle; so, to disable the automatic tabbing, deselect the check box.

Determining the Cursor Position when Clicking on a Field

SAP users can decide how they want the cursor to behave when clicking on the blank area of an input field. For instance, the cursor could automatically position itself at the beginning of the field when the user clicks anywhere in a blank field, or it could position itself to the right of any text already entered in the field, considering blank spaces as if they were nulls. Alternatively, users can decide to leave the normal behavior of the cursor positioning, which is to appear exactly where they place it in the field, whether there are blank spaces or not.

Determining the behavior of the cursor positioning depends on the type of tasks users perform most frequently. For example, when the screens they most often use require entering data in many empty fields, it is advisable to make the cursor appear at the end of any text when clicking anywhere behind the text. In such cases, if the input fields are empty, the cursor will position automatically at the beginning of the field, ready for entering data. This is the default setting.

The other setting is to place the cursor exactly in the field position that the user clicks on with the mouse, whether the field is empty or not. This is more suitable for making lots of modifications in fields that already contain data and when users move across fields using the arrow keys instead of the TAB or the mouse.

Cursor behavior is set by selecting the Cursor tabstrip in the Options menu. In this folder there is a check box with the caption *Position cursor to end of text*. If this box is checked, the cursor will be positioned at the end of the text of the input field. Otherwise, the cursor will be positioned wherever the user clicks on a field.

If you select (check) the option Note Cursor Position in Field at TAB, then the system will position the cursor exactly where you last clicked within an input field.

Resetting the Default Windows Size

The option Default Size under the Customizing of Local Layout menu adjusts the size of the SAP GUI window to the default window size. This feature, however, flashes an error message in the status bar if the user does not have the correct windows resolution. And it won't have any effect if the windows still have the default size. The windows size can be changed by following the normal procedures used in any other screen of other windows applications.

Using the Clipboard

You can transfer the contents of fields onto the clipboard of your windows environment and then paste them into other fields of the SAP systems or into other windows applications. You can move or copy the contents of fields by using the functions of the Clipboard option located in the menu.

The SAP GUI clipboard functions work very similarly to the clipboard functions of the Windows environment. In many SAP screens and applications, for example, when working with the ABAP editor, you also have copy and paste functions below the Edit menu. However, options under the Edit menu only work inside the SAP system and cannot be transferred to other windows applications. The Edit menu usually contains more extensive options than the clipboard.

The SAP GUI clipboard presents four options: Mark, Copy, Cut, and Paste. The Mark option is useful when selecting several fields to copy and paste. Otherwise, just select a field by clicking and dragging the pointer over the text field and select the most appropriate option. When the Mark option is selected, the cursor changes automatically to a crosshair sign. The selection is made by clicking on a corner of the area to copy and holding the mouse and dragging to the opposite corner. The SAP system will display a rectangle indicating the selected area.

In display-only fields (which cannot be changed) you can *copy* the contents to other fields, but you cannot *cut* them.

Other Options

Since latest releases of the SAP GUI, the Customizing of Local Layout menu includes many more advanced options, which are typically set up by system managers and distributed to the end user population because normally they are not used except in special situations. Some of these advanced options are as follows:

- History and Cache setting in users workstations, which can be found under the Options and Local Data tabstrips.
- Multitype support functionality for displaying multiple character sets. This can be found under the Options and I18N tabstrips.
- The tabstrips Trace, Scripting, and Expert serve the main purpose of debugging and tracing errors of the interface between SAP GUI and the application server.

Personalizing the Favorites

You can create a Favorites list of the transactions, reports, files, Web sites, and other objects you use most. You can add items to your Favorites list by using the Favorites menu option, by dragging and dropping, or by using the right-click feature on most transactions. You can also create your own folders in the Favorites list, move Favorites, and change their text as desired. Figure 4-14 shows an example of Favorites.

In addition to selecting functions from a Favorites list, User menu, SAP standard menu, or the menu bar, you can still select functions using transaction codes.

In order to include other type of objects, such as those from a Knowledge Warehouse, BSP applications, and so on, select Favorites | Add Other Objects from the main menu. You get a dialog screen similar to the one shown in Figure 4-15. Select the appropriate radio button and then enter the appropriate information, such as the title and the link to the actual object you want to include in your list of Favorites.

Role-Based Scenarios

A growing majority of SAP users are no longer just the professional users. Rather, an ever-increasing percentage of companies' employees are using SAP products as occasional users. Realizing that these occasional users come from different departments and perform different jobs leads to the creation of user roles. Interfaces are tailored to the user in each case, but ultimately use the same back-end functionality.

From classical SAP R/3, role-specific scenarios were extended into SAP's New Dimensions and ultimately into all SAP solutions within the mySAP Business Suite and SAP NetWeaver, and a key concept for a proper configuration and deployment of the SAP Enterprise Portal. Yet role-specific scenarios can be individually used in classical SAP GUI-based SAP solutions.

A role describes a set of logically linked transactions. These transactions represent the range of functions users typically need at their workstations. Users who have been assigned

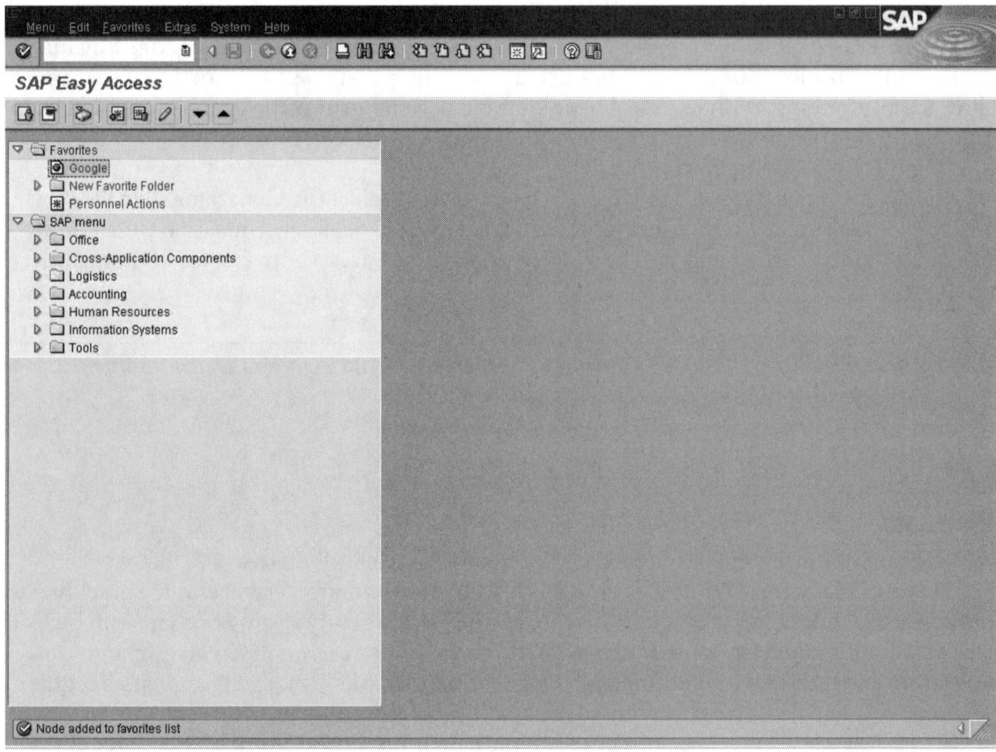

FIGURE 4-14 Example of Favorites (Copyright by SAP AG)

FIGURE 4-15 Selecting the appropriate radio button and entering the appropriate information (Copyright by SAP AG)

Add additional objects

Select which type of object you want to add

- Web address or file
- Predefined URLs from directory
- BSP Application
- Generic Web Address (URL Template)
- Web source from Drag&&Relate Servlet
- External mail system
- Knowledge Warehouse
- SAPScript (Texts defined with SE61)

to an activity group can choose between the User menu and the SAP standard menu. Selecting the User menu icon displays the User menu in place of the SAP standard menu.

The authorizations for the activities listed in the menus are also assigned to the users using activity groups. With release 4.6, predefined activity groups (user roles) from all application areas are included in the standard system. These can be displayed and used by selecting the Other Menu button.

Activity groups (user roles) have to be set up using the Profile Generator so that users of the SAP system can work with user-specific or position-related menus. The Create Role, Assign Users, and Documentation buttons provide access to Activity Group Maintenance functions.

NOTE *The availability of the Other Menu, Create Menu, Assign Users, and Documentation buttons depends on the user's authorizations.*

More information about roles and profiles is provided in Chapter 8.

Shortcuts

Shortcuts are a component of the SAP GUI, available since Basis release 4.5, that work in the Windows platforms (Windows 98, 2000, NT, XP, etc.) and are very useful for quickly running those functions or transactions that are more frequently used. Shortcuts can be created from the standard toolbar of the SAP GUI, or can be manually created (using program sapshcut.exe with parameters). Once they are created, shortcuts appear as regular desktop icons that can be included in other Windows documents or even sent by e-mail.

The easiest way to create a shortcut for a particular application is to go to the required screen with regular SAP menu functions or transaction codes. Once in the transaction for which a shortcut is desired, click on the Create Shortcut icon on the standard toolbar. Figure 4-16 shows the dialog box for creating shortcuts. Enter the requested logon data and click OK.

The system automatically creates a SAP shortcut on the user's desktop. To run the SAP shortcut, just double-click on the icon. For security reasons the system will display a dialog box requesting the username and password. After a successful logon, the shortcut will take you automatically to the defined transaction or report. You can also include logon data while creating a new shortcut; however, this is not recommended for security reasons.

Shortcuts can also be used in the current SAP GUI sessions, which eliminates having to enter username and password. There are three options:

- If you drag and drop the shortcut on the existing session, the system will automatically go to the defined shortcut transaction.
- To run the shortcut on a new session, press CTRL while dragging the shortcut to the SAP window.
- To change the shortcut parameters, press SHIFT while dragging the shortcut to the SAP window.

System Status Information

In every SAP GUI window, users have the option of displaying important information about the System, the user, the transaction, and other data, which can be extremely helpful on many occasions.

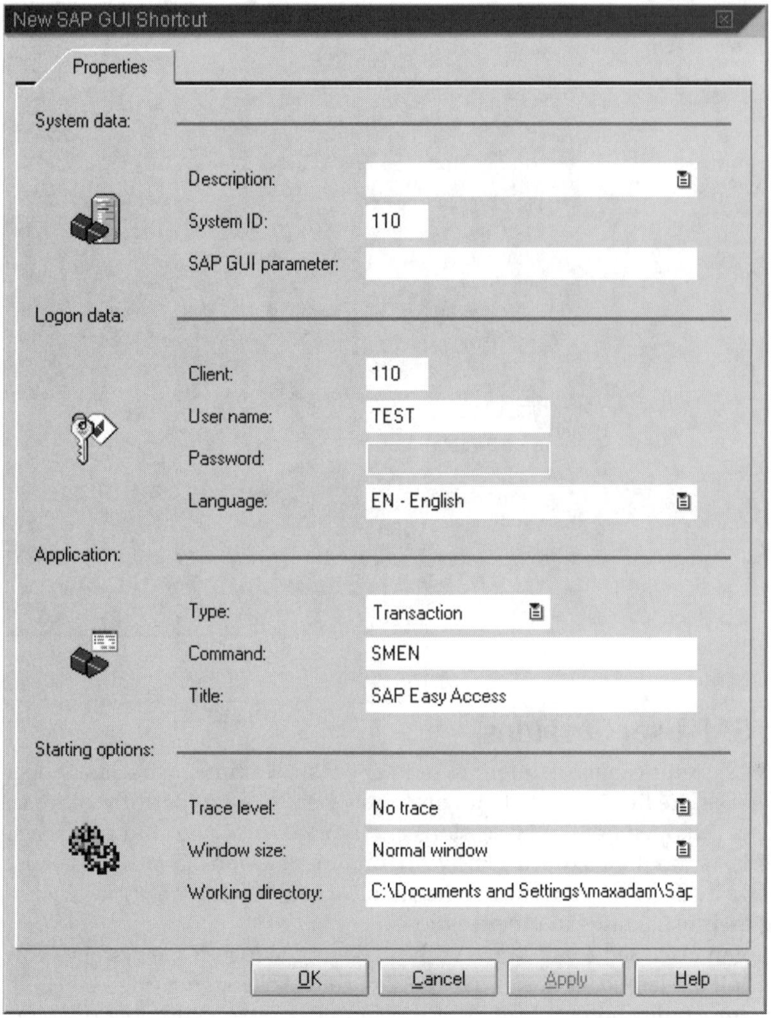

New SAP GUI Shortcut

Properties

System data:

Description:	
System ID:	110
SAP GUI parameter:	

Logon data:

Client:	110
User name:	TEST
Password:	
Language:	EN - English

Application:

Type:	Transaction
Command:	SMEN
Title:	SAP Easy Access

Starting options:

Trace level:	No trace
Window size:	Normal window
Working directory:	C:\Documents and Settings\maxadam\Sap

OK Cancel Apply Help

FIGURE 4-16 Creating Shortcut window (Copyright by SAP AG)

The Status screen can be accessed by choosing System | Status from any SAP window. In the Status window, under the Usage data box, you can see what the actual user name, client, language, date, and time are. Most important, though, is the Repository Data, where the system displays the transaction, program, and screen number. This is the way users can locate the transactions they are working on and developers or support personnel can easily locate the specific programs or menus that might have errors.

Since SAP GUI release 4.5 and later, part of the status information can also be displayed from the status bar by clicking on the possible entries arrow on the system box.

An example of a Status window is shown in Figure 4-17.

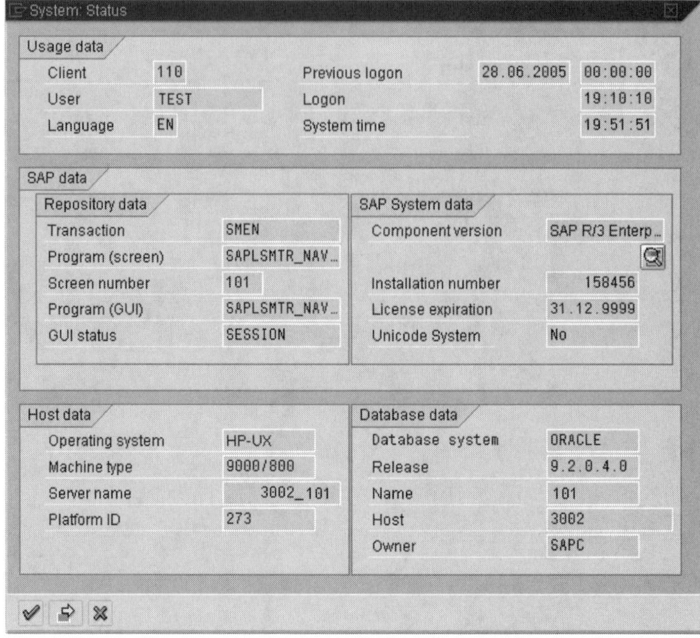

FIGURE 4-17 Status window (Copyright by SAP AG)

Working with SAP User Sessions

Users of SAP systems can work on more than one task at a time by means of opening new sessions. *Sessions* are like independent windows where you can perform other tasks. By default, a user can open up to nine sessions and work or move around all open sessions at the same time, without interrupting the work on other sessions. For example, users might decide to have a session open to watch the status of background or printing jobs while performing their usual tasks in other sessions.

Sessions can be closed at any time, without having to log off the system. However, when a user closes off the last session, this has the same effect as logging off.

The system administrator might decide to limit the allowed number of open sessions to less than nine because the workload caused by open sessions is virtually the same as having additional users logged on to the system.

Users can create new sessions from anywhere because the Create Session function is under the System menu. Or, also, there is an icon in the standard toolbar, available in every SAP GUI window.

To create a new session, click on the Create Session icon, or, from the menu bar, select System | Create Session. The system will open a new window with a new session and will place it in front of all other windows, immediately making it the active session. The status bar at the bottom of the screen shows the session number in parentheses beside the SAP system name (SID). The new session will be either the initial SAP window or the user-assigned initial menu. There is, however, a faster way to create a new session and a task (transaction) in a single step by using transaction codes in the command field. In order to do that, users have to know the needed transaction code.

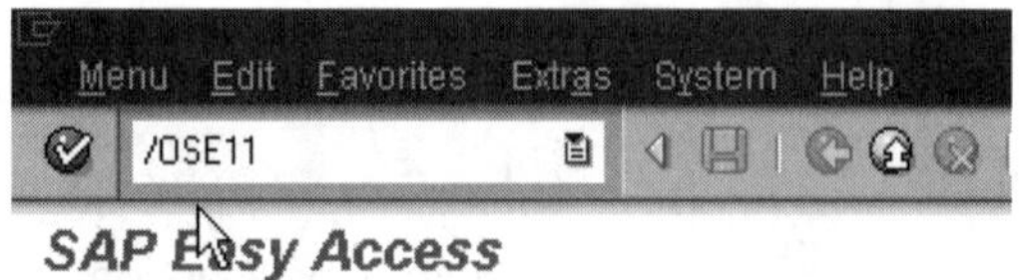

FIGURE 4-18 Opening a new session from the command field (Copyright by SAP AG)

The SAP system includes some utilities to help users find the needed transaction codes. When opening a new session with a transaction code, the system displays the initial screen of the transaction in a new session. To create a new session with a specific transaction at once, you must enter /O<TCODE> in the command field: front slash (/), the letter *O*, and <TCODE>, which stands for transaction code. For example, typing /OSE11 in the command field and pressing ENTER will start a new session with the initial screen of the task belonging to transaction SE11 (ABAP Data Dictionary). Figure 4-18 shows the command field with the example described.

Moving among sessions is like moving among windows in the Windows environment: with your mouse just click on any part of the window to make that session the active one. In the Microsoft Windows environment, you could also use the popular key combination ALT-TAB. Likewise, you can iconize or maximize your windows as you would with any other application.

Ending sessions is easy; however, users should be careful to save data before ending sessions because the system will not prompt them to save the data unless they are in the last open session—in which case, ending it is the same as logging off the system. When working in different sessions you don't lose any data as long as you don't log off without saving data first.

There are several ways to end sessions:

1. Select System | End Session from the menu bar.

2. Press the Exit button on the standard toolbar when located in the higher-level task (for instance, the transaction you first called when opening the session or the SAP main menu). Note that ending a session is not the same as logging off. The system behaves in that way only when you are in your last open session.
3. Log off the system completely, in which case all open sessions for the current user are ended.

Moving Around the SAP Systems

Users of the SAP solutions need to move around to perform their usual work. The SAP system includes several ways to move around. The most usual is by selecting options from the hierarchy tree menu at the left of the screen, or from application menus and submenus. This allows users to navigate and choose from the available functions to perform their tasks without the need to memorize keyboard combinations or transactions codes. Navigation in application menus is possible either with the mouse or with the keyboard. Selecting options is just like any other typical windows application: just drag around the menus and click the function you want to start.

Selecting functions just with the keyboard might not be very convenient, but it's easy. Pressing F10 takes you to the menu bar. From there, you can navigate with the arrow keys: right, left, down, and up.

Once you are located over the needed option, just press ENTER. To cancel a selection, press ESC. To cancel the menu bar selection, press F10 again. To move around the SAP work area, press TAB to go forward from field to field or SHIFT-TAB to move backward.

Once users working on particular tasks decide to finish their work and go to another application function, they have to move back through the menus and locate their new menus.

Within each specific application screen, usually the most common functions are directly accessible through the pushbuttons on the standard toolbar and the application toolbar. For example, when working in the initial screen for user administration, you will see the buttons for functions such as Create, Copy, Display, Lock/Unlock, and Change Password, which are the most common ones.

Likewise, clicking and holding the right-hand pushbutton of the mouse (for right-handed people) shows a pop-up box with those usual functions and the equivalent keyboard combinations. This is known as the Function Key menu. The options available under the Function Key menu differ among tasks. Figure 4-19 shows an example of a Function Key menu.

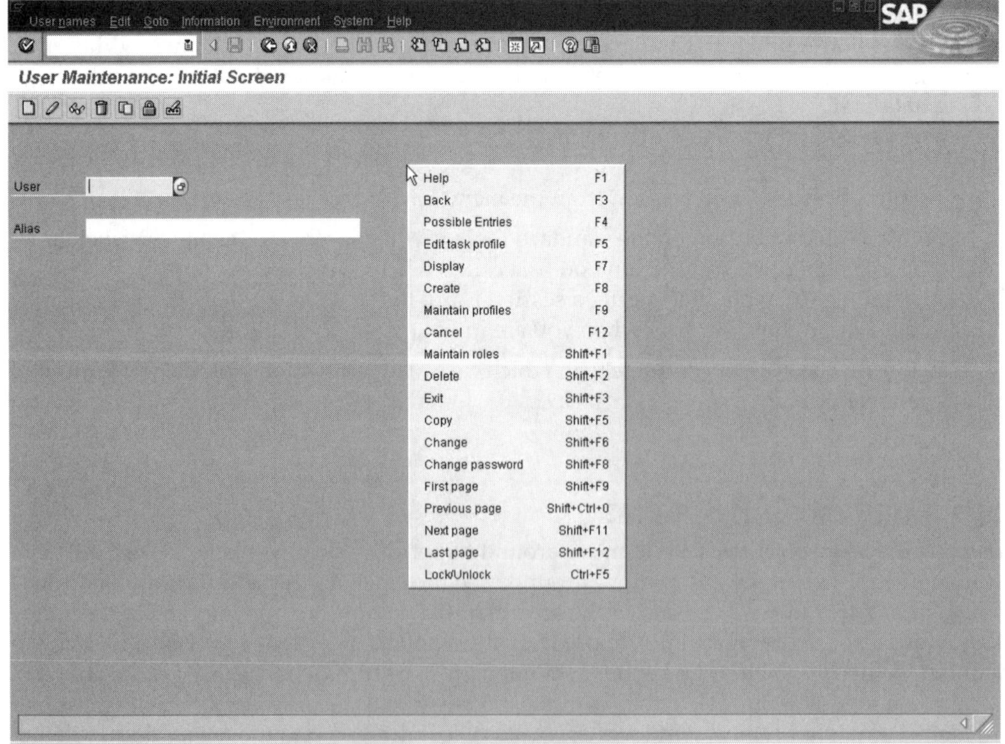

FIGURE 4-19 Example of Function Key menu (Copyright by SAP AG)

Another way to move around, often used by expert users, is by entering transaction codes in the command field. With this method, users can go directly to a task without navigating through the application menus.

Moving Around with Transaction Codes

The SAP system provides an alternative way of selecting menu options for moving around the tasks and functions of the SAP system by using transaction codes directly in the command field.

Using transaction codes gives users the advantage of moving faster to other transactions and also creating a new session with another function at once. When moving with transactions, you can go to any part of the SAP system, not just the application you are working with. There is, of course, the need for the necessary authorization in order to execute the task.

The disadvantage is that in order to use this method, users have to memorize cryptic transaction codes. A *transaction code* is an alphanumeric code, up to 20 characters, associated with a SAP task. By typing the transaction code in the command field and pressing ENTER, the system takes you directly to the initial screen for that transaction. Every function within the SAP system has a transaction code associated with it. There are two main ways to find the transaction code you want to use.

The first way is to navigate with the menu functions and reach the desired screen. When in the screen, select System | Status. You get the status window, which contains the transaction code in the transaction field.

Another way to find a transaction code is by selecting from the main menu Extras | Settings and checking the option Display Technical Names. With this option, every time you move in the hierarchical tree menu, you will be able to see the transaction code preceding every menu option.

Finally, you can also use transaction code SE93 (maintain transactions) and then use the search help to look for the transaction code.

To move around by entering transaction codes, position the cursor in the command field. Then enter /N followed by the transaction code, for example, /NSM37, where /N indicates to end the current task, and SM37 is the transaction code, in this case, corresponding to Simple Job Selection. When you are in the initial screen you don't have to enter /N before the transaction code because there is no task to end. Upon pressing ENTER, the current task is finished and the system takes you automatically to the specified task.

Another way to work with transaction codes but not end the current task is to create a new session and a new task at once, as stated previously and shown in Figure 4-18. To do that, you must enter /O and the transaction code. For example, typing /OSE09 in the command field opens a new session in a new SAP window with the initial screen of the transport organizer, which is transaction SE09. The command field includes an entries list indicated by the down arrow on the right side, which is a history list of transaction codes previously entered since you logged on. You could also press the history list and select a transaction from that list. Clicking on a transaction from the list and pressing ENTER displays the initial screen associated with the transaction. A history list display is shown in Figure 4-20.

When using the System | Status function to find the transaction code for the current task, you must be aware that many transactions have several screens associated with them. So, when using transaction codes to move to a task, you can only reach the initial screen for the transaction.

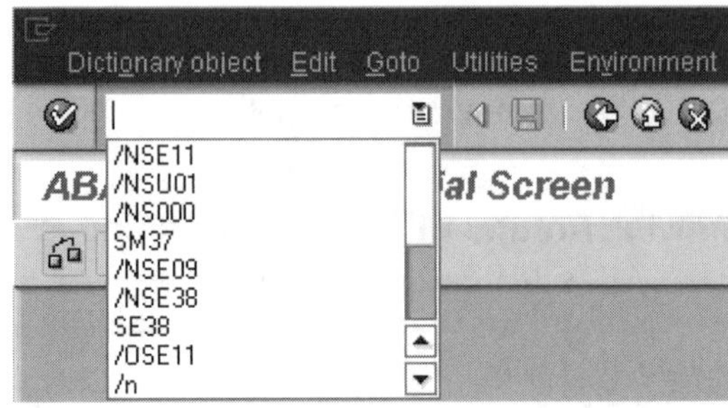

FIGURE 4-20 History list of transaction codes (Copyright by SAP AG)

Working with Information

User work on the SAP systems normally involves entering data into the system or displaying information from it. To perform those functions, users select options from menus, enter data in the input fields, send jobs to the printer, and interact with the system through dialog boxes.

A *field* is a single unit of information, such as a zip code or a last name. Fields have a *field name* (a description) and *field data* (actual data). Figure 4-21 shows an example of some fields in a SAP window, where *User* is the field name and *SMITH* is the actual data.

There are two field types in the SAP GUI windows: display fields and input fields. Display fields are fields that show information to the users. Input fields are fields where users can enter data.

Fields have different lengths limiting the amount of allowed characters. In the SAP windows, the field length is determined by the length shown on the screen, or by the length of the database field.

When entering data, users have two common methods available in standard windows applications that require entering information: overwrite (replace) and insert. The default in SAP is set to replace. The status bar shows the mode (OVR or INS) in which a user is working. To switch methods, just press INS on the keyboard. It works like a toggle.

To enter data in a field, just position the cursor and type it in. When finished and the field is full, the cursor moves to the next field automatically when autoTAB is enabled. Otherwise, just press TAB or click on the next field.

Possible Entries for an Input Field

The SAP system provides several types of facilities for helping users fill the data in fields. Input fields sometimes show a possible entries arrow, where the system can display a list of possible entries. Users select the entry, and the system transfers them automatically to the field.

Another method of finding entries is with *search helps* (in older releases they were known as *matchcodes*). As their names state, these are methods for helping users find possible entries using different search criteria, that is, using other related fields.

Figure 4-22 shows fields with possible entries (*Industry Sector* and *Material Type*) and with a search help (*Material*).

FIGURE 4-21 Example of field description and field data (Copyright by SAP AG)

To display a list of values, position the cursor on the field, click on the possible entries arrow, or press F4. If the field is associated with a search help, a dialog box for selecting the search criteria will appear where you can restrict the values of the search or modifying the maximum number of hits. An example of such a dialog box is shown in Figure 4-23.

To select an entry, double-click on it, or click once and press ENTER. Value is transferred to the field. To change the data in an input field, normally just type over it. If the field is for display only, no change is possible, unless you have a button that can switch between display and change modes. Display-only fields have the same color background as the screen's background.

When working in the SAP system, some input fields are *required*. If a particular screen contains a required field, you must enter data into it in order to proceed to the next screen in the task or transaction.

Sometimes users find screens without required fields. In such cases, users can proceed without entering any data. However, in some situations, if data are entered in nonrequired fields, users might have to deal with any required fields associated with them.

Trying to proceed to the next screen when a required field has not been filled out triggers an error message in the status bar, and the cursor is automatically positioned in the required field. Often you can get help on values to enter in input fields that do not have an associated search help but do have a possible entries list sign.

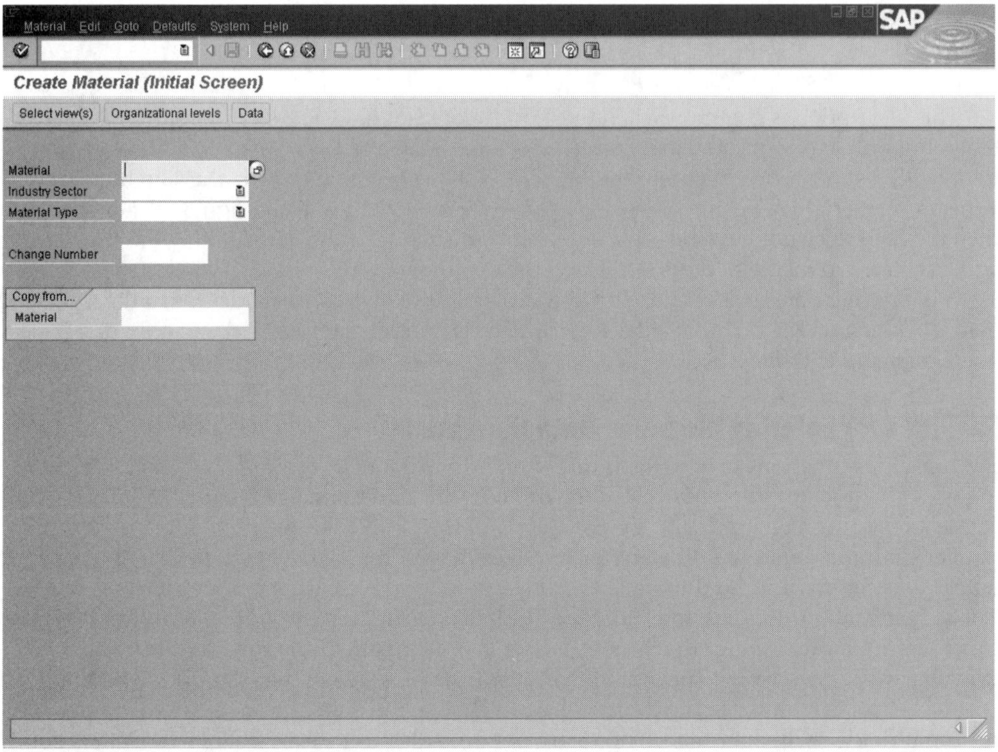

FIGURE 4-22 Example of possible entries and search help (Copyright by SAP AG)

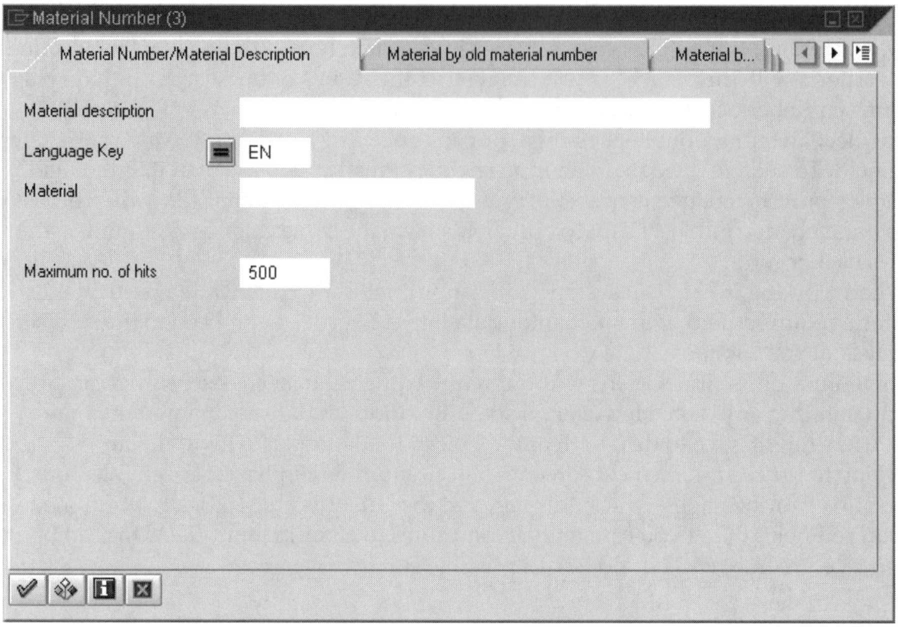

FIGURE 4-23 Restricting Search Values dialog box (Copyright by SAP AG)

This last option is common when the search does not have to mix different views or tables but only has to use the main table associated with a field. To display a list of entries for a field, just position the cursor on the field. If it has possible entries, the sign button appears to the right. Clicking on it displays the possible values. If the sign does not show, then the field does not have possible entries. To select one of the values shown in the list and transfer it to the field, double-click on the desired value.

If the number of entries is very long, it can be limited by using wildcards in the field before clicking on the possible entries arrow. For example, entering *ma** will only display values starting with *ma*.

Facilities for Entering the Same Data Repeatedly

SAP provides functions to ease the input of repetitive data, for example, when filling out invoices, material master records, orders, or even when creating users with similar data. Those facilities can be used with the Set Data and the Hold Data functions.

For example, suppose you want to create users with the same role or profile. You can enter the data once and hold them, using these data for the creation of the rest of the users. The system can transfer automatically the held data to the corresponding input fields. These functions are located under the System | User Profile menu. These functions are not available in all the screens. The system will display a message in the status bar when this occurs. With the Hold Data function, users can change the data after data are transferred to the input fields. With Set Data, changes are not possible. This means that Hold Data is good for occasions when there are small differences in the fields. Set Data has the advantage that the cursor skips over input fields with held data, so you don't have to move among fields.

Data are held on a screen until a user decides to delete the held data or when the user logs off from the SAP system. To hold the data on the screen, you first enter the data to be held in the input fields. Then, select System | User Profile from the menu bar. If you want to hold the data with the ability to change the data, choose Hold Data. If you want to hold the data without changing the data and to skip the fields with held data, select Set Data. If Hold Data and Set Data are not available, a message is displayed in the status bar.

To delete the data held on a screen, go to the screen containing the held data to be deleted and choose System | User Profile | Delete Data from the menu bar.

Input Field Default Values with User Parameters

User parameters are other facilities that the R/3 system offers for fast data input. User parameters are associated with certain common fields of the system, but not all. For example, common input fields in many SAP business applications are Company Code, Plant, Purchasing Group, and so forth. When you define a user parameter for a field, every time and in every screen that the same field appears, it will have the default value specified.

In order to define these parameters, you have to know the technical details of the fields you want to set. To get the parameter name (PID), press F1 for the field for which you want to set the value. This function displays a help screen for the field that includes the Technical Info button in a dialog box.

Clicking this button, you get the Technical Information screen for this field: table name, field name, and so on. Figure 4-24 shows an example of this screen. On the field data

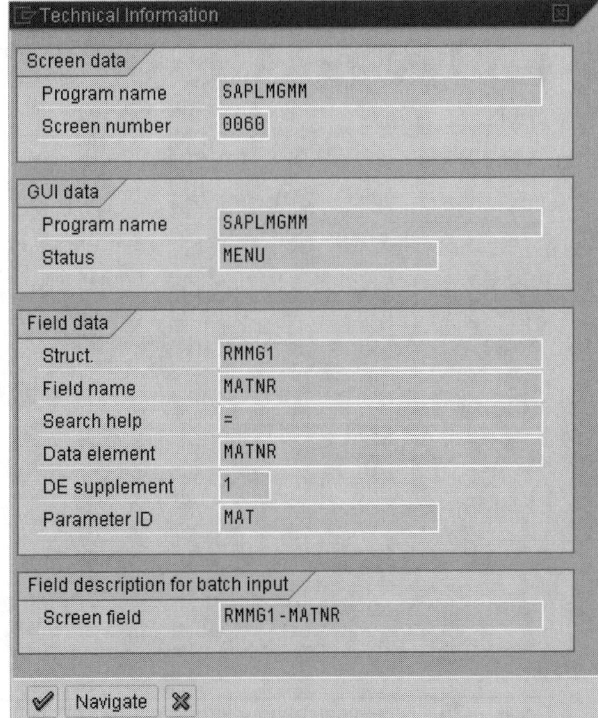

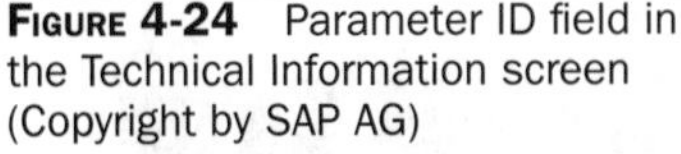

FIGURE 4-24 Parameter ID field in the Technical Information screen (Copyright by SAP AG)

section, you can see the Parameter ID field. In the example, this parameter is MAT, which corresponds to *material*. If you always work with the same material, you can enter this parameter in your defaults. To do so, select System | User Profile | Own Data from the main menu. On this screen, click on the Parameters tabstrip, and enter the parameter ID code and the default value. Upon pressing ENTER, the system will automatically display the definition for the parameter. Here, users can enter as many parameters IDs as they like.

Getting Help in SAP Systems

SAP GUI interface and SAP applications provide an extensive help system, with a large amount of information, documentation, and good contextual help links.

Use F1 for help on fields, menus, functions, and messages. The F1 help also provides a link to the technical information on the relevant field. This includes, for example, the parameter ID, which you can use to assign values to the field for your user, as we explained in the previous section.

SAP applications includes many possibilities to get online help for almost every element of the system. Users can get help with entire applications, for specific functions, for glossary terms, fields, reports, messages, and so on.

One of the standard menus in every SAP window is the Help menu, from which users have several options to obtain help.

Finally, users can obtain help when entering data in fields. The system often displays many fields either with possible entries lists or with search helps associated with them. Figure 4-25 shows the Help menu. Options included in the menu are as follows:

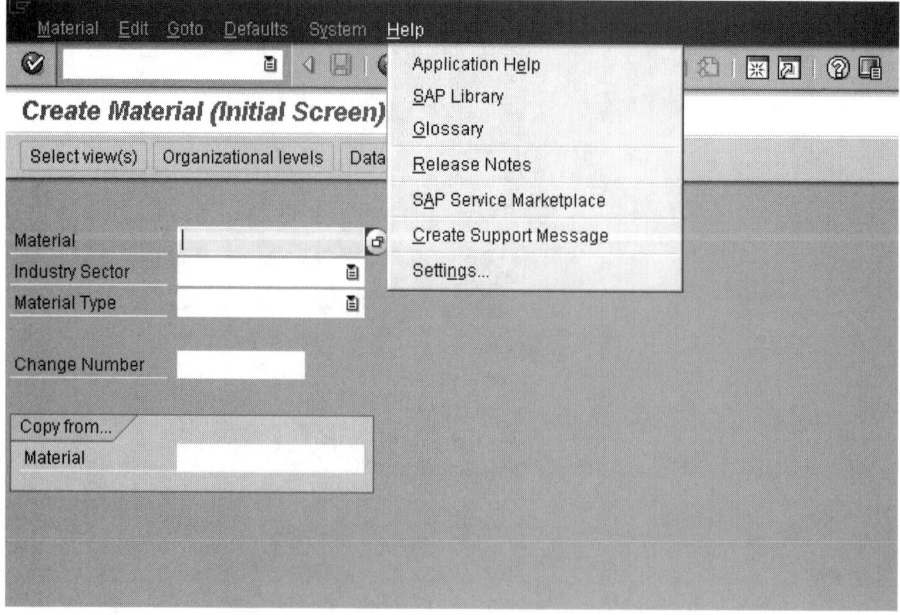

FIGURE 4-25 Help menu options (Copyright by SAP AG)

- *Application Help.* Links with detailed instructions for the tasks, normally calling the online documentation.
- *SAP Library.* Links with the initial screen for the online documentation library.
- *Glossary.* Contains definitions of common SAP terms related to the current task.
- *Release Notes.* Includes the release notes for the latest SAP versions.
- *SAP Service Marketplace.* Allows access to the SAP Service Marketplace (http://service.sap.com) directly from the SAP GUI.
- *Create Support Message.* Can be used to create internal support messages.
- *Settings.* For deciding whether to display help in a classical modal R/3 window or use an external help viewer.

The online documentation can be always be looked up to see the available help for a specific SAP application or the Technology system (whether Basis or the Web Application Server). The online documentation is provided in a CD-ROM that comes bundled with the SAP kit and must be installed by the administrator either directly in a CD-ROM drive or can be copied to a LAN server so all users can access it.

The Application Help option is meant to display step-by-step instructions for the task or application you are currently working on. If, when selecting Help | Application Help, there is no extended help available, you get the initial SAP Library screen.

The option SAP Library from the Help menu links directly with the online documentation and is presented in HTML or compressed CHM format depending on how the online help was installed and the front end used. From the main menu you can proceed by choosing any application, topic, or area of your interest and then navigate the documentation with the windows hypertext utilities.

With the Help | Glossary function, users can look up the meaning of terms related to the current task they are working on. When the meaning of a word or term used by SAP in some application is not clear, choosing the Glossary option from the Help menu shows a dialog box with related terms. If it is a long list, use the scroll bars to find the needed term. To display the definition for the term, double-click on it.

The SAP system provides help on most fields, input fields, or messages that appear in the SAP screen. Not all fields have related help available.

To get help on a particular field, position the cursor over it and press the Help button or F1. You get a Help screen in which some terms in the Help field might appear highlighted. This means those terms are defined in the online glossary. Double-clicking on those highlighted terms shows their definitions.

Another way in which the SAP system provides help is when system or error messages are displayed in the status bar. Double-clicking on the status bar shows additional information about the message. Sometimes the additional help on the message includes a hypertext link that can take you directly to a transaction to solve the problem. Another way to get help about the message in the status bar is by positioning the cursor over the message and pressing F1.

When specifying or executing a report, from the execution screen you can get additional information on the report by choosing Help | Extended Help.

The Help option to display the SAP Solution Release Notes can be very useful when upgrading the system or when you want to see what has changed or what is new in the current release compared to previous releases.

The Help | Release Notes option allows you to search notes by full text or attributes. Or you can see all the notes by clicking on the mySAP Release Notes: Entire List button.

Release notes can be very long, depending on the particular version. To search for release notes, the SAP system permits users to specify search criteria or attributes. *Attributes* are the types of information contained in the release notes—for example, whether it is a correction or a new function, what version it is, if it has an effect on interfaces or batch input, and so forth.

Finally, when you have error or doubts and would like to try to find a solution yourself, before entering a note with SAP Service, you can access the SAP Service Marketplace directly from a SAP GUI by selecting Help | SAP Service Marketplace. You need to have a valid OSS username and password in order to be able to log on to the SAP Service Marketplace and use the available options.

Working with Reports

Reports in the SAP systems are typically ABAP programs whose function is to look up information in the database and display it or print it. When end users perform their usual work with the SAP systems, they often need to look up information to analyze, to see business results, to make decisions, or simply to continue the work. This type of extracting, collecting, and formatting of the data held on the database is performed by the SAP reports.

SAP distinguishes two terms in this environment: a *report* is the program itself, and a *list* is the result (the output) of the report.

End users don't have to program the reports themselves because the SAP system includes virtually thousands of preprogrammed reports. These reports can be the result of normal menu function selections, and often users don't even know that they are executing reports, except for the result displayed on the screen or sent to the printer. In these cases, the data already entered in the fields of a screen act as search terms for the reports.

However, sometimes end users, and administrators too, have the need to call a report manually using the functions and facilities provided by the SAP system. How to work with reports managing these manual calls is the purpose of this section.

The general reporting facilities of the SAP systems can be found under the System | Services | Reporting menu (transaction code SA38). With this function, users can start reports when they know the name of the reports. Figure 4-26 shows the aspects of the report selection screen.

To start the report, enter the report name in the field and click on the Execute button. Most reports have selection criteria to delimit the scope of the search and the expected results. Some reports, however, do not have selection criteria, so when executing the report, the results are shown immediately.

If the report includes selection criteria, the corresponding screen appears, where users must enter the criteria they want to use for the report results. Criteria are the search terms, and the use of wildcards is allowed.

Once the criteria are entered, press the Execute button again or select Program | Execute in Background from the main menu to submit the report as a background job.

A common way to enter selection criteria automatically is with the use of variants. A *variant* is a collection of predefined criteria to use in reports. When using variants, users can execute reports with any variant available for that report, in which case, they don't have to enter selection criteria. For example, regional sales managers executing a report to see the sales evolution in their territory can use the same report but with different variants. The

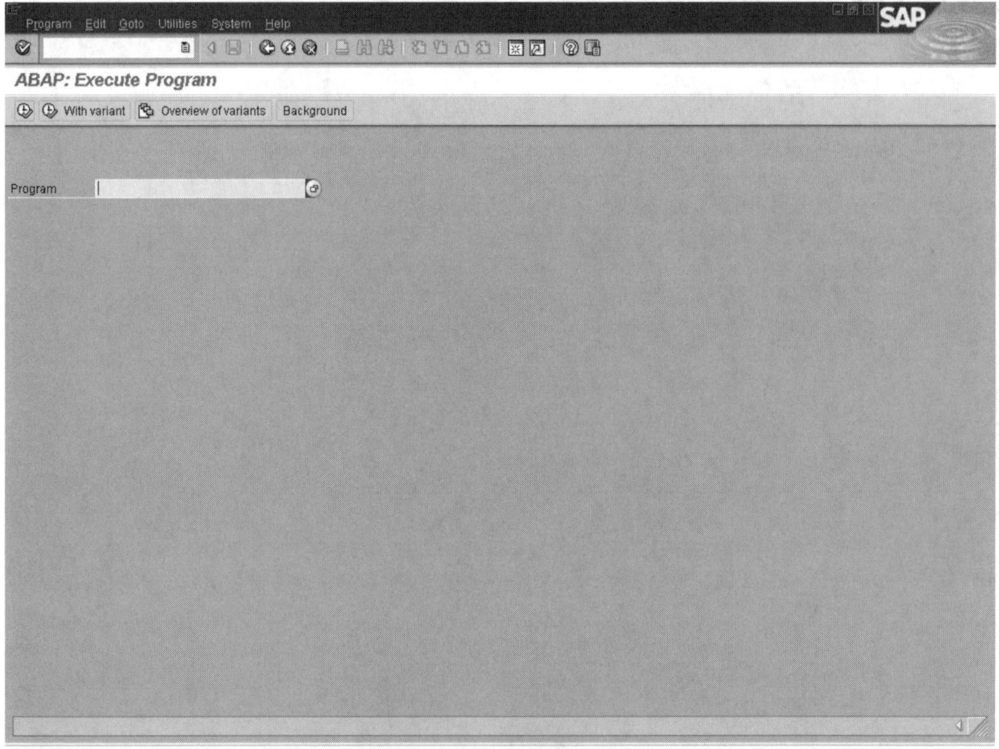

FIGURE 4-26 Report selection screen (Copyright by SAP AG)

only difference in the variants is that in the selection criteria one has region A and another one has region B.

Looking for Reports

To start a report manually with the reporting functions, users must know the report name. In the SAP system, most standard report names start with letter *R*. However, customer-created reports should start with letters *Y* or *Z*.

Reports are grouped in classes, for example, sales reports, stock movements, and projects. Report classes can be very useful for finding report names.

To find report names, from the reporting screen select Utilities | Find Program from the menu. The system shows the ABAP program directory search screen, like the one in Figure 4-27. The report search screen (titled ABAP Program Directory) appears.

In the Program field enter the part of the report name to search for and use wildcards (* or +). The * wildcard replaces multiple characters, whereas the + wildcard replaces a single character. For example, RSM* will find all reports starting with RSM, and RS++V46* will find all reports starting with RS and having the string V46 after two characters.

Wildcards can be used anywhere in the field and as often as you want. For example, Z*PS* will find all reports starting with *Z* (customer-developed reports) and having PS anywhere in the middle strings.

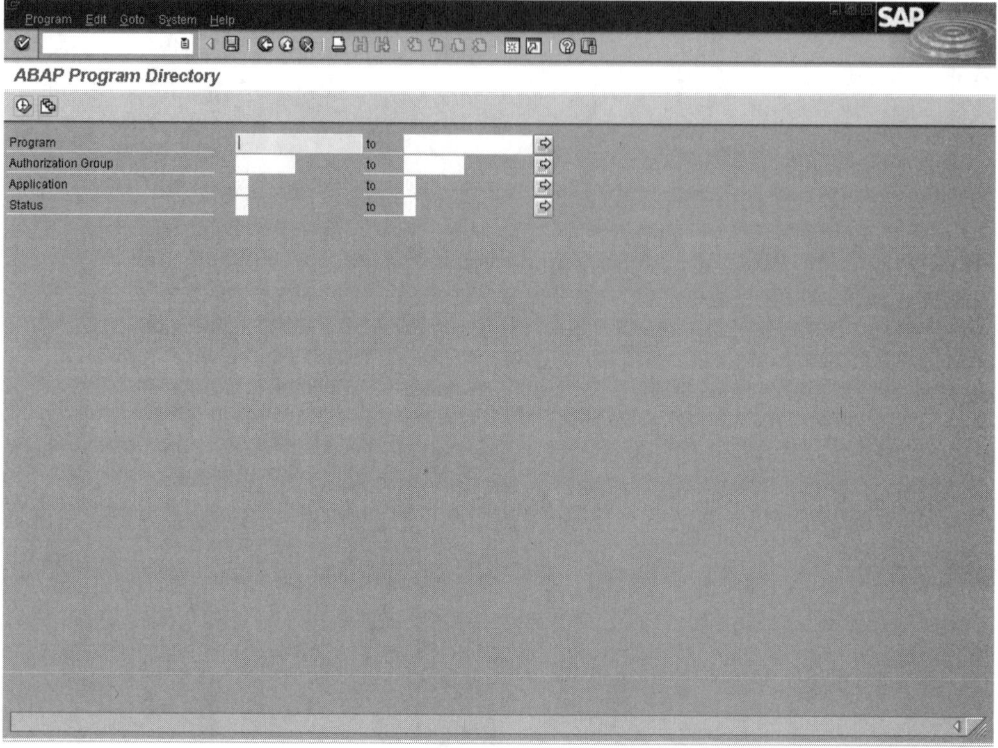

FIGURE 4-27 Program directory selection screen (Copyright by SAP AG)

Executing Reports

Once the Program field is specified, press the Execute button. The system will display a list of reports matching your criteria or a list of report classes. If the latter is displayed, you have to double-click on any line to display a list of reports belonging to the class. Repeat the process until you find the report needed. Once the report is found, it can be directly called from this screen by positioning the cursor over the line and pressing the Execute button or by choosing the Program | Execute function from the menu bar. The difference with this process in respect to the reporting screen is that if the report requires a variant, it won't allow the execution from this screen.

Users can find the name of the report directly within their usual tasks and so are able to call it even when they are working on different menus or applications. To find the name of the report, first call the report within the normal tasks and select System | Status from the menu bar. The name of the report appears in the Program field.

Using Selection Criteria

The selection criteria are input fields that allow users to delimit the type and amount of information they want the report to process. If no criteria are specified, the result of the report execution can be a long list including data that are not needed for the users. For example, to analyze materials movements in a warehouse, users should enter the warehouse ID as the criteria. The report will process and display only lists matching the selection criteria specified.

Selection criteria are not limited to specific values for the input fields. Some input fields permit the introduction of value ranges and multiple ranges, for example, if you want to display those customers that have been billed between $1000 and $5000 or if you want to search for customers in the states starting with A and C, plus Pennsylvania. As more values are entered in the selection criteria fields, the output can be more specific and the lists will be smaller.

If the system can't return all data because of processing limitations (for example, because it exceeds the maximum time for online processing), it displays a message in the status bar.

Often in a report you find two types of selection criteria

- *Database selections,* which determine which records are selected from the database
- *Program selections,* which are an additional filter to tell the system which of the fields from the records selected will be displayed on the list

You can get the additional selection options by positioning the cursor in the input field and clicking on the Selection Options button on the application toolbar. By using the selection options and the multiple selection arrow, users can specify complex search criteria, including multiple value ranges, AND and OR conditions, and so forth.

Working with Reports Variants

A variant is a group of values used as selection criteria or as parameters when calling a report or another type of ABAP program. Variants are attached to a report, which means that a variant cannot be used except for the report for which it was created. The group of values for the selection criteria is saved and assigned a variant name; so every time you want to call a program or a report, instead of specifying the selection criteria, you could call a previously saved variant, thus avoiding having to type the criteria over again. In fact, when using variants, the screen for entering the selection criteria does not appear.

Variants are a great help for simplifying data input when launching reports, and they ensure that reports have some selection criteria to limit the results. Users can have as many variants for a report as they wish.

Each variant can be used to retrieve different types of information. For example, the same report that retrieves the monthly warehouse inventory could have different variants—one for each warehouse location—so each manager uses the variant according to his or her location.

At the initial reporting screen, when users don't know which variants are available, they can display a list of the variants that are attached to the report, and they can also see the values assigned to the selection criteria. To do that, users just have to enter the report name and click on the Overview of Variants button on the application toolbar. The system displays the available variants. To see the contents, click on one variant to select it, and click on the Display button on the application toolbar, or choose Edit | Display Values from the main menu.

To enter a variant for a report, after calling the reporting function and specifying the report name, click on the Execute with Variant button, or in most standard application reports, click on the Get Variant . . . button. The system displays a dialog box to specify the variant name from the Variant Directory of the specific program or report, as shown in Figure 4-28. According to your specific report, you can either enter the variant name, select the variant from the list, or click on the possible entries arrow to find which variants are available for the report. Once you select the variant, click on the Execute button in the same dialog box.

Creating Variants

To create variants for reports, go to the main reporting screen (System | Services | Reporting), enter the name of the report for which you want to create the variants, and select Goto | Variants | Save as Variant from the menu. The system displays the initial screen for the ABAP variants, or you might get a Change Screen Assignment dialog box in cases where the program includes more than one selection screen.

Enter a name for the variant and click on the Create button. At this moment, SAP shows the selection criteria screen for the report specified previously.

In the input fields, enter the criteria and click on the Attributes button. The system displays the screen for specifying the attributes for the variant. In the Description field, enter a brief description for the variant so that you can distinguish the purpose of the variant when looking at the variants overview.

In this screen there are three check boxes where users can specify environment options for the variant:

- By selecting Only for Background Processing, you tell the system to send the processing of the variant to the background processing system.
- With the Protect Variant option, only the user who created the variant can modify it or delete it.

FIGURE 4-28 Variant directory (Copyright by SAP AG)

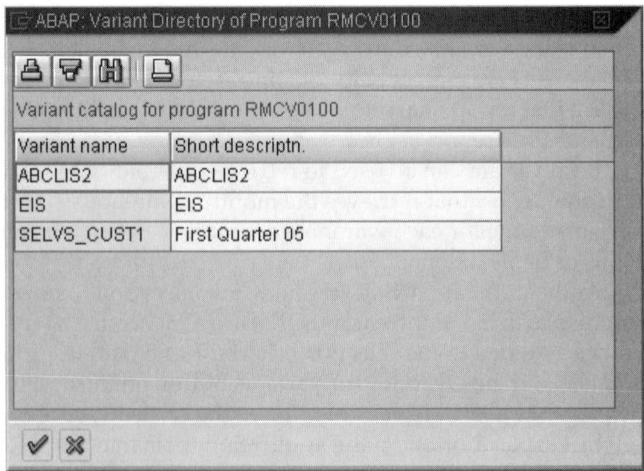

- By selecting the check box next to Only Display in Catalog, you tell the system that the variant name will appear in the variant catalog, but not in the input help.

The bottom part of this screen shows additional field attributes corresponding to the specific report for which the variants are being created.

Once all needed values are specified, click on the Save button in the standard toolbar to save the variant.

Working with Background Jobs

In this section, the use and basic management of background jobs are introduced. More advanced options and information about the background processing system are explained in Chapter 9.

Background jobs are definitions of programs, printing specifications, and start times to be processed by the SAP background processing system. The programs can be either ABAP reports or external programs.

With background processing, the system automatically runs the programs specified in the job at the scheduled time for its execution. There are facilities to monitor the background jobs and for displaying the job's results.

Background jobs have the advantage over traditional online processing that once the job is defined, the background processing system takes care of running it. Otherwise, launching a program interactively locks your session for further input until the program is finished. Remember that in interactive dialog work processes there is a limit on the time a process can be running. If the programs surpass this limit, the system displays an error and the program is canceled. In cases of long-running reports, background jobs are the only way to execute those programs.

Because background jobs can be scheduled to run at any time, another of their advantages is that the execution of long reports can be specified to run at periods with less system load, such as nighttime or weekends. The background jobs offer a great advantage for defining automatic and periodic execution of the jobs, for example, periodic database cleaning jobs or the system performance collector, which runs hourly as a background job. System administrators have to define these jobs only once, and then they are regularly executed at the scheduled times. A report defined in a background job generates the same output as one run interactively. The output list can be either printed directly or sent to the output controller.

Because job definitions are held on the SAP database, jobs are available even when the whole SAP system or the computer itself is restarted. Jobs that were running at the time of a shutdown are canceled by the system, and the owner of the job has to schedule it back. There are several ways to define and schedule programs for background execution:

- In some of the tasks within the SAP applications, the system automatically schedules long-running reports or programs for background execution.
- From within the ABAP workbench program editor and from several other SAP application screens where programs can be executed, the menu bar or the application toolbar often contain the option to execute the program either online or in the background. Within the ABAP editor, this function is under Program | Execute | Execute in Background. Upon choosing this option, the system displays the screen for defining and scheduling the job. At any time and anywhere in the SAP system,

a job can be defined by selecting System | Services | Jobs | Define Job. Alternatively, system administrators can also go to the job definition screen by selecting Tools | CCMS | Jobs | Definition or directly with transaction SM36, where the job information must be specified. This screen is shown in Figure 4-29.

Scheduling Background Jobs

The system offers several ways to define background jobs as stated earlier. A job definition basically consists of the following:

- Entering a name for the job
- Entering the date and time of when to execute the programs
- Entering the program or programs to be executed in the background. Programs can also contain variants
- Entering printing information
- Entering the names of recipients of the spool list

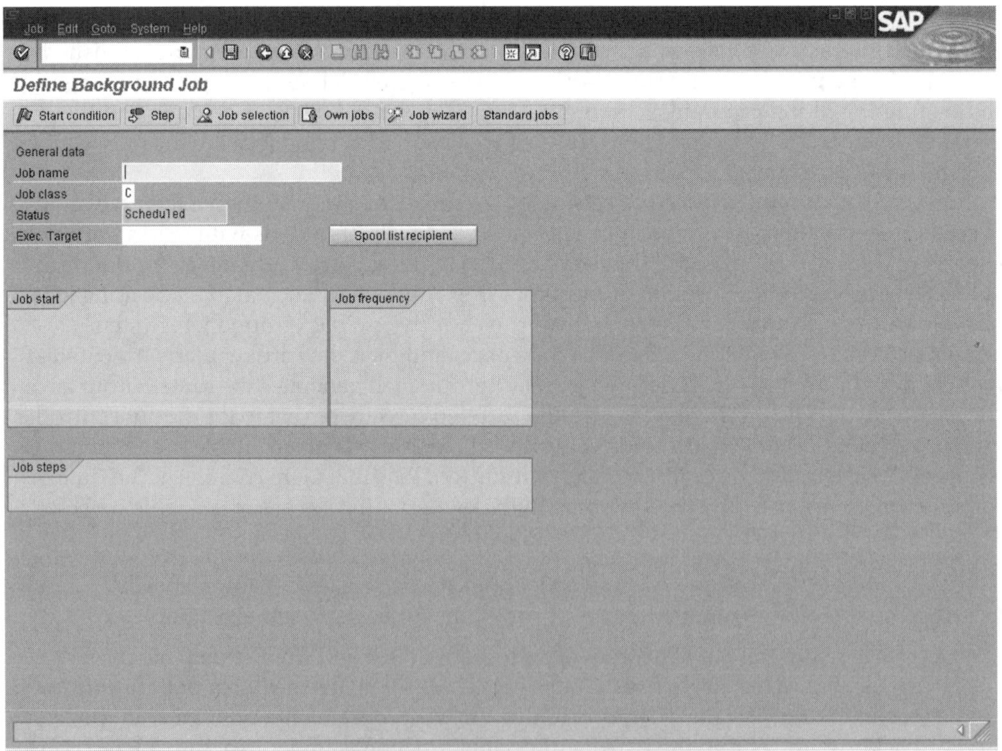

FIGURE 4-29 Initial Job Definition screen (Copyright by SAP AG)

There are many other options when scheduling a job, such as specifying the host to execute the job, indicating the priority, deciding whether to execute it periodically, specifying a system event instead of time, and so on.

Since release 4.6 of SAP R/3 and other SAP Basis–based solutions, you can also find a *Job wizard*, which will guide you step by step in the process of defining a background job.

To schedule a job, go to the job definition screen by selecting System | Services | Jobs | Define Job from any menu. On this screen, enter a name for the job first. You can choose any meaningful name.

In the Job Class input field, you can specify *A*, *B*, or *C*. Job class *C* is the normal and default value. *A* and *B* are higher-priority classes, and users must have authorization for those classes.

Users can enter a target host (Exec. Target) for background processing or leave it blank for executing it on the default background server. Clicking on the possible entries arrow displays a list of available background servers. Select the start time for the job by clicking on the Start Condition button. The screen for specifying the start time has many available options. Normal options are either Immediate, which schedules the job as soon as you save it, or Date/Time, which schedules the job for the date and time specified. The other options follow.

- *After job.* The job will start when another job that must be specified has been completed. In order to use this option, you must know the name of the other job. If you check the box next to Start Status Depend, the job will only start if the previous job finished successfully. Otherwise, the job will not start.
- *After event.* The job will start when the background processing system receives a signal with the event specified. You can see the available events by clicking on the possible entries arrow.
- *At operation mode.* The job will start as soon as the operation mode becomes the active one. Operation modes are a way of configuring how the SAP system distributes the work processes.
- *Start on work day.* The job will start on the day of the month you specify. Upon clicking on the possible entries arrow, the system displays the SAP factory calendar from which you can choose a workday of the month. For example, entering 07 will cause the job to start on the seventh work day of the month. You can specify additional restrictions, such as not starting before a specific date and so on.

Check your entries with the Check button and, if the system does not complain, save your entries. The system then takes you back to the job definition screen. Now, you must specify the program or programs to execute. Because a job might contain several programs (either ABAP or external programs), the system names them as *steps*.

Click on the Define Steps button on the application toolbar. The system displays the Create Step screen. Initially, the input fields of the screen are grayed out until you either press the ABAP Program, External Command, or External Program buttons, depending on the type of program being sent to the background. Clicking on one of the buttons changes the color of the associated input fields. Select over one of the fields and fill in the needed information:

- Enter the user ID under whose authorization the SAP system will run this background job. By default it uses the current user ID under which the user has logged on.
- Enter the name of the program. If the program has a variant, the system will request that it be entered.
- Enter the language in which you want to receive the output for the report. Remember that SAP Solutions supports many different languages.
- Finally, using the Print Specifications button, you can specify how to print the results of the programs.

When specifying external programs, such as C programs, shell scripts, or other supported types, the full pathname must be specified together with the parameters the program might need, such as options or filenames, and the hostname where the program will be executed. Make sure the system can access the specified host and path and that it has the right permissions.

Press the Save button to save the job. At this moment, the job is scheduled to be processed by the background system at the specified start date and time.

A job that has been scheduled does not actually run until it is also released. To release a job, the user must have the right authorizations. If the user is not authorized to release jobs, then administrators must release the jobs for him or her. This is a security measure to better monitor and control the background processing system.

To check the status of your background jobs, select System | Own Jobs from any SAP screen in the system. If you see a job with status Cancelled, it means the job has terminated abnormally. Press the Log button to find out the reason for the failure. System administrators can monitor background jobs graphically from the facilities of the CCMS.

User Printing

All the output lists and almost every other screen in the SAP system include a printing function. The most common way to access the printing function is either by clicking on the Print button on the standard toolbar or application toolbar or by selecting System | List | Print from any SAP window.

Up to release 4.6 of SAP R/3 and SAP Basis–based solutions, printing in the SAP systems was normally a two-step process that should not confuse users: first they select the print function, which displays the print screen. This screen must be filled out, and then it will send the list to the output controller and to the printer.

Since release 4.7 of R/3 and the Web Application–based solutions, the printing functions have been simplified, although previous specific functions can still be accessed and modified according to user's printing needs.

The system will display the Print Screen List dialog box. In this abbreviated screen, users only have to fill out the basic information required by the SAP spooling system: *output device* (name of the printer), number of copies, and number of pages. By default the system will send the print information immediately to the printer selected. If you want to define additional attributes for the print request, click on the Properties button of the Print Screen List dialog box. Figure 4-30 shows an example of this dialog screen.

Some applications require users to enter some printing information on a special screen and will not show the print screen.

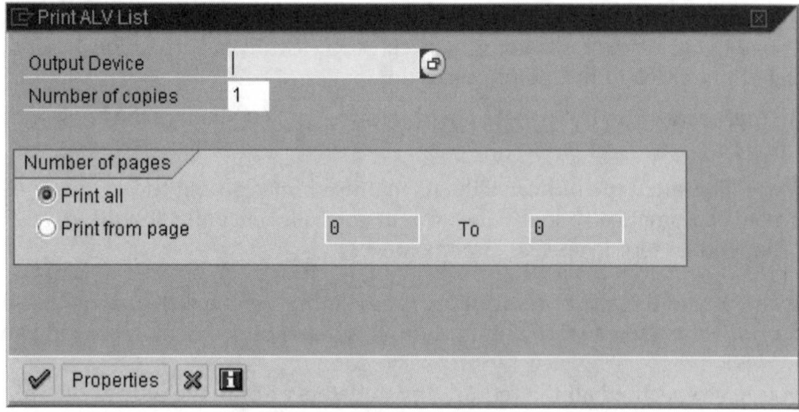

FIGURE 4-30 Print Screen List dialog box (Copyright by SAP AG)

Print Attributes

Figure 4-31 shows an example of the print or spool request attributes. As indicated by the help in the same screen, you can double-click on a line to change its value, or choose default values.

Some of the available attributes for a spool request are as follows:

- *Name.* This field identifies the print request in the SAP output controller. This field is automatically set by the system, but users can change it if they wish, by selecting the Spool Request folder and double-clicking on the Name. The system will present an input field where you can define your own spool name.
- *Title.* Users can enter here a short description of the print request, so they can easily identify it. This is also located under the Spool Request folder.
- *Authorization.* This field can contain an authorization code previously defined by the system administrator. It is used to protect users looking at printed data that can be sensitive or confidential.
- *Time of printing.* This attribute is found under the General Attributes folder. If you need your job to be printed immediately, you have to select this option and in the Time of Print list box, select Print Immediately. When this option is selected, the system sends the output immediately to the printer. This is a key option because users often forget to select it, and nothing comes out of the printer. If this attribute is not selected, the print job is sent to the output controller, where you can later print it. Users can have this option selected by default by modifying their own user parameters. To do this, go to System | User Profile | Own Data, select the Defaults tabstrip, and click on the check mark next to Output Immediately in the Spool Control section. However, deselecting this option can be useful when you want to print just a few pages from a long listing because you can specify pages to print from the output controller but not from the print screen.

- *Delete immediately after printing.* Select this attribute to tell the SAP system to remove the print request after it has been successfully printed. This attribute is located under the Output Options folder.
- *SAP cover sheet.* You can use this field to print a cover sheet at the beginning of the print job.
- *Format.* This attribute indicates the format used for printing the report or list. The format is automatically set by the system, and users usually should leave this option unchanged, except in special circumstances.

If you want any of the attributes to show on the initial screen, select the check box *Show select print parameters on initial screen* found when modifying or specifying any of the attributes.

Once you have specified all the required parameters or only the output device, click on the Continue icon. Clicking on it creates the output request. If the Print Immediately option was sent, the job is sent directly to the printer.

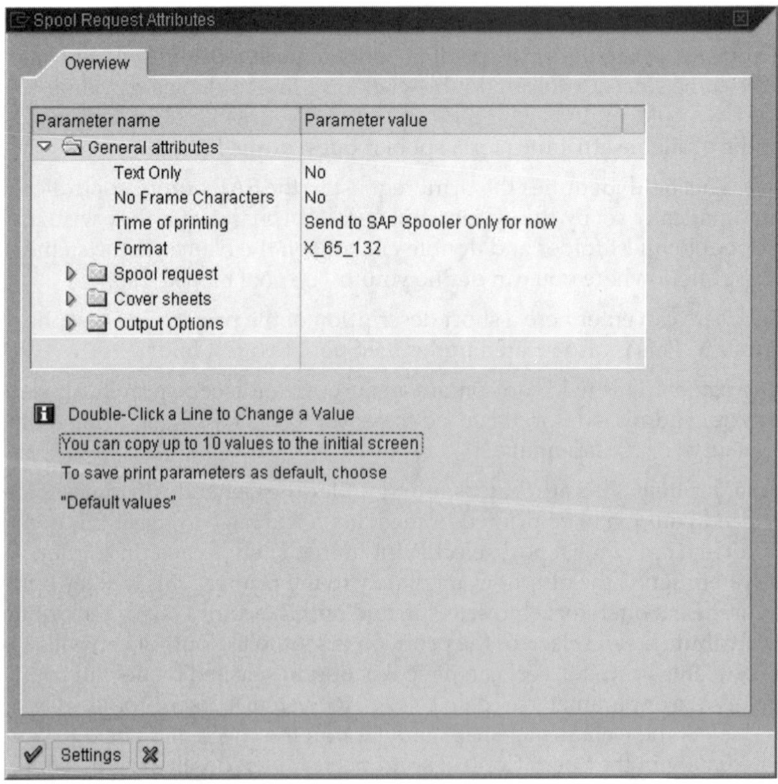

FIGURE 4-31 Specifying spool request attributes (Copyright by SAP AG)

Monitoring the Status of Your Print Requests

By selecting System | Services | Output Control from any SAP screen, the system displays the Spool Request selection screen, where users can select and check the status of their print jobs. On this screen, enter the criteria for the print request you want to search and click the Execute button.

The system will display the Spool Request screen. The most important information on this screen is *output status,* where users can check whether the job has been printed or if any problems have arisen. Possible values of the output status field are as follows:

- *—(Dash).* The print request has been created but has not been sent to the printer yet. This is the normal case when the Print Immediately check box was not selected. You can send the print request to the printer by selecting the request and clicking on the Print icon on the application toolbar.
- *Compl.* The print job has completed successfully and should be at the printer.
- *Wait, Problem, or another colored message.* There is a problem with completing the print request. To see the problem details, select the print request by checking the box next to it and press the Output Request button. On the next screen, select the line again and press the Output Request Log button.

Common problems relating to the print functions include *Printer is offline* and *Local PC where the printer is attached is not turned on.* The output controller also allows users to perform additional functions besides looking at the status of their requests and printing held jobs. For example, they can remove jobs from the system by clicking on the Delete button or can display the job output on the screen by selecting the Display button.

Additional User Utilities

The SAP system menu includes some more additional utilities that users can find helpful and that they might need from time to time, for example, sending messages to other users, downloading/uploading lists or documents to/from PC files from/to the SAP system, checking problems with authorization objects, performing debugging, showing table contents, recording transactions, and several more. The following two sections explain briefly two of these options. For more information about other services and utilities within the System menu, please refer to the SAP online documentation.

Sending Short Messages

To send a short message to another SAP user on the same system, select System | Short Message from any screen. The system displays a screen similar to the one shown in Figure 4-32. Just write the message in the Note area of the screen and specify the recipient name in the input fields below. When you are done, just click on the Send button to deliver your message. This is a fast way to call the basic Business Workplace function for sending messages between SAP users. For more extensive information about the functions of Business Workplace, please refer to the SAP online documentation.

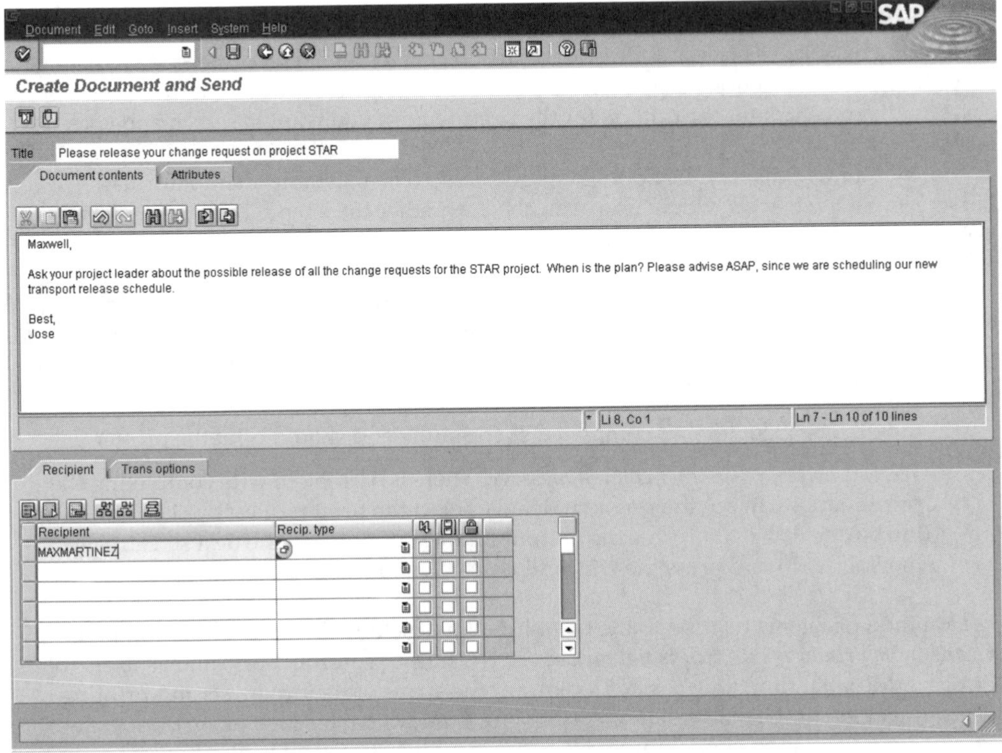

FIGURE 4-32 Sending a short message (Copyright by SAP AG)

Downloading Files to Your Desktop Workstation

Every list generated in the system as well as most screens that generate a print screen can be downloaded to PC files for further treatment or for other analysis or documentation purposes. Similarly, you can upload files from the PC, for example, ABAP source code. While in the ABAP editor, you can find the upload and download functions under the Utilities menu.

When the screen displays a printable list, you can decide to save it to a local file. To do so, from any SAP screen, select System | List | Save | Local File. The system will display a dialog box with four options from which you can choose your output format. Select the one that best suits your needs and press the Continue button.

The system will display another dialog box (Save as) requesting the path and name of the file in your local PC. It normally shows the work directory path where the SAP GUI is installed. Enter the filename and press the OK button. The list will be transferred to your local PC.

5

CHAPTER

Upgrading to SAP R/3 Enterprise: The First Step into SAP NetWeaver

A SAP upgrade or any other software upgrade is the process of changing an application software release to a newer, more current release, such as upgrading from SAP R/3 4.5B to SAP R/3 4.7.

SAP software upgrades, in most cases, and particularly when upgrading R/3 to SAP Enterprise, should be considered as projects. Upgrading is not necessarily a complex or critical project, but it should be treated as such, with provision of a project team, careful planning, and the required expertise to accomplish it successfully.

As such, in this chapter we will analyze the reasons and motivations for upgrading; the key issues in how to approach the project; and the technical implications, tools, and techniques involved.

We will also discuss what is to be found once SAP R/3 Enterprise is in place, and therefore the SAP Web Application Server (WAS), as introduced in Chapter 4. With the SAP WAS you will have the technological and application foundation of the SAP NetWeaver integration platform.

This chapter presents those technical enhancements in the upgrade process and the new tools that SAP has made available for customers to simplify or better control the overall upgrade project.

Why Upgrade?

A SAP release upgrade is a serious project, a project that will require time and organizational resources and might also require external consulting help. Therefore time, resources, and budget must be allocated for the project.

From a very general point of view, upgrading is either necessary because companies want to get the advantages of the newer release or they want to solve the issues implied by having an old release, from outdated maintenance to technical shortcomings. Either of the two general factors, and whether they are operational, economic, or strategic, must be recognized by customers to determine if an upgrade is needed.

Let's review in more detail some of the reasons influencing a customer's need for a SAP upgrade:

- *End of maintenance.* Every SAP release has a deadline, meaning that SAP will not provide additional corrections or fixes in Support Packages. Normally it also implies having to pay additional maintenance fees for regular support.
- *Need for new functionality.* It might happen that the new release contains important new functionality that would solve some of the business or technical requirements, whether these are new, or whether they were previously solved with local programming or third-party tools.
- *Need to have the latest release and latest technology.* Many companies prefer to be updated as soon as possible (normally starting to plan the upgrade after general availability is released) and so choose to be updated not only with new functionalities, but with all the new technical possibilities (for instance, to take advantage of the SAP NetWeaver integration capabilities or all the Web development options).
- *Technical limitations with current release.* Similar to the previous reason, customers might find that the current release is limiting system's growth, compatibility with other solutions, or increased effort for evolving or adapting the business.
- *Reduction in the number of interfaces.* Older releases include fewer BAPIs, which might have led to the local development of interfaces with other systems or external applications. It normally happens that newer SAP releases include additional BAPIs and additional interface or integration technologies that most likely will reduce the current number of interfaces.
- *Standardization.* Customers with several SAP systems can clearly see an improvement in efficiency, support, and maintenance costs when all their systems are on the same release.
- *Stepping into newer product suites.* Upgrading to SAP R/3 Enterprise, thus having the SAP Web Application Server as the application platform, will make customers technologically ready for SAP NetWeaver and newer integrated solutions such as mySAP ERP or mySAP Business Suite.

In any case, there will be a recognition process for upgrading, followed by a justification process, which can be based in one or several of the aforementioned reasons.

Justifying an upgrade project will also involve closely analyzing objectives, planning, risks, return on investment, and expected benefits. When too many risks and too little gain are identified, and if the reasons are mainly based on functionality gain, the customer might look at alternatives before proceeding with the upgrade project.

There is, however, a theory in the SAP world that the longer a customer makes a decision for an upgrade, the harder and more costly it becomes.

Considerations for an Upgrade Project

Customers will have to deal with a project that will be time consuming and costly, not only for the internal or external resources required, but also because it might involve the acquisition and procurement of new hardware. A SAP upgrade is not just a question of running a program; there are other issues to be considered:

- *Project methodology.* A methodology is recommended for any project, so customers must have a framework or roadmap of the necessary phases, activities, and steps required to achieve the goals. SAP provides the ASAP Upgrade Roadmap, now integrated within SAP Solution Manager (available with release 3.2).
- *Upgrade project planning.* First a generic plan and then a more detailed project planning will be required. Examples or templates can be found within the SAP Upgrade Roadmap within ASAP or SAP Solution Manager.
- *Functionality.* An extremely important factor to consider for an upgrade project is the analysis of the current and future business processes. Even if it is not the objective of the upgrade project to gain new functionality, this must be carefully analyzed to adjust any changes to current business processes in the newer release.
- *Technical upgrade.* The technical upgrade will be also a time-consuming process that will require several tests and adjustments, as well as careful planning to minimize the downtime that will be required. SAP provides many new tools that have largely improved the technical mechanics of the upgrade.
- *Modification adjustments.* A very important task for a SAP upgrade is analyzing whether adjustments will be required, specifically for repository objects that have been modified by customers.
- *Testing.* As in any other project, different types of testing will be absolutely required to minimize the risks of the upgrade. Testing will include technical tests of the upgrade and functionality, and likely regression, volume, or stress tests.
- *Training.* Training is an issue largely ignored by many project teams, but it has a very big impact on when the system is activated and on ongoing support. Training will be initially required by the project team, but more importantly by end users, who should be familiar with the way business processes work in the newer release. Therefore, user training must be planned and new documentation and training material must be prepared.
- *Going live with newer release.* When careful planning, testing, and training have been provided, going live with a newer release should be a minor issue. This process requires the preparation of what often is called a "mini test," which is a script that can be run in just a few hours and that will lead to the "Go–No Go" of the upgrade.
- *Supporting the new release.* Last but not least, the organization must be prepared to provide maintenance and support to the new SAP release. This means that system managers are trained and familiar with newer features, and the persons in charge of the application support have been trained in the new changes in SAP technology.

Upgrading to SAP R/3 Enterprise: What Is New?

Depending on what release you come from, you will find many or few changes in your systems. The new architecture, based on the Web Application Server, as well as the option of running the Java engine, J2EE, was discussed in detail in Chapter 2.

If you have overlooked that chapter because it might have seemed too technical, this section introduces some of the new items you can find in the SAP R/3 Enterprise, as well as an overview of the new upgrade tools, which are later discussed in this chapter.

This is a brief list of what you will find with the SAP Enterprise release 4.7:

- SAP R/3 4.7 includes an Enterprise Core 4.7 functionality, Extension Sets (2.0 or later), and the SAP Web Application Server as the application platform. Refer to Chapters 1 and 2 for more information.
- With the SAP Web Application Server you get a Web-ready SAP system except for some specific applications. However, SAP Web AS does not replace ITS until version 6.40. Understanding HTTP/S does not mean that you can use SAP Web AS the same way as you do ITS. SAP can work both as a Web server and as a Web client (refer to Chapter 2).
- A new upgrade strategy, where you can choose whether you want to minimize the downtime or the resources required for the upgrade.
- Enhancements to the ABAP development environment, including the possibility of developing Web applications based on Business Server Pages (BSPs), which combine ABAP code with embedded HTML and Javascript (refer to Chapter 7 for more information).
- The Enterprise Extension Sets or Add-Ons can be freely activated. This is the first option you will see now in the Customizing transaction.
- SAP Enterprise is ready for Unicode and includes Unicode programming code check. You can decide whether to install the Unicode version or not.
- You can find also specific industry solutions business processes within the SAP Enterprise Extensions.
- The SAP Web Application Server includes native support for many standards, for instance, the SMTP protocol used by e-mail and messaging system, which makes the installation and configuration of previous connectors either not required or much simpler.
- The provided functionality of SAP R/3 Enterprise is the core functionality of mySAP ERP and all Industry Solutions, and the provided technical background is the core technology of SAP NetWeaver.
- Basically you will find the same Transport System and Administration tools, except for the fact that you have newer processes, such as the ICM and optionally the Java Engine (J2EE).
- You will find some changes in the naming convention of the menu options, and now the classical "R/3" name has been changed to just "SAP."
- The core application functionality of SAP R/3 4.7 is mostly the same as release 4.6C, except for the new business processes included in the extension set.

Visit the "Release Info" section within the SAP Service Marketplace for updated and specific information on new functionality and features of the SAP Solution being upgraded.

SAP Upgrade Projects

As stated, a SAP upgrade is a project that is going to involve many tasks, but the most important activity of the upgrade project is the gap analysis and adaptation of the current functionally and business processes with the new features of the new SAP release. This will involve not only changes or adjustments to the repository or the customizing, but also new menus, screens, or ways of performing a business process by end users, as well as the new functionality that system managers will have in the newer SAP release.

Overall an upgrade project will require a detailed project planning that can be easily followed by the project team and conducted by a project manager. The project plan will be the roadmap to a successful project completion.

The degree of difficulty of the upgrade project can range from simple to very complex, and the main variable that determines this is the degree and quantity of modifications to standard SAP applications as well as to local developments based on standard SAP programs.

Regarding upgrade project timing and difficulty, there are other variables, such as the number and size of the systems and volume of the database, on the technical side.

On the business application side, an upgrade can be used for solving business processes that were not fully covered or not covered at all in previous version. Therefore, focusing on and analyzing the gaps will be critical in the overall project.

Because an upgrade means changes, some of the *change management activities* must be undertaken, such as risk assessment, training, communications, and knowledge transfer. This means that organizations must prepare for a new change.

A very important factor in any upgrade project that also becomes critical for realizing the upgrade in productive systems is the *time needed for completion* because this will affect system availability and therefore business operations.

A new release might require additional infrastructure such as disk space or processing power. So in the planning phases of the upgrade project, a *new systems sizing* should be requested.

With respect to the roles and resources needed for duty, when upgrading SAP releases, or any other previous SAP solution, there is the need to have a team similar to the team that performed the initial implementation. The team will be in charge of analyzing the impact of possible business changes; setting up new configuration parameters; developing or modifying ABAP programs, reports, transaction and interfaces; and preparing the technical infrastructure for the new release.

An upgrade can be different in many aspects when performed on a development system or the production system. Though the process will start by upgrading the development system, it can be very helpful to have a similar system, or a test system where the actual productive upgrade can be carried out and *business functions tested* with the real data. If the goal of the upgrade does not initially involve a *functional gain,* then those test are known as *regression testing,* the process of ensuring that the result or output of the business processes transactions are the same as in the source release of the upgrade.

An additional factor to consider, already mentioned, is what *training* will be needed for both end users and the project team. Customers must plan for time and resources to gain skills on new functions, changes, or enhancements as provided by a new version.

Let's have a closer look to some of the issues and what are the available tools and help to facilitate the upgrade process.

Key Success Factors in an Upgrade Project

The key success factors in a SAP upgrade project are no different than in any other type of project where the organization, the business processes, and a great deal of technical work is involved. These are as follows:

- Clear goals and objectives, based on the justification process for an upgrade.
- Project methodology, project planning, and project management.
- Commitment and sponsorship by upper management.
- Focusing on the gaps: what are the changes between releases and how will they affect business processes and end users?
- Teamwork, because there are many interrelated activities that involve not only technical or business configuration work, but a close collaboration with different parts of the company, including management, key users, and end users. Most likely you will also use some expert consulting services from SAP or its partners.
- A tested upgrade script, which can be used for a quick checkup of the final system status before the "go" decision.

Methodology: The Upgrade Roadmap

SAP has set in place an Upgrade Roadmap as the central guiding point for any SAP upgrade project. The Roadmap provides the methodologies and tools that facilitate and simplify both the plan and execution of an upgrade project.

The Upgrade Roadmap used to be part of ASAP and ValueSAP, and it is included in release 3.2 of the SAP Solution Manager. Additionally, you can access the Roadmap in the SAP Service Marketplace, in the Upgrade Center, at http://service.sap.com/upgrade. You have also the option to download it in HTML format and install it locally in your desktop. Figure 5-1 shows the local version of the Upgrade Roadmap.

The Upgrade Roadmap includes five phases:

- *Phase 1: Project preparation.* Includes all the initial activities to set the project, such as the objectives, initial project planning, and analysis of the current and required IT infrastructure for the upgrade project, and includes a comprehensive set of tools (accelerators) to help organize and manage the project. Among other tools, you can find a template of project plan.
- *Phase 2: Upgrade blueprint.* This is the functional or design phase of the upgrade project. Available work packages for this phase include the design of business processes in the newer release, the future IT infrastructure, the security concept, the test planning, the upgrade process design, and the planning for the end user training.
- *Phase 3: Upgrade realization.* During this phase, the previous design is actually performed and implemented, normally in a test environment. The result is an upgraded test environment where all testing can be performed and the team can agree on the results, and avoid further problems in the actual upgrade of the productive systems.
- *Phase 4: Final preparation for cutover.* This phase is meant basically to reassure that the productive system is ready for the actual upgrade, the end users are trained,

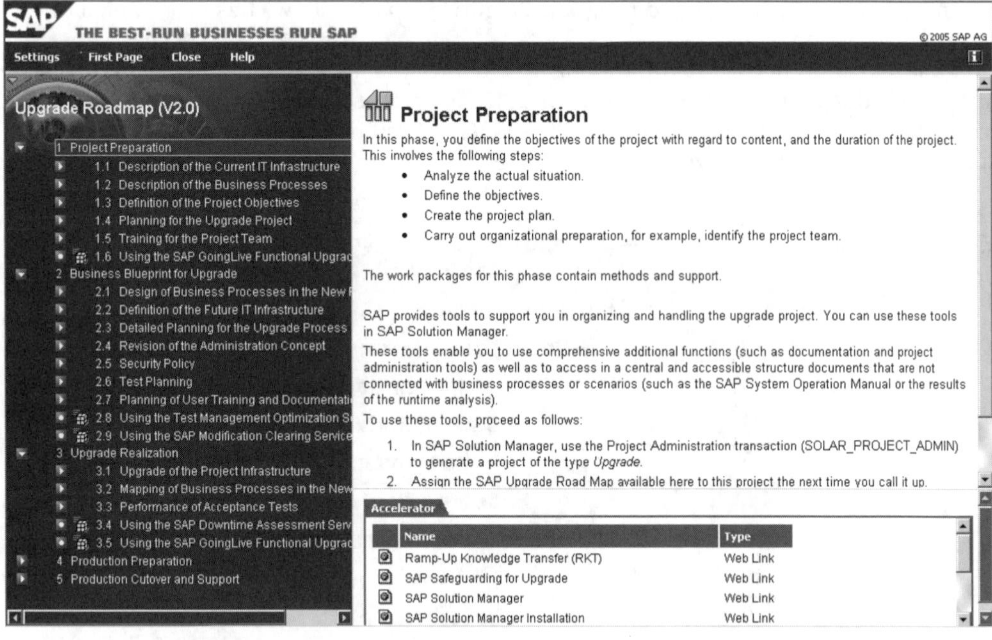

FIGURE 5-1 SAP Upgrade Roadmap: local HTML version (Copyright by SAP AG)

and documentation prepared. Most activities include comprehensive integration and system testing.

- *Phase 5: Production cutover and support.* The last phase in an upgrade project is the actual upgrade of the production system and the support after go live. This will include providing support to the first days of operation, specifically for end users, and other technical issues that are typical after changing a system release.

All phases of the Roadmap are supported by comprehensive instructions and a collection of tools, documents, templates, and presentations. SAP recommends using the SAP Solution Manager to handle the upgrade project as the central platform for implementation or upgrade of SAP Solutions. Refer to Chapter 11 for more details.

Upgrade Project Plan

There is no general rule or precise estimate on how long an upgrade project might take. Technical upgrades can take as little as a couple of weeks; however, other more complicated upgrade projects involving many software and hardware changes can take several months.

In any case, as already mentioned, careful planning is needed that considers the special circumstances regarding the inhouse development and customized business processes.

An approach to an upgrade project plan can be found in the ASAP Upgrade Roadmap; specifically you can find a template in the WBS number 1.4.2. The plan, tasks, and activities are normally limited to projects whose previous implementation did not include enhancements based on standard programs. Figure 5-2 partly shows this project plan without date assignments.

Time and effort needed for upgrading each of the systems will probably not be comparable due to hardware differences and size of database. However, problems and errors detected on previous upgrades will be better solved on following updates. The order of the upgrade is very important.

FIGURE 5-2 Sample SAP upgrade project plan (Copyright by SAP AG)

	ℹ	Task Name
1		⊟ **Upgrade Roadmap (V2.0)**
2		⊟ **Project Preparation**
3		⊟ **Current IT Infrastructure**
4		⊟ **Current Software Components**
5		Documentation for Software Components
6		⊟ **Current Hardware Components**
7		Documentation for Hardware Components
8		Create a Load Overview
9		⊟ **Description of Current Interfaces**
10		Interface Documentation
11		⊟ **Description of Business Processes**
12		⊟ **Overview of Business Processes**
13		Catalog of Business Processes
14		Business Processes Documentation
15		Customer Developments and Modifications
16		⊟ **Definition of the Project Objective**
17		⊟ **Functional Analysis and Determination of the T**
18		Information on Availability of New Component Ve
19		Check Compatibility
20		⊟ **Definition of Target Platform Required**
21		Requirements of Hardware Architecture
22		Rough Estimation of Additional Hardware
23		Dependency With Other Projects
24		⊟ **Analyze Downtime for the Upgrade**
25		Define Acceptable Downtime for Production Syst
26		Combine Activities During the Downtime
27		⊟ **Define Target for the Upgrade**
28		Analysis of Business Processes
29		Identification of New Functionality

During the actual realization of a SAP R/3 or other SAP solution release upgrade, each of the systems in the landscape is upgraded in the order defined within the transport routes: usually start with development, then quality assurance system, and then production. However, it more normal to copy a productive system into a test environment and perform the initial upgrade tests, upgrade design, and realization in this system.

Besides the ASAP Upgrade Roadmap, planning for an upgrade involves also preparing all the documentation and material needed for the upgrade, including the Upgrade Manuals and the related SAP Notes, and organizing the project team.

The Upgrade Script

From the upgrade project plan and with the specific tasks that you will define for the project with the help of the Upgrade Roadmap, you should create an *upgrade script*.

The upgrade script is a sequential and chronological task list that specifies the processes and activities of the upgrade for your specific installation or system landscape.

The upgrade script should contain detailed tasks for each project team member, and it becomes very useful, first for the project blueprint and realization, but more importantly for the final phases and go live.

With the upgrade script, the project team, the tasks, and roles to be done are completely documented and assigned, so that no steps are forgotten during the process. The upgrade script is probably the best way to organize tasks by project members.

Typically, the final productive upgrade is performed during weekends or holidays, and the timing is usually limited; therefore, following a script (tested previously in upgraded test systems) is critical so that no step is forgotten, which could avoid the "go" decision. It is assumed that this script must have been performed at least once or twice before the actual productive upgrade.

For the technical part of the upgrade, there is an upgrade checklist within the specific Upgrade Manual (depending on your hardware and database platforms). This checklist must be closely analyzed and performed, and every required task must be included within the Upgrade script and in the right order.

Using the checklist in the manual, you must create your own script according to your specific installation. For instance, some of the differences between customers installations have to do with the following:

- Users and passwords
- Hardware platforms and directory names
- Storage and file systems
- Databases engine
- System names
- Directories locations and syntax
- File names and locations
- Maybe others, such as interfaces

The tasks specified in the upgrade script must be assigned to project team members, and it is very important to include what are the expected results for some of the critical tasks of the upgrade and which are the decision points for the go/no-go decision.

It is very useful to include in the upgrade timing indicators (start-finish dates or time) from previous runs, so that the whole process can be better planned, and a status field to indicate whether the tasks has been completed.

Remember that the purpose of the upgrade script is to be able to repeat the process, so that the final productive upgrade is as free of errors or problems as possible and there is a much greater chance of the "go" decision.

Gap Analysis

As stated in a previous section, a proper gap analysis is a critical factor for a successful upgrade project. It must be observed that a gap analysis in an upgrade project is similar in methodology to an initial implementation project, but quite different in scope.

The *gap analysis* can be defined as a work of comparison of what is currently implemented in the SAP release and what new functionality is included within the new release of the SAP system to be upgraded.

If you still have the documentation of the gap analysis during previous implementation, the upgrade project can be used to assess whether the original gaps could be replaced by the functionality included within the upgraded SAP system. For instance, the new release can avoid many of the local developed programs, or might include additional BAPIs, so that some interfaces can be replaced.

Checking and analyzing the release notes for each of the components on the new version can be of great help to understand and test the new release.

An additional help is to procure and install an IDES system with the new release. Although IDES generally will differ from your current implementation, IDES can be used for project team training, and even some short-scale testing of new functionality.

Upgrading to SAP R/3 Enterprise: An Organizational View

An upgrade project requires setting up a comprehensive project team that is committed to the successful completion of the project and is well informed of the objectives.

A SAP upgrade is more than just a technology task, and normally the technical activities of the project take less time than other critical phases, such as the upgrade blueprint.

The upgrade team is made up of different groups, among them the following:

- SAP technical consultants, commonly known as the Basis personnel (can be internal, external or both)
- Other internal IT staff, such as network, security, and system managers
- Business process staff, or functional consultants (internal, external)
- Key users, which are typically the process owners
- SAP and partners contacts
- End users; they are not part of the upgrade team, but consider them when planning because they will need to receive training and updated user documentation

The previous groups are organized by functions, but in many customers, some of the roles are assumed by the same persons; for instance, we typically find key users as internal business process owners, or they do the customizing themselves. In small installations we also find that the IT persons can cover themselves for full support of the technical aspects of SAP systems, including performing the technical upgrade.

However, large companies and large system landscapes may need an army of partners or consultants working side by side with customer personnel. These partners or consultants can typically provide previous expertise or technical knowledge in upgrade projects.

Let's briefly describe in the next sections two very important roles within the SAP upgrade project.

Key Users and the Functional Team

The key users, or business process owners, are the representatives of the different departments or organizations within the companies, for instance, order processing, accounts payable, treasury, production planning, purchasing, and many others. The function of the key users is to verify that the business processes within the SAP applications work the way they are supposed to, according to the business requirements and to end users. Key users are involved during the systems and integration tests, and often they are also in charge of training end users.

The functional or business process team is made of members with knowledge and experience with different SAP application modules, such as MM (Materials Management), FI (Financial Accounting), CO (Controlling), or any other within the scope of the previous SAP implement functionality. It is also recommended that a technical expert handle tasks related to cross-application activities such as workflow and BAS.

This team is comprised of users and key users of the different organization units or departments related with the upgrade project, and often is complemented by functional SAP consultants.

Often the functional team is also composed of one or several ABAP programmers, which can help during the modification adjustment process, review, or modification of previously developed local programs.

Activities and functions of the business process team include the following:

- Gap analysis and business process reengineering. If the new functionality included in the new release affects the business processes, the functional team is responsible for analyzing the system to adapt those changes.
- Adjusting the modifications. As a result of the gap analysis and according to the new repository objects included in the new release, the changes will have to be adjusted. Refer to the section "Modification Adjustment" later in this chapter.
- Integration and regression testing to ensure that all the business processes still work properly after the upgrade.
- Often, the functional team is also responsible for creating end user training material and documentation.
- Providing the functional support during the go live, and later.

Upgrading to SAP R/3 Enterprise: Technical Point of View

The following sections will cover those upgrade tools and procedures that have to do with the technical part of the upgrade project, which is intrinsically a very important part of the upgrade.

Factors Influencing the Technical Upgrade

Several factors may influence the upgrade and they all may be different for your situation, depending on *what* you consider the technical part of an upgrade project.

Downtime influences the length of time necessary to complete the upgrade. *Downtime* is defined differently by different customers, but a common definition is the elapsed time that the systems are not serving the purpose for which they were designed and implemented.

The hardware configuration and power of such hardware and the sizing of the systems may affect the speed of the upgrade. The database size may affect the time before the upgrade is running.

However, there are other factors that influence the upgrade technically and that we tend to forget or put aside, such as the number of modifications in a system and the number of customizations. SAP repository objects that have been modified must be reconciled and custom-developed programs must be tested, especially when they use SAP objects.

These and other postupgrade activities, such as creating new authorizations, or moving additional transports to production, add time to the actual upgrade.

Depending on your front-end rollout strategy, you may need to upgrade the front end all across. In the near future, when all the SAP user interfaces are Web based, this will not be a real consideration.

The network bandwidth will likely be much higher than in your source release, especially if you are upgrading from an older release, such as R/3 4.5 and below.

Planning very carefully the timing on each and every action in a detailed project plan and upgrade script and extensively testing the upgrade process are the real keys to a successful upgrade.

Appropriate planning will also help you to invest where it is necessary (for example, you may need additional testing time) and to save wherever possible (i.e., you may not need additional hardware).

A common and constant question is, "How long does the upgrade last?" Often we are just thinking about the actual time that it takes to insert the CDs and upgrade the software and that is all. Try to plan the *project* and *all* the factors that may influence implementation, based on previous experience, customer references, SAP's assistance, and so on.

The more prepared you are, the better. It is essential to become familiar with all the SAP Notes that help in troubleshooting the upgrade. Other customers that have previously upgraded and run into issues may have reported them to SAP, and a collection of available SAP Notes to upgrade to SAP R/3 Enterprise is available in the SAP Service Marketplace. Early fixes to certain bugs, necessary versions of the executables to run, necessary downloads, specific SAP Notes related to your database and operating system platform, additions to the documentations, and so on are included in such SAP Notes.

Study carefully the SAP Upgrade Guide that you can download from the SAP Service Marketplace. Familiarize yourself with all the service offerings that are included in your maintenance and how SAP can further assist you, and find all the documentation available under the alias/upgrade.

The Upgrade Process

Technically, at the time of upgrading to SAP R/3 Enterprise, there are two major parts of this process: the upgrade preparation executing PREPARE and the upgrade itself executing R3UP.exe. Each part of the upgrade, PREPARE and R3UP.exe, goes through several different phases, and every phase must be successful.

Prepare before PREPARE

Without being redundant, we need to emphasize that preparation is key for a successful upgrade. In this section you will find a few tips and reminders that will help you prepare more efficiently for your upgrade.

For the upgrade preparation and execution, you need to create a directory in the file system of the server that contains the central instance named "usr\sap\put" (note that in this example the naming convention used was UNIX back slashes and it is different in Windows platforms, where forward slashes are used). The upgrade directory must have sufficient free space configured in order to avoid errors and must be empty before starting any phase of PREPARE. The SAP system administrator <sapsid>adm must be the owner of the upgrade directly and all subdirectories.

Ensure that you have blocked a timeframe to upgrade the front-end software *before* the upgrade runs, because once the *new* system is up and you need to log on to perform postupgrade activities, you need to log on with the new front-end release!

Check whether you have enough hardware resources to handle the upgrade and production operations in SAP R/3 Enterprise. See the next section for a more detailed explanation and tips to estimate your hardware requirements.

Back up your database and operating system completely before starting the upgrade. This way you will ensure that you can always go back to your previous stable state if a disaster occurs.

Also, back up your database and logs whenever it makes sense, essentially, before and after the upgrade. But if you choose a different strategy, just make sure that such times are added according to the project plan.

If you have SAP Add-Ons, make sure that their release is in synch with SAP R/3 Enterprise and if you need to upgrade them or not. Search for SAP Notes to gather the necessary information and for consulting assistance, if you need to.

TIP *When searching for SAP Notes that relate to your SAP Add-On while upgrading, use a combination of strings that include the name of your add on and upgrade, for example.*

In addition, if you have third-party add-ons, check with your software vendor for dependencies and if an upgrade of such add-on is necessary.

R/3 Plug-Ins are essential to connect to other SAP systems, such as SAP CRM or SAP APO. R/3 Plug-Ins must be upgraded during the upgrade as well and R3UP will prompt you for the Upgrade Plug In CD. Check the alias */r3plug-in* in the SAP Service Marketplace for the most up-to-date information about R/3 Plug-Ins and their availability, as well as Support Packages.

Hardware Requirements

Very early in the upgrade process, it is essential that you check whether your current hardware configuration can handle the upgrade and the production operations in SAP R/3 Enterprise.

The main hardware components that you must check are the CPU, physical memory, and disk space of your servers, as well as your network capacity and infrastructure.

SAP can assist you greatly figuring out whether you need to upgrade your hardware or not. In addition, there are several SAP Notes that can also be of great help, because they provide information on the increase in hardware resource consumption from your target release to SAP R/3 Enterprise. These SAP Notes are as follows:

- 517085 (resource requirements upgrading from SAP R/3 4.6C to SAP R/3 Enterprise)
- 323263 (upgrading from 4.5B to 4.6C)
- 113795 (upgrading from 4.0B to 4.5B)
- 89305 (upgrading from 3.x to 4.0B)

Depending on your source release, you may need to add the increases that each SAP Note reveals one by one.

For example, if your source release is SAP R/3 4.0B and you are upgrading to SAP R/3 Enterprise, following the aforementioned SAP Notes, you would need to add 20% more CPU from 4.0B to 4.5B, 10% more CPU from 4.5B to 4.6C, and 5% more CPU from 4.6C to 4.7. This results in expecting a total of a 35% increase in CPU consumption in each application server.

If your central instance and database server are installed in the same physical server, add an extra 10% from release to release to handle the database processes. This would result in our example of expecting a 65% increase in CPU consumption in such a server with a SAP Instance and a database.

The SAP Notes also help to figure out the increase consumption in physical memory and in disk space. These SAP Notes are built upon experience from the SAP installed base and are averages that are supposed to assist you figuring out roughly the resource consumption increase in your servers. Depending on your functionality and many other factors, these figures will vary more or less.

In addition, it has been noticed that if you upgrade to a 64-bit environment, an additional 5% of resource consumption in CPU and memory may also apply. This is the case if you are upgrading SAP to a core Unicode system.

Remember that these are rough estimates and that you should contact your hardware partner to size your system according to your needs. SAP can also assist with the services that are part of your maintenance or additional offerings, if available.

Upgrade Strategy and System Switch

The new features of and upgrade to SAP R/3 Enterprise include a new way to substitute the repository that replaces the old *A_on, A_off, A_Switch* strategy.

A new "shadow system" is installed in the central instance of your system. You may choose to install this system in a different application server as well and run in parallel. The resources that you need are basically those of your central instance.

During this process, a SAP Web Application Server 6.20 or above is installed (created) and runs in parallel to your production system in whichever release it is. The database of the new release is imported and all the shadow objects point to the original objects in the production database. Import of SAP Support Packages is also included.

Next, you must run a modification adjustment of the dictionary objects executing transaction SPDD. You can do this, again, while the system is up. You can also choose to convert tables using transaction ICNV (Incremental Conversion).

At this point, though, you cannot transport anything else; the system must be completely locked.

Then the system must be shut down and the shadow system takes over. The kernel and the repository are switched, the central instance restarts, and afterward, all the dialog instances restart.

When performing an upgrade process using SAP tools, there are different upgrade strategies available that will affect the total downtime of the process. These strategies are based on the *system switch* as introduced previously.

The upgrade strategy determines whether the substitution set is imported into the shadow tables during production operation of the system. The Repository Switch procedure can be divided into two parts:

- The database tables that make up the substitution set include almost the complete SAP repository. This substitution set is imported into the shadow tables. The substitution set does not influence and is not recognized by the productive SAP system, and therefore the substitution set part of the upgrade can be performed during the operation of the SAP systems.
- At a certain important point of the upgrade, the repository is switched by deleting the old repository and renaming the shadow tables. When this upgrade phase is going to occur, users cannot use the system productively.

There are two available upgrade strategies:

- *Downtime minimized.* Most upgrade phases and actions are performed to reduce the downtime it will take to finalize the upgrade. With this strategy, systems require the use of more memory and CPU. Although the total productive downtime is reduced, the total runtime of the upgrade is longer.
- *Resource minimized.* Using this upgrade strategy, the shadow repository system is not started in parallel to the productive system. The production system and operations will have to be stopped before the shadow system can be started.

The decision between the strategies is mainly based on the maximum possible downtime, which must take into consideration the time needed for a recovery of the system in case serious problems arise.

NOTE *If you choose the strategy "downtime minimized," the system switch happens as mentioned previously, but if you choose the strategy "resource minimized," the production system is down for all the steps mentioned. Choose wisely one strategy or another depending on your resources and how long you can afford to have your system down. Check SAP Note 398100 for more information about the shadow system.*

Upgrade Preparation: PREPARE Program

Because extensive checks are required for the upgrade, SAP provides the PREPARE program as a collection of checks to support the preparation of the upgrade without affecting productive operation, because the program can be run while the systems are running. It's an independent program that can and must be used previous to the actual upgrade.

The PREPARE program automatically checks all the requirements for the upgrade, provides information for further steps, and imports several tools in the database.

PREPARE has four different levels of execution:

- Level 1 can be started at any time.
- Level 2 is performed only once.
- Level 3 performs all the checks requiring short runtimes.
- Level 4 includes long-running jobs, such as the estimation of the modification adjustments, an extended space check, or the repository transfer.

You can execute PREPARE as many times as you want and as early in the upgrade process as you want or need.

PREPARE checks the disk space that is necessary for the upgrade to run, if there are open modifications and transports in your system, and if you need to upgrade your database or operating system versions, among other checks.

The Product Availability Matrix is published in the SAP Service Marketplace under the alias /PAM or you can also check the alias /platforms, which can redirect you to the Product Availability Matrix. This way you can check whether your operating system and database versions can be a possible combination for your target SAP R/3 release, SAP R/3 Enterprise.

If a database or an operating system upgrade is necessary, plan ahead the necessary steps to take and to consider, such as technical platform upgrade, testing, short production downtime, and so on.

The number of clients and your database size may influence the disk space that you need to have free for the upgrade to execute without running out of space. If there are many tables that need conversion (the structure changed from release to release), this may add additional space requirements as well. If you are a global organization that has several languages installed, ditto.

Finally, if you need to, a Unicode conversion requires quite some time in preparation and execution.

In addition, during the PREPARE execution, you are prompted the switch the new SAP R/3 Kernel, if necessary. Ensure, though, that you have the minimum necessary patch level specified in the SAP Notes, which you should have checked before starting PREPARE.

Check that you have the latest SPAM update for the application of SAP Support Packages. Search for SAP Notes that may reflect problems encountered related to the SPAM updates.

During PREPARE the necessary tools are imported to the system. You can also configure the upgrade phases in which the SAP Support Packages that you need to import can be bound (bundled together) and the strategy to install multiple languages.

As introduced in the previous section, a new feature coming with SAP R/3 Enterprise is the *system switch upgrade*. This new feature consists of installing a new SAP Instance and a database with the target release that will help in running the upgrade operations. You can choose where to install this Instance (e.g., a parallel server, or the same server as the central instance). This is called a *shadow system* and will run completely in parallel with the production system.

While the production system's database contains all the repository objects, so-called shadow objects will be created in the shadow system that point to the actual objects in the production repository. In the last phase of the upgrade, these shadows are activated and the old repository eliminated.

This process can be performed during regular production operation, if you choose the strategy *downtime minimized*. If you choose the strategy *runtime minimized*, this switch will happen during system downtime.

During PREPARE you can decide whether to use one strategy or another during the actual system switch. This is a very important step in the upgrade and you must choose carefully your options.

As stated in the previous section, the strategy *downtime minimized* allows you to run production operation for a longer period of time, because you can log on the shadow system and perform postupgrade activities in it. However, it will demand more resources out of the system and performance for the users will be impaired, as you can imagine. The actual system switch, though, requires the system to be shut down.

If you choose this strategy, you can run the modification of adjustments, activate the dictionary objects, import transports and SAP Support Packages, as well as use the Incremental Table Conversion functions in the shadow system while the old production system is still up.

Runtime minimized is more similar to the old upgrade strategy in which the system is down during the switch and therefore there is less resource consumption. However, production cannot go on until the system is up again.

You may execute PREPARE from the Upgrade Assistant (see the brief explanation later on) or from the command prompt.

You need to enter data to start the phases of PREPARE, such as the language in which the tests from R3UP must appear; for example, in English-E or German-D. Database-specific entries must be made as well, such as necessary passwords, profiles, and other specifications related to your database platform.

You must enter the mount points of the CDs with the software and whether they are directories in the local file system or CD drives (you may have to change CDs, as prompted).

Specify the number of background processes to run in parallel and the number of parallel import processes. The hardware capacity of the machine influences greatly these decisions. The defaults are fairly conservative.

Ensure that you have downloaded all the necessary SAP Support Packages (of all types that you need for your applications and SAP Add-Ons) and that they are uncompressed into the correct directory (usr\sap\trans\EPS\in). You can bundle them together to import them, which saves great time. This is a new feature with SAP R/3 Enterprise. In addition, binding SAP Support Packages together ensures that you do not miss important fixes that come with the corresponding level.

These are the most important phases of PREPARE. Ensure that all phases are completed successfully. The results of PREPARE are written in a file called CHECKS.LOG in the upgrade directory.

You can repeat each PREPARE phase until it successfully completes, but you may not skip PREPARE before running R3UP.

Additional Upgrade Tools

There are some additional upgrade tools, besides PREPARE and R3UP, that are basic to control and monitor the upgrade. Additionally, there are standard transactions and utilities within the SAP system that are also used in upgrade runs. The following sections discuss the Upgrade Assistant and the Upgrade Monitor, as well as the ICNV transaction.

Other key transactions required for the Modification Adjustment phases, such as SPDD and SPAU, are introduced later in this chapter.

The Upgrade Assistant

The Upgrade Assistant is a Java tool that can help you to control and execute all the phases of PREPARE and R3UP and monitor their status. It can be started in SCROLL mode or in SERVER mode (this is the default and also recommended mode).

This tool is meant to provide support to run the upgrade remotely. The advantage of using the Upgrade Assistant is that the front-end and the upgrade processes are separated so that the entire upgrade does not terminate abnormally if a connection fails.

To run the Upgrade Assistant, you need to install and start up the Upgrade Assistant server. In order to do this, at the operating system level, you need to execute the command jview /cp <your upgrade directory>\UA\ua.jar UaServer.

Afterward, you can start the Upgrade Assistant GUI from a Web browser (recommended) executing a URL such as http://<upgrade server hostname>:4239/ua/UaGui.html (you need to include the full Internet name as the upgrade server hostname) or you can start it up from the command prompt with Java commands.

Log on using the default user and password (Administrator/admin) and you are ready to go.

You will be prompted to start (initialize) each phase of the PREPARE and once PREPARE has been executed successfully and you have done everything you need to start R3UP, you can start this program with the Upgrade Assistant and, as before, control the upgrade phases and progress.

The Upgrade Monitor

From the Upgrade Assistant, you can start the Upgrade Monitor, which can assist you to monitor the different phases of the upgrade, their runtimes, their activity, if there are processes hanging, and other system conditions.

The Upgrade Monitor estimates when the upgrade and important phases of the upgrade will be finished. These estimates are based on SAP reference timings as well as on the duration of previously run phases.

The runtime statistics are refreshed once every minute only and they can be used as reference to what the upgrade is supposed to last. However, do not take these times for granted or totally "by the book," because they will vary greatly from system to system and environment to environment, depending on all the factors previously discussed. You may see green bars all the time or red bars, and this may or may not mean a problem all the time.

Additionally, you can start the Upgrade Monitor from the operating system calling "R3UP.exe monitor."

Use this monitor to check whether processes are stopped and the upgrade is "not moving" while you are executing the phases of the upgrade.

An animated graphic displays the activity of the upgrade processes. If the graphic is not moving, one of the upgrade processes is stopped. The upgrade processes that are running appear under *Current activities*. The monitor does not recognize any subprocesses of these processes, and therefore cannot display them.

Incremental Conversion (ICNV)

The structure of the tables in the SAP database might change with each new release, and therefore one of the activities performed by some of the upgrade phases is to convert these tables.

Traditionally these table conversions happened only during the upgrade downtime, which usually was one of the longest processes to run. However, by using incremental conversion, you can convert many of the tables before the upgrade, using the transaction ICNV.

With this mechanism, you can clearly have some advantages, such as a reduced downtime during the upgrade, because a large number of tables are converted while the productive system is still running.

With transaction ICNV you have the following functions:

- Display tables flagged for conversion as determined by the PREPARE tool.
- Select the tables you want to convert incrementally.
- Execute and monitor the conversion process.
- Estimate the runtime of the conversion.

ICNV provides users with information about the progress of the conversion and estimates finish runtime.

The Software Upgrade: R3UP

R3UP.exe is the program that upgrades the SAP software, performs the actual system switch according to your chosen strategy, and shuts down the system when it is time. You may execute R3UP from the command prompt or from the Upgrade Assistant. Ensure that you run it, though, in the central instance.

R3UP can also be stopped at the end of each phase before starting executing the next using the Upgrade Assistant or the command prompt. You may need to do stop and restart R3UP, if a SAP Note tells you so to correct a situation or if you encounter a problem that must be solved before continuing. Afterward, the upgrade can be restarted.

The R3UP phases leave their logs in the directory \usr\sap\put\logs. Check these logs to analyze errors. The program's TP also leaves logs in this directory; look for the "SLOG" logs.

R3UP needs input, as PREPARE needed, and you will be prompted to enter the necessary data for the phases to run. You can use the Upgrade Assistant and the Upgrade Monitor to check the progress of the upgrade.

In each phase you will be prompted to enter the necessary data and at the end of each phase you should check the success.

You must enter the chosen upgrade strategy, downtime minimized or runtime minimized. Execute a complete backup, if you choose the strategy resource minimized, so you can ensure that you can come back to this point, in case of a disaster.

Certain phases are critical. For example, the upgrade program checks whether the necessary SAP Support Packages are ready to be imported in the correct order. If you still have SAP Support Packages from the old release to confirm, release the open repairs and lock transports to avoid conflicts.

After R3UP

Certain activities must be performed once R3UP has successfully finished. Of course, to start, a database backup cannot be missed. Many parameter settings will need to be changed, especially those for memory management, for example, or those related to the new components, such as the ICM, the SAP J2EE Engine, and so on.

Database-specific actions, such as updating statistics, must also be performed at this time.

Run transaction SGEN to generate ABAP loads of programs that don't exist and to generate BPS applications.

New authorizations and changes in the existing profiles for the users must be done at this point so the users are ready to log on in the new system and perform their transactions.

Imports of transports with new developments can be done now as well and some new SAP Support Packages, if necessary, as well.

All the adjustments from SPDD and SPAU run before and marked for transport can be imported to production as well.

ABAP Load Generation with SGEN

SGEN is the SAP transaction that is used to generate the ABAP loads and that replaced the report RDDGENLD, found in SAP R/3 releases before 4.6.

Due to the fact that SAP systems are based on a concept of integration and activation of structures and programs, when in an upgrade, many ABAP loads for transactions and business application are not automatically generated during the upgrade. This happens automatically as soon as a program, transaction, or menu function is selected, but if the loads are not previously generated, this will impact system performance the first time users enter the specific transaction or application. Load generation requires a large amount of system resources. This may, however, reduce production system performance, and to avoid this, you can use transaction SGEN to generate the missing loads.

One of the advantages of the new SGEN transaction with SAP Web Application Server is that it allows users to generate loads in parallel.

With the new release, SGEN can not only generate ABAP reports and programs, but also BSPs (business server page applications) or function groups.

It is recommended that users generate the ABAP loads immediately after running the upgrade.

Modification Adjustment

When you upgrade a SAP system, the standard process will make you lose any modifications made to objects that conflict with SAP modifications in the new release. You must modify your code to Unicode. The modification adjustment process lets you make your modifications to the appropriate new objects in the upgrade.

The normal order in which you upgrade a SAP environment starts upgrading the development system, which contains the version management, the utility that keeps track of all changes to all the objects in the SAP repository. Thanks to the version management and the utilities SPDD and SPAU, the modification adjustment can be performed to avoid conflicts and ease the risk of losing important customer functionality.

You can find five different types of changes or modification within SAP systems:

- *Local customer developments.* These are programs or other repository objects that customers create or develop, by using the proper naming conventions, such as starting with Y or Z, or by reserving a name space. Refer to Chapter 6 for more information on the transport system.
- *Customizing.* This is the process of setting and defining system parameters using the Customizing transactions within the IMG. Customizing is a basic and mandatory process of any SAP system implementation. Typically it does not affect directly repository objects.
- *Modifications to SAP standard.* These are customer-specific changes to SAP repository objects. When standard SAP objects are changed during an upgrade process (also during the installation of Support Packages), the customer version has to be modified to match the new SAP version.
- *Enhancements.* These are customer changes to SAP repository objects without the need for modifications to the standard. The most common enhancements are are the advantages of the new Business Add-In technology that replaces the user exists.
- *Advanced corrections.* These corrections are meant for applying fixes to programs or other repository objects from SAP directly to the customer SAP system. The corrections are provided from the SAP Service Marketplace in the form of Support Packages, which avoids customers having to modify those SAP objects manually.

If you have modified objects in the SAP standard software, such as programs and objects in the dictionary, you must run an adjustment to compare if the new release is bringing over those objects that you needed to modify in the past. Maybe you performed that modification because the standard did not provide with such functionality or object in the previous release and now it is included. You can choose to go back to the standard or to keep your modification.

When you choose either to return to the SAP standard object or to keep your modification, those objects are included in a transport request that you will import to the test system later on and to the production system finally.

To perform this adjustment, you must execute transaction SPDD to adjust objects in the SAP dictionary and SPAU to adjust programs in the repository.

If you choose the strategy downtime minimized, you can do this while the system is up, but in the strategy resource minimized it is done during actual downtime of the system.

Adjustments with SPAU must be performed at the end of the upgrade, after the switch has finished and the new programs have been actually imported.

SAP includes two main modification adjustment transactions, SPDD and SPAU, that are used for adjusting dictionary and program objects that could have been modified on customer systems before the upgrade.

In good upgrade projects the adjustments are performed only on development systems to be later transported to QAS (quality assurance system) and PRD (production system).

The adjustment of modifications is performed first during the actual upgrade, where the tool will stop so that developers and consultants can analyze the differences between modified objects and new objects. When doing this process, customers can decide to keep the old modifications and adjust them to new objects, or can just decide to keep new objects, overwriting previous ones. The SPDD and SPAU transactions show a list of the modified SAP objects.

Especially in those installations with complex modifications, the adjustment process can be one of the more time-consuming activities of the upgrade projects. Therefore, it is very important to perform adjustments in the development system so that these objects can be automatically transported to the production system. Sometimes landscapes are different in each system, so the process has to be reviewed after finishing the upgrade phase.

Usually the upgrade is limited to maintain the operation and business processes as they were before the upgrade. The main problems are the locally developed transactions, especially those that were first copied from standard and then modified and enhanced. After the upgrade, the company might decide to perform additional customizing.

The objects list that must be adjusted in your SAP system will be determined in the ADJUSTPRP phase of the upgrade. This phase is included within the PREPARE and runs in the upgrade between the import of the substitution set and the end of the production.

To perform the adjustments correctly, it is very important that the original authors review the modifications. The original authors of those changes can be found in the log file UMODPROT.<SID>, located in the log subdirectory of the upgrade directory.

The ABAP dictionary objects (tables, data elements, domains, and so on) are adjusted during downtime before the activation of the ABAP dictionary. The adjusted objects are collected in a transport request, but you cannot release this transport request; instead it must be flagged for export in transaction SPDD.

In one of the last phases of the upgrade, the upgrade program R3UP exports this transport request into the transport directory (/usr/sap/trans) and registers the request for transport in the file *umodauto.lst*.

Repository objects (reports, screens, and so on) are adjusted toward the end of the upgrade. At this stage, the import of SAP objects has already been completed. However, the old, modified version is still available in the versions database. As with ABAP dictionary objects, all adjustments are released to a transport request that is noted and then exported and registered by R3UP. Activation will be carried out automatically after the adjustment.

After you have completed the upgrade, you have a maximum of 14 days to execute transaction SPAU without a key check (SAP Software Change Registration) for the objects that you changed.

SPDD and SPAU

SPDD and SPAU are the two main transactions and utilities to complete the process of adjusting modifications so that the upgrade process does not overwrite any important customer objects.

- SPDD is used to adjust dictionary objects (table structures, domains, data elements, and so on).
- SPAU is used to adjust all other repository objects that are not dictionary (reports, function modules and so on).

At the start of the adjustment process, SAP R/3 repository objects from the preupgrade repository are compared with objects from the repository of the new release.

For each object, transactions SPDD and SPAU guide users through the adjustment process by offering the options of performing the modification adjustment or returning to the SAP standard. Normally, as team members work through the list of objects flagged for adjustment, they should mark each object once they finish with the adjustment.

The adjusted objects will be collected in a change request. However, notice that there can be only one transportable change request for SPDD adjustments and only another one for SPAU adjustments.

Once all modified objects are marked as processed, the change request is ready for export. By transporting the change request, you avoid needing to make the same adjustments again in each system. It might happen, however, that the repository of the systems in the landscape is not completely identical; for instance, some modifications made in the development system were not transported onto subsequent systems in the landscape. Therefore, and unfortunately, the final adjustments will have to be verified after the completion of the upgrade.

There are several ways of adopting and adjusting modifications:

- *Automatic modifications.* Using this option, the customer modification can be automatically adopted.
- *Semiautomatic adjustment. Semiautomatic* means that each tool will individually offer you support during the adjustment process. When adjusting programs, the splitscreen editor is called, whereas in the other tools any entries made in the collision dialog box lead to the necessary adjustments being made automatically. As with the green traffic light, the semiautomatic adjustment icon only appears in the with Modification Assistant category.
- *Manual adjustment.* Objects in the "Without Modification Assistant" subtree can only be postprocessed manually after the adjustment process. Manual adjustment means that you must make modifications without any special support from the system. Use the log as a help. Using Version Management, you can retrieve old versions or use your recordings to process the newly imported objects. In rare cases, the red traffic light may also appear in the With Modification Assistant category.
- *Unknown adjustment mode.* The adjustment mode (manual, semiautomatic, automatic) for at least one of the objects in question could not be determined for modification adjustment with the Modification Assistant. If this is the case and you start transaction SPAU, a dialog box informs you that you can start a background process by choosing the appropriate pushbutton that determines the adjustment modes for all objects.
- *Reset to original.* If you choose Reset to original for an object displayed in the overview, no modifications are adopted for this object. The original is the version that was last imported into the SAP R/3 system during an upgrade or the application of a Support Package.

To adjust objects without the Modification Assistant, use version management wherever possible. When modifying objects where version management cannot be used, carefully document any changes that you make. This documentation can be of great assistance the next time the object needs to be adjusted. Choose Change from the maintenance transactions of the individual ABAP Workbench tools to adjust objects without the Modification Assistant.

Troubleshooting the Upgrade

A few tips and tricks that can ease your upgrade are as follows:

- Prepare yourself very well and check all the documentation available.
- Always check the log files left in each phase of PREPARE (CHECK.LOG) and R3UP.log in the log directory (check the phase log summaries, which contain a list of all errors during the phase). Especially check the log for the shadow instance, STARTSFI.LOG.
- Reserve port numbers for the upgrade to avoid conflicts.
- Check the developer traces logs in the "work" directory for the work processes involved in the upgrade.
- Check that the profile parameters and their settings are correct.
- Check that the DDIC password has not been changed.
- Avoid manual calls to R3LOAD, R3TRANS, and TP, because they can damage the system if used with the wrong settings.
- Remember, TP will use a different profile (pf path) for its TPPARAM parameter file, so be careful!
- Perform a full backup when is necessary to avoid disasters and losses of data.
- Test, test, and test again. Perform at least two full test upgrades with a system as close to production as possible before starting the final actual production upgrade.

Unicode Conversion

Nowadays, especially with the Internet as one of our daily tools to communicate business to business, people to people, systems have some trouble to translating properly characters from one language to another. This limits the potential use of some languages and it makes more difficult to make systems "talk."

Unicode is a standard that allows you to support almost all of the languages used worldwide. SAP Solutions may be converted to Unicode as well, and this is somewhat of an effort to be made.

SAP R/3 Enterprise is Unicode enabled (and other SAP components as well). That means that you when you upgrade to SAP R/3 Enterprise you can also convert your system to a Unicode system. This is because SAP R/3 Enterprise is based on SAP Web Application server 6.20.

During a Unicode conversion, there is high hardware resources consumption and the system must be down during the database conversion. After the upgrade to Unicode, regression and validation testing must be performed.

As requisites to start a Unicode conversion, the front-end servers must be of release 6.20 or higher and the database version used must be Unicode enabled.

6

CHAPTER

The Change and Transport System

SAP systems, and specifically the SAP Web Application Server (formerly known as the SAP Basis), include a collection of tools for managing the changes across a group of related SAP systems. These tools are linked to the ABAP workbench and the customizing functions, which are very important for managing and coordinating development and customizing work within a group of SAP systems. These tools form the overall *Change and Transport System (CTS)*. Figure 6-1 shows a typical diagram of the CTS components, which are explained throughout the following sections of this chapter.

The CTS components are in charge of performing essential functions in the overall development and customization environment, and thus in the implementation process as well as in the operation and support after productive start.

Among the functions of the CTS tools are the following:

- Administering and controlling of new development requests
- Modifying and correcting repository objects
- Recording and auditing of all configuration settings and changes
- Managing the transport of development packages
- Locking of objects to avoid parallel work
- Performing version management
- Documenting changes
- Assuring teamwork development and workflow control
- Transporting of objects and settings changes among systems
- Logging of transport results
- Setting the system and client change options
- Performing client copy functions
- Recording of where and by whom changes are made

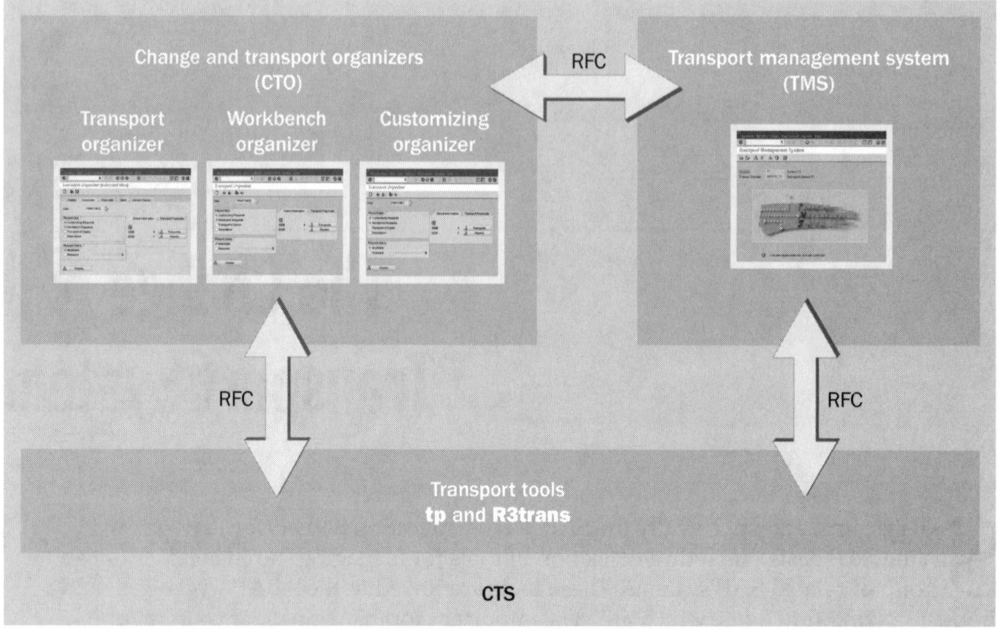

FIGURE 6-1 Overview of the Change and Transport System

- Configuring the systems landscape
- Assisting in maintaining consistency of changes throughout the SAP landscape

Additionally, the CTS tools are extensively used and play a fundamental role in the release upgrade process and tools. These tools can further be utilized when applying SAP maintenance including plug-ins and support packages.

The CTS components are made up of the following:

- *Change and Transport Organizers (CTOs).* The organizer is the main tool for managing, browsing, and registering the modifications done on repository and customizing objects. It's the central point for organizing the development projects. The main transaction is now SE01 (the extended view of the Transport Organizer). In previous releases there was a separation between SE09 (Workbench Organizer) and SE10 (Customizing Organizer). With 4.7 you can still call these transactions and the system will open the Transport Organizer in the standard view.
- *Transport Management System (TMS).* In distributed SAP system environments, the Change and Transport Organizer use the Transport Management System for managing, controlling, copying, or moving, in an orderly manner, the development objects or customization settings among different SAP systems. This process is usually performed between the systems used for development and testing and the productive systems, using predefined transport routes. The transport process consists of exporting objects out of the source SAP system and importing them into the SAP target system or systems.

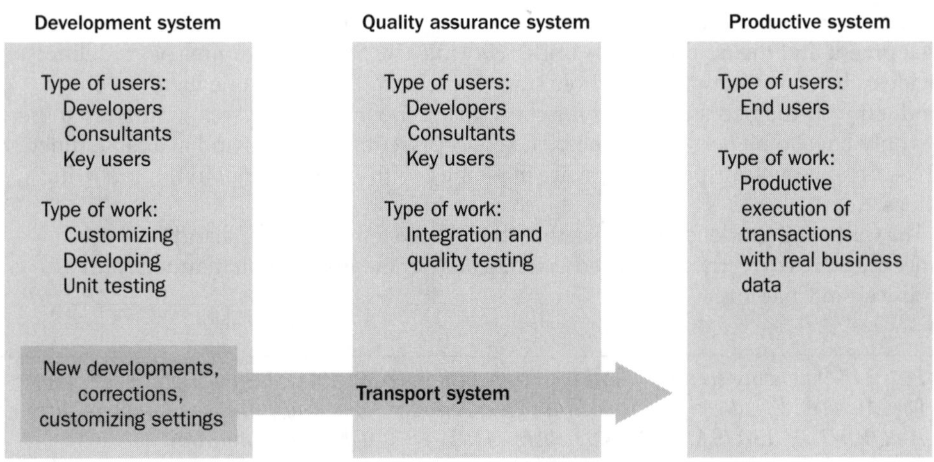

FIGURE 6-2 Simple illustration of the transport process in a three-system landscape

- *Transport tools at the operating system level.* The actual transport (copying) process is performed at the operating system level using the transport tools. These tools are part of the SAP kernel and include the program *R3trans* and the transport control program *tp*. The TMS is linked to those programs so that the SAP system allows transports (exports and imports) to be performed within the system using RFC calls. Figure 6-2 shows a simple diagram of the transport process.

What's New in the Transport System with the Web Application Server?

For those SAP system managers or other professionals accustomed to previous SAP R/3 releases and the Basis system, the following shows the main changes in the transport system since previous releases, as well as other useful hints:

- Development classes are now packages.
- Since first release of the SAP Web Application Server, there is no difference in the transactions SE09 (Customizing Organizer) and SE10 (Workbench Organizer), and they have been combined into the Transport Organizer (transaction SE01).
- The transport system works the same in every SAP solution based on the SAP Web Application Server.
- For the same reason, and very evidently, those menu options that previously showed "R/3 system" have been changed to "SAP system."

Overview of the Complete Process of Transporting Objects from a Source System to a Target System

The transport system together with the Transport Organizer is one of the most puzzling parts of the technical environment of SAP systems; this is probably because there is no place for chaotic and unorganized software development or customization. The transport system and Transport Organizer are actually intended as help functions for having the system development and the modifications under control. The following summary guideline provides a brief overview of the whole transport chain. This guideline includes an introduction of the necessary steps for configuring the transport system, although these steps only have to be performed once. The concepts, configuration, and available functions and features of the transport system are explained with further detail in the following sections.

The following guideline assumes that the SAP systems landscape and network connections are correctly configured, as indicated in the installation manuals, and as introduced in Chapter 3.

NOTE *In the following sections, the directory notation represents Unix-flavors file system types. For Microsoft Windows platforms, it works exactly the same way, but the notation for directories is <DRIVE>:/USR/SAP/TRANS, where <DRIVE> is a disk or volume unit.*

Configuration steps are made of these basic tasks:

1. *If needed, configure the transport directory and configuration file TPPARAM.* The transport directory (/usr/sap/trans) is created by the installation program. You have to make sure that this directory can be accessed correctly among systems within a transport group. Within the bin subdirectory, there are two global configuration files TP_DOMAIN_<SID>.PFL and TPPARAM (transport parameter file) that must include entries for each of the SAP systems taking part in transports. This file must be correctly configured for the transport control program tp to function properly.
2. *If required, initialize the Transport Organizer.* This is accomplished by transaction SE06 (there is no direct menu point entry to this transaction) and is one of the first tasks to perform after the installation of the SAP systems as part of the postinstallation activities, especially if the system is based on a copy of a previous system. This transaction initializes the basic settings for the Transport Organizer and can also be used for specifying the system change option—that is, which objects and configuration settings can be modified or not within the system. This transaction distinguishes whether this R/3 system comes from a standard installation or from a systems or database copy.
3. *Configure transport systems and routes.* This configuration step is performed using transaction *STMS* (Tools | Administration | Transports | Transport Management System) from client 000. The first time this transaction is called, the system creates a *transport domain controller,* a central system where all configurations is done and then transferred to other systems in the group. The easiest way to configure the systems landscape and transport routes is to select a standard configuration. This can be done by first entering the SAP systems (Overview | Systems) and then back in STMS main screen, selecting Overview | Transport Routes and Configuration | Standard Config. In this case the TMS will request the roles of the defined systems and set up the transport layer and transport routes for each. For nonstandard configurations or complex system landscapes this process must be performed manually.

In addition to these configuration tasks, it is also important to set the system change options as well as to check the system client settings. These settings define what parts of the system can be changed and recorded by the organizers.

The next steps typically are as follows:

4. *Create a package.* Packages (formerly development classes) act as a way to group together objects belonging to the same development project (programs, transactions, tables, etc.). Only objects with an appropriate package can be transported to other systems. To be able to transport development objects, you must define a package that is not local (such as $TMP) or for test purposes (all starting with *T*). You should define the package with a name within the range allowed for customers.
5. *Create or modify an object.* The process of creating a new object (a table or a report, for example) or making a customization setting automatically asks for the creation of a change request. This request will be transportable as long as the assigned package, the transport route, and/or the type permit it.

NOTE *The automatic creation of a change request is allowed by the SAP client settings. You can disable this function and the ability to make changes in the system client-independent objects. However, in the rest of this chapter and other chapters, it is assumed that the client allows for changes in the repository and client-independent objects.*

6. *Release and export the transport.* Access the Transport Organizer (SE01) and find the transportable change requests that have not yet been released. Expand the folder to access the change tasks. Change requests are composed by one or more *tasks*. First release the tasks and then release the change request. When the change requests are released, the system performs an export and creates several files at the operating system level.
7. *Import into the target system.* When the group of SAP systems shares the same common transport directory, files that have been exported are directly accessed by the target system. Imports are performed within the TMS by accessing the system import queues and performing the imports.

   Imports can also be performed with the tp program at the operating system level by logging onto the target system as user <sid>adm, going to the /usr/sap/trans/bin directory, and performing the corresponding call to the program. For example,

   ```
   tp import <transportable change request number> <target SID>
   ```

   Imports can also be performed within the TMS by accessing the system import queues and performing the imports.

   Lastly, transport requests can be imports running function module trint_tp_interface in SE37. At runtime, the following are specified:

   - *Import* is specified at the IV_TP_COMMAND parameter.
   - *Target system* is specified at the IV_SYSTEM_NAME parameter.
   - *Transport Req* is specified at the IV_TRANSPORT_REQUEST parameter.

- *Client* is specified at the IV_CLIENT parameter.
- *Unconditional modes ("umodes")* are specified without the *U* at the IV_UMODES parameter.

8. *Check log files.* You can check the log files (transport logs) from inside SAP or at the operating system level. Ultimately, try to display the objects you just imported in the target system.

With these steps, a whole transport process is accomplished. The next sections discuss the concepts, details, options, and possibilities of all the SAP functions involved.

Transport System Concepts

The Change and Transport Organizers and the transport system deal with topics and concepts, some of which are the same as those used within the ABAP workbench, and some of which are specific to the functions these systems perform. In order to better understand this chapter, the main concepts are introduced in the next sections.

Repository and Development Objects

The Transport Organizer records and controls changes to current or new development objects. A *development object* is any object created (developed) within the SAP system.

The collection of development objects that are either cross-client or client-independent (behave and act exactly the same regardless of logon client) is known as the repository.

Examples of development objects within the repository are as follows:

- ABAP dictionary objects—tables, domains, search helps, data elements, and so forth
- ABAP programs, functions modules, menus, and screens
- Documentation
- Application-defined transport objects

The Transport Organizer (SE01) is used to manage the repository and development objects changes.

Customizing

For customers to adapt a SAP system to their business environment, they "customize" it. To perform the customizing of the SAP application, users and consultants use the Implementation Guide (IMG), from which they can access specific customizing transactions. The IMG is accessed by transaction SPRO. The Transport Organizer (SE01) is used in conjunction with the IMG to manage changes by user.

The Two Main Types of Change Requests

There are two main types or categories of change requests, SYST and CUST.

SYST changes record a version of the ABAP Objects and general customizing object when the request is released. These changes also lock all the objects in the request, which prevents users from making changes to the objects from the time of change until the release of the request.

CUST requests are comprised of client-dependent customizing changes. Each object of a CUST request contains a table key. The key has the *client,* where the data are stored; the *table name,* where the data are stored; and the *key,* which defines what rows of the table are stored in the request. CUST changes do not lock the objects (table rows) at anytime. So it's important that access to customizing changes is controlled properly.

The Transport Organizer is fully integrated into the ABAP development workbench and the customizing tools to manage both types of change requests. This integration allows users to access the Transport Organizer functions directly from the ABAP development workbench. It also allows users to jump directly to the IMG customizing objects from the Transport Organizer.

Clients and Type of Data in SAP Systems

As introduced in Chapter 2, a client is a technical and organizational independent entity or unit within SAP systems. Clients include their own set of data, such as the master data, the customizing data, and the application or operational data.

Clients are useful for creating "separated" environments within a single SAP system without the need to use several physical databases.

From a technical point of view, a client is defined using a three-digit numeric code, and this client code, is always used as the first field, named "MANDT," and part of the primary key for every SAP table that is client dependent. This means that physically that data are still stored in the same database tables but are separated by the functions within the SAP kernel and the database interface, which restrict the access to only client-dependent or cross-client data. The system selects and processes the data according to the client the users are logged on.

Figure 6-3 shows the types of data that are always found in SAP systems.

Among client-specific data, there are the following types:

- *User master data* contain the user login information, including the username, the password, the user defaults, the authorization profiles or roles, and other useful and auxiliary information such as user groups, communication, and so on. These data are physically contained in a specific set of tables (the USR* tables). More information can be found in Chapter 8.
- *Customizing data* contain the configuration settings that made up the actual application implementation of the organizational structure and the business processes for companies implementing SAP. These data are client dependent and are physically stored in tables known as customizing tables.
- *Application data* are also client dependent, and normally users distinguish two types: master data or transactional data. Master data, such as material master, vendor master, and so on, are data that are often loaded at the beginning of the project and later changes less often than operational or transactional data, such as posting financial documents, sales orders, production orders, and so on.

Besides the Repository, there is also a type of data, known as *cross-client customizing,* which are specific data contained in a set of configuration tables and which are valid and shared by all the clients within a SAP system.

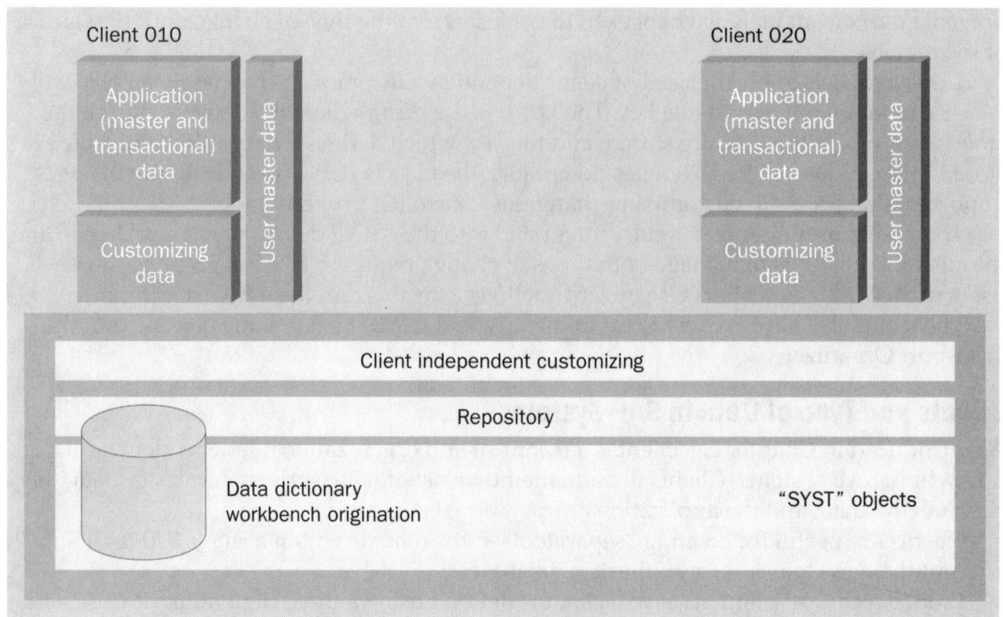

FIGURE 6-3 Data types in SAP systems and clients

Only customizing data and repository (workbench) objects are transportable. The system settings prevent user master and application data from being transported.

Table 6-1 shows where and how the different types of data are changed.

The Application, User Masters, and Customizing data types exist solely in tables. How then does the SAP system determine if a table's data are transportable or not? This is determined by a few attributes of the table: its *class, maintenance settings,* and if a *table maintenance dialog* exists. An introduction to the SAP Data Dictionary can be found in Chapter 7, but for more information on table classes and table maintenance dialog, please refer to the SAP Online Help.

TIP *You can identify cross-client customizing in the IMG by selecting Additional Information | Technical Data, then Client Dependencies. All cross-client customizing will be labeled Cross-Client and client-dependent data by Client-Specific.*

Roles Involved in the Transport Process

The functions of the Change and Transport Organizers allow developers and project team members to have the organization and coordination of individual or team development projects. Within the environment of the organizers and transport system, there are three points of view concerning the roles of individuals in charge of controlling and managing the system:

- The team leaders or project managers are responsible for creating change requests and assigning them to team members (developers or customizers). As we will see in

Data Type	Data Entered by	Type of Change (if it's transportable)	Client Dependent/ Independent	Example
Application/ transaction	End users by transactions	Not transportable	Client dependent	Sales invoice, purchase order
Application/ master	Data load programs (during system setup)	Not transportable	Client dependent	Vendor, employee, or customer data
User authorization, profiles, and roles	Creating transport requests for authorization/ profiles/role data	CUST	Client dependent	User ID
User master data	Security administration by transactions or CATT scripts	Not transportable	Client dependent	User ID and its values
Cross-client customizing		CUST or SYST	Client independent	SAP calendar
Customizing	IMG in development system	CUST	Client dependent	Yes
Repository	Object Navigator (SE80) and other workbench transactions in development system	SYST	Client independent	ABAP program, table, data element

TABLE 6-1 Where and How Data Are Changed

following sections in this chapter, the system will create a *task* for every customizer or developer, which will record the additions or modifications they do in the system. The project manager is usually in charge of releasing the change requests for transport to other systems. With the quality assurance process and the transport workflow, the team leaders can also be assigned the role of approving transports.

- The developers and/or the people doing the customizing work are in charge of creating or correcting development objects as well as customizing the system, and thus will create the change requests or use common change requests in a project. (Project managers and team leaders or authorized personnel should approve and release change requests.) Releasing the change requests actually performs the export phase of a transport. When doing this, the project team should also check the log of the export phase as well as inform the administrator of the status and possibly request that the administrator make the import.

- The SAP system manager or transport administrators set up the transport systems, perform or schedule the imports, check the result of imports, and finally inform the developers or customizers. Administrators have to work both at the SAP application level and sometimes at the operating system level using the transport control program (tp). Since the introduction of the STMS, the most common transport functions, including imports, are performed within SAP.

SAP System Group

With the CTO, SAP has established a safer and more controlled environment for the development work among SAP systems. An important concept for the whole process is the SAP *system group,* which is a group of related SAP systems, each with its own database (its own SID) and its own role in the development and implementation process. Normally, the SAP system group is defined by a common configuration of the TMS (configuration tables) and a common configuration at the operating system level where the group of systems share the transport directory (/usr/sap/trans).

Transports can still be performed when directories are not shared. However, in such cases, administrators must either configure specific RFC connections and transport domains or manually copy the export and import files into the corresponding transport directories of the target systems and use special functions of the tp program to perform imports.

Within the Transport Management System, a SAP system group creates a *transport group,* which shares a configuration file TP_DOMAIN_<SID>.PFL, where <SID> is the three-letter system ID, located in the common transport directory. A SAP system group is also referred to as a SAP system landscape. Within a system group there will be one production system. This is important as it relates to SAP licensing. SAP licenses by installations or system group. Within SAP licensing allowances, an installation can have at most eight SAP systems and only one production system.

Transport Layer

A transport layer is used for grouping all the development objects that will always use the same transport routes within the same development system. Transport layers are assigned to all the objects that come from a specified development system.

Grouping objects is a central concept for the Transport Management System and is a requirement to create a transport layer before any development project can start.

Normally there is no need to have more than one transport layer within a SAP system group, except in those cases where there is more than one development system.

Transport Routes

The transport routes are used for defining the different routes that exist between two systems within the same system group. There are two types of transport routes:

- *Consolidation routes* link a source system, such as the integration (development) system, with a target system, such as the consolidation (quality assurance) system. Every consolidation route is assigned to a transport layer. A consolidation route defines where a change request goes after *export* from the development system.
- *Delivery routes* are used for linking a source system, such as consolidation (quality assurance) systems, with a target system such as the recipient (productive) systems.

The delivery routes are not assigned to a transport layer, but every object that arrives at a consolidation system via a consolidation route (transport layer) that is also the source of a delivery route is automatically sent to the specified target system using the delivery route. The delivery route defines where change requests go after *import* into the consolidation system.

Consolidation routes are related to the export of change requests. When a request is exported from SAP, it follows a consolidation route to the target system. Delivery routes are related to the import of requests. As the request is imported into the quality assurance system, the change request will be added to the import buffer of the productive system.

Since release 4.x, any system from the group can be the source of a delivery route, which allows complex transport routes to be established among a group of SAP systems. If no consolidation route is assigned to a transport layer, or if the transport layer does not exist for the system where objects are modified or repaired, then these modifications are considered local and therefore cannot be transported to other systems.

A well-defined transport and development strategy within a systems group, including the configuration of the transport routes, is extremely important for SAP system implementation and support. The configuration of the transport system is used for managing and automating the process of distributing the development or customization objects among the systems belonging to a group. Configuration is also very important when planning an upgrade project in a systems group, because modifications must be made in several systems and then transported among the various systems to be upgraded.

Extended Transport Control

Extended transport control, available since v4.5x, allows multiple clients of a system to be defined in a transport route in STMS. Without it one client is defined per system in STMS.

Before extended transport control, operating system scripts, using the tp program, were used to import into multiple clients of a system. With extended transport control, all the clients of a landscape can be defined in a transport route within STMS.

Extended transport control is enabled by setting the parameter CTC = 1 in the TMS configuration. It is accessed by transaction STMS. Overview | Systems and then choosing the desired system and selecting SAP | Display in the application menu. The parameter can be fixed in the Transport Tool tag.

Change Requests

A *change request* or *transport request* is a list in the system containing the objects to be transported and information on the purpose of the transport, the transport type, the request category, and the target system. A change request is made up of one or more *tasks* or *change tasks*.

When a change request is created, either manually or automatically, the system assigns a number to it automatically, known as the *change request number*. The format of this number is normally <SID>K<number>, for example, DD1K900030, where DD1 is the system identification (SID), *K* is a keyword, and the number is automatically range generated by the system, which starts at 900001 and does not need to be maintained by the system administrators.

When using the Transport Organizer, providing it has been correctly configured, the target system and the type of transport are assigned automatically. The change requests record all modifications made to development objects or to the customizing settings. The development objects from the ABAP workbench and customizing are recorded in different request types.

When the changes have been made and the change tasks have been released, the list of objects is complete and the change request can be released. Transportable change requests are released to the transport system, which exports the objects and keeps a record of the transport in logs. When a change request is released, a transport log is automatically created.

A change request becomes a transportable change request, also known as a transport request, at the time of export. At the time of export, the SAP system copies the objects and table entries of the request to a data file and writes a descriptor file, called a cofile. The export then adds the request to the buffer of the target system.

To display and check change requests, use the initial screen (request overview screen) from the Transport Organizer.

To access this screen, from the main menu tree, choose Tools | Administration | Transports | Transport Organizer (or call transaction SE01 from the command field). Figure 6-4 shows an example of Transport Organizer initial screen. Click on the check boxes to delimit your criteria for displaying change requests and press the Display button.

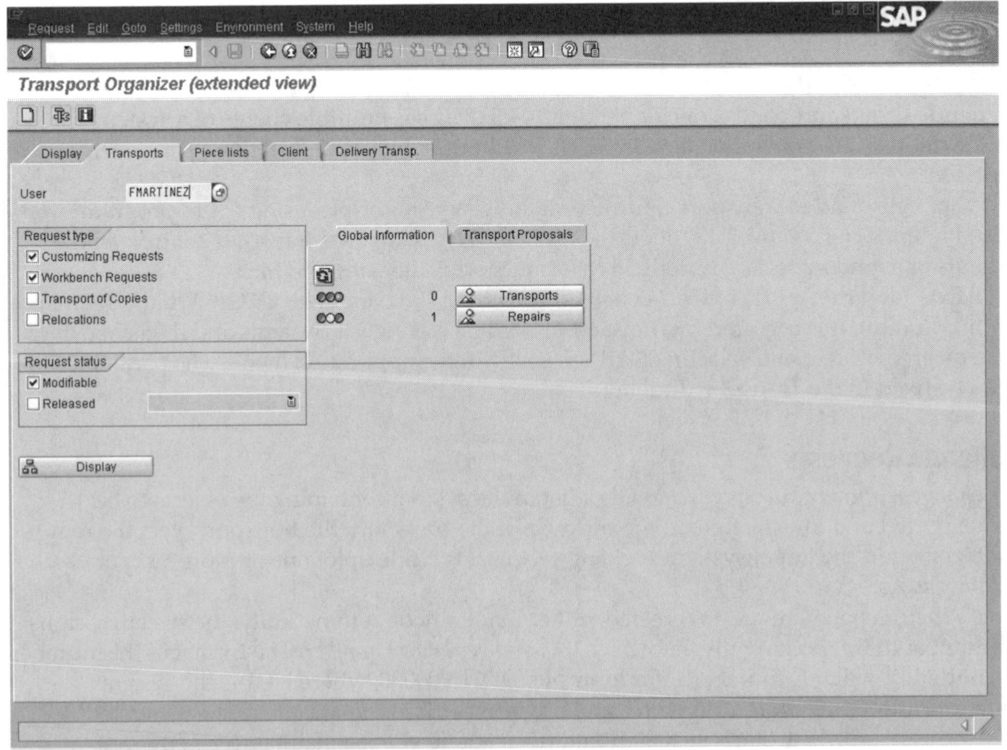

FIGURE 6-4 Transport Organizer main screen (Copyright by SAP AG)

Let's review the two main types of change requests:

- *Workbench requests,* which contains repository objects and cross-client customizing (customizing for all clients). These requests are in charge of recording changes to the Repository, that is, ABAP workbench objects. Within workbench requests, we can distinguish another two types: local or transportable. The difference is that the local ones do not need to have a target SAP system. Whether a workbench request is local or transportable is determined by the *package* it belongs, because it is in the package definition where the transport route is set. A transportable request will always belong to a package that has a transport layer assigned to it. A local request will always belong to the $TMP package, which is not transportable. Within workbench requests there are also Not Assigned and Unclassified requests. Both of these types are requests have no changes assigned to them.
- *Customizing requests,* which contain objects that belong to client-specific customizing. According to the client settings, these types of requests are automatically recorded when users perform customizing settings. The system also assigns automatically the target system according to the defined transport layer.

There are other types of requests, which are also managed from the Transport Organizer, such as the transport of copies or the so-called relocations, which can be used to perform special transport functions with packages or with a collection of change requests. These types are described in the Transport Organizer section, later in this chapter.

Tasks

A *task* or *change task* in the Transport Organizer is a list of objects that are created or modified by a user. Within the organizer, tasks can be either development, correction, or repair tasks.

Tasks are held individually by single users. A change request, on the contrary, can contain tasks belonging to different users. Tasks are not transportable by themselves, but only as part of a change request.

Tasks also have a task number, which uses the same number range as change requests and is consecutive. This means that you cannot distinguish tasks from change requests by their numbers.

If you want to search just for tasks within requests, from the initial Transport Organizer screen, select Request | Find Requests. In the request type, make sure to check only the entries belonging to Tasks and uncheck the rest. Enter other selection criteria, such as username, date, and status, and click the Execute button on the application toolbar. The system will show the list of change requests in hierarchical form, with tasks located one level lower than change requests. You can view tasks by clicking on the + folder sign.

Another option is to select the Transport Organizer Tools icon on the application toolbar (transaction code SE03) and then select some of the reports to find tasks and requests within the Requests/Tasks folder.

When development work starts, usually a system administrator, a development leader, or a project manager creates a change request to define tasks for all users involved in the project. Modification of objects and the creation of new objects that are registered as tasks belong to the change request. Once users finish working on their tasks, they must release them. Only when all tasks under the same change request are released can the change request be released and exported.

It is important to distinguish between the release and export of a change request. The release of a request relinquishes locks and creates a new version for SYST type requests. Before the release of all the tasks, the request must be documented.

Development Teams

The method of grouping tasks together in a common change request is what makes the process of having several users working in the same development project possible. The system uses the authorization object S_TRANSPRT to protect the Change and Transport Organizer functions and S_CTS_ADMI for the administration and management of the transport system.

To define tasks and requests for other users, a project leader must have the authorization S_CTS_PROJEC.

Developers or people in charge of customization need the authorization S_CTS _DEVELO to work at the task level.

There are some standard superuser profiles containing these authorizations. Superuser profiles are profiles that describe a superuser for the system.

Objects included in tasks or requests become locked against other development work on the same objects until the requests have been released. If this occurs, the lock is removed from the objects. Users on the same team can display and change the objects of other users working on the same project sharing the same change request.

Packages (Formerly Development Classes)

A *package* (formerly known as development class) is a way of classifying objects belonging to the same development project, or, in other words, for grouping repository objects that are functionally related. Every repository object in the system is assigned a package.

The packages are objects themselves and, apart from grouping together related objects; also include the consolidation route for the objects belonging to the package. The packages form the main structure on which the ABAP workbench is based to start development work and can be also used to control the naming of the objects.

Packages are based on a hierarchy with a primary container for all the development objects that are grouped together and share the same system, customer delivery status, and transport layer. Packages can be maintained using the Object Navigator (transaction SE80), using transactions SE21 or SPACKAGE.

As of SAP Web Application Server, "nesting" of packages is possible. Nesting allows packages to have other packages embedded in them.

Version Management

Both the ABAP workbench and the organizer provide a version management facility for all the development objects in the system. With version management, users can compare the current version of an object with previous versions; this enables developers to display or restore previously released versions of objects.

To display the version for a particular object, first locate your object by navigating through the change requests and tasks of the Transport Organizer. Click on the object to select it, and from the menu select Object | Versions. With this facility, administrators have the ability to monitor the development work by seeing what has been modified when and who did it.

Version management is very useful for developers and also very important when performing upgrades, because it allows users to compare previous programs or customer-created programs or tables with those of the new SAP release. Developers can check or create versions from SE80, then select the object Utilities | Versions | Version.

The system stores all versions of objects; they would occupy a lot of space. However, the SAP system stores them in the *form of delta sets*. This means that the system actually has one full version and the differences with the other versions. One version state is rebuilt by applying the deltas over the full version.

Hint

- *To back out code changes, use the Retrieve pushbutton in the version management screen for SYST objects.*
- *To view code of another SAP system, use the Remote Compare pushbutton. This is helpful when doing SPAU/SPDD adjustments during maintenance or troubleshooting problems.*

Requests Documentation

In order to have complete control over the development process, the Workbench Organizer system requires that the developers write some structured documentation for each request. The documentation screen appears automatically when releasing a task.

To display a task or change request associated documentation, just click, select the transport request (double-click) and the Documentation tabstrip within the screen for displaying requests.

Repairs and Original Objects

An *object original* is a key concept in the Transport Organizer and the transport system, and a correct understanding of it will help you understand the inner workings of the software logistics around SAP systems.

SAP repository objects are held in the table TADIR. This table includes the field *SRCSYSTEM,* indicating the source system for the object.

The source system is the attribute that is used by the system to determine whether the object is original or not. An original object is a development object (table, report, form, screen, etc.) that has been created in the system in which you are working. When you receive your system and install it, you do not have any original objects in your own system: all objects contained in the repository have been *originally created* at SAP.

When the development team members create new reports, tables, or other development objects, then they have originals, as long as they work on them in the same system in which they were created.

For example, you have a report program called ZRSP0001 that was created in system DD1. This means that the *system owner* (the source system) of the report is DD1. If you make modifications to this program in system DD1, you are making a *correction* to the program. However, suppose you transport this report to system PP1 without changing the source system or system owner of the object. Then, if anyone in system PP1 tries to modify the program, he or she will be making a *repair* to the object, because among the properties or attributes of the program, there is one (SRCSYSTEM) that says that the original system for that object is DD1 and not PP1. This is exactly the case when anyone tries to modify original SAP objects in his or her system. Those object modifications are always repairs because the originals are at SAP systems, where they were developed.

The objects' original location is a security measure to ensure that development objects remain consistent for all systems in which they are used, thus preventing parallel work on the same objects and ensuring that an original of each object exists in only one system.

Corrections and development work can normally only be carried out on original objects in the original system they were created. This is a key concept because it makes a fundamental distinction between a correction/development task and a repair task:

- If you modify an object in a system in which it was not created, then you are making a *repair task.*
- If you modify an object in a system in which the object was created, then you are making a *development/correction task.*

NOTE *There are procedures to make objects appear as originals even if they were not created in the same system where they are being modified. That is one of the purposes of the relocations.*

The next sections describe in detail the procedures for handling repairs and change requests and how to change the system owner of a particular object.

You can easily find whether a particular object is original in the system you are working. To do so, find the object by navigating either in the Workbench Organizer or by means of the Object Navigator (transaction code SE80) or directly from the ABAP Editor (transaction code SE38).

From the ABAP Editor you can see the original by choosing Goto | Object Directory Entry. The Original System field shows clearly the system in which the object was originally created. Notice that table entries do not have this field, because inserting or updating table entries is allowed in any system. Figure 6-5 shows an example of the Object Directory Entry.

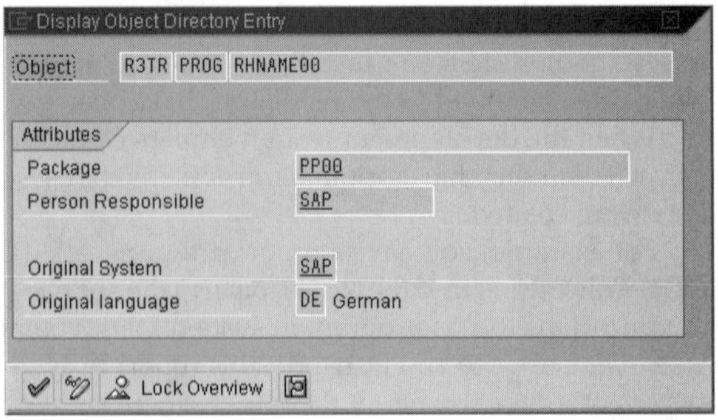

FIGURE 6-5 Object Directory Entry (Copyright by SAP AG)

System Types

Depending on the size of your SAP implementation (number of users and business modules to deploy) and the projects planned, you will install several SAP systems that serve different purposes in your system group.

Normally, the implementation of SAP R/3 in a company requires the installation of several systems (meaning a different SID, which implies a different database server), each of which will serve a particular function.

For instance, normally one system is used to carry out development and customizing work; this is later transported to the productive environment, which is the real system where end users connect and do their work.

Sometimes, though, you also need another system for testing special functions or new modules without affecting either the production or the development environments.

The first distinction to make is that there are two perspectives when talking about system types:

1. The perspective of their function—what they are used for in our installation: development, production, testing, training, quality assurance, and so on
2. The perspective of Transport Organizer and transport system settings—consolidation, integration, recipient, special development systems

The transport system allows a complex group of SAP systems to be set up. For instance, you can set up several systems for distributing the development projects among them. You can also transfer special development work to another system, or you can finish and freeze the development work and make the transport system automatically distribute it to several other systems.

Of course, if the needs are not so demanding, a classical three-systems landscape—one for development, one for quality assurance, and another for productive operation—will suffice to organize development and testing and productive operation.

System types can be set to special change options to protect them from unwanted development or modifications. To do this, the Transport Organizer includes a utility that allows administrators to set the system change options.

System Change Options

With the System Change options, the project leaders or administrators decide how to set up the systems for new developments or customizing, ensuring the integrity of the systems. The available options are suitable for different types of systems and directly affect the functions allowed in the Transport Organizers and transport system.

In order to reach and set the system change options, the user must have all the authorizations for the Workbench Organizer.

To reach the system change options screen, enter transaction SE06 in the command field, and then click on the System Change option button on the application toolbar. Alternatively, you can also get to the System Change options from the Transport Organizer tools (transaction SE03). On this screen, you will see a collection of functions and utilities to perform special transport tasks. The Set System Change Options function is located in the Administration folder. Open the folder and double-click on the Set System Change Options line. You get a new screen as shown in Figure 6-6.

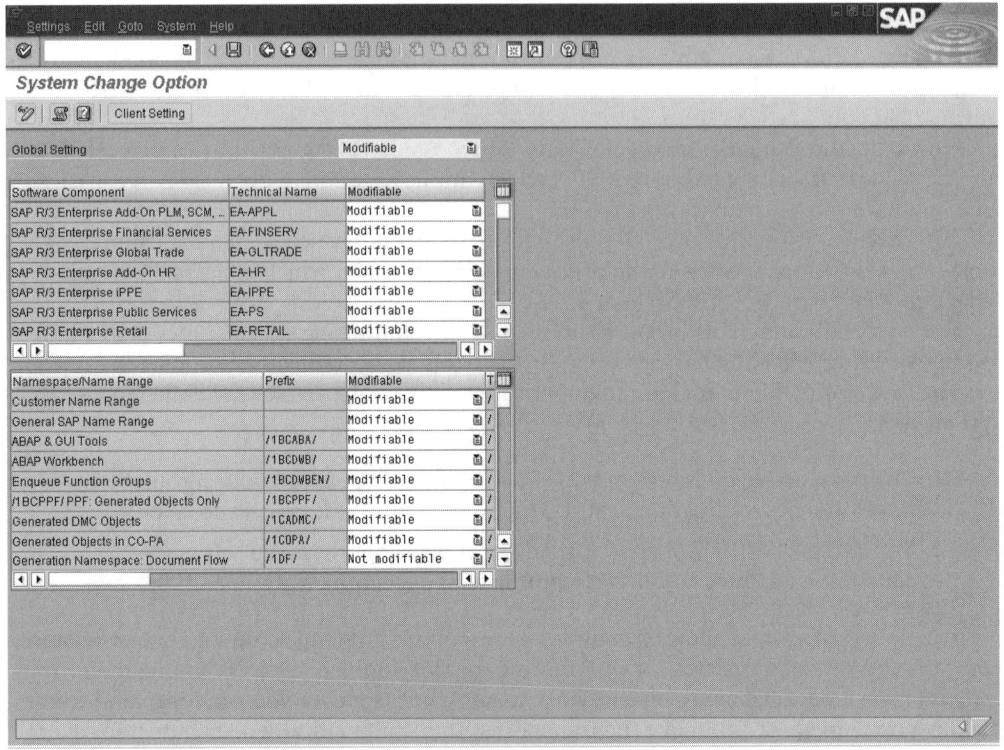

FIGURE 6-6 Set System Change Options screen (Copyright by SAP AG)

The system displays two column tables, one for software components and the other one with the name ranges or namespaces for different types of objects. In order to enable modifications on any type of objects, you must first select the Global Setting option to indicate whether the objects from the repository or client-independent customization can be modified. You can only change System Change options in the name ranges when the Global Setting option is set to Modifiable. If you want to modify the Global Setting, just make sure you are in Change mode. If not, just toggle between Display and Change by clicking the Display/Change button in the application toolbar. If you want to enable modifications in any of the name ranges, just select the check box under the Modifiable column.

You can either set up each option individually to Modifiable or Not Modifiable, or from the Edit menu you can select subsets, for example, Software Components Not Modifiable, Own Namespace Modifiable, and so on.

System Change options can also be set using special command options of the transport control program tp. For example, to set the system to *objects cannot be changed* in system DD1, as a sapdd1 user you can issue the command: tp lock_eu DD1.

Functions of the Systems

The type, function, and number of systems are a matter of factors such as budget, size of implementation, critical needs, and so on. However, even in the smallest installations a second system is almost a must, because it is really not a good practice and not recommended by SAP to do the customizing or development work in a productive system.

From the point of view of the Transport Organizers and the transport system, the function of the systems as described previously is not really needed. What the Transport Organizer needs in the settings is to know which objects can be modified in every system, which system contains the original of the object, and how these changes should be transported to other systems.

Usually development or customization is not carried out directly in productive systems, because the risk of problems is high: a wrong program, a change in a table structure, or an incorrect customization can cause total system unavailability.

However, where there are several systems available, the developers can isolate their work from real production work, minimizing the risk of impacting the productive work of the end users. When the development work is completed and tested, the new or modified objects and programs can then be transported. This object transport can further be tested for integration purposes in another system, or, if that step is not necessary and tests were successful, development objects can be transferred directly to the productive system.

From the point of view of functionality, a training system is often needed as well, although often a different client in the development or test system would normally suffice. If training is going to be intensive, for many users and parallel sessions, then an additional system could be the most convenient option. This training system could be built by performing a copy of the production system. Sometimes, it is also convenient to install a sandbox system for administrators.

Development Systems

As the name says, the development systems are where the development work takes place. Normally, the development is carried out for your own objects, making these objects originals from these systems. The development system is also used for customizing work, which includes functions to create automatically transportable change requests.

From the point of view of the Transport Organizer, the development system is the *integration system* for the packages defined for your own objects. Original SAP objects can also be modified in these types of systems.

You should only do modifications to SAP objects when you need to change the functionality or you receive indications from SAP (OSS or hotline) to correct a bug. If this is the case, then you are making a repair.

HINT *OSS note 170183 details many types of modifications.*

In development systems, if repairs are permitted, the System Change option is normally set to enable modifications on all name ranges, including both customer and SAP objects.

Production Systems

The production system is where the end users enter real business data and where the actual business processes run.

The production system only contains released versions of your development work. No development takes place in this system, or better, no development should be made in this system. Set the System Change option for your production system to Not Modifiable in the global settings.

The production system is normally the consolidation system for your own packages and receives transportable change requests with your own development work from the development system.

If for any critical reason you need to perform repairs to the production system, then temporarily change the global settings of the System Change option to Modifiable to allow modifications in the required name range or namespace.

Test Systems

Test systems, normally known as *quality assurance systems,* are used to test the new developments and the customizing settings. Also, they can be used as distribution points of new developments. This does not mean that tests are not performed on the development system; what happens is that test systems often use real data for the integration tests.

Test systems are useful both for preparing the productive environment and for testing new developments with real data after the beginning of production. Often in SAP implementations, not every module or application becomes productive at once; it's a phased project where some applications become productive before others.

When tests are validated, the development objects or customizing work can be transported from the test system to the productive environment.

System and client settings enforce strict adherence by SAP users that development and customizing is done only in the development system and not in the quality or production systems. This initialization is done at system setup before users are allowed in.

Table 6-2 shows recommended system and client change settings for a SAP landscape. Note that the global system change setting is done in SE06. The client role, changes to client-specific objects, and cross-client object changes are done in SCC4.

Table 6-2 shows a simplistic SAP landscape where there is only one client in both development and quality. In a typical landscape, the development system will have multiple clients. For these clients different SCC4 setting should be used. For example, for a sandbox client you might have "Changes without automatic recording" and "No changes

System	Global System Change Setting	Client Role	Changes to Client-Specific Objects	Cross-Client Object Changes
Development	Modifiable	Customizing	Automatic recording of changes	Changes to repository and cross-client customizing allowed
Test systems	Not Modifiable	Test	No changes allowed	No changes for repository and cross-client customizing objects
Production systems	Not Modifiable	Production	No changes allowed	No changes for repository and cross-client customizing objects

TABLE 6-2 A Simplistic SAP Landscape

for Repository and Cross-Client Customizing Objects." Nonetheless the global system setting for test and production systems should always be "Not Modifiable."

HINT *The production client role allows some activities not allowed in other systems. Some transactions allow data to be changed within a transaction whereas on test systems a change request is needed.*

Managing Packages

Packages are used by the SAP system for grouping together related development objects that belong to the same or similar application areas or similar functions. Packages are a way in which objects are classified and allow the system to perform certain functions on all objects belonging to the same packages.

Packages are held and defined in table TDEVC, which can be maintained from the Object Navigator (transaction SE80) or, better yet, using the transaction SPACKAGE.

To create a new package, go to the Object Navigator, and then select the Edit Object button on the application toolbar.

On the new dialog screen, select the Development Coordination tabstrip and enter the name of the new package in the Package input field and click the Create icon. If the name follows naming conventions, it will automatically include the transport layer and will be linked to the Workbench Organizer. Enter a short text describing the new package and save your entries.

Alternatively, you use the context menus. Select the object tree, then right-click and select Create | Package. A package can also be created by choosing Package from the ComboBox on the left of the screen and introducing a name in the text box and then pressing ENTER.

Notice how important the definition of the package for the transport system is. Every package is assigned a transport layer, which defines the route for transports coming from the same development system.

When defining new packages, carefully follow SAP's recommended naming convention:

- Customer objects and test objects should belong to packages beginning with *Y* or *Z*. This ensures that changes to objects belonging to those classes are recorded in the Workbench Organizer and therefore can be transported.
- Packages beginning with $ are known as local packages and the changes in these objects are not recorded and cannot be transported because the package does not have any transport layer assigned.
- Packages that begins with a *T* are considered private test classes. SAP systems always include the TEST package. When creating a new class of this type, you can specify whether the Workbench Organizer should control the objects belonging to that class. If you want the Workbench Organizer to manage that class, select the check box next to Link to Workbench Organizer when creating the package. However, objects belonging to these classes are not intended for transport and are treated as local objects. When creating such a class, the system does not assign a transport layer. If in any case you want to transport objects belonging to those

classes, you have two options: special transport as copies or modify the TADIR entry for the object.

- Packages beginning with A-S or U-X are for SAP standard objects, and customers cannot create repository objects within them. If you make any changes in objects within these packages (repairs), changes are maintained with the transport system and can be transported.
- Finally, you can have packages beginning with a namespace prefix, which you can reserve through the OSS. These packages and the objects are considered just as customer objects and can be transported across systems.

Every time a new object is created by a developer, it must be assigned to a package. Actually, the ABAP workbench requests that the user enter the package as soon as the Create Object Catalog Entry dialog box appears, as shown in Figure 6-5. This information is automatically entered in the TADIR table, which is the catalog for the SAP repository objects.

Packages can also be the entry point for navigating through the Object Navigator (transaction SE80).

NOTE *Be extremely careful when modifying the catalog entry for a particular object because the catalog entry can cause inconsistencies in the system. Follow SAP Notes or the instructions of SAP specialists.*

Configuration of the Transport System

The process of configuring from scratch the transport system for a group of SAP systems includes the following activities:

1. Initializing the Change and Transport Organizer
2. Setting up the transport directory and the tp program
3. Configuring the TMS, which includes
   a. Configuring the transport domain controller
   b. Adding systems
   c. Setting up system groups (if extended transport control enabled)
   d. Configuring the transport routes
4. Setting the System Change option

When configuring a group of related SAP systems in which the customization, development, and transport systems are organized, there is some information you must know beforehand. This information is basic system landscape design information and involves the following:

- Which systems are in the group and what their roles are: production, testing, development, other
- What clients will be created and with what purpose

- Which objects can be modified in the systems
- What will be transported and what the transport routes are
- Whether recipients' systems will be defined to receive transports when these have been imported into consolidation systems

The next sections explain the most important configuration settings for each of these activities.

Step 1. Initializing the Change and Transport Organizer

This initialization is known as *installation follow-up work* or processing after installation because it has to be performed as one of the first activities after the R/3 installation is finished.

This step is accomplished by executing transaction SE06 (Postinstallation Actions for Transport Organizer). Figure 6-7 shows an example of this screen.

This transaction initializes the basic settings for the CTO and distinguishes whether this SAP system was created from a standard installation or from a copy of an existing system. It can only be executed once.

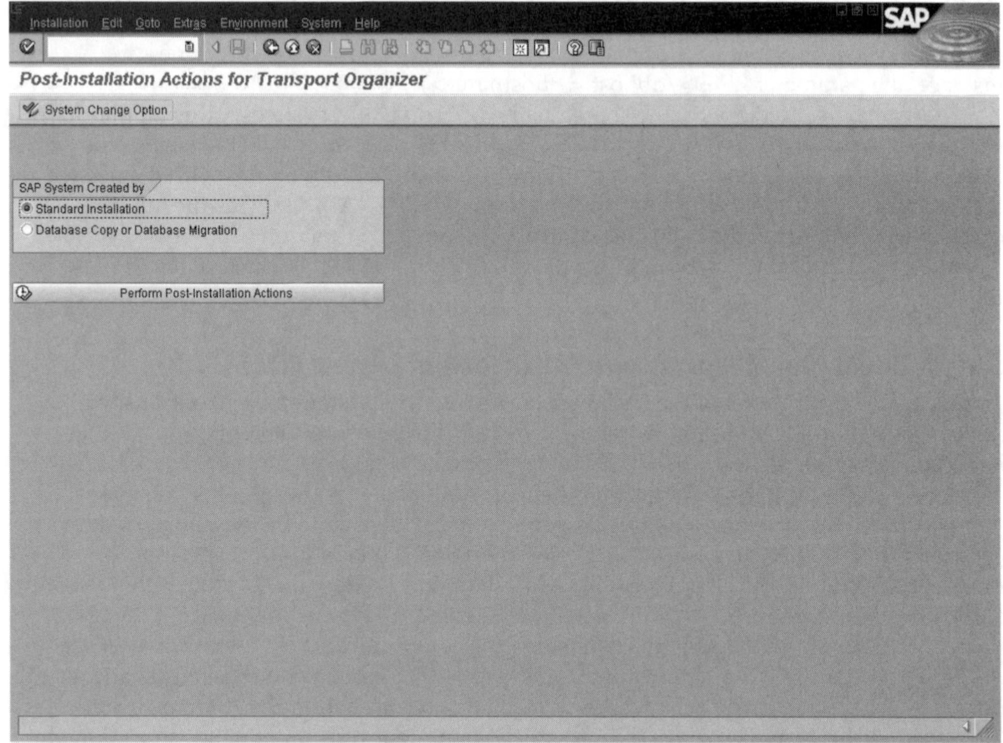

FIGURE 6-7 Transaction SE06 (Copyright by SAP AG)

On the SE06 screen, specify how the system was installed and click on the Execute pushbutton (Perform Post-Installation Actions).

When Standard Installation is selected, the system assumes that it has been installed using the standard SAP software kits. In this case the program will initialize some basic CTO tables, and there is no need to adjust requests or repairs, because no changes exist. This option should not be used if the system was originated from a copy, because the option will create many problems with the Change and Transport Organizer when transports or even upgrades are performed.

When the selection is Database Copy or Database Migration, it means that the SAP system has been created from a copy. In this case it is very important that the system name does not match any other system name within the SAP system group. Systems coming from copies are normally assigned a different role within a group of SAP systems.

When this option is executed, the system will request the name of the source system and will ask whether the objects are to be kept as original (new role) or changed to the new system (assuming role from copied system).

Step 2. Setting Up the Transport Directory and the tp Program (TPPARAM)

This second step consists of ensuring that the transport directory (/usr/sap/trans) is shared among a SAP system group. All systems taking part in the group are included in the global configuration file TPPARAM (transport parameter file), located under the bin subdirectory of /usr/sap/trans. You must edit this file and make sure all systems have a corresponding entry. If a system is missing, copy another systems entry and change the values (for instance, the parameter <SID>/dbhost = <hostname>).

The transport directory can be shared using NFS on UNIX systems, or using file shares and the alias SAPTRANSHOST or SAPGLOBALHOST on Windows NT systems. The installation program creates the transport directories and subdirectories with the needed files, including an initial configuration or a template TPPARAM file. This file must be correctly configured for the transport control program tp to function properly.

Additional information about the tp program and TPPARAM is included in the following sections of this chapter.

Step 3. Configuring the Transport Management System (TMS)

One of the main functions of the TMS is to create a central system for global transport system configuration and administration. This is achieved using RFC communications between SAP systems.

The first time a SAP system group is being installed, one of the systems must be set as *transport domain controller*. To do this, log on to the SAP system to be the transport domain controller in client 000, and enter transaction code STMS (Tools | Administration | Transports | Transport Management System). If there is no domain controller, the system automatically prompts you to create one. It will generate RFC destinations and the TMSADM user, which is used for establishing the communication.

Now you have to include the other SAP systems. The easiest and most automatic way to do this is to log on to each of the SAP systems and run transaction STMS from client 000. If the transport directory is shared, the systems will automatically join the transport domain. Once they join, from the domain controller, select the new system and from the menu select

SAP System | Approve. Finally, distribute the TMS configuration to all systems in the group by selecting Extras | Distribute and Activate Configuration.

Once the systems are configured, the transport routes must be set up to establish consolidation and delivery routes. In regular three-system landscapes, the easiest way is to select a standard configuration. This can be done by first entering the SAP systems and then back in the STMS main screen selecting Overview | Transport Routes and then Configuration | Standard Configuration. In this case the TMS will request the role of each of the defined systems and set up the transport layer and transport routes for each. For nonstandard configurations or complex system landscapes, this process must be performed manually.

Step 4. Setting the System Change Option and the Client Settings

Client settings and System Change options define the parts of the system that can be modified and automatically recorded by the organizers. Basically, both configurations must allow changes to take place and must be linked with the Workbench or Customizing Organizers. System Change options are explained in a previous section. Client maintenance, copy, and settings are explained in Chapter 9.

The Transport Management System (TMS)

The TMS is the transport tool that complements the Change and Transport Organizers for central management of all transport functions. The TMS is used for performing the following functions:

- Defining a central transport domain controller for managing transport configuration in a group of related SAP systems
- Configuring the SAP system landscape by assigning roles
- Defining the transport routes among systems within the landscape
- Displaying and managing import queues on each of the systems
- Performing imports of request queues or specific requests
- Performing transports between systems that do not share a common transport directory
- Distributing a configuration
- Testing the configuration
- Displaying the transport logs and parameter files

Within a SAP transport domain, all systems share a common or reference configuration held in the transport domain controller. Other SAP systems contain a copy of this reference configuration.

Normally all systems within a transport domain share a common transport directory (usr/sap/trans), although there are situations where this directory is not shared, such as in slow WAN connections, in heterogeneous hardware platforms, or for security reasons. Because of this possibility, there is the concept of the transport group, which indicates a group of SAP systems that share the common transport directory. A transport domain can have more than one transport group.

The next sections explain the main functions and options of the TMS in configuring systems or domains and defining transport routes. The functionality related to managing imports and transport using the TMS is explained in the next section.

Configuring Systems and Domains

The transport domain will contain the SAP system landscape whose transports are being managed jointly. One of the systems will have the role of domain controller and will hold the main reference configuration. For availability and security reasons, this system is normally the production system.

When transaction STMS is started in client 000 on a SAP system, the following happens:

- If the system is already assigned to a transport domain, the initial screen shows the system's role in the domain.
- If the system has not yet been assigned to a transport domain, it will look for file DOMAIN.CFG in the transport directory to locate an existing transport domain.
  - If a domain exists, the system will prompt to join the domain.
  - If a domain does not exist, a new transport domain is created and the current SAP system is assigned as the transport domain controller.

When a transport domain is first created, the TMS system performs several configuration actions:

- Creating a transport domain and a transport group
- Creating the user TMSADM
- Generating RFC destinations required for R/3 communications
- Creating the file DOMAIN.CFG in the bin directory of the common transport directory

This file contains the TMS configuration and is used by systems joining groups and domains for checking existing configurations. Figure 6-8 shows the TMS initial screen.

The TMS allows the definition of a backup domain controller that can take over the functions of the transport domain controller in case of failures.

To define a backup domain controller, select the main transport domain controller system, change its definition (SAP System | Change), then select the Communication tab and enter the system to be used as backup domain controller. Save your entries and distribute your configuration (Extras | Distribute and Activate Configuration).

When configuring the TMS on a SAP system consisting of several application servers, you can specify the application server to be used for TMS functions. Normally you should select the application server with the highest availability, such as the central instance (the one running the message and/or enqueue server).

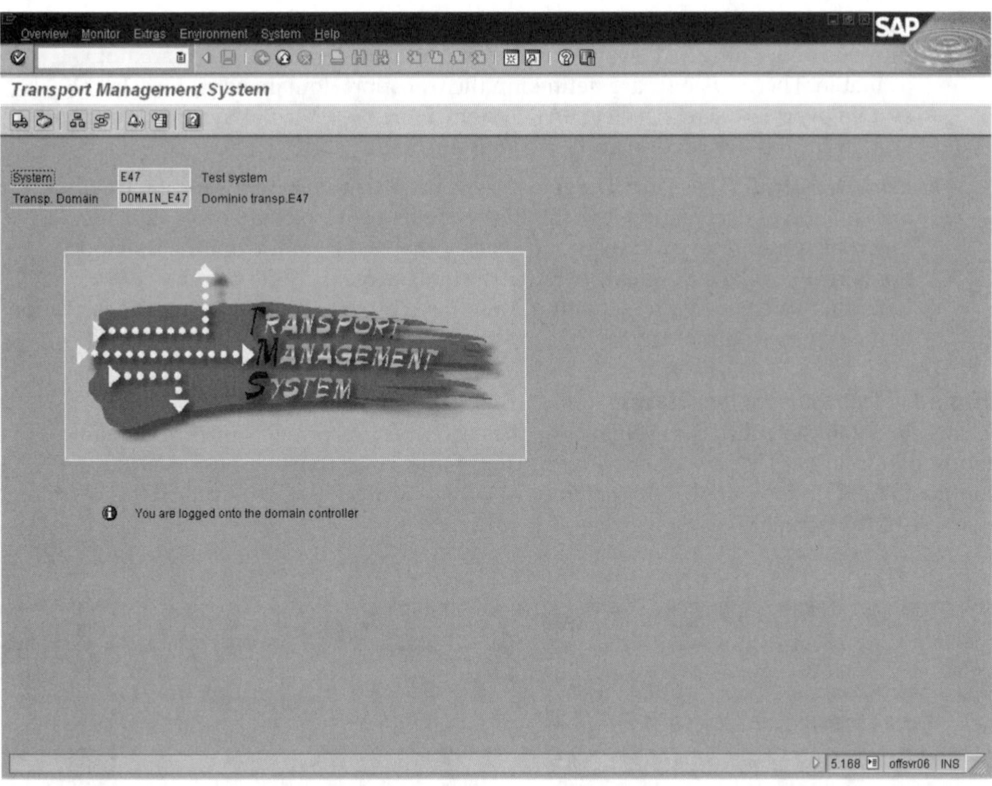

FIGURE 6-8 Transport Management System initial screen (Copyright by SAP AG)

Adding SAP Systems to a Transport Domain

Once the transport domain controller is configured, you have to add other SAP systems within the landscape. TMS allows the definition of the following:

- *Regular SAP systems sharing the common transport directory.* To include these systems, log on to the system to be included in client 000 and start transaction STMS. The TMS will check for the configuration file DOMAIN.CFG and will automatically propose to join the domain. Select the proposal and save your entries. The system status will be waiting to be included in the transport domain. For security reasons, inclusion of systems still needs to be accepted by the transport domain controller. So, log on to the domain controller and go to Systems. The screen will display the new system. Select this new system, and choose from the menu SAP System | Approve.
- *SAP systems without common transport directory.* To include these systems, log on to the system to be included in client 000 and start transaction STMS. In the Configure Transport Domain dialog box, select Other Configuration | Include System in Domain, then enter the hostname and system number. Save your entries. The system status will be waiting to be included in the transport domain. As in the previous case, this system must be accepted by the transport domain controller to be active.

- *Virtual systems.* The TMS includes the functionality of adding virtual systems for the purpose of defining SAP systems that have not yet been installed or are not yet available. These systems are defined in the transport domain controller. In the system overview screen, select SAP System | Create | Virtual System. Enter the system ID and description and save your entries.
- *External systems.* These are like virtual systems but are used for sending transport information or exchanging it with other systems using exchangeable data media. External systems have a transport directory that is different from the transport domain controller's. To create external systems, select SAP System | Create | External System. Enter the system ID and description, and the path and description of the transport directory.

Displaying Transport System Status

At any time you can check the systems and the current status of the transport domain configuration in the TMS systems overview. To do this, enter transaction STMS in the command field. In the initial TMS screen, select Overview | Systems. Figure 6-9 shows an example of this screen.

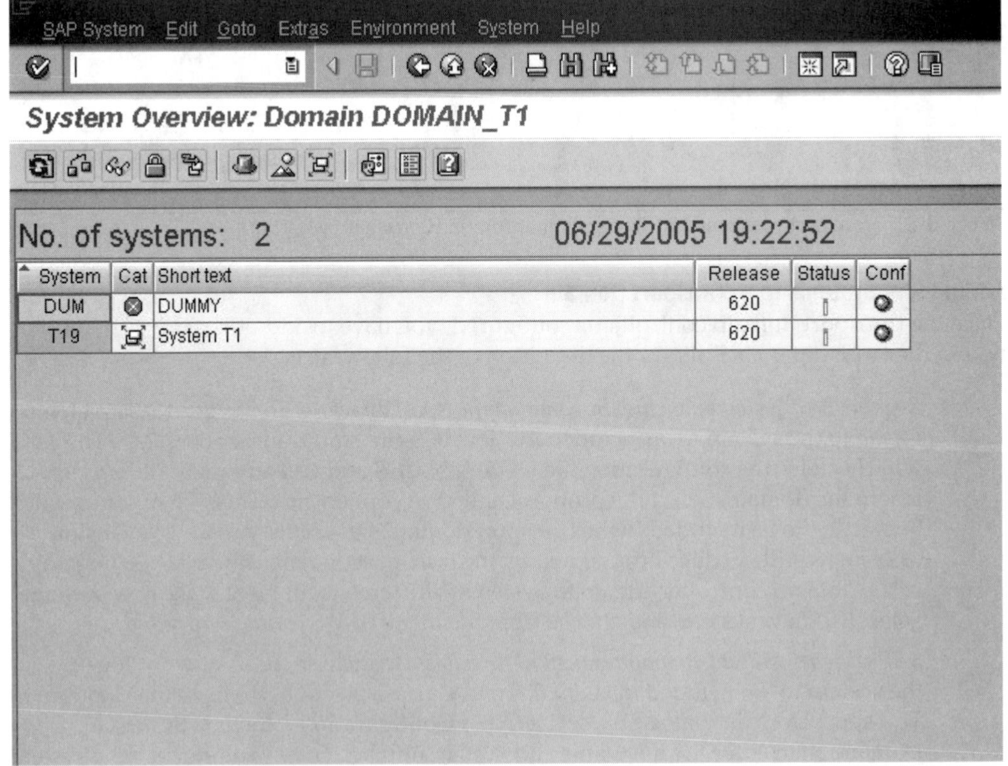

FIGURE 6-9 TMS systems overview (Copyright by SAP AG)

The systems overview shows the current status of each of the systems in the Status column. You can see whether the configuration is up to date and active or whether there was any error in distributing the configuration.

You can display the meaning of the icon symbols by selecting Extras | Legend or by clicking on the Legend icon on the application toolbar. Figure 6-10 shows the meaning of each symbol.

Configuring Transport Routes

Once the domain and systems are configured, you have to specify the transport routes that will be used by the systems. Because many customers' systems landscapes fall into the same categories, the TMS provides some standard system groups that can be used for easily defining routes. When standard system groups are used, the system automatically generates the transport routes. You can select the following standard system groups:

- Single system
- Two-system landscape: development and production
- Three-system landscape: development system, quality assurance system, and production system

Transport routes are configured by selecting Overview | Transport Routes from the initial TMS screen. To define transport routes or use a standard configuration, you have to be in change mode. If you are in display mode, switch by clicking on the Display/Change icon.

If you select the standard configuration, the current configuration of the SAP systems will be replaced by these standard settings, although existing objects or packages will

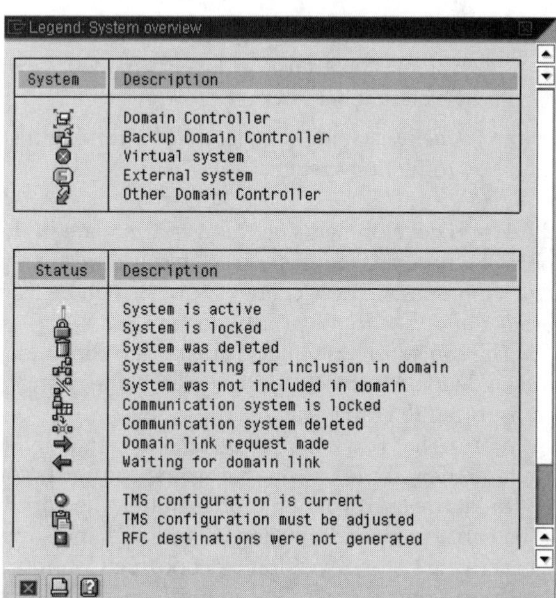

FIGURE 6-10 STMS icon legend (Copyright by SAP AG)

not be deleted. To define a standard configuration, select Configuration | Standard Configuration and then whether it is a Single System, Development and Production System, or Three Systems in Group. Enter your selection and click Continue. Depending on selection, the system will then ask which systems play which role: development, production, or quality assurance. It will then generate the transport routes according to user entries.

If you are not using standard configuration but need to define complex transport systems, you can also use standard settings for initial transport routes and then define additional consolidations or delivery routes.

The TMS includes two types of editors (you can configure editor settings in the Graphical Editor and using the Transport Routes Editor option from Settings in the main menu) for defining and configuring transport routes:

- A *hierarchical list editor,* where systems and transport routes are displayed in a tree structure. To create transport routes in this editor, from the initial TMS screen select Overview | Transport Routes and then, while in change mode, select the Create button on the application toolbar.
- A *graphical editor,* where systems and transport routes are displayed graphically and editing can be performed using the mouse. For accessing the graphical editor, from the hierarchical list editor screen, select Goto | Graphical Editor.

Information on the display areas and on working with the graphical editor can be found in the online documentation. As introduced in the section on transport system concepts, transport routes can either be of the *consolidation* or *delivery* type. For a standard three-system landscape (development, quality assurance, and production), the transport routes are as follows:

- The *consolidation route* links the development system and the quality assurance system. This transport layer is named Z<SID>, where <SID> is the system ID of the development system.
- A *delivery route* is generated for linking the quality assurance system and the production system.

When developments or changes are made in the development system that include objects whose package refers to the standard transport layer, these changes are recorded in change requests. These change requests will be transported first to the quality assurance system and then to the production system.

The transport system also creates the consolidation route SAP that is used when changes are made to SAP objects. In these cases, the changes are recorded in *repair tasks* that can be transported the same way.

Notice that you will only be able to create delivery routes for existing consolidation routes. An example of transport route configuration is shown in Figure 6-11.

In Figure 6-11, you will notice in the title bar that the system includes a version number. When an active configuration is modified and saved, the system creates a new version. You can activate a stored version by choosing Configuration | Get Other Version from the transport domain controller on the Transport Route screen.

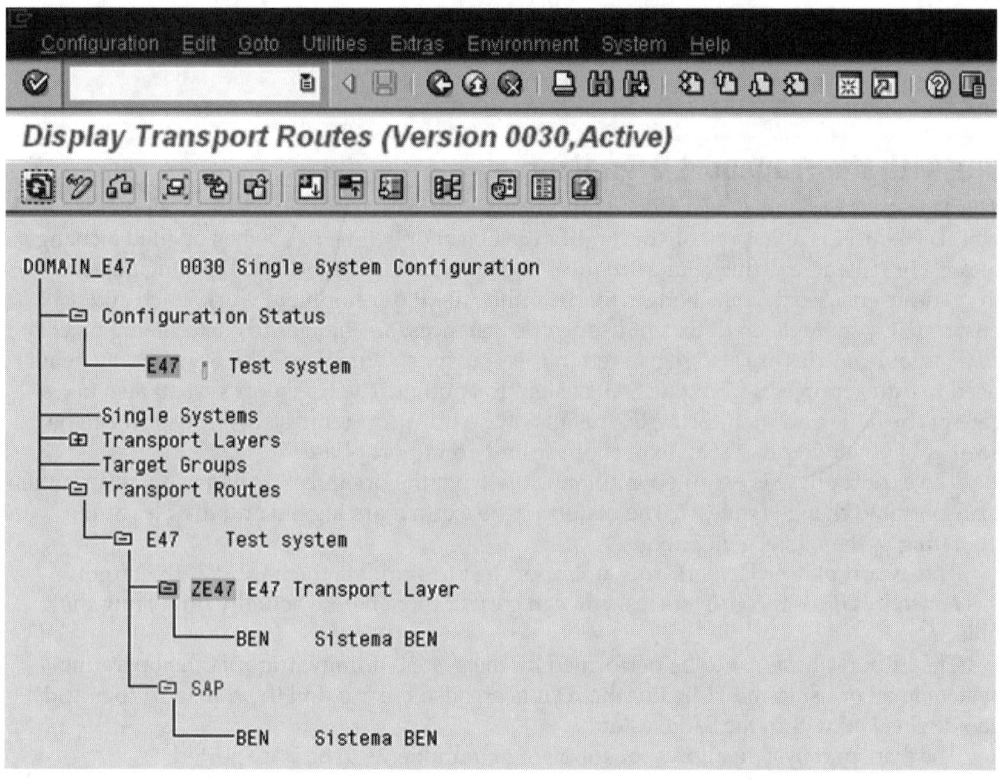

FIGURE 6-11 Transport route configuration (Copyright by SAP AG)

Distributing and Verifying TMS Configuration

Before distributing the TMS configuration to other systems in the group, you should first check the configuration. There are several checking options available that should behave without errors before the TMS can function properly. If any errors are found, review your configuration or network settings before proceeding.

Within the Transport Routes Overview screen, select Configuration | Check | Request Consistency and then either Local or All Systems.

Because all SAP systems in a transport domain communicate using RFC connections, you should also check these RFC connections in the TMS system overview. Select Overview | Systems, and then from the Systems screen, select SAP System | Check | Connection Test.

To check whether the transport control program tp and the TPPARAM file are correctly configured, select SAP System | Check | Transport Tool from the Systems Overview screen.

Additionally, you should also verify the availability of the transport directories in all systems within the transport domain. Select SAP System | Check | Transport Directory from the Systems Overview screen.

When the configuration of the transport domain controller is complete, the next step is to distribute the configuration to all other R/3 systems within the transport domain. To do this, select Configuration | Distribute and Activate from the Transport Routes Overview screen. You can also select Extras | Distribute and Activate Configuration from the Systems Overview screen.

Working with the Transport Organizer

The Transport Organizer is activated automatically every time a user edits a repository object. The user is able to create or modify the object only if he or she has opened a change request or uses an existing change request in the Transport Organizer. Entering objects in requests ensures that all changes made in the ABAP development workbench and customizing are registered. Except in specific instances, all changes to customizing objects such as table entries are also registered in the Transport Organizer. The transport system is used to transfer objects from one SAP system to another. The transport system also takes care of checking and monitoring the results of the transport requests. A transport can be seen as having two phases: an export phase and an import phase.

The export phase is executed automatically from the organizers when users release their transportable change requests. The results of the exports are logged and the files at the operating system level generated.

The export phase also performs an import test to simulate the import at the target system so if it finds inconsistencies, you can correct them before actually importing the objects.

The import phase has to be performed by the system administrator at the operating system level or using the TMS, but the results are also recorded in the transport logs and can be checked within the SAP system.

The transport system allows the following components to be transported:

- New or corrected objects created by customers
- Standard objects from the SAP system
- Table entries

The transportable objects are virtually any SAP objects, including programs, function modules, forms, documentation, table definitions (structure), data elements, domains, screens, menus, print definitions, and number ranges; also, as stated in the preceding list, table entries that are not by themselves development objects, but data, are included, too.

Objects or table entries can be transported whether they have been modified or not.

The following sections explain how to proceed to perform transports successfully by observing the available options and restrictions of the SAP system.

The transport control program tp, which ultimately performs imports and exports at the operating system level, is explained later in this chapter.

Creating Change Requests

Although there are two main types or categories of change requests, SYST (workbench) and CUST (customizing), the flexibility and features of the Change and Transport Organizers are further enhanced, with the possibility of relocating objects, instituting packages, copying objects, including requests within requests, and so on. All of these special functions are performed using the Transport Organizer (SE01).

The following sections and examples deal with the most common and typical tasks to be performed when working with regular workbench and customization tasks and change requests.

There are two basic ways to create a change request:

- *Automatically.* When creating or modifying an object, or when performing customization settings, the system displays the dialog box for creating a change request. It is important to note that any users who need to perform development on the system or modification to SAP object originals must be registered using the SAP Software Change Registration (SSCR).
- *Manually.* Create the request from the Transport Organizer, and then enter required attributes and insert objects.

The manual creation of transports is sometimes very useful when transporting copies of objects to systems outside the system group, when copying specific table entries among systems, or for solving synchronization problems. To create a change request manually in the initial Transport Organizer requests screen, click on the Create icon on the application toolbar. The system will display a new dialog screen in which it will ask to specify a type of request. Figure 6-12 shows this dialog box. The two main types of requests are as follows:

- *Workbench requests.* Regular workbench requests (category SYST) that will contain objects with the correct packages, and that will have a transport layer and a target system
- *Customizing requests.* Change requests that will contain customization settings that can either be client dependent (CUST category) or applicable to all clients (SYST category)

Other types of requests that you can manually create are as follows:

- *Copy of transports.* Change requests that can be used to merge objects of different change requests or select a smaller set of objects of another request.
- *Relocations.* Allows you to move development with three options: (1) Transport objects without package change. This can be done to develop objects in another system on a temporary basis. (2) Transport objects with package change allow reassignment of objects in the current and imported systems. (3) Relocation of complete package allows all objects to be organized in one transport.

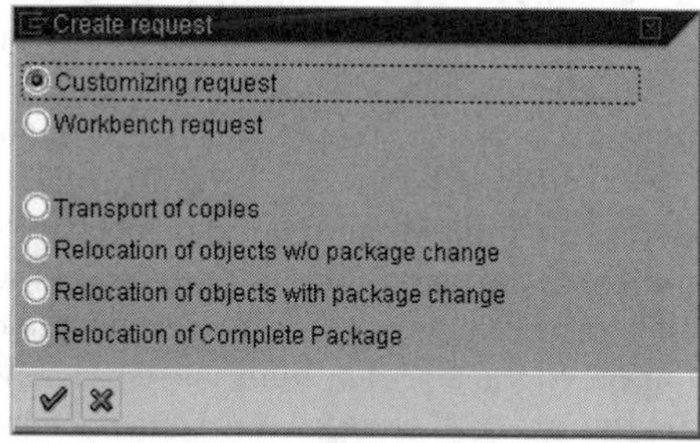

FIGURE 6-12 Create request dialog box (Copyright by SAP AG)

- *Piece lists.* Lists that allow a user-defined request name. The lists cannot be released or transported. They can be used as a template to add objects to another request by using the Include Objects function in SE01.

You will also see the following two types of requests in the Transport Organizer:

- *Local requests.* Requests that will not be transported, mostly because they are meant for use in editing or creating objects for test purposes.
- *Unclassified requests.* Requests whose type is not initially assigned or empty but will be manually entered when appropriate. This option is only visible on the requests overview lists.

To manually create a change request and associated tasks, click on the Create icon and specify a type of request. The system will display a dialog box like the one shown in Figure 6-12. Normally you only have to specify a short descriptive text and enter the usernames to participate in this request. The system will create a task for each of the usernames.

You can also specify special request attributes for qualifying and evaluating change requests. SAP provides several standard attributes, like SAPCORR, SAPNOTE, and so on. You can add your own by editing table WBOATTR using transaction SM30.

Releasing Tasks and Requests

When new developments, corrections, or customizing work is complete, team leaders or project managers must release their tasks. To release a task, go to the initial Transport Organizer screen. As request types, select the Transportable and Modifiable check boxes, and deselect other options. Then, click on the Display pushbutton, or press ENTER. The system will display a list with the change requests that have not yet been released. To list the tasks, open up the change requests by clicking the + sign on the folder signs. The system shows a screen similar to the one shown in Figure 6-13. Position the cursor on the task to be released and click on the Release button on the application toolbar. You can figure out which tasks have been already released by the color coding (Utilities | Legend). If the task is a repair, the system will display a dialog box asking whether to confirm the repair automatically.

When releasing a task, the system will automatically show the documentation screen for entering whatever descriptive text should be held with the tasks. Enter your documentation in the editor screen, click the Save button, and then click the Back icon. The system will inform you that the task is being released in response to the change request. If there were any locks on development objects included within the task, those locks are transferred to the change request, along with the documentation for the tasks.

When developers finish working on their tasks and have released them, then requests themselves can be released. This process is almost the same as releasing tasks. Just position the cursor on a transportable change request whose tasks have already been released, and click the Release button on the application toolbar. The system will display a message on the screen indicating that the objects are being exported, or you might get an error message if there is any problem with the objects within the change request. If the release is normal, an export run takes place, exporting the object data to operating system files in which the import to the target system takes place. When the request is released the locks on the objects are removed, allowing users to make further changes.

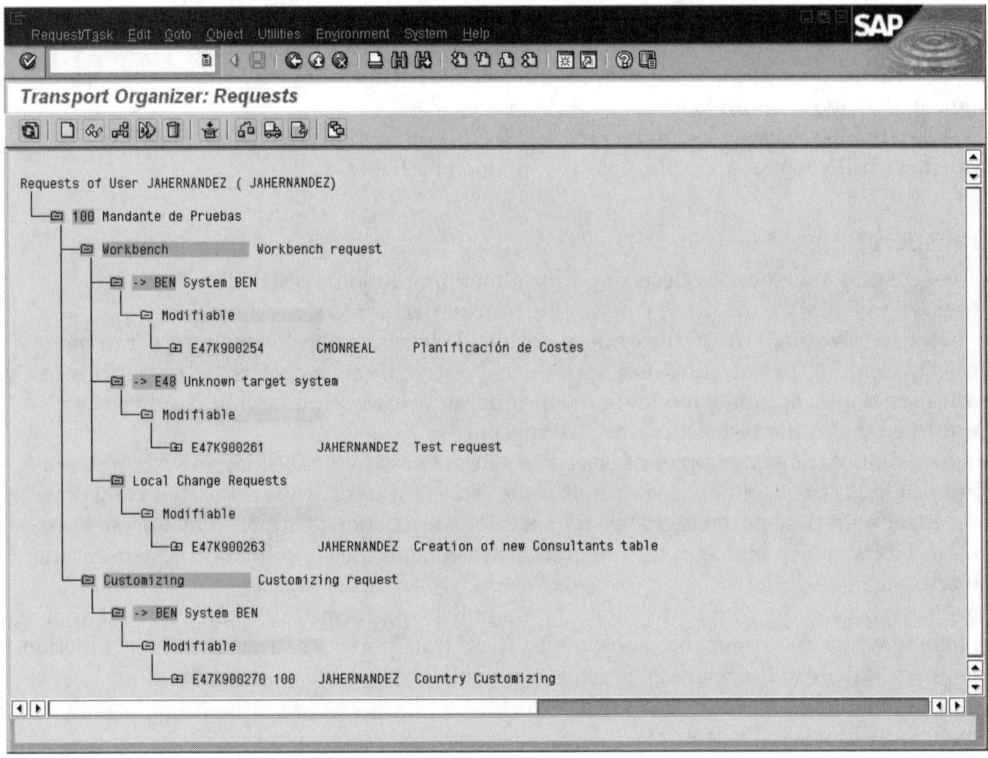

FIGURE 6-13 Requests display screen (Copyright by SAP AG)

Monitoring Transports and Repairs

The square box Global Information on the right side of the initial Transport Organizer screen in extended view (transaction SE01) contains two stoplights with a summary of the transports and repairs performed in and out of the system. Click the pushbuttons to display the associated change requests.

The change requests corresponding to the selected categories are displayed in a hierarchical list. You can navigate this list, from which you can see the transport logs at the last level of the hierarchy. Double-clicking on the line will display the transport log screen, in which you can select the level of detail to be displayed.

An example of the transport log and the codes is shown later in the section entitled "Checking Transport Results," where the return codes of the logs are also explained. If you find the reason for the error and have corrected it, you can select Transport/Repair | Error Corrected from the menu bar of this screen, which will delete the error from the display. This function is recorded in the transport action log. To see the action log, select Goto | Action Log from the menu bar.

You can enter criteria for searching and displaying different types of change requests. To display an individual change request or task, or to perform a search, select the Display tabstrip on the main Transport Organizer screen. In the input field you can enter a request or task number and click ENTER. If you click the possible entries arrow on this dialog box, the system shows an additional screen for entering criteria and searching requests.

You can also select the request from different user. This is done by entering the user name in the Owner input field.

From the list display, also in hierarchical form, you can navigate and expand the branches until you reach specific objects contained in the tasks.

Transport Rules

When creating transport requests or performing imports, some restrictions must be observed to maintain the consistency of the transported objects.

Transports cannot overwrite or delete original objects or objects under repair in the target system. In special situations, imports that overwrite such objects can be performed with special unconditional modes of the tp program. However, this should only be performed under the instructions of SAP specialists.

You cannot transport copies of objects to a target system (consolidation system) that is not included the consolidation transport route. This is automatically set by the Transport Organizer with transportable change requests. The restriction is imposed by the package of the objects, which indicates the integration system and the consolidation system for the objects.

Transports to any recipient system should only be performed from the consolidation system to which the system has subscribed. These transports are automatically included in the import queue of the recipient systems, as defined in the delivery routes.

Specifying Objects to Transport

When working with tasks and change requests directly with the Workbench Organizer, the object list is generated automatically when the tasks are released. The task numbers are included within the object list of the transportable change requests.

But you can also enter objects to be transported using the organizer object list maintenance tools, which provide utilities for creating objects lists, copying and pasting, and so on.

To create or modify an object list, select the change request from the request overview screen. You can either include the object directly in the change request or in tasks. Position your cursor on the change request or task, and double-click on it.

The Transport Organizer shows the Change Request/Task screen. Select the Objects tabstrip. Click on the Display/Change icon to access the edit mode. The system displays the Maintain Object List window as shown in Figure 6-14.

In this screen you can manually enter the objects you wish to transport. There are eight columns:

- *Short Description.* This is filled automatically once the object is entered and is taken from the object description.
- *Program ID.* The program ID is part of the name of an object type for its use in the Workbench Organizer and the transport system. Press F4 or click on the possible entries arrow to display a list of allowable values. Normally, the R3TR value is used for ensuring the consistency of all related objects in a transport. For example, if you want to transport a new table between systems, the R3TR program ID ensures the

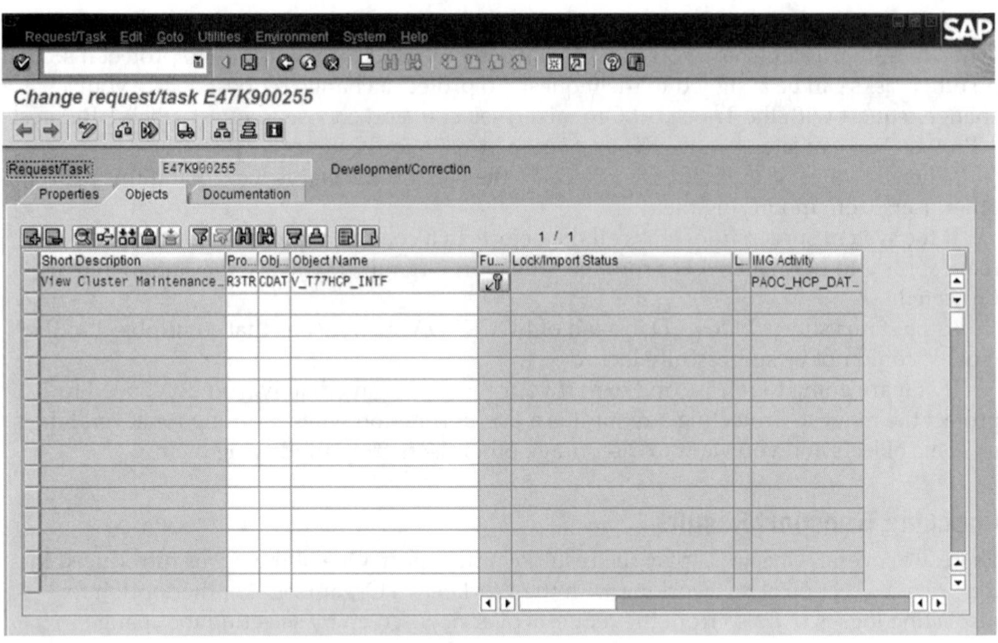

Figure 6-14 Object list maintenance screen (Copyright by SAP AG)

transport of all the needed and related objects for the table, including the data elements and domains.

- *Object Type.* This is the object type. The system uses this type to perform the needed operations at the target system. There are hundreds of types, which you can look up by pressing the F4 function key. Most typical are *PROG*, which means ABAP source code and CUA definitions; *TABL* for table definitions; and *TABU* for table contents.
- *Object Name.* This is the object name, for example, a table name, a program name, a view name, and so forth.
- *Function.* The function column is normally grayed out. It can be used to specify special functions for an object entry. For example, suppose you want to transport the contents of a long table, but only want to transport those entries that match a particular key value. You can do this with function K. To access this field, click over the Function icon. Some object types do not have any object function.
- *Lock/Import Status.* The Object Status field is automatically maintained by the system and is mainly a lock indicator.
- *Language.* This is either blank or filled out automatically to denote the language used for the object definition.
- *IMG Activity.* If the object has been included from an IMG (Implementation Guide) activity, this would be filled out automatically with the activity that wrote the object in the request.

Protecting a Transport Request

When temporarily finished working on a change request, you can decide to protect it so that no other tasks can be assigned to the request. To protect a change request, locate your change request with the Transport Organizer, select it, and choose Request/Task | Request | Protect. You can later remove the protection at your convenience.

When a request is *protected,* the objects in the lists get the status locked and this prevents other users from modifying them.

If the system successfully locks all the objects in a change request, the status of the request is set to LOCKEDALL. From the Transport Organizer, you see the status as Protected.

If the status shows LOCKED instead of LOCKEDALL, it means that some object in the request could not be successfully locked.

If you are going to release and export your requests immediately, you don't need to protect the request. Protecting a request is a useful function when working for several days on some objects and you want to discourage other users from modifying them.

Checking Transport Results

There are several ways to display the result of a transport. One of them was introduced in the previous section about working with the Workbench Organizer. Another option for displaying logs is to do so from the requests overview screen by selecting the change requests and then choosing Goto | Transport Log. Figure 6-15 shows an example of the overview of transport logs for a request. Transport logs only exist when the release of the change request has been performed.

There are two main types of logs:

- *Action log,* which logs and displays actions that have taken place: export, test import, import, and so forth
- *Transport log,* which keeps a record of the log files generated by the transport steps

The transport log includes several levels of detail, from a summary information screen to a more detailed output where you can even see exactly which objects have been transported, how long it took, and possible warnings or errors. Figure 6-16 shows an example of a transport log.

Transport logs have several levels of details that you can expand or compress using the icons in the application toolbar. In Figure 6-16 the transport log for the main import in the production system is completely expanded. Additionally, the upper line on the display shows the location of the log file at the operating system level.

The most important information on the transport log is the return code, which indicates whether the transport was successfully performed. The codes have the following meanings:

- *0.* The transport was successful.
- *4.* The transport has at least one warning message. The objects in the request have been transported but the system warns that some action might have been improperly set in the transport, for example, when importing an object to a system that was not the original target system.

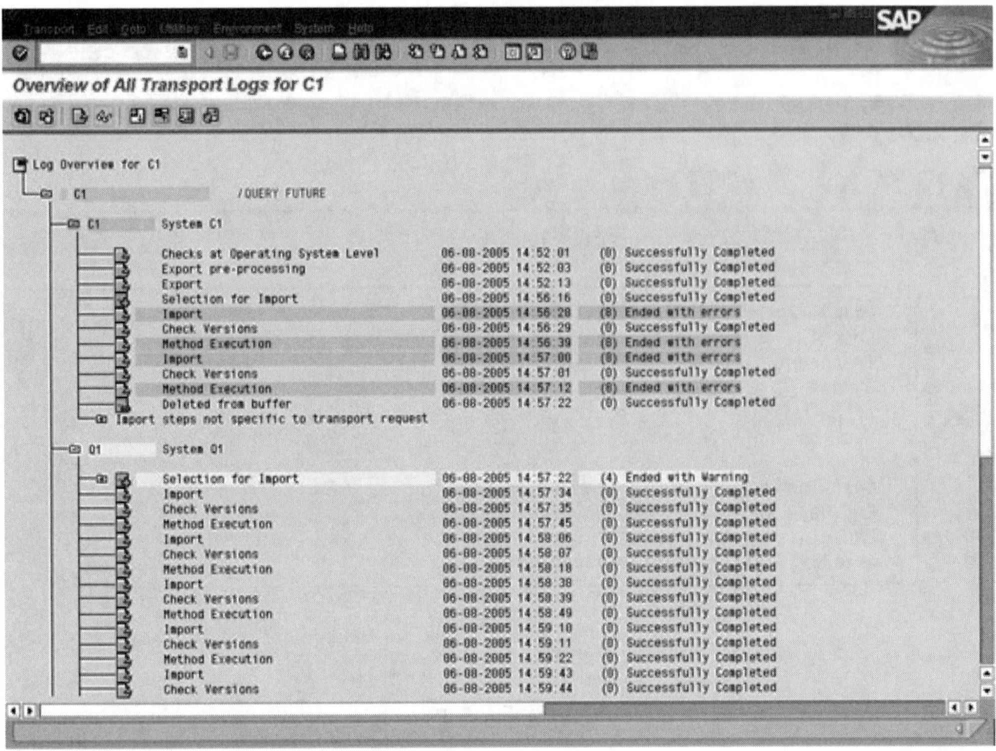

FIGURE 6-15 Overview of transport logs for a request (Copyright by SAP AG)

- *8.* The transport has some severe errors that prevented the objects from being transported. You should look at the error messages and take a corrective action before performing the transport again.
- *12 or higher.* The system has flagged a fatal error. These errors normally are not related to the transport content itself but to some SAP system error that can be related to the operating system or to the database system. In such cases, perform the basic troubleshooting with the CCMS tools and contact the SAP hotline or look up your error messages in SAPnet.

Object Attributes

As mentioned earlier, the attributes of an object offer important information that directly relates to the way the object can be handled by the Workbench Organizer and the transport system.

The attributes for all objects in the system are held in the TADIR table, which is the repository object directory. This table can be displayed from the general table maintenance function (transactions SM30) or from the data browser (transaction SE16). Only authorized users can maintain this table, however; modifying entries from this table could have

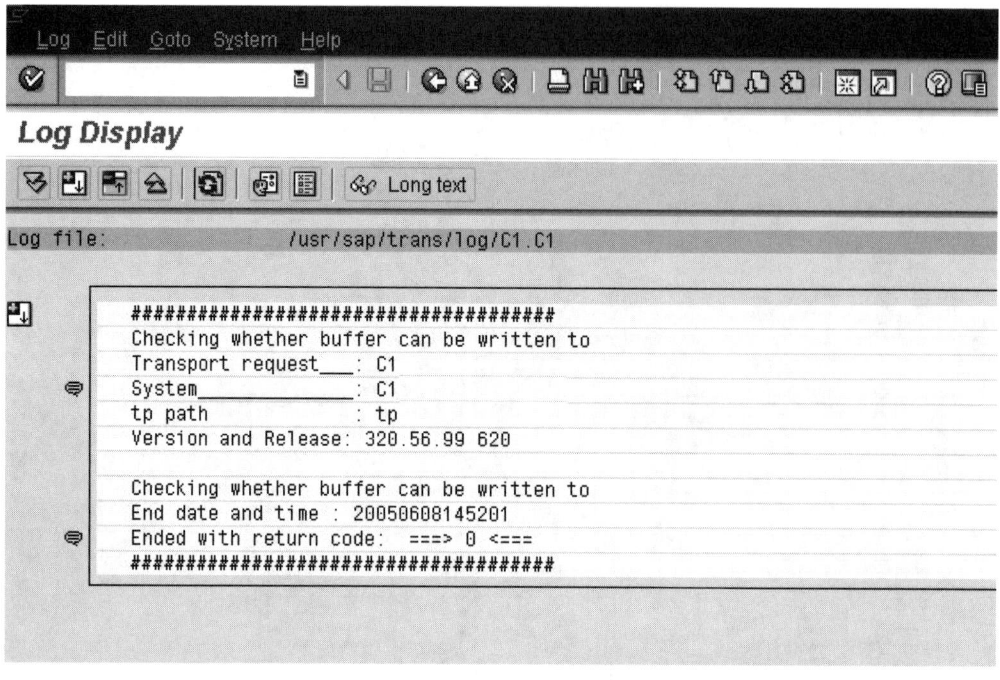

FIGURE 6-16 Example of a transport log (Copyright by SAP AG)

unexpected results and should be avoided except if instructed by a SAP note or by SAP support personnel.

From the transport system there are other menu options to display the TADIR table or only the records containing the attributes related to a particular object. For example,

- Selecting Object | Object Directory Entry from the request overview screen, when an object has been previously selected
- From the menu of the object list maintenance screen, selecting an object and then choosing Goto | Transport Organizer Tool.

Selecting an object and using one of these options allows you to see the following attributes:

- *Program ID, object type,* and *object name.* The identification of an object for the Workbench Organizer and the transport system. The meaning of these fields is explained in the previous section entitled "Specifying Objects to Transport."
- *Author.* The user ID of the person who created the object or is responsible for it.
- *Package.* The package of the object, which specifies the integration and consolidation system for the object; therefore, it restricts the allowable transport routes to other systems.

- *Original system (SRCSYSTEM),* for which the object is considered original. It could be the same system in which it was originally created or can be another one if the object was transported changing the authorization.
- An *entry flag (SRCDEP),* which indicates whether the object is under repair or is system specific. In these cases, the object is protected from being overwritten by other transports.

To find additional information or get reports on tasks, change requests, repairs, and so forth, use the Workbench Organizer tools (transaction SE03), which are available as an icon in the application toolbar on the organizer screens.

Transport Organizer Tools

The utilities tools for the transport system provide a collection of standard and expert functions, mainly for use by the system administrator, and provide facilities for reporting, unlocking, setting the system change options, and other advanced functions over the objects controlled by the Workbench Organizer.

To use some of the expert functions included within these tools, users need the CTS _ALL authorization. This screen can be accessed from the initial Workbench Organizer menu by selecting Goto | Transport Organizer Tools. Alternatively, use transaction SE03 in the command field.

To get additional information about the actions or report that each of the functions perform, click on a line and select Goto | Documentation from the menu bar.

Performing Transports with the TMS

Up to release SAP R/3 3.1H, the import phase of transports was always performed at the operating system level. Since the introduction of the TMS, there is a full suite of functions for managing transports and performing imports from within the SAP systems. The TMS uses the tp program for performing imports and other functions.

You can still use all the functionality available with the transport control program tp and even with R3trans. The following sections cover these programs in great detail.

The TMS includes all the security measures to ensure the proper order of imports. It does allow special preliminary transports and the use of unconditional modes, and other special queue functions, similar to the ones found when using tp.

All the transportable change requests that have been released are now displayed in the import queues of the target systems. When releasing change requests, the system creates several files in the transport directory (data, control file) and inserts an entry in the import queue of the target system. The import queue is the same as the system import buffer, and as such the file is located under the buffer directory.

To access the import queues, access the initial TMS screen Tools | Administration | Transports | Transport Management System (transaction code STMS) and then click on the Imports icon on the application toolbar, or select Overview | Imports. The system will display the import overview screen, with several columns including the system within the transport domain, the description, the number of requests in the queue, and the status.

To display the contents of an import queue, double-click on one of the systems. Figure 6-17 shows an example of an import queue. For performance reasons the TMS only reads

Requests for C19: 57 / 173 06-08-2005 09:43:37

Number	Request	Owner	Short Text	St
115	SAPKVSDF61	SAPUSER	Default	
116	L9CK178572	C5055248	BSI 6.0 TUB 299 (T5UTN, T5UTT, BTXAUTH, BTXFORM)	
117	L9CK178140	C5057955	BSI 6.0 TUB 297 (BTXTAXC) for all clients	
118	L9CK178470	C5055248	BSI 6.0 TUB 298 (T5UTX) for all clients	
119	L9CK178571	C5055248	BSI 6.0 TUB 299 (T5UTA, B, R, W, D) for all rel(CUM)	
120	L9CK178139	C5057955	BSI 6.0 TUB 297 (T5UTZ) for release 46 and up (CUM)	
121	L9CK178570	C5055248		
122	L9CK178795	C5055248	BSI 6.0 TUB 300 (T5UTN, T5UTT, BTXAUTH, BTXFORM)	
123	L9CK178794	C5055248	BSI 6.0 TUB 300 (T5UTA, B, R, W, D) for all rel(CUM)	
124	L9CK178939	C5055248	BSI 6.0 TUB 301 (T5UTA, B, R, W, D) for all rel(CUM)	
125	L9CK178940	C5055248	BSI 6.0 TUB 301 (T5UTN, T5UTT, BTXAUTH, BTXFORM)	
126	L9CK178942	C5055248	BSI 6.0 TUB 301 (T5UTZ) for release 46 and up (CUM)	
127	L9CK178943	C5055248	BSI 6.0 TUB 301 (BTXTAXC) for all clients	
128	L9CK179175	C5055248	BSI 6.0 TUB 302 (T5UTA, B, R, W, D) for all rel(CUM)	
129	L9CK179176	C5055248	BSI 6.0 TUB 302 (T5UTN, T5UTT, BTXAUTH, BTXFORM)	
130	L9CK179178	C5055248	BSI 6.0 TUB 302 (T5UTZ) for release 46 and up (CUM)	
131	L9CK179179	C5055248	BSI 6.0 TUB 302 (BTXTAXC) for all clients	
132	L9CK179313	C5055248	BSI 6.0 TUB 303 (T5UTA, B, R, W, D) for all rel(CUM)	
133	L9CK179314	C5055248	BSI 6.0 TUB 303 (T5UTN, T5UTT, BTXAUTH, BTXFORM)	
134	L9CK179316	C5055248	BSI 6.0 TUB 303 (T5UTZ) for release 46 and up (CUM)	
135	L9CK179317	C5055248	BSI 6.0 TUB 303 (BTXTAXC) for all clients	
136	L9CK179802	C5055248		
137	L9CK179803	C5055248	BSI 6.0 TUB 304 (T5UTN, T5UTT, BTXAUTH, BTXFORM)	
138	L9CK179805	C5055248		
139	L9CK179806	C5055248	BSI 6.0 TUB 304 (BTXTAXC) for all clients	
140	L9CK179943	C5055248		
141	L9CK179944	C5055248	BSI 6.0 TUB 305 (T5UTN, T5UTT, BTXAUTH, BTXFORM)	
142	L9CK180029	C5055248	BSI 6.0 TUB 306 (T5UTA, B, R, W, D) for all rel(CUM)	
143	L9CK180030	C5055248	BSI 6.0 TUB 306 (T5UTN, T5UTT, BTXAUTH, BTXFORM)	
144	L9CK180032	C5055248	BSI 6.0 TUB 306 (T5UTZ) for release 46 and up (CUM)	
145	L9CK180033	C5055248	BSI 6.0 TUB 306 (BTXTAXC) for all clients	

FIGURE 6-17 Import queue (Copyright by SAP AG)

import queues the first time it accesses them. If you need the latest queue status, select the Refresh function.

From the import queue you can display the object list, the logs, the documentation, or the owner. You can do this from the Request | Display menu.

To begin the transport process, transport all the requests in the import queue into the quality assurance system. This will automatically insert these requests into the import queue of the delivery systems (normally production systems). Then users should check and test what has been transported into the quality assurance system. If tests are verified, the next step is to transport the full import queue into the production system. Transport administrators will normally select the Start Import function, which will request the target client and start importing the queue in the order in which the change requests were previously released. This function is equivalent to the tp import all command.

Imports can be started from any R/3 system within the transport domain; however, if you are logged onto any system but the target system, TMS will show a logon window for providing logon information. TMS will establish an RFC connection and start the tp program in the target system.

When tp starts the import, the system closes the RFC connection. When imports have been successful, they are automatically inserted in the import queue for the next system in the transport route.

The status column of an import queue can show different statuses. You can display these statuses by clicking on the Key icon on the application toolbar. The queue can have the following statuses:

- *Open* for new requests being added
- *Closed,* meaning that the newly added requests will not be imported during the next full import
- *Running*
- *Errors occurred during import*
- *Import terminated*
- *Import queue could not be read*

Besides importing all requests in the queue with the Start Import function, the TMS includes many other options. Following is a list of the main functions that can be performed using the TMS import facilities:

- *Closing an import queue.* This is the function of setting a stop mark for preventing imports of change requests that were released and added to the queue after a certain time. To do this, select the queue and choose Queue | Close from the menu. The TMS then sets a mark so that new requests are positioned after the mark and only requests before the mark will be imported in the next import.
- *Opening the import queue.* Select Queue | Open to delete the stop mark.
- *Adding requests to the queue.* You can manually add a change request to an import queue by selecting Extras | Other Requests | Add. Normally this function should not be used because requests are automatically added. This is equivalent to the tp addtobuffer command.
- *Removing requests from the queue.* You can also remove a particular request from the import queue. Select the request, and from the menu choose Request | Delete. SAP's recommendation is not to delete, but to create a new change request with the correction.
- *Performing single imports.* This process is known as performing preliminary imports, as opposed to standard import, in which the full queue would be included. To perform the import of an individual change request, click on its line in the import queue and select Request | Import. The system displays a dialog box for entering some information. Figure 6-18 shows an example that also displays the expert mode. With the expert mode you can set unconditional modes just as with the tp program. Options are as follows:
  - Ignore that the transport request has already been imported (unconditional mode 1)
  - Overwrite originals (unconditional mode 2)
  - Overwrite objects in unconfirmed repairs (unconditional mode 6)
  - Ignore invalid transport type (unconditional mode 9)

Enter the system client and options and click the Start Import icon.

FIGURE 6-18 Transport request import options (Copyright by SAP AG)

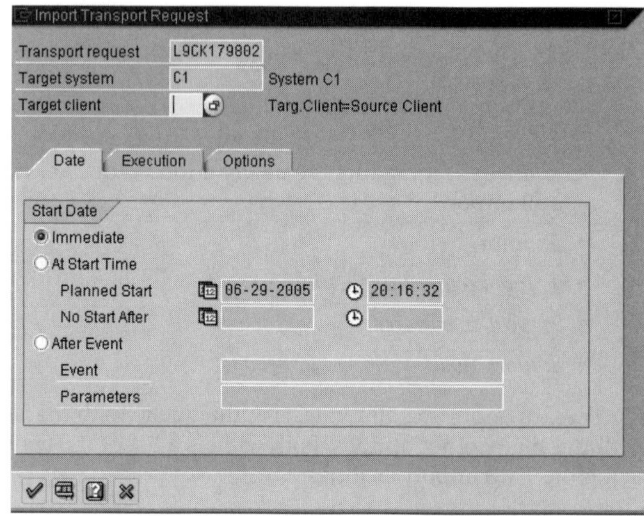

SAP does not recommend this process because there is some risk of creating inconsistencies. However, to minimize the risk, when a single import is performed it remains in the queue and will be reimported the next time the full queue is imported. This guarantees that exports and imports are performed in the correct order.

- *Forwarding a change request.* On certain occasions, you can select the function Request | Forward to send a change request to a system outside the predefined transport routes.
- *Transporting between transport groups or foreign domains.* Under the Extras | Other Request menu, you have several options for reading the import queues on systems whose transport directories are not shared and that therefore are located on other transport groups or domains. You can still perform transports among these systems, but the import queues of target systems must first be adjusted.

Using tp, the Transport Control Program

The transport control program tp is the SAP program that administrators use for performing and planning transports between systems and also in upgrades of the SAP systems. The tp program is used by the CTO and the TMS.

The tp program uses other special programs and utilities to perform its functions. Mainly, it calls the R3trans utility program. However, tp offers a more extensive control of the transport process, ensuring the correct sequence of the exported/imported objects, because the wrong order can cause severe inconsistencies in the system.

Administrators normally use tp for performing imports; it can also be used for exports, although the normal export process is automatic when releasing change requests. The export phase extracts the objects from the database and places them on files at the operating system level, together with a control file and a transport log. The export phase is done in the source system.

The import phase has to be performed in the target system. In this phase, the exported objects are inserted into the database following the instructions on the control file that came along with the data files of the export.

Importing data causes a refresh (a synchronization) of the SAP buffers, which can cause performance problems if this is done often. For that reason, it is a good practice to schedule imports at times of less interactive work, such as at night or on weekends.

Before you can start using the tp program, you should ensure that the tp program is set up correctly and the requirements met. The next section explains how to set up the tp program.

Setting Up the tp Program

The tp program is located in the standard runtime directory of the SAP system. This directory is /usr/sap/SYS/<SID>/exe/run. It is automatically copied in the SAP installation process.

The requirements for using the tp program are as follows:

- The transport directory /usr/sap/trans must exist. This is a requirement for the SAP system installation, so it should be there. Watch out for the correct ownership, which you set to the SAP administrator user account, <sid>adm.
- The transport directory must be accessible by every R/3 system taking part in the transport process. This also includes all the application servers. If an application server cannot access the /usr/sap/trans directory, then you must make sure that the background process for imports doesn't run in this system; otherwise it will fail because it will not find the needed files in the directory.
- The Workbench Organizer and the transport system must be initialized as indicated in a previous section with transaction SE06, which initializes and updates the needed control tables for transports.
- Transports are only allowed between systems with different names (different SIDs).
- Both the source system and the target system must have at least two background processes each. This is because the transport process automatically schedules and releases the needed jobs.
- You must log on as user <sid>adm to perform transports. Imports with tp always have to be performed in the target system, whereas exports with tp must be done in the source systems.
- The tp global parameter file, TPPARAM, must be maintained, specifying at least the hostname of the systems taking part in the transport process. This file is explained in a later in this section of this chapter.
- The import dispatcher process RDDIMPDP and RDDIMPD_ CLIENT_<nnn> should be scheduled as background jobs in every system where imports will be performed. These jobs are automatically scheduled by the system when performing a client copy. If for any reason they are deleted, you can schedule these jobs by running report RDDNEWPP. These jobs are defined as periodic event triggered, meaning that tp sends a signal (an event) to the R/3 system and the job starts. These events are SAP_TRIGGER_RDDIMPDP and SAP_TRIGGER_RDDIMPDP_CLIENT.

The Transport System at the Operating System Level: Users and Directories

In a group of related SAP systems that are going to perform transports among themselves, a correct configuration of users at operating system level and of the file directory structure is essential. In a standard R/3 installation, the system correctly sets both the users and the directories. There might be, however, some circumstances where the configuration might change unintentionally or from previous system settings.

The standard transport directory is /usr/sap/trans and is shared by all the systems. Normally, one of the systems holds it physically while others access it via NFS (network file system) or with file shares. This is done so all the systems have access to the exported files and transport logs. Otherwise, a manual copy of the needed files must be performed.

It is equally important to give the right system authorization for accessing this directory. All the subdirectories should have <sid>adm as the owner. To avoid permissions problems, the normal setting is to give read, write, and execute access both to the owner and to the SAP administrator group number, *sapsys*. At the same time, this group should be defined the same in all SAP servers. If the group number has been manually created, modified, or previously used by other applications, problems might arise.

Exports are always automatically performed by SAP systems using <sid>adm. Imports are performed at the operating system level in the target system and users must be logged on as user <sid>adm to guarantee correct file permissions.

The installation creates the subdirectory structure beneath /usr/sap/trans. The subdirectories are as follows:

- *bin.* Contains the TPPARAM file, which is the global transport parameter file. Normally, the <sid>adm user positions in this directory to perform imports so that the tp program locates the TPPARAM at the default directory. Otherwise, the call to tp must include the location of the parameter file. Optionally, this directory might contain other files such as T_OFF.ALL or T_OFF.<SID>. These files can be used to deactivate permission for all or a particular system to perform exports.
- *data.* This directory contains the transport data files.
- *log.* Under this directory, all the individual and general transport logs, statistics, and trace files are located. Administrators should refer to this directory for troubleshooting functions.
- *buffer.* Contains special buffer files with the SID of every system in the transport group. These files include control information on the transports that will be imported into other systems and the order of them. A good monitoring and display of the buffers improves the management of all the transport processes.
- *cofiles.* This is the control file directory containing information about the steps of the transportable change requests as well as the return codes.
- *sapnames.* Contains information on SAP users performing exports and keeps track of the status for each change request.
- *tmp.* This is the temporary directory containing some auxiliary temporary files with control flags, semaphores, and so forth.

- *actlog.* This directory includes action log files for all the tasks and change requests. These files are only accessed and modified by the R/3 system.
- *olddata.* Contains archived transport files from other transport directories that are generated when the administrators perform the tp clearold command.

Additionally, the system might have two more optional directories:

- *backup.* This directory is used if you are going to perform logical backups with the R3trans program.
- *serial.* This optional directory is needed in the case that the serialization option of tp is used.

TPPARAM: tp Global Parameter File

The tp program uses a parameter file, TPPARAM, located in the bin subdirectory under the transport main directory (/usr/sap/trans) that defines many important parameters that directly affect the way tp works for performing exports or imports.

Every time tp is executed, it has to know the location of the TPPARAM file. For this reason, administrators call tp from the bin directory. Otherwise, the location must be specified with the option pf =. If this option is not specified, then tp must search for the TPPARAM in the current directory. This allows for the creation of different parameter files, when administrators wish to perform special functions or wish to call the tp program from a different location than /usr/sap/trans/bin.

The TPPARAM file can contain lots of parameters that can be either

- *Global,* which are then valid for all the SAP systems in a group.
- *Local,* which are only valid for each SAP system. These parameters are preceded by the system name. For example: DD1/impdp_by_event = yes.
- *Operating system dependent,* in which case these parameters are preceded by a keyword corresponding to the specific operating system.
- *Database dependent,* which means the parameters contain a prefixed keyword corresponding to the specific database system.

Because there are many allowed parameters in TPPARAM, as with instance profiles, the parameters that are not specified will take a default value.

Local parameters have precedence over global parameters. This system of precedence allows for having at the same time local and global parameters, which can be used for specifying different parameter values for special systems.

The syntax on the file is very simple: comments are preceded by a # sign whereas parameters have the form of <Parameter> = <Value> for global values.

If the parameter is preceded by a SAP system name and a forward slash (/), then the value only applies for that system. For example: DD1/dbhost = copi01.

When the parameters are only valid for a particular operating system, then you enter the keyword or acronym for the operating system and the | sign, for example, as4 | transdir = . . . Valid keywords for operating systems are aix, hp-ux, osf1, sinix, sunos, wnt (Windows), and as4 (AS/400).

Finally, when the parameters are database system dependent, the parameters are preceded by a database system acronym and the : sign. For example: ora: <parameter> = <value>. Supported acronyms of databases are ora (Oracle), inf (Informix), ada (Adabas D), mss (Microsoft SQL Server), db4 (DB2/400), and db6 (DB2 for AIX).

Additionally, TPPARAM provides predefined variables that can be used when specifying parameters and that are converted at runtime. These variables must be specified with the format $(var_name), for example, $(dbname). For a list of predefined variables, refer to the online help documentation.

Because there are so many possible parameters in the tp configuration file, only the most important ones are described here:

- *TRANSDIR.* This parameter indicates the transport directory that should be accessible by all the systems in a SAP group and with the same name. All the transport data files and log files are stored in different subdirectories beneath TRANSDIR. In UNIX systems, this parameter is TRANSDIR = /usr/sap/trans/. In Windows NT systems, this parameter is TRANSDIR = \<transport host> \sapmnt\trans\.
- *R3TRANSPATH.* Sets the name and location of the R3trans program that is used by the tp control program. The system will find the correct program as long as the imports are performed by the <sid>adm user in the target system, because the SAP administrator user profile includes the right path accesses. In UNIX systems, this parameter is R3TRANSPATH = R3trans. In Windows NT systems, this parameter is R3TRANSPATH = R3trans.exe.

Following are database-dependent parameters that the tp program needs to establish communication with the SAP system database. Only relevant Oracle parameters are introduced here:

- *DBHOST.* The name of the host with the database server. Both in UNIX and Windows NT systems, this would be DBHOST = <hostname>. For example: DBHOST = copi02.
- *DBNAME.* This parameter sets the name of the database instance, which normally matches that of the SAP system.

Two other global parameters that are always present in TPPARAM are

- *ALLLOG.* This parameter is used to specify the name of the log file that keeps information of the steps for all transports in the system. This file is always located in the /usr/sap/trans/log directory. Default value is ALOG $(syear) $(yweek), which indicates that an ALOG file is generated for every calendar week. For example: ALOG9705.
- *SYSLOG.* This parameter specifies the name of the file in which the transport control program keeps information about the imports performed to a certain system. Default value is SLOG $ (syear) $ (yweek). $ (system). This generates a SLOG file every calendar week and with the name of the import system as the file extension. These files are also located in the transport log directory. For example: SLOG9708.TT1.

Two useful parameters in TPPARAM for common functions of tp when communicating with the background import job of R/3 are

- *IMPDP_BY_EVENT.* This is a boolean parameter that is either true or false. The default value is true and it means that the tp program will trigger the import background job of the SAP system (RDDIMPDP) whenever an import takes place. If it's set to false, then the import background job must be scheduled to run periodically to check if there are pending imports. You leave it set to the default true value to avoid hundreds of background job logs. This requires that the additional parameter SAPEVTPATH be set.
- *SAPEVTPATH.* Must contain the complete path to the sapevt program. This program is the SAP event trigger program, which can send signals to the R/3 system. This parameter is only used if IMPDB_BY_EVENT is set to true. For example: DD1/ sapevtpath = /usr/sap/$ (system)/SYS/exe/run/sapevt.

When tp is called with special option put, there are some parameters in TPPARAM that control the command files for starting and stopping both the R/3 system and/or the R/3 database. These parameters are

- *STARTSAP.* This is the location for the program that starts the SAP system. The default value is " ", which will not start the system when tp is called with the put function, unless you are performing a SAP system upgrade, in which case, the upgrade program will modify it when needed. Similarly, the other three parameters, which also default to " ", are as follows:
  - *STOPSAP.* This is the parameter for stopping the SAP system.
  - *STARTDB.* This is the parameter for starting the SAP database.
  - *STOPDB.* This is the parameter for stopping the SAP database.

To display the values of the TPPARAM parameters for a particular SAP system, issue this command: tp showparams <sid>. For example: tp showparams DD1.

Additionally, with the use of the "-D = <value>" option when calling the tp program, you can temporarily change individual parameter values, only valid for the current tp call. For example: tp import DD1K900052 PP1 "-D stoponerror = 1."

For other TPPARAM parameters, please refer to the SAP online documentation under the transport control section.

Overview of Options for the tp Program

The tp transport control program allows system or transport administrators to perform all the management functions for the transport system. These functions are specified by entering options when calling tp. The list of available options can be obtained by issuing a tp help command.

To display help for a particular option of the tp program, call the tp <command> where <command> is a valid option.

The program tp includes functions for exporting, importing, performing buffer actions, managing disk space of the transport system, organizing information, and performing special functions. Only those options that are more useful in normal daily operative tasks are included here. More information about all available options can be obtained from the SAP online documentation library.

Informative options are as follows:

- *tp showbuffer <sid>.* This displays the transportable change requests ready for import to the <SID> system. For example: tp showbuffer TT1.
- *tp count <sid>.* This command option displays the number of requests in the <SID> buffer waiting for import. For example: tp count TT1.
- *tp go <sid>.* This command is just informative, and it shows the environment variables needed for the connection to the database of the <SID> system. This command is executed automatically by tp before logging on to the database. Issuing this command, however, does not log on. For example: tp go TT1.
- *tp connect <sid>.* This is another informative option to check whether the connection to the <SID> database is successful. It logs on to the database and then logs off. It displays a message on the screen displaying the result of the connection.
- *tp checkimpdp <sid>.* The output of this command shows the type of background job that is scheduled in the <SID> system: whether it is event periodic, just periodic, or not scheduled at all. For example: tp checkimpdp TT1.
- *tp showinfo <transport request>.* This informative option shows the header information of the transport request. You don't need to specify a <SID> system. For example: tp showinfo DD1K900052.

Main options for cleaning up the transport subdirectories data, log, and cofiles are as follows:

- *tp check all.* This checks the transport directories looking for files that are not needed (not waiting for imports) and have exceeded a minimum age specified by parameters in TPPARAM. These parameters are DATALIFETIME, OLDDATALIFETIME, COFILELIFE, TIME, and LOGFILELIFETIME. This parameter displays a list of files that can be deleted and generates a temporary file with the list.
- *tp clearold.* This uses the list file generated by the tp check all command and deletes the files included in the list.

Command options for handling the transport buffer are as follows:

- *tp addtobuffer <transport request> <sid>.* Adds the transport request to the buffer for the <SID> system and places it as the last request to be imported. If this request was already in the buffer, it modifies its order and places it as the last request. For example: tp addtobuffer DD1K900052 PP1.

CAUTION *Changing the order of transport requests might have unpredictable results.*

- *tp delfrombuffer <transport request> <sid>.* The transport request is deleted from the buffer queue of the specified <SID> system. It does not delete the transport files from the directory. For example: tp delfrombuffer DD1K900052 PP1.

CAUTION *This command can cause changes in the import sequence and therefore might produce unpredictable results.*

- *tp setstopmark <sid>.* This command option sets a special mark in the import buffer for the specified <SID> system. This is useful when issuing the import commands tp import all or tp put, in which cases the importing only processes those requested before the mark. When the system processes the import of all objects before the mark, it stops itself and deletes the mark.
- *tp delstopmark <sid>.* Deletes a stop mark from the <SID> buffer if it exists.
- *tp locksys <sid>.* This command locks the <SID> system preventing users other than DDIC or SAP* from logging on. This command is normally issued by upgrade utilities. However, users already logged on will not be affected by the call.
- *tp unlocksys <sid>.* Removes the lock on the <SID> system set by a previous tp locksys command.
- *tp lock_eu <sid>.* Sets the system change option of the specified <SID> to *cannot be changed.*
- *tp unlock_eu <sid>.* Sets the system change option of the specified system to the value it had before a previous tp lock_eu command.

The main import tp command options are detailed in the following section.

Working with Imports Using tp

Although transport administration and performing imports has become much easier using the TMS import functions, it is still necessary to know how the tp control program can be used for performing imports.

There are many available command options for performing imports in the R/3 system. Most of them are used for special purposes, such as importing only certain objects, performing activations, and so on.

The main and most commonly used commands for the tp program when performing imports are as follows:

- *tp import <transport request> | all <sid> [options...].* The tp import command has a more complex syntax than the other tp commands, because it allows many options to be specified. The command allows the import of a single transport request or the import of all requests waiting for import in the buffer of the <SID> system (up to a stop mark). Examples are import of a single transport request: tp import DD1K900052 PP1; and import of all pending transport requests for system PP1: tp import all PP1. Available options for the tp import command are as follows:
  - *U<n>[<m>..].* To specify one or more unconditional modes. The next section describes the unconditional modes available. For example: tp import all DD1 U1.
  - *client<n> or client = <n>.* Imports to a specified client. For example: tp import all DD1 client007 or tp import all DD1 client = 007.
  - *pf = <TPPARAM>.* Specifies the exact path of the tp parameter file if it does not use the default one located under /usr/sap/trans/bin.

- *D "<parameter value."* Changes a TPPARAM value for the current call.
- *silent.* Writes the output of the command to the dev_tp file located under the SAP instance work directory.
- *tp put <sid>.* Imports all the transport requests registered for import in the SID buffer up to a stop mark. This option will perform a start and stop of the SAP system as specified in the parameters for TPPARAM. If the default values of the STARTSAP and STOPSAP parameters are set to " ", the call to tp put won't stop the system.

This option is mainly used when upgrading SAP systems. When the default parameters are set, then tp put is the same as issuing a tp import all.

In order to perform imports, the administrator in charge of importing the objects into the target systems has to log on at the operating system level as user <sid>adm. Normally, the administrator imports all objects that are in the buffer waiting for an import. Because importing objects might reset the buffers, it is not convenient to launch imports during normal working hours. An alternative is to include a tp import all <sid> call in a shell script that can be scheduled using system utilities or specialized software for scheduling the import at more appropriate times.

When performing imports, the tp program performs all the necessary steps depending on the nature of the objects or data being transferred. It will perform the following steps:

- ABAP dictionary import. The tp program calls the R3trans utility to import the dictionary objects into the target system. The data are imported inactively so as not to disrupt the normal work in the target SAP system.
- ABAP dictionary activation. During this phase, the nametabs (runtime dictionary objects) are written inactively, so that the system can keep running. Enqueue modules are not activated during this phase for consistency reasons.
- A distribution program checks whether there are any pending actions to move the new and inactive runtime objects into the active system.
- Next, the tp program performs any required structure conversion for the objects in the transport.
- At this moment, the system can move the new dictionary runtime objects to the active runtime environment. Some inconsistencies could occur if the objects are being accessed by active users.
- The next step is the main import phase where all the data are imported with the R3trans utility. If the data are successfully imported and consistent, an automatic transport to another subscribed recipient system can take place.
- Then the tp program takes care of activating any enqueue modules present in the transport which cannot be handled as other dictionary objects. These modules are directly passed onto the runtime environment.
- The final steps are to import any application-defined objects, set version flags for the imported objects, execute XPRA reports in case of puts, generate any report or screen, and remove the transport request number from the system buffer.

If you get error messages during any phase of the import, tp will stop any further actions. After looking at the log files and finding the cause for the error and solving the problem, you normally can start the import again. The tp program records the point at which the processing should be restarted.

Unconditional Modes in the tp Program

Unconditional modes are options that can be specified for exports or imports with the tp program and are intended for performing special actions on transport requests.

CAUTION *Use only unconditional options when you are sure of what you are doing. Otherwise, this can cause severe inconsistencies in the systems.*

The unconditional modes tell the tp program to overwrite the rules imposed by the objects as defined in the Workbench Organizer. For example, they allow the import of original objects when that's not permitted by the package.

Unconditional modes are numbers from 0 to 9, and they can be used in the options part of the tp call. They are always preceded by the letter *U*. Several unconditional modes can be used in the same command. For example: tp import DD1K900052 PP1 U18. This tells the tp to activate unconditional modes 1 and 8.

When using unconditional modes, the transport log usually issues warning messages. These are functions for every unconditional mode:

- *0.* Known as *overtaker.* It can be used for importing from the buffer without deleting it and then it uses unconditional mode 1 to allow another import in the correct location.
- *1.* During an import, the system ignores that this request was already imported, and it can be imported again.
- *2.* During an import, this permits the overwriting of original objects.
- *3.* During import, this allows the transport program to overwrite system-specific objects.
- *6.* This allows for overwriting objects that are unconfirmed repairs.
- *8.* This mode ignores transport restrictions based on the table classes.
- *9.* This mode ignores whether the system is locked for this type of transport.

Managing Special Transports

Usually administrators should perform imports for all the change requests that have been exported for a particular system. This is accomplished by a tp import all command. This is the only way that tp can guarantee the right order for importing objects, avoiding some newer versions being overwritten by older ones.

There are occasions, however, when special and individual transports must be used, for example, when performing urgent imports or for transferring client-specific data from different clients. In these cases, you must be extremely careful not to change the order of the individual change requests. These types of transports require the import for individual transport requests. For example: tp import DD1K900054 PP1.

When performing individual transports, have a look at the buffer (tp showbuffer <sid>) and ensure that no other older change requests contain the objects that you are going to import individually. This process can take some time and requires the use of the transport information system.

For performing individual imports, SAP recommends using the unconditional mode 0, which does not delete the change request from the buffer and will be imported again in a normal import, but ensures the correct release order for all change requests of a system. For example: tp import DD1K900078 PP1 U0.

Normally, the data exported from a source client are imported into the client with the same number; however, the tp program permits specifying a different target client on the command line. For example: tp import DD1K900078 PP1 client = 007. This type of transport is valid for all the objects in the change requests that are client specific in the source client.

You should be careful when issuing a tp import all command when trying to transport to more than one client. In those cases, the only way is to transport individually every change request to the required target clients.

The Interface between tp and ABAP

The actions that the tp control program performs are not performed alone. The tp program communicates with the ABAP runtime to execute the needed actions over the transported objects (for example, structure conversion, screen generation, and so forth).

The interface between the tp program and ABAP is handled by the import dispatcher background jobs and the use of two system tables: TRBAT and TRJOB. By looking at the contents of these tables while an import is going on, administrators have another way of monitoring the transports online.

The dispatcher background jobs, as explained earlier, are RDDIMPD and RDDIMPDP _CLIENT_<nnn>, which schedule further jobs when needed. These jobs schedule themselves back to wait for further import steps or new imports.

When a tp command is issued at the operating system level, it sends a signal to the background processing system for the RDDIMPDP to start, makes an entry in the TRBAT table for each transport request to import, and inserts the number of the background jobs in table TRJOB. At that moment, RDDIMPDP starts processing, first checking the TRBAT table to see if there are any pending imports. If it finds an entry, it launches additional ABAP programs as background jobs that will perform the necessary actions on the transport objects. If any step is canceled, RDDIMPDP checks for entries still existing in table TRJOB and tries to restart the action. For this reason, the system needs to have at least two free background work processes.

Table TRBAT contains several fields, including the change request number, function, return code, time stamp, client, special function, and log, which logs online the actions being performed during import. The unction and the return code indicate the step being performed and the status. Refer to the SAP online documentation in the transport control section for a description of the function keys and return codes of the TRBAT table.

Overview of the R3trans Program

R3trans is the SAP system transport program that can be used for transporting data between different SAP systems, even when they don't belong to the same group. For example, it can be used to transport change requests created at SAP that are bug corrections to current programs or new developments. R3trans normally is not used directly but called from the tp control program or by the SAP upgrade utilities.

R3trans is only directly used in certain circumstances, such as for exporting or importing data to or from other SAP systems and also for performing special functions such as SAP logical backups or for managing imports or exports with data from other SAP versions. This, however, can be done only when you are sure that no logical inconsistencies will occur in the transported data.

R3trans supports transporting data between different operating systems or even different database systems.

The syntax for calling the R3trans program is R3trans [<options>] <control file>. Options are parameters that indicate what function the program will execute. You can use several options at the same time. At least one option must be specified. The control file further specifies the actions that the R3trans will perform. This is a normal text file with special commands.

R3trans must be called by the SAP system administrator, <sid>adm.

Some of the useful options available are as follows:

- *R3trans -d,* which checks whether it's possible to connect to the database.
- *R3trans -i <file>*, which imports directly the data from the <file> without the need for a control file.
- *R3trans -t <control_file>*, which performs the functions on test mode. Modifications are not written in the database.
- *R3trans -w <file>*, which writes the transport log to the specified file. If none is specified, the default is trans.log in the current directory.

Information on additional options and how to write control files can be found in SAP online documentation.

CHAPTER 7

Development Options with SAP Solutions: ABAP Engine

The development environment of the SAP systems was traditionally based on a fully integrated set of development tools, functions, programming languages, and a data dictionary, grouped together under the name *ABAP Workbench*.

With the Internet Business Framework, the ITS, and the connectors, the development environment around SAP was quite extensive, but with SAP Web Application Server, R/3 Enterprise, and SAP NetWeaver, the options have been heavily enlarged and enhanced, with the two fundamental additions of the J2EE engine and the including of native HTML code and JavaScript with the ABAP language.

This chapter provides an overview of all the possibilities for development of SAP systems around the ABAP engine and provides examples that will show the possibilities according to the nature of the development. However, to get acquainted with the diverse programming options, you must refer to specific programming documentation on SAP online help and other books.

In any case, you must not overlook the fact the ABAP and the ABAP Workbench have been, are and will most likely be, for the coming years, the main and most important programming environment around SAP development. Java developments and services are key areas for the future. For this reason, we will start this chapter with an overview of the Data Dictionary and the ABAP Workbench.

For an introduction and overview of the development options for the Java Engine and the SAP NetWeaver Developer Studio, including a Web Dynpro example, refer to Chapter 11 on this book.

The ABAP Workbench

The ABAP Workbench is the kernel for all the SAP system business applications and the foundation for developing additional functions and applications for SAP Solutions based in ABAP.

The ABAP Workbench is intended as a development environment that can cover all the phases of a development project, allowing teamwork, organization, and version management even across SAP systems.

The ABAP Workbench permits easy transfer of developments among systems, which makes it completely portable among SAP ABAP engine–based systems and thus ensures information integrity.

For example, a large part of a SAP system upgrade is made up of a big collection of programs, function modules, tables, and so forth, which are developed at SAP and are transferred to customer systems using the transport tools. This process is quite automatic and almost transparent to administrators.

The main features of the ABAP Workbench architecture are as follows:

- Distribution of applications among servers, where the same application runs across different underlying hardware platforms without modification
- Support of common and standard GUIs
- Transparent communication with other systems, with the interfaces provided by SAP middleware
- Transparent handling of underlying database systems with ABAP Open SQL or Native SQL
- Communication with external applications using RFCs and with desktop applications using RFC, OLE2, and ODBC

The development work is based on an object repository, which contains the following:

- Facilities to create and maintain database definitions, application defaults, and business rules that can be viewed graphically
- The ABAP dictionary, which does central, active management of all application-related descriptive data, including table definitions, foreign key relations, and views

The full integration of the components means that changes in any part have a direct and immediate effect on all applications using those components.

SAP is based on standards: user interface, database development, communications, and programming. It provides the data model for SAP Solutions, which contains the relationships between the business applications. The workbench contains a major library of business functions. You can precisely fine-tune SAP to your special needs.

Basic Concepts of the Development Environment

The development environment includes virtually hundreds of functions, many of which are common in other types of applications, especially the features concerning a programming language, such as a sensitive editor, a data dictionary, a function library, and debugging facilities.

The SAP ABAP engine development environment has, however, many of its own functions and features. Within the whole environment there are two basic concepts that have particular importance: development objects and packages (formerly development classes).

Development objects are all the components of an ABAP application: program elements (events, global fields, variants, subroutines, includes), program code (function modules, reports, module pools), transactions, message classes, dictionary objects (tables, data elements, domains, etc.), packages, and ABAP Classes or Interfaces, BSPs, and Internet services.

Packages are logical groups of development objects that are related and are normally deployed for the same application module, related reports, and so on. This concept was introduced in Chapter 6. Packages are particularly important for team development, the transport system, and use within the repository browser, application hierarchy, and so forth.

The ABAP Workbench is made up of a very extensive set of transactions and tools. The following is a list of the most important transactions in release SAP Web AS 6.20:

- *Overview*
  - SE81 SAP Application Hierarchy
  - SE82 Customer Application Hierarchy
  - SE80 Object Navigator
  - SWO2 Business Object Repository Browser
  - SE95 Modification Browser
  - SE83 Reuse Library
  - SE84 Repository Information System
  - SE16 Data Browser
  - SE09 Transport Organizer
  - BAPI BAPI Explorer
- *Development*
  - SE11 ABAP Dictionary
  - SD11 Data Modeler
  - SE41 Menu Painter
  - SE51 Screen Painter
  - SE38 ABAP Editor
  - SE37 Function Builder
  - SE24 Class Builder
  - SE33 Context Builder
  - SE32 Text Elements Maintenance
  - SE36 Logical Database Builder
  - SE91 Messages
  - SE92 System Log Messages
  - SE39 ABAP SplitScreen Editor
  - SE35 Maintain Dialog Modules
  - SWO1 Business Object Builder
  - SE54 General Table Maintenance Dialog
  - SE93 Transactions
  - SE43N Area Menu Maintenance

- *Test*
  - SE30 ABAP Runtime Analysis
  - ST05 SQL Trace
  - SECATT Extended CATT
  - CATT CATT
  - SCOV Coverage Analyzer
  - SCI Code Inspector
  - SRTM Runtime Monitor
  - SM21 System log
  - ST22 Dump Analysis
  - SLIN Extended Check
- *Utilities*
  - SE61 R/3 Documentation
  - SE63 Standard Translation Environment
  - SQ07 Language comparison of SAP Query Objects
  - SPAM Support Package Manager
  - SPDD Dictionary Compare
  - SPAU Program Compare
  - SQVI QuickViewer
  - SQ01 SAP Query, Queries
  - SQ02 SAP Query, Infoset
  - SQ03 SAP Query, User Groups
  - SE18 BADIs, definition
  - SE19 BADIs, Implementation
  - SMOD Enhancements. Definition
  - CMOD Enhancements. Project Management

NOTE *Some of the transactions that can be seen from the Easy Access menu have been excluded from the preceding list, because those transactions are not related with the ABAP development.*

The ABAP Dictionary

The ABAP Dictionary, known usually as data dictionary, is the central workbench repository utility providing the data definitions and the information relationships that are later used in all the SAP business applications.

The ABAP dictionary can be seen as a logical representation or a superior layer over the physical underlying database. The supported database engines must comply with the relational data model. This model is strictly followed by the ABAP dictionary.

A *data dictionary* in computing terms is the source of information in which the system data are defined in a logical way. The data dictionary is the centralized and structured source of information for business applications and the core of a well-structured development environment.

Around a data dictionary, you can assemble other components of a development environment as a programming language, of context-sensitive editors, screen painters and handlers, and so forth.

The elements that make up a dictionary are known as *metadata*. Metadata is the computing term for the data whose function is to describe other data. Actually, the data of the dictionary are not the operational data that tell a customer's address or an article price, but rather a type of data whose function is to define the semantic or syntactic properties of the operational data, such as the type, length, and relationships.

Currently, the relational databases and the transactional systems in general all have and all use a data dictionary as the system core. An advantage of having a data dictionary is avoiding inconsistencies when defining data types that will later be used in different parts of an application; this avoids redundancies and considerably decreases the cost of maintenance.

When a type of data is defined in the dictionary, it is available to any program or function module in the application. A change in the definition of a type of data in the dictionary automatically affects any other data, module, function, or program that has data or variables defined using that modified data type. This can be useful when you want to modify all related data types, but at the same time and for the same reason, you must be extremely careful not to negatively affect other system parts (other types or programs) using those data types.

The data dictionary allows developers and system managers to create, modify, or delete data definitions (data types). At the same time, it's a great source of information, not only for the development environment but also for the user—it is a fast and efficient way to answer questions such as which entries exist in a table of the database; what the structure of this table is; this view . . . ; and what the relation between two different dictionary objects is.

The ABAP Dictionary in SAP Systems

The ABAP dictionary data is the core of the ABAP development environment. It is the source of every definition within SAP applications, from the very basic domains to the company model. It is totally integrated with the other tools of the development environment.

The integration of the ABAP dictionary with the development workbench is an *active* integration. Activating any modification in the data definitions has an immediate effect in all related ABAP programs, function modules, menus, and screens.

Some of the main available functions in the ABAP dictionary are the following:

- It allows you to add, delete, modify, and, in general terms, manage the definitions of the dictionary data (activation, version handling, etc.).
- It allows you to reserve the data integrity.
- It is a central source of information. From the dictionary, you can get information about the defined relations between the system tables.

- It allows direct access to the data in the underlying database system. The dictionary tells whether a table is active, empty, or contains data, and so forth.
- It acts as the central layer for software development. The ABAP dictionary is an active component of the SAP environment. Every created or modified element of the data dictionary (every definition) can simultaneously and automatically be used in every software component that includes that definition.
- The ABAP dictionary is integrated in the development environment and in the SAP application environment using *call interfaces*. With those call interfaces, the programs can directly access the information stored in the dictionary. At the same time, all the development workbench tools can directly access the data dictionary for creating menu definitions, generating screens, reporting functions, and other activities that always have up-to-date data definition information. For example, when declaring a table inside an ABAP report, there is no need to declare the structure of the table—you only need to declare the name of the table itself. At program generation time, the system directly accesses the data dictionary to look for its structure and properties.
- The ABAP dictionary permits the documentation of the system data.
- The dictionary also provides some services that are not directly related to the database for supporting the development environment, for instance, the online documentation associated with the screen fields (accessed when pressing the F1 help key) or the possible entries list for a field (when selecting the F4 function key).
- The objects created in the ABAP dictionary are themselves data objects within the underlying database. In general, the database tables related to the dictionary start with "DD."
- The dictionary ensures that the data definitions are flexible and can be updated. Because the SAP system uses an interpretative method, instead of working with original objects, it actually works with internal representations of objects. With this type of operation the system performance is enhanced and has the advantage that the development tools, screen interpreters, database interface, and so forth always access the most current data.

When any of the data dictionary objects are used in other parts of the development workbench, for example, within a source code program or in a screen, the developers only have to enter a table name or position the corresponding field in the screen. The system automatically knows all the object properties and information and automatically creates and initializes all the work areas, symbol tables, and so on.

Entering one or more table names with the X TABLES keyword allows the system to automatically know, even in the program edition phase, the properties for the tables and fields making up those tables. For example, if an ABAP report contains the declaration TABLES: TABNA, all information about this table, such as primary key, indexes, field names, and data types, that are all defined in the data dictionary is retrieved when the program is generated. Any changes to the table do not require the source code for the program to be modified except when explicitly using field names that have been removed from the table structure. When the programs are called after a table structure change, they are automatically regenerated without user intervention, always making the most updated information available by retrieving it from the ABAP dictionary.

Before entering the definition of the object types and services of the data dictionary, let's briefly review some important concept and tools of the Dictionary.

Object Activation

There will be many occasions where there is a need to change some objects, which are already being used by other objects within the repository. When the modifications are not simple, that is, when you have to modify many related objects (domains, structures, tables, etc.), you could end up with some inconsistencies in the system. To avoid that unwanted circumstance, the system includes the *activation* concept, by which two versions of the objects are maintained. The "active" version is the one being used by the other repository objects, and a "saved" version is not used by them. When we are finished modifying all the repository objects, we can activate the set of related objects, guaranteeing a stable environment.

Sometimes the system also activates repository objects indirectly when they use other objects or elements that were previously modified and activated.

Where-Used List

On some occasions, before modifying an element of the DDIC, you need to know whether there is dependence between objects. For example, if you modify the structure of a table, you need to compile the whole ABAP processes that use such a table to verify if the update will create inconsistencies in the system. To facilitate this labor, there is a tool in the system that you can use, known as a "Where-Used List."

To access this utility, from the main Data Dictionary screen, select the menu option Utilities | Where-Used List.

The system shows a dialog box with a selection screen to mark the different types of objects for which we want to perform the search. Figure 7-1 shows an example.

Once the object types are selected, press ENTER, and you will get a list of references from which you can perform further navigation. Figure 7-2 shows the result.

Repository Information System

The Repository Info System, transaction code SE84, is a very useful reporting engine for the whole development environment. Within this tool we have a subtree for finding information about the data dictionary. See Figure 7-3.

From this tool, we can look for cross references of any dictionary object. For example, if we want to find all *domains* (we'll discuss the domain concept later in this chapter) that start with "kn" and of the alphanumeric type, we would do the following:

Open the ABAP Dictionary menu tree by clicking on the arrow in the left panel, and then select Domains by double-clicking over it.

The system will show new selection fields in the right panel. Enter "kn*" in the Domain field and the value "CHAR" in the Data Type field, as shown in Figure 7-4. Next press the Execute button.

The system will show a listing with all the hits, as shown in Figure 7-5.

From the list we can select those "domains" we want to display. Just mark the corresponding check box and click the Display button.

The system shows a screen with the first object selected as if we were using the SE11 transaction (initial ABAP Dictionary screen) and also shows in the lower window the list of

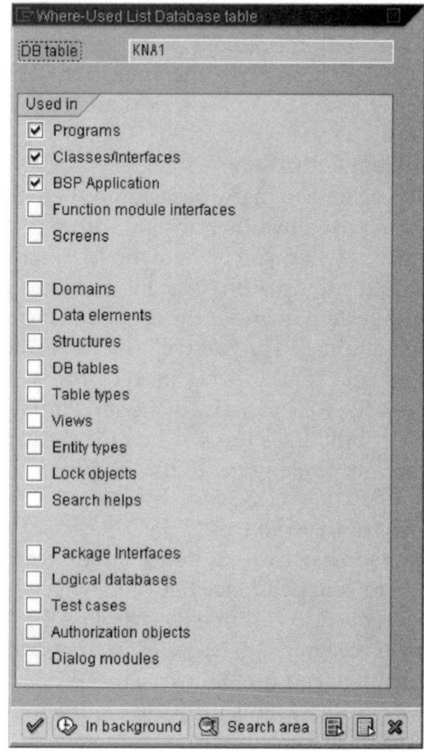

FIGURE 7-1 Where-Used List dialog box (Copyright by SAP AG)

all selected objects in the previous screen. Double-click on the element to navigate the objects. The action buttons of this new window can be used to remove previously selected objects.

ABAP Dictionary Objects

The objects that can be defined and managed with the ABAP dictionary are as follows:

- Domains
- Data elements
- Structures
- Table types
- Tables
- Views
- Indexes

The services that can be defined with the dictionary are as follows:

- Search helps for field data entry
- Field help (documentation)
- Lock objects

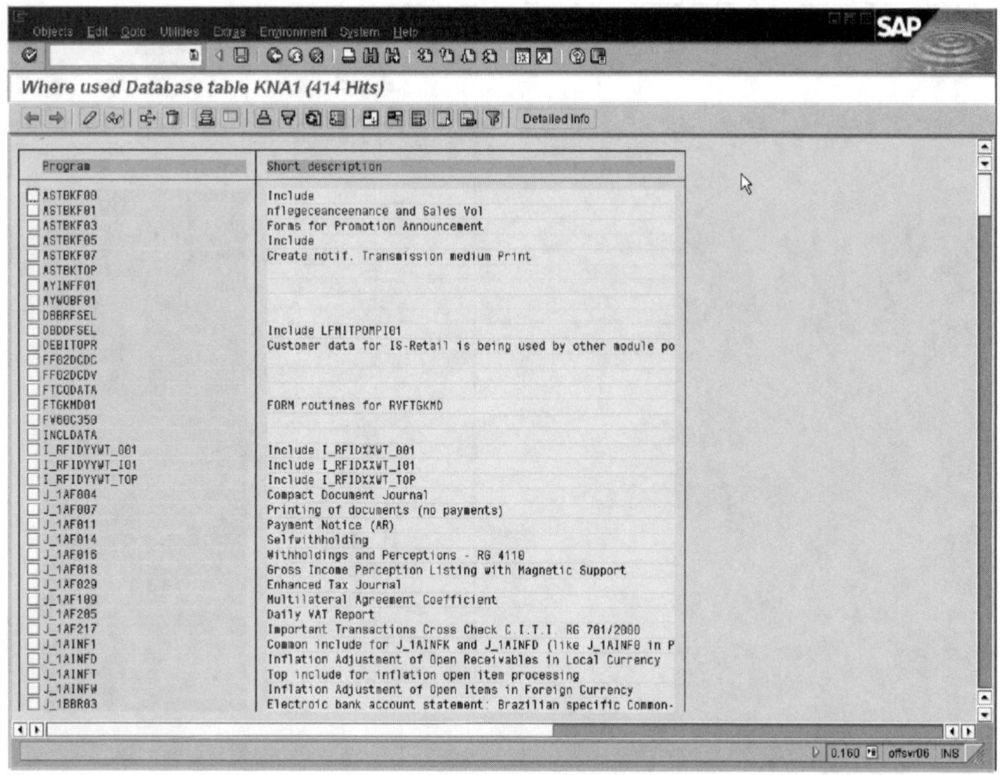

FIGURE 7-2 Where-used list example (Copyright by SAP AG)

Domains

Domains are used to make technical definitions that are used by the data elements. The technical attributes defined within a domain are as follows:

- Field type
- Length
- Decimal positions

It's not strictly mandatory to use a domain when defining a data element. We can directly define the type and length; however, the type must be a predefined one. Figure 7-6 shows an example of domain definition.

Domains can also be used to define the range of valid values for the field to which they reference, but exclusively when they are used in screen fields. That means that these values do not restrict, for instance, updated SQL statements in programs.

Value restrictions for a field can be performed in two ways:

- By means of the introduction of fixed values. We can introduce both individual values as well as a range of values. To carry out these inputs, we must select the Value Range tabstrip.

FIGURE 7-3 Repository Info System (Copyright by SAP AG)

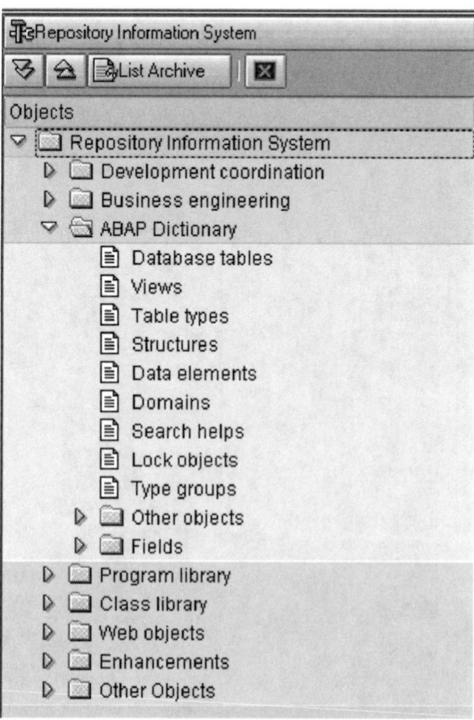

FIGURE 7-4 Finding domains in the Repository Info System (Copyright by SAP AG)

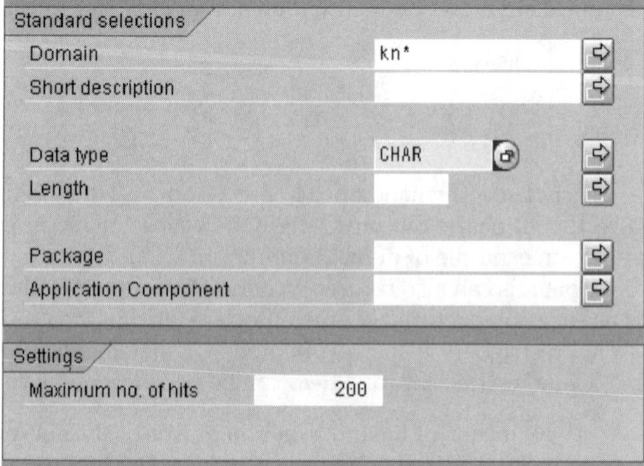

Domain name	Short Description
KNART	Dependency type
KNART2	Dependency type supplement
KNBDR	Indicator: print kanban
KNBEO	Authorization to maintain dependencies
KNEGA	Control ID for sign
KNFAK	Customer factory calendar
KNGRP	Dependency group
KNNAM	Name of dependency
KNNAM_CL	Name of dependency
KNOJT	Object ID for dependency maintenance
KNOTN	Points
KNPRS	Pricing type
KNRDD	Free goods category
KNREF	Customer-specific description of partner (plant, warehouse)
KNSTA	Knowledge status
KNTAB	Table ID for object
KNTDY	Indicator: Account assignment screen
KNTTP	Account assignment category
KNTTYP	Account category
KNTYP	Condition type: Freight, tax, cost,,......
KNUMA	Agreement
KNUMB	Sequential number
KNUMB_CL	Sequence number
KNUMH	Number of the condition record
KNUMV	No.of condition in the document
KNVTP	CAPP rule indicator
KNZVV	Version category, assortment list

FIGURE 7-5 Hit list of domains (Copyright by SAP AG)

- Specifying the name of a value table. This input is also performed on the Value Range tabstrip. Unlike the previous method, it is not necessary to carry out this input in the definition of domain. It is necessary to specify the foreign key in the field of the table that uses this domain. The advantage of defining the table in the domain is that when we want to create a foreign key, the system detects this definition and proposes to accept such table.

The foreign keys are used to secure the integrity of the information. To update the foreign keys of a field in a table we must first select the field to treat (clicking the first field of the definition of the field) and press the Foreign Keys icon. Refer to Figures 7-7 and 7-8.

Before analyzing the properties of the foreign keys, we must define some concepts:

- *Unique primary key.* The definition of a table requires a combination of fields that secure the personalized identification of the table fields. This combination of fields is known as unique primary key.
- *Candidate keys.* A table, besides having a unique primary key, can have other candidate keys. This means fields of a candidate key also form the registers of a table.
- *Foreign key table.* Table used for the definition of a foreign key field.

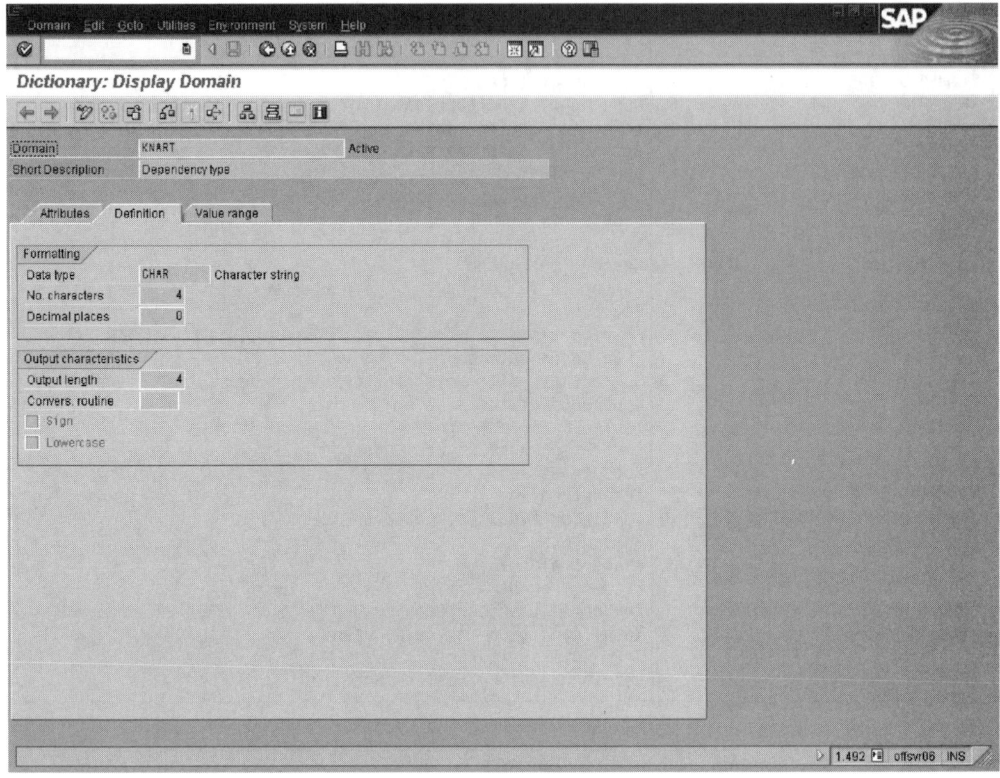

FIGURE 7-6 Displaying domain definition (Copyright by SAP AG)

- *Verification table.* Table used for verifications of consistency of the foreign key field.
- *Foreign key fields.* The set of fields that allows accesses to a table of verification from a foreign key field.

The more significant properties in this type of definition are the following:

- *Cardinality.* The cardinality describes the existent relationship between the foreign key and the table of possible values of verification. The cardinality always is defined from the point of view of the verification table and the possible values are the following:
    - 1:1—Univocal relationship between the verification table and the table of the foreign key field.
    - 1:N—An entry in the check table can have more than one entry in the foreign key field table.

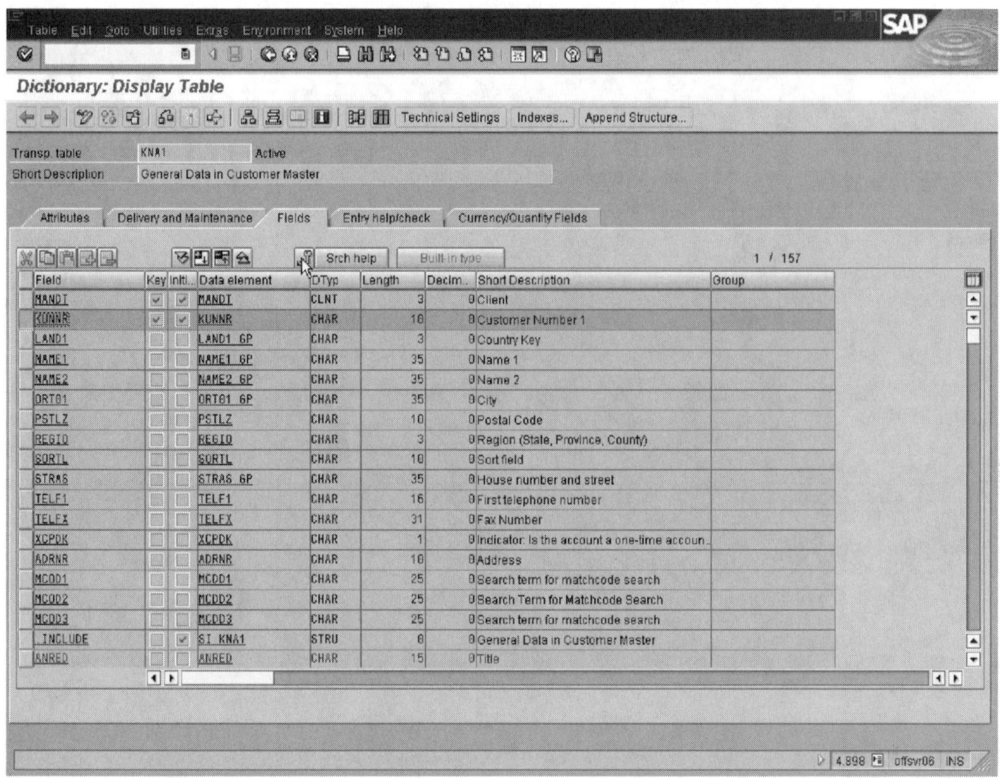

FIGURE 7-7 Foreign keys reference (Copyright by SAP AG)

- 1:C—An entry in the check table can only correspond with an entry in the foreign key field table, although there can be entries in the check table without correspondence.
- 1: CN—An entry in the check table can correspond with more than one entry in the foreign key field table, although there can be entries in the check table without correspondence.

- *Field type.* This property defines the type of field. The permitted values are the following:
  - *Not specified.* The field type is not specified.
  - *Nonkey fields/candidates.* The foreign key fields are not identified by the foreign key table. Therefore, the foreign key fields are not key fields nor are they candidate fields of the foreign key table.
  - *Key fields/candidates.* The foreign key fields are identified by the foreign key table. A register of the foreign key table uniquely identifies the entries in the foreign key fields.

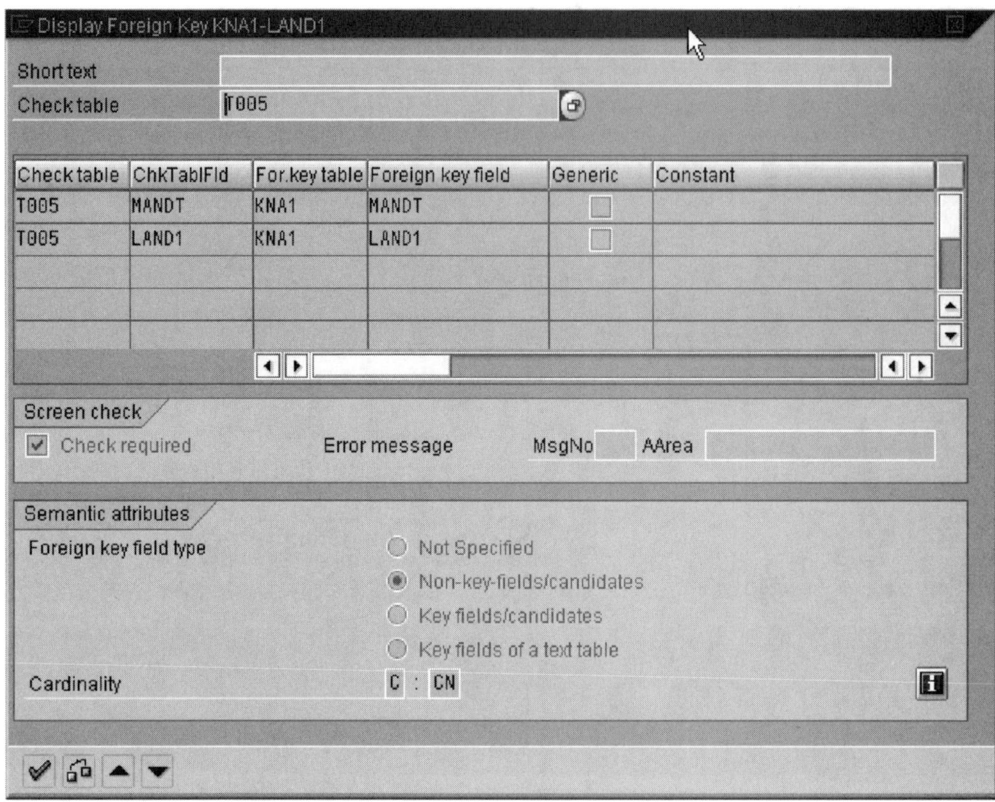

FIGURE 7-8 Displaying foreign keys (Copyright by SAP AG)

- *Key fields of a text table.* The foreign key table is a "text table" of the check table. This is a subtype of the previous type, key fields/candidates. Text tables is a type of table very often used in SAP systems that is used to maintain multilanguage definitions for the business objects defined in the systems.

Data Elements

Data elements are used to make semantic definitions of fields. They describe an elementary data type that can be used in other dictionary elements, for instance, in tables or data structures. Data elements provide meaning to the domain definitions. The direct attributes for data elements are the following:

- Search help
- Labels for screen fields

Using the domain, the data elements acquire the technical settings such as data type, length, and decimal places (if needed).

It is not mandatory to use data elements in the definition of a field (structure, table, etc.). We can directly enter the data type and length. This type of definition is known as "direct type."

The Hierarchy Domain | Data Element | Field allows the creation of structures that simplifies the definition of the database within the SAP systems. The advantages of making the field definitions using this mechanism are the following:

- When we modify a domain and activate the changes, all the data elements related to that domain are automatically updated.
- When a data element is modified (for instance, by means of their associated domain) and we activate those changes, the system will update all the fields of the dictionary that use that domain.
- When a table field is affected by a change in its related data element or domain, the structure (for instance, a table) is also updated automatically.

As we can see, a simple change in a domain allows us to update multiple changes in the database automatically. Therefore, it is very important to create and define domains and data elements for every application object to be defined in the SAP systems.

Structures

Structures are sets of components of any type. The fields of a structure, and also those of a table, have no entity by themselves, contrary to the definition of domains or data elements.

The structures do not have physical correspondence at the database level. These definitions allow us to globally define structured fields that can be used in other dictionary objects or within ABAP programs.

Structures can be used in tables or within other structures, which can avoid redundancies when defining these structures.

Table Types

Table types describe the structure of an internal table that can be later used within an ABAP program. This is the way that the system allows for defining internal tables on a global way, that is, that can be used in any type of ABAP program.

Tables

The tables of the ABAP dictionary are an image of the set of tables within the database, and therefore tables are the most important objects within the dictionary. The main characteristics of the tables are the following:

- Tables are identified by a unique name within the system.
- A table is made up of columns (fields) and rows (table entries).
- Fields within a table have a unique name in that table and some attributes are as follows:
  - Whether the field is a key or not. A table can have one or more key fields. The values of the key fields uniquely identify an entry in a table.
  - Field type. The field types of a table are defined using data elements. For the fields of type CURR (currency) and QUAN (quantity) we must specify a

reference field and reference table (it can be the same table). The reference field for the currency type must be of type CUKY and for the quantity must be of type UNIT. These references are made field by field.

Technical parameters for a table are the following:

- Data class
- Size category
- Buffering
- Logging

Before saving or activating a table of the dictionary, you must enter those technical parameters, and these are very important to optimize the table performance regarding their storage and the access to the table data.

To access the technical parameters, from the menu, select Goto | Technical Settings, or just press the Technical Settings button on the application toolbar. Figure 7-9 shows an example.

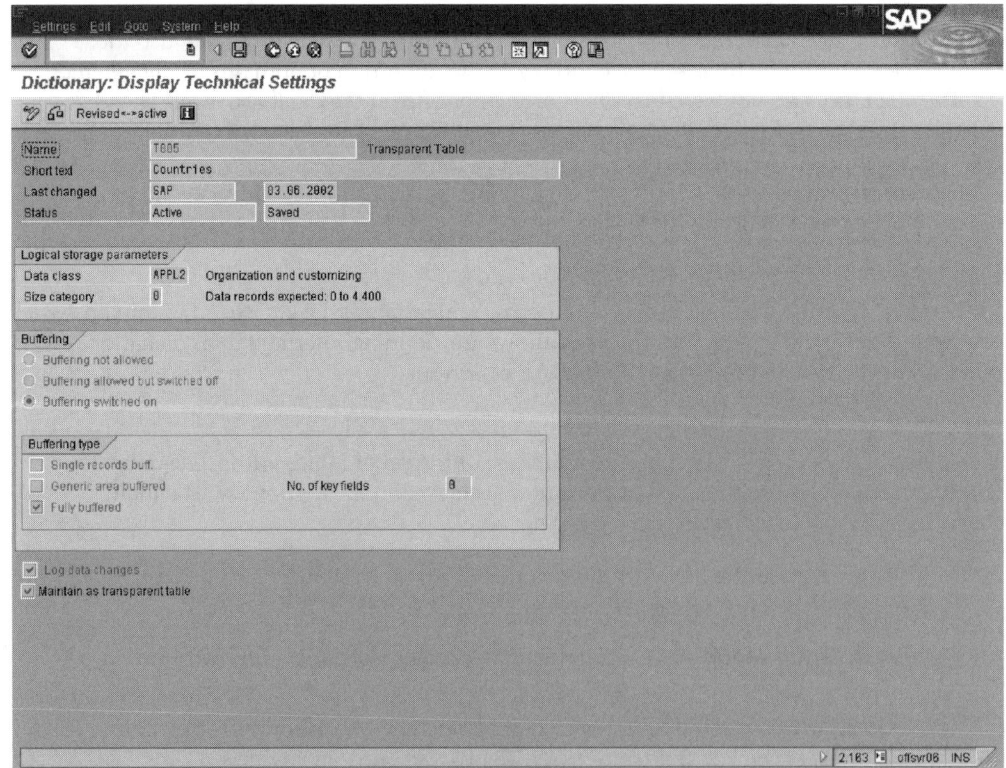

FIGURE 7-9 Table technical settings (Copyright by SAP AG)

Data Class

With the data class parameters you can define the physical area of the database where the data are going to be stored. For instance, for the Oracle database, we are referring to the Tablespace. The possible data classes or storage areas are the following:

- APPL0 — Master data (transparent tables)
- APPL1 — Transactional data (transparent tables)
- APPL2 — Customizing and organizational data
- USER (USER*) — Client data

The physical division of the data according to their nature is established based on the typical use for them. For instance, master data (materials, vendors . . .) normally have few modifications, whereas transactional data (accounting posting, sales orders . . .) are frequently modified. Organizational data, for instance, currencies, are normally only updated during system implementation or customizing, but once systems are in productive operation, they are rarely modified.

It must be noted that customer tables must be assigned to client data classes (USER, USER1, . . .) because if they are incorrectly assigned to other class, this can affect the performance of the systems.

Size Category

The size category defines an estimate for the number of rows that the table can have. According to the setting of the size category, the database will decide the value of the storage area. When we create a table, the database reserves physical space, fixed by category to store the table rows. If more space is required, the database will use the size category to determine the size for the extension.

It is also important to set this parameter properly because an incorrect value could cause a high number of table extensions. You must take into consideration that the number of extensions can be limited depending on the underlying database engine. This can lead to frequent database reorganizations, and conversely, if the setting is too high for smaller tables, you can have too much unused database storage.

Buffering

Buffering is the feature of the systems to store table rows in the memory of the application servers. With this procedure the access time to the data is much faster, normally when tables are not heavily updated. The procedure for access to buffered table data is the following:

- A program requests a database data row.
- The application server looks for that data in the specific memory for that data type.
- If the data record is stored within the buffer, the search is done and the system returns the data to the program.
- If the data record is not in the memory buffer, the regular process of accessing the physical database takes place. Once the program gets the record, it will be kept in the buffer for future access.

A statistical approach used to improve performance estimates is a ratio of 1 to 10, when data are accessed in the application server buffer instead of the database. In any case, the database engines also have some optimization techniques including buffering.

When the application server tries to store data rows in the data buffer and there is no more available space, what it does is the asynchronous switching or swapping of the data, letting out of the buffer those data rows that are accessed less frequently. It's very important to control this type of event because excessive swapping might create performance problems on the application server. There might be also performance problems when doing massive updates on the data located in the buffer.

There are three types of buffering:

- *Single records buffer.* Only the accessed record is stored in the buffer. In large tables, this might be the only type of buffering permitted.
- *Generic area buffer.* The buffer will store all the table entries that correspond to a specific part of the key that has been selected. For example, if the primary key of the table is made up of the first three fields and the generic buffering is established using the first two fields, only the records that match the first two fields of the primary key will be stored in the memory buffers.
- *Fully buffered.* The whole table is stored in the buffer. Logically, this type of buffering can only be performed with small tables.

When a data record is modified from an application server process, the system includes a synchronization process, in order to avoid inconsistencies within the system. Therefore, the buffering technique is only recommended for those tables that are not frequently modified. The process includes the following phases (for instance, in the case of a full buffering):

- Initial situation: The data buffer of an application server (let's call it server A) does not have those table records stored because there has not been any accesses to that data since the application server was started. The SAP system has other application servers (for instance, B, C, D, . . .) with their corresponding local buffers, which can or cannot have those data records.
- A program from the application server A accesses some of the records of the table.
- Because the table has the "buffering" parameter active and we have defined a full buffer, all the entries of the table are stored in the data buffer of that application server A. In this first access, the system will need to request all the information from the database.
- From that moment, the accesses to that table from that application server will be performed using the data in the buffer, which will increase the performance.
- We will suppose that the same process happens from another application server (let's call it server B). A program requests access to that table data. Because those data are not in the local data buffer of server B, the system will also access the data from the database, but after that access, the buffer will have all the table records for future accesses.
- A program or process from server A performs an update to that table, for instance, deletes a record. This server will update a synchronization table (system table) to notify all the other application servers that the table has been modified. This

synchronization table reflects which application server performed the update, as well as the entries of the modified table. Additionally, it updates the data buffer with the modifications.

- At this point, the application server A has the data from the buffer in sync with the database, but this is not the case yet with the other application servers.
- A program of the application server B accesses some of the data records of the table. Because all the rows of the table are in the buffer, it accesses that information and retrieves the records, which are not actually in the database (deleted in the previous step).
- At this point, we don't have synchronized data among the application server. The system is providing information that is not current. If this last access to the data was performed from server A, it would not be any problem, because the data buffer is in sync with the database.
- Now it's time for the *synchronization*. Every certain period of time, which can be set with a parameter, each application server checks the consistency of its own buffer with the existing entries of the synchronization table. In this way, server B detects that server A made some updates on a table that server B has in its own buffer and sets those entries in its data buffer as "not usable." The last step in the synchronization consists of cleaning the records of the synchronization table. From that moment on, any access to the data rows of the table in any of the application servers will be consistent with the actual contents of the table in the physical database, although the same process will happen every time the table is modified or updated by any of the application servers.
- A program in server B can access the data of the table. Because the table has been marked as invalid in the buffer, the server will access the database and will regenerate the entries in the buffer with the new situation found in the physical database.

The main advantage of this technique is that it minimizes the load in the network. However, if the all the buffers are synchronized every time an update is performed, we would have very significant impact on overall performance. Another disadvantage is that during a short time, some of the data buffers might become obsolete.

As a summary for this technique, we must comment that tables with a high number of updates should not have active the "buffering" parameters because this can cause important impacts on the performance due to a high load and swapping of the records in the buffers.

In the transaction code field (OK-CODE) we can enter the command $TAB to reset the content of the data buffer in the application server where the command is executed. We should only use this command when we are aware that there is a synchronization problem in the buffer. In systems with a very large data volume, the process of loading the buffer can last up to several hours, and therefore the use of this command should be restricted with the corresponding authorizations.

Logging

This technical parameter is used to activate the creation of a log over the updated on the table. We should only activate this parameter on a table when we need to analyze the update process on a particular table.

Before checking and activating this parameter, and in order for the system to perform the table "logging," it is necessary that the profile instance parameter "rec/client" has a value different from "OFF." Possible values for this parameter are as follows:

- ALL "Logging" is performed in every system client.
- 000 . . . "Logging" is performed in the specified system clients.
- OFF No "logging" is performed even if the table has the Logging setting activated.

Table logs can be displayed using transaction SCU2, Analysis of Changed Customizing Objects and Tables. When we run this transaction, if the instance profile parameter is not active, we will get a warning message like the one shown in Figure 7-10.

From transaction SCU3 we can not only analyze the modification logs of tables, but we can also display a list of the dictionary tables that have the logging parameter set.

Finally, it is very important to observe that this parameter should be only used in special cases and for short periods because it can create performance bottlenecks.

Performance

In order to improve the performance of table access, we can use two techniques:

- *Indexes.* This is described in a later section of this chapter.
- *Buffering.* We have seen the positive effects of buffering in the previous sections.

In the majority of occasions, the creation of indexes with good criteria will improve the performance of the database, but indexes have the disadvantage that it will make the database grow and will also impact the performance in database updates because every new update will have to update also the index.

Likewise, the buffering technique can improve the performance of the accesses of a particular table, but it can also impact the general performance of the system.

In conclusion, we see that performance is a complicated issue comprised of the balance between benefits and disadvantages and therefore requires continuous and periodic checking and tuning.

Table Definition Modifications

A very important aspect for the maintenance of the table in the dictionary is the updating or modification of the table definitions.

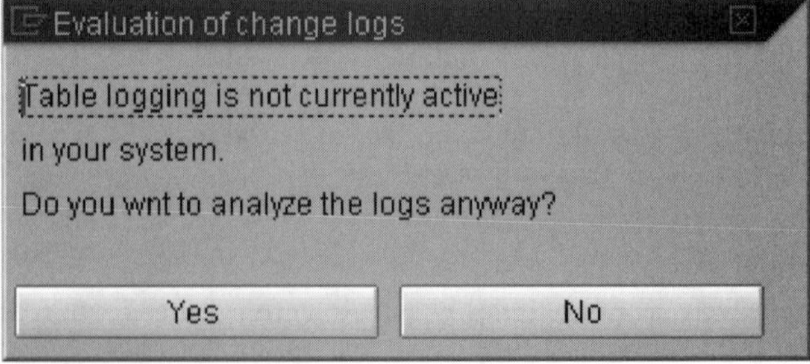

FIGURE 7-10 Evaluation of change logs (Copyright by SAP AG)

There are some modifications that will not alter the structure of the table at the physical database level. We will deal in this section with those modifications that alter the structure. In these cases, the following situations can happen:

- *Tables without data.* There is no problem in this case because the table is deleted (DROP TABLE) and re-created (CREATE TABLE).
- *Tables with data.* Under this circumstance, we can have two situations:
  - The table can be modified with an ALTER TABLE statement. In this case, the process is finished without further intervention.
  - The table cannot be modified with an ALTER TABLE statement. In this circumstance, the system will need to perform a conversion process.

When we try to carry out a manual activation of the table, the system detects that we cannot carry out the activation for the circumstances previously mentioned and does not allow it, but it proposes a conversion process.

The steps carried out during a process of conversion are the following:

- Initial situation: The table has been modified in the dictionary. We have, for example, modified the length of a field. In this situation the system keeps two definitions of table: the active and the saved. The difference between both is the length of one of the table fields. The table contains data and also has indexes that use the modified field. In the database we have, therefore, a table and indexes with a length of one of the fields that has to be modified (converted).
- The first thing that the system does during the process of conversion is to lock the table so that its structure cannot be modified by any user, even the one that carried out the modification. If this were not the case, we could find the unpleasant situation of loss of data.
- The table of the database is renamed. The name of the new table follows the naming convention "QCMxxxxx," with "QCM" a fixed value and "xxxxx" the previous name of the table. Also in this step all the secondary indexes defined for the table are erased. It also removes the views that refer to this table. Any program using the initial table cannot use it because it was renamed.
- Renaming the table activates the version of the new table, that is, it generates the table at the database level but not with the initial name of the table. In this occasion the naming convention is the following: "QCM8xxxxx," with "QCM8" a fixed value and "xxxxx" the previous name of the table. Renaming also creates the primary key of the created table. The created table has no data yet.
- Now there is a movement or transfer of data between the "QCMxxxxx" and "QCM8xxxxx" tables. For simplifying the description of this step, let's say that the system carries out a type of MOVES-CORRESPONDING using the fields of both structures. Obviously, this is the longest process of the conversion because it requires extra storage space and it is the only step that could create other problems. The more frequent problems that could happen up to this point are the following:
  - Overflow in tablespace. Because there is the need for extra storage, we could have problems with the tablespaces (or similar objects in different database

engines). To solve this problem we must increase the storage space of tablespaces.

- Loss of information if the length of one of the key fields is decreased. When reducing the size of a key field, we could have, logically, lost records for duplicity of keys. We cannot influence the registers that the system will discard. Therefore, if we want to have certain control of this, we must carry out a filter process before beginning the process of conversion.
- Invalid modification of type. This type of error is not desirable because the situation of the process of conversion reaches a dead end. We must manually recover the original situation of the table before launching the conversion process and discard this type of modification because the system won't be capable of carrying out the conversion. Refer to the online SAP documentation to see more information for this point.

- Next the system renames the "QCM8xxxxx" table back to the original name, "xxxxx." The secondary indexes are created again. Also, the system creates the views that refer to this table.
- The "QCMxxxxx" table is erased in the database.
- The lock of the table is deleted.
- Analysis of the process. It is always advisable to analyze the result of the process. The system provides the following tools:
  - Transaction SE14—Objects log
  - Transaction SM21—System log analysis (system log, local analysis)
  - Transaction ST22—System dump analysis (ABAP runtime errors)

Obviously, we must review all the ABAP programs that use the modified table because they could be acting in an incorrect way.

Append Structures

The append structures permit us to add client fields to standard tables without having to modify the standard definition of the tables. The append structures are structures of the dictionary that are assigned to one table. If we use the specific customer naming conventions (which is the correct way of doing it), we will ensure that an upgrade process of any type will modify our definitions.

When we activate a where table with added append structures, the system adds the fields defined in the append within the database. As happens with other types of structures, the append structures can also be used in ABAP programs in the data object or data types definitions. It is important to emphasize that the name of the fields for fields of the append structures of clients must begin with "ZZ" or "YY."

Unfortunately, the use of append structures is restricted to the following:

- Transparent tables. You cannot use transparent tables with pool tables or cluster tables.
- Tables without fields of LCHR or LRAW type. Given the variable characteristics of these fields, they don't permit the compatibility with append structures.

Table Types

The possible types of tables in the dictionary are the following:

- Transparent type. They are the most frequently used in SAP systems.
- Pool type.
- Cluster type.

Transparent Tables

When we activate a transparent table in the dictionary, the database system creates the same table with that definition. The definition in the dictionary is independent of the underlying database configured with the SAP installation (Oracle, MS SQL Server, DB2, and others). The name of the table in the database matches the name used in the definition of the dictionary. The data types used in the definition (dictionary) are converted to the corresponding data types of the used underlying database.

The order of the fields in the dictionary can differ from the physical order of the fields in the table of the database. This permits us to insert fields in the definition without the need of converting the table of the database. Technically, when we add a field in the definition of a table, what is executed in the database is an ALTER TABLE statement.

The ABAP programs can access the data stored in these tables in two ways:

- By means of the statements known as Open SQL. There is a whole of set of ABAP statements that allow us to carry out the common operations with the data of a table, such as reading (SELECT), modifications (UPDATE), new entries (INSERT), or erasing (DELETE) of data. These statements are independent of the underlying database.
- By means of native statements (Native SQL). We can execute any SQL statements particular to the underlying database engine. To do this, we must include the Native SQL statements between the ABAP sentences SQL EXEC and SQL END.

Views

Often, the data of a business object, for normalization reasons, are distributed in several tables of the database. The database systems provide the possibility of creating objects that relates fields of different tables of the system. These objects are called "views."

We can access to the definition of the views from the initial screen of the dictionary, as shown in Figure 7-11.

When defining a view we will find the following technical characteristics:

- *Join of tables.* This defines the set of tables that will be related in the view.
- *Projection.* This permits us to select the fields (columns) that we want to be part of the definition of the view.
- *Selection.* This permits us to select the registers (rows) that we want to use in the view.

There are also other important features of the views that are worth comment. The views can be as follows:

- *Inner joins.* The view will only include those entries that exist in both tables. The database views implement this type of joins.

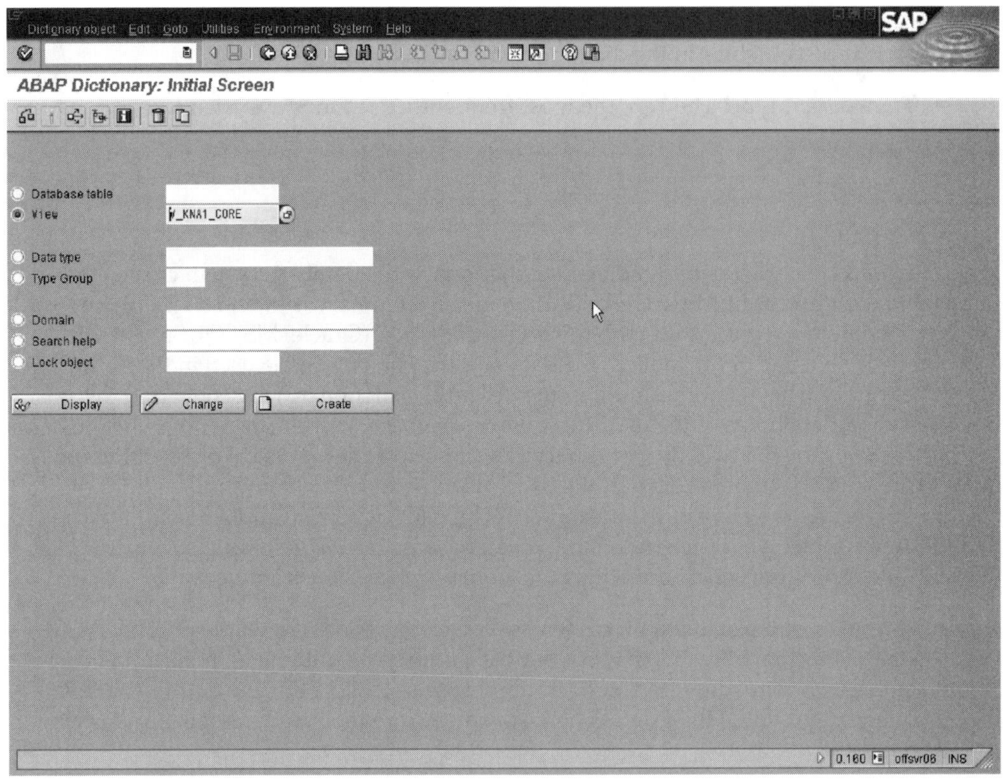

FIGURE 7-11 Views (Copyright by SAP AG)

- *Outer joins.* The table will include all the entries of all the tables in the view, even in the case that there are no entries in some tables. The maintenance views implement this type of join.

We can create four types of views in the system:

- *Database views.* They permit us to combine fields of several tables to be used in ABAP programs.
- *Projection views.* They permit us to make a select (a projection) of a certain table. This type of view allows for hiding the complete content of a table to certain users.
- *Maintenance views.* These are views that allow a more simple maintenance of complex objects within the application.
- *Help views.* These are views that can be used in the search helps. These objects are also created in the dictionary.

In the Table/Join Conditions tabstrip we can enter the name of the tables involved in the definition of the view, as well as the relation conditions between the tables to establish the combination of entries of the tables. Figure 7-12 shows this screen.

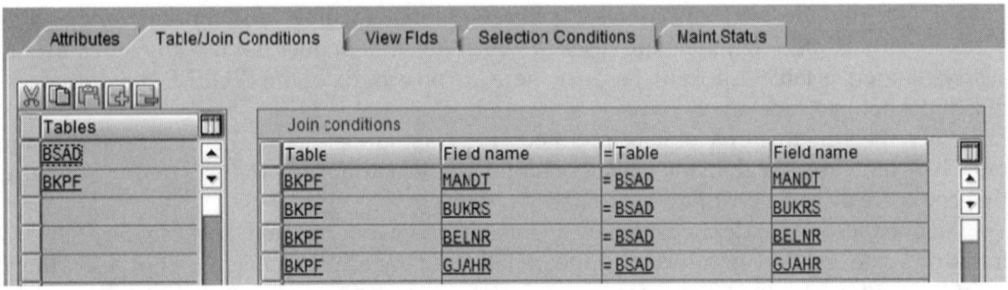

FIGURE 7-12 Table/Join conditions (Copyright by SAP AG)

In the tabstrip for the view fields, we have to define the settings for the projection. That is, we have to define the fields to be included in the view. Logically, those fields must belong to the specified tables in the Table/Join Conditions tabstrip.

In the Selection Conditions tabstrip we have to enter the selection criteria for the data in the view. That is, we have to enter the conditions that must be met to select those records from the database.

The last tabstrip (Maintenance Status) is used to define whether the view is read only or if we allow it to be both read and update access. For the views that can be updated, we can also define whether data maintenance is allowed or not.

Indexes

We can define indexes in the dictionary to increase the performance for data access. These indexes are also created in the underlying database. We can consider an index like a copy of the table, but only including the columns of the table that are defined by the index. The data of the indexes are classified according to the key defined for that index. Given this classification, accessing the data using the index reduces considerably the time to get and read that information, because the system can perform quick binary search using the index key.

We can access the definition and management of the indexes by selecting the menu option Goto | Indexes or just clicking Indexes from the application toolbar.

When we create and activate a table, the system creates the table and also an index that is known as "primary", where the key fields of the index matches the key fields of the table. This index can be used when we perform access to the table using key fields for the selection criteria. The remaining indexes are known as secondary indexes.

The table indexes are identified by three characters. The code "0" is reserved for the primary index. The customer indexes must begin with "Z" or "Y."

Besides the fields defined within an index (key fields and nonkey fields) the system adds a field with the address (pointer) of the corresponding table.

Indexes can be unique or nonunique. A unique index defines which values of the key cannot be duplicated. An example of unique key is the primary key of the table. The nonunique indexes can accept duplicates values in the combination of the key fields.

We can also decide whether the index will be created for some databases. In some circumstances we might consider whether an index is recommended for a particular database; however, it could be not so good for other types of database engines.

Fields within the WHERE clause set whether the index will be used for searching and accessing tables, although there are cases in which the system does not use any index for the search (known as table full scan), because there are no criteria of the WHERE clause that match the defined indexes.

When the structure of a table is modified, the system must perform an adjustment of the table indexes. Tables with many updates should not have too many indexes defined because that could create some type of performance bottleneck.

We must also try to define table indexes that are somehow related, because the indiscriminate creation of indexes can mean that the database optimizer will not select the right index to use for the table access.

Dictionary Services

Services included in the dictionary are the following:

- Search helps (F4)
- Field help documentation (F1)

Field Search Helps (F4)

Field search helps are a common and standard function of the SAP system. They allow the user to enter values for an entry field by selecting them from a list of possible values. The system shows the Possible Entries icon to the right of the field to indicate to the user that the field includes a search help. In order to use that help, we have two options: when in the field, clicking on the Possible Entries button, or just pressing F4.

On many occasions, the list of possible entries of a field can be so large that it becomes necessary to perform additional restrictions for the search. One of these restrictions is the number of entries to show, which by default is typically restricted to value "200."

If there is no search help defined, the Restriction dialog box is directly related to the field. For instance, when we search for possible values on a date field, pressing the F4 key will show up a calendar, like the one shown in Figure 7-13.

An easy way to create a field help, without the need to use the search helps, is the following:

1. In the definition of a domain, in the tabstrip for the value range, we can enter the list of allowed values, a value range, or a reference table.
    a. In the first section we can enter individual values. We can attach a descriptive text of the value that will appear when the user clicks on the Help button.
    b. We can also enter a value range, which also allows including a descriptive text.
    c. The other possibility is to include a table with reference values. When using this last option, we must perform some additional operations.

Let's look at an example. The standard domain "BLART" does not have individual values or ranges but includes the reference table "T003," which is a standard table for Document Types. We are going to use the domain in the definition of the text elements. For example, the data element "BLART" uses the domain "BLART." You can see this in Figure 7-14.

As we already saw, the data element is used to define the fields of the tables. For example, standard table BKPF includes a field that uses the BLART data element. In the

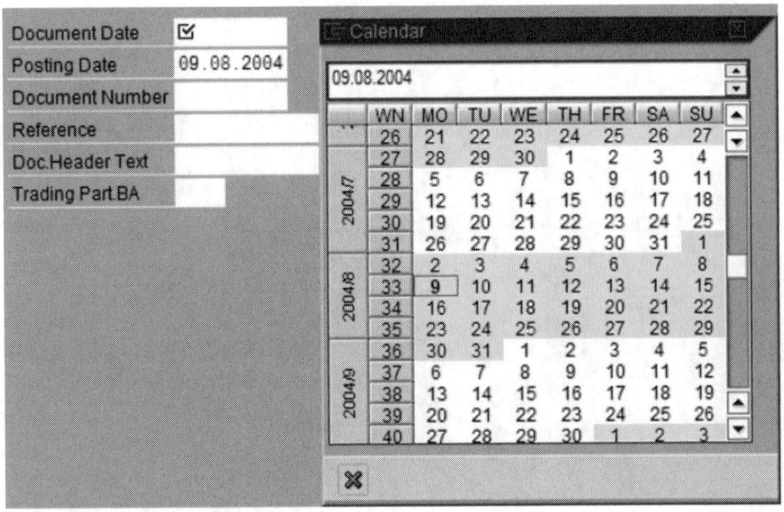

FIGURE 7-13 Calendar as search help (Copyright by SAP AG)

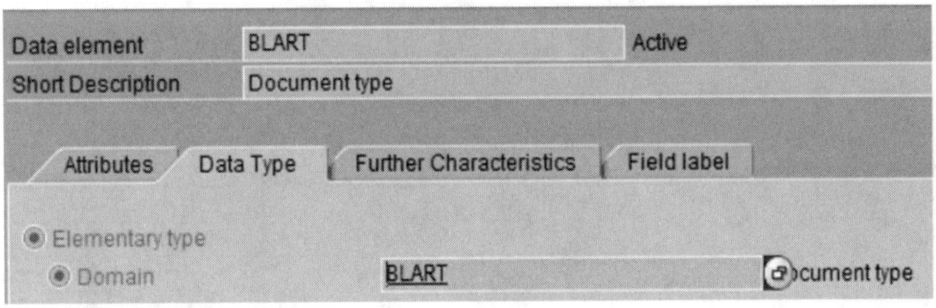

FIGURE 7-14 Domain BLART with data element (Copyright by SAP AG)

definition of the table we also must define a "foreign key" that allows us to relate the field to a reference table of possible values. To access to this screen, just click on the Foreign Keys button. For example, in the table BKPF, field BLART has a foreign key against the table T003. The system detects that table T003 has been included in the data element used, and therefore it automatically proposes to use the related fields between the reference table (T003) and the foreign key table (BKPF), as shown in Figure 7-15.

We define fields in ABAP screens (Dynpros) that make direct reference to the fields of the tables in the data dictionary, as shown in Figure 7-16. For example, the initial screen for the FB01 (*Post Document, Header Data*) is technically known as SAPMF05A-100 and includes the field BLART defined with the reference we described previously.

With these steps we have created a simple field help. In the example, the user will be able to see the entries from table T003 when pressing F4, over the BLART field, in the initial screen of transaction FB01, as shown in Figure 7-17.

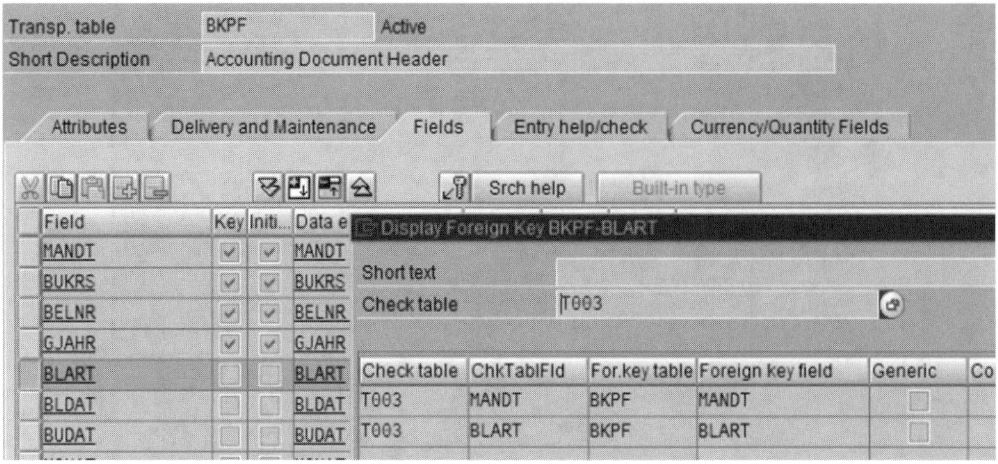

FIGURE 7-15 Example of foreign keys relations (Copyright by SAP AG)

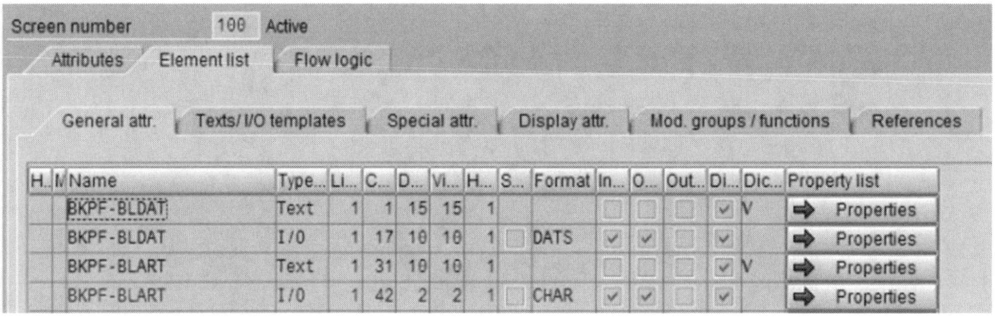

FIGURE 7-16 Attributes for Dynpros (Copyright by SAP AG)

Search Helps

The other possibility for field helps are known as search helps, formerly known in SAP systems as matchcodes. Search helps allow for defining more extensive helps for entering values in screen fields.

You can access the maintenance screen for search helps from the initial dictionary transaction SE11.

There are two types of search helps:

- *Collectives,* which are used to define a set of elementary helps
- *Elementary,* used for defining specifics settings for a search help

Collective Search Helps When we associate to a field a collective search help, the system will show every elementary search help as a tabstrip in the help window.

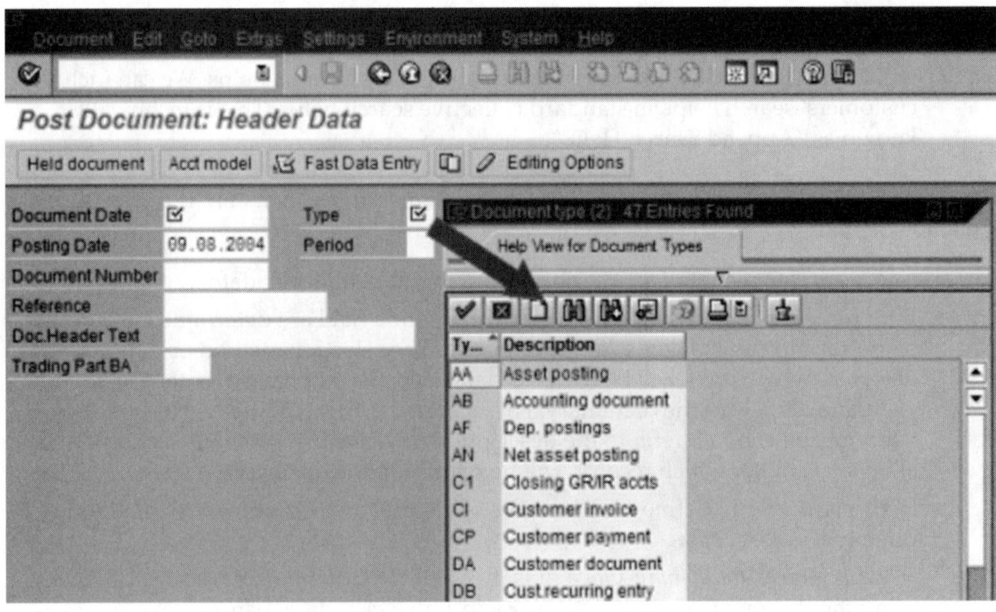

FIGURE 7-17 Simple search help (Copyright by SAP AG)

The information entered in a collective search help is the following:

- *Set of parameters for the search help.* These are the fields that we will use to associate the help to another element of the ABAP repository, for instance, a field in a table of the dictionary or a screen field. We can enter a default value in the parameters by setting a reference to a memory parameter GET/SET. In the example shown in Figure 7-18, we can see the standard DEBI with two defined parameters: Customer number (KUNNR) and Company (BUKRS).

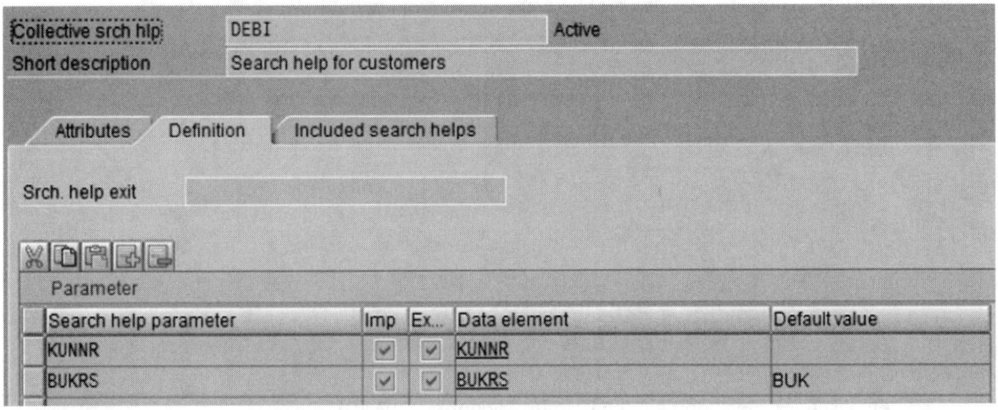

Collective srch hlp: DEBI Active
Short description: Search help for customers

Attributes | Definition | Included search helps

Srch. help exit

Parameter

Search help parameter	Imp	Ex...	Data element	Default value
KUNNR	✓	✓	KUNNR	
BUKRS	✓	✓	BUKRS	BUK

FIGURE 7-18 Example of collective search help (Copyright by SAP AG)

- *Individual search help.* Figure 7-19 shows some of the individual search helps defined for the standard search help DEBI. By double-clicking on the helps, we will "navigate" to the individual definitions of those search helps. We can include customers' search helps in standard collective search helps. This is technically known as "Append Search Help."

Elementary Search Helps Information related to an elementary search help is comprised of the following parts:

- *Name and short description.* The short description field is mandatory.
- *Data collection.* The possible values or entries for a field are determined at runtime by performing a read access to the database. The selection method or data collection describes which rows will be read. As data collection we have to enter the name of a table or view of the dictionary. For example, using a view we could perform a "previous selection" (refer to the description of views in a previous section), which allows us to filter which records will be read from the database.
- *Dialog behavior.* To define the behaviors of a search help window, we can define three types of dialogs:
  - *Immediate value display.* Once F4 is pressed, the system displays a list of values without showing the restriction or additional criteria screen.
  - *Dialog with value restriction.* The screen for value restriction is the first one shown. Once a user enters the restrictions or criteria, the system will show the values that match the established restrictions.
  - *Dialog depends on value set.* This is the most interesting form because the first action that the system does is to evaluate the number of entries to show without any restriction. If the number of entries is less than 100, the list of values will

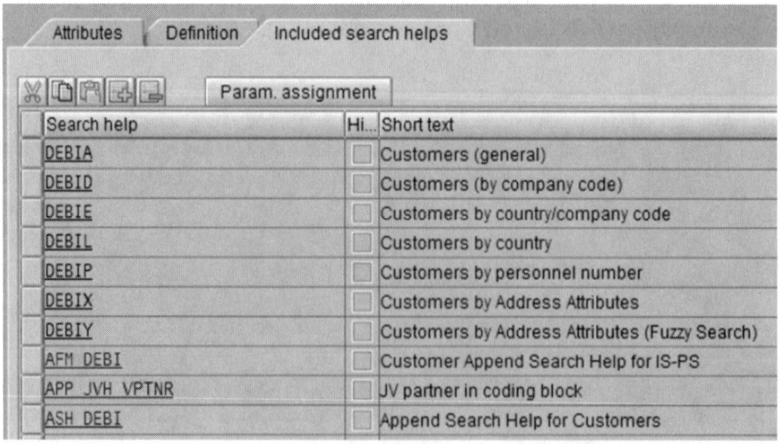

Attributes | Definition | Included search helps

Param. assignment

Search help	Hi...	Short text
DEBIA		Customers (general)
DEBID		Customers (by company code)
DEBIE		Customers by country/company code
DEBIL		Customers by country
DEBIP		Customers by personnel number
DEBIX		Customers by Address Attributes
DEBIY		Customers by Address Attributes (Fuzzy Search)
AFM_DEBI		Customer Append Search Help for IS-PS
APP_JVH_VPTNR		JV partner in coding block
ASH_DEBI		Append Search Help for Customers

FIGURE 7-19 Included search help (Copyright by SAP AG)

be immediately shown. However, if the number of entries is above 100, then the system will show the restriction value dialog first.

- *"Hot key."* This method allows using a search help usually known as "direct notation." This type allows for entering directly in the possible entries field the condition for restricting the search. An example is described in the next section.
- *Parameters.* As a general rule, we can say that the parameters defined in this section are the field that are shown in the restricting value dialog and also correspond to the columns of the proposed entries display. There is one exception, when we enter values that can be used in one "search help exit" (see the following entry). Figure 7-20 shows an example of parameters.
- *Search help exit.* These "exits" allow us to enhance the standard features of the search help. Technically, a search help exit corresponds to an ABAP function module. For instance, we could create more complex restrictions; define more dynamic columns in the hit list display, and so on. One of the few exceptions that the SAP systems have when verifying user authorizations are found in the search help exists. If we have several companies running under the same client, a user of a company could see some master data of clients of other companies with these types of exits. In order to avoid this type of potential security problem, we can also implement an AUTHORITY-CHECK function within the exit. Implementing this type of search help exit is not an easy task, and therefore SAP has included some reference examples, such as the function module F4IF_SHLP_EXIT_EXAMPLE.

Example of Hot Key for Search Help In this section we will show an example of using brief or direct notation for finding possible entries for a field, and we will use the search for customers. The elementary search help DEBIA has the letter *A* as associated hot key. In the parameters defined, the order is very important.

The syntax for hot keys to use as search help for a field is the following:

= <hot_key_letter>.<field_value_1>.<field_value_2>., . . .

where

"="	Activates the use of the hot key.
<hot_key_letter>	Is an identifier of the elementary search help or hot key.
"."	Allows for separating the values for each field. If we don't want to enter any value for this field, we can enter two periods together. After the first period, we have to enter the value for the first parameter defined in the search help. After the next period, we have to enter the value for the second parameter, and so on.
<field_value_n>	Is a restrictive value for field "n."

For example, if in the field for a client code in transaction XD03 (Display customer) we enter the value "=A..12045", the system will show every customer with Zip code matching the value "12045," as you can see in Figure 7-21.

Search help parameter	IMP	EXP	LPos	SPos	SDis	Data element	M...	Default va
SORTL			1	1		SORTL		
PSTLZ			2	2		PSTLZ		
MCOD3			3	3		MCDD3		
MCOD1			4	4		MCDD1		
KUNNR	✓	✓	5	5		KUNNR		

Figure 7-20 Search help parameters (Copyright by SAP AG)

Field Help (Documentation)

Objects or services are used to provide documentation help in dictionary fields, which can be later called from any screen where they are used. The definition of the help can be defined using the dictionary data elements.

From a data element, we can maintain its associated documentation using the Documentation button in the maintenance screen for the data elements, as shown in Figure 7-22.

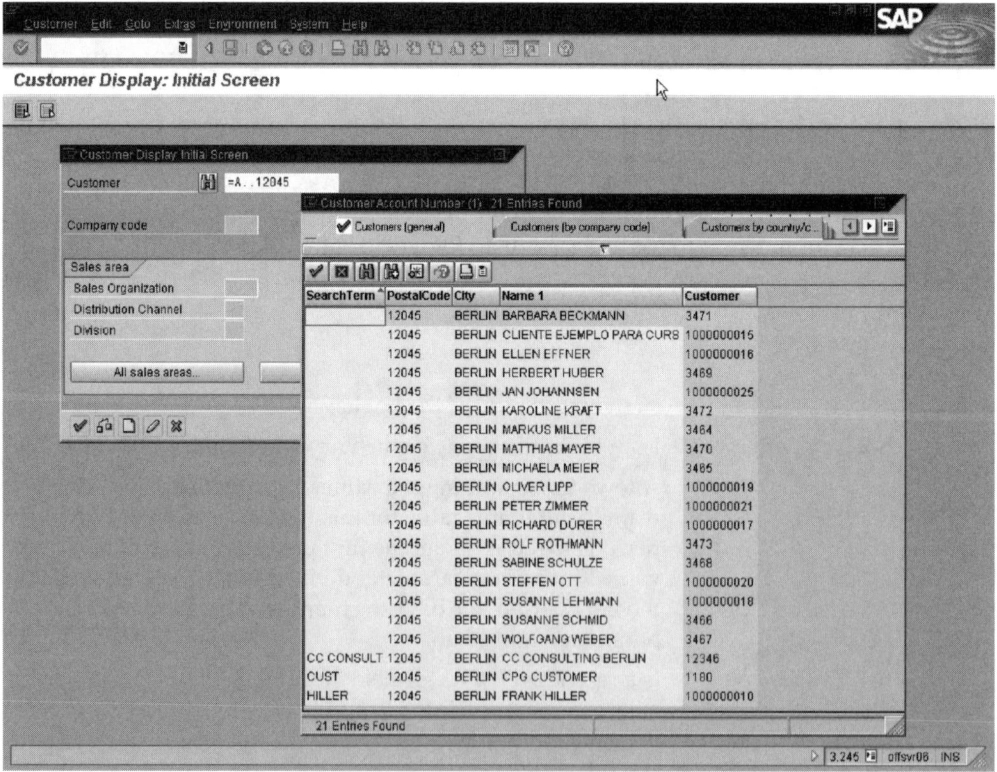

SearchTerm	PostalCode	City	Name 1	Customer
	12045	BERLIN	BARBARA BECKMANN	3471
	12045	BERLIN	CLIENTE EJEMPLO PARA CURS	1000000015
	12045	BERLIN	ELLEN EFFNER	1000000016
	12045	BERLIN	HERBERT HUBER	3469
	12045	BERLIN	JAN JOHANNSEN	1000000025
	12045	BERLIN	KAROLINE KRAFT	3472
	12045	BERLIN	MARKUS MILLER	3464
	12045	BERLIN	MATTHIAS MAYER	3470
	12045	BERLIN	MICHAELA MEIER	3465
	12045	BERLIN	OLIVER LIPP	1000000019
	12045	BERLIN	PETER ZIMMER	1000000021
	12045	BERLIN	RICHARD DÜRER	1000000017
	12045	BERLIN	ROLF ROTHMANN	3473
	12045	BERLIN	SABINE SCHULZE	3468
	12045	BERLIN	STEFFEN OTT	1000000020
	12045	BERLIN	SUSANNE LEHMANN	1000000018
	12045	BERLIN	SUSANNE SCHMID	3466
	12045	BERLIN	WOLFGANG WEBER	3467
CC CONSULT	12045	BERLIN	CC CONSULTING BERLIN	12346
CUST	12045	BERLIN	CPG CUSTOMER	1180
HILLER	12045	BERLIN	FRANK HILLER	1000000010

Figure 7-21 Example of hot key search help (Copyright by SAP AG)

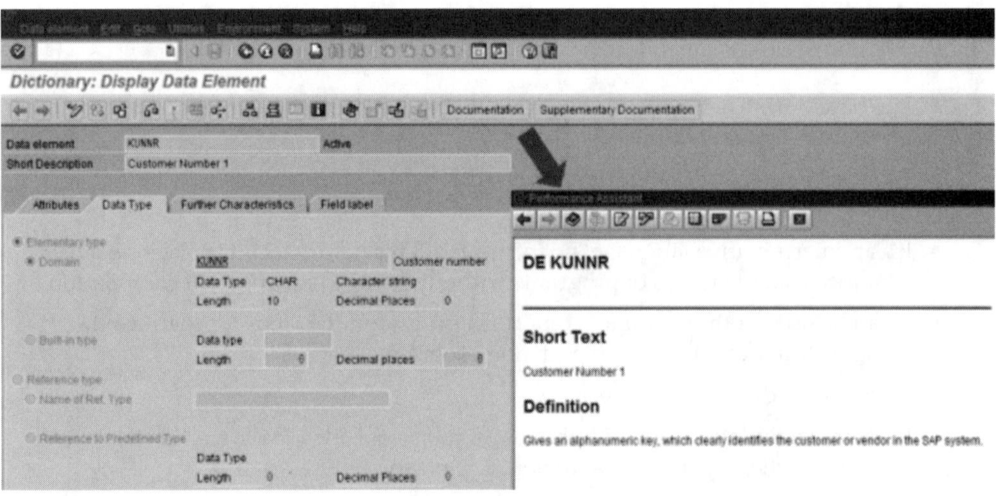

FIGURE 7-22 Data element documentation (Copyright by SAP AG)

Lock Objects

The lock objects within the ABAP dictionary provide the basic service for creating or releasing logical locks for the elements of the database.

Lock objects automatically generate function modules to perform the locking and releasing for the objects. It's very important to understand that these are logical locks. They can be used to include in ABAP programs, so that you can have a further level of control; however, you must remember that the database engine already uses its own locking mechanisms, which are the ones that actually guarantee the consistency of the database at a physical level.

Introduction to the ABAP Programming Language

ABAP stands for Advanced Business Application Programming. Before release 4.0 of SAP R/3, the language was known as ABAP/4 (the 4 meant it was a fourth-generation language). With release 4.0B, back in 1998, the name was changed to simply ABAP because, although the language maintains most of the best fourth-generation language features and previous syntax and keywords, many object-oriented features have been incorporated in a move to make it a fully capable object-oriented language.

ABAP is the programming language that SAP has used to develop all the SAP R/3 business modules and applications, including the system management functions. It is available to customers and developers to extend SAP functionality for their particular needs.

ABAP programs are created and maintained using the workbench tools discussed in previous sections.

Because of its origin and evolution, ABAP retains many of the fourth-generation language features such as the following:

- It is based on structured programming methodologies, allowing modular programming and reutilization of code.
- It resembles natural English language, making ABAP programs easy to read and understand.
- It's an interpretative language, not compiled. This nature facilitates testing and running earlier versions of programs without the need for constant compilation.
- It can be used both from single report list programming (report programs) to complex transaction processing (dialog programs).
- It's an event-driven language.
- It's completely integrated with the rest of the workbench tools, such as the screen painter, the menu painter, the dictionary, and so on.
- It supports multilanguage text elements. This means that you can create text elements in several languages without modifying the program source code.
- Similar to many programming languages, it includes elements for
  - Variable and data type declarations
  - Flow control elements
  - Operational elements
  - Event elements
  - Functions and subroutines, which can be managed by a central library
- It contains a subset of standard SQL statements enabling transparent database table access independently of the underlying database system being used.
- It provides extensive functions for handling and operating with data types such as dates, strings, floating point numbers, and so on.

The ABAP object-oriented features started together with SAP's strategic and technological move toward working with business objects and the introduction of Business Application Program Interfaces (BAPIs) within the Business Framework architecture. The business objects are included within the ABAP Workbench in the business object repository (BOR).

As an object-oriented language, the new ABAP, from release 4.x onward, incorporates technology principles such as inheritance, encapsulations, and polymorphism to provide the language with advantages such as lower maintenance costs and greater ease in reusing code.

Basic concepts and features of the ABAP object-oriented programming language are the same as those of other object-oriented languages. The most important are as follows:

- A business object, or simply an object, represents a type of entity—a customer, a business unit, an account, and so on—containing all its properties. Every object has an identity that allows it to be distinguished from other objects.

- Object classes, or simply classes, specify the structure of the objects belonging to a given class and the definition of the interfaces. Classes are useful for grouping objects with the same structure (attributes, methods, events). Generally, objects are defined using classes. The term *instance* is used for a specific object belonging to a class.
- The object's attributes provide the object with its characteristics, describing the current object state.
- Methods are the actions that can be performed with the object, indicating the behavior of the object.
- Events are used so that the object can inform or be informed of any event or state change on the system to enable the system to react to those events.
- Interfaces are another very important feature of objects. They define the method in which objects can be used independently of their internal implementation.

Basics of the Syntax of the ABAP Programming Language

In the next few sections we will introduce the basic elements of the ABAP programming language, with the objective of providing an overall description of the most important features of the ABAP syntax, such as data types, comments, naming conventions, operators, program flow control, and so on. We will also provide the classical example with the first ABAP program *"Hello World."*

ABAP Data Objects

When defining a data object within an ABAP program, there are two possibilities: using the keywords LIKE or the keyword TYPE. This type of definition is static. At runtime, we cannot modify the type of the data object. There are other possible syntax options, but they are not supported with ABAP objects.

With the LIKE keyword, what we are indicating is that the type of the data object being defined is the same that the data object referenced in the clause. For example,

```
DATA field1 TYPE C.
DATA field2 LIKE field1.
```

In the example data object field2 is of type C (field of one position) because that is the type of data object field1.

With the keyword TYPE we have three options for defining the data object:

- Reference to a predefined ABAP type
- Reference to a global type, that is, a type defined in the ABAP dictionary
- Reference to a type defined with the TYPES keyword (local types)

There is also the possibility of defining complex structure types based on the elementary types.

Data Types

The following table shows the current ABAP predefined data types:

Type	Type Length and Bytes	Description
I	Fixed, 4	Integer
F	Fixed, 8	Floating number
P	Fixed, 1 . . . 16	Packed number
N	Fixed, 1 . . . 65535	Alphanumeric, numeric digits
C	Fixed, 1 . . . 65535	Alphanumeric, characters
D	Fixed, 8	Alphanumeric, date
T	Fixed, 6	Alphanumeric, time
X	Fixed, 1 . . . 65535	Hexadecimal
String	Variable	Character sequence
Xstring	Variable	Hexadecimal

The length of variable fields is established at runtime, and therefore it is not required to specify their length when defining the fields.

It is necessary to specify the length for the fields of type "c," "n," "x," or "p." You cannot specify length for type "D" or "t" because the length is predefined for the standard type.

Type Groups

We can also define type groups in the ABAP dictionary. The main features of the type groups are the following:

- The name of the type group can only have five characters.
- Statement TYPE-POOL defines the group within the dictionary.
- In a type group (Figure 7-23), we can define types and constants, but following the convention that the name bust start with a prefix including the same characters that the name of the group.
- Constants are defined using the keyword CONSTANTS, like any other ABAP program.
- Types are defined with keyword TYPES, like in any other ABAP program. In order to define this global types we can use predefined types or types that have been previously defined within the type group (Figure 7-24).
- This is the only way to define global constants within SAP systems.

Integer Types

The features of the integer data type are the following:

- The type identifier is "I."
- Length is 4 bytes.

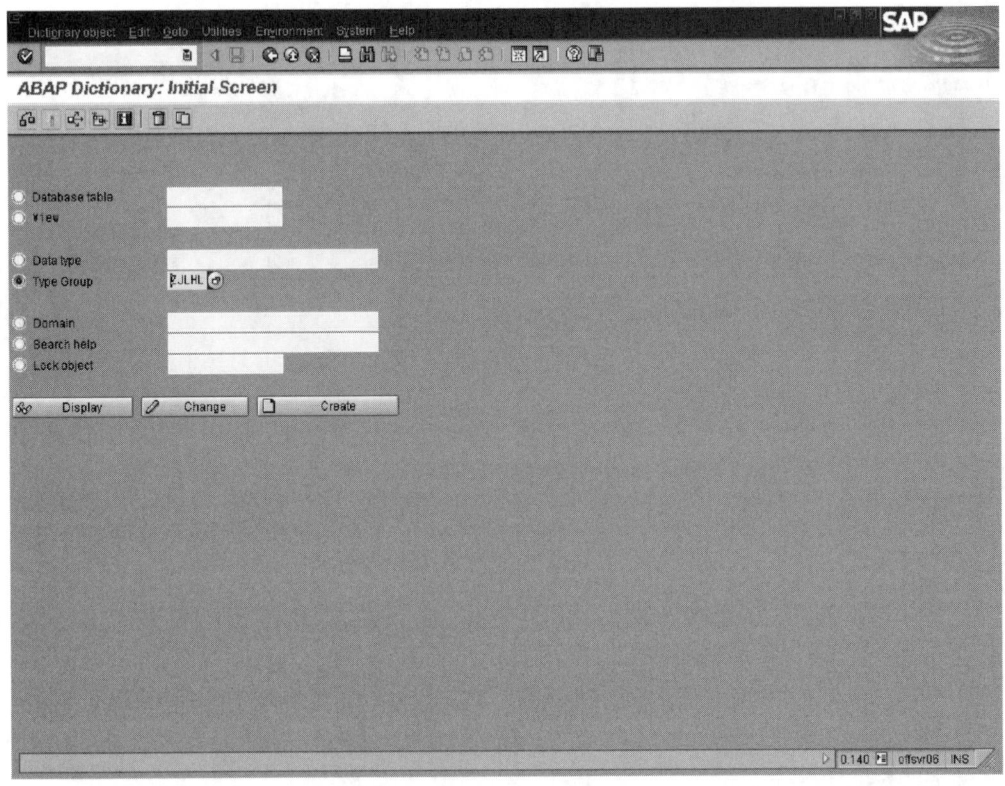

FIGURE 7-23 Type group (Copyright by SAP AG)

- Value range goes from 2147843648 to –2147843648.
- Arithmetic operations using integer types present a much better performance than operations performed with other numeric types.

This is the arithmetic used by integer number types:

- All the auxiliary fields required to perform internal operations are also of the same type, integer.
- Results are always rounded to an I type.
- Arithmetic operators are as follows:

Operator	Meaning
+	Addition
–	Subtraction
*	Multiplication
/	Division
DIV	Integer division

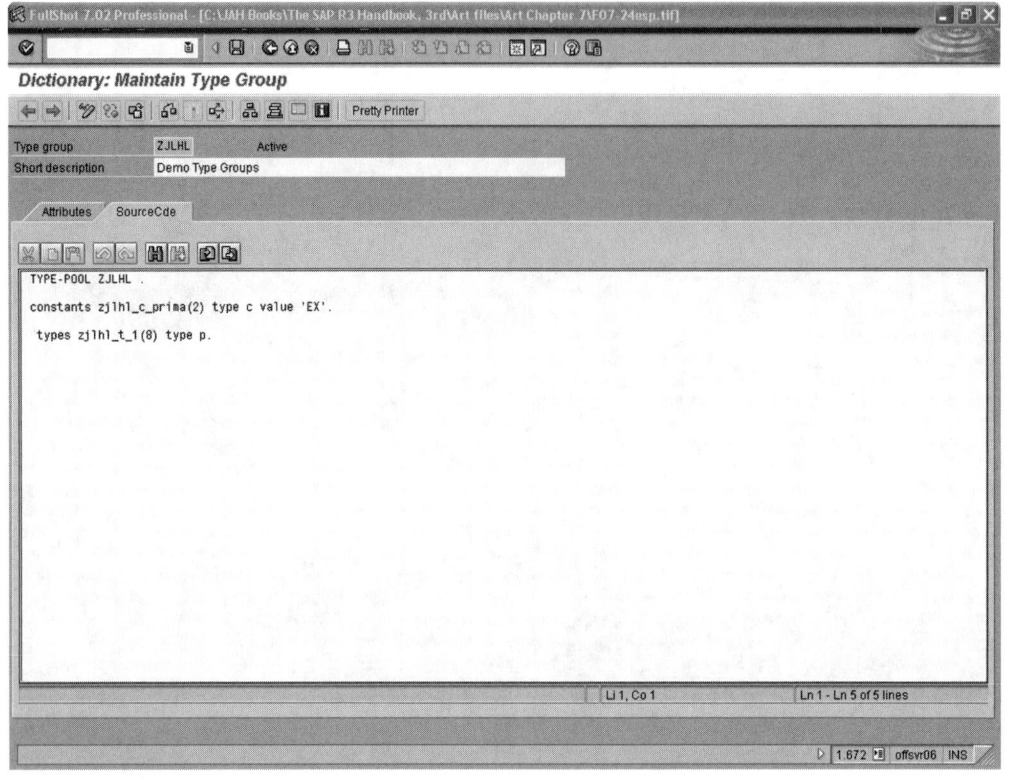

FIGURE 7-24 Maintaining a type group (Copyright by SAP AG)

MOD	Rest of the integer division
**	Exponentiation

- You can also perform operations with the COMPUTE clause.

For example:

```
DATA integer TYPE i.
Integer = 4 / 10 "Result is 0.
Integer = 5 / 10 "Result is 1.
```

Packed Types

The main features and arithmetic of the packed number types are the following:

- The length in the definition of the data object describes the length in bytes of the field.
- The DECIMALS keyword established the number of decimal positions within the field, but it's only relevant when showing the field in the screen or printed.

- The length allows lengths from 1 to 16 bytes. For this reason, packaged types can include numbers from 1 to 31 digits, because the last byte is used to store the sign (+ or –).
- Logically, the number of decimal positions cannot be larger than the number of digits, so it never has more than 15 digits.

The arithmetic of the packed type is as follows:

- The intermediate results from arithmetic operations are kept in fields with maximum length.
- Type is the data type to be used with operations on business fields.

For example:

```
DATA field(3) TYPE p DECIMALS 2 VALUE '234.20'
```

Floating Comma Numeric Type

The features of this type are the following:

- In packed numbers the floating comma types are represented by addition of binary fractions. Both the exponent and the mantissa are stored in this way.
- Packed numbers should not be used.

The arithmetic of this type is the following:

- Fields of this type keep the approximation of the real number. Therefore, they should not be used when a exact precision is needed.
- Packed numbers can only be used for approximations, because the number that the system stores might not be the one expected.
- The main advantage of this type of fields is the range of values accepted, from 2,2250738585072014E–308 to 1,7976931348623157E+308.
- Packed numbers is the only valid type for operations of aggregation of the SELECT statement.

For example:

```
DATA field(8) TYPE f.
```

String Character Type

Main features of the string type are the following:

- The range of values accepted by the string character data type depends on the page code that the system is using. The code page contains all the characters supported by means of a code number. From transaction SPAD (Figure 7-25), you can validate the code page of your system.
- The initial value of all string types is ***.

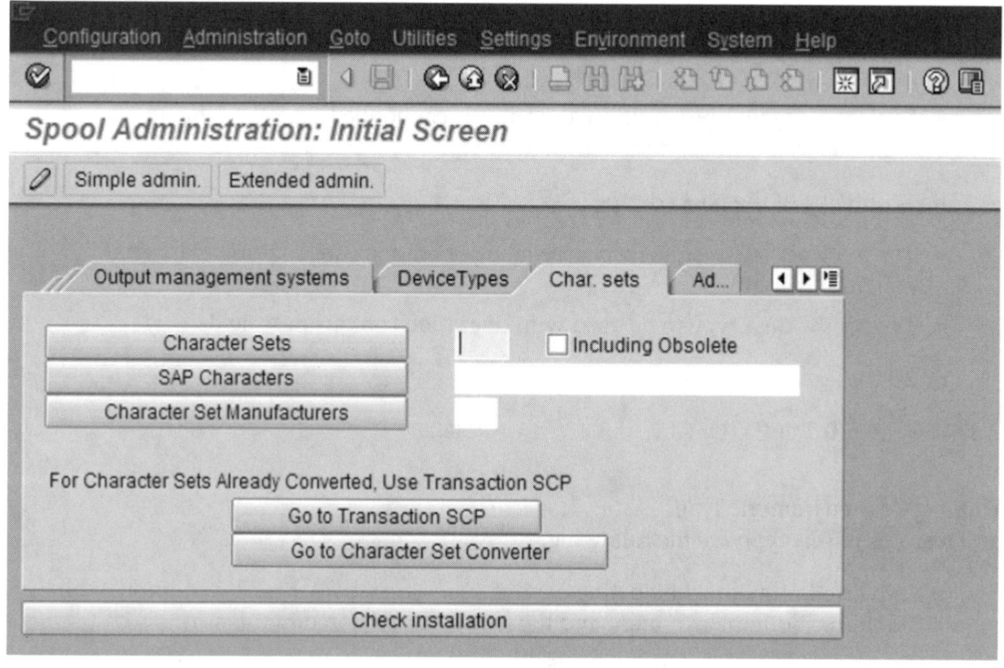

FIGURE 7-25 SPAD transaction (Copyright by SAP AG)

Comments in ABAP

Comments in ABAP are easy to include in the programs. The two types of comments that we can enter in our ABAP programs are

- Line comments
- Partial line comments

Line Comments ABAP provides a way to mark a line as a comment. The method consists of entering an asterisk sign (*) in the first column of the line. For example:

```
*&---------------------------------------------------------------------
*& Report ZTALLER_ABAPUNIT
*&
*&---------------------------------------------------------------------
*&
*&
*&---------------------------------------------------------------------
```

Partial Line Comments The partial line comments allow for making a comment only in a part of a line. In order to enter one of these types of comments, you have to code double quotes (") in any column of the line. The compiler will not take into consideration anything that is entered after the quotes.

It is important to note that the ABAP comments are entered using quotes (") whereas literal values are identified by a single quote sign ('). For example:

```
Select *  from bkpf "Read all the columns from the table
...
```

Conventions in ABAP

The ABAP programming language is not restrictive when defining identifiers, but it has some rules that must be closely observed.

The names of the components of classes (attributes, methods, events, and so on) can only be made up of characters A–Z, a–z, 0–9 and character _. Additionally, the first character cannot be a numeric digit. You cannot use special characters in the identifiers because, on some occasions, these have special meaning for the system.

For example: The first DATA statement is wrong, whereas the second one is correct:

```
DATA:  field-name TYPE, . . .
       1name TYPE . . .
DATA:  field_name TYPE, . . .
       name1 TYPE . . .
```

Although there are other elements of the ABAP language less restrictive, it is recommended to use the same conventions as those used in ABAP objects.

ABAP Operators

Relational Operators for Any Data Type

Operator	Description	Example	
=, EQ	Equals	a = b	a EQ b
<>, NE	Not equal	a <> b	a NE b
>, GT	Greater than	a > b	a GT b
<, LT	Less than	a < b	a LT b
>=, GE	Greater than or equal to	a >= b	a GE b
<=, LE	Less than or equal to	a <= b	a LE b

Relational Operators for String Character Types

Operator	Description	Example
CO	Contains only	`'ABCDE' CO 'XYZ'` is false; `SY-FDPOS` = 0.
		`'ABCDE' CO 'AB'` is false; `SY-FDPOS` = 2.
		`'ABCDE' CO 'ABCDE'` is true; `SY-FDPOS` = 5.
CN	Contains not only	Previous examples would have opposite results.

(*continued*)

Operator	Description	Example
CA	Contains any	`'ABCDE' CA 'CY'` is true; `SY-FDPOS` = 2. `'ABCDE' CA 'XY'` is false; `SY-FDPOS` = 5.
NA	Does not contain any	Previous examples would have opposite results.
CS	Contains the string	`'ABCDE' CS 'CD'` is true; `SY-FDPOS` = 2. `'ABCDE' CS 'XY'` is false; `SY-FDPOS` = 5. `'ABAAA' CS 'AB'` is true; `SY-FDPOS` = 0. `'ABC' CS 'AB'` is true; `SY-FDPOS` = 1. `'ABC DEF' CS ' '` is true; but `SY-FDPOS` = 0, since `' '` is interpreted as a blank space.
NS	Does not contain the string	Previous examples would have opposite results.
CP	Contains template	`'ABCDE' CP '*CD*'` is true; `SY-FDPOS` = 2. `'ABCDE' CP '*CD'` is false; `SY-FDPOS` = 5. `'ABCDE' CP '++CD+'` is true; `SY-FDPOS` = 0. `'ABCDE' CP '+CD*'` is false; `SY-FDPOS` = 5. `'ABCDE' CP '*B*D*'` is true; `SY-FDPOS` = 1.
NP	Does not contain template	Previous examples would have opposite results.

Relational Operations for Fields of Byte Type Data of type byte are of type X (fixed length) and XSTRING (variable length).

Operator	Description	Example

BYTE-CO	Contains only	`x1 = '01020304'.`
		`x2 = 'FEFF'.`
		`x3 = '0102'.`
		`x1 BYTE-CO x2` is false; `SY-FDPOS` = 0.
		`x1 BYTE-CO x3` is false; `SY-FDPOS` = 2.
		`x1 BYTE-CO x1` is true; `SY-FDPOS` = 4.

BYTE-CN	Contains not only	Previous examples would have opposite results.

BYTE-CA	Contains any	`x1 = '01020304'.`
		`x2 = '03FF'.`
		`x3 = 'FEFF'.`
		`x1 BYTE-CA x2` is true; `SY-FDPOS` = 2.
		`x1 BYTE-CA x3` is false; `SY-FDPOS` = 4.

BYTE-NA	Does not contain any	Previous examples would have opposite results.

BYTE-CS	Contains string	`x1 = '01020304'.`
		`x2 = '0304'.`
		`x3 = 'FEFF'.`
		`x1 BYTE-CS x2` is true; `SY-FDPOS` = 2.
		`x1 BYTE-CS x3` is false; `SY-FDPOS` = 4.
		`x1 = '00000102'.`
		`x2 = '000102'.`
		`x1 BYTE-CS x2` is true; `SY-FDPOS` = 1.

BYTE-NS	Does not contain string	Previous examples would have opposite results.

Relational Operators for Bit Masks

Operator	Description
O	The expression is true if f1 contains a 1 in those positions in which there is a 1 in f2.
Z	Expression is true when f1 contains a 0 in those positions in which there is a 0 in f2.
M	Expression is true when f1 contains at least a 1 and a 0 in those positions where there is a 1 in f2.

Other Relational Operators

Operator	Description	Example
[NOT] BETWEEN AND	Verifies if a value is/is not between two values.	f1 [NOT] BETWEEN f2 AND f3.
IS [NOT] INITIAL	Compares a field with the default value of the field, depending on the field type.	f1 IS [NOT] INITIAL.
IS [NOT] ASSIGNED	Verifies if the field symbol is assigned (points to) a field.	<fs1> IS [NOT] ASSIGNED.

IS [NOT] BOUND	Verifies if a reference variable has a valid reference.	data DREF type ref to DATA.
		start-of-selection.
		  perform: TEST,
		           CREATE,
		           TEST.
		form CREATE.
		  data INT type I.
		  get reference of INT into DREF.
		  perform TEST.
		endform.
		form TEST.
		  if DREF is bound.
		    write / 'Bound'.
		  else.
		    write / 'Unbound'.
		  endif.
		endform.

IS [NOT] REQUESTED	Used to verify if a formal parameter in a call has been specified in a call within a function module. It is "true" if it has been specified, and "false" if not. This operator has been enahnced with method verification with the IS SUPPLIED clause. It is recommended to use this last form.	...
		IF TEXT IS REQUESTED.
		  SELECT SINGLE * FROM
		...
		  TEXT = ...
		ENDIF.

(*continued*)

Operator	Description	Example

IS [NOT] SUPPLIED	Used to verify (or not) whether a parameter was passed at runtime as an input parameter (importing) or output parameter (exporting) in in function modules or in methods.	`CLASS test DEFINITION.`
		`  PUBLIC SECTION.`
		`    METHODS meth`
		`IMPORTING  op TYPE i`
		`OPTIONAL`
		
		`EXCEPTIONS excp.`
		`ENDCLASS.`
		
		`CLASS test`
		`IMPLEMENTATION.`
		`  METHOD meth.`
		`    DATA: feld TYPE i.`
		`    IF op IS SUPPLIED.`
		`      CASE op.`
		`        WHEN 1.`
		`          feld = 100.`
		`        WHEN 2.`
		`          feld = 200.`
		`        WHEN OTHERS.`
		`          RAISE excp.`
		`      ENDCASE.`
		`    ENDIF.`
		`  ENDMETHOD.`
		`ENDCLASS.`

[NOT] IN	Verifies if a parameter is contained in a selection criteria. Instead of being a selection criteria (SELECT OPTIONS), a range can be used (RANGES) or any internal table that stores the corresponding structure.	fIN so_client

My First ABAP Program, Hello SAP World!!!

As it cannot be any other way, we will show a very easy example that will show the message *Hello world!!!* in the screen. The result of this practical example is shown in Figure 7-26.

The ABAP Language Editor is included within the SAP systems, and it can be accessed from transaction SE38.

When in main screen of transaction SE38, enter the name of the program (ZLESSON1) in the Program field, and click on the Create button. Refer to Figure 7-27.

In the next screen, enter the following information, as shown in Figure 7-28.

- *Title.* Enter the program title.
- *Type.* Enter Executable Program.
- *Status.* Enter Test Program although we could enter some other types.

Leave default values in the rest of the fields and click on Save.

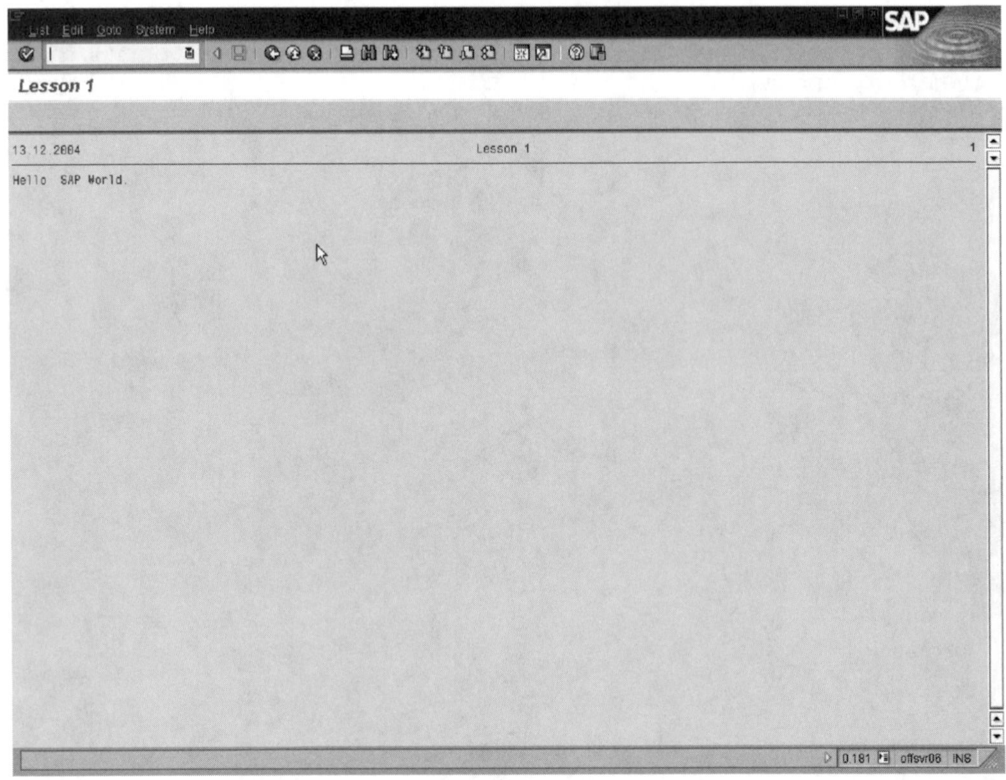

FIGURE 7-26 Hello SAP World result (Copyright by SAP AG)

Next the system will show up the ABAP Editor. In this next screen is where we write the ABAP code that will generate the output as we have shown previously.

The source code is shown in Figure 7-29.

After entering the code we must verify the syntax by clicking on the fm:see file in this email button, saving the changes in the program by clicking on the Save button, and then activating the program to be able to run it by clicking on the Activate button.

We can run the program by clicking on the Direct Processing button. After pressing this button, and if there was no error on the code, we will get the output as shown in Figure 7-29.

Easy, isn't it?

Testing and Debugging ABAP

This section introduces some of the most important utilities within the ABAP Workbench to test and debug ABAP programs.

ABAP is a powerful programming language for developing sophisticated business applications, and for the very same reason it is important to be able to test those developments and avoid errors during runtime that might have not been initially foreseen, such as unexpected messages, incorrect return codes, performance errors, and others.

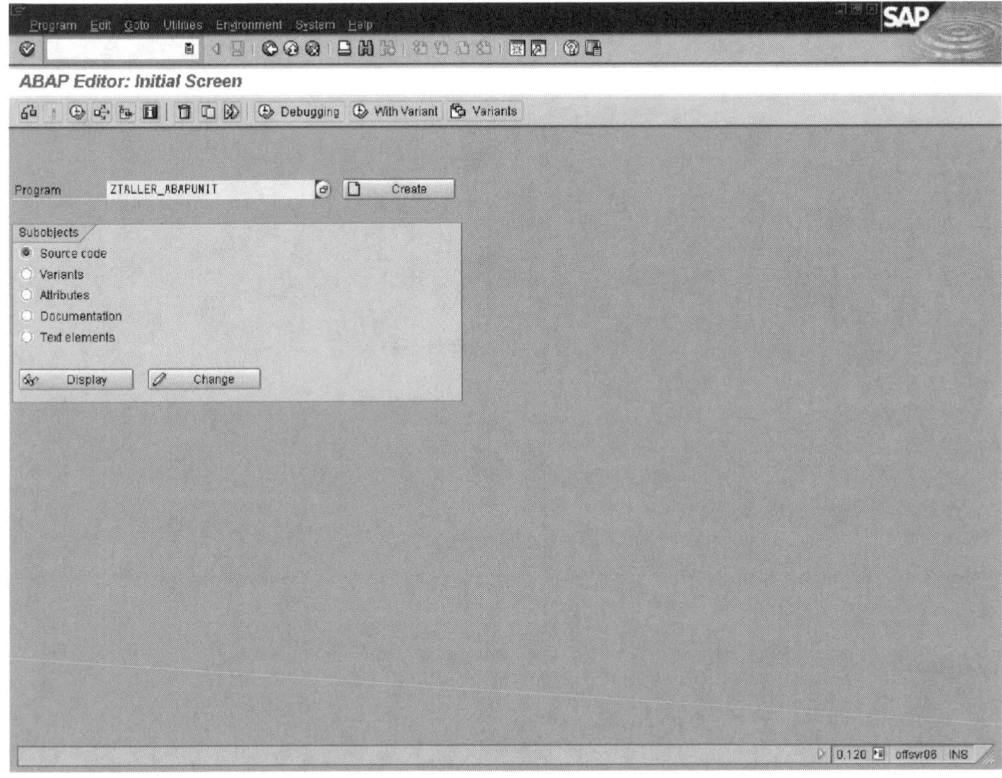

FIGURE 7-27 Main Screen of transaction SE38 (Copyright by SAP AG)

A single tool would not be enough to detect all types of situations that could happen during the development of a SAP application. The ABAP Debugger can be used to see the content of an internal table at runtime, but it is not the proper tool to detect performance problems.

SAP, within the Web Application Server, provides a collection of tools that can be used to perform code verification in a static manner, as well as more detailed analyses of system events, analysis of processes with errors, setup of traces at runtime, as well as perform debugging at runtime.

As a starting point, we will assume that the programs being analyzed are free of syntactical errors, and therefore we can activate and run them. For the most part, if there are initial syntax errors, the programs cannot even be activated. However, even with these premises, we cannot guarantee that there will be no errors at runtime.

The main transactions and tools within the ABAP Workbench that can be used to debug and test ABAP programs are as follows:

- ABAP Debugger
- Runtime analysis

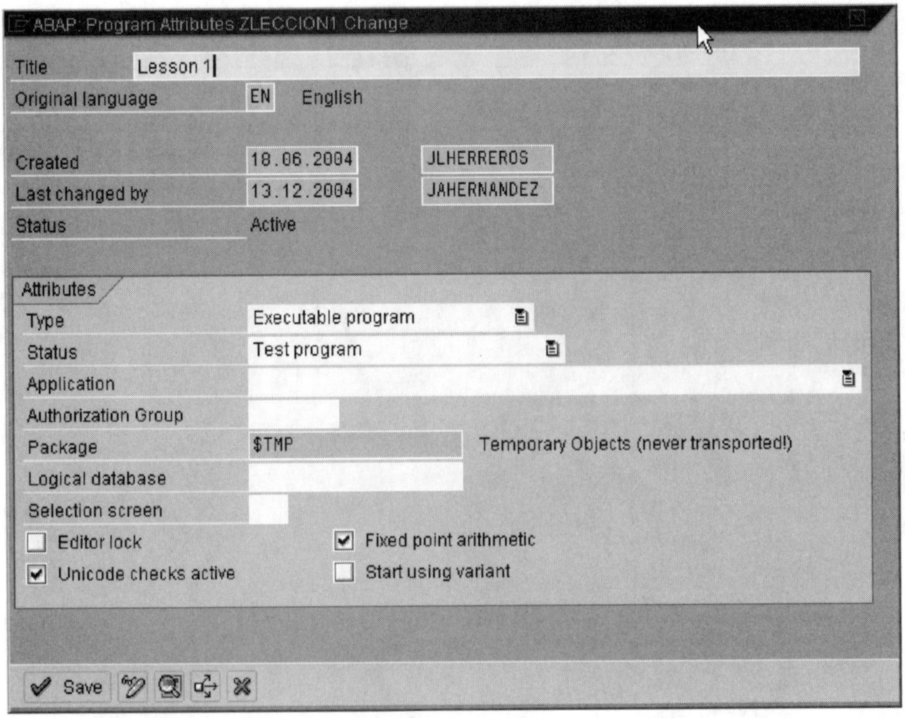

FIGURE 7-28 Program attributes (Copyright by SAP AG)

- Performance Trace
- Extended program check
- Code Inspector
- ABAP Unit
- eCATTs
- Coverage Analyzer

The next sections briefly introduce three of these tools. For more detailed information on these topics, please refer to the SAP online documentation or the SAP Help Web site.

ABAP Debugger

The ABAP Debugger can be activated from any transaction by entering the /H code in the transaction command field (also known as the OK-CODE).

You can also activate the debugger by including the statement BREAK-POINT within the ABAP code. When the system processes the statement, the debugger is automatically

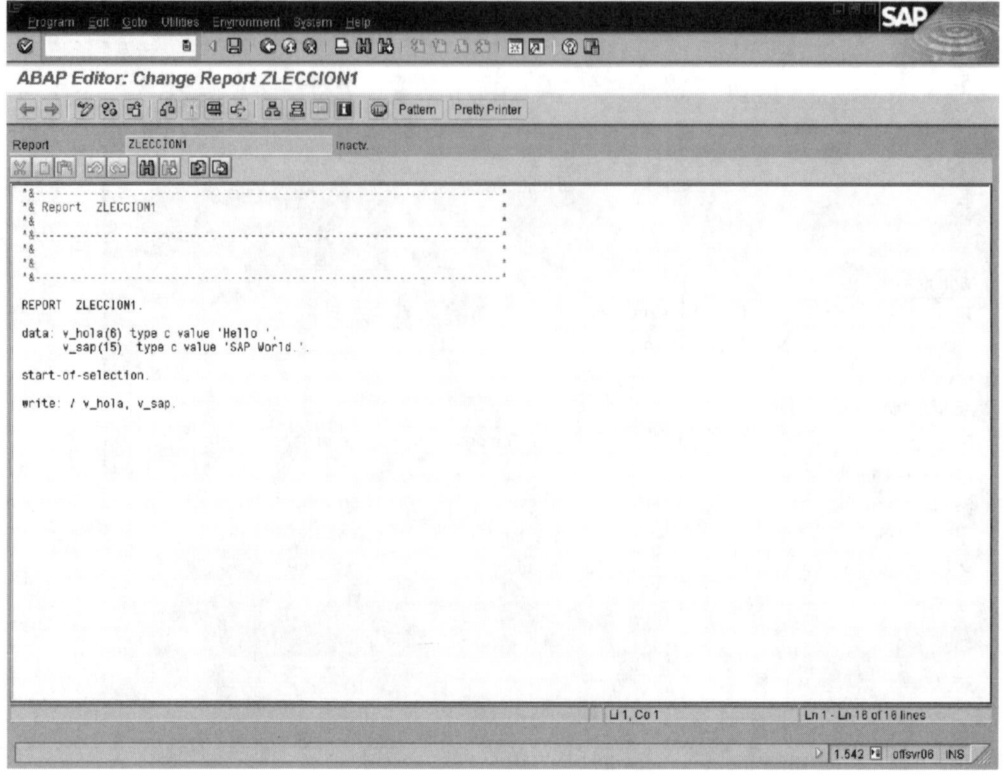

FIGURE 7-29 ABAP source code (Copyright by SAP AG)

activated. You can also use the macro keyword BREAK <username>. The debugger will only be activated when the program is run by the username in the program.

Another more elegant way of setting up breakpoints is by using the options within the ABAP Editor, as you can see in Figure 7-30.

In Figure 7-30, the developer has just located the cursor over the WRITE sentence and pressed the Stop button. At runtime, when the statement is processed, the system activates the debugger. Figure 7-31 shows the ABAP Debugger.

If we enter the name of a data object of the program in the fields in the lower part of the debugger, the system will show the current contents of the field.

With the Table button, we can see the content of an internal table.

The Breakpoints button can be used to see all the existing control points within the program.

The Watchpoints button allows seeing the watch points defined in the debugging process. A watchpoint is a conditional break point. There are many possible conditions for setting watchpoints, but the most common one is comparing a field value with the value of a constant or another program variable.

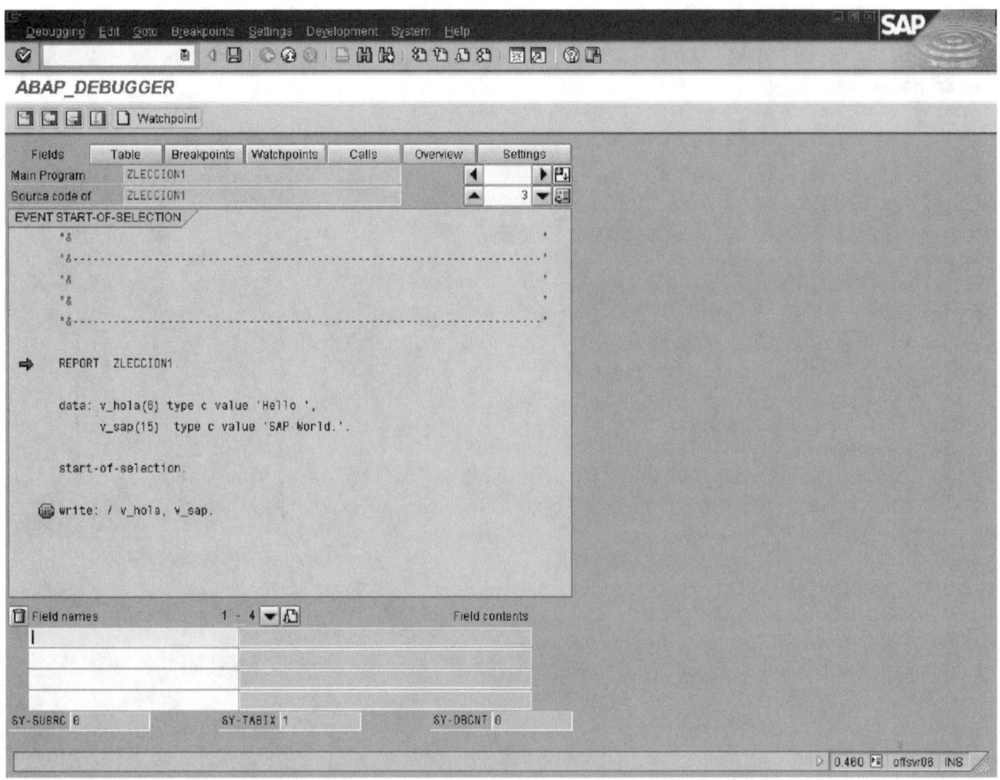

FIGURE 7-30 Setting breakpoints in the ABAP Debugger (Copyright by SAP AG)

The Call button can be used to see the sequence of the current calls in the program. This sequence allows us to see the nesting of the calls between programs, function modules, ABAP processes, and so on.

The Overview button is used to see the process blocks executed from the main program.

With the Settings button we can configure how the debugger will behave. For example, we can set whether we also want to debug the system sentences.

Extended Program Check

The extended program check, invoked with transaction SLIN, is a tool that can be used to perform a comprehensive verification of our program. Figures 7-32 and 7-33 show the functions that can be included with the transaction as well as some of the results of running it over a program.

In the initial field, we have to enter the name of the program to be analyzed. Next, we check those verifications to be performed. Figure 7-32 shows the default values for these verifications.

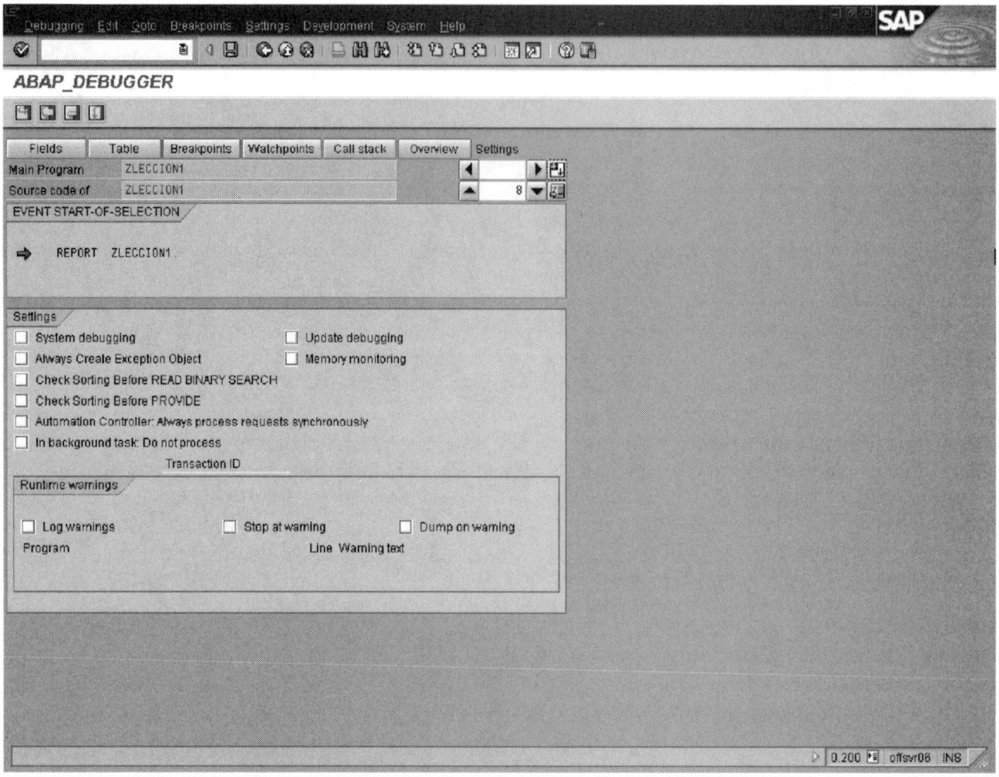

FIGURE 7-31 Example of ABAP Debugger (Copyright by SAP AG)

We could, for example, analyze those sentences that SAP already considers obsolete, or those that could create errors or dumps at runtime.

In the resulting screen after running the analysis, we can identify the potential problems that might arise at runtime.

You can exclude part of the program code if you include the following statements (during an extended syntax check, you can ignore these statements by using the additional function Include Suppressed Fields):

```
SET EXTENDED CHECK OFF.
<ABAP code>
SET EXTENDED CHECK ON.
```

ABAP Units

The concept of unit testing is very common among Java developers, and the tool that normally is used for that type of testing is known as *Junit*. ABAP Units work with a similar concept, but it is significantly different in its forms.

The most important concept of a test unit is to run a simple modularization unit of a program under certain valid testing conditions (specifically for input data) so that output

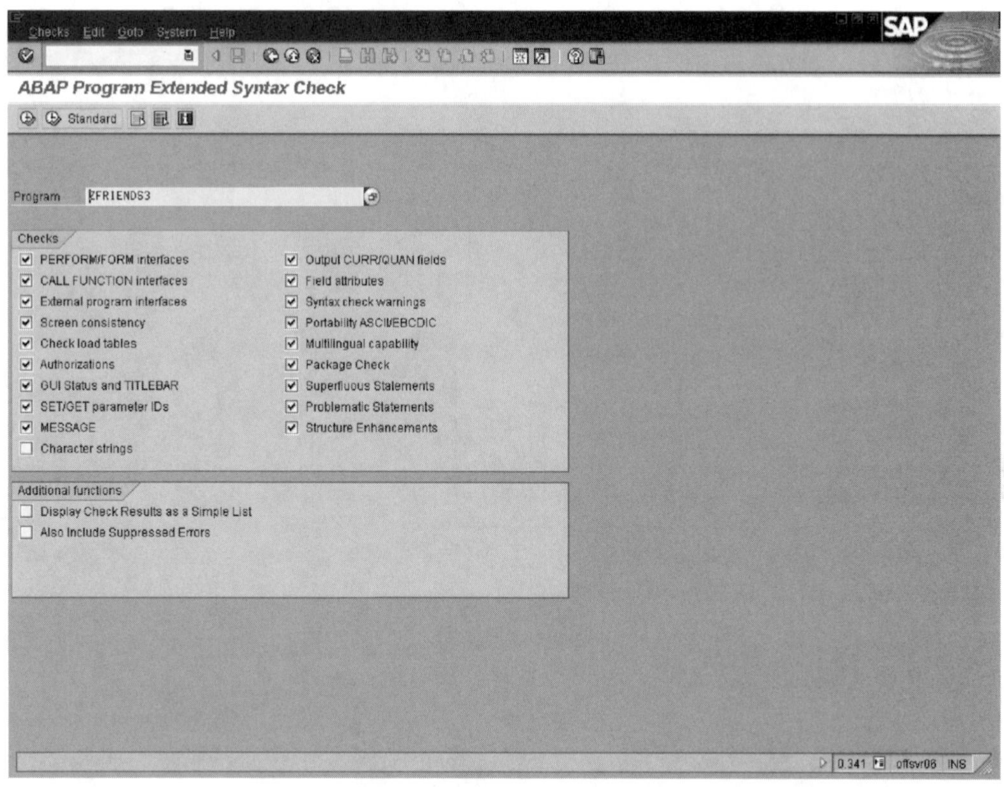

Figure 7-32 Extended program check (Copyright by SAP AG)

can be analyzed. In this context, the routines (FORMS), function modules, and methods are units of an ABAP program.

Steps to perform unit testing are the following:

- Customize the input data for the ABAP modularization units.
- Run the ABAP modularization unit.
- Get and analyze the output data from the ABAP Unit.

The test units are implemented as local ABAP object classes within a main program. This does not mean that we can only test classes or instances methods. As indicated previously, we can test other usual object types, such as FORMS or function modules.

Connectors

This section includes a description of the main SAP connectors that can be used to communicate and integrate SAP systems with other SAP or non-SAP systems.

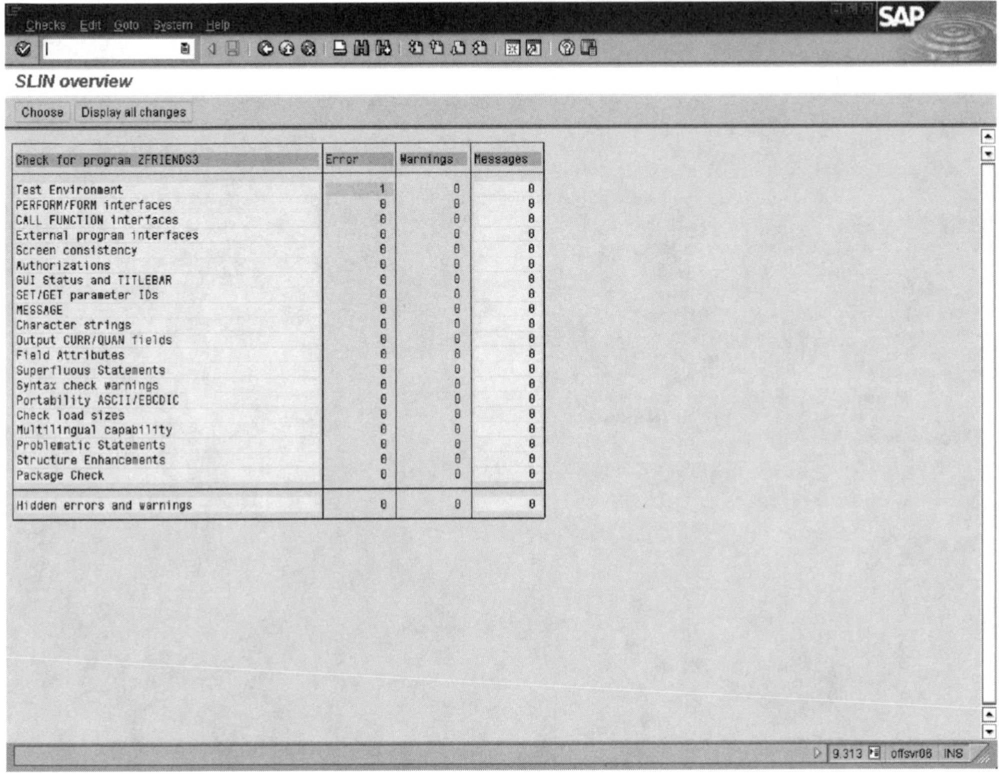

FIGURE 7-33 SLIN overview (Copyright by SAP AG)

Besides the options explained next, and in the context of the SAP NetWeaver integration platform, there is a new and advanced process integration tool, known as XI. For more information, refer to the corresponding section in Chapter 11.

SAP Business Connector

The SAP Business Connector, also known as SAP BC, allows for a high degree of automation and extends the business process to the Internet using nonproprietary standards. SAP BC is bidirectional, which means that we can invoke SAP objects, such as function modules, BAPIs, or IDOCS from external systems, and conversely we can use it from a SAP process to call a remote system's functions. These calls can be both synchronous and asynchronous.

SAP Marketplace Connector

SAP Marketplace Connector is a connectivity tool that allows the connection between SAP back-end systems with a SAP Marketplace, using standard Internet protocols. It can use IDOCs or xCBL as data format and HTTP (HTTPS/SSL) as communication protocol.

This connector is being used less frequently because the SAP Marketplaces are being migrated or changed to others based on SAP Enterprise Portals (SAP EP).

SAP Java Connector

SAP Java Connector, known commonly as JCO, is a set of classes (Java packets) that allow us to connect Java applications with SAP systems. The API provided is simple to manage, with a high degree of flexibility and performance. The JCO is bidirectional like in the other types of connectors; that is, you can make calls from Java to ABAP programs, as well as from ABAP to Java.

SAP .Net Connector

SAP .Net Connector offers application developers accustomed to the Microsoft .NET framework architecture the possibility of invoking BAPIs and functional modules from any .NET programming language, such as C#, VB .NET and others. With this connector there is also the possibility of accessing or calling .NET Components from SAP systems.

SAP DCOM Connector

DCOM connector is a SAP development with support from Microsoft that enables the Windows COM world to access any BAPI or RFC-module in a SAP system. DCOM means Distributed COM, and it means you can also access objects remotely defined in another server.

Since release 3.0 of the SAP Basis (R/3), ABAP can access COM objects from SAP. In this way ABAP has implemented instructions like CREATE OBJECT, SET/GET PROPERTY, and CALL METHOD and the programmer can access Windows objects and invoke the methods with this. These instructions are executed through the SAP GUI; this means that the ABAP sends a RFC to the SAP GUI and the SAP GUI executes the COM method. The biggest problem with this method is that it needs a user interface to be executed; for example, it will not work in a batch program.

Since release 4.6D of the SAP Basis (before the SAP Web Application Server) the DCOM suite has a bidirectional interface and you can access COM objects from ABAP through a new component called COM4ABAP (COM for ABAP) that allows you to invoke COM objects without SAP GUI. In the last section of this chapter bidirectional DCOM will be presented.

There are different ways to access a BAPI from the external SAP world. In the lower level you could use all the RFC available platforms, like RFC-API in DLL, C library in all the SAP-supported platforms including Windows, different UNIX and Linux, OS400 and OS/390, C++ library, or JAVA-RFC. In this level you can call directly the Function module that implements the BAPI.

But SAP supports also object-oriented programming and has implemented ActiveX controls, JAVA-BAPI, and also CORBA support in order to call BAPIs.

You can use the ActiveX controls in VB or ASP or in any Windows object-oriented programming language. The ActiveX controls are also called SAP Automation, and it is a simple approach to start programming BAPIs from VB, for example. SAP Automation is included in the Desktop Development Kit option from SAP GUI installation and is also available for download from saplabs.com.

If your preferred programming language is Java, you have also available a Java-BAPI (with the SAP GUI installation) and there are CORBA implementations for BAPI programming, such as Visual-Edge.

In the Windows world you should choose between ActiveX and DCOM and .Net connector programming. ActiveX is a simple starting point, but if you need hundreds of connections to SAP, DCOM connector allows you the Microsoft Transaction Server, which defines pools of connections instead of a connection for a single user like the SAP Automation controls.

DCOM connector allows you to access the SAP objects like local objects in your programming environment. All the facilities in object-oriented programming languages like the Intellisense editor in VB, where you can see objects, select one and see the methods, and select one and see the properties, are available with the DCOM connector.

With the optional use of Microsoft Transaction Server (MTS), DCOM connector enables you to define use the dispatching and queue possibilities of MTS.

The first thing that should be clear for you is that DCOM connector is a development environment, from which you can decide which SAP objects you want to use, and creates C code and compiles it for your developer later use. In the case of MTS DCOM connector creates MTS classes for you.

RFC Library

The RFC library offers yet another and one of the oldest interfaces to connect with SAP systems. This is the integration component that has been typically more used in SAP installations. The interface allows for performing calls to any RFC function available in a SAP system from an external system. We can also create a program that acts as an RFC server, which can be invoked from any SAP system or even from external applications. Many of the SAP connectors frequently use this library as the underlying platform for communication with the SAP systems.

SOAP Processor

The SOAP processor is an integral component in the SAP Web Application Server and provides all the required mechanisms in order to use the SOAP protocol to synchronize the accesses and the calls to RFC function modules that complies with the SOAP 1.1 standards. A Web Service browser can be used for the searching and generation of WSDL 1.1 descriptors. The SAP Web Application Server also provides a SOAP client API that represents the function modules that can be called synchronously using SOAP 1.1.

What Is New in the ABAP Development Environment with the SAP WAS

In this section we review most of the new features of the developing environment with release 6.20 of the SAP Web Application Server.

What Is New in the ABAP Development Environment

In the following sections we present the most important new features of the ABAP development environment and the new system features that are closely related to the ABAP Object Repository. Among these are the following:

- Description of the new options within the Object Navigator
- Properties for the new development element: the package
- Description of the new transaction Code Inspector
- New screen for the print dialog
- Process for mass update of the print parameters

New Options in the Object Navigator

With release SAP Web AS 6.20, there are several new buttons within the Object Navigator (transaction SE80). Figure 7-34 shows these new figures.

With the MIME Repository button you can access the MIME objects of the repository. This allows for easier and friendlier development of BSP applications, because you can access MIME objects and BSP applications from the same transaction.

The second button that you can see is Tag Browser, which allows you to use "drag and drop" techniques for any significant tag you need to use for the development of BSP applications. This is shown in Figure 7-35.

From the settings transaction, which you can reach by selecting Utilities | Settings from the menu, you can configure the buttons that you need to appear within the Object Navigator transaction.

Under the Workbench (General) tabstrip in the section Browser Selection, you can see the rows with all the buttons of the transaction. If you don't want to see a particular button in the transaction, you only have to uncheck the corresponding check box. Refer to Figure 7-36.

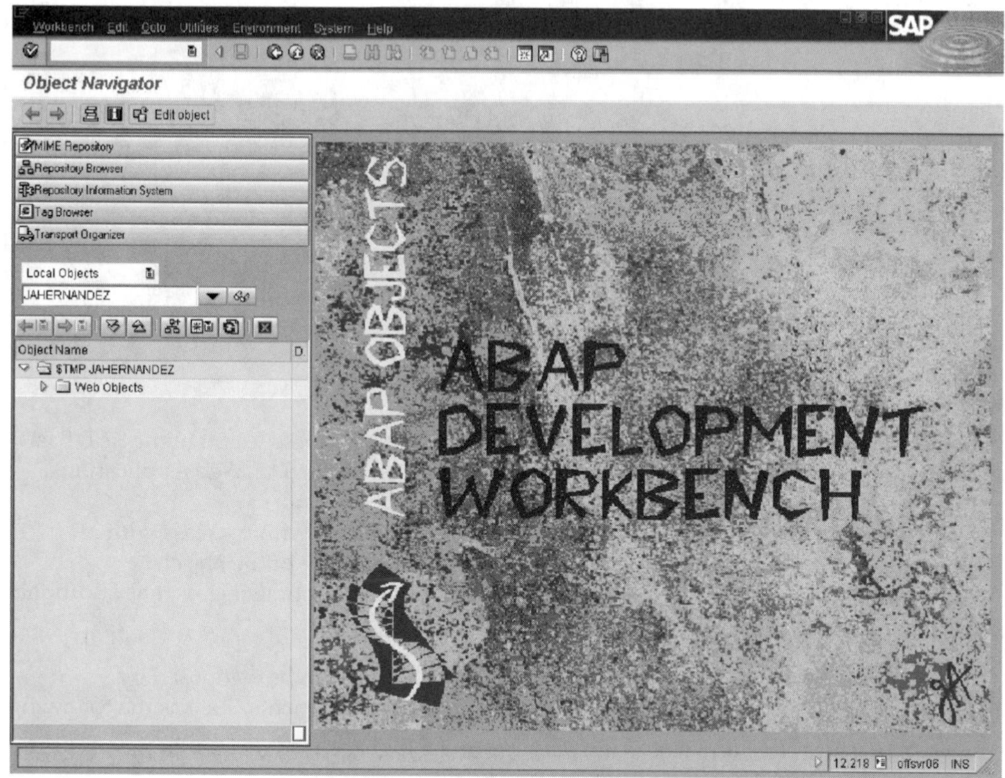

Figure 7-34 SE80—Object Navigator (Copyright by SAP AG)

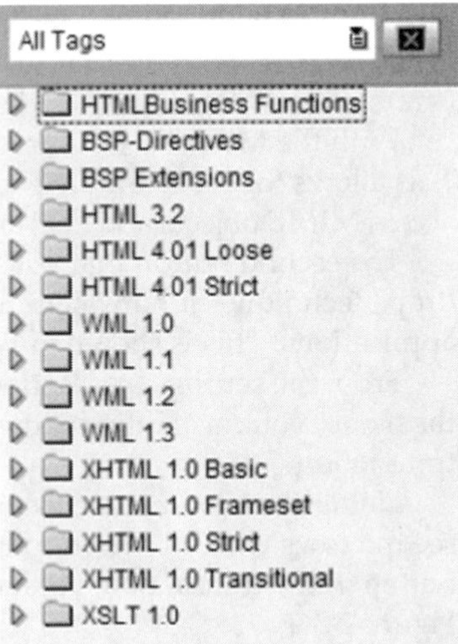

FIGURE 7-35 Tag Browser (Copyright by SAP AG)

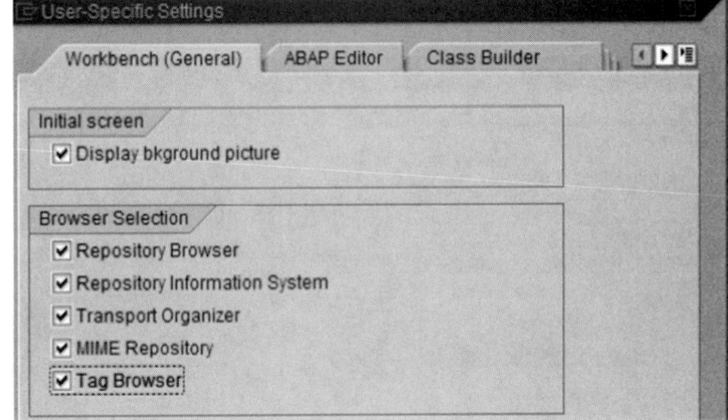

FIGURE 7-36 Workbench settings (Copyright by SAP AG)

Package

As we explained in Chapter 5, the concept of the development class found in the SAP Basis has been substituted by the package with the introduction of the SAP Web Application Server.

The development class was used to relate associated objects within a class with a transport layer, which was used to determine the transport route of the objects.

The package, besides serving the same purpose of the development class, has additional functionality, such as the following:

- Allows for the *nesting* of packages. That is, a package can be composed by subpackages. Therefore, we can see some additional elements, such as the following:
  - *Package structure:* This is the package of the highest level defined in the package hierarchy.
  - *Main package:* Main packages can only be composed by other packages.

- There is a new *visibility* concept regarding the objects within a package. For an object to be used outside the scope of a package, you have to define it as visible and define also its interface for accessing the objects.
- It is necessary also to define the *rights of use,* which establish that other packages can use the objects of a package.

As a general rule, these verifications that the system can perform before doing transports are deactivated. In order to activate these verifications, you have to access the PAKPARAM table. You can find an entry with the name "GLOBAL_SWITCH" that by default has the value "OFF." To activate the validations or verifications, you must either set the values "RESTRICTED" or "R3ENTERPRISE."

Even if you have activated this flag, it is also necessary to define in the packages that the validations will be activated.

There are several ways to create packages in the SAP Web Application Server. The easiest way is selecting the package category within the object navigator transaction by entering the name of the package. The system will detect if the package does not exist and will display a dialog window for creating the package. By selecting Yes, the system will show a new window with the attributes for the package. Because this is a customer package, the software component must be "HOME." In the Package Type field we can enter whether the package is not a main package, that is, a package that will be composed just by objects, or whether it is a main package or a structure package.

After entering the basic information of the package, the system will pop up for the creation of a change request and then creates it. From that moment, we can access that object from the Object Navigator and modify any of its attributes. The administration of the packages is performed within a window with several tabstrips:

- The Attributes tabstrip is used to manage the main properties of the package.
- Package Interface allows for the definition of the interface for accessing the objects of the package.
- Use Access is used for defining the packages that will have access to the objects of this package.
- Package Included is used to define the subpackages in the case that this is a main package.

Figure 7-37 shows an example of package definition.

Code Inspector

The Code Inspector (Figure 7-38) is a new utility that allow users to perform complex checks on ABAP code, as well as massive checks, that is, several programs at the same time. You can access from transaction code SCI.

From the Code Inspector initial screen, and before you can perform an inspection, let's look at the main concepts and elements of this utility:

- *Check variant.* In a check variant we have to define what type of inspection we want to perform. The check types are grouped into categories. In most occasions, the checking provided by the standard system will be enough, but you can also define

Package ZPAK Saved

Attributes | Package interfaces | Use access | Packages included

Short Description	Package		
Person responsible	JLHERREROS		
Created By	JLHERREROS	Created on	11.08.2004
Last changed by	JLHERREROS	Changed On	11.08.2004
Appl. component	LO	Logistics - General	

Package properties

- [ ] Main Package

Surrounding package

Allowed object types: No restrictions

- [ ] Package not extendable

Transport attributes

Transport Layer: ZE47 E47 Transport Layer

Software Component: HOME

- [x] Changes are recorded

FIGURE 7-37 Example of packages (Copyright by SAP AG)

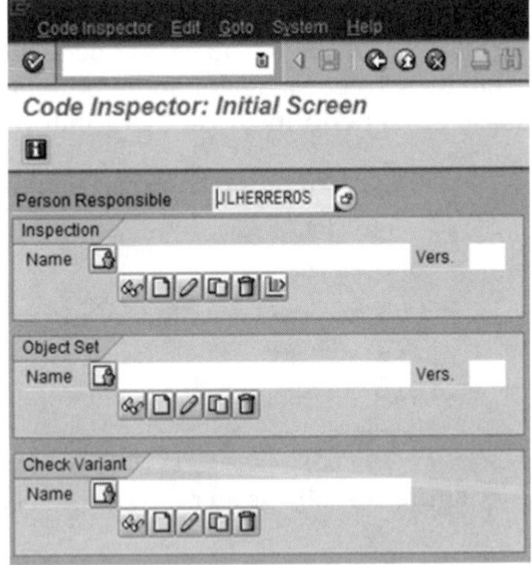

FIGURE 7-38 Code Inspector initial screen (Copyright by SAP AG)

user check variants. The following sections will show you how to create user checks and new customer categories. Figure 7-39 shows an example of the check variant.

- *Data sets.* The data sets are used to define the set of objects to be analyzed and inspected. These objects can be programs, include objects, and even ABAP dictionary objects. Figure 7-40 shows an example of this screen.

In Figure 7-40 we are defining a data set to analyze all the programs starting with "Z."

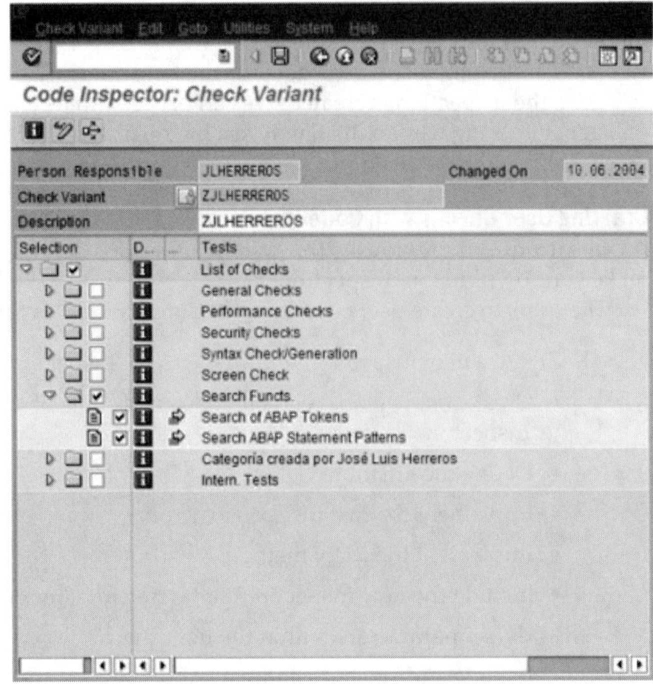

FIGURE 7-39 Check variants in the Code Inspector (Copyright by SAP AG)

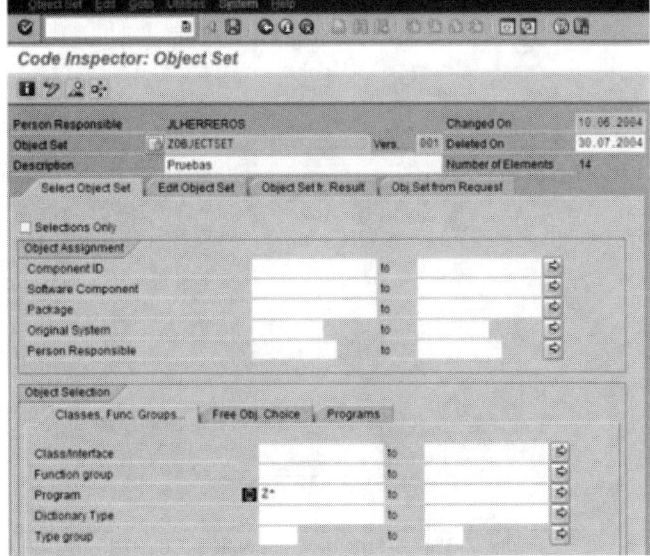

FIGURE 7-40 Code Inspector object set (Copyright by SAP AG)

Once the check variant and the data sets are defined, we can perform our first inspection. In the field for the object set, we have to enter the set defined in the previous step, and accordingly enter the data for the field check variant.

Once the inspection is created, we can proceed to its execution. Running an inspection will generate a log we can display to see the results, and we can look up this log at any time by clicking on the results button. Refer to Figure 7-41.

Creating User Checks with Code Inspector

As we introduced previously, the system allows for defining user checks so that you can make your own custom inspections.

The steps to create user checks can be summarized as follows:

1. Create a new inspection within the Code Inspector.
   - Create a new global class that extends some of the existing classes of the Code Inspector.
   - Define the attribute C_MY_NAME.
   - Implement the instance constructor.
   - Implement the RUN method.
   - Include the new inspection in the tree for checks variants.
2. Add user parameters within the new check.
   - Include additional instance attributes.
   - Modify the constructor method.

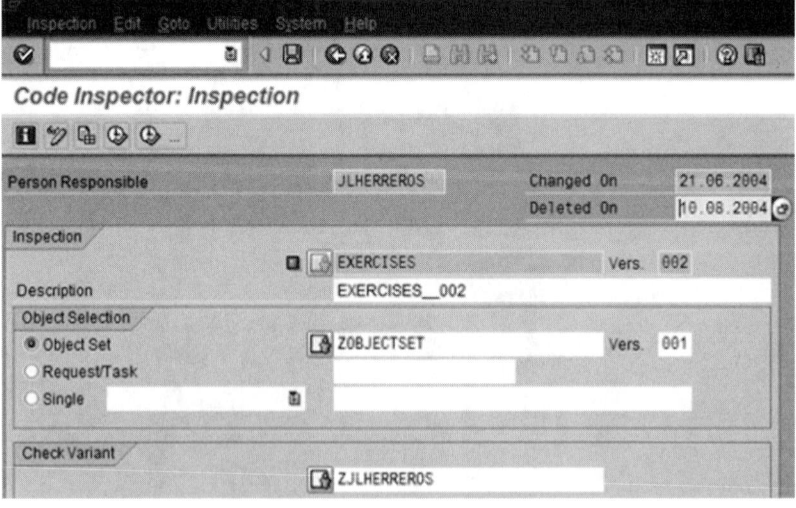

FIGURE 7-41 Example of inspection (Copyright by SAP AG)

- Implement the methods PUT_ATTRIBUTES and GET_ATTRIBUTES.
- Implement the method QUERY_ATTRIBUTES.

3. Document the messages for the new inspection.

Create a new global class that extends some of the existing classes of the Code Inspector. To create a new class, you have the following possibilities:

- Create it from scratch.
- Copy from a template: CL_CI_TEST_SCAN_TEMPLATE or CL_CI_TEST_ROOT _TEMPLATE.
- Copy from standard classes already implemented and then modify it. This is the recommended method. For instance, copy from package S_CODE_INSPECTOR (Figure 7-42). Display from the Class Builder utility (transaction SE24) all classes starting with "CL_CI."

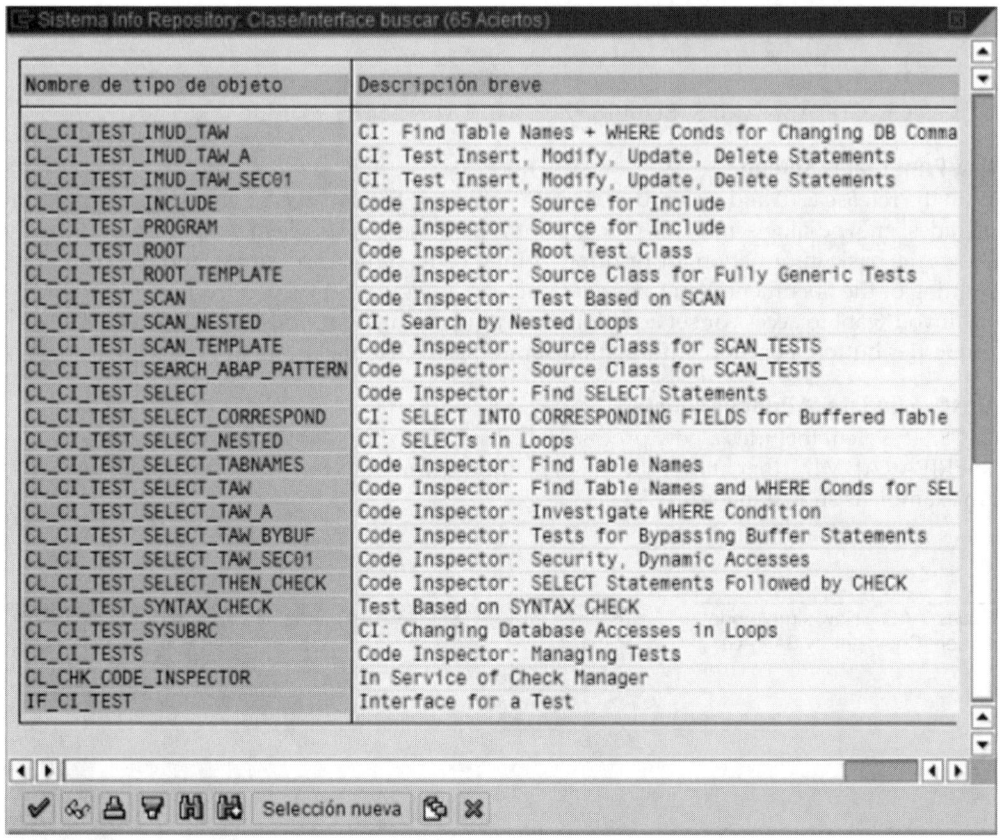

FIGURE 7-42 Class info system (Copyright by SAP AG)

Even if you cannot see it in the previous figure, the system includes the class CL_CI _CATEGORY, which represents the various existing categories within the Code Inspector.

The classes' hierarchy is represented in the following structure. Each class within the hierarchy specializes in a different inspection or check type:

CL_CI_TEST_ROOT

↓

CL_CI_TEST_PROGRAM

↓

CL_CI_TEST_INCLUDE

CL_CI_TEST_SCAN

↓

CL_CI_TEST_SELECT

↓

CL_CI_TEST_SELECT_TABNAMES

↓

CL_CI_TABNAMES_PUBLIC (ZCL_CI_TABNAMES_PUBLIC)

New Print Dialog Screen

With the release 6.10 and upward of the SAP Web Application Server, the SAP system includes a new dialog screen for report printing. The screen has been simplified, and it only shows the basic information for printing: printer code, number of copies, and total or partial printing of the document. You can see this screen in Figure 7-43.

If you want to access or set additional printing parameters, you must click on the Properties button. For more information about these attributes, refer to Chapter 9.

Massive Update of Print Parameters

The SAP system includes a new process, which can be run using the ABAP program RSPRIPARADMIN, that allows the massive update (for all users) of print parameters. An example is shown in Figure 7-44.

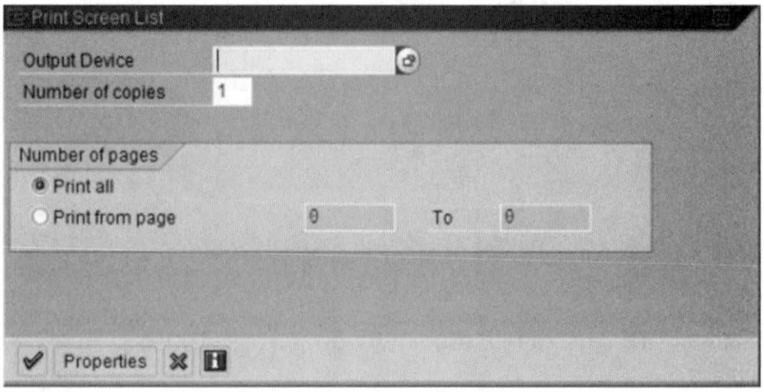

Figure 7-43 New simple print screen (Copyright by SAP AG)

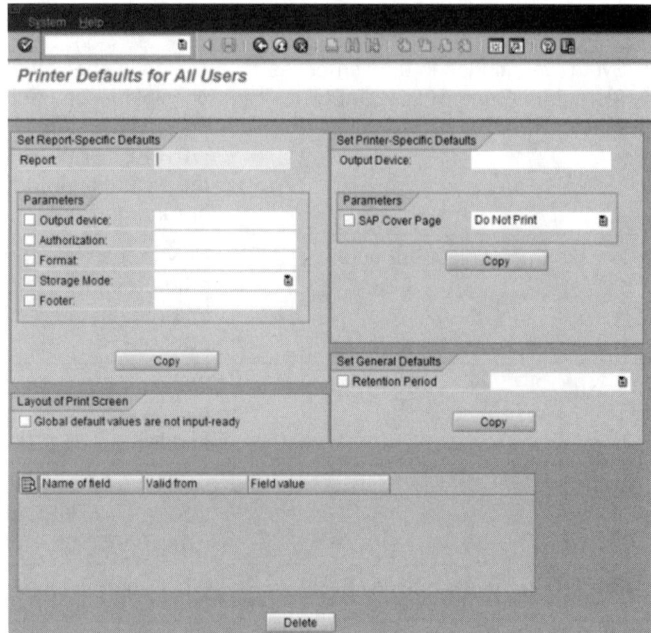

FIGURE 7-44 Printer defaults (Copyright by SAP AG)

New Elements of the ABAP Programming Language

SAP has been constantly enhancing the ABAP programming language, and in this section we show these new features, sentences, and enhancements. This section is meant mostly for those users accustomed to previous ABAP releases. Because the number of new features is very extensive with the SAP Web Application Server, we will summarize the most significant ones, such as the following:

- Those new elements related with internal tables
- Update with the string data types
- New ways of handling files in the application servers
- News in the SQL sentences
- News in the sentences for report creation
- New system fields

News with Internal Tables

The following table describes the most important news when dealing with internal tables from ABAP.

New Feature	Description
Possibility of creating internal tables at runtime	Sentence CREATE TABLE allows developers to create any type of internal table at runtime.

(*continued*)

New Feature	Description
Syntax verification in the sentences READ TABLE and DELETE TABLE	The code check feature is enhanced to detect possible incompatibilities when using READ TABLE and DELETE TABLE sentences, with the keywords WITH KEY or WITH TABLE KEY. In previous releases, the exception MOVE_NOT_SUPPORTED was activated at runtime.
Access to an object attributes	Now we can use the clause COMPARING with object attributes that are part of the definition of an internal table. For example, COMPARING object -> attribute.
TEXTPOOL	We can use tables of type SORTED and HASHED in the sentences READ TEXTPOOL, DELETE TEXTPOOL, and INSERT TEXTPOOL.
IN operator	We can use the IN operator in the read sentence LOOP . . . WHERE independent of the table type (STANDARD, SORTED, or HASHED).
Overflow for fields of type "F"	When there is an overflow status with a field of type "F," because of a COLLECT or SUM sentences, these can now be captured with the exception CX _SY_ARITHMETIC_OVERFLOW using the sentence TRY.
ASSIGNING and REFERENCE INTO	The clauses ASSIGNING and REFERENCE INTO can now be used with the sentences READ, LOOP, INSERT, APPEND, MODIFY, and COLLECT.
SORT . . . BY	We can now use both capital letters or lowercase letters when identifying a dynamic component in the clause SORT . . . BY <component>.
Function LINES	There is a new function, LINES, that can be used to obtain the attributes of an internal table. This is a replacement for the DESCRIBE TABLE sentence.
Offset and length when specifying a table	The system will trigger a syntax error if a table is declared specifying offsets and lengths.

News with the String Data Type

The following table describes the most important news when dealing with string data types in ABAP programs.

New Feature	Description
Function CHARLEN	Function CHARLEN provides the length (note that it does not have to match the number of characters because of the Unicode code page) of the string contained in any field of character type.

New Feature	Description
Function NUMOFCHAR	Function NUMOFCHAR provides the number of characters (note that it does not have to match the length because of the Unicode code page) of the string contained in any field of character type.
Function DBMAXLEN	This function obtains the maximum length of the string that can be stored in the ABAP dictionary.
Sentence FIND	This sentence allows for searching in a string. This sentence replaces the sentence SEARCH.
Sentence REPLACE	This has been enhanced to allow replacing characters according to the character position or in bytes (IN BYTE MODE, IN CHARACTER MODE).
Access by offset/length	The quickest way to access a string, character by character, is by using offsets and lengths.
STRINGs and RAWSTRINGs in the database	We can use the types STRING and RAWSTRING to store strings in the database for short and long texts.
Constants	The type STRING can be now used to define a constant.
String literal	There is a new type of literal, known as the string literal, that is coded with the apostrophe " ' ". For example, `DATA: str type string value 'AFG'` We can obtain the length of the string literal including the blank spaces at the end of the string, something that does not happen with the regular literals.

News when Dealing with Files in the Application Server

The following table describes the most important news when dealing with handling files in the application servers.

New Feature	Description
Sentence GET DATASET	With this sentence you can obtain information of a file, for instance, its properties or the current position for reading.
Sentence SET DATASET	This can be use to update some properties of a file being treated, and it is also possible to modify the position of the reading on the file.
Class CL_ABAP_CONV_IN_CE	Using instances of this class allows for converting an external file of binary data in a valid ABAP data object.
Class CL_ABAP_CONV_OUT_CE	Using instances of this class allows for converting an ABAP data object in binary data.
Class CL_ABAP_CONV_X2X_CE	Using instances of this class allows for converting a text data type (for several character sets) in numeric data (for several numeric formats).

(*continued*)

New Feature	Description
Handling large files	Except for the OS/390 and AS/400, we can now handle files with a size larger than 2 GB.
Read limit	Using the clause MAXIMUM LENGTH of the sentence READ DATASET, we can limit the maximum number of characters or bytes that are to be read. The open mode will define whether they are characters or bytes being specified.

News with SQL Sentences

The following table describes the most important news when dealing with SQL sentences in ABAP programs.

New Feature	Description
Additional syntax verifications	Subqueries are only allowed in the WHERE clause of a SQL Sentence if the source table is transparent. Clause GROUP BY is only allowed with transparent tables. Clause FOR ALL ENTRIES now requires two internal tables, one for input data and another one for output data. Clause INTO CORRESPONDING can only be used to move data with structured data areas or internal tables. There is now the clause ESCAPE that is attached to the LIKE clause to indicate that the escape character that is being used within a search string (or field).

Dynamic SQL	You can now perform dynamic specification in the following situations:
	• ABAP variables in the WHERE, HAVING, FROM, and SET classes of the SELECT sentence
	• ABAP variables in the WHERE clause for the sentences DELETE and UPDATE
	• Dynamic SET clause in the UPDATE sentence
	• Functions for dynamic aggregation in the clause HAVING
	• Dynamic FROM in the SELECT sentence
	Example:
	`PARAMETERS: airline(2) TYPE C,`
	`            date       TYPE D.`
	`DATA: where_clause TYPE STRING,`
	`      connid       TYPE sflight-connid.`
	`CONCATENATE 'carrid = ''' airline ''''`
	`            ' AND fldate = ''' date ''''`
	`   INTO where_clause.`
	`SELECT connid FROM sflight INTO connid`
	`WHERE (where_clause).`
	`        WRITE: / date, airline, connid.`
	`ENDSELECT.`

New Feature	Description
DISTINCT	You cannot combine the DISTINCT clause with tables of type pool or cluster. If you perform this combination statically (direct coding) a syntax error is triggered, but if the sentence is created dynamically (at runtime), a short dump will be generated. The new feature means that you can capture the exception at runtime: CX_SY_DYNAMIC_OSQL_SEMANTICS.
Read only views	With previous releases, when you modified the database using a read only view, there was a runtime error. Now the system detects the syntax error and activates an error message before runtime.
Exception handling	There are many exceptions as a result of SQL sentences that have been now assigned to exception classes that you can capture. You can now capture exceptions generated with Native SQL sentences using the statements TRY . . . ENDTRY. For the Open SQL sentences, the system includes new exceptions to the class: DUPLICATE KEY, SQL ERROR, STATEMENT TOO LARGE, LOBLENGTH EXCEEDED, CONVERSION ERROR, and INVALID CURSOR.
INSERT/ UPDATE TRDIR	Now the system generates a syntax error when you try to update the table TRDIR using the sentences INSERT or UPDATE. It is still valid to use the sentence MODIFY TRDIR [FROM].
FOR ALL ENTRIES	You can now use the same internal table in the INTO clause and the FOR ALL ENTRIES clause. Example: SELECT . . . INTO itab1 FOR ALL ENTRIES IN itab1 . . .
Pool or cluster tables	When using tables of type POOL or CLUSTER in subqueries, joins, aggregation functions using the clause GROUP BY, the system generates the exception ILLEGAL_TABLE_TYPE that you can capture.
Strings in the database	Now you can store fields of type string on fields (columns) of the database of that type.

News in Sentences for Creating Reports

The following table describes the most important news when dealing with SQL sentences in ABAP programs.

New Feature	Description
FRAME ON/OFF	This new sentence can be used to prevent printing special characters that are used to draw frames on the window. With the option OFF this feature is deactivated. Deactivating this feature can be very practical both in performance and cost.

New System Fields

The following table describes the most important news when dealing with SQL sentences in ABAP programs.

New Feature	Description
SY-CALLD	Now the system field SY-CALLD will contain a space if the program is the first or the only one in the call sequence, and it will contain an "X" if the program was called by another program. Previously it did not work this way when the call was performed with a SUBMIT without RETURN.
SY-REPID	The system field SY-REPID and the field of the structure SYST of the Data Dictionary do not exist anymore. Now, when an ABAP program is executed, the system includes a program constant with the same name: SY-REPID (also SYST-REPID) whose value is the same that the name of the program at runtime. Because the name is the same, we can keep our data definitions: TYPE SY-REPID or LIKE SYST-REPID.

MESSAGE Sentence

There is now a new variant of the MESSAGE sentence:

```
MESSAGE <string> TYPE <kind1> [ DISPLAY LIKE <kind2> ]
```

With this sentence variant we can now activate messages that are not defined in any message class (table T100). The message type <kind1> establishes the type of message: warning, informative, error, and so on. Additionally, we can add the way we want to display the message with the optional parameter DISPLAY LIKE <kind2>, which establishes how the message is displayed.

Enhancements Related to Data Types

For constants definition we can now used structure types, as in the following example:

```
types:
  begin of structure,
    ITAB type standard table of SPFLI with non-unique key CARRID,
    MREF type ref to OBJECT,
  end of structure.

constants:
  CONST  type structure value is initial.
```

For the elementary field symbols and the formal parameters in the routine definitions (FORM), functions (FUNCTION), or methods (METHODS), we can use now generic types that will be converted to their definitive types at runtime. The new generic types are described in the following table:

	Includes Generic Type	Includes Elementary Type
SIMPLE	CLIKE, XSEQUENCE and NUMERIC	
CLIKE	CSEQUENCE, structures	N, D, T
CSEQUENCE		C, STRING
XSEQUENCE		X, XSTRING
NUMERIC		I, P, F

The final elementary data types (established at runtime) must be one of the types that are included within the generic data type. If this was not the case, an exception will be raised.

New Methods

Some of the new features related to new methods are as follows:

- *GET_PROPERTY.* The system includes now the GET_PROPERTY method within the class CL_ABAP_TYPEDESCR to obtain properties at runtime.
- *GET_FRIEND_TYPES.* The system also includes now the GET_FRIEND_TYPES method within the CL_ABAP_CLASSDESCR class to obtain the description of the objects defined as FRIENDS within a class.

For more new features related to methods, please refer to the online SAP documentation.

New Features with Logical Expressions

The following table includes the new features with logical expressions, including relational operators:

New Feature	Description
IS [NOT] BOUND	Returns whether a reference variable referenced in an expression has a valid reference.
IS [NOT] SUPPLIED	Returns whether an IMPORTING or EXPORTING parameter was passed in a method or function module.
IS [NOT] INITIAL	Can make comparison with an initial value.
IS [NOT] ASSIGNED	Returns whether a field symbol was assigned or not.
IS [NOT] REQUESTED	Establishes whether a formal parameter was specified in the call to the routine.
IS [NOT] IN	Determines the existence of a value in a selection criteria.
IS [NOT] BETWEEN	Returns whether a value exists within a value range.

For other changes in logical expressions or relational operators, please refer to the SAP online help.

Web Development with ABAP: Business Server Page (BSP)

As we already explained in Chapter 2, with the appearance of the SAP Web Application Server 6.10 back in 2001, SAP replaced the SAP Basis System as the underlying platform for SAP Solutions. The SAP Web Application Server, commonly referred to as SAP WAS, is the technological foundation and platform for the SAP R/3 Enterprise, as well as most of the other SAP Solutions within mySAP Business Suite and the SAP NetWeaver integration platform.

The main difference between the SAP WAS and SAP Basis is that the SAP Web Application Server supports natively Web protocols such as HTTP(s), SMTP, SOAP, and others, which allows users to avoid using the traditional Internet gateway used in SAP installations, namely the Internet Transaction Server (ITS).

Another big difference is that the system includes a new development model, known as *Business Server Pages (BSPs)*. With BSPs you can know build Web applications to for access to data and information on the SAP systems.

A BSP application is made up of a set of HTML pages that contain server scripts and ABAP code. They can include, for example, SELECT statements that access the system database, BAPI calls to run processes, or interfaces with any SAP component, such as R/3 systems, BW, and others.

In order to code server side scripts, we can use two development languages: ABAP and JavaScript. We can also use JavaScript to create client side scripts. Compatibility with the browser is the only limit to including code that runs on the client. For instance, if the Web browser that we use includes the plug-in of Macromedia Flash, we could include flash animations within our pages.

Once you decide which server side language to use (ABAP or JavaScript), you will have to add special tags in order to combine the code with HTML (Hypertext Markup) or WML (Wireless Markup Language).

Developing a BSP

Web applications developed using the BSP model are built using the Web Application Builder, which is a transaction integrated within the ABAP Workbench. For this reason, traditional ABAP developers will be able to adapt quickly to the look and feel of this new transaction.

The way to develop these Web applications is quite similar to the traditional programming model for some of the ABAP applications on SAP systems. Often, even the same transactions are used, like the Class Builder (transaction code SE24).

We can access the development environment of BSPs from transaction SE80 (Object Navigator). From this screen we will be able to access also other tools needed for the development, such as the ABAP Editor or the Debugger.

The system does not impose limitations for developing Web applications with the ABAP Editor. We can also use some more specific editors for this type of applications, as long as they meet the Web DAV standard, which allows for the exchanging information between different systems. SAP follows this standard, and you could, for instance, develop Web pages with external editors such as Macromedia DreamWeaver MX, Microsoft FrontPage, and others, and automatically transfer those pages to the SAP Web Application Server.

In transaction SE80, select the option BSP Application, and enter the name of the BSP to me created or maintained, as shown in Figure 7-45.

In this small practical example, we are going to develop step by step a BSP application with flow logic. This was the only option in the initial SAP WAS release 6.10, but it had a lot of limitations. With the introduction of 6.20 and later 6.40, there are other development and enhanced development options such as the Model-View-Controller (MVC) and the BSP Extensions, well known in other programming environments that include the tab libraries.

As a brief summary, we can describe a BSP application as follows:

- It contains one or several HTML pages.
- Each page can include any HTML or WML tag.
- You can dynamically include SAP data or data from non-SAP systems.
- The business logic can be entered using *tags* and *scripts* in the HTML pages. These server side scripts are used to generate static pages which are then passed to the client.
- SAP and non-SAP data are retrieved, processed, and formatted.

We can find many similarities between the BSP development in SAP systems and the Web development of the Java environment (JSPs) or in the Microsoft environment (ASPs).

We consider a first practical example in the next section.

Your First BSP: Hello World!!!

In order to show in a simple way how to create BSP applications, we will show a very simple BSP that will display the message *Hello world!!!* in a HTML page using different font sizes. The static HTML code will contain the dynamic ABAP code on the server side.

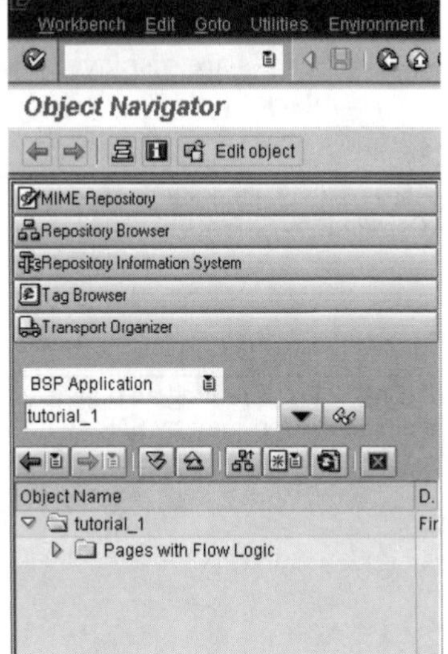

FIGURE 7-45 BSP option within the Object Navigator (Copyright by SAP AG)

Step 1: Create the BSP Application

From transaction SE80, enter the name of the BSP in the corresponding field. In our example we will use "ZSAMPLE1," as shown in Figure 7-46.

When pressing ENTER, the system will detect that the BSP application does not exist and will pop up a dialog box proposing its creation, as shown in Figure 7-47.

Click on Yes. The system will request to enter a short description in a new dialog box. Enter some descriptive test and click on the Create button.

As with other repository objects, we have to enter the package. In this example (which will be different in real development) we will define the object as local by clicking on the Local Object button of the Create Object Directory entry dialog box.

For the moment, we have created the BSP object.

Step 2: Create the BSP Page

We should carefully differentiate between BSP application and BSP page. The application is a set of pages with some logic, whereas a BSP page is just one of the pages within a BSP application.

To create a BSP page, right-click on the BSP application, and from the function menu, select Create | Page as shown in Figure 7-48.

The system shows a new dialog screen, where you should enter the name of the page to be created, for example, *default.htm*. We also have to enter a short description and the type of page, which by default is *Page with flow logic*. We will leave the default option in the example.

The system will add the page in the hierarchical structure of the BSP application and shows on the right side of the screen the layout editor for the page. As you can see in Figure 7-49, it also has generated automatically some HTML code.

On the layout editor, we are going to make some changes to include a script in ABAP that will perform the objective of this example, and also remove some elements that we don't need at this time. The final code is shown in Figure 7-50.

The code in the figure shows some new elements that need some description:

- Scripts are displayed in the editor in a blue color, whereas the HTML code is in black.

FIGURE 7-46 Entering the BSP name (Copyright by SAP AG)

FIGURE 7-47 Creating an object dialog box (Copyright by SAP AG)

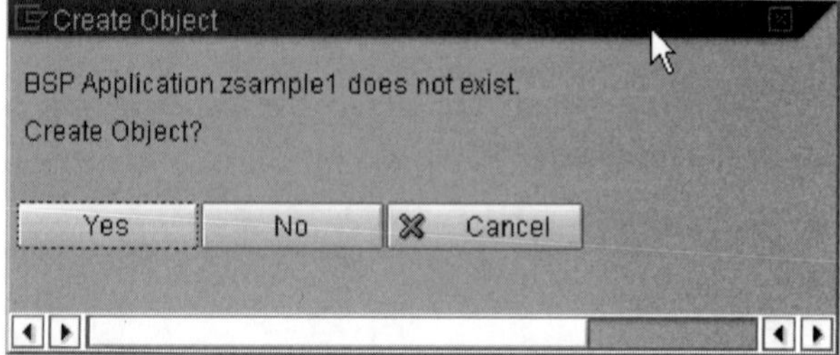

FIGURE 7-48 Creating a BSP page (Copyright by SAP AG)

```
<%@page language="abap"%>
<html>

  <head>
    <link rel="stylesheet" href="../../sap/public/bc/bsp/styles/sapbsp.css">
    <title> Initial BSP page </title>
  </head>

  <body class="bspBody1">

  </body>

</html>
```

FIGURE 7-49 Creating a BSP page (Copyright by SAP AG)

FIGURE 7-50 BSP code (Copyright by SAP AG)

```
<%@page language="abap"%>
<html>
<% data: fontsize type I value 1. %>
  <head>
    <title> Initial BSP page </title>
  </head>

  <body>
      <P ALIGN="CENTER">Different font sizes:<BR><BR>
      <% do 7 times. %>
          <font color = "black" size = <%= fontsize %>
              <P ALIGN="CENTER"> Hello world...!!!<BR>
          </font>
          <% add 1 to fontsize. %>
      <% enddo. %>

  </body>

</html>
```

- Observe that the script code used has been ABAP as indicated in the first sentence.
- In order to include ABAP within the layout you have to use directives, as with other programming languages. The following table shows the directives that can be used.
- Basically, the program modifies the font size of the shown text.

Directive	Comments
<%@page . . . %>	Page directive. It is used to indicate which programming language is being used. In this case is ABAP, but we could have used JavaScript.
<%@include . . . %>	Include directive. It allows by means of a relative URL to include any element to the code.
<% . . . %>	"On line" directive. It allows entering ABAP code between two tags.
<%= . . . %>	Directive used for transferring variables.
<%— . . . %>	Comments directive. These comments are not transferred to the client (browser) contrary to what happens with the HTML comments.
<%extension . . . %>	Directive used to include extensions.
<otr> . . . </otr>	Directive used to enter texts from the Online Text Repository (OTR).

We will not go into detail in this example about the meaning of the HTML elements. Please refer to diverse HTML and Web manuals or the SAP online help.

Remember to save the page.

Step 3: Running the BSP

In order to run the BSP, the first thing we have to do is to activate it. The activation concept is the same as for the other repository objects. Refer to initial sections of this chapter.

First, leave the editor screen of the BSP page; otherwise the activation will fail. Then, place your cursor on the name of the BSP application, and click on the Activate button (you could also use CTRL-F3) to activate the BSP application and the created BSP.

To run the application, click the Direct Processing button, or, alternatively, press F8.

Because we have not defined the page as public, the system will request the SAP username and password, as shown in Figure 7-51. Enter the information requested and click OK. We could have alternatively defined the page as public. Look up the SAP online help the description of transaction SICF (service maintenance).

Next the system will display the generated HTML page in the browser as shown in Figure 7-52.

If you look up the source code from the browser (with Microsoft Internet Explorer, select View | Source), as shown in the Figure 7-53, you can actually see that the whole code is static, and the font text "Hello world . . . " changes from 1 to 7.

After this first success, let's have a closer look to each of the elements that make up a BSP application.

Overview of BSP Concepts

The elements that make up a BSP application are the following:

- Properties.
- Navigation.
- Navigation modeler. This model allows for designing different browsing models between HTML pages. We will not deal with further details about this element.
- BSP pages.

You can see this option in the tabstrips in the right-hand side of the screen of a BSP application.

FIGURE 7-51 Entering username and password for BSP (Copyright by SAP AG)

Connect to offsvr06.offilog.com

SAP Web Application Server [E47]

User name: jahernandez

Password: •••••

Remember my password

OK Cancel

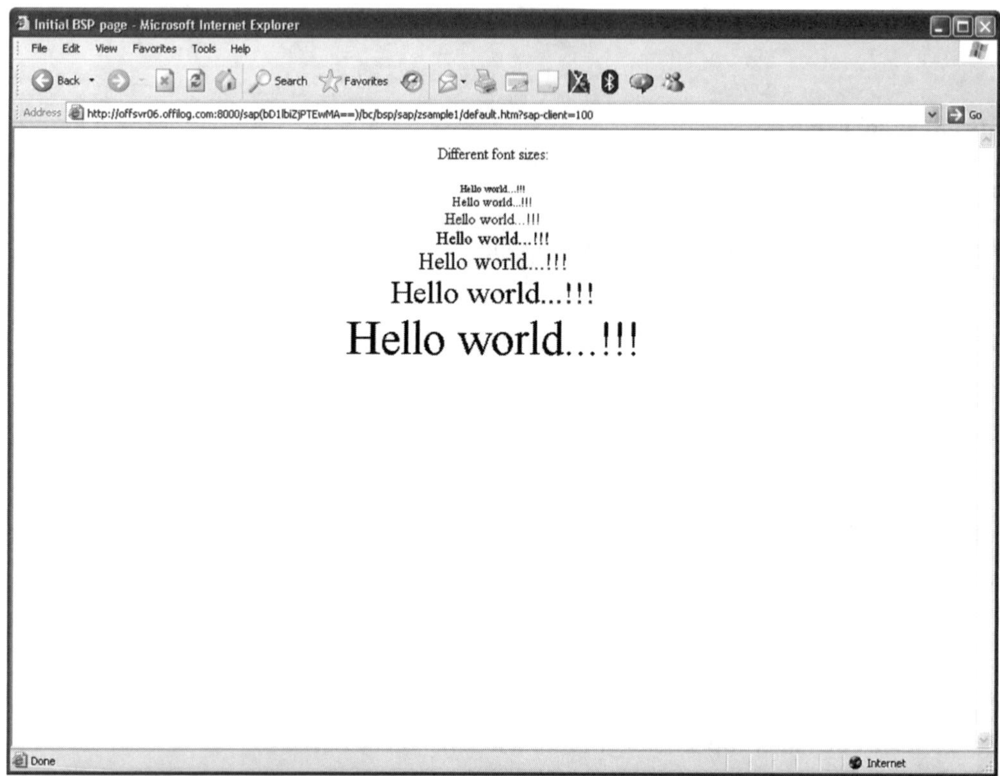

FIGURE 7-52 Result from our first BSP application (Copyright by SAP AG)

default[1] - Notepad

File Edit Format View Help

```
<html>

  <head>
    <title> Initial BSP page </title>
  </head>

  <body>
      <P ALIGN="CENTER">Different font sizes:<BR><BR>

           <font color = "black" size = 1
               <P ALIGN="CENTER"> Hello world...!!!<BR>
           </font>


           <font color = "black" size = 2
               <P ALIGN="CENTER"> Hello world...!!!<BR>
           </font>


           <font color = "black" size = 3
               <P ALIGN="CENTER"> Hello world...!!!<BR>
           </font>


           <font color = "black" size = 4
               <P ALIGN="CENTER"> Hello world...!!!<BR>
           </font>
```

FIGURE 7-53 HTML source code (Copyright by SAP AG)

BSP Properties

In the section for the properties, the system shows the administrative data for the application. These include the user, creation and modification dates, and package. You can enter the following information:

- *Initial BSP page.* This is useful for the system to know which is the first page to run when the application is executed.
- *Application class.* For professional BSP application, you should use an application class to implement all the business logic.
- *Theme.* With the theme you can personalize the output for an application without the need of modifying the code.
- *Type of state.* In contrast to other Web development environments, with SAP we can decide whether the application keeps the *state* (all the variable information of an application) between the execution of the pages. The usual way is to make *stateless* applications.
- *Portal support.* With this check box you can indicate that the application could be used for execution within the SAP Enterprise Portal.

Navigation

Navigation allows for defining calling routes between HTML pages. In this way, if a page is called from several other pages and we have the need to modify the name of the page, we would only have to perform the change in one single place.

The column *Start* is used to enter the name of the source page. In the column *Navigation Request* we enter the alias used in the page, and the column *Target* is used to enter the name of the target page. As can be seen, this is a procedure for indirect calls.

BSP Pages

The BSP pages are the main components of the BSP applications. BSP pages are also made of the following elements:

- Properties
- Layout
- Event handler
- Page attributes
- Type definitions
- Preview

Let's take a closer look at each of these elements.

Page Properties

As in the BSP applications, there is a tabstrip in the application to enter the main properties or attributes of the BSP pages. The most important properties are as follows:

- *Description.* Field used to enter a brief description of the page.
- *MIME type.* Generally, the type of the pages are text/html.
- *Compression type.* Normally, pages do not use any type of compression, but you could decide whether you want trailing spaces removed.
- *With or without server scripting.* By using the W/O Server Code check box, you can decide whether to allow scripting on the server side. This check is verified at runtime.
- *Page type.* The different type of pages that we can create are as follows:
  - *View.* This type is used when developing an application following the Model-View-Controller.
  - *Page with flow logic.* This is the example of the page we have created in the previous example. This type is a page that will have a set of events associated, which will be executed before and after the execution of the page.
  - *Page fragment.* These fragments can be used like "includes" for other pages. This is a utility that can be useful for building page modules. For instance, you can create one page of this type with the foot page that you want to show in every page of the application.
- *Error handling and error page.* You can assign here a page that the system will show in case of error at runtime.
- *Status.* This section is to describe the status characteristics (stateless or statefull) of the page.
- *Caching.* You can decide the duration or time of residence of the pages in the server and/or browser caches.
- *Transfer options.* In this section you can define some of the options for compression and security, for example, deciding on HTTPS (HTML over SSL).
- *Additional administrative information.* In this section you can see username and the creation and modification dates of the BSP page.

Event Handler

This option only appears in pages with flow logic. This section can be used to code the actions to be performed for each of the system events. In this case, the only valid language is ABAP.

When selecting an event in the first input field, the system will show the editor for the code corresponding to that event.

Possible events are as follows:

- *OnCreate.* This event is run the first time when the page is generated, just in applications that keep the status (statefull). It's used to initialize once the data objects.
- *OnRequest.* This event is run when there is a request of the page by an user. This event is run before other events such as *OnInitialization* or *OnInputProcessing.* It is used to restore internal data in application which do not keep the state (stateless).

- *OnInitialization.* This event is executed when a page is processed. If this action is necessary, then it is used to restore data.
- *OnManipulation.* This event is used for postprocessing of an http data stream.
- *OnInputProcessing.* This event is activated when a dialog with a user is established. This event can be used to implement verifications of input fields and activate the navigation according to the user entries.
- *OnDestroy.* This event is run immediately before the instance of the page is destroyed. It is used to perform some "cleaning" actions so that no obsolete data are kept in the system memory.

Page Attributes

This tabstrip is used to enter any "data object" that we need to share for the layout and the events. To create a page attribute, we have to enter the following information:

- *Attribute name.* This first column is used to specify the name for the attribute.
- *Typing method.* You can either set TYPE for regular data objects or TYPE REF TO for the creation of object instances.
- *Associated type.* This is the ABAP reference type for the page attribute. The reference type must be either a global type of the dictionary, a global object type, a predefined ABAP type, or a type defined in the Type Definition tabstrip of the BSP page.
- *Description.* Brief description of the attribute.
- *Auto.* If you check this flat, the system will automatically update the value of the attribute if the system already has an attribute with the same name.

Type Definitions

In this tabstrip, the system shows an editor that can be used to enter type definitions (like the ones used with the TYPES sentence). We have the option to create any type likewise a traditional ABAP program.

Preview

The preview tabstrip can be used to display approximately how the page layout will appear when the HTML page is called, but only of the static code. The scripts for dynamic content are not run in preview mode.

CHAPTER

User Management and Security in SAP Environments

Security is increasingly being considered one of the key points to boost electronic commerce over the Web. SAP has always established security as one of the critical topics both for the implementation and correct deployment of SAP Solutions and any of the SAP Web-enabled applications. Every professional involved in modern SAP projects is aware that leveraging security technology and measures and a sound security policy is mandatory.

The information stored in the systems we support ranks among a company's most important and valuable assets. Moreover, addressing security during and after a SAP implementation not only protects valuable business information; it ensures continuous and stable systems operations.

Most of the concepts around the SAP and SAP NetWeaver security infrastructure are based on the sound security services typically available in R/3 systems plus the latest security technology. Therefore, this chapter first includes an introduction to traditional SAPs and other general security concepts and options and the second part of the chapter deals with the user administration and the role and authorization concept.

The chapter then takes a deeper approach into Single Sign-On Solutions, the SNC (Secure Network Communications) interface, Digital Signatures, Data Encryption, Public Key Infrastructure (PKI) technologies, and Privacy protection for user data. There are additional sections explaining available security options for user authentication such as cookies, X.509 certificates for Internet connections, standards such as HTTP-SSL (Secure Service Layer), and new Web security services.

It is impossible to cover in one chapter all the topics around the SAP NetWeaver and Java technologies security options. Should you need additional information, you can find comprehensive security documentation at the SAP Service Marketplace in the quick link *Security* (service.sap.com/security).

With the SAP NetWeaver Security Infrastructure, based on market standards, SAP has set in place a full range of security measures and technologies so that business data integrity and privacy are protected against unauthorized access. Security is more than ever increasingly important considering how data and business processes expand beyond intranet levels into Web collaborative scenarios often quite transparent to end users.

With these and many other considerations, SAP and its partners provide a full range of security services to make SAP Solutions a secure place to do business.

Objectives of SAP security are as follows:

- Set up private communication channels.
- Use strong authentication mechanisms.
- Implement group concept in Java.
- Provide evidence of business transactions.
- Enforce auditing and logging.

Among these objectives the security services available for SAP environments are as follows:

- The use of client and server certificates for user *authentication*
- Single Sign-On solutions to access the full range of SAP components and solution
- The *role-based* concept, which involves activity groups and authorizations
- Deployment of firewalls between systems and networks, as well as secure protocols such as HTTPS (HTTP over SSL)
- SNC (Secure Network Communications) and SSF (Secure Store and Forward) for compliance with security standards

Before discussing the specifics of available options and implementation considerations for SAP security, the following sections introduce readers to common security concepts as well as to the background of traditional SAP Security Services from the R/3 age, most of which still apply and have evolved into newer scenarios.

Overview of Security Concepts

Traditional SAP implementation projects usually considered security just as the design and realization of the authorization concept. At the *application level* the authorization concept (user masters, profiles, authorizations, activity groups, roles) is key to provide access to needed transactions and ensure secure access to sensitive data and as such is extremely important within the SAP security infrastructure. However, systems within mySAP Business Suite applications and SAP NetWeaver do have many other *levels* that could be attacked, and therefore a consistent security strategy must also consider all these other layers and components of the SAP systems.

Security can be defined from two different perspectives that have in common the objective of protecting the company systems and information assets. These two perspectives are as follows:

- *Security* as the protection measures and policies against *unauthorized accesses* by illegitimate users (both internal and external). An internal attack is considered when a SAP user tries to access or perform functions for which he or she is not allowed.
- *Security* as protection measures against hardware, software, or any other type of environmental *failures* (disasters, fires, earthquakes, and others) using safety technologies (backup/restore/disaster recovery/standby systems/archiving and so on).

In this chapter only the first perspective is dealt with: explaining some of the most common and practical concepts of SAP security components and security infrastructure from the first perspective to protect SAP systems from unauthorized accesses. It must be noted that a global security policy includes other "non-SAP" related components that can be defined as "peripheral security," such as the measures that must be taken to protect workstations, servers, and networks from the many types of outside attacks (e.g., viruses, denial of services, password cracking, sniffers).

Security Policy Basics

Companies must implement some type of security policy to protect their assets, but also they are required to comply with their country's legal obligations, business agreements, and industry laws and regulations. For instance, many countries have some forms of laws for protecting confidential data of employees. It is also very important to keep all financial records for tax authorities. And in terms of business partners, it is of great importance to ensure the confidentiality of commercial agreements with vendors or customers.

Modern information systems and technologies are both the means and the containers of the strategic and operative business information. They are the known but hidden treasures of companies, and companies need to keep their treasures secure.

The *Security Policy* is the set of procedures, standards, roles, and responsibilities covering and specifying all the security and organizational measures that companies must follow to protect their business from threats and vulnerabilities. An approach to security will have the objective of building a strong security policy and should start by assessing a risk analysis to implement, monitor, and enforce such policy. It is important to realize that security implementation never ends and must be continually updated, reviewed, communicated, implemented, monitored, and enforced.

The security strategy and risk analysis must first consider these basic issues:

a. *What is to be protected?* Companies must identify those assets—such as critical information (customer list, employee personal data, contracts), hardware, software, intangibles (hours of operation, cost of nonrevenue, nonproduction) or others—that require some type and some degree of protection against unwanted and unauthorized access, which could damage or destroy to some degree such assets.

b. *Which are the possible threats?* The second security issue is to identify the possible sources of attack and the degree of vulnerability of infrastructure. Threats are of different type and nature and sometimes unknown. They are often intentional, but can also be unintentional. They can be external threats or can be internal (for instance, by other geographical locations or by burned-out or frustrated employees).

c. *What protection measures can be taken?* Finally, the risk analysis and the security policy must identify the best security measures to implement and enforce such policy efficiently. Measures can be standard measures included in the information system capabilities, additional and external security infrastructure, and behavioral rules. For instance, a basic and strong security measure is the *password* that users must provide to access systems; however, it is almost impossible with technical means to know whether someone told his or her password to someone else.

Efficiency in security policy means that measures do not include awkward procedures that would obstruct or make users' jobs more difficult. Security policies always follow a principle of controls, which means that the security strategy must approach the balance between risks and control measures.

As indicated, security is a continuous process due to the fact that new assets, new threats, or new technology can be identified as well as some threats or assets that are obsolete and no longer need protection. These facts will make the security policy a living entity that also includes the retraining of employees.

In the following sections, the SAP security infrastructure is discussed so that you can better identify threats and vulnerabilities as well as the standard and nonstandard measures that can be applied to better protect and secure your assets.

Risks and Vulnerabilities

The increasing need for broad and open connectivity within complex SAP system landscapes and the increasing number of components within the architecture combined with options for external communications increase the risk of being attacked.

Systems are more vulnerable when a security policy is either insufficient or nonexistent. In these cases people trust that standard measures will be enough, but normally this is not the case.

The following is a brief list of threat types:

- External network attacks to set systems unavailable
- External password cracking attacks
- Internal sabotage to set systems unavailable
- Internal attacks for collecting confidential data
- Unintentional internal attacks or misbehavior
- Trojan programs
- Intentional internal breach of security policy
- Unintentional breach of security policy
- Unknown attacks

The main point is that the greater the number of risks and the fewer security measures in place, the greater the vulnerability of systems and therefore company assets.

Basic Security Processes

The following sections introduce some of the basic processes that are common when dealing with security and that you will find referenced continuously during this chapter.

Authentication

Authentication is the process that is used for verifying that users, programs, or services are actually who they say they are. Authentication is the cornerstone of any security infrastructure or technology.

SAP's standard User Authentication verifies a user's identity through the use of logon passwords. (Unsuccessful logon attempts will cause the session to terminate and activate user locks.) As standard security measures, SAP provides several login profile parameters and an initial set of password rules that you can expand on according to your needs. Standard security measures already provide a moderate to high degree of protection. User Authentication applies mainly at the presentation level, but a breach will affect other layers as well.

Limitations on SAP standard authentication pertain to the legal export rules of different countries regarding encryption software and algorithms. SAP included SNC in the kernel to overcome these limitations.

Additional security measures to raise your system to the highest protection level include the following:

- Using external security products that support encryption. Any such products however must be SNC compliant (see the discussion later in this chapter on SNC).
- Using techniques such as client certificates or logon tickets for Web User Authentication security. However, these methods can only work if other security layers, such as the network and Internet, are also properly protected over secure protocols such as SSL.

Further references for SAP user authentication can be found on the SAP online help, the Security Guide, and the SNC user's guide, which can be found at http://service.sap.com/security.

Smart-Card Authentication

SAP's standard smart-card authentication allows a "safer" authentication process. The users use cards, "smart cards," instead of passwords to log on to the security system. No password information is transmitted over the communication lines. Because the smart cards are often protected with a password or PIN, it is much more difficult for someone to compromise a user's authentication information.

The use of hardware devices such as smart cards is normally configured using an external security system based on the SNC interface.

The smart cards that can be used for login into the SAP Enterprise Portal are actually holders of the private keys of users, so the cards work as digital certificates that authenticate the holder.

Authorization

Authorization is the process that is used for determining what accesses or privileges are allowed for users. Authorizations are enforced by means of *access controls*, which are in charge of restricting user accesses.

SAP's User Authorization Concept

SAP's standard User Authorization secures user access to business data and transactions, ensuring that only preauthorized users gain access to data and processes. User authorizations are defined by Authorization administrators in coordination with key business users in authorization profiles that are stored in the SAP user master records. An initial set of authorization profiles is predefined by SAP; you can modify/add to these profiles and you can use the Profile Generator to create new profiles automatically based on user activity information. Authorization applies to the application level mainly, but remote communications, operating system commands, and the Change and Transport System must also be taken into account.

The SAP authorization system is very comprehensive but difficult to implement fully to achieve the strictest security standards. It is difficult to implement and maintain because it has a great deal of organizational projects in which users, key users, managers, and technical consultants are involved. Therefore, it is necessary to audit and monitor critical system authorizations. The SAP online documentation as well as the SAP security guide provides a good basic understanding and methodology for implementing the authorization concept.

You can increase the security level of SAP's User Authorization system by including well-defined developing standards along with a quality control that filters programs that do not implement the necessary security and authorization checks.

Privacy

Privacy is the process that can be used for ensuring that data or information sent over a network or communication line is not accessed or read by unauthorized persons. A usual way of granting privacy is by using *cryptography* technology. Both authorization and privacy ensure the confidentiality of data and information.

Within SAP landscapes *privacy* can be considered the highest security level that can be set by technological means and can be enforced by means of digital signatures, digital envelopes, and the use of the SNC and SSF components.

Integrity

Integrity is the process that verifies that nothing or nobody modifies data from a source to a target. Similar to the privacy within mySAP landscapes, *integrity* can be enforced by means of digital signatures, digital envelopes, and the use of the SNC and SSF components.

Proof of Obligation

Obligation or proof of obligation is necessary for confirming and guaranteeing that a business message is correct so it can be considered a business transaction between business partners. For this reason in electronic commerce there must be enough security mechanisms to guarantee the *nonrepudiation* of business messages.

Auditing

Auditing is the process of collecting and analyzing security data for verifying that the security policy and rules are complied with. *Accounting* is a way of measuring and/or restricting the use of system resources and as such is a form of authorization.

Cryptography

Cryptography is the technique based on mathematical algorithms and other methods to encode data and thus prevent data from being read or disclosed. Cryptography is commonly defined as the science of secret writing.

SAP's encrypted communications secure the exchange of critical data. This is an important security aspect in e-commerce communications. You can use SAP's SNC (Secure Network Communications) or SSF (Secure Store and Forward) solutions and the SSL (Secure Sockets Layer) protocol to encrypt the data being transferred via HTTPS connections. Data encryption ensures that the data being exchanged are secured end-to-end and protected from being intercepted.

SAP does not directly include encryption software within their solutions but provides the possibility of external security products that are compliant with SNC and SSF so it can be used for authentication, for single sign-on, for digital signatures and envelopes, and so on.

If security measures are not taken seriously, the manipulation and disclosure of information or digital documents is relatively easy with the aid of the current technology. Most of the advanced security measures are based on cryptography technologies. The following sections discuss common topics in modern cryptography applied to information technology.

Public Key Cryptography

Public key cryptography is based on mathematical functions of one direction, meaning that it is impossible to observe the results.

With this type of system each user that originates communications or messages has two keys:

- A private one (secret)
- A public one that is distributed to their communication partners

Every message that is sent with public key can only be decrypted using the private key.

Let's consider an example of how this system works. Suppose that these keys are the keys for a wooden box: from one of the keys there is only a master copy that you have securely kept; from the other one you have as many copies as you want and you give them to all people who want to communicate with you. The messages are boxes that have two locks (one opens with the secret key and the other one opens with the public one), with the special feature that if the box is closed using one of the keys it can only be opened using the other one.

Because of this procedure each communication partner has its own private key and the public keys from other partners.

If a person (sender A) wants to send a private message to another person (receiver B), the procedure would be as follows: it will introduce the message in a box that would be locked with the public key of the receiver so that only the receiver will be able to open it with his or her private key.

Then there is the following question: once the message is received, how does the receiver know that the message comes from the person (sender A) and not from another person that has his or her public key? This is the type of problem that digital signatures try to solve.

Digital Signatures

Digital signatures are special appendixes that are added to the digital documents to show the authenticity of the origin and the integrity of those documents.

A digital signature is equivalent to the traditional hand-written signatures on paper documents. When someone tries to modify a handwritten signature illegally, there are usually clues that can be detected by physical means. This is usually what guarantees the authenticity and integrity of data and information contained.

The digital signature must guarantee the same elements although using technological means. The first important point is that each digital signature will be different in every document. Otherwise it could be easy to copy and falsify digital signatures. For this reason the digital signature will depend on the document that is being signed using a mathematical function. This mathematical relationship allows for later verification of the validity and authenticity of the document.

The impossibility to falsify any type of digital signature is based on using characteristics or knowledge owned by the sender (the one that signs). Every time a person uses its analogical (handwritten) signature it generates a very similar graphic using its inherent graphological characteristics. In the case of digital signatures the signatory uses its secret private key. This is a very secure mechanism because even if the message is intercepted and someone wants to modify its content, he or she must also modify the signature and that cannot be done without knowing the secret private key.

To guarantee the security of digital signatures, the following points must be applied:

- Digital signatures must be unique: only the signatory can generate them.
- They cannot be falsified: in order to distort the signature the criminal should resolve very complex mathematical algorithms (considered computational safe).
- Verifiable: they should be easily verifiable by the receiver or by a competent authority.
- Nondeniable: the signatory cannot deny its own signature.
- Feasible: digital signatures should be easily generated by the signatory.

Several different protocols based on private key cryptography were proposed in standard organizations. However, currently it has been concluded that the public key cryptography is safer. Digital signatures in use and according to the aforementioned characteristics are based on the RSA signature and the DSS signature (Digital Signature Standard).

In certain countries digital signatures can be used legally as if they were handwritten. In terms of security this means proof of obligation and nonrepudiation. For this reason the use of digital signatures based on public key infrastructure can raise the system to a high degree of security.

Cryptography in SAP Systems

Since release 4.0 of SAP Basis R/3 in 1998, SAP systems have included the SSF (Secure Store and Forward) as a mechanism for protecting some of the data within the system. The SAP applications can use the SSF layer for securing the integrity, authenticity, and privacy of certain data. The key point of the SSF is that the data are still protected when they leave the SAP systems. The first applications using SSF are as follows:

- Production planning–process industry
- Product data management
- ArchiveLink II

SAP is committed to providing further applications that support SSF. SSF uses digital signature and *digital envelopes* for securing data. The digital signature identifies the sender and ensures the data integrity whereas the digital envelope ensures that the message can only be opened by the receiver.

Besides those features the Secure Store and Forward includes others that are relevant and important for electronic transactions:

- SSF is asynchronous: the creation, transmission, reception, process, and confirmation of business transactions are different steps that can take place at different times without locking or affecting the applications in charge of the process.
- Independence of the transport so that it should be possible to use different transfer mechanisms such as public networks, Internet, online services, magnetic disks, and so on as well as different protocols and communication services such as HTTP, FTP, e-mail, and EDI.

In order to perform these functions SSF requires the use of a third-party security product. Since release 4.5 of SAP R/3, the system has included the SAPSECULIB (SAP Security Library) as default provider for SSF services. SAPSECULIB is a software solution, but the functionality is limited to digital signatures. In order to support specific cryptographic hardware such as smart cards or for supporting digital envelopes, SSF needs to be complemented by an external product that must be certified by SAP.

To use digital signatures effectively, it is necessary to maintain a public key infrastructure (PKI). Because there is no accepted worldwide PKI, it is required for this infrastructure to be established in a secure provider domain.

Digital signatures are available in SAP systems and the SAP Business Connector and XI and can be used to secure business documents in SAP environments.

SAP's standard digital signatures authenticate the SAP systems data that are being transmitted and ensure that the senders (signatories) can be clearly determined. The subsequently assigned *digital envelope* ensures that the data contents will only be visible to the intended recipients. On SAP systems digital signatures are based on SSF.

Single Sign-On (SSO)

With SAP's standard Single Sign-On solution, users only need to enter their passwords once when they initially log on to the security system or the operating system. The security system then generates "credential" information so that the users can later automatically log on to other systems, such as R/3 or other mySAP Business Suite components, without any password information being transmitted over the communication lines.

With SAP R/3 and further with the SAP Web Application Server systems, there are many possibilities for Single Sign-On, although not all of them provide the same level of service. Some of these are as follows:

- External security product compliant with the SNC interface
- Use of central administration
- Trusted systems
- Microsoft Windows security provider
- Cookies
- Client certificates (X.509)

- Integration with LDAP servers
- SAP logon tickets

You can find extensive information on Single Sign-On solution on the security page of the SAP Service Marketplace (http://service.sap.com/security) and in the online documentation, as well as a set of SAP Notes.

LDAP

LDAP is the abbreviation of **L**ightweight **D**irectory **A**ccess **P**rotocol. A directory access protocol provides defined criteria to search, read, or write within a directory. Known for a long time (e.g., Novel Directory Services NDS, Netscape Directory Server) directories are having a comeback with the introduction of PKIs that require a LDAP server to store users and certificates and have them accessible for search and verification requests. Microsoft introduced LDAP functionality with Windows 2000 and its ability to use Active Directory Services.

Originating from the OSI Directory Access Protocol (DAP) introduced to the Internet community in August 1991, the X.500 Lightweight Directory Access Protocol is specified in RFC1777 from March 1995 as a read-only access protocol to the X.500 protocol suite (LDAP v2). The lightweight is derived from the fact that this directory access protocol provides read-only access to the main topics, variables, or features using TCP or other transport. This means that not all accessible values are represented using LDAP and that the corresponding layer is the transport layer bypassing much of the session/presentation overhead required for DAP. An update of LDAP can be found in RFC2251 from December 1997, which specifies LDAP v3 that has, in addition to other enhancements, writing capabilities within the directory.

Secure Socket Layer Protocol (SSL)

HTTP is the default protocol for transferring files on the World Wide Web. HTTP transports Web sites as plain-text files. So it is possible that a third party having access to the network can read or alter the data sent. The protocol has no proper mechanisms to ensure authentication and confidentiality for the data. For that purpose SSL encryption can be used. The HTTPS protocol transfers HTTP over an SSL connection. HTTPS offers options to encrypt the data and to identify the other party by its digital certificate.

SSL/HTTPS provides confidentiality and integrity of the data transmitted and authentication of the user.

- Confidentiality is ensured through strong encryption. So the information transmitted cannot be decrypted by anyone else and the intended recipient and is unreadable to third parties.
- Data integrity ensures that a third party did not alter data sent through the network.
- Authentication is provided through digital certificates that are very difficult to falsify.

When an HTTPS communication is set up, client and server first agree on a protocol version and define the encryption algorithms. Then they authenticate each other and use encryption techniques to generate the session information.

The following sections provide an overview over the steps required to set up a HTTPS connection:

1. The client sends a request to the SSL-enabled server.
2. The server sends its public key and its certificate to the client.
3. The client checks if the certificate of the server was signed by a certificate authority whom the client trusts. Otherwise the client will abort the connection to the server.
4. The client compares the information from the certificate with those it just received about the server: domain name and public key. If the information matches, the client accepts the server as authenticated. At this point the server might request a certificate from the client as well.
5. The client creates a session key, encrypts it with the public key of the server, and sends it to the server.
6. The server receives the session key and encrypts it with its private key.
7. Client and server use the session key to encrypt and decrypt the data they send and receive.

SAP Security Infrastructure

As indicated previously, SAP systems security often is only seen as the implementation of the authorization/role concept. However, SAP solutions based on open, multitiered client/server and Web-based architecture include many components that can exchange or are used for exchanging data and information with other components, applications, or systems. Each of the elements needed for the communication and exchange of information is a layer of the SAP security infrastructure also known as a security service.

Security must be addressed at all these layers. Here is an introduction to each of them; these will be further covered in following sections:

- The presentation level is represented by all forms of front ends used for accessing SAP systems. This is typically the SAP GUI for Windows although other options are available, such as the SAP GUI for HTML, SAP Enterprise Portals, the SAP GUI Shortcuts, and other front ends that can be programmed with the SAP Automation and other utilities. At the presentation level the main security service is the *user authentification.*
- The application level includes the application logic that is run by the ABAP programs. The role-based and authorization concept is the main security service located at this level.
- The SAP databases are the containers of all the business information as well as the metadata, data models, and object repository. SAP databases must be protected against unauthorized accesses, which can come from direct or remote accesses. It is very important to recognize and protect the most critical system tables. This is the level of data access protection.
- The network is the de facto backbone of computing, and there is no business or collaborative application that can work without it. SAP solutions and systems are a

complex set of networked servers and applications both inside and outside the companies and as such the network is the enabler that must be protected. Since SAP R/3 release 3.1G the system includes the SNC interface that can be complemented with third-party security products to further enhance and protect the SAP network communications. The network is located at the access security level.

- Remote communications. The natural openness of the SAP systems and the endless possibilities of communicating and exchanging data between them and other systems require a security analysis from the point of view of external or remote communications mainly on the areas of the RFC and CPIC protocols, which are used in other interfacing techniques such as the BAPIs.
- Internet. The Internet represents the biggest opportunity and natural marketplace for e-business and at the same time the riskiest place if security measures are not in place. More and more SAP solutions are extensively based on Web technology and they are Internet enabled. Internet security is very extensive and would require a book on its own. In case of SAP systems care, must be taken to use firewalls; protect ITS, SAP WAS, or SAP Enterprise Portal servers; and use SNC and other cryptographic technologies.
- Operating system. SAP solutions include naturally a large collection of software applications. Access protection to SAP files and directories as well as the operating system commands must be also be in place.

Security must also address the overall system landscape: development system, quality assurance system, productive system, and any connected complementary system whether belonging to the SAP Business Framework architecture or not. Security also implies the Change and Transport System.

All security aspects on SAP systems components are based on restricting the access to each of the system's layers to authorized users or authorized external systems only.

A security infrastructure must also include all the logging and auditing possibilities because these mechanisms are required for monitoring and enforcing the security policy.

What Type of Security Is Standard on SAP Systems?

SAP NetWeaver and the mySAP Business Suite systems include many security features, the majority of which are not often applied in most customer's installations. On one hand, it is easy to think that in order to reach SAP systems you must first leak into the network, the operating system, or the database. And whereas somehow this is true it is also true that if internal threats are considered, then standard security measures will certainly not be enough.

The SAP Basis Middleware (R/3) as well as the SAP Web Application Server includes basic and generic security measures based mostly on passwords for user authentication as well as the authorization concept for user access to business data and transactions. SAP Basis comes with other powerful security features, such as support for Secure Network Communications (SNC), Secure Store and Forward (SSF), and digital signatures and allows the use of external security products, Single Sign-On solutions, smart cards, and many other options to suit the needs of the most exigent businesses and chief security officers.

How Can SAP Security Be Improved?

If you understand the security components and infrastructure, there is a lot you can do to improve SAP systems security without compromising normal users' operation.

You can improve security by

- Designing and implementing a secure systems infrastructure by means of firewalls and setting password policies and parameters
- Setting the most appropriate values for security-related instance profile parameters
- Using external security products
- Establishing a security policy and efficiently communicating it
- Creating a security checklist that can be periodically tested either manually or automatically so you can evaluate the efficiency of your security policy
- Enforcing the security policy by means of logging and auditing
- Monitoring security alerts and locating threats
- Establishing a procedure for constant update of the security policies

The Multilayer SAP Security Infrastructure

Layers of the SAP security infrastructure must interoperate to form a cohesive security strategy. This interoperation cannot happen unless you understand what each layer is supposed to do. We explore these functions in the following sections.

Security at the Presentation Level

Presentation-level security addresses all forms of front ends used for accessing SAP systems. This is typically the SAP GUI, though other options are available, such as the SAP GUI for HTML, SAP GUI for Java, the SAP GUI shortcuts, the SAP Enterprise Portal, and other front ends or logon programs that can be programmed with SAP Automation and other utilities. The primary security service at the presentation level is User Authentication. When security fails at this level it is typically because

- The security policy is weak, not well communicated or enforced, or not existing at all.
- The profile parameters that enforce basic security measures are not set.
- You have not changed the passwords of standard users.
- Basic protection measures at the workstation are not taken.
- You have not implemented advanced security methods such as SNC, Single Sign-On, client certificates that allows encryption, or smart login devices.
- Security auditing and monitoring is scarce.

As a result you see unauthorized users logging in with privileged user accounts, many unsuccessful logon attempts, or users using other persons' accounts.

Once I was starting a security analysis for a customer and he gave me access to a PC. I asked him for a username and password to enter the SAP systems (they had many systems) and he went out a few minutes to ask someone else for a username. When he came back I had successfully logged into every SAP system using the well-known privileged user and password. I said, "What SAP instance do you want me to stop?"

It is mainly the job of the Basis administrators and User administrators together with the IT department and the security manager to define a clear authentication policy, to set in place all the standard SAP security measures, and if needed to add any advanced measures to protect the system at the presentation level.

Application-Level Security

Security at this level addresses the application logic that is run by the ABAP programs. Here the main security service is the User Authorization concept, which grants or denies access to business objects and transactions based upon a user's authorization profiles. When security fails at this level it is typically because

- The authorization system has been poorly implemented.
- Critical authorizations have not been defined.
- Local development did not include appropriate authority checks.
- Administration of authorizations and profiles are not properly distributed and protected.
- The user and authorization information system is rarely used.

As a result you see unintentional transaction executions by unauthorized users, performance problems, display or modification of confidential information by unauthorized users, or even deletion of important data.

Several times it happened to me that a user that was not supposed to have such an authorization had unintentionally deleted or changed parts of the number range table (NRIV) and due to the legal implications of this we had to make a point-in-time recovery of the whole system.

It is the Application administrators' job to define which users have access to what data and transactions. These definitions must later be technically implemented by the User and Authorization administrators. It is also very important that every developer follows a programming methodology that includes security checks.

Security at the Database Level

The SAP systems databases are the container for all the business information as well as the metadata, data models, and object repository. These databases must be protected against unauthorized accesses. At this level security services must grant access protection to SAP systems data. When security fails at this level it is typically because

- Standard passwords have not been changed.
- Access to the operating system is not properly protected.
- Remote access to the database is not secure.
- Auditing has not been activated on critical tables.
- The authorization system at SAP level is poorly implemented.

As a result you see modifications at the database level that compromise systems integrity and consistency, uncontrolled access to confidential information below the application level, or systems unavailability.

In one of my customer installations the operator (who additionally did not understand very good English) started a tablespace reorganization instead of adding a new data file to a tablespace. The system was stopped for some hours.

It is the job of the Database administrators together with the OS system managers and the Basis administrators to take appropriate security measures at this level. Some of the measures are changing the passwords of privileged DB users, protecting SAPDBA with expert mode, restricting external remote access to read-only mode, auditing critical tables, setting correctly the S_TABU_DIS authorization object.

Operating System–Level Security

Security services must guarantee access protection to SAP files and directories as well as the operating system commands and programs. At this level security services are provided by the operating system features themselves. When security fails at this level it is typically because

- Permissions on files and directories are not properly set.
- The password and user policy at the OS level is static and widely known.
- Logging and monitoring is scarce.

As a result you see deletion of important system and application files, software malfunctions, or system unavailability.

I have seen a system operator deleting critical system files like the database files by mistake that were fully unprotected. A restore and recovery was necessary in order to have the system up and running again.

It is the job of the Operating System manager to implement security measures at the operating system and to monitor the main log files of the audit system. Measures include implementing a security password policy at user level, taking care not to create unnecessary users or services, monitoring SETUID programs, setting ACLs (Access Control Lists) in critical files and directories, and protecting external commands from being executed from SAP.

Network-Level Security

Networks are the de facto backbones of computing. There is no business or collaborative application that can work without one. SAP systems based on a client/server architecture are no exception. With release 3.1G SAP Basis (R/3), SAP systems included the SNC interface (Secure Network Connections), which can and in most cases should be complemented with third-party security products to further protect network communications. When security fails at this level it is typically because

- There are too many unprotected network services.
- Network topology is poorly designed.
- There is little or no network monitoring.

- Routers, filters, or firewalls are not correctly configured.
- SAP router configuration is not properly set.
- There is no automatic intrusion detection system.
- Data are not traveling in encrypted form.

As a result you see users or programs trying to log on to unauthorized systems like hackers, users logging on to the wrong servers, unbalanced system loads, or even sniffing.

One example of security violations in the network environment is when end users log on directly to the database server when this has an administrative instance. Another one I have seen many times is when the *rlogin* service is completely unprotected and users have logged on through the network and stopped the wrong servers.

It is the Network administrators' responsibility to design and implement a security network topology that takes into consideration an automatic monitoring and intrusion detection system.

Transport System–Level Security

SAP has provided the TMS (Transport Management System) as an environment for coordinated customizing and team development that protects the modification of objects and settings across a SAP landscape. Unfortunately the TMS is a facet of the SAP enterprise that is often undersecured.

When security fails at this level it is typically because

- System landscape settings are not properly configured.
- Repairs are freely allowed.
- There are no filters that control which objects are being transported.
- Authorizations are not completely implemented.
- Transport monitoring is not a periodic task.

As a result you see software failures, transport of copied programs without security checks, or problems when upgrading your system.

It is the task of the Basis administrator together with users in charge of customizing and developers to properly set the system to basic security standards and to define a security policy that makes sure that there is some type of filtering and monitoring within the transport system.

Secure Network Communications (SNC)

SAP's standard Secure Network Communications provides protection for the communication links between the distributed components of a SAP system. SNC is built on the SAP WAS kernel based on standard GSS API V2 and allows you to increase the level of your SAP security via external security products (e.g., Single Sign-On, smart-card authentication, and encrypted communications). SNC can raise your system to high security standards because it can cover several layers such as the presentation (authentication and Single Sign-On) layer, the remote communications layer, the network layer, and even the Internet layer.

Remote Communications-Level Security

The natural openness of the SAP systems and the endless possibilities of communicating with and exchanging data between SAP and other systems require stringent security analysis from the point of view of external or remote communications mainly in the areas of the RFC and CPIC protocols, which are used in other interfacing techniques such as ALE or BAPIs.

When security fails at this level it is typically because

- The authorization system is poorly implemented for remote communications.
- RFC communications include the passwords in their definitions.
- There is scarce monitoring at the gateways.
- OS and network security is also weak.
- No encryption software has been used.

As a result you see unexpected connections or program executions from other systems, software failures, or access to confidential information.

It is the job of Basis administrators together with Network administrators and developers to implement standard security measures to avoid leaving holes at the remote communication level.

Some standard measures are as follows: do not create more RFC destinations than those necessary, include AUTHORITY-CHECK within the programs that can be remotely called, protect table RFCDES, use standard interface techniques, provide periodic monitoring of the gateway server, and ensure that the *secinfo* file exits.

Document Transfer-Level Security

SAP security services must guarantee the integrity, confidentiality, and authenticity of any type of business documents such as electronic files, mail messages, and others. At this level SAP provides Secure Store and Forward (SSF) mechanisms, which include digital signatures and digital envelopes based on public key technology. And these mechanisms can be deployed using external security services like digital certificates and digital envelopes.

When security fails at this level it is typically because

- Certificates and encryption are not used/implemented.
- Private keys are not properly protected.
- There is scarce tracing and monitoring.

As a result you see documents intercepted by unauthorized persons or access to confidential information.

It is the job of the Basis administrators and expert security consultants with the help of the legal department to define and implement secure mechanisms like encryption methods for protecting the secure transfer of documents.

Introduction to SSF (Secure Store and Forward)

SAP's standard Secure Store and Forward provides the required support to protect SAP systems data and documents as independent data units. You can use the SSF functions to "wrap" SAP systems data in secure formats before the data are transmitted over insecure communications links. These secure formats are based on public and private keys using cryptographic algorithms.

While SAP provides a Security Library (SAPSECULIB) as a software solution for digital signatures as well as standard support for SSF in certain application modules such as PDM or ArchiveLink, a high degree of protection is achieved only when private keys are secured using hardware devices such as smart cards.

Despite the fact that the communication infrastructure might be well protected, it is also necessary to protect the private keys that are used in digital signatures and envelopes because if this information is intercepted, the cryptographical strategy will be useless.

This includes SAP components such as the application servers when these act as the senders of the messages and therefore hold the private keys.

In addition to the risk that exists in case the private key falls into the wrong hands, it must also be considered that criminals can be interested in sabotaging the communications and could modify the public keys repository for the partners with whom the company system communicates.

Protecting Private Keys

There are two main ways for storing and protecting private keys:

- *Via hardware.* The best solution for protecting SAP users' private keys is the use of an individual smart card for every user. With this there is no way to reveal the private key that the smart card holds. Additionally users must be identified in their smart cards using biometric means (such as a fingerprint, the eyeprint, etc.) or by the use of a secret number such as a PIN, a password, a question that only the user knows, and so on. Users are responsible for securing their cards.

  If this method of protecting private keys is selected, companies should develop a communication campaign so that users are informed of the importance of not sharing or letting others use their smart cards.

  From the point of view of the server and in order to improve performance, the recommendation is the use of a crypto box instead of a smart card.
- *Via software.* The software solution is not as safe as when specific hardware is used. If a file holding the keys is used, then it is very important to protect this file from unauthorized accesses.

Protecting Public Keys

If the security products use an address book for holding the public keys just in the case of the private keys, then the files must be protected from unauthorized access or modifications.

An alternative is to use certificates that are issued by a trusted Certification Authority (CA) to grant the authenticity of those certificates.

There are several countries that have regulated the use of cryptography and digital signatures. However, these rules or laws frequently generate a big amount of controversy and even change. Some countries already accept the digital signatures as a valid proof of obligation and therefore digital signatures can be used for secure business.

Internet-Level Security

A critical component is what I call the "Internet level," which addresses the interactions that take place between a SAP system and browsers, Web servers, SAP Web Application Server, ITS, SAP EP, firewalls, and so on.

When security fails at this level it is typically because

- Secure protocols are not properly set.
- Encryption and certificates are not used.
- Remote debugging of ITS is not disabled.
- Service files are not protected.
- Firewalls and authentication might not be properly configured.
- Security measures at Web servers are weak.
- Monitoring is scarce.

As a result you see many types of attacks on Web servers that might make systems unavailable or compromise critical information.

There are thousands of Internet security incidents and break-ins reported; some of them make the CNN headlines. There are dozens of books and hundreds of Web sites covering security, hacking, and protection software. You could start at http://www.securitynews.org.

It is the job of the Basis administrator, Network administrator, and Web administrator to set in place a system design for implementing the best security measures that protect against attacks to the SAP systems that are tightly connected to the Internet.

A comprehensive security strategy limits access at each of these security layers to only authorized users and/or authorized external systems. It also accounts for the overall *system landscape*: development systems, quality assurance system, productive system, and the transport system that operates between them as well as any connected complementary systems whether they belong to the SAP NetWeaver infrastructure architecture or not. You want to be sure that certain protective procedures are set in place to guard against insecure programs or Trojan horses that may travel from one system to another.

Logging and Auditing

Last but not least, a security infrastructure must include robust *logging and auditing* capabilities; the mechanisms you will need to monitor and enforce your security policies. Logging and monitoring address the efficiency of the security measures and the capacities of the system for detecting weaknesses, vulnerabilities, and any other security problem. There are logging and auditing facilities in the SAP security infrastructure at every level. These facilities are implemented mainly in the Security Audit Log, the Audit Info System (AIS), the security alerts within CCMS, and the Users and Authorization Info System (SUIM). These tools are complemented by other logging facilities such as those available at operating system level, database auditing statements, network and Internet monitoring and management, and others.

The difficulty for monitoring the whole SAP security infrastructure is that there is no single tool for doing that automatically although the evolution of the CCMS and the AIS tools make us think that it might happen.

You can find extensive information and checklists for auditing security in the diverse SAP Security Guides at the SAP Service Marketplace (http://service.sap.com/security).

SAP Trust Center Services

The focus of the SAP Trust Center Service is to provide global one-step authentication and digital signature technology for enabling collaborative business scenarios. The trust infrastructure relies on already existing business relationships between SAP and its customers. The SAP Trust Center provides more trust than any other existing trust center because these do not typically rely on existing business relationships. This service provides a smooth migration from password-based authentication to certificate-based authentication.

The Trust Center Service works with the customer's internal Portal to distribute digital certificates—called SAP Passports—to individual users. The SAP Passport is based on the X.509 certificate standard and enables data to be encrypted and transmitted safely over intranets and open Internet connections. SAP customers using the Trust Center Services can be sure that only authorized partners and employees are accessing information and conducting business in Marketplaces.

If SAP users wish to apply for a SAP Passport when they log on to their Portal, their UID and password is used. The Portal Server transfers the user as well as the company's identity to the Web browser of the user. The Web browser then automatically generates an asymmetric public/private key pair. After receiving and verifying the certificate request containing the user's and the company's identity and the public key from the Web browser, the Portal Server approves the certificate request with its digital signature. The Web browser then sends the approved certificate request to the SAP Trust Center Service. The SAP Trust Center Service verifies the certificate request against the agreed naming convention. Then the Trust Center Service Certification Authority (CA) creates a X.509 certificate and transfers the certificate back to the Web browser. The SAP Passport is now ready for use.

Management of Users, Authorizations, and Roles

The users of the SAP systems are defined internally within the same SAP systems and there is no need for user management at the operating system or database level, except for those special users defined in the standard installations, such as <sid>adm, SAPServices<adm>, ora<dbsid>, or others, depending on the operating system and database platform.

The users are defined and maintained, and the security of the system is enforced in the user master records with the use of the SAP authorizations and role concept.

The following sections deal with the general management of user master records and the most important available fields and options, just on the SAP Web Application Server with the ABAP engine.

But the main concern for system administrators and project managers when implementing the SAP solutions is how to enforce the right security methods for users' access to the business information. As we have seen in the first part of this chapter, the SAP system provides a comprehensive and flexible way to protect data and transactions against unauthorized use.

In the user master records, users are assigned one or more *roles* and *authorization profiles*. These authorization profiles are made of a set of *authorizations*, which give access privileges for the different elements of the system. Further down, authorizations refer to *authorization objects*, which contain a range of permitted values for different system or business entities within SAP systems.

Managing roles, profiles, and authorizations is a complex and time-consuming task within SAP implementation projects and later maintenance and support. SAP has designed a tool that reduces the time needed for implementing and managing the authorizations, thus decreasing the implementation costs. This tool is known as the *Role Maintenance* based on the classical *Profile Generator*. The Profile Generator is a SAP utility available since release 3.0F of the R/3 Basis kernel, with the goal of making easier the configuration and management of authorizations, profiles, and roles. It can be used for automatically creating roles, authorizations, and profiles and assigning them easily to users. The definition of profiles using the Profile Generator is based on the possibility of grouping functions by *roles* (known as *activity groups* in releases of SAP Basis before 4.6C) in a company menu. This menu will be generated using customizing settings and will only include those functions selected by the customers. *Roles* form a set of tasks or activities that can be performed in the system, such as running programs, transactions, and other functions that generally represent a job description or job role.

In the following sections, all the concepts are introduced with some practical examples dealing with the process of granting access rights and protecting the system elements. A final section of the chapter covers the topic of organizing the user master record management from the point of view of tasks involved in granting access rights to the users.

Overview of User Administration

As a SAP administrator or support personnel, user handling should not be of major concern if certain rules and guidelines are followed from the beginning of the project. This, however, does not apply to authorization and role maintenance, which are matters of joint projects and efforts between the SAP functional and technical people. The reason is that usually SAP system managers do not have to deal with such things as granting access to certain users for specific general ledger accounts, cost centers, or production plants. It is the role of the customization specialists, developers, or business consultants to define entities that should be protected by means of authorization objects and to assign or create the corresponding roles or profiles.

This task is really important, and it might become a puzzle that can take a lot of time to solve, depending on the degree of security protection desired and the number of users and modules being implemented.

The easy part of user administration deals with such things as creating user master records, changing passwords, helping users define their own default values, and organizing the user maintenance tasks.

Managing User Master Records

Similar to the rest of the SAP systems based on the SAP WAS for ABAP, where there is a material master, a vendor master, and so on, the user administrative and management functions also have a user master. The *user master records* define the user accounts for enabling access to the system. They contain other screens with additional fields apart from the user ID, some of which are just for information purposes (but are nevertheless important) and others that can make life easier for both users and administrators.

The user master records contain all the access information needed by the system to validate a user logon and assign users access rights to the system, such as passwords, roles, and authorization profiles.

There is a lot of extra information in a user master record, including which start menu the users will see when they first log on, what printer is assigned by default, and the addresses and phone numbers of users. Some of the fields are just for information purposes, whereas others have a direct effect on the working environment for the users.

To reach the user maintenance functions via menu options, from the SAP Easy Access menu select Tools | Administration | User Maintenance | Users, or type the transaction code SU01 in the command field. Figure 8-1 shows the user maintenance initial screen.

This screen shows the input field for specifying an individual user for which to perform administrative actions.

To find a particular user when you don't know the proper user ID, you can select the possible entries list arrow and then click on the List icon on the dialog box.

To perform functions over a group of users, the system includes some options under the menu Environment | Mass Changes. This is introduced in a later section.

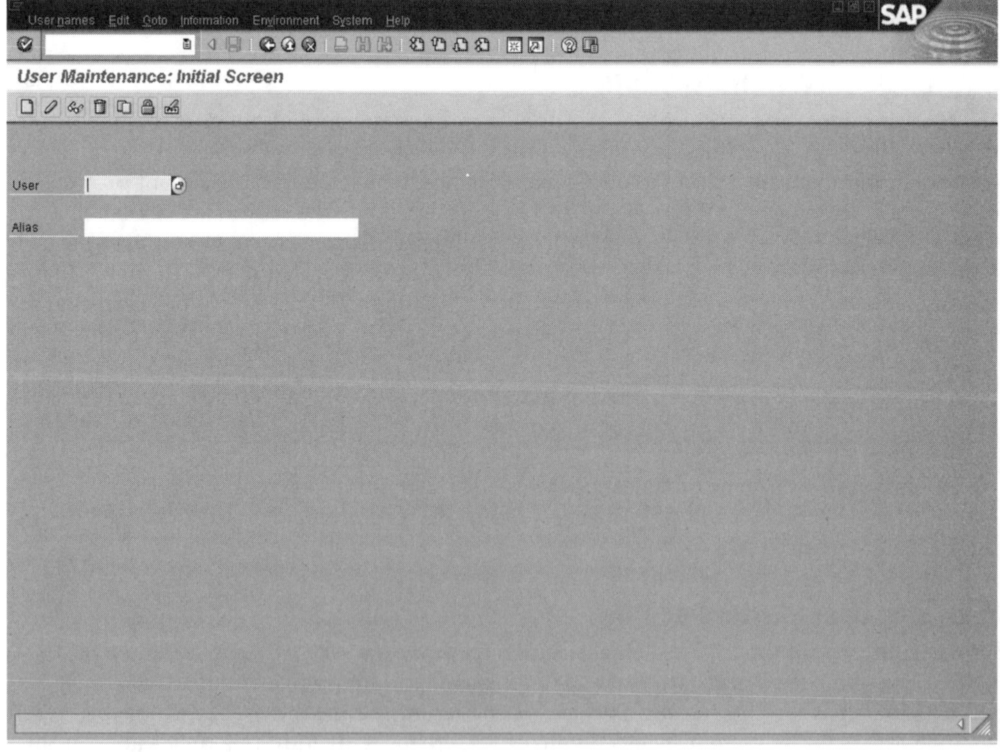

FIGURE 8-1 Initial screen for user management (Copyright by SAP AG)

Creating Users

From the User Maintenance initial screen, as shown in Figure 8-1 there are many options available. Normally, the input field for the user field is empty, except if you have been working in other user management functions previously in the same session.

User master records are client dependent, which means that they are separately defined for each client in the SAP system. For example, if user *FREDSMITH* is defined on client 003, but not on client 005, he won't be able to log on in client 005.

To create a user master record you have two options: either define it completely from scratch or copy it from another user or from a reference user you had previously defined. The next list explains both methods.

- *Creating new users from scratch.* From the User Maintenance menu, enter the name for the new user and click on the Create icon, or with the right mouse button select the F8 function key, or select User Names | Create from the menu bar. Figure 8-2 shows a screen similar to the one you will get. The system displays the different sections of the user master records within the different tabstrips. You might get additional tabstrips if you have security interfaces installed, such as with an SNC compatible product.

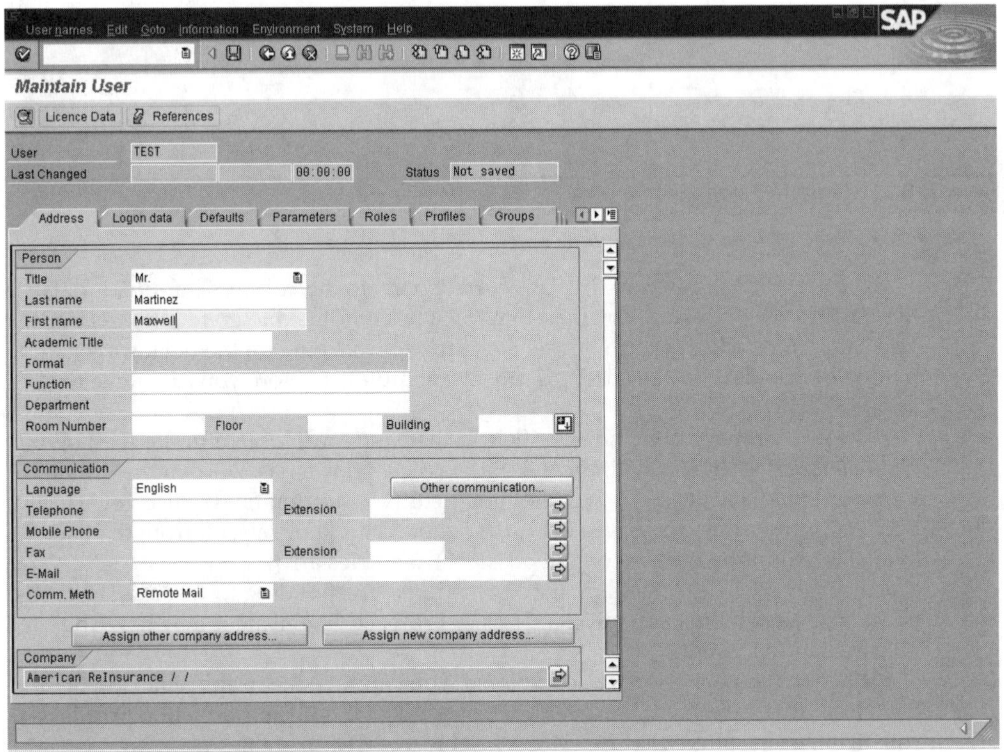

FIGURE 8-2 Creating users from scratch (Copyright by SAP AG)

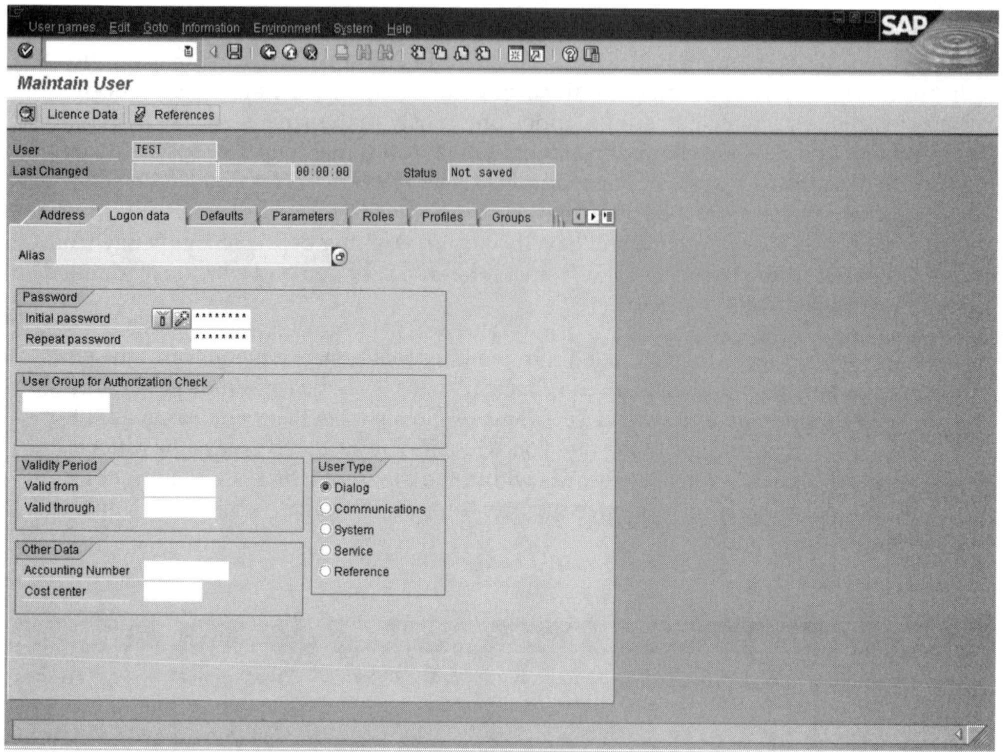

FIGURE 8-3 Logon data (Copyright by SAP AG)

The first data the system displays corresponds to the Address information. Here the Last Name is a mandatory field that must be completed to go to other sections. You can move back and forth between tabstrips by clicking on them. However, any mandatory fields on these tabstrips must be completed before you can move to another section.

The most important mandatory field is the password, located under the Logon Data tabstrip, as shown in Figure 8-3. Enter or generate a password in the Initial Password field and retype it in the second field (verification field). Also you can optionally enter the user group for authorization check, or select it from the list of available groups by clicking on the possible list entries arrow.

Users themselves can maintain information corresponding to Address, Defaults, and Parameters by selecting System | User Profile | Own Data if they have the required authorizations.

When mandatory fields are completed, you can save the user by clicking on the Save icon. It is important, however, to assign at least some authorization profiles or role to the users; otherwise they won't be able to perform any task.

After a user has been created, any modification to the user master fields is performed by entering the user ID in the User input field of the initial User Maintenance screen and clicking on the Change icon on the application toolbar.

- *Copying users from reference master records.* Instead of defining the SAP users one by one from scratch, it is usually better to define some template user master records and to create new users by copying these templates and changing only some of the fields. Doing it this way reduces the time needed to create users, especially at the beginning of the system life. These models or reference users can be regular SAP system users. For example, suppose your company is implementing a SAP R/3 Enterprise for managing the sales and distribution, the materials management, and the finances. Possibly there will be users who just take orders in the system, others doing accounting work, and others with different tasks. In these cases, you can create a reference user for the sales module and use that user master record as a reference for creating the rest. The same process can be done for the users of other modules.

  To create a new user by copying from a reference user, from the initial user maintenance screen, enter the name of the new user in the input field and press the Copy function button from the application toolbar. The system displays a dialog box similar to the one shown in Figure 8-4.

  As you can see from Figure 8-4, you can decide what parts of the user master record to copy. You might want to copy just the profiles or just the address, in case you want to reuse any of the company address, or even just the defaults. In any case, you will have to specify a new password for the new user. The other values for the following screens can be modified just as if you were creating a new user. To modify any input field value, just write over the field while in Overwrite mode.

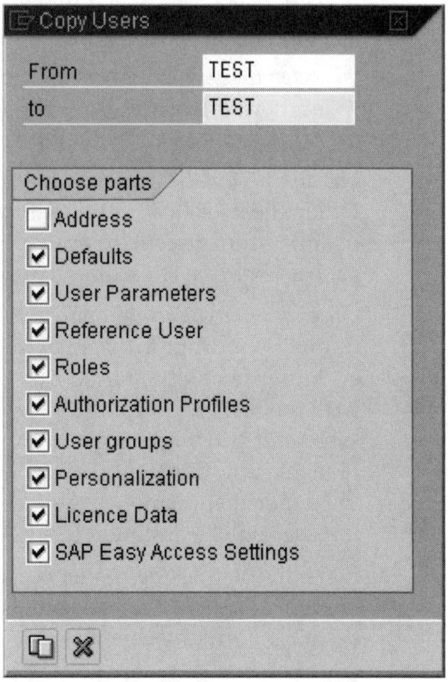

FIGURE 8-4 Dialog box for copying users (Copyright by SAP AG)

User Master Records Fields

Whether you are creating or modifying user master records, the SAP system screens for the user maintenance transaction show several input fields.

There are many, and some of the most important fields are the following:

- *Initial password.* The password for the first logon with the user ID. The password must be entered twice in a verification field, to make sure there were no typing errors. The next section explains password management from the point of view of the administrator. For an introduction and guide for users, refer to the section on password rules in Chapter 5.
- *User group.* Located under the Groups tabstrip, the name of the user master record groups to which this user can be assigned. This is a useful field for dividing user maintenance among groups or for performing changes on all users belonging to a group. For example, you can create user administrator master records in charge of a particular group but not of others. Before you can assign a group, it must have been created first.
- *User type.* Located on the Logon Data tabstrip, there are five user types available, each of which provides special access privileges depending on the type of processing. The normal interactive or ordinary user must be of type *Dialog,* which is the default. Other types of users are
  - *System,* which provides access privileges for processing background jobs and for internal RFC calls.
  - *Communication,* which is used for communication between systems not requiring dialog, such as ALE, RFC, or the TMS.
  - *Service,* a very special type of user, which can be assigned to a large group of anonymous users, which allows multiple logons.
  - *Reference,* which is an additional user type for assigning additional and identical authorizations to users. No online access to the system is allowed with this type of users. A user can only be assigned to a user type.
- *Validity period.* In this optional field, administrators can enter a period of time in which the user ID is valid. Although this field is often left empty, it can be very useful within a security policy, especially when setting accounts for occasional users such as external consultants or business partners.
- *Other data: accounting number.* You can enter in this optional field any name or number you want to assign to a user as his or her user account. It can be unique for each user or can be shared by a group of users. This field is useful when working with the SAP user accounting system, which performs statistics of the usage of the system. If you want to get individual usage statistics, you could enter the same user ID name into this field. For group statistics, a possibility is to enter the cost center, the department name, and so forth. If you leave it blank, the accounting statistics for the user will be assigned to a collective *No account* category.
- *Roles.* In the roles tab page, you can enter any number of predefined roles, which is one collective way of assigning specific authorizations to users for accessing SAP systems. Formerly this was known as *task profile.*

- *Profiles.* A profile gives the user the permission to access specific system functions. *Profiles* are made of a group of authorizations and authorization objects. Profiles can be simple or composite. Composite profiles are groups of profiles (either simple or composite).

SAP systems include a large number of predefined roles and profiles matching most common user needs for the different SAP application modules and also for the development and system management functions. To get the list of predefined roles you can click on the possible entries arrow of the input field for profile. Looking for specific predefined profiles can be done by either looking in the application documentation or by searching the implementation guide (IMG). There are other ways to search for profiles by tracing authorizations and then using the authorization information system.

The system provides facilities for creating your own roles and profiles, using the Role Maintenance and the Profile Generator, when the predefined profiles or roles are not enough.

Available Defaults and Options for User Master Records

After the first initial screen for user maintenance, the system provides additional screens for entering other user information. You can set, for example, the default printer for a user, the user's address, and values for user field defaults (parameters). The three available screens are Address, Defaults, and Parameters. These subscreens are accessed by clicking on the corresponding tabstrip within the User Maintenance screen.

Users can set their own values and defaults by themselves in the System | User Profile | Own Data menu. The following sections show the available options that can be set by users.

Specifying User Address

The information in user addresses is only used by the SAP system for documentation purposes. It can be very useful, however, for system administrators when trying to locate a user by her or his name, phone number, and so on. Often companies assign user IDs using letters and numbers which are coded so that it is easier to locate or assign user IDs to system users. The address data for a user includes three main information boxes, corresponding to *Person, Communication,* and *Company*. Some of the most important fields in those boxes are as follows:

- *Last Name.* In this field you must enter the surname of the user. This is a mandatory field that has an additional use when using the SAP Business Workplace.
- *Telephone No., Fax, and E-mail.* These fields can be used for entering the phone number, fax number, and e-mail address, which are important, especially the fax and the e-mail, when connecting the SAP systems with external fax systems or Internet e-mail.
- *Company.* You can also enter and maintain the company information for users.

Setting User Default Values

Administrators or users by themselves can set some fixed or default values for some common functions or input fields that they find often while working in SAP systems. Figure 8-5 shows an example of this screen. Here, you can set the following:

- *Start menu.* You can set the name of the menu or the transaction, which will be started automatically when a user logs on.

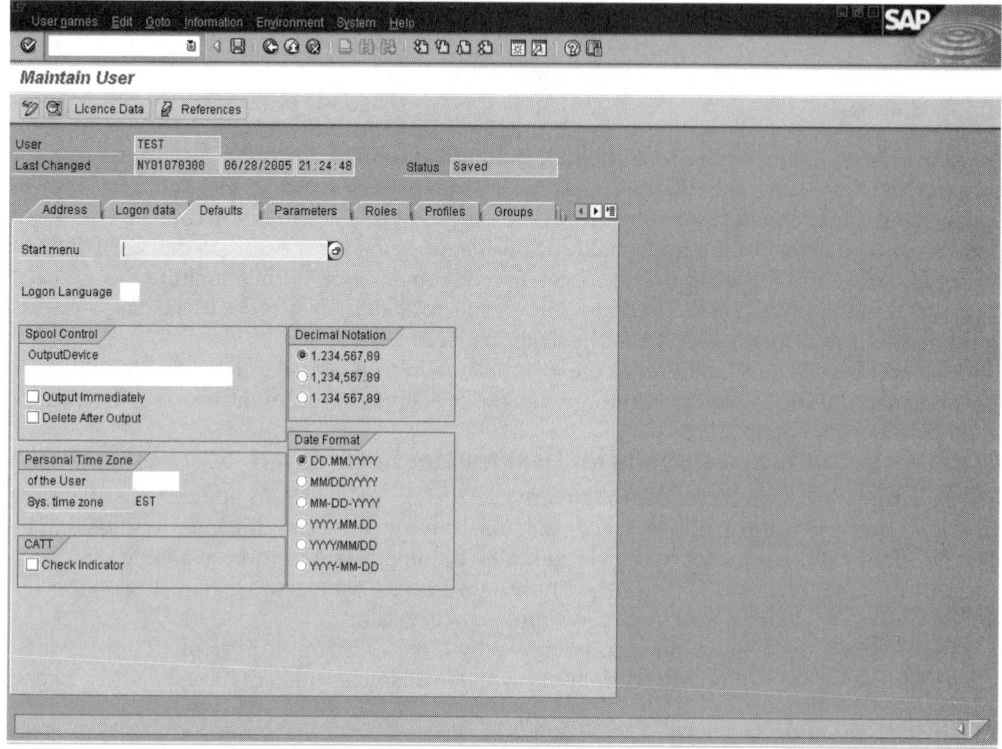

FIGURE 8-5 Maintaining user default values (Copyright by SAP AG)

- *Logon language.* Setting this field for a user will overwrite the system default when the user logs on. If the language field for the initial logon window of the SAP system is empty, the language specified in this field is used.
- *The default printer for a user.* This is assigned in the Output Device field. You can click on the possible entries arrow to display a list of printers.
- *The output controller check boxes.* These are particularly important for handling user print requests. Check the box next to Print immediately to have a print job sent directly to the printer; otherwise, it will just send it to the output controller where users can print it later. Setting the box next to Delete after output tells the system to delete the job from the spool database after it has been printed.
- *The format for date and decimal points.* The last check box, CATT, is used for special test functions within the computer-aided test tool provided in the SAP system. For information on CATT, look it up in the SAP online documentation.

Setting User Default Values for Parameters

The parameters that can be set on this screen match some fields of the SAP systems. Setting default values using these parameters offers the advantage that every time a user is presented with a screen containing any of those fields, the value is automatically entered in the input field.

This concept is explained in Chapter 5. Remember that at any time users can overwrite those values or change the parameter values by selecting System | User Profile | Own Data.

The parameter screen has two fields:

- *Parameter ID* refers to the parameter ID, which you can find using the technical information for the field (remember: place your cursor on the field, press F1 and then Technical Info). You can also list the available parameters by clicking on the possible entries arrow next to the parameter input field.
- In the Value field, enter the value you want to assign as the default any time a SAP screen presents that field.

Managing User Groups

User groups within the SAP user maintenance functions basically serve as a way to divide administration tasks. To reach the user group screen, from the initial user maintenance, select Environment | User Groups and then you can either Maintain or Display them.

User groups are just assigned a name. So the only two basic functions to perform are either *create* a group or *delete* a group. To create or delete a group, position the cursor over the group name and click on the corresponding function button.

Clients 000 and 001 include a special privilege group, SUPER, which is normally assigned to superusers SAP* and DDIC. To delete the group SUPER, users need special authorization.

Modifying User Master Records

Changes to user master records can be performed by the system administrator with the corresponding authorization or by the users themselves to their own address, defaults, or parameters values. Normal privileged users cannot change, for example, their roles or authorization profiles. They can do that only if they have additional access rights to perform that operation.

The modifications made to a user master record (like a password, a locking, a time period validity, etc.) are only effective the next time a user logs on. Current logged-on users are not affected by those changes. But administrators can make some changes to the users' access permission by modifying and then activating authorizations and profiles.

Changes made to profiles are not effective until the users log on again; however, a modified and reactivated authorization has an immediate effect, even on logged-on users. So, for instance, if an authorization has been changed and then activated, it will immediately affect all users with profiles containing that authorization.

Deleting Users

To delete a single user master record, just enter it in the input box of the initial user maintenance screen and press DELETE on the application toolbar.

Locking and Unlocking Users

Administrators can temporarily set a lock in user master records that prevents a particular user from logging on to the SAP system. To lock a user, enter the user name in the input field and select the Lock/Unlock button on the application toolbar, or select User Names | Lock/Unlock from the main menu. Locking and unlocking functions work in a toggle fashion. A lock won't have an effect on users who are currently logged on.

The system also enters automatic locks in user master records after 12 consecutive unsuccessful logon attempts. The default value is 12, but administrators can change that by setting an instance profile parameter. Refer to the section on technical details at the end of this chapter.

A user who has been automatically locked out by the system because of unsuccessful logon attempts is also automatically unlocked by the system at midnight. However, a manual lock on a user master record will remain in place until you explicitly delete it.

Making Modifications to a Group of Users

The SAP system includes many functions to perform over a group of users. The options available are as follows:

- *Deleting, creating, locking, and unlocking several users from the current client.* From the initial User Maintenance screen, select Environment | Mass Changes. In the new screen you select users by using the possible entries list box, or by Address or Authorization criteria.
- *Modifying profiles or roles for all selected users.* To do this, select Environment | Mass Changes. First select the users in the Mass Change initial screen manually or by using criteria, and then click on the Change button on the application toolbar. You can not only modify profiles, but many other information for the group of users which can be applied to all of them at the same time, such as validity period, user type, defaults, and so on.

User Information System

The user maintenance functions of the SAP system include a comprehensive information system where you can look up, display, and analyze the users, profiles, or authorizations of the system. The system permits extensive navigation among the information: from users to profiles, from there to authorizations, and so on.

To reach the user and authorization information system, from the main user maintenance menu, select Information | Information System. The system displays a report tree corresponding to the authorization information system. These report trees contain several folders, each of which contains different reports. Figure 8-6 shows this report tree. By running different reports from the report tree folders, you can get a list of users, profiles, objects, authorizations, and so forth. The system presents several selection screens to permit searching for different criteria.

Another very useful report collection is the Change Documents folder reports, which can be used for displaying any modifications made to authorizations, users, or profiles and tells who did the modification.

Password Management

To change a password for a user, click the Change Password pushbutton on the application toolbar from the initial user maintenance screen. The system will display the New Password dialog box where you have to enter the password twice to verify that you didn't make any typing mistakes.

When system managers change the password for other users, the system requests these users to enter the new password when they log on. Administrators can change their

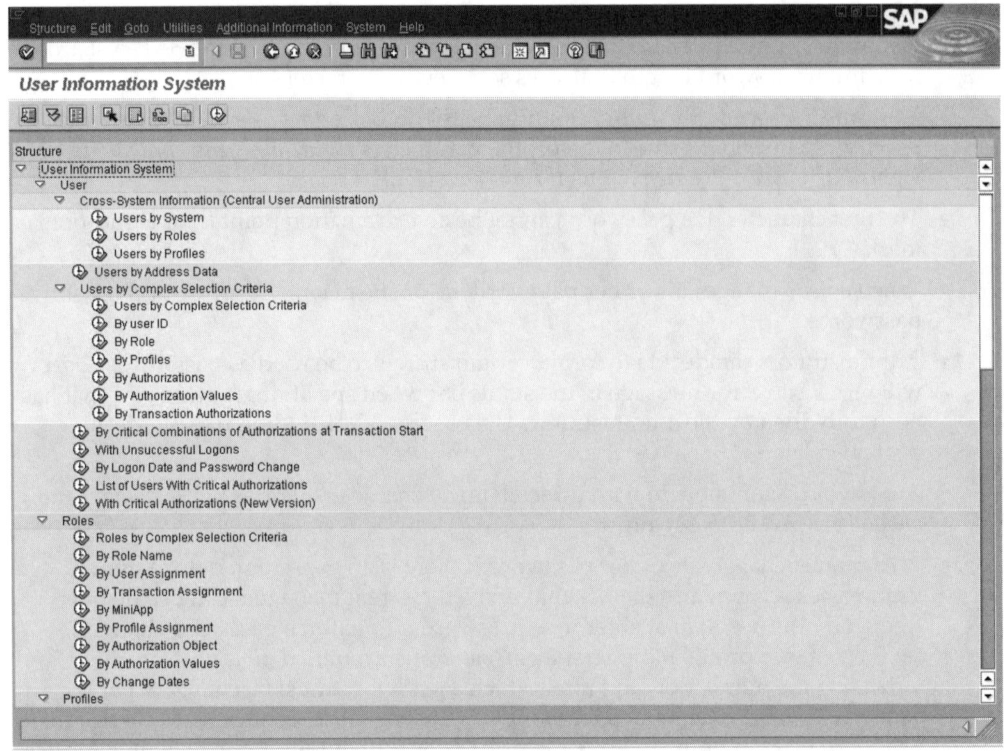

FIGURE 8-6 Authorization info system report tree (Copyright by SAP AG)

passwords and other users' passwords as many times as they wish; however, normal privileged users can only change their passwords once a day.

By default and right from installation, there are some standard requirements concerning passwords. Some of the restrictions are set up in the system code and cannot be changed, while others can be changed as required by setting some instance profile parameters or by configuring system tables.

For example, system administrators might decide to set up a minimum password length or enter a character string as a nonpermitted password.

On the other hand, passwords are not case sensitive, so uppercase and lowercase passwords or a mix and match of both cases behave exactly the same.

Password Restrictions and Requirements

The passwords restrictions and requirements are as follows:

- The password cannot be the word *pass*.
- Minimum password length is set by default to three characters. Administrators can change this setting by specifying a greater value in the instance profile parameter

login/min_password_lng. If you change this parameter, be sure to do it in the common DEFAULT.PFL so that it has effect on every instance of the SAP system. Maximum password length is always set to eight characters.

- You can also specify the minimum number of digits, letters or special characters, by specifying a number value in the profile parameters *login/min_password_digits, login/min_password_letters*, or *login/min_password_specials*.
- The first character of a password cannot be an exclamation point (!) or a question mark (?).
- When a user changes his or her password, he or she may not use any of the last five passwords.
- Administrators can decide to forbid certain strings to be used as passwords. Users will receive an error message in the status bar when specifying a password that has been forbidden by the administrator. The process of forbidding passwords is explained later.
- A password cannot begin with three identical characters. For example, *aaamy* and *bbbyou* are invalid passwords.
- A user must change his or her password if there is an expiration date in the user master account and the date has arrived. System managers can decide how frequently the users must enter new passwords. To enforce password changes, set the instance profile parameter *login/password_expiration_time* with a value indicating the number of days after which a password must be changed. For example, if the profile parameter is set to 30, users will be requested to change their password every month. To leave the passwords without limit, the default value *0* is used for this parameter.

With the previous restrictions and other user master records rules, the process of logging on to SAP systems based on SAP WAS requires some more work for the system code to do besides checking the password. For instance, when a user tries to log on with a correct password, the system first checks whether the user is locked. If the user is locked either manually by the system manager or automatically after 12 unsuccessful logon attempts or by a system upgrade, the system displays an error message.

If the user is not locked, then the system checks whether the current password has expired. In this case, the system requests the user to enter a new password.

Restricting Password Strings

System administrators can forbid passwords or password strings by entering them in the table USR40. This is useful, for example, to avoid the use of passwords that start with similar words as the name of the company, the river that crosses nearby, and so forth. Table USR40 is maintained with standard table maintenance transactions such as SM30 (System | Services | Table Maintenance | Extended Table Maintenance).

To specify a nonpermitted password string, you can enter the typical wildcards, * and ?, where the * substitutes a group of characters, and the ?, a single character. Figure 8-7 shows an example of this table with some of the forbidden password strings. In this example, all passwords starting with the characters *SAP*, containing *R3*, or ending with *2005* are forbidden. This table is client independent and, therefore, the password restrictions are applied to any system client.

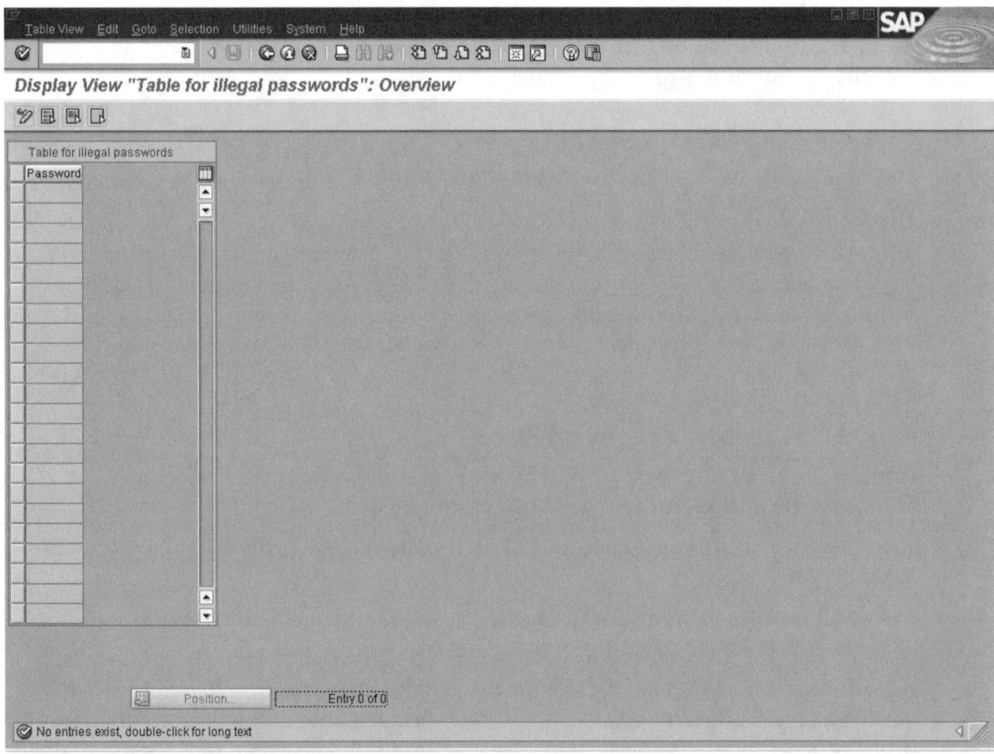

FIGURE 8-7 Maintaining forbidden password character strings in table USR40 (Copyright by SAP AG)

Managing SAP System Superusers

The SAP WAS system includes in the default installation two special users: DDIC and SAP*. These users have special privileges and must be protected to avoid unauthorized access. System administrators should consider a good strategy for managing the superusers of SAP systems for security reasons and to ensure system integrity.

The standard installation creates the system clients 000, 001, and 066. The SAP* and DDIC users are created in clients 000 and 001 with standard names and passwords.

User SAP*

SAP* is the standard SAP system superuser, and it's the only system user who does not require a user master record because it's defined in the code itself. When a new client is created for doing a client copy, SAP* is created by default in the new client with a standard password *PASS* and unlimited access rights. In the standard installation, SAP* has the password 06071992 in clients 000 and 001.

The special properties of the SAP* user can be deactivated. To deactivate the properties of the SAP* superuser, you must create a user master record for it, in which case it will have just the authorizations given in the profiles of the user master record.

If a user master record exists for SAP* and then it is deleted, it recovers the special properties assigned by the system code and has the password *PASS* again. When SAP* does not have a user master record, the password is always *PASS*; it cannot be changed, and it's not subject to any authorization check.

Some of the measures to protect SAP* are as follows:

- Change the password in client 000 and 001.
- Create a user master record for SAP* in 000, 001, 066, and the possible new clients you create in the system.
- Turn off the special status of SAP* by setting the instance profile parameter *login/no_automatic_user_sapstar* to a value greater than zero in the common default profile, DEFAULT.PFL. If the parameter is set, then SAP* has no special default properties. If there is no SAP* user master record, then SAP* cannot be used to log on. Be sure to have a user master record for SAP* even when this parameter is set because, if the parameter is reset to the value *0*, the system will again allow the logins by SAP* with the password *PASS*.
- Having a user master record, SAP* behaves like any other user subject to authorization checks. Its password can be changed.
- Create your own superuser account in each system client. This is explained in the next section.
- Delete all profiles from the SAP* profile list so that it has no authorizations.
- Be sure that SAP* is assigned to the user group SUPER, which protects the master records from being deleted by anyone not having authorization to delete SUPER master records. The user group SUPER has special status in the user maintenance profiles as delivered by the system. Users within this group can only be maintained or deleted by new superusers, as defined by the SAP standard authorization profiles.

Defining a New Superuser

Defining a new superuser just requires giving him or her a superuser profile with all authorizations in the user master record. The standard profile with full authorization, which is the only one needed to define a new superuser to replace SAP*, is the SAP_ALL profile. SAP_ALL contains all SAP authorizations, including the new authorizations as released in the SAP_NEW profile. SAP_NEW is a standard profile that ensures upward compatibility in access privileges. It's the way to protect users against authorization problems after a new system upgrade. If the upgrade of the system includes new access tests, this profile ensures the inclusion of those new authorization objects needed to validate the new access tests.

User DDIC

User DDIC (from *data dictionary*) is the maintenance user for the ABAP dictionary and for software logistics. It's the user required to perform special functions in system upgrades. Like SAP*, user DDIC is a user with special privileges.

The user master record for user DDIC is automatically created in clients 000 and 001 when you install your SAP system. It has, by default, the password 19920706. Its difference from SAP* is that it has its own user master record.

To secure DDIC against unauthorized use, you must change the password for the user in clients 000 and 001 in your SAP system. User DDIC is required for certain installation and setup tasks in the system, so you should not delete DDIC.

The Authorization System in SAP WAS

The authorization system of the SAP system is the general term that groups all the technical and management elements for granting access privileges to users to enforce the SAP system security.

An *access privilege* is permission to perform a particular operation in the SAP system. Access privileges in SAP systems are granted to users by assigning them authorizations, profiles or roles. By entering such roles and profiles in user master records, you enable users to use the system.

The main features and concepts of the SAP authorization system can be summarized as follows:

- The authorization system is based on complex system objects with multiconditional testing of system access privileges. The authorization system tests multiple conditions before granting users the permission to perform a task in the system. A multiconditional access test is defined in an authorization object. A multiconditional testing is, for example, to allow users to create, display, or delete information from one purchasing center, but only display information in another purchasing center. The following list shows this concept:

User	Purchasing Center	Permissions
FREDSMITH	001	Create, Delete, Display
FREDSMITH	002	Display
JGALPJR	002	Create, Delete, Display

- The authorization system uses authorization profiles and roles, together with the Role Maintenance (former Profile Generator) tool, to make the maintenance of the user master records easier. Authorization profiles are groups of authorizations. Instead of entering every authorization in the user master records, administrators only have to enter either roles, profiles, or both.
- Authorization profiles can be either simple or composite. Composite profiles contain other profiles.
- The authorization system uses an activation method. When authorization or profiles are created or modified, they must be activated to become effective.
- The SAP authorization system provides mechanisms for the distribution of the maintenance tasks related with users and access privileges, such as assigning authorizations, roles, activating profiles, managing new authorizations, and so on. These tasks can be done by a single superuser or they can be divided among several administrators.

SAP systems include many predefined authorizations, profiles, and roles that cover most of the usual needs for assigning access privileges to users. Before creating a new role or profile, you should try to use an existing predefined one.

The complex objects of the SAP authorization system are structured in a hierarchical but flexible way, as shown in Figure 8-8. The next section introduces the main elements of the authorization system.

In order to aid understanding of the authorization system, basic concepts are explained first. Then the manual procedure for creating profiles and authorizations is introduced, and finally the Role Maintenance tool and how to work with it are covered.

Authorization Profiles

An authorization profile contains a group of authorizations, that is, a group of access privileges. Profiles are assigned to users in the user master records. A profile could represent a simple job position since it defines the tasks for which a user has access privileges. Every profile might have as many access privileges (authorizations) as desired. Profiles can contain authorization objects and authorizations.

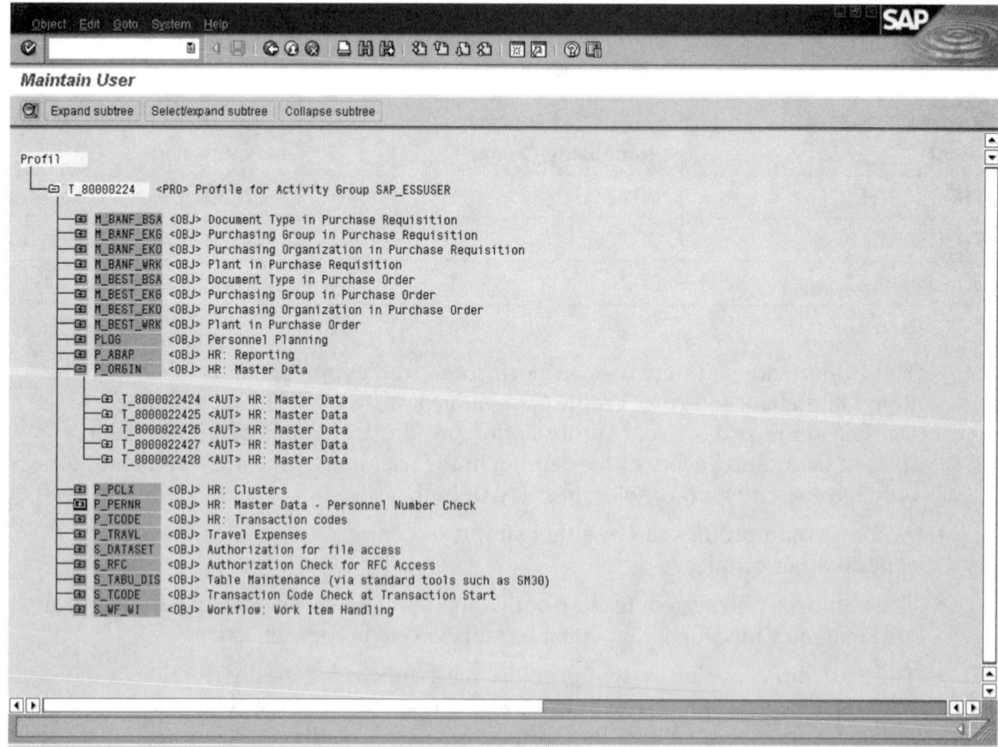

FIGURE 8-8 Hierarchy of authorization system (Copyright by SAP AG)

Changing the list or contents of the authorizations inside a profile affects all users that are given that profile when this is activated. It becomes effective the next time the user logs on. The change is not effective for users currently logged on.

Composite Profiles

Composite profiles are sets of authorization profiles, both simple and composite. A composite profile can contain an unlimited number of profiles. They can be assigned to users just as profiles in the user master records are.

Composite profiles are suitable for users who have different responsibilities or job tasks in the system. These profiles are sometimes known as *reference* profiles for assigning a larger group of access privileges and having the possibility to better match users with several responsibilities.

Making modifications to any of the profiles in the list included in the composite profile directly affects the access privileges of all users having that composite profile in the user master record.

When displaying profiles on the different SAP screens, there is a description indicating whether the profile is simple or composite.

Authorizations

The SAP system uses authorizations to define the permitted values for the fields of an authorization object. An authorization might contain one or more values for each field of the authorization object.

An authorization object is like a template for testing access privileges, consisting of authorization fields that finally define the permitted values for the authorization. Both authorization objects and fields are explained in the next two sections.

An authorization is identified with the name of an authorization object and the name of the authorization created for the object. An authorization can have many values or ranges of values for a single field. It is also possible to authorize for every value (by entering an asterisk, *) or for none (by leaving the field blank). In the example shown in Figure 8-9, you can see that for the object, *Batch processing: Batch administrator,* there are several authorizations. Each of these authorizations can have different values for the authorization fields within the object.

Authorizations are entered in authorization profiles with the corresponding authorization object. When an authorization is changed and then activated, it immediately affects all users having a profile containing that authorization in their user master records.

The technical names for authorizations and authorization objects have a maximum of 12 positions, but usually they are displayed in the system using short descriptive texts. For customer-created authorizations, the only name restriction is to not place an underscore in the second position of the technical name. Additionally, every customer-created system object should comply with SAP standard style guide and begin either with a *Z* or a *Y* to distinguish it from the SAP original objects, thus avoiding the possibility of being overwritten by a system upgrade.

Authorization Objects

An *authorization object* identifies an element or object within the SAP system that needs to be protected. These objects work like templates for granting access rights by means of authorization fields that allow for performing complex tests of access privileges. An

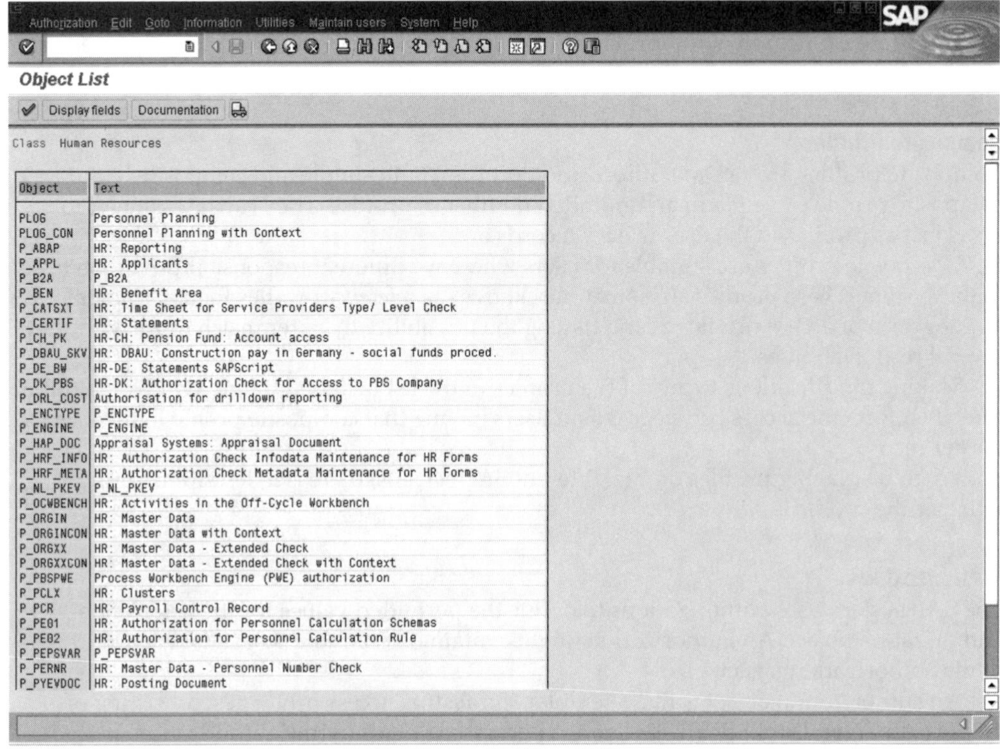

FIGURE 8-9 Example of authorization list for an authorization object (Copyright by SAP AG)

authorization object can contain a maximum of 10 authorization fields. Users are permitted to perform a system function only after passing the test for every field in the authorization object. The verification against the field contents is done with the logical AND operator. With this mechanism, the system can perform multiconditional tests.

As with authorizations, when maintaining authorization objects, the system does not display the names but descriptive text for each object.

Authorization objects are grouped in object classes belonging to different application areas that are used to limit the search for objects, thus making it faster to navigate among the many SAP system objects.

SAP predefined authorization objects should not be modified or deleted, except if instructed by the SAP support personnel or a SAP note. Deleting or changing standard authorization objects can cause severe errors in the programs that check those objects.

Before an authorization object is modified, all authorizations defined for that object must first be deleted.

If you want to use the OR logic to give users access to certain functions, you can define several authorizations for the same object, each time with different values. In the user master records, you assign each of these profiles, which are linked with the OR login. So, when the system tests whether the user has access privileges, it checks each authorization to see if the assigned values comply with the access condition. The system allows access with the first authorization that passes the test.

Authorization Fields

Authorization fields identify the elements of the system that are to be protected by assigning them access tests. An authorization field can be, for example, a user group, a company code, a purchasing group, a development class, or an application area. There is one authorization field that is found in most authorization objects which is the *Activity*. The Activity field in an authorization object defines the possible actions that could be performed over a particular application object. For example, activity *03* is always *Display*, so if an authorization contains two fields such as *company code* and *activity* and if the company code field is * (meaning all company codes), the user with that authorization can only display the company codes.

The list of standard activities in the system is held on the SAP standard table TACT, which can be displayed using standard transactions such as SM30 (Extended Table Maintenance), or SE16 (Data Browser).

The relationship between the authorization objects and the activities is held in table TACTZ. Not all authorization objects have the Activity authorization field. Authorization fields are the components of authorization objects as stated previously. And also, fields are part of the standard ABAP function call AUTHORITY-CHECK.

When maintaining authorizations, the system does not display the real names (technical names) for the fields; instead it shows a description for each field. Table TOBJ contains the fields that are associated with each authorization object; this is how the SAP system knows which fields belong to an authorization object. The fields in an object are associated with data elements in the ABAP data dictionary.

Authorization fields are not maintained from the user maintenance menu, but have to be defined within the development environment. Normally users do not need to change standard authorization fields, except if adding or modifying system elements and they want those elements to be tested with authorizations.

Roles

Roles form a set of tasks or activities that can be performed in the system, such as running programs, transactions, as well as access to Web sites, files and other functions that generally represent job roles. When you assign roles to users, the system will automatically present a specific menu for that role when the users log on to the SAP system.

The roles and the information they include are what makes the profiles able to be automatically generated.

Roles are the basic components needed for working with the Role Maintenance tool (transaction PFCG), based on the Profile Generator, which uses them to generate authorization profiles. You can also access the Role Maintenance tool, by clicking on the Create Role button on the application toolbar from the initial SAP Easy Access screen.

Roles resemble a job description, such as sales representative, accountant, treasurer, system administrator, and so on. Roles can include as many single system activities as needed. Single system activities can be transactions, reports and access to other types of objects such as Web sites, files, BSPs, and others.

Role administrators select transactions or reports from a menu tree or can select authorizations and save this information as an activity group. This selection is used by the profile generator for determining the necessary authorizations and generating the profiles, which can then be assigned to users.

You can also assign roles to organizational objects, such as organizational units, jobs, positions, users, and so on. This can be done with the Organizational Management pushbutton, but you will only see this function if you have defined what it's known as an active plan variant, which is configure through the Customizing of HR. Please refer to the SAP online help for guidance on how to set up Roles for Organizational Management in HR.

User master records can be assigned to one or more roles. When this type of assignment takes place, the updating of the user master records can be performed manually or automatically by running a background job. When this happens, the system combines the functions in the user menu when she or he logs on.

Roles can be temporarily assigned to users, which means that they can have multiple validity periods that cannot overlap. Date dependency assignment of profiles to user master records can be enforced by scheduling background jobs for that purpose.

User Buffers

User buffers are special areas (tables) containing all the authorizations for the user. These buffers are specific for individual users, and are actually built when the users log on, based on the authorizations contained in the profiles included in the user master record. When users try to perform activities in the system, the application programs and transaction are checked against the authorization objects and values contained within the user buffer.

The number of entries in the user buffer can be controlled using the profile parameter *auth/new_buffering*.

You can see the context of the user buffer by selecting Tools | Administration | Monitor | User Buffer from the main menu, or by running transaction SU56.

The Activation Concept in Profiles and Authorizations

The authorization system allows two versions of authorizations or profiles: an active version and a modified, or maintenance, version. A new or modified authorization or profile cannot be used until it has been activated, since user master records can only contain active versions of profiles.

The activation concept is useful for preventing mistakes when creating new authorizations or modifying existing ones, since the maintenance versions will not affect the system. It is also helpful for dividing the maintenance tasks among several users. For example, some users can define or edit authorizations, while an activation administrator can be in charge of activating the maintenance versions previously created.

The system verification for access privileges is only performed against active versions. Active versions are the only ones that have real effect in the system. When administrators create or modify an authorization or a profile, then they are working with a maintenance version. In this state, the system displays the status *Revised* in the header of the authorization or profile being modified. When the activation is performed, the maintenance version becomes the active one and replaces automatically the existing version if it exists. The system changes the status to *Active*.

Working with the Role Maintenance Tool

The Role Maintenance tool is an evolution of the Profile Generator available in releases of SAP R/3 since 4.6 that aids in facilitating the management of roles, user authorizations, and profiles. Previous to the Role Maintenance and Profile Generator, there was a great deal of effort involved in the implementation and support of the authorization concept, and this was a costly activity within projects.

The Role Maintenance tool was designed by SAP with the objective of reducing the time needed for implementing and managing the user menus and authorizations associated with a job description, thus decreasing the implementation costs. SAP recommends using the Role Maintenance and Profile Generator to set up authorizations.

Using the Role Maintenance is very different from manual profile management, where authorization objects must be selected, authorizations defined, and profiles created to be assigned to users later. With the Role Maintenance, the management of profiles and authorizations is based on the functions and tasks that users will perform with the SAP systems, and the Profile Generator is in charge of selecting and grouping the authorization objects (Figure 8-10).

The definition of roles with the Role Maintenance is based on grouping functions or tasks user menu that generates the profiles and authorizations selected by the customers.

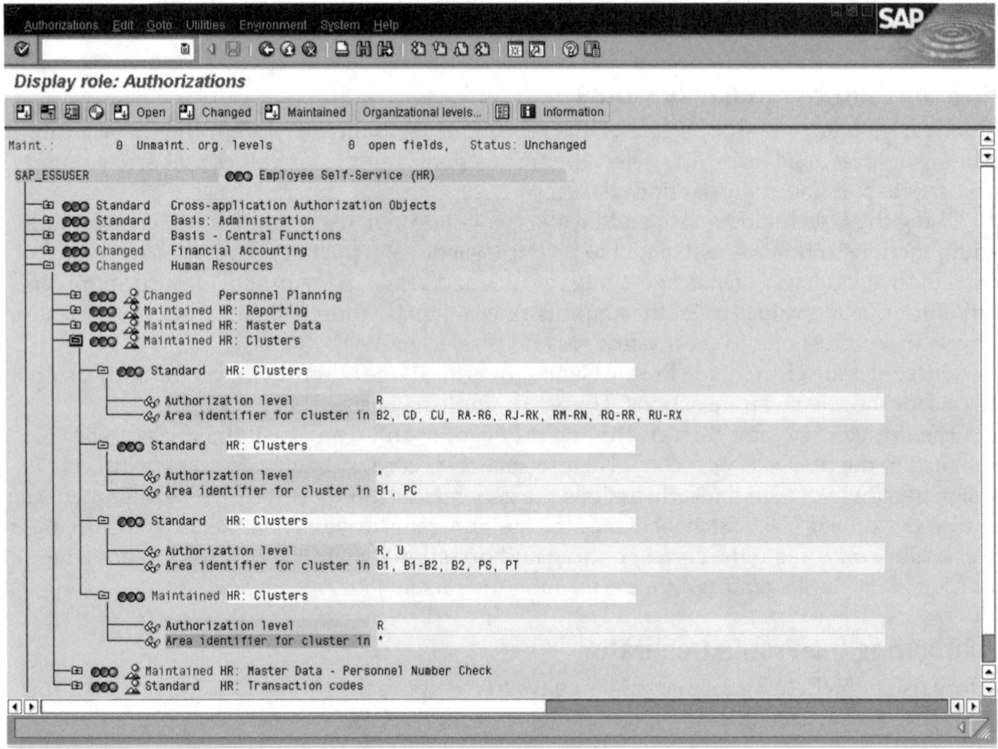

FIGURE 8-10 Assigning authorizations to the new profile (Copyright by SAP AG)

As introduced in a previous section, *roles* form a set of tasks or activities that can be performed in the system, such as running programs, transactions, and other functions that generally represent job roles. SAP systems already include a very large number of predefined roles that can be freely selected, or copied and then modified to accommodate specific needs.

In summary, the Role Maintenance tool and the Profile Generator

- Can be used to automatically create profiles and assign them easily to users
- Only select and use the necessary authorization objects, avoiding excessive validations in the system and thereby improving performance
- Facilitate functional communication between security or the authorization administrator and end users or consultants
- Make defining and maintaining authorization profiles easier

The Role Maintenance and Profile Generator can be accessed from the initial SAP Easy Access screen by clicking on the Create Role pushbutton on the application toolbar; or, from the main menu tree by selecting Tools | Administration | User Maintenance | Role Administration | Roles or alternatively by entering transaction code PFCG in the command field.

The following sections introduce how the Role Maintenance works, how to configure it, and a basic example of creating roles and using automatically generated profiles to assign those roles to user master records.

How the Role Maintenance Works

Based on a job role, or group of tasks that represents what the users are trying to perform, administrators can identify and select the transactions, reports, or values that are required for users to pass the authorization checks.

Using the Role Maintenance and Profile Generator tool, the administrator creates roles with functions and tasks, associated to SAP transactions, reports, and other object types, that automatically will create a generate profiles and select the required authorizations, and sets authorization values or let the administrator maintain those values for the authorization objects that correspond to the specific functions selected.

Once roles are created, the Profile Generator is in charge of retrieving all the authorization objects for the selected transactions. This is accomplished using special check tables.

The Profile Generator then creates the profile or profiles, and then the roles can be assigned to the user master record. The user master record is then updated by a direct assignment, which automatically assigns the generated profiles as well. This assignment can be also performed via a batch job. Once the assignment is done, when the users log on, their user buffer will contain the corresponding authorization that will allow them to pass the authorization checks required for performing their usual jobs.

Configuring the Profile Generator

Before using the Role Maintenance, you have to configure the Profile Generator for the first time. The steps required to configure and work with the Profile Generator tool are the following:

1. *Activate the Profile Generator.* The activation of the Profile Generator is based on the instance profile parameter *auth/no_check_in_some_cases* = *Y*. If this value is

not set, users won't be able to see the Authorization pushbutton within the role maintenance screen. This is the default value since R/3 Basis release 4.0. This profile parameter tells the system to allow certain authorization checks to be ignored in a program. With this setting the profiles will only contain the necessary authorizations. For example, if the installation includes only one company code, administrators don't want to worry about setting authorizations for company code.

2. *Set up the initial copy of Profile Generator configuration tables.* You must run transaction SU25 to transfer the SAP transactions and authorization objects from SAP tables USOBT and USOBX to the customer tables USOBT_C and USOBX_C. You can then maintain these tables using transaction SU24. Table USOBT includes the relation between the transactions and the authorization objects. If it is a new installation, just click on the button next to option 1, *Initially fill the customer tables*. If you are upgrading from a previous release, you must use the lower options, but first look up the most recent information concerning your release in the online documentation.
3. *Maintain the scope of authorization object checks in transactions.* This is performed using transaction SU24 (also the last button on the screen for transaction SU25) in order to maintain customer tables USOBX_C (transactions and authorization objects) and USOBT_C (proposed values for authorization objects). This is not a mandatory step, but can be used by customers to maintain their own authorization checks as well as to assign SAP authorization objects to custom transactions. You can also maintain the assignment for a single transaction, and enforce or suppress the authorization check for any transaction. Additionally, it is possible to maintain the field assignments for the transactions. In any case there is always the possibility of comparing these settings with the SAP standard settings. The purpose of this transaction is for the administrator to be able to maintain the scope of authorization checks in transactions by
   - Assigning the authorization objects that are relevant to a transaction
   - Assigning default values and organizational level defaults for authorization object fields

Basic Concepts for Working with Roles

Access the Role Maintenance screen by clicking on the Create Role pushbutton in the initial screen of the SAP Easy Access, or enter transaction PFCG in the command field. The system will display a screen like the one in Figure 8-11.

Role maintenance includes three different views, which you can select from the initial screen by choosing Goto | Settings:

- The Simple Maintenance View is used only to maintain the Role menu.
- The Basic Maintenance View allows additional functions for defining and maintaining roles, not only for maintaining the menu, but also the profile and authorizations.
- The Complete View includes all the functions for the basic maintenance plus the organizational management link and the workflow. This is the more comprehensive view that can display all the assignments for a role. This view is tightly related

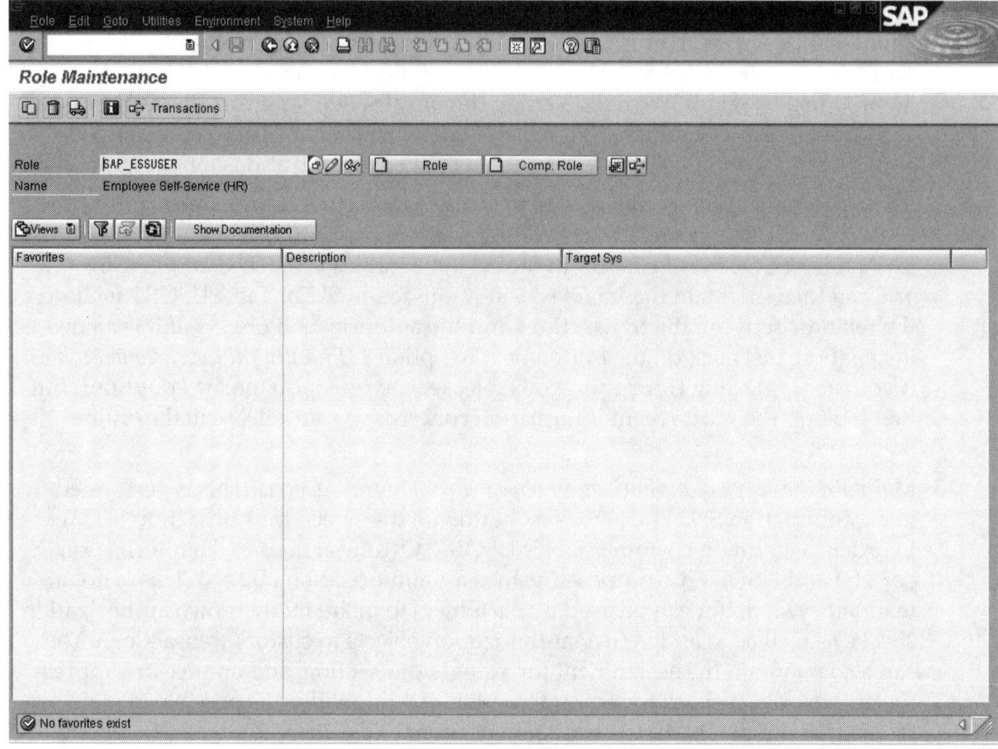

FIGURE 8-11 Role Maintenance initial screen in complete view (Copyright by SAP AG)

to the personnel development HR application, so it is useful for users working in organizational management.

When implementing structural authorizations, that is, roles linked with HR organizational management, roles are assigned to *agents*. There are several types of agents, being the most common the *user master record;* however, there are other types of organizational agents that can be created within the Human Resource module, such as *organizational units, positions, jobs, persons,* or *work centers.*

Creating Roles

The basic steps for creating a new role are, in a simplified way:

1. Enter a role name in the input field and press the Create pushbutton to the right of the name or the Comp. Role if wishing to create a composite role. Remember to follow the naming convention, starting the role name with Z_ or Y_.
2. Save the role, click on the Menu tabstrip and select the transactions from the SAP menu, from other role, or insert individual transactions or objects by clicking on the corresponding pushbutton. The process is very easy and intuitive.

3. Next, go to the Authorizations tab, and enter a profile name, or let the system propose one for you. Click on Change Authorization Data. The system will present the Change Role: Authorization screen. Complete the authorizations for chosen activities: those marked with an orange light.
4. Select Authorizations | Generate the Profiles.
5. Assign the role to users and press User Comparison to transfer profiles to the user master record.

The following example shows how to create a simple role for the purchasing department users, providing them with authorizations for creating purchasing orders when the vendor is known (transaction code ME21) and for changing and displaying purchasing orders (transaction codes ME22 and ME23). These are the steps:

1. Access the main Role Maintenance screen by entering transaction code PFCG in the command field. The system will display the Role Maintenance initial screen.
2. Enter the name for the activity group, and click the Create icon located to the right of the name. Enter a description, or even some sort of documentation in the space provided at the bottom of the screen.
3. Click on the Menu tabstrip. The system will display the main Change Roles screen, full of options to create a menu for this specific role. In this case, we will do it from a standard SAP menu.
4. Click on the From the SAP Menu pushbutton located on the right of the screen. The system will show a dialog box with the standard SAP Menu tree. In our example, click on the plus signs on Logistics, Materials Management, Purchasing, Purchase Order, Create. Finally, mark the square box next to Vendor/Supplying Plant Known. On the same level as Create and below, mark the square box next to Change and Display. Save your selection by clicking on the Transfer icon.
5. You will return to the previous screen. The next step is to maintain the Authorizations, by clicking on the Authorizations tabstrip. Click on the small icon to the right of the Profile Name field, so that the system will propose a profile name. Then click on the Change Authorization Data pushbutton in the lower part of the screen. Save the role.
6. Next, the system first displays a new screen where you have to maintain the organizational levels. In this case, these are the Purchasing Group, Purchasing Organization, and Plant. You can input simple values or ranges, or enter a wildcard such as * to indicate all organizations. Fill in the fields or click on the Full Authorization pushbutton if you want to allow authorization on all organizational levels and save it. The system will display the Change Role: Authorizations screen, as shown in Figure 8-12.
7. Expand the nodes by clicking on the folders or by positioning the cursor on the line and clicking on the Expand icon. Notice how the browser view is presented in four levels: authorization object class, authorization object, authorizations, and field values. The system automatically selects the objects and values according to the previous selections. Select Utilities | Technical Names On to display the familiar authorization objects. Notice also how the Profile Generator tool has selected the

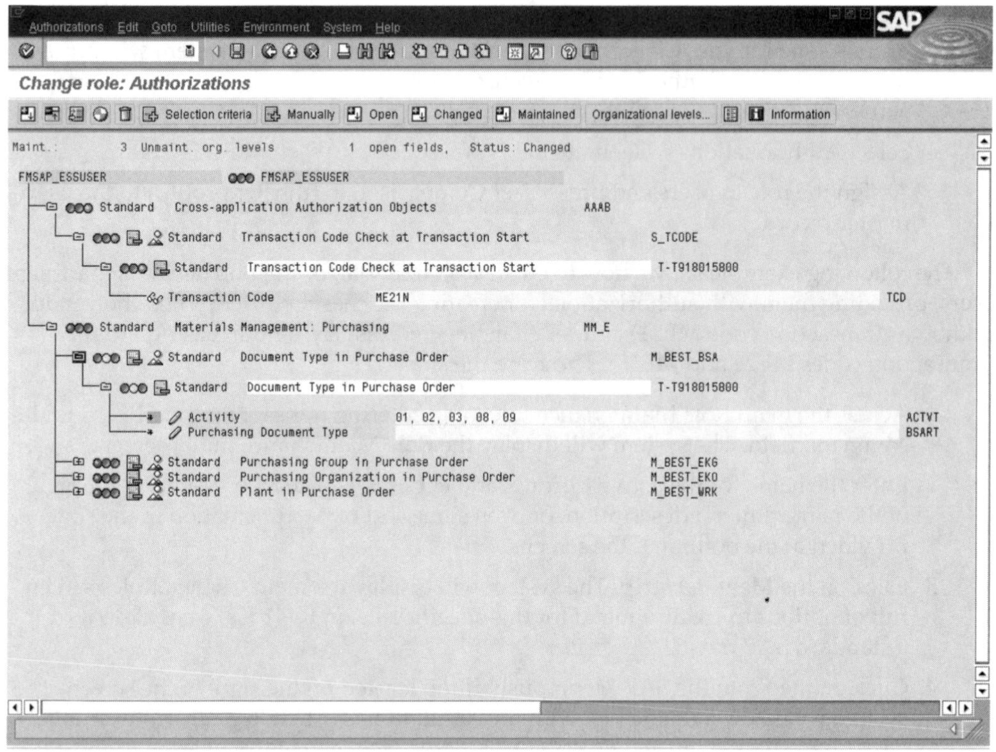

FIGURE 8-12 Activity group browser view (Copyright by SAP AG)

authorization object S_TCODE (authorization for transaction start) and provided it with the values of the selected transactions.

8. You have to maintain all pending authorizations before you can generate the complete profile. The maintenance status of the authorizations at every level is shown using traffic lights: green indicates that all values are maintained, yellow that there is some value that is not yet maintained, and red that at least an organizational level is missing. In order to maintain pending or open values, you can click on the individual level so the system will display a new dialog box for entering required field values.

   Or, you can click on a traffic light and maintain all outstanding fields below, or assign full authorizations. For this example, you can assign complete authorizations for the subtree by clicking the stoplight on the *Standard: Document type in purchase order* line. On the dialog box, click the Enter icon.

9. Next, click the Generate icon on the application toolbar. If you did not define previously, the system will display a dialog box for entering the profile name and a short text. You can keep the proposed system name or change it to your own standards. Continue by pressing ENTER. The system will now generate the profile.

10. Go back to the initial activity group maintenance screen. The screen will show green traffic lights for both Menu and Authorizations. Now assign this profile to one or more user master records by clicking on the User tabstrip.
11. In this part of the role maintenance, you could simply assign this role to one or several users, or associated with other type of agents, by clicking on the Organizational Management pushbutton (you will only see this pushbutton if in complete view). Enter the name of the user or users you want to assign the new created role.
12. If you want the profiles to be transferred to the actual user master records, click the User Comparison pushbutton. The system will display the use comparison program.

You can verify that the role and profiles have been effectively transferred by looking up the user master records using transaction SU01. There is the possibility of running a general report for updating all user masters and pending assignments of activity groups by using transaction PFUD.

The Role Maintenance and Profile Generator tools include many additional functions to facilitate the creation and maintenance of roles, authorizations and profiles, such as using single roles as templates, collections of authorization objects that can be included within roles.

Tracing Authorizations

The SAP system includes some options to find the authorization for any transaction or function a user performs in the system. This is quite useful when looking for an authorization denial problem or when defining profiles when you want to specify exactly what authorization objects a particular transaction checks. The two methods available in SAP systems for finding authorizations are the authorization check transaction (SU53) and using the system trace.

The *system trace* is a more general-purpose tool used mainly by developers or system administrators which can provide a great detail of information and can be used to trace other user sessions.

Transaction SU53 is more specific for authorization error analysis but can only be used for the current user sessions. However, SU53 is a faster and more direct method for finding an authorization denial problem. Transaction SU53 can be accessed from the menu System | Utilities | Display Authorization Check.

Using the System Trace for Tracing Authorizations

The SAP system includes extensive tracing and debugging utilities. You can find more information about tracing in Chapter 10. This section covers just the simple process of activating and displaying a trace concerning authorization checks.

To start the system trace, from the main menu select Tools | Administration | Monitor | Traces | System Trace. The system displays the available trace options and switches, one of which is the Authorization Check. Make sure you mark the check box next to Authorization Check.

To limit the trace to your own user ID or another user ID, enter the name of the user ID you want to trace in the General Filter field by clicking on the possible entries arrow and then selecting it from the list.

To activate and start the tracing process, select Trace On from the application toolbar. The trace will start recording every system function you or the entered user performs. So, if you are looking for an authorization problem or just want to find a particular authorization check, open a new session and go to the screen, function, or transaction you want to analyze.

Once you are finished you should stop the system trace. Go back to the session where you activated the trace, and if you are on the tracing screen, stop the trace by selecting Trace Off.

Now you should look at the trace file generated. To analyze the trace click on the Analysis pushbutton on the application toolbar, and enter the criteria for the analysis.

The trace file contains the authorization objects, authorization fields, and values that have been tested while you have been performing system functions. Authorization tests are displayed in the following format:

<Authorization object>:<Field>=<Value tested>

But you can display a more legible view of the authorization check by clicking over the entry.

Using the SU53 Transaction

The transaction SU53 can be used to analyze a function when getting the error *You are not authorized to* in the status bar. When you get this message, enter SU53 or /NSU53 in the command field. Alternatively, you can select System | Utilities | Display Authorization Check from any SAP screen. The system will display the authorization object and value for which you were not authorized.

Transaction SU53 can also be used from any of your open sessions and not only from the one in which you got the authorization error message. However, you cannot use SU53 to analyze other users' authorization errors. In those cases, administrators should instruct users to reproduce the error and then to enter the transaction SU53 in the command field to receive information about the authorization error messages they got.

Organizing the Maintenance of the Authorization System

The SAP authorization system offers many options for organizing the administration of users, authorizations, and profiles, making it quite flexible when defining roles. Depending on the type, size, and security restrictions, an installation can have a single superuser for all users and authorization system maintenance to several decentralized administrators with different maintenance functions and limited authorizations.

SAP recommends that for enforcing maximum system security customers divide the maintenance of the user and authorization system among three types of users:

- *User administrators.* They are in charge of creating and modifying user master records. User administrators can set user parameters, edit the list of assigned profiles, and so forth. User administrators cannot create or activate roles, authorizations or profiles. User administrators can be further divided by assigning them authorization maintenance to certain user groups.

- *Authorization administrators.* These users are able to define or modify roles, authorizations and profiles; however, they are not permitted to activate authorizations or profiles. Authorization administrators only work with *active* versions of authorizations and profiles.
- *Activation administrators.* They are in charge of activating profiles and authorizations. This type of administrator is no longer able to change the authorizations or profiles but can only activate existing revised versions of profiles and authorizations.

Dividing the maintenance responsibilities among different administrators can increase the security of the system against unwanted actions over user master records, authorizations, and profiles. Another advantage is the decentralization of the user administration. In big installations with hundreds of users, it can be a good practice to divide up user maintenance functions by department, building, regional office, and so forth.

To implement these administrative roles, the superuser uses authorizations to limit which user groups are maintained by user administrators and which authorizations and profiles can be maintained or activated by which administrators. Because the superuser can limit and restrict the access rights, the decentralized administrators do not need to be high-level technical staff. They can be normal company users.

As a superuser, you can define new profiles for these administrators using the standard S_A.ADMIN profile as a template and changing the allowed field values corresponding to authorization objects such as *user group, authorizations, authorization profiles,* and mainly setting the Activity field values.

Refer to the SAP online documentation in the "Users and Authorization" help file for details on setting values for dividing up administrative roles.

Creating New Authorization Checks

Although the SAP Web Application Server systems includes virtually all authorization objects and checks to test whether users can access the system functions, customers might add new development objects and functions to extend the system capabilities. In such cases, customers might also need to include a new authorization check.

SAP provides several ways to include new authorization checks for custom-developed objects or transactions, the most important being:

- By programming the authorization check using the ABAP standard statement AUTHORITY-CHECK
- By assigning authorization groups to tables, maintaining table TDDAT, and using authorization object S_TABU_DIS
- By using authorization object S_PROGRAM and using program authorization groups by maintaining table TPGP

For specific details about these procedures, please refer to the SAP online documentation.

9

CHAPTER

Web Application Server System Management

This chapter covers all those administrative areas and management tasks that are basic and typical in SAP systems, both SAP Basis and SAP Web Application based. Differences were covered extensively in Chapter 2.

These administrative tasks deal with the basic monitoring and management of the components that make up the SAP system. SAP systems offer a very extensive collection of programs, menus, and utilities for performing administrative tasks. Most of them are located under the functions provided from the Tools | Administration menu.

This chapter concentrates on the basic monitoring facilities, background processing, and printing system, and it introduces database administration. Both the performance and troubleshooting issues are described in the next chapter. The basic SAP management utilities include the following:

- Checking the consistency of the system installation
- Displaying and monitoring systems and application servers
- Displaying and monitoring the system work processes
- Displaying and monitoring the user sessions
- Posting system messages to all logged-on users of a SAP system to inform them of any particular events such as closing the system for upgrades, backups, and so on
- Managing the SAP update records in charge of performing the changes in the database
- Displaying and managing the SAP lock entries on the database objects
- Using the client copy functions

General SAP System Management

The functions available for the basic administration of the SAP system form the group of transactions that should be performed on a regular basis in the daily operation and management of the system. These functions are the responsibility of the SAP system administrator and/or the system operator. Whenever a problem is detected while doing basic administration, it has to be reported and solved as soon as possible.

Administrators can help prevent problems from occurring by following certain monitoring practices. In the event that problems are detected, the monitoring and administration facilities can help to isolate the problem and solve it more quickly. Having an operator or administrator manual and maintaining an internal incidence log will greatly reduce the time it takes to solve a particular problem in cases where it has happened previously.

In case a problem cannot be solved quickly enough, SAP system administrators should contact the SAP hotline or enter the problem in the SAP Service Marketplace support services (formerly OSS).

Checking the Installation

Every time a SAP instance is started, the system automatically checks whether there are any inconsistencies. You can manually check the system status for inconsistencies by selecting Tools | Administration | Administration | Installation Check.

When you call the Installation Check, the system looks into the table that collects system events and performs the following checks:

- That the critical database structure definitions are identical in the data dictionary and in the SAP kernel, including tables such as SYST, T100, TFDIR, TSTC, and so on
- That the SAP kernel release number matches the number stored in the database

Displaying and Monitoring the SAP Instances and Application Servers

Using transaction code SM51 in the command field or by selecting Tools | Administration | Monitor | System Monitoring | Servers from the menu options, you can display the instances or application servers of the SAP system, as shown in Figure 9-1. In the figure only one server is defined for this system.

This should be one of the first monitoring tasks run by the administration to determine whether all application servers are up and running.

The application servers shown on the screen are the ones that have registered themselves—the ones that have connected to—the message server. If for any reason the message server process dies, you won't be able to see the servers.

On the application server display, you can see several fields that give specific information about the SAP instances. These are standard fields. You can also configure your own layout using the Current Layout icon or CTRL-F8. These fields are as follows:

- *Server name.* It's the name of the SAP instance. The name is made up of the hostname of the server, the SAP system name (SID), and the SAP system number.
- *Host.* It's the hostname in which the SAP instance is running.
- *Type.* The type of work processes for which the application server is configured.
- *Status.* Shows whether the instance is active or not.

From this monitoring screen you can further display which users are connected to any of the instances shown on the screen or see what processes are running by selecting the User

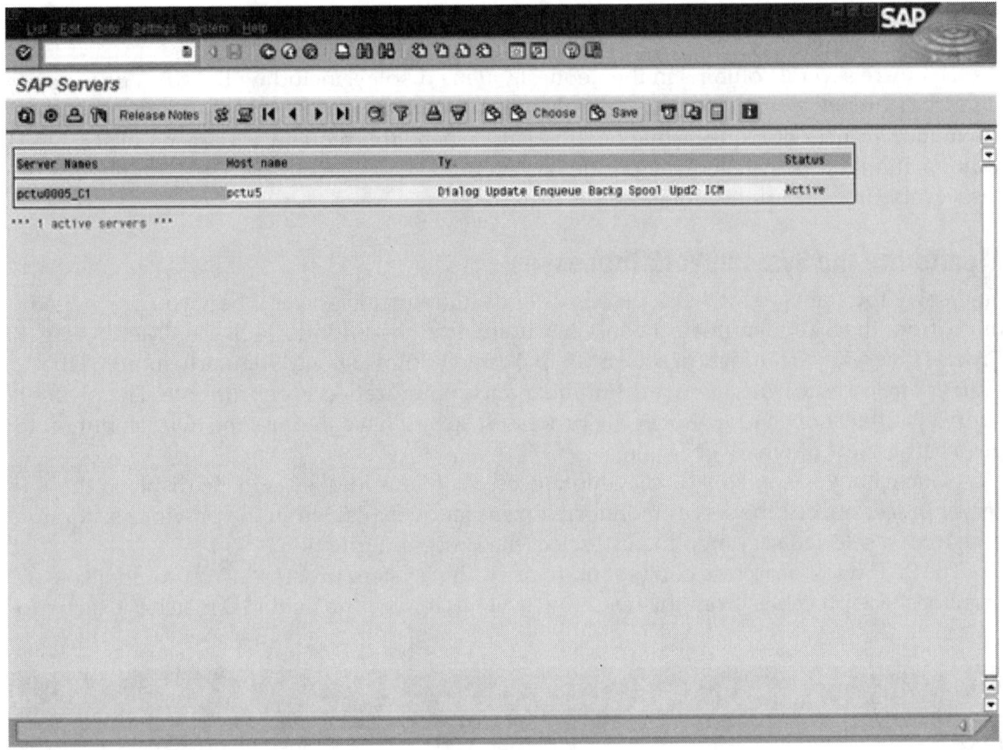

FIGURE 9-1 Server monitoring display (Copyright by SAP AG)

or Processes icons on the application toolbar. By using these functions, the system takes you to exactly the same transaction as if you were going directly to the user or work process monitoring transactions.

On this screen, there are additional options that you can access from the Goto menu or directly by clicking on the pushbuttons on the application toolbar. Main options are as follows:

- *System log.* Displays an instance system log.
- *OS monitor.* Calls the operating system Performance Monitor for summary statistics on the status of the host platform on which a SAP instance is running.
- *Remote logon.* Performs a SAP remote logon to any of the servers in the system.
- *SAP directories.* For displaying the main files and directories associated with the SAP instance. You can navigate the directories by double-clicking on the corresponding line.

From the SM51 transaction, an interesting and very useful option for system administrators when monitoring, tuning, and troubleshooting the system is to look up the status of the dispatcher queue. This information can be obtained by selecting the application server and then choosing Goto | Server Information | Queue Information. Figure 9-2 shows an example of this screen.

There are several columns in the Request Queue display, including the work process type, the number of requests waiting in the dispatcher queue to be processed, and the maximum number of requests that had to wait. If there are frequently many requests waiting, it might indicate locking problems or too few work processes. These numbers are reset every time the application server is restarted.

Monitoring the System Work Processes

To display the status of the work processes of the application server where you are logged on to, from the SAP menu, select Tools | Administration | Monitor | System Monitoring | Process Overview (transaction code SM50). Administrators should regularly monitor the system processes to determine if the number and configuration is appropriate. The process overview offers only a snapshot of the processes, so you have to press the Refresh button to get a better view of what's going on.

Notice that you can only display the processes of your local system. To display other server processes, call the server monitoring transaction explained in the previous section and, from a selected server on the list, select the Processes function.

The SAP work processes correspond to operating system processes. You could also monitor these processes from the operating system. In fact, the field PID matches exactly to

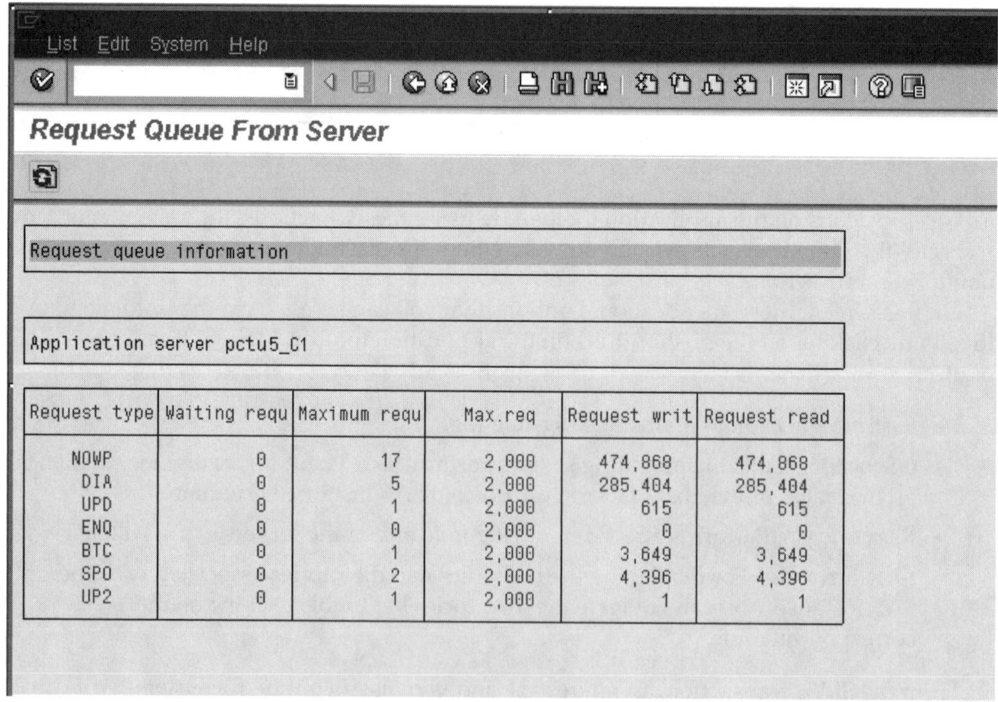

Request type	Waiting requ	Maximum requ	Max.req	Request writ	Request read
NOWP	0	17	2,000	474,868	474,868
DIA	0	5	2,000	285,404	285,404
UPD	0	1	2,000	615	615
ENQ	0	0	2,000	0	0
BTC	0	1	2,000	3,649	3,649
SPO	0	2	2,000	4,396	4,396
UP2	0	1	2,000	1	1

FIGURE 9-2 Request Queue information display (Copyright by SAP AG)

the Process ID of the underlying operating system. With a UNIX command such as `ps-eaf|grep dw`, you can see the SAP processes. On Windows NT systems you can see the processes from the Task Manager as disp+work.

The SAP runtime directory (/usr/sap/<SID>/SYS/exe/run) contains some monitor programs that allow you to see some of the work processes and the dispatcher from the operating system.

The work process overview presents detailed information in different columns. Notice that in order to see all the available columns you might have to scroll horizontally using the scrolling buttons on the bottom part of the screen. The columns in the Work Process Overview screen show the following information. Although this is a standard layout, you can design your own layout selecting these desired fields:

- *No.* Refers to the internal ID number of a process. It is useful for identifying messages in the system log belonging to a work process.
- *Ty.* It's the type of work process. Chapter 2 explains in detail each of the SAP work process types. On this screen, you can find the following types:
    - *DIA.* Dialog work processes, in charge of executing interactive dialog steps.
    - *UPD.* Update work process for executing U1 update components (refer to Chapter 2 for more information). In charge of critical updates on the database.
    - *UP2.* Update work process for executing U2 update components. In charge of performing secondary updates on the database.
    - *ENQ.* Enqueue work process in charge of setting and releasing lock objects.
    - *BGD.* Background work processes, in charge of executing background jobs.
    - *SPO.* Spool work process in charge of the SAP spooling system (formatting and printing).
- *PID.* Process identification number of the work process that matches the PID of the operating system process.
- *Status.* Shows the current state of the work process. Observe that the Process Overview screen always offers a snapshot of the processes. So, upon pressing the Refresh icon, it can change. Possible process status are as follows:
    - *Running.* The process is executing a system request.
    - *Waiting.* The process is idle and waiting for any system request.
    - *Hold.* The process is held by a single user. Although a Hold state can be normal, having too many processes in a Hold state affects the system performance.
    - *Killed or Complete.* The process has been aborted with the restart option set to *No.*
    - *Stopped.* Due to system or application error, the process has stopped and could not restart automatically.

  When the process overview displays many processes with status Waiting, it means that the system load is low. When this happens, the SAP dispatcher will try to allocate the same work process for a user, and thus avoid rolling in and out the user contexts.

- *Reason.* This column displays a mnemonic code displaying the reason for a work process with a Hold status. Some of the reasons can be activities performed by the lock mechanism, the update process, debugging, CPIC tasks, or RFC requests. If the reason columns display *Priv*, a dialog work process will be used by that particular user executing the transaction already started without possibility of switching the user context to another Dialog work process. A dialog work process will be in this status when the "heap" memory allocation is reached (see the section on memory management in the next chapter), which could happen in case that such transaction or program is very resource consuming. *Note:* This status only applies to dialog work processes.
- *Start.* This column has either the values *Yes* or *No* and indicates whether the work process will be automatically restarted in the event of an abnormal termination. Normally, this field is set to *Yes* but you can switch the restart status by selecting the function Restart After Error from the Process menu.
- *Err.* Contains the number of times a work process has terminated abnormally. Generally, this counter increases when, for example, a system administrator kills a work process from transaction SM50.
- *Sem.* This column can contain the number of the semaphore on which a work process is waiting. Normally, this field is empty. However if you notice that a semaphore number appears often, it might indicate some performance problems in the system and might need some parameter adjustments. For information on semaphores used in a SAP system, check SAP Note 33873.
- *CPU.* Contains in number of seconds the CPU time consumed by a work process.
- *Time.* Indicates the elapsed execution time used by the work process for the dialog step that it is currently processing. This column usually contains a small figure. When it displays a large figure, it might indicate that the process is being held in a debugging session.
- *Program.* This column contains the ABAP program that is currently executing.
- *Client.* Indicates the SAP system client where the session is being executed.
- *User.* Contains the user ID whose request is being processed.
- *Action.* Under this field the system shows the actions being performed by the running program. These actions are the same as those recorded by the system Performance Monitor, which is activated by default with the profile parameter *stat/level.* This column might display actions such as Sequential Read, Insert, or Direct Read.
- *Table.* This column displays the name of the tables being accessed, if any.

There is more detailed information available from the Process Overview screen, which you can display by selecting the work processes and then clicking on the Details icon on the application toolbar. With this option, in addition to all the information from the Process Overview screen, the system displays statistical information about the work process such as the memory, development environment, and database usage.

From the Process Overview display, you can perform additional options by selecting them from the menu item Process.

You can terminate a work process with or without generating a core dump file in the operating systems, which can be used for debugging.

Before canceling a work process, you should select the menu function Restart After Error, either with options *Yes* or *No*, to indicate whether the process which is to be canceled should restart or not, after being manually terminated.

By selecting a work process and then selecting the Process | Trace | Active Components option from the menu, you can activate a trace and choose what is to be traced in the work process, which is stored in the so-called low-level *developer traces* files (dev files). Figure 9-3 shows the available tracing options for the work processes, where you can decide the level of tracing information to get.

To display a trace, choose the work process and, from the menu, select Process | Trace | Display File. More information about the system tracing facilities is provided in the next chapter.

By selecting the work process and selecting Program/Mode | End Session from the menu, you can also delete a user session and release the work process. However, you should avoid performing this function from this overview, since the work processes can be attending several users, and you could unintentionally affect other users' work. Rather, you should delete a user session from the User Overview screen, as explained in the next section.

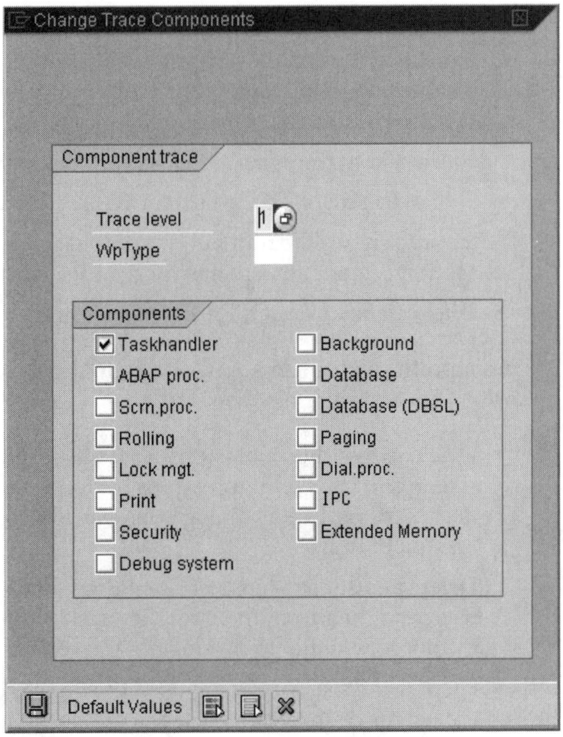

FIGURE 9-3 Tracing options from the work process display (Copyright by SAP AG)

Finally, by selecting any work process that is currently executing a program, you can decide to put that program into debugging mode. To do this, select the line of the work process and from the menu select Program/Mode | Program | Debugging. The system displays the ABAP debugging facility and locks the work process for exclusive use. Refer to the online SAP documentation for more information on this facility.

Monitoring and Managing User Sessions

To display the users that are active in your current system, you can directly use the transaction code SM04 in the command field or, from the menu options, select Tools | Administration | Monitor | System Monitoring | User Overview. Notice that with this transaction you can only see which users are active in the same server where you are logged on. There are several ways to see which users logged on to other application servers:

- Select the User function from the SAP servers overview display.
- From the main menu, select Tools | Administration | Monitor | Performance | Exceptions/Users | Active Users | Users, Global. Alternatively, use transaction code AL08.

The User Overview screen includes the following fields (the display can different depending on the layout you selected. You can configure this report using CTRL+F8 and select the desired fields):

- *Cl.* displays the SAP system client the user is logged on to.
- *User* contains the name of the user ID. Sometimes this field might appear blank when users are in the process of connecting, and also when the system itself is performing special functions with users SAPSYS or SAPCPIC.
- *Terminal* displays the name or address of the desktop from which the user is connected to the application server.
- *Transaction* displays the current transaction code in which the user is working.
- *Sessions* shows the number of external sessions opened by the user. An external session is manually created by the user with the System | Create Session option.
- *Trace* can be ON or OFF, indicating whether the user has an active trace.

Besides monitoring the users' activity, from the User Overview screen you can perform the following functions among others:

- Delete external user sessions. To do this, select the user from the User Overview screen and click on the Sessions button. The system displays a dialog box with the user sessions. In this dialog box, select the session to delete and click on the End Session button.
- Delete all user sessions at once. From the User Overview screen menu, select the user, and then from the User menu, select Logoff. The system will display a dialog to choose whether to delete only the *poold* sessions or *system wide*.
- Display the memory being used by the logged-on users or the terminal from where the user is connected by selecting Goto | Memory.

- Display brief information about the user by selecting it from the overview list and clicking on the User Info icon. The system will show the information as entered in the Address screen of the user master record.

Posting System Messages

The system manager often has the need to post messages to all users connected to the system for administrative functions, such as for informing them of the time the system will be shut down for maintenance, backups, and so on. For that purpose, the SAP system includes a utility for administrators to post brief messages to users by selecting Administration | System Messages from the main administration menu. Alternatively, they can enter transaction code SM02 in the command field. If there are no messages created, the system will display the screen indicating that the system message list is empty.

To create a system message, click on the Create icon on the application toolbar. The system displays a dialog box like the one shown in Figure 9-4.

Enter the message in the input text lines provided for that purpose. Users can create as many messages as they wish, with a maximum length of three lines.

You can decide to display the messages to all logged-on users in the whole SAP system or only to the users logged on to a particular application server.

By using the expiration fields provided, you can decide when a message will automatically be deleted from the system.

The system displays the message as a pop-up box in the user sessions. It will display it only once to each user, either when they log on or, for users who are already logged on, as soon as they interact with the application server.

Before continuing to work, users must clear the messages by pressing ENTER or by clicking on the Continue icon. When there are messages already created, users can change the message either to modify the text, change the expiration date, or the server.

Individual messages or all posted messages can be deleted from the system by selecting them and pressing DELETE. This transaction, by default, is not protected with any authorization objects, so any user in the system is allowed to post a message.

This function is not intended for sending messages or notices to particular users. To do that, use the Short Message function available from the System menu. This is actually a fast path to SAP office functions and it's available to all authorized users.

FIGURE 9-4 Creating a System Message dialog box (Copyright by SAP AG)

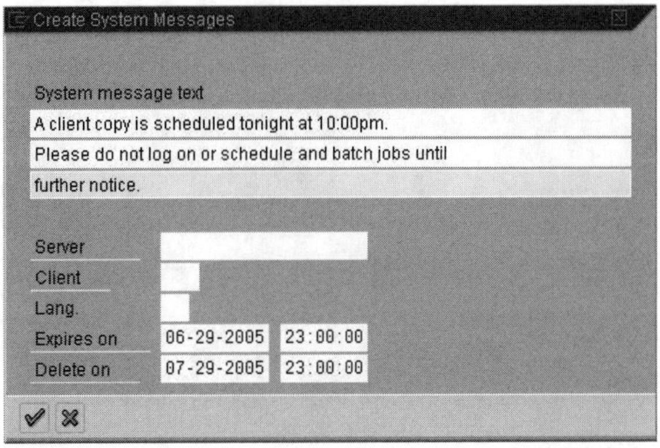

Displaying and Managing Update Records

The update work processes are in charge of making and recording the changes in the SAP underlying database as users work normally in the system.

The update work processes perform their functions when the ABAP applications are programmed with the statement IN UPDATE TASK. This type of updating is performed asynchronously in the system, meaning that the programs leave update records in a queue to be processed and then continue the execution. The following section discusses the main concepts related to the update processes.

Normally, the updating processes run without management intervention; nevertheless, the SAP system includes utilities to monitor, check, and perform management operations on the updating process, which can be very useful in case problems arise. When updating errors occur, normally the user requesting the update receives an express SAP message and an alert is triggered in the CCMS monitor.

The update functions are located under the administration menu, and then Monitor | Update. Alternatively, enter transaction code SM13 in the command field. The system displays the Initial Update screen as shown in Figure 9-5. From the Initial Update screen, you can perform the following functions:

- Display the system update records with error status or that have not yet been processed or to be processed.

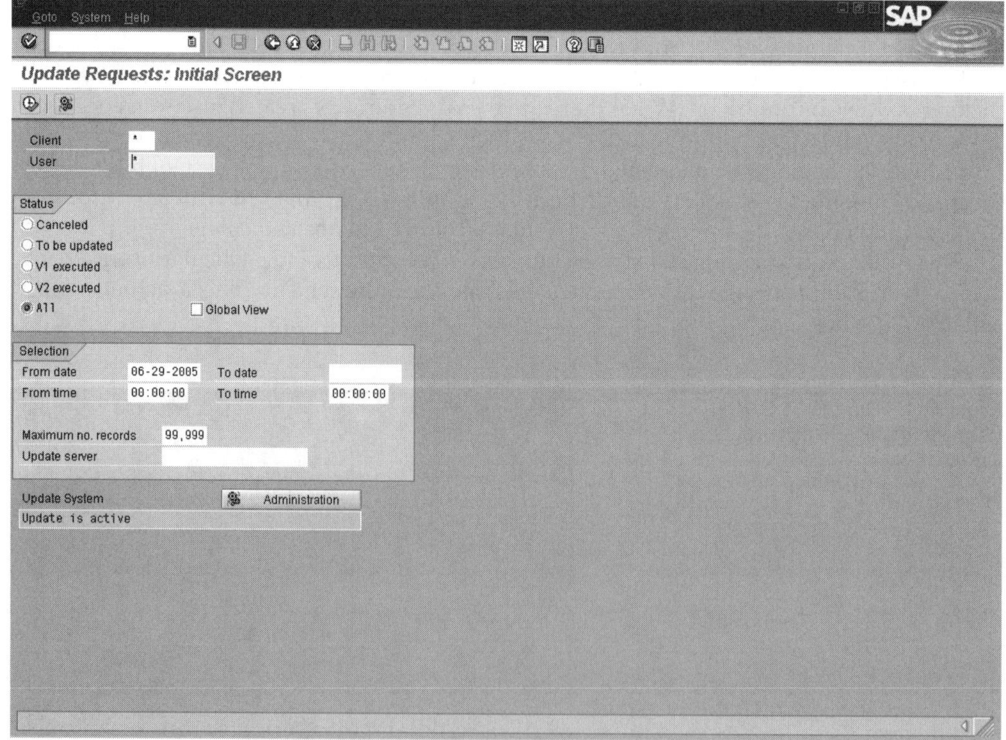

FIGURE 9-5 Update process monitoring initial display (Copyright by SAP AG)

- Activate and deactivate the updating in the whole SAP system.
- Display update statistics from the updated administration.
- Display the data on the erroneous update records and reprocess them, either in real or in test mode.
- Send waiting update records for processing after a deactivation/activation of the updating.
- Delete update records.

Be sure to understand clearly how the updating process can affect the system before performing any management options on update records.

Update Process Concepts

Several of the work process types of the SAP system update the database. The dialog and background work processes include a database interface that can directly update the database. But these processes might also make use of the update work processes for updating the physical database in an asynchronous way. This section deals with the updating as performed by the update work processes.

If the transactions programmed in the ABAP business applications have been designed for asynchronous updating, then in the database commit phases, the transactions pass the update records to the update work processes, which finally perform the changes in the database.

The update records contain both the data and the instructions on how to modify the database. These update records also have an update record header that is created by the transaction requesting the update. The headers of the update records are used for monitoring and managing the update processes.

An update record might have several update components in charge of making different changes to the database. Update component types modify different database objects. The SAP system distinguishes between primary (U1 or V1) and secondary (U2 or V2) update components.

Primary update components, known as *UI components*, are in charge of the critical updates of the database and have priority over the secondary update components, U2.

Critical updates of the database are the most usual, including posting financial documents, receiving sales orders, launching a production order, and so on. Secondary updates are lower priority changes such as calculating totals or preparing statistical information.

The SAP dispatcher always assigns a higher priority to U1 components to perform the update as soon as possible; they are always processed before the U2 components.

These types of update components are completely transparent to users and system managers, since they are programmed in the application transactions. However, developers must consider the update components when defining new customer transactions. A group of update components of both types in an update record is processed sequentially by a single work process of an application server.

U2 update components are always processed by the U2 update work processes. Should no U2 update work process be available in the application server, then the U2 components are processed by the U1 update work process.

Distribution of Update Work Processes

The profile parameters *rdisp/wp_no_vb* and *rdisp/wp_no_vb2* define the number of update work processes running in an instance. A U2 work process can only process U2 update components.

The update work processes can be running on more than one server, in which case the system will perform server load balancing to distribute the update requests among the available work processes. For performance reasons, many installations define most of their update work processes as "close" to the database as possible, that is, on the same server as the database server.

Every 10 minutes or whenever period that is selected (this is customizable), the system checks the availability of the update servers and refreshes the information for the application servers. When a server is down, the update requests are reallocated to active update servers.

As a security measure to ensure that the update process does not get saturated with update records, the update servers process synchronously every 100th update. When this happens, the program that requested the update will wait until all pending updates have been processed. Then the program will resume execution.

This is particularly useful for large data load programs or background jobs that perform many updates and that could potentially fill up the processing capacity of the update server.

Monitoring Update Records

From the main menu for monitoring the update records, as shown in Figure 9-5, there are several input fields and radio buttons for selecting update records. When entering selection criteria, you can use wildcards for selecting all update records. You can select using the following criteria:

- *Client.* Enter here the SAP system client or an * to indicate all clients.
- *User.* You can specify the user ID whose transaction generated the update record.
- *Status.* With this radio button, you can indicate the type of update record:
  - *Canceled.* Indicates that the update records terminated with errors. This status corresponds to internal status ERR.
  - *To be updated.* Will show records that have not yet been processed.
  - *V1 executed.* With this status, you select those update records for which the U1 part has been successfully processed.
  - *V2 executed.* It's the status for selecting those update records which have successfully processed the U2 component.
  - *All.* To display all the update records regardless of their status.
- *From date and From time.* These are used to specify the date and time range in which to display update records. Successfully processed update records are automatically deleted by the system and will not appear.
- *Maximum no. records.* This is used to limit the number of update records to be displayed.

- *Update server.* This is used to indicate which update server is in use in case there is more than one update server configured in the SAP system.

After executing the report of update request, you get a list of canceled or terminated update records, and there are several actions you can take. From this screen, by selecting the record and then choosing Goto | Update Header from the menu, you can display the header of the update record, needed by the update process to manage the records. The update header includes management data that show specific information about the update record and that can be useful for finding the problem in the system log as transaction/ report that caused the error and error details and navigate the source code.

Available Update Functions

From the Monitoring Update menu, there are functions to help you locate the causes of updating problems, functions for looking at the data that were contained in the update record, and also utilities for processing or repeating update records.

The next section contains an overview of the management options within the Update Monitoring menu.

Processing and Repeating Update Records

From the Updated Records menu, you have the option to manually start, restart, continue, or repeat the processing of update records. This function is performed with the Repeat Update option.

With the Repeat Update option, you can decide to update records which have not yet been committed and which are waiting to be processed. These records have either the status INIT or AUTO.

INIT status indicates that an update record has all the needed components: header, update function modules, and the data, but has not yet been processed.

Records with AUTO status are flagged in update records that have been marked for processing as the update process restarts. This situation might happen when the updating process has been deactivated.

Within the Post menu option, select whether you want to process *all records* or a *single* update record.

With the Repeat Update function, you can request the system to reprocess update records carrying status ERR, which means they have terminated abnormally. You should, however, analyze the cause of the error before proceeding. You cannot reprocess an update with those records with status Error (No Retry), which is indicated by a Stop icon.

When an update record terminates abnormally, it automatically releases the lock held on the objects for updating. This means that the user who got the error might have tried to manually enter the same data again and therefore update the database. If you, as administrator, are not aware of that fact and repeat an update, you can cause severe inconsistencies in the database. Therefore, as a step before repeating an update record, contact the user or users with the update errors to see if they can reenter the data in the system. If the users do not know or do not remember the data, you can help them by looking at the actual data fields and tables with the update records. Select Goto | Update Modules | Display Data | Display RF Documents functions.

When repeating the processing of an update record, you can select either the U1 or U2 update components. However, the U2 components will not be processed unless the U1 have been successfully processed. Normally, the U2 update takes place immediately after the U1 update, but it's not asynchronously performed from the U1.

From the Repeat Update menu you can decide whether to select All Records or Single to repeat abnormally terminated update records.

Deleting Update Records

Once you are sure the update record has been processed, either by manually reentering the data or by repeating the update process, you can delete the update records (if the record was processed successfully, it is automatically deleted from the list of pending update processes). To do that, from the Update menu, first enter the criteria for selecting the records to delete. The system will display a list with the update records that met the criteria. On this new screen from the Updated Records menu, select Delete and then either All Records or Single to delete just the one you have selected.

When deleting update records, the system releases any locks held on the objects.

Displaying and Resetting Update Statistics

You can display a report for the update activity in the SAP instance where you are currently logged on. This report can be seen by selecting Goto | Administration of Update System from the first Update Monitoring screen, and then clicking on the Statistics icon or directly from the Update Request initial screen Goto | Administration of Updated System.

In this report, you can see information such as number and status of update requests, database activity involved in the update processing, and runtime statistics.

You can reset the statistics to zero. From the Statistics screen, select Edit | Statistics | Reset and then you can either choose *local*, for resetting the statistics just on the current application server, or *global*, for resetting the statistics in all update servers.

Activating and Deactivating Updating

If a severe system error takes place but the system did not crash, such as, for example, a tablespace overflow, it sometimes might be useful to deactivate the updating as a security measure to prevent all coming update records to be aborted by the system, in which case users must enter the data back and process again the erroneous transactions. You could deactivate the updating, correct the system problem, and then activate it again and reprocess all the pending update records.

To deactivate updating systemwide, from the initial Monitoring Update menu, select the Administration of Update System function, located as an icon in the application toolbar, and from the next screen, select the Deactivate button. When performing this function, users will get a message in the status bar indicating that updating has been paused.

When the system updating is deactivated, all the transactions in the system, including background processing, are paused and users are disabled from generating update requests; however, when updating is reactivated, they can continue to work without losing any data. Background jobs continue from the point they were paused.

To reactivate the updating process, from the Update Administration screen, select the Activate button.

Displaying and Managing Lock Entries

Lock entries are system objects in charge of protecting the integrity of the data by synchronizing the access, so users cannot modify the same data at the same time. The lock objects are defined in the ABAP dictionary as a way of locking a data object.

To display and perform some basic operations on lock entries, from the main administration menu, select Administration | Monitor | Lock Entries (transaction code SM12). Figure 9-6 shows this display.

This screen works like a selection criteria display. You can select lock entries for displaying by client, user, specific tables that have locked rows, and by lock entry arguments. By entering the wildcard * in the client and user, the system displays all current lock entries.

Clicking on the Continue button will display the list of current lock entries, if any. The display includes the following columns:

- *Cli* refers to the SAP system client.
- *User* shows the SAP user ID holding the lock.
- *Time* indicates the time when the lock was generated.

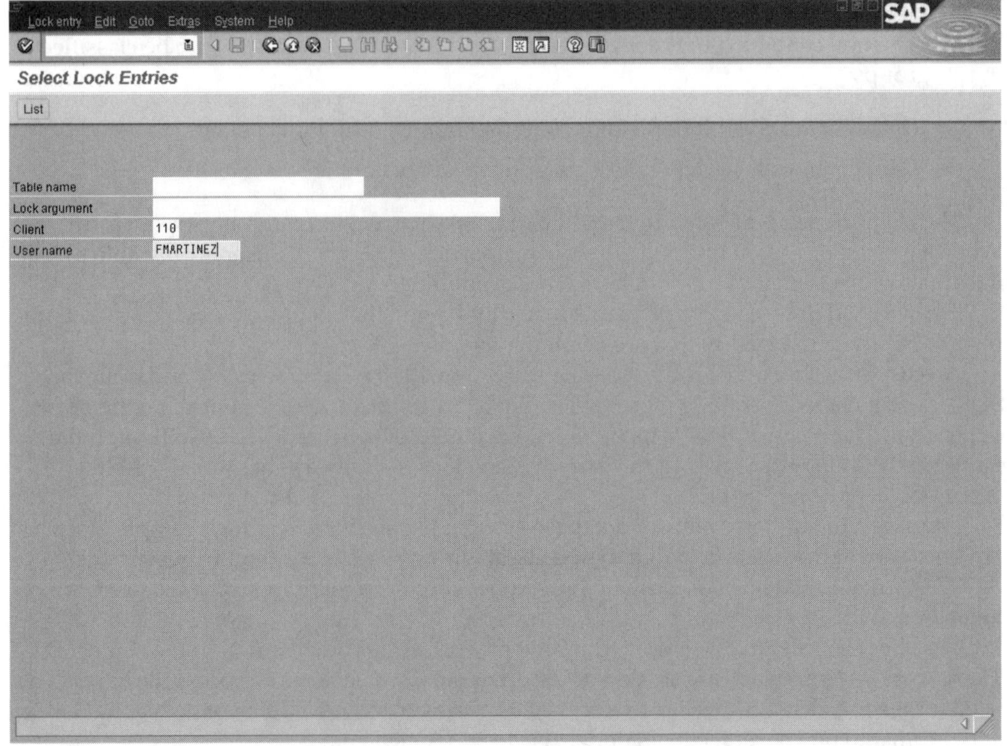

FIGURE 9-6 Lock entries initial selection screen (Copyright by SAP AG)

- *Shared* is an indicator that tells whether the lock object is shared or exclusive. With shared lock objects, more than one user might lock the same data.
- *Table* includes the name of the table with locked rows.
- *Lock argument* shows the fields used by the lock entry.

Lock entries are deleted automatically by the system when the programs release the data objects. However, it might sometimes be useful to display and possibly manually delete the lock entries when a system error has occurred and the dispatcher cannot release the lock. For example, this might happen in cases where users shut down their systems without logging off from the SAP system in an orderly manner. If this happens, users will not be able to access the locked data or mostly by an erroneous user development. It is advisable to contact the previous user to unlock the entry.

To display additional information about a lock entry, click on any of the entries from the list and select the Details button on the application toolbar. This window shows interesting information such as the transaction code being performed by the user, the application server hostname, and the lock object name.

For troubleshooting lock entries refer to the section in Chapter 10.

Client Copies

The information contained in the SAP systems, and thus in the database, can be classified in two groups:

- Data that are client independent, and therefore valid for all clients
- Data that are client dependent, and only available in the specific client

The client-dependent data are treated by the SAP system in their own special form. When a user is logged on in a SAP session in a particular client, the user is only able to see data that belong to that client or data that are client independent.

The way SAP internally implements this is by having the client field as a key field in the records that belong to tables that are client dependent.

An easy way to test this is by accessing directly with the database tools and doing an SQL select statement in one of those tables. There are a few thousand tables that are client dependent. These tables always include the client field (known as *MANDT* although the name can be different) as part of the primary key. This field always has table T000 (the clients table) as a check table.

Internally, the underlying SAP database system, like in the preceding example, does not know about the limits imposed by the client within the SAP system. However, the ABAP Open SQL statements normally only know about the client in which the users are logged on.

The client concept allows for having several work environments within the same SID. These work environments are treated as different business entities, although they are often used for testing, demo, training, different customizing modules, and so on, which makes it very normal to find several clients under the same SAP system.

The SAP system, as was introduced in previous chapters, includes three standard clients from the standard installation: clients 000, 001, and 066. In new installations, there are two standard clients 000 and 066.

Client 000 is the reference client with a complete society model and with sample data. SAP recommends not working in this client for productive purposes, except for those administrative tasks that are performed in client 000.

Client 001 is a copy of client 000, which customers can use to start the customizing work or use also as a reference client.

Client 066 is a special client used by the SAP service personnel to perform the preventive maintenance service, EarlyWatch.

Apart from the standard SAP clients, customers can create their own, as many as they consider necessary. Pay attention, however, to the storage needed for having too many clients.

The SAP system includes functions for creating, copying, and deleting clients, as well as the necessary options to access the client data without altering the consistency or integrity of the database. It's important to use the SAP-provided functions for managing clients and not to perform them with database utilities because there is a high risk of creating inconsistencies in the system.

Right after installation, to start working with the SAP system, one of the first post-installation steps is to create a new client. When the client is initially created it contains no data. From this newly empty client, administrators have to decide whether to fully copy another client into it or copy just parts. Initially, your reference clients for copying are the SAP standards. Then when your installation has more clients, the source client for the copy can be any of the existing ones in the system.

The next section explains the functions that SAP makes available for doing client copy management functions.

Client Copy Tools

The system includes five tools to perform client copy functions. All these tools are available from the Tools | Administration | Administration | Client Administration menu. Figure 9-7 contains the menu tree client administration. Options under this menu are as follows:

- *Client Maintenance*, transaction SCC4. It's the function for maintaining system clients: creating new ones, modifying attributes, and so on.
- *Client Copy.* It's the main client copy function and includes two options:
  - *Local Client Copy*, transaction SCCL. It's the function for copying clients within the same SAP system.
  - *Remote Client Copy*, transaction SCC9. It's the function for copying clients among different but connected SAP systems.
- *Special functions.* Includes special functions for client maintenance such as deleting clients, comparing tables between clients, or copying a client in base to transport request. Menu options are as follows:
  - *Copy Transport Requests*, transaction SCC1. Used for "internal" transports.
  - *Delete Client*, transaction SCC5.
- *Client Transport.* It's the function for performing client copy transport functions and includes two options:
  - *Client Export*, transaction SCC8.
  - *Import Editing*, transaction SCC7.

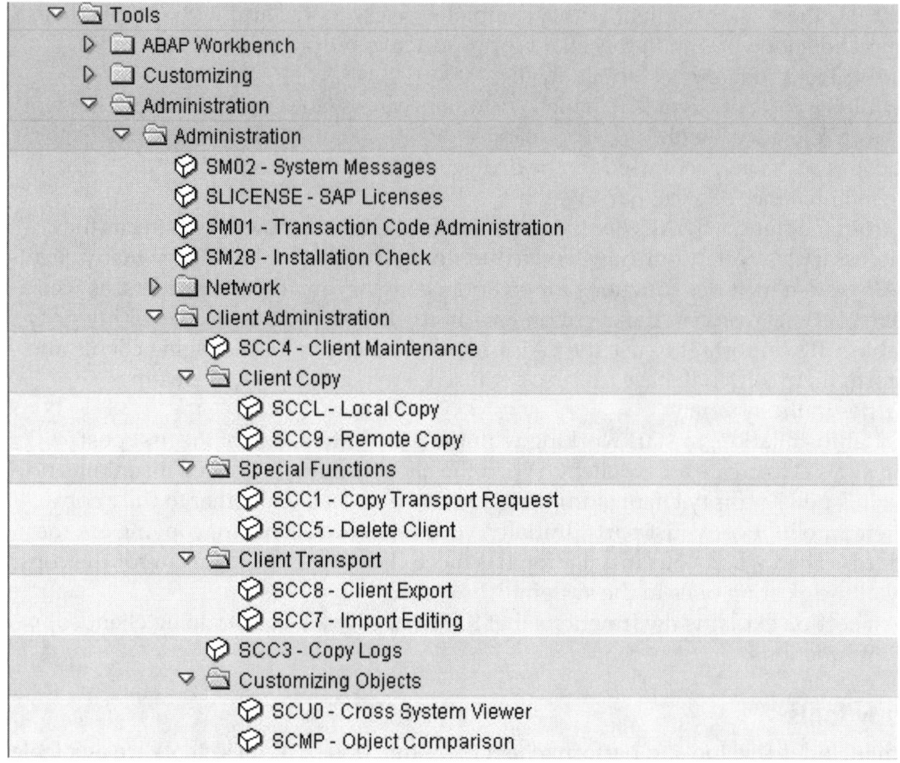

FIGURE 9-7 Client administration options (Copyright by SAP AG)

- *Copy Logs*, transaction SCC3. This option presents the list of the client copy logs and allows copy progress to be monitored.
- *Customizing objects:*
  - *Cross System Viewer*, transaction SCU0.
  - *Object Comparison*, transaction SCMP.

The main options for client copy and maintenance are explained in the following sections.

Creating a New Client

To create a new client for being the target of a client copy, you first have to define that client. The client definition is performed by selecting Administration | Client Administration | Client Maintenance from the initial administration menu or, alternatively, by entering SCC4 transaction code in the command field.

The system displays the client table, T000. In this table you can define additional clients or modify the information of the already-defined clients.

If the table is in display-only mode, click on the Display/Change icon to set the table to maintenance mode. The system displays a message warning that you are going to update a table that is client independent and will show the Client table overview. Figure 9-8 shows this screen.

To create a new client, click on the New Entries button. You get a screen like the one shown in Figure 9-9.

On that screen, you must enter the client number in the corresponding required input field. Enter a descriptive text and other optional information in the available fields. When your input is complete, click on the Save button to save the new entry.

Changes and Transports for Client-Specific Objects

When creating new clients, there are four options to consider for client-dependent objects according to the possibility of changing client customization and possible transport to another clients or systems. These options are as follows:

- *Changes without automatic recording.* When setting this option the client can be customized, although the system will not automatically generate *change requests.* If users later wish to transport customizations performed on this client, the transport requests must be manually created. This flag is not usually set except for test or demo clients and is not suitable for development and customization.
- *Automatic recording of changes.* With this option, customizing is allowed on the client, and all changes are included on *change requests* that can later be transported to other clients or systems. This is the usual configuration for developing and customizing clients on development systems.
- *No changes allowed.* This option does not allow any modifications to be performed on the client. In this case the client is protected (locked). This is a usual configuration for productive clients where customization should not be performed. It is possible,

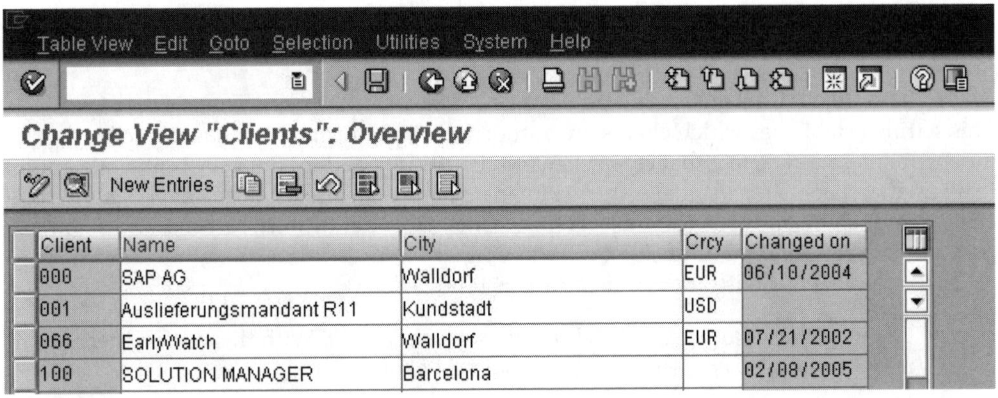

Table View Edit Goto Selection Utilities System Help

Change View "Clients": Overview

New Entries

Client	Name	City	Crcy	Changed on
000	SAP AG	Walldorf	EUR	06/10/2004
001	Auslieferungsmandant R11	Kundstadt	USD	
066	EarlyWatch	Walldorf	EUR	07/21/2002
100	SOLUTION MANAGER	Barcelona		02/08/2005

FIGURE 9-8 Client table T000 (Copyright by SAP AG)

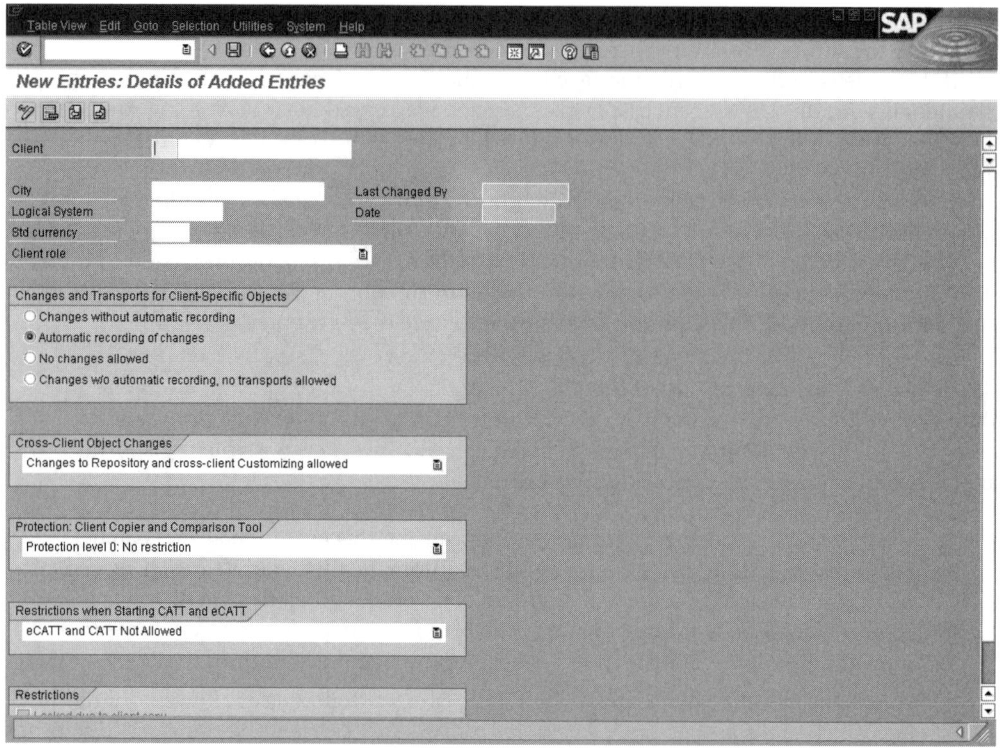

FIGURE 9-9 Defining a new system client (Copyright by SAP AG)

however, to export the customization settings of this type of client using manual generation of a transport request.

- *Changes without automatic recording, no transports allowed.* Changes are allowed with this option; however, customization settings cannot be transported either automatically or manually.

Cross-Client Object Changes

This setting establishes which clients are authorized to perform maintenance of client-independent data. The fact that cross-client or client-independent data exists and is common to all existing clients means that a change in any of this data affects all system clients. Cross-client data include all repository objects (programs, table definitions, screens, and so on) as well as some common types of client customizing.

Four possible options for this setting are as follows:

- *Changes to repository and cross-client customizing allowed.* With this option there are no restrictions on this client for changes and development.
- *No changes to cross-client Customizing objects.* This option allows for development on repository objects but not on client-independent customizing.

- *No changes to Repository objects.* This option lets users perform client-independent customizing but no development or modifications to repository objects.
- *No changes to Repository and cross-client Customizing objects.* This setting prohibits any client-independent modifications and is common on productive systems.

Protection: Client Copier and Comparison Tool

This option is a security measure used for avoiding undesired client copies or client overwriting and for prohibiting access for the purpose of comparing customization settings with those of other external clients. The three options are as follows:

- *Protection level 0: No restriction.* There are no restrictions, so a copy could be duplicated or compared.
- *Protection level 1: No overwriting.* Client cannot be overwritten by a client copy. This should be the standard setting for productive clients.
- *Protection level 2: No overwriting, no external availability.* Client is protected against read access by other clients—for example, comparing the customization settings using client comparison tools.

Restrictions

Client definition can additionally include several special restrictions:

- *Restriction when starting CATT and eCATT.* Within this box, you can decide among several options to allow or deny access to this client in order to be used as a test client for the SAP Computer Aided Test Tool (CATT) and the eCATT tool.
- *Currently locked due to client copy.* The system sets this flag automatically when a client copy is in process, thus disabling work on this client temporarily until the client copy is complete. When the copy is finished, the program releases the lock and unsets this flag.
- *Protection against SAP upgrade.* This flag can be used for preventing a SAP upgrade from overwriting customization settings on this client. This is a very special option that should be carefully used in accordance with SAP upgrade instructions and particular installations.

Requirements for Creating Clients and for the Copy Process

When creating new clients there are some requirements that must be considered. One of the main factors is the storage requirement. Creating a new client is like creating a new structure inside the database. So, before actually creating and copying the client, you should ensure there is enough space for it. This can be done by executing a client copy in *test mode*, which outputs the database space requirements for the new client in the copy log. SAP recommends at least 500 MB of free space for a client with no application data.

Other restrictions that apply during a client copy process are as follows:

- No users should be working on either the source or target clients, because this might cause inconsistencies. Administrators should lock users on the source client for entering the system. Only SAP* and DDIC are allowed to log on to the system.

- The client copy should run in background and if possible at night. In this case, ensure that no background process is scheduled to run in the source client that could modify the database at the time the client copy process is running because it can cause inconsistencies in the database just as normal logged-on users would.
- In order to launch a client copy, the following authorizations are needed:
  - S_TABU_CLI allows the table maintenance in all system clients.
  - S_TABU_DIS permits the content of the CCCFLOW table to be modified.
  - S_CLIENT_IMP permits data import when doing a client copy.
  - S_DATASET_ALL allows log files to be written in the file system.
  - S_USER_PRO permits copying user profiles.
  - S_USER_GRP permits the user master records to be copied.

When users need to create and export object lists for a client export, the following authorization also might be required:

- S_CTS_ADMI is the authorization for performing administrative functions on the transport system.
- S_TABU_RFC is the authorization allowing access to tables in a remote system, and required for a remote copy.

As the system superuser, SAP* has all the needed privileges to launch a client copy. SAP recommends performing the operation with SAP* or with a self-defined superuser having all the system access privileges.

Be careful when copying a source client over an existing client, because the process will first delete all the tables' contents in the target client before importing the new data from the source client.

If the source client includes very large tables, it can result in long runtimes and also there is the risk of rollback segments overflow. When possible, enlarge rollback segments before performing a client copy.

When copying clients between different SAP systems, copy only the client-dependent tables. Copying cross-client (client-independent) tables can only be performed when the target system has not been customized yet; otherwise, the copy process will overwrite the existing tables and this might leave the target client in an inconsistent state.

Depending on how—what is copied—the client copy is performed, you must watch out for the system number ranges. SAP distinguishes three different situations:

- When customizing and application data are copied, the number ranges are copied together with data because application data refer to number ranges.
- When only customizing data are copied and application data are deleted, the number ranges are reset.
- When only customizing data are copied but the application data are not deleted, the number ranges and application data are retained.

According to the table and table class selection, these are selected based on *delivery class*. This setting determines whether the entire table or only part of it (the client-dependent part) is copied. You can see it on transaction SE11, then select the table name and Delivery and Maintenance tag. The Delivery class field shows this table attribute. All customizing tables will be copied except those with the following delivery classes:

- *L*. These tables should be empty on the target system.
- *A*. Application tables.
- *W*. System tables, which are internally filled.

Copying a Client in the Same System

Copying a client requires the following steps that we will explain further in detail. You should check and restrain users from actually logging into the system:

- Defining the new client
- Logging into the new client with user SAP* and password PASS
- Selecting a copy profile and a source client and launching the client copy
- Checking the copy log

When you have defined a new client as indicated in the previous section, you can automatically log on to the new client with user ID SAP* and password PASS.

Once logged on in the target client, from the main menu, select Tools | Administration | Administration | Client Administration | Client Copy | Local Copy or, alternatively, enter transaction code SCCL in the command field.

In the Selected Profile input field, you have to enter a profile that tells the function what to copy. The SAP system includes a group of predefined profiles. Click on the possible entries list arrow to display a list of the available copy profiles. Figure 9-10 shows the resulting dialog box.

If you want to copy the whole client, including users, customizing, master, and transaction data, select the SAP_ALL profile.

If the profile selected includes user master data, enter the source client for the user master in the Source Client User Masters field. In the Source Client input field, enter the source client for the copy.

It is advisable to perform a *test run* before the real execution of the copy. The test run informs you about storage requirements and possible problems when copying clients.

Finally, you have to execute the copy. Depending on the chosen copy profile, these functions can take a considerable amount of time. Therefore, it is recommended to execute the client copy functions in the background. You should only execute them online when copying users' master data only.

Deleting Clients

There are several possibilities in the SAP Web Application Sever systems for deleting a whole client. The first one is by using the standard Client Delete transaction, SCC5. Log on in the client to be deleted and make sure no users are logged on to this client. Then, from the main menu, select Tools | Administration | Administration | Client Administration | Special functions | Delete Client or enter transaction code SCC5 in the command field. This function also gives you the possibility of specifying whether you also want to delete the entry from the client table T000.

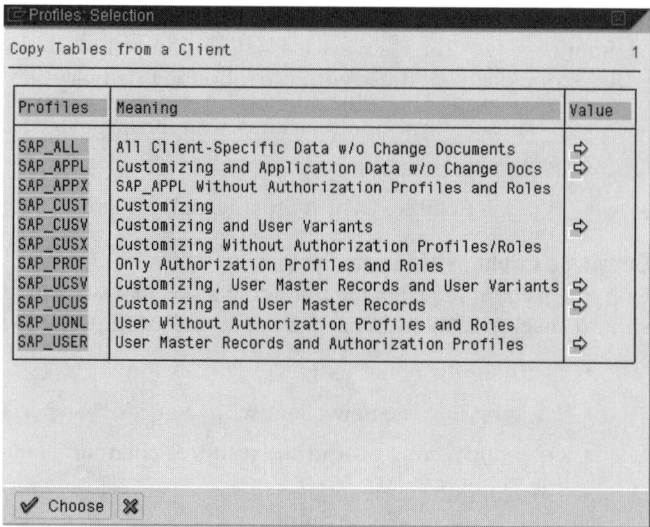

FIGURE 9-10 Entries list for copy profiles (Copyright by SAP AG)

You can execute this function online or launch it in the background. You can check the client deletion process by looking at the log with transaction SCC3.

Deleting a Client with R3trans

Clients can also be deleted using the R3trans programs, which can be the fastest way. For example, suppose that the SAP system name is TT1 and the client to delete is 010. To delete this client, log on at the operating system level as user tt1adm and access the /usr/sap/trans/bin directory (i.e., cd/usr/sap/trans/bin).

Using a standard editor, create a control file, for example, delcli.ctl, with the following text:

```
clientremove
client=010
select *
```

where *010* is the client number to be deleted. Save the file and execute the command:

```
R3trans -w delcli.log -u 1 delcli.ctl
```

Status after Deletion

After deleting a client, the space is not automatically freed from the database, although these free areas can be filled up with new data. When a client has been deleted and a new client is created and then copied, the space that was freed can be reused by the new client.

To restore the free space immediately after a client delete, you should perform a database reorganization. This is only recommended in cases where the deleted client had a lot of data and you don't expect to reuse that space. And also in case, for performance reasons, you want to fill up the gaps left for the deleted data.

Client Copy Logs

Any of the client copy functions generate a log file that can be displayed by using transaction SCC3. From the administration initial menu, select Administration | Client Administration | Copy Logs. The system displays a list with the target clients for the copies, number of runs, and date of last run, and a short status text.

From the initial screen you can select the copy log you want to display and navigate to see the full details of a copy process. To do this, double-click on the needed client line. The system displays the list of logs. Select one to display the client copy log analysis. Then to display the details or the full file copy log, select Choose from the application toolbar. In the next screen, you can select the Details or the File Log.

Restarting a Client Copy Process

If for any reason (such as database storage problems) the copying process has been canceled, when trying to reexecute the same copy process, the system allows you to restart the copy at the point where it was previously terminated, using the same parameters as before.

The client copy programs use the client copy control flow table, CCCFLOW, which includes checkpoints. When you are presented with the option of restarting the copy process but you don't want to use the restart option, select the NEWSTART option.

Transporting Clients between Two SAP Systems

This process can be useful in cases where there is no direct network connection between two systems; otherwise, a remote copy is preferable.

For example, suppose you want to copy client 005 from a source system TT1 to target system DD1. The target client can be 005 or any other client. If the client does not exist in the target system, DD1, first log on to the target system in any existing client and create the new client by using the standard function, for example, Tools | Administration | Administration | Client Administration | Client Maintenance.

If the client already exists in the target system, you should first delete it. Refer to the previous section on deleting clients.

Log on in the source system in the client you want to copy (to export). In this example, system TT1 and client 005. Enter transaction SCC8 in the command field or, alternatively, select Administration | Client Administration | Client Transport | Client Export from the initial administration menu. Enter the same copy profile as you would in a normal copy procedure between clients in the same system. You must select what you wish to transport by using one of the existing copy profiles, as shown in Figure 9-10.

Copy profile management is explained in the next section. Execute the copy in the background.

When the export is finished, and depending on the chosen copy profile, you get the following transport requests:

- TT1KOnnnnnn (cross-client objects)
- TT1KXnnnnnn (client-dependent long texts)
- TT1KTnnnnnn (client-dependent tables)

where TT1 is the SID and <nnnnnn> is a system-generated transport number.

Now you have to import those transport files manually using the Transport Management system in the target system.

After importing the KO and KT, you have to run transaction SCC7 in the target system for the import postprocessing, in which text files are automatically imported. Check the transport log for errors.

Because client transports and export/import options vary between different releases of the Basis system and the WAS, please refer to the latest version of SAP Note 70547 for updated information and known problems.

Copying Individual Tables Entries between Clients

In addition to the previous functions and transactions used when performing client copy functions and the associated reports, SAP provides additional reports that can be very useful when managing information among system clients.

You can use transaction SCC1, which allows you to "transport" an object list from a source client to the current logon client. Watch out with certain restrictions for long tables, and refer to SAP Note 45796.

Other possibilities for copying individual table entries between clients include, for example, programming in ABAP the transfer of the data to a file and then loading that file on to the target client. And finally, you could transport the table contents by creating a transportable change request and entering the table contents in the transport editor. For table contents, use the R3TR TABU <table name> option. However, you should avoid using these last two options, which can cause inconsistencies in the system data.

Copying Tables Entries between Two Different Systems

There are several ways to copy table entries between two different SAP systems. One of the most efficient is by using the R3trans utility. The tp program could also be used; however, the transport control program tp performs many additional checks and imposes some restrictions on the table types to be transported.

For example, assume that, after a client copy between two SAP systems, a table content could not be completely copied to the target system (import phase) because the table reached the maximum number of extents in the underlying database. You can avoid having to perform a whole import again by transporting a single table with R3trans. The general procedure to do this is as follows:

1. Create the control file for the export.
2. Run the control file in the source system.
3. Check the export log.
4. Create the import control file in the target system.
5. Run the import control file in the target system.
6. Check the import log and the data in the target system.

Example of Copying Table Entries between Clients and Systems

The following example shows the copying process of the contents of a table from the client 002 in system C12 to client 010 in system T12. After verifying the client copy log, due to some storage problems in table MOFF, this table could not be completely copied. To avoid having to perform the whole client copy process, just the entries on table MOFF from the source client will be copied to the table MOFF on the target client 010 in the target system T12.

1. In the source system (C12), create a control file, for example, expmoff.ctrl with the following content:

```
export
client=002
select * from moff where mandt = '002'
```

2. Run the R3trans utility with the previous control file: R3trans -w expmoff.log -u 18 expmoff.ctrl.

   The R3trans syntax and options are discussed in Chapter 6. While the -w flag indicates the log file, the -u flag sets unconditional modes for the transport. In the export phase, unconditional mode 1 indicates the system to ignore the wrong status of transport requests. Mode 8 allows direct selection of tables when the default modes are not allowed.

   By default, the previous command generates the data file trans.dat in the directory where the export has been executed. If both source and target systems share the transport directory, it won't be necessary to copy the trans.dat file. Otherwise, you must use available tools for file transfer, for example, ftp.
3. Check the export log file, expmoff.log, and verify it did not contain any errors.
4. Once in the target system, create the import control file, for example, impmoff.ctrl, with the following content:

```
import
client=010
```

5. Then execute it with the R3trans tool: `R3trans -w impmoff.log -u 248 impmoff.ctrl.` By default it uses the data file trans.dat generated by the previous command file.

   The unconditional modes used in the import phase are 2 for enabling the overwriting of the original; 4, which ignores that the transport request was intended for a different target system; and 8, which allows for importing tables that are restricted by their table types.

   If you use the default options for the import, you do not need a control file. The import can be performed directly with R3trans -i <file>.
6. Check the import log file, impmoff.log, to check that the import runs fine without errors. You can also log on to the target client, 010, in the target system and look up the table contents with standard dictionary utilities, such as the data browser (transaction code SE16).

Managing the Background System

The SAP system includes functions that allow users to work noninteractively, or offline. These functions are handled by the background processing system.

Users normally work interactively with the SAP system. *Interactively* means they are working online, they input data into the application screens, and the system responds. The interactive service is provided to the users through the dialog work processes.

There is, however, the option of working noninteractively, or offline. *Noninteractively* means that instead of executing programs and waiting for an answer, users can submit those programs for execution at a more convenient, planned time. This type of work is performed by the background work processes.

Introduction to Background Processing

The execution of programs in the background are submitted in the form of *background jobs*, or simply *jobs*.

There are several reasons to submit programs for background execution: The interactive user sessions are always *fighting* to get a free dialog work process for their requests.

The maximum allowed time for online execution is defined in a SAP parameter profile (rdisp/max_wprun_time), which normally should not exceed 300 seconds. This means that for ABAP programs whose processing time would exceed that parameter, users would get a TIMEOUT error and an aborted transaction. To avoid these types of errors, you could submit jobs for background processing.

You can continue to work in the system while your program is executing—this is the most important reason to run background processing jobs. When working online with a long processing report, you cannot interact with the system and have to wait until it finishes or the dispatcher throws you out if you exceed the time limit.

This does not mean that interactive or online work is not useful. Both types of processing have their purposes. Online work is the most common one: entering business data, displaying information, printing small reports, managing the system, and so on. Working interactively or online requires the person to be present to interact with the system. However, with background jobs, the system does not need user input or users have already provided the input in the job definition.

Background jobs are used mainly for the following tasks:

- To process large amounts of data, for example, to get a quarterly report of sales, a monthly warehouse movement report, data load from external systems, and so on.
- To execute periodic jobs without human intervention. A couple of easy examples are jobs needing everyday reports of the total incoming payments or periodic cleaning jobs submitted by the SAP system manager that take care of deleting obsolete data, such as old log files, ABAP dumps, and so on.
- To run programs at a more convenient, planned time other than during normal working hours, for example, at night and on weekends, when there are usually less interactive users.

For example, if interactively running a report that takes two or three minutes to finish, the SAP session in which the report is executing will be busy until the report execution ends. During that time, the user cannot interact with the session. Instead, the user could have scheduled it for background processing, creating a background job and specifying the name of the report. When releasing the job, the system will execute it in the background but will give the user the control of the SAP session so he or she can keep on working and interacting with the system.

Jobs executing in the background are working online with the SAP system, so any actions performed by the program steps, such as locking a table or updating the database, will have an immediate effect just as if an interactive user was running the same program.

Background jobs execution is handled with the background work processes. The way to implement the background work processes depends on the particular needs of the SAP installation.

In any case, when installing a SAP system for the first time, the system configures by default the background processing system in the central SAP instance with a number of background work processes depending on the hardware configuration.

The number and location of background work processes is configurable both with SAP system profile parameters and with the use of the CCMS operation modes. With operation modes, system managers can define some work processes to work as dialog during certain hours and then switch automatically to background processes without the need to restart the application server instances.

Background Jobs

A SAP background job defines the program or group of programs that are going to be executed by the background work processes. In order to do this, the job must be defined. SAP includes several utilities to define, manage, monitor, and troubleshoot the background jobs. Figure 9-11 shows the initial screen for job definition. You can get to this screen from many different places: by entering transaction code SM36 in the command field, by selecting from the initial SAP screen Tools | CCMS | Jobs | Definition, or by selecting System | Services | Jobs | Define jobs from any SAP screen.

Components of the Background Jobs

A background job has the following components:

- *Job name.* Defines the name assigned to the job.
- *Job class.* Indicates the type of background processing priority assigned to the job.
- *Status.* Refers to the status of job status and is set automatically by the system. Refer to the next section about job status.
- *Exec. target.* It's the SAP instance where the job will be executed.
- *Job steps.* A job step defines the program (either ABAP or external) that will be executed.
- *Job start time and Job frequency.* Define when the job will be started and whether it should be periodically executed.
- *Job print lists.* These lists specify the printing parameters for the job output.
- *Job log.* The logs for the jobs include log information about the job execution, such as starting time or any other information coded in the programs.
- *Job spool recipient list.* A recipient list can be used for specifying one or more recipients who will receive automatically the spool list generated by the job.

All these components of background jobs are explained in greater detail in the following sections of this chapter.

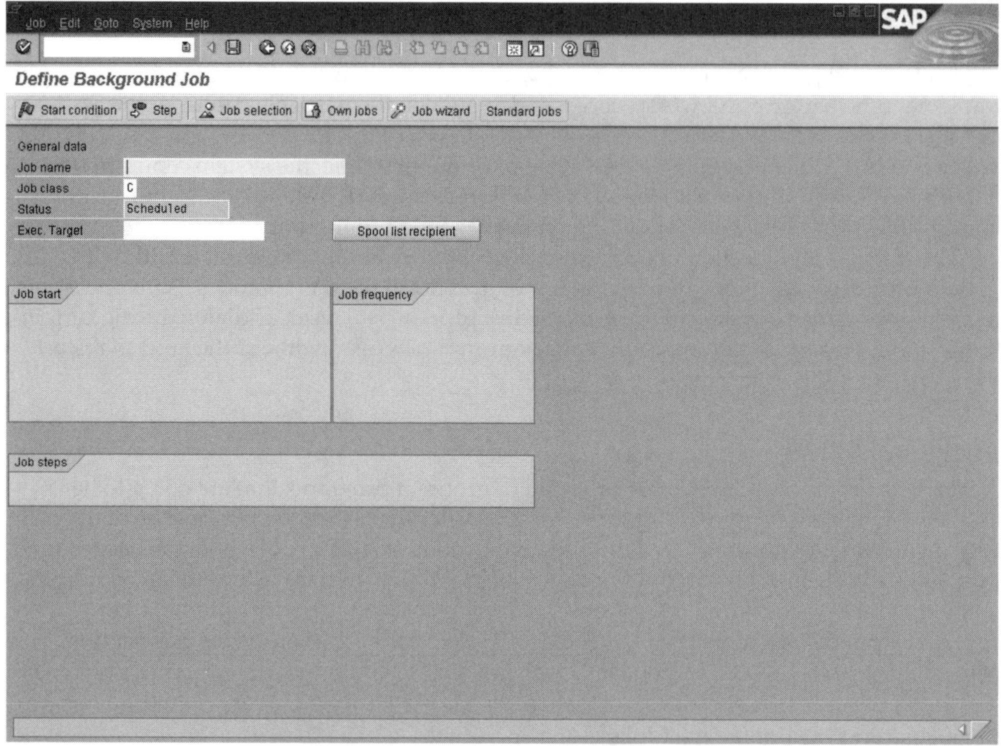

FIGURE 9-11 Initial screen for defining jobs (Copyright by SAP AG)

Starting Background Processing

Starting background processing means reaching any type of job definition screen in order to specify the needed data for the background execution of programs. There are several ways to start the background processing system:

- From the initial job definition screen as shown in Figure 9-11.
- From the ABAP Reporting Service screen. From any menu, you can select System | Services | Reporting, then enter the report name. The reporting screen includes the option for background execution by selecting Program | Background from the menu.
- From the ABAP Workbench Editor. On the editor initial screen, enter the name of the program in the input field and select Program | Execute | Background from the menu.
- Sometimes working with business applications, especially navigating through the many information system and reporting functions, the system allows for background execution.

The last three methods mentioned are virtually the same thing, though the system can display different selection screens. With these three methods of starting background processing, after indicating Background Execution, the SAP system displays the Execute Report in Background screen.

The job will have automatically included the report as the first job step, whereas the user has to enter additional job definition fields, such as the job class, target host, start time, and so on.

Defining Background Jobs

Starting background jobs is a two-step process: you first define the job and then you have to release it.

When users define a job and save it, they are actually *scheduling* the report, that is, specifying the job components, the steps, the start time, and the print parameters. So to schedule a job is the same thing as to define it.

More precisely, a *scheduled* job is a job definition that has been saved. When users schedule programs for background processing, they are instructing the system to execute an ABAP report or an external program in the background.

Scheduled background jobs, however, are not actually executed until they are released. When jobs are released, they are sent for execution to the background processing system at the specified start time.

Jobs are released automatically if the user is authorized to release jobs, and they automatically start the execution in the background system if the user has chosen the Start Immediately option.

Both the scheduling and the releasing of jobs require authorizations. Standard SAP users have authorization that allows them to schedule jobs; however, releasing jobs is a task normally assigned to the system administration and requires another authorization. Protecting the releasing of jobs with authorization enables system administrators to better monitor and maintain the background system and allows the available resources to be better distributed. The drawback is that scheduling jobs is such a common task that it can surpass the administrator's ability to maintain the whole system. Therefore, reserve some time for studying which users should be allowed to release their own jobs.

When users do not have release authorization, the start time or frequency they specify does not have any affect at all, except for informing the administrator in charge of releasing them of their preference for executing the job. Administrators or users with authorization for releasing jobs can change the start time specifications and the interval.

The authorization objects that control the background jobs are described later in this chapter.

When scheduling jobs, users can specify several steps, each having a different report or program. Each step has its own attributes, such as authorized users or print parameters. The same job can contain steps with ABAP reports and steps with external programs or commands (this is explained more fully in a later section).

When defining jobs, users also have the option of scheduling a program as a separate job or modifying an existing job which has not yet been processed and adding it to the list of job steps.

Users, and especially administrators, should avoid having too many released jobs during normal, operative working hours, because the system processes the background jobs during online operation where there are available background work processes. Remember that a background job will perform the same tasks as if the functions were performed online. So, if a background job does lock a table or updates the database, it will have an immediate result and can affect the work of online users.

Job Definition Fields

As introduced earlier, to schedule or define a background job, there are some input fields that must be filled. From the initial job definition screen as shown in Figure 9-11, you can see in greater detail which are the job definition fields and what their intended functions are.

Job Name The job name identifies the job. You can specify up to 32 characters for the name, including letters, numbers, and space characters. Try to give a name which will easily identify the function of the job; also, you could use the same starting letters of words for related types of jobs, since the name will often be used to display lists of jobs.

Job Class The job class determines the priority of a job. The background system admits three types of job classes or priorities: A, B, and C, which correspond to job priority. Class A is the highest priority class; class B is the next priority class; and normal jobs have the C class, which is the lowest and default priority for most jobs. To schedule jobs with higher priority, users must have special authorizations or request the administrator to change the priority of the job. Job classes are very useful when you need to reserve some of the background work processes for scheduling important or more critical jobs.

You can reserve background work processes for class A jobs. This can ensure that class A jobs will always have free processes so that they can be executed (in case there are no more class A jobs waiting for work processes reserved for class A). Class A jobs can be processed as well by normal background processes, and they have priority over regular class C or class B jobs.

With this method, administrators can decide how they want to use background processes of type A:

- Work processes for critical tasks, such as type A, and two-level priority for job classes B and C
- No background work processes reserved for class A jobs, so that regular three-level priority is used

The advantage of having work processes reserved for class A jobs is that even when there are many released jobs of class C waiting to be processed because all work processes are busy with other jobs, these normal-priority jobs will not use the reserved work processes intended for jobs with the class A. Therefore, even in high-load background situations, administrators can release important jobs by assigning a higher priority job class.

To reserve background work processes for class A jobs, you have to configure the instance operation modes with the CCMS utilities.

Exec. Target This field is used to specify the server instance where the background job is to run. You can select the instance by clicking on the possible entries list arrow and choosing one of the hosts from the list. However, this field is normally left blank, which instructs the system to execute the job in the system with the lightest work.

Because of the possibilities for distributing the SAP systems services, not all servers might offer background services (run background work processes), and it's also possible to configure one or several servers just for background processing.

The target field is used mainly when, for any reason, a job must be processed on a particular server. Some of the reasons to do that might be: a job will read operating system files only accessible from a particular server, the printer defined for the job output is only defined in that server, and so forth. For example, you should be particularly careful when performing change request imports in a system with several servers. In order for the background job RDDIMPDP not to fail the first time, all SAP servers where background jobs might run should have access to the common /usr/sap/trans directory; otherwise, you should specify a target host for the importing jobs.

Commonly, jobs do not require a target instance for being executed, because the CCMS system with the help of the message server is responsible for distributing the load among the available background servers.

NOTE *Do not confuse this target host instance, which specifies a host running background work processes, with the target host as specified when defining external programs as job steps. It can be the same, but not necessarily.*

Job Steps

Once the general job definition fields are entered, you have to click on the Steps function button to define the programs that will be executed as part of the job. Figure 9-12 shows an example of the initial Create Step screen.

There are three types of steps that can be defined depending on the nature of the program to be executed. You can notice these types by looking at the buttons on the program values box shown in Figure 9-12. These types are as follows:

- *ABAP programs.* With this option, you can specify the execution of ABAP reports as steps of a background job. Module pools or functions groups are not allowed for definition as steps.
- *External commands.* These are predefined commands that should have been previously defined by the system administrator. Normal users with the required authorization can schedule these job steps. Because this is a way of executing programs or commands outside SAP, for security reasons users have to specify the operating system type and cannot change the predefined arguments.
- *External programs.* These programs are unrestricted operating system programs or shell scripts that require batch administrator privileges. There is no need to define these commands using transaction SM69. The requirement is that the computer must be reached from within the SAP server and have either remote shell support, a running SAP gateway, or a SAP instance that is on the reach of a SAP gateway.

Clicking on the command function buttons for the type of step actually changes the available command buttons on the lower part of the screen.

The following sections explain how to schedule steps and the requirements and parameters which can be used.

Scheduling ABAP Programs as Job Steps

When scheduling ABAP reports as job steps, there are several type parameters which can be specified. The most important one is usually the selection criteria for the execution of the report as it would be normally specified when launching the report online. A group of selection criteria is saved in variants. Refer to Chapter 4 for a description of report variants.

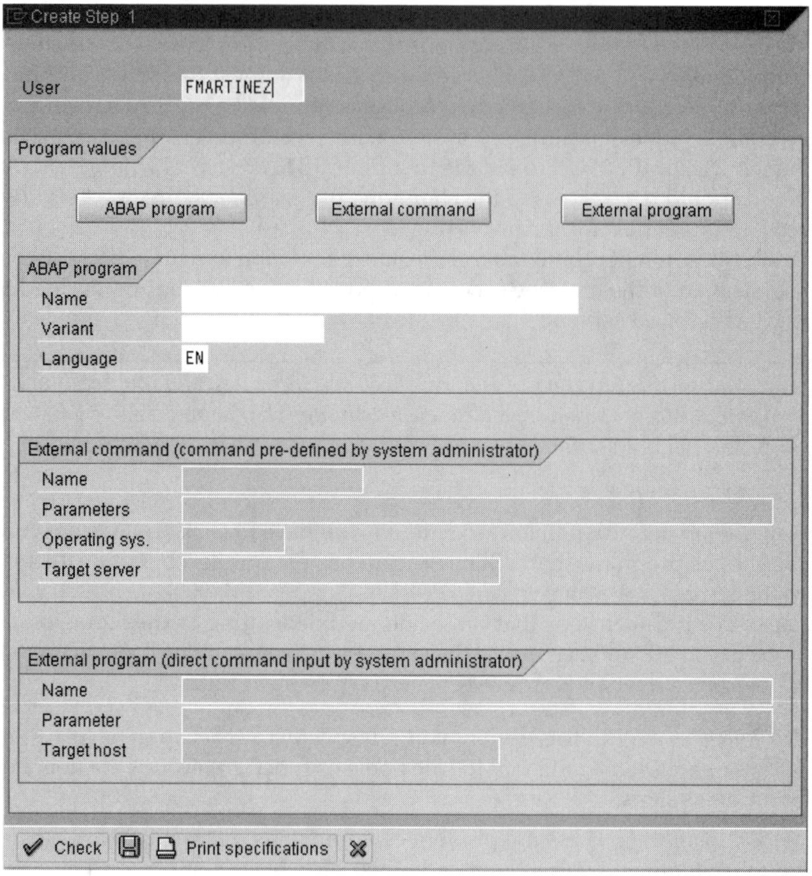

FIGURE 9-12 Screen for creating a job step (Copyright by SAP AG)

When an ABAP program is specified as part of a background job, if it needs selection criteria, the variant must have been previously created; otherwise you will not be able to save the ABAP step.

To define an ABAP program as a job step, from the initial job definition screen, press the Define Steps button on the application toolbar, and then click on the ABAP Program button on the Create Step screen. Then proceed as follows:

- The User input field will be filled automatically with your own username. But you can select another username that will be used by the system to check the authorizations for the running job. You can only enter another username if your own user is authorized to do so.
- Enter the name of the ABAP program in the Name input field.
- If the ABAP program has selection fields, you must enter a variant in the Variant input field. If you don't know the name of the variant, click on the Variant List

button and select one. If you don't have any variant defined, you have to first define at least one variant; otherwise the system will not let you schedule the job. You can leave this field blank only in the case that the program does not require variants.

- Finally, in the Language input field, you can select a different language than the default, which is the one used when logging in to the system. Because SAP solutions are multilanguage systems, there might be some language-dependent texts in the program that will be affected by the value of the Language field.

In the definition of steps with ABAP programs, you can also specify print parameters to instruct the system on where and how to print the job output.

When finished entering the needed information in the input fields, you can check your definition by clicking on the Check button. The system will display a message in the status bar if it finds any errors in the job definition. If there are no errors, click the Save icon to save your step.

Scheduling External Commands

Both external commands and external programs are executed by means of the sapxpg program. This program is called either by a remote shell (rsh, remsh, and others) or by the SAP gateway (the usual way under Microsoft Windows platforms).

External commands to be scheduled must have been previously defined by the system administrator (transaction code SM69 or Tools | CCMS | Configuration | External Commands).

To define these commands as job steps, first click on the External Command pushbutton on the Create Step dialog box.

On the Name input field, click on the possible entries arrow to select one of the available external commands. Only the commands available for the target operating system can be successfully executed.

The Parameters input field is used for specifying additional flags or parameters for the command.

Select Operating System from the available options, and the Target Server where the command will be executed.

Finally, verify the definition by clicking on the Check icon. If no errors are found, proceed by saving the step definition.

Scheduling External Programs

You can schedule external programs as job steps. These external programs can be of any type as long as they can be reached from the SAP server and the host where the program resides can execute the program itself. It can be any compiled or executable program, shell script, and so forth.

The step definition for external programs allows you to include any parameters the program needs in a complete transparent way. The error messages generated by external programs are included in the log file for the background job.

To enter an external program as part of a job, when on the Create Step screen, click on the external program. The system will change the colors for the relevant input fields while graying out the field for the ABAP programs.

Notice how the command buttons in the lower part of the screen change as well, depending on the type of program.

Enter the following information for the external program:

- *Name.* Enter the name and path of the external program. You should enter the path to ensure that the program can be found in the target system except if the program is in the search path of the SAP user with which the SAP gateway was started (normally the <sid>adm user). For example, enter */home/dd1adm/copy.sh*, instead of entering just *copy.sh*.
- *Parameter.* Enter here any parameters, flags, or options that the external program might need. For example, if the program /usr/bin/ps needs the option *-eaf*, enter this value in the parameter field.
- *Target host.* You have to enter here the hostname of the server where the external program is to be executed. This host must be reachable from the SAP server.

The SAP system includes some special options for submitting external commands or external programs, which can be reached by clicking on the Control Flags button that appears on the screen for creating a step with external programs.

Figure 9-13 includes the new dialog box shown by the system when selecting this function.

With the Control Flag options, you can activate a trace for the external programs, and also direct the output and error information to the job log.

But the most interesting option within the Control Flags is the *Job to wait for ext. termination*. By selecting the Check button option, the SAP system will start the external programs as service programs in the host where they are started, which means that they will remain active in the system.

When starting these types of service program which do not terminate, these programs return control to the SAP background system which terminates the job as soon as it has been started.

Defining the Start Conditions for the Job

For background jobs to execute, you have to specify their start time. SAP systems provide many options that virtually cover most needs both for defining start-time criteria and for defining a repeat interval. In any case, jobs are not executed until they are released, independently of the start time defined.

Start time can be defined before or after the definition of the job steps. However, if no start time is specified, the job will be saved but will never be executed unless the system or job administrator modifies a job and defines a start time and then releases it.

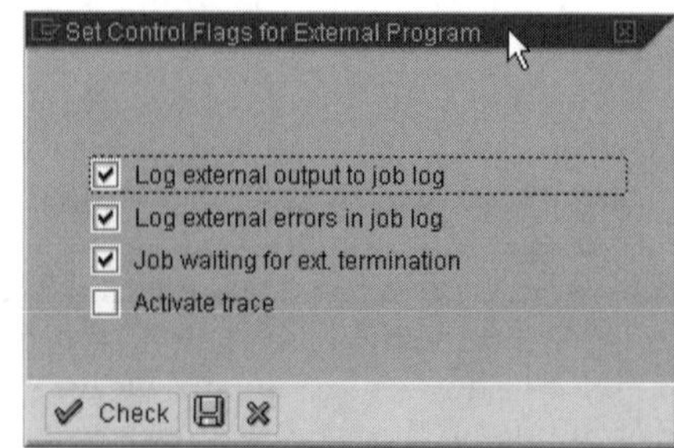

FIGURE 9-13 The Control Flag display for external programs (Copyright by SAP AG)

To define a start time, click on the Start Condition button on the initial job definition screen. Figure 9-14 shows the resulting display. The system provides the following start options:

- Immediate start
- At a specified date and time
- After receiving a system event
- At change of operating mode
- After termination of a preceding job
- On a specific work day

For those jobs which need to be periodically executed, SAP also provides the facility to specify a repeat interval, which can be assigned to every start option.

The following sections cover available start options one by one.

Immediate For immediate start jobs, the background processing system sends the jobs for execution as soon as they are released. The immediate start jobs are released by clicking on the Save icon. When users define *immediate* as the start option, the background scheduler processes the job immediately if there are available background work processes. If there are

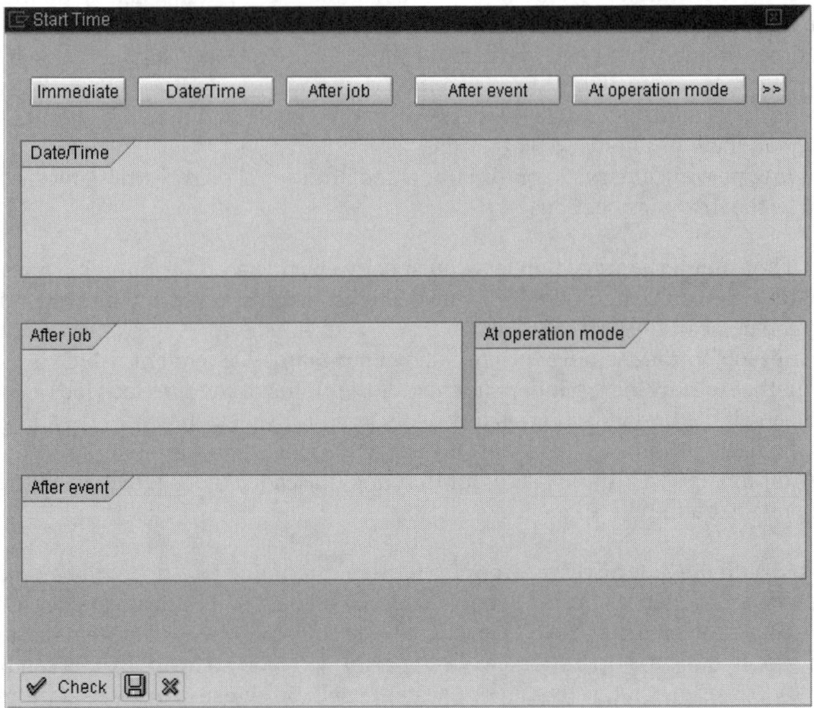

FIGURE 9-14 Job start options (Copyright by SAP AG)

no background work processes available, the job will wait in Released status until one of the background work processes becomes free. This also applies if the job class is B or C (normal priority) and the free work processes are reserved for class A.

If, when defining the job, the user specifies a target host, immediate start jobs will also wait for execution if there is no free background work process in the specified host, even if there are free background work processes in other hosts.

When no target host is specified, immediate start jobs are evenly distributed among the available background processing servers.

When selecting the Immediate option, the system includes this information within the Date/Time box and presents additional options on the same screen, such as the check box to specify whether it's going to be a periodic job and whether you want to specify additional restrictions for the start time of the job.

Users not having authorization for releasing jobs cannot use the Immediate start option.

Date and Time The Date/Time option allows you to specify the date and the time when the job will be processed. When you click on the Date/Time button, the system opens input fields under the Date/Time box to allow for entering the start data, and also automatically shows the Periodic Job check box and additional function buttons on the bottom part of the screen.

In the input fields, enter the requested start date and time. You can either type the requested information or click on the possible entries arrow to choose a value. In this case, when selecting dates and time, similar to the rest of the SAP system, clicking on the arrow for a date will display a dialog box with a calendar.

Sometimes, it might not be convenient for the job to be released for execution if there are no free work processes available at the specified date and time. In these cases, the system allows for restricting the job not to start after a specified date and time by entering that information in the input field No Start After.

Specifying periodic intervals for execution and additional start restrictions are explained in the following sections.

After Job The After Job start option lets you specify starting a background job after the execution of a previous job. Figure 9-15 shows the list box displayed by the system in which you enter the name of the previous job.

The After Job option includes the check box Start Status-Dependent, which is used to specify whether to start the job independently of the status of the previous job or only execute the job if the previous job was finished successfully. Selecting the check box indicates the background system to start the job only if the previous job was successful.

The After Job option is quite useful for defining "cascaded" jobs which need to be executed one after another.

After Event With the After Event start option, users can define jobs that will be executed when the system triggers a specific event. *Events* are signals that indicate that a certain condition, phase, or stage has been reached, for example, that the SAP system has just been started, a certain database operation has been performed, and so forth. Events can be triggered by ABAP programs, by the SAP system itself, or by using the sapevt program from the operating system.

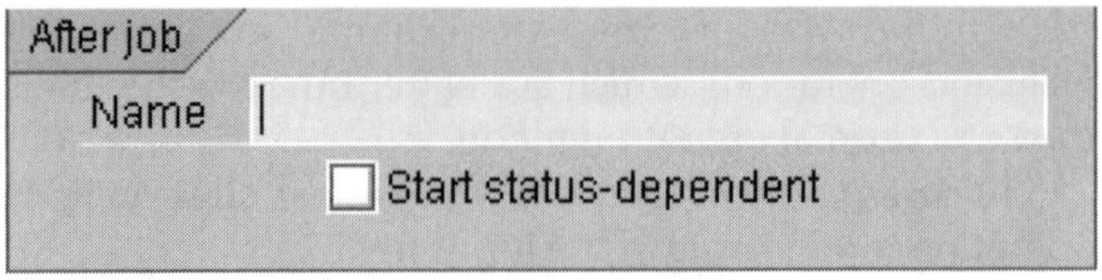

Figure 9-15 Specifying a job after a predecessor (Copyright by SAP AG)

Starting background jobs by sending events is quite useful especially in situations where there is an interface or relation between operating system processes and SAP. Two typical examples are as follows:

- When imports are performed with the transport management programs, the operating system process sends the SAP_TRIGGER_RDDIMPDP event. When the SAP system receives the event, the background job RDDIMPDP is automatically started, because it is scheduled to run after receiving this event.
- When receiving sequential files for processing by a batch input session in the background, you can have a shell script or program that periodically looks for the requested file. When it finds the needed sequential file, it can trigger an event to the SAP system to start the background job that processes the batch input program.

It is also possible to specify the jobs started after events to be periodic. This means that when the job is triggered, the first thing it does is to automatically reschedule itself for the next time it receives the event.

You can display a list of available events by clicking on the possible entries arrow. Or you can create your own events. To do that, from the main menu, select Tools | CCMS | Jobs | Maintain Events. Alternatively, run transaction SM62.

A practical example is as follows:

1. Create a new event, for example, MY_TEST_EVENT.
2. Define a job with a simple ABAP report and select the After Event start option.
3. Click on the event possible list arrow and select your newly defined event. Save the job. It will be released.
4. Login at the operating system level as user <sid>adm and trigger the event by using the command `sapevt "MY_TEST_EVENT" pf=/usr/sap/<SID>/SYS/profile/<instance_profile>`, for example, if the <SID> is DD1 and the instance profile DD1_DVEBMGS00, the full command is `sapevt "MY_TEST_EVENT" pf=/usr/sap/DD1/SYS/profile/DD1_DVEBMGS00`.
5. In the SAP system, check that the job has been started.

At Operation Mode Change Another option for starting background jobs is when the system changes the operation mode. This option can be quite useful for system or job administrators when having to reschedule many jobs for other users at a more convenient time in order to optimize system resources and performance. For example, when changing the operation mode, the system is configured to switch many dialog processes to background work processes (for example, in operation modes defined for nightly or weekend operation), which is a better time to schedule the jobs that could not be processed during a normal operation mode.

To define a job *at operation mode change*, click on its function button and enter the operation mode name in the input field.

Additional Start Restrictions The system includes an option to restrict the job start time to a specific workday linked with a factory calendar. This option can be useful when jobs are not needed on holidays or weekends, but only on certain workdays, for example, background jobs that generate production orders or project worksheets that are only required for operative users who do not work on holidays or weekends. Restrictions on workdays and the factory calendar can only be applied to jobs with the Date/Time start option. To specify start restrictions, when in the Date/Time option, click on the Restrictions button. Figure 9-16 shows the dialog box that the system displays.

In the restrictions for the Start Date dialog box, you can define jobs to execute only on workdays and decide how the background system will behave in case the scheduled job's planned start is on a nonworking day. The system allows you to either cancel the job, always execute it, move it to the next workday, or move it backward to the previous workday.

Relative Start Option The last available start option is to specify the number of workdays relative to the beginning or end of a month when a job should be started. As with every option in the system that uses workdays, it must be linked with a factory calendar. To display the dialog box for specifying relative start times, press on the >> icon on the initial Start Date/Time screen. The Period input box is specified in number of months. For instance, *02* means that the job will be repeated every two months.

Defining a Repeat Interval Period

The background processing system allows for defining a repeat interval for jobs that you want to execute periodically. For example, administrators can run cleaning background jobs everyday, sales managers can have a sales report run in the background every month, and so on.

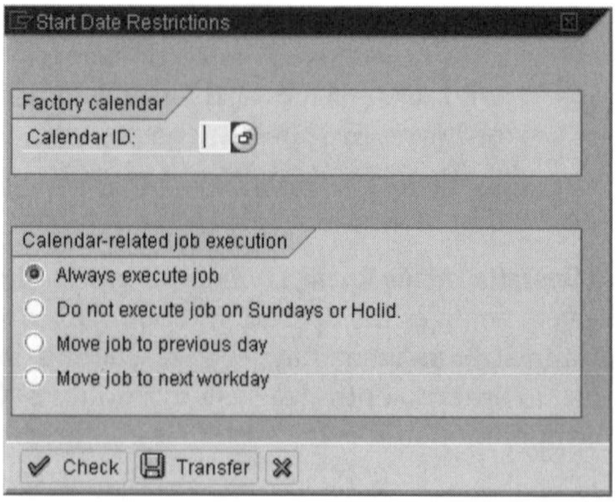

FIGURE 9-16 Specifying start restrictions (Copyright by SAP AG)

To define a repeat interval period, you first define a start option. The dialog box automatically shows the Periodic Job check box. Select this box and then click on the period values. The system displays a new pop-up box like the one shown in Figure 9-17. This figure has five standard options: hourly, daily, weekly, monthly, and other. To select any of the periodic values, just click the pushbutton.

With the fifth option, Other Period, you can specify virtually any repeat period option. Enter the desired values in the corresponding input fields. When specifying a repeat interval for jobs started with the After Event option, you cannot specify a repeat time value; instead, when the job is defined as *periodic*, the system will reschedule it every time it is processed.

Specifying Job Print Parameters

Often, the result of an ABAP program or external program makes database modifications that are not output in lists. Often, too, the result of a background job is a report list, which can be passed directly to the printing system, either as an output request or directly sent to the printer. You can also send the spool output to a list of recipients.

When defining ABAP reports that generate report lists, you can decide to define the print parameters for the background jobs. To do that, click on the Print Specifications button, which appears in the dialog box for ABAP step creation. The Background Print Parameter screen is virtually the same as any other print request generated in the SAP system. Enter the requested print specifications and save the settings.

Specifying the Spool List Recipient

The system includes the possibility of automatically sending to a group of recipients the result of a job that includes a spool request. The system allows this output to be sent both to internal users or by other external means (Internet mail, fax, and so on) if these communication types have been previously configured in the system.

To send the output of a job to a recipient or group, click on the Spool List Recipient pushbutton on the initial job definition screen. The system will display a dialog box for determination of recipients, as well as additional flags that will be attached to the message. Clicking on the possible entries arrow in the Recipient input field opens an additional dialog box for selecting the type of user or messaging system. Figure 9-18 shows these screens.

Make your required entries and press the Copy icon to transfer the information to the job definition.

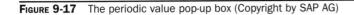

FIGURE 9-17 The periodic value pop-up box (Copyright by SAP AG)

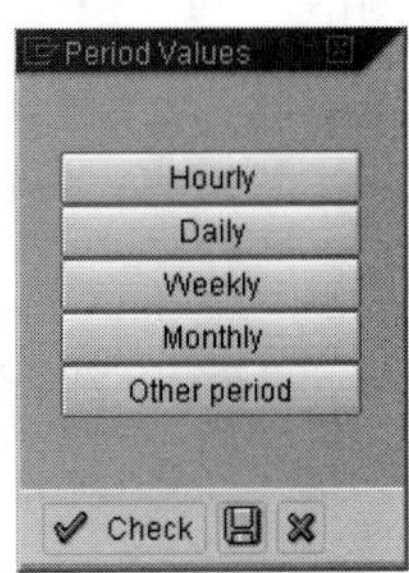

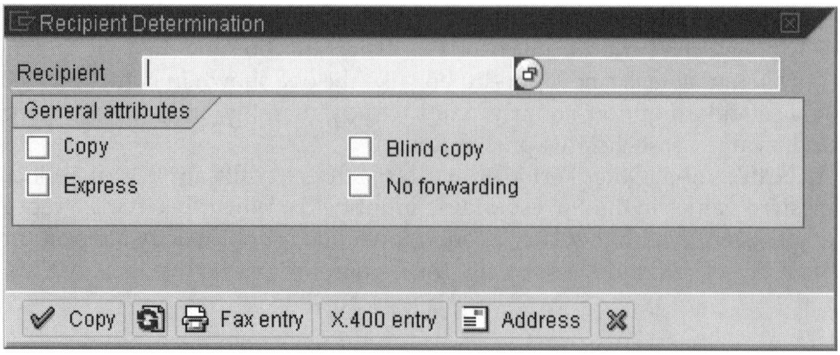

FIGURE 9-18 Spool List Recipient options (Copyright by SAP AG)

Management Operations on Background Jobs

Previous sections explained the process of defining and scheduling jobs. This section covers additional management options to handle modifying, monitoring, and controlling background jobs. Users can display a list of their own jobs by selecting System | Own Jobs from any SAP window.

The most important background job managing operations are as follows:

- *Checking the status of jobs.*
- *Modifying jobs.*
- *Deleting jobs.* Some time after a job has been processed, you should delete it to release system resources. You have two options for deleting a job: manually, job-by-job, or automatically, using a reorganization program that deletes jobs that are beyond a date line.
- *Viewing the job log.* If a job has been aborted, you should view the job log for the cause of the failure.

Most basic management operations are performed from the Job Overview screen. To reach the Job Overview screen, first, from the main menu select System | Services | Jobs | Job Overview or, alternatively, enter transaction code SM37 in the command field. Figure 9-19 shows the initial screen for selecting jobs.

On the initial screen, enter the selection criteria for the jobs you want to look for. On the job selection screen, you can specify job name, user name, a date and time interval, job status, and so forth. Wildcards, such as the asterisk sign (*) are allowed. Do not forget to enter the event name or an * to select jobs which are started after event, even when they are already finished in the date and time range.

Once the criteria are specified, press ENTER to display the job overview for the requested selection. Figure 9-20 shows an example of a Job Overview screen. This screen includes several menu options that allow you to perform common monitoring and management tasks over a job or a group of selected jobs.

The next sections explain some of these common tasks.

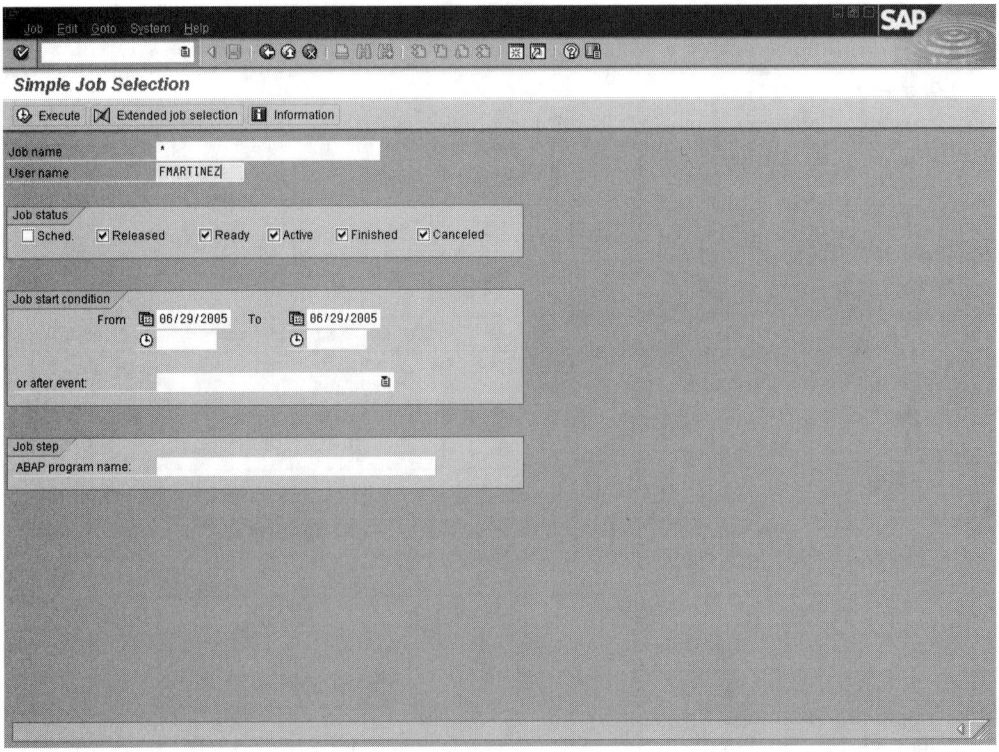

FIGURE 9-19 Background jobs main selection screen (Copyright by SAP AG)

The Job Status

A job can have one of the following statuses: scheduled, released, ready, active, finished, canceled. They indicate the following conditions:

- *Scheduled.* The job has been created but still has not been released to run. A scheduled job will never execute unless it is released.
- *Released.* The job is released to run at the time or condition specified in the start options.
- *Ready.* The start date and time has arrived and the job is waiting to be executed. This status is not seen very often. It is a short period of time before the job changes to an active status.
- *Active.* The job is running, being executed.
- *Finished.* The job has ended successfully.
- *Canceled.* The job has ended with errors.

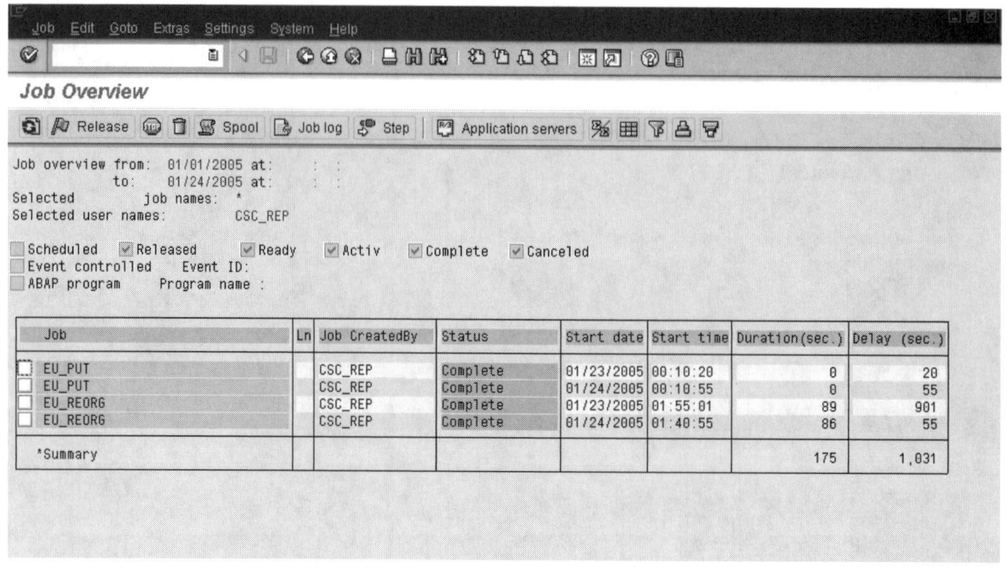

Job	Ln	Job CreatedBy	Status	Start date	Start time	Duration(sec.)	Delay (sec.)
EU_PUT		CSC_REP	Complete	01/23/2005	00:10:20	0	20
EU_PUT		CSC_REP	Complete	01/24/2005	00:10:55	0	55
EU_REORG		CSC_REP	Complete	01/23/2005	01:55:01	89	901
EU_REORG		CSC_REP	Complete	01/24/2005	01:40:55	86	55
*Summary						175	1,031

FIGURE 9-20 Job Overview list (Copyright by SAP AG)

Modifying Scheduled Jobs

A job that has been released can be canceled, which reverts its status to Scheduled. To do this, from the Job Overview list, select the job, and then, from the menu, choose Job | Released | Scheduled.

To release a scheduled job, from the menu, click on the Release Job button on the application toolbar.

From the Job Overview screen, administrators can also change the definition of a job that has not yet been processed. By selecting the job and then choosing Job | Change from the menu, authorized users can modify the start time, the steps, print lists, restrictions, and so on.

Other available options under the Job menu are as follows:

- *Copy* is used to copy a job with another name.
- *Move to different server* is the option available for changing the target host of a job, useful if there are no available background work processes in the server where it was defined to run.
- *Capture: active job* is a function to intervene in an active job in order to interrupt it or put it under debugging mode.
- *Check status* is useful in situations where, due to system failures, shutdowns, and the like, it's not clear that the status of the job is the real one.

For jobs that are already finished or have been canceled, you can display the job log by selecting the job and clicking on the Job Log function button on the application toolbar.

To display the details of individual jobs, select the job and double-click on it or select Job | Job Details from the menu. From the Job Display screen, you can look further at the rest of the job information like the steps, start time, repeat interval, print specifications, and so forth.

Deleting Jobs

Background jobs become very numerous in productive SAP installation and so do the number of job logs and job-related information. It is a good practice to periodically delete all the jobs that have already been processed and are no longer needed. Deleting jobs removes the associated job log and the internal table entries.

There are two ways to delete jobs: manually, by selecting jobs from the job list display and then choosing the Delete function from the menu, or automatically, by defining one or several jobs which periodically clean up old jobs. The standard ABAP report RSBTCDEL is used for this purpose.

You can create several variants that delete only those jobs specified in the selection criteria. You can find more information about other useful cleaning jobs in the SAP Notes.

When deleting jobs, be careful to determine which are predecessors of other jobs, because those jobs will no longer be started, although you have the option of rescheduling them by assigning a different start option.

Displaying Job Logs Every background job generates a job log after execution; job logs are only available for finished or canceled jobs. They record the messages that are issued by the programs specified in the job steps. The messages of the job log are language dependent. These logs can be very useful for finding the cause of errors, problems, and failures or for tracing important parts of a job. If no problem occurs in the job execution, the job log simply contains the start time and finish time of the job and an indication of the start of every job step.

Sometimes, depending on the nature of the executed program, job logs might also contain internal program information, such as statistical information.

These messages are output to the log file using the MESSAGE keyword of ABAP.

To display the log for a job, select the job from the Job Overview list and double-click on it or click on the Job Log button on the application toolbar.

For each job log a job file is created at the operating system level. These are usually located under the SAP system global directory (/usr/sap/<SID>/SYS/global) and are managed within the TemSe (temporary sequential objects) database. These log files should not be deleted manually in the operating system, because they are managed by the SAP system and their deletion can cause inconsistencies in the TemSe database. The log files are automatically deleted by the system when the jobs are deleted.

The Graphical Job Monitoring Tool

Within the CCMS monitoring functions, the SAP system includes a utility for graphical job monitoring. To display the job scheduling graphical monitor, from the main menu, select Tools | CCMS | Control/Monitoring | Job Scheduling Monitor or transaction code RZ01. Figure 9-21 shows an example of the SAP graphics display for monitoring jobs.

The graphical Job Monitor is quite useful for looking at the available resources for background, the status of jobs, estimated runtime, operation mode switch, and so forth.

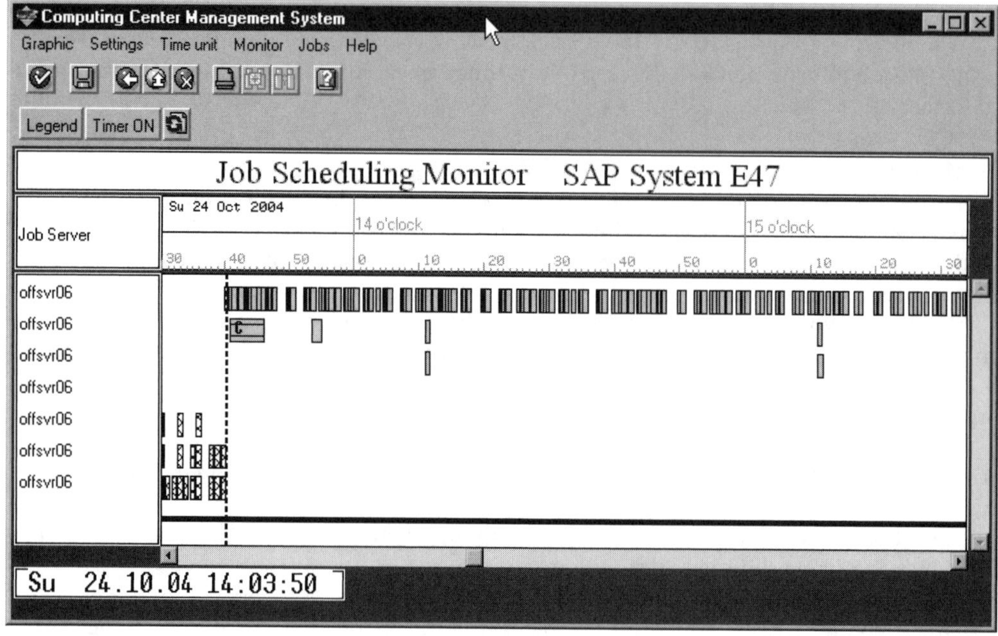

FIGURE 9-21 The Job Scheduling Monitor main screen (Copyright by SAP AG)

The background processing system manages a statistics database used for making estimates of job processing times. This is particularly useful with periodic jobs. For jobs without runtime statistics, the monitor shows an estimate with the minimum length.

In the left column of the display under Job Server, the monitor shows how many background work processes are available identified with the name of the host system.

The ruled horizontal line on top of the display shows the time unit used for monitoring. The broken vertical line shows the current time. The Monitoring tool shows the jobs as rectangles where you can click to display an overview with information about the particular job. The length of a job rectangle shows the approximate amount of time that the job requires for processing. For a finished job, it actually shows the time it took to complete.

The status of a job is indicated by its colors. To display a legend of the meaning of each color, click on the Key button on the display toolbar.

Watch out for long yellow bars with shading, which might indicate a problem in the background scheduler or blocked work processes. Many red bars with >>> shading (estimated runtime exceeded) might indicate that the program is not running correctly.

The graphical Job Monitoring tool can quickly give an idea of the load distribution among the available background work processes. From a general display, you can see if the system is executing jobs evenly among the available background servers.

The Job Monitor uses an additional Alert Monitor, which automatically reports any errors related to the background processing such as canceled jobs.

Since release 4.5 or the SAP Basis system, the background processing system was integrated into the new alert architecture and CCMS monitors.

To the right of the current time, the rectangles are for jobs that are waiting to be processed.

On the menu bar of the graphical display, there are several functions available to configure the monitoring utility, as well as for displaying and managing jobs. The time unit menu allows you to change the time measurements on the display. By default it is set to minutes, but you can compress or expand the display by selecting another time unit such as hours or days.

With the Jobs menu, administrators can display job logs and job overview information and can change the job information. To perform any function under this menu, first select the function and then click on the job. For example, you can select Check Job Status from the Jobs menu and then click on any job in the display. The system shows a dialog box indicating whether the job status is OK or not.

By clicking on the Timer On button, the system automatically updates the job display every three minutes.

Using the Monitor | Customize function, you can decide to set some standard values for displaying jobs under the monitoring tool. For example, you can decide how many hours you want to have for displaying canceled jobs, what the standard expected runtime assigned to jobs without statistics is, and so forth.

SAP Printing System

SAP provides its own spooling and printing system within the SAP applications to enable a uniform interface for all printing functions, independently of the system platforms supporting both the printing devices and the application services. This is one of the features of the traditional open client/server architecture of the SAP Basis system.

Printing is an issue within SAP systems that should be seriously considered and carefully planned in the early technical implementation phases any SAP solutions. After the SAP system starts in productive operation, system managers should monitor and manage all the operations related to printing.

Printing functions are intimately associated with and supported by the SAP spool work processes as well as by the operating system spool system.

When a SAP application server is configured for running at least one spool work process, then it's considered a *spool server.* This does not mean that the application server is not running other types of SAP services. However, there might be installations where there is a heavy printing demand, and one or more dedicated spool servers might be required.

These servers can be small, dedicated workstations with a high-speed network connection to the other servers, which are used for connecting and configuring the host printers used by the SAP system.

The following sections introduce the SAP spool system architecture, the management and definition of the printing devices and spool servers, and the spool system troubleshooting and planning considerations for a printing strategy.

Among the basic features of the SAP spool system are the following:

- Manages the output requests for printing, for the SAP communication server, and for the archiving devices
- Provides a uniform interface for different host spool systems

- Supports local, remote, and PC printing
- Supports multiple print and output devices, formats, paper types, and character sets

Additional features that in latest releases have improved the SAP spool system functionality are as follows:

- Better look of spool administration transactions
- Multiple spool work processes per instance
- Open interface to external output management system (OMS)
- Spool accounting exit
- Workload balancing
- Advanced management facilities

Printing from the user's point of view is covered in Chapter 4.

Concepts of the SAP Spool System Architecture

Printing in the SAP system is accomplished by the SAP spool system. The SAP spool system is in charge of handling all the system print requests, as well as managing the output for other SAP components such as the communication server, which can be used for EDI and fax devices or for the optical archiving systems. The SAP spool system can also be integrated with external output management systems (OMSs). More information about the *access method E* that implements the spool system's XOM interface to external OMSs can be found in the *SAP Printing Guide*, within the SAP Online Library, under the section *Computer Center Management System.*

Handling print requests basically involves the following:

- Formatting the data according to the specified print parameters and for a specific device type.
- Sending the formatted data for output to the host system where the printing or faxing device is connected. Figure 9-22 shows a diagram of the spool system operation. This diagram represents how several SAP system components can generate different types of information output ready for printing, such as reports, mail messages, lists, and graphics. When users request printing for the output generated, they are actually sending the request to the SAP spool system. This process is known as generating a *spool request*. These spool requests can either be sent to the host spool, or they can be held in the SAP spool system for later printing.

When a spool request is actually sent to a printer or fax device, it is first passed to the SAP spool work process, which is in charge of formatting the output and then sending this print job to the host spool system.

If the SAP application server where the spool work process is running and the host system are actually the same server, then this is considered *local printing;* when these systems are different, then it's considered *remote printing.* A special type of remote printing is when the host system is a Windows PC running the SAPLPD transfer program; this type

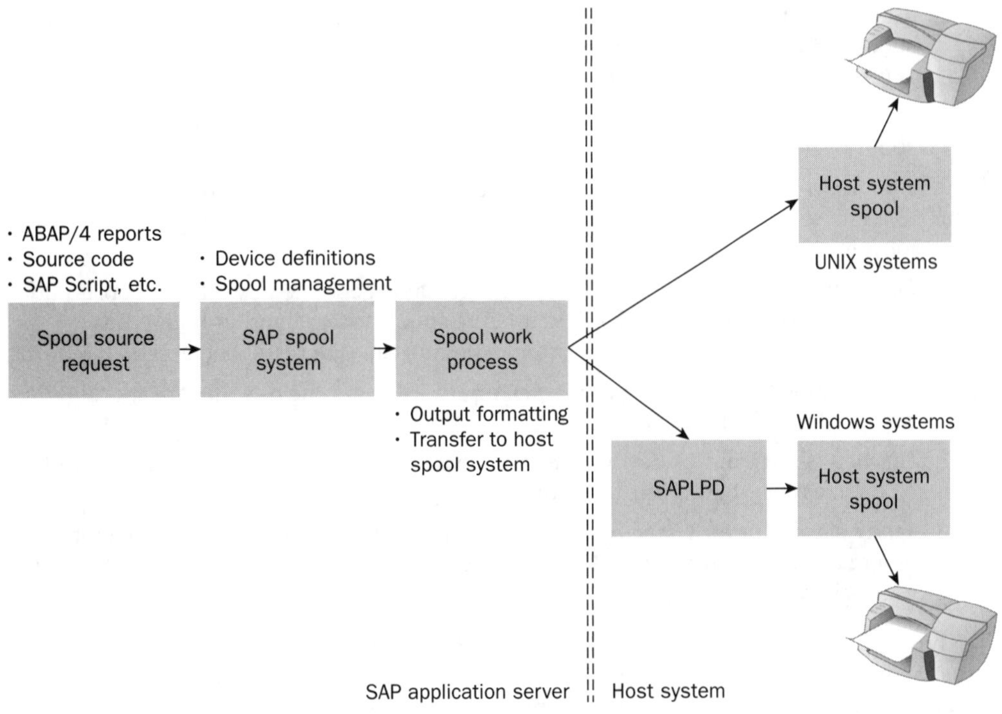

FIGURE 9-22 The SAP spool system operation

of printing is known as *PC printing*. These types of connections are important for defining the output devices within the spool system and are defined using the SAP access methods.

Printers or other output devices defined in the SAP spool system have a primary spool server designated—that is, a server with one or more spool work processes running on it. This server is in charge of processing spool requests for those printers and devices. If the primary spool server becomes unavailable, it is possible to specify an alternate spool server in order to process the spool requests from those printers and devices.

The host spool system is the ultimate component in charge of sending the print job to the physical printer. This is basically how the printing system works in SAP WAS. However, even if it might seem very simple, it is actually a little bit more complicated, especially when defining new device types, print controls, formats, and so on. The following is a closer look at the basic spool and printing system concepts:

- *Spool request* is the SAP naming convention for *output job* or *print job*, but in SAP terms, a *spool request* is made up of the spool request record (administrative information to manage the print jobs), the data that are sent to the printing device, and the actual output requests. A spool request is not necessarily meant just for printing; it can also be generated for other communication or archiving devices.
- *Output requests* are the component of the spool request which actually formats the output data and sends it to the host spool system to be printed. You can submit

multiple output requests for a single spool request. You can, for example, have a spool request printed on different printers or reprint a request if it could not be printed successfully the first time.

- *Access methods* are how the SAP spool work process communicates with the host spool system.
- *SAP Script* is SAP's own text editor, which is used for creating and formatting documentation in SAP, such as online help, forms, implementation guide texts, mail messages, and so on.
- *List output* is a generic name for the output that is generated by ABAP reports and that is not formatted using SAP Script. The spool system handles both types of output: that generated by SAP Script text editor and the results of an ABAP report.
- *Forms* define the page layout for texts, report lists, and the like that are specially prepared for display or for printing.
- *Layout sets* are maps of the output pages that specify where the text is placed (filled) on a page and what its attributes are.
- *TemSe* stands for the *temporary sequential* object database, which is a special place where the SAP system stores the spool request data and other SAP objects such as the background job logs.

The SAP spool system is not only responsible for handling the spool and output requests, but it's also the SAP component containing the functions for managing output devices, device types, device drivers and initialization, device formats, character sets, and so forth. It's actually a complete interface which converts all types of SAP output into the required output device format.

The Spool Work Process

Every printer or other type of output device defined in the spool system requires the availability of an associated spool work process, which will take care of handling all spool requests for the specific devices. It's also possible to have the same printer defined (with different names) for being managed by different spool work processes. This is sometimes done for contingency situations when an application server might be stopped.

As introduced both in Chapter 2 and in the previous section, the spool work process is one of several types of SAP work processes running on an application server that formats the data in a spool request and then sends it to the host spool system.

Actually, the spool request contains a reference to the data, the specific output device (printer), and the printing format. The data itself is kept in the TemSe database.

When the spool system sends the request for actual printing, it then generates an *output request* (or print request), which is handled by the spool work process. To generate the output request, the spool work process converts the spool request into a device-specific (printer-specific) output stream. Performing this conversion requires the following:

- Translating (resolving) SAP device print controls into actual printer commands, adding initialization strings corresponding to specific device types
- If needed, converting the character set used within the SAP system to the character set understood by the output device

- Formatting the data for generating the output request using the printer driver assigned to the device type for SAP Script output

The spool work process will finally send the data to the host spool system, and, in the case of PC printing, to the SAPLPD program, which communicates directly with the Windows print manager.

The SAP profile parameter that controls the number of spool work processes per instance is *rdisp/wp_no_spo*, which can be maintained from the CCMS instance profile maintenance utility.

You can define more than one spool work process per server even if there is only one instance installed in the application server. One big advantage of enabling the definition of more than one spool work process is the possibility of sending parallel output requests from the same SAP instance.

Having several spool work processes per instance avoids bottlenecks caused by such things as communication problems between spool work processes and printing devices (PCs, network printers, LAN connections, and others) that could be temporarily turned off or unavailable. With multiple spool work processes, these other requests can be handled by additional free spool work processes.

Before SAP Basis (R/3) release 4.0, the spool server assignment and spool server work process were static, so that each device was assigned to a specific server that only had one spool work process. Since release 4.0, it is possible to implement spool load balancing by using spool server groups. This is known as *dynamic spool assignment*.

Spool Servers, Hierarchies, and Load Balancing

Dynamic spool server assignment was introduced with R/3 release 4.0, allowing for printing load balancing. *Spool servers* provide greater flexibility in defining and configuring printing systems in SAP installations. Spool servers can be configured on the basis of different attributes, and there is also the possibility of defining different types of spool servers. There are two types of general spool servers:

- Real or physical
- Logical

A logical server is mapped directly or indirectly to a real spool server. Logical servers are given a name pointing to another logical server or to a real server. Relationships between spool servers, whether logical or real, define different hierarchies.

A hierarchy is a dependency relationship of different levels that define priorities when spool requests are being managed by the spool servers within the hierarchy.

A hierarchy is established when a spool server, whether logical or real, is assigned an alternative spool server. Hierarchies can be as complex as required.

There is a relationship between a spool server and its alternate spool server. If the server is logical, then there is an additional relationship between the logical server and the server it is pointing to, which can also be either physical or logical. Output requests assigned to logical servers are processed by the real server.

For example, a SAP system made of two application servers, ntsap_NT1_00 and ntsap _NT2_00, has two logical spool servers Logical_ NT1 and Logical_NT2. These logical servers are defined as *nonexclusive spool servers*, have Production print (type P) as their server class, and are mapped to real spool servers ntsap_NT1_00 and ntsap_NT2_00, respectively. Additionally, logical server Logical_NT1 has Logical_NT2 as an alternate server. Figure 9-23 shows the hierarchy relationship. The horizontal relationship represents the mapping between a logical server and another server (either logical or real). The vertical relationship links the logical server with an alternate server (either logical or real).

The definition and configuration of logical spool servers can be performed and tested on development system, then transported to production systems at a later time with minimal and quick adjustments.

When logical servers are defined as *nonexclusive spool servers*, they are enabled for the process of load balancing, which means that the system will take into consideration both the logical server and the alternate server when calculating and finding the most appropriate server for processing output requests.

Server Selection

When the SAP printing system is going to process an output request, one of the steps to be performed is selecting the spool server. By default, SAP commonly has the static selection option for choosing the spool server, meaning that this is a constant definition and does not allow for load balancing.

Using dynamic spool server selection, the system can automatically balance the load of the spool processes by means of assigning alternate servers.

Dynamic selection of servers has certain limitations when using local SAP printing, such as access methods C and L. Refer to the latest SAP Notes and the online printing guide for current status.

Defining Spool Server

To create a new spool server, go to the main spool administration menu by selecting Tools | CCMS | Spool | Spool Administration from the initial menu (transaction code SPAD). Then select Configuration | Spool Server or click on the Spool Server pushbutton. Switch to change mode by clicking on the Change icon. Then click on the Create icon on the application toolbar or select Spool Server | Create from the menu.

Fields on this new screen have the following function:

- *Server name.* This is the name of the server. You can assign any name, although SAP systems normally default to hostname_SID_instance_ number—for example, k2p001_K2P_00.
- *Short text.* This is located right below the system name for entering a brief description of the server being defined.

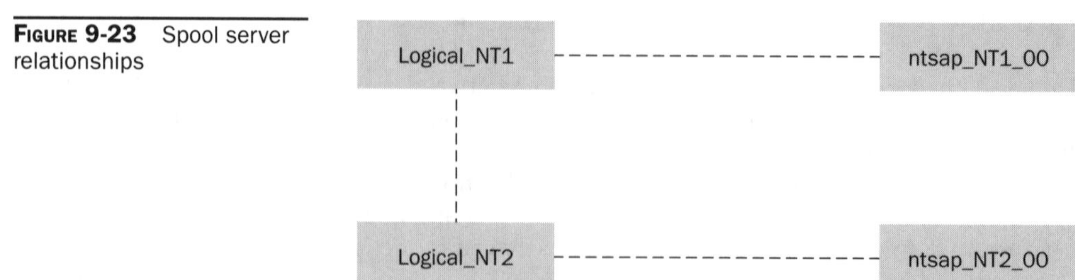

FIGURE 9-23 Spool server relationships

- *Server class.* Indicates the class of server. There are many values that basically classify the servers according to its intended used. Figure 9-24 includes some of them that you see when you click on the possible entries list.
- *Logical server.* Selecting this flag defines the spool server as a logical spool server. This selection will force users to define the Mapping field that will appear when the ENTER is pressed or the definition is saved.
- *Mapping.* Only appears when defining logical servers, in which case users must select the server to which a logical server must be mapped.
- *Allow load balancing.* Activating this option removes the static spool server selection. By default all output devices are handled exclusively by a single spool server. This flag is useful when the primary spool server is unavailable, because the system can redirect the spool requests to an alternative server. This flag is also selected for enabling printing load balancing. The system will look for the best or least loaded spool server based on the defined spool server hierarchy.
- *Alt. Server.* This is the name of the alternate spool server. It can be used by the system if the primary spool server assigned is not available, so it will be able to process pending spool requests. This alternate spool server can be either real or logical.

Managing Spool Requests

There are several ways of calling the spool request management functions:

- From the main menu, select Tools | CCMS | Spool | Output Controller.
- From any menu, select System | Services | Output Control.
- Directly enter transaction code SP01 in the command field.

Figure 9-25 shows an example of this screen.

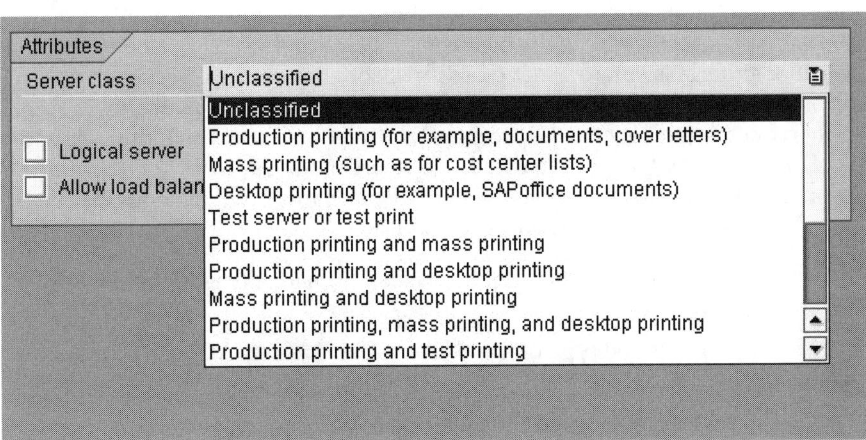

FIGURE 9-24 Server classes (Copyright by SAP AG)

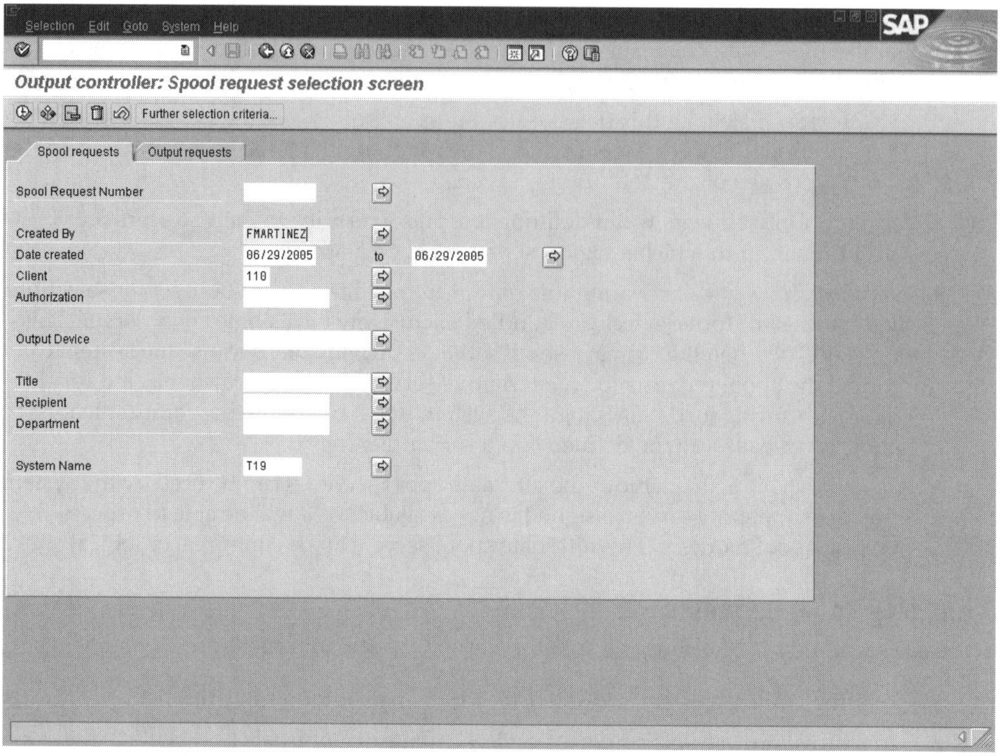

FIGURE 9-25 Initial output controller display (SP01 transaction) (Copyright by SAP AG)

This initial output controller display behaves like a selection screen, where you can search spool requests by spool request number, spool request name (in the extended view), user name, date, client, and so forth. By default, the screen always presents the logon user name, the logon client, and the system current date—but these parameters can all be overwritten. You can also select further selection using the button Further Selection Criteria.

Once the selection criteria is entered, just press ENTER or click on the Overview (Continue) icon on the standard toolbar to display a list of spool requests matching the criteria. The spool requests that have been successfully printed and for which the user had selected the flag *Delete after print* are automatically deleted from the system, and therefore will not appear on this list. On this screen, the system displays information about the spool requests arranged by columns. These columns are as follows:

- *Spool no.* The spool request number as it has been automatically assigned by the system.
- *Type.* Shows an icon with the type of spool request, such as ABAP lists, forms and so on.
- *Date.* Date in which the spool request was generated.
- *Time.* Time when the spool request was generated.

- *Status.* Indicates what the status is of the spool request. The system can display the following output statuses:
  - For this spool request no output request (order to print) has been generated.
  - *Wait.* The output request is waiting to be processed by the spool system. It has not yet been sent to the host spool system.
  - *Process.* The spool work process is formatting the spool request to be sent to the printer.
  - *Print.* The host system spool is processing (printing) the SAP output request.
  - *Compl.* The output request has been completed and successfully printed.
  - *<F5>.* This status indicates that there is more than one output request for the same spool request. You can double-click on this status field to show all the associated output requests or, alternatively, select the check box to the left and click on the Output Request pushbutton on the application toolbar.
  - *Problem.* A problem has occurred during the output request processing. The printing might have been generated; however, it might not be correct or correspond actually to the expected printed format.
  - *Error.* There is a severe printing error. No output request is generated at the physical printer.
  - *Archive.* For spool requests that were sent to an archiving device. The spool request has been processed by the spool system and is waiting for archiving.
- *Pages.* Indicates the number of pages of the output request.
- *Title.* Displays the title of the spool request if the user entered one when submitting a spool request; otherwise the system by default shows as the title the type of request, the device name, the program, and the first three characters of the user name.

From the Spool Request screen, you can perform several useful functions as introduced in the following sections.

Printing and Displaying Spool Requests

To create an output request (to actually send to the printer device), select the spool request from the list by marking the check box to the left of the entry, and then just click on the Print icon in the application toolbar or, from the menu, select Spool Request | Print.

There is also the option of sending the output to the printer after actually displaying the spool request on the screen. To do this, from the spool request list, select the entry by marking the check box, and click on the Display icon. The system will show the Spool Request <number> screen.

From this new screen, you also have a print icon in the application toolbar. On the Display of Spool Request screen, you can specify displaying the spool request in graphical, raw, or hexadecimal format by clicking on the corresponding pushbuttons on the application tool bar, except for spool types.

By default, the maximum number of lines displayed in this mode is 1000 or, alternatively, 10 pages of a SAP Script document. You can, however, specify a different number by selecting Settings in the application toolbar.

Displaying and Modifying the Spool Request Attributes

When in the Spool Request List screen, you can display the attributes for any request by double-clicking on the entry, or selecting it and clicking on the Attributes icon in the toolbar. The spool system includes several types of attributes to show *spool attributes, output attributes*, and *TemSe attributes*. You can toggle between the attributes by clicking on the corresponding tabstrip. Figure 9-26 shows a screen with spool request attributes.

From the attributes screen, you can modify the spool request attributes if you want to send the spool request to the printer again (generating a new output request). And, as an interesting point, notice that the attributes display includes an authorization field which can be used to limit which users can access the output request for displaying or printing it again. The Output Attributes tabstrip includes information such as the number of copies, priority, cover page, or the Storage mode.

Displaying Output Request Log Files

If any errors occur during the processing of the spool requests, you can display the log information from the Spool Request List screen. To do that, double-click on the entry to select it, and then select the option Display Log. You can display more information about the error by clicking on the More Info pushbutton on the application toolbar.

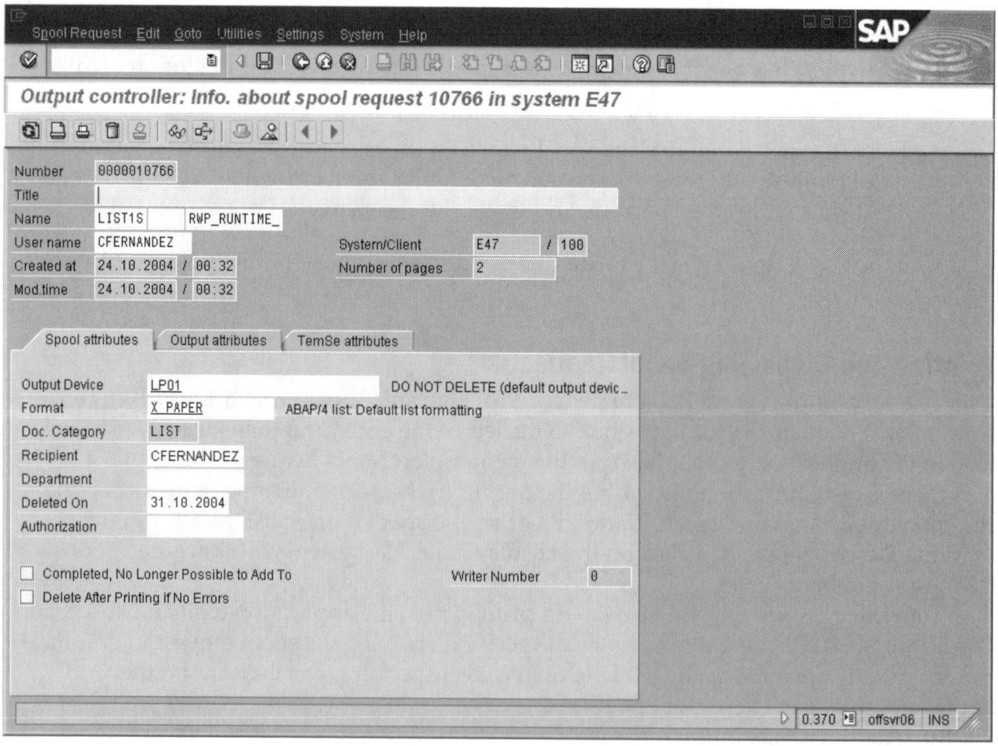

FIGURE 9-26 Spool request attributes display (Copyright by SAP AG)

Deleting Spool Requests

There are several ways to delete spool requests:

- Automatically, by setting the flag Delete After Print when creating output requests.
- Interactively, from the spool request list, by selecting the required entries and clicking on the Delete icon.
- Calling the Spool | Spool Administration menu from the CCMS initial screen, then selecting the Administration tabstrip and clicking the Delete Old Spool Request pushbutton. The system displays a new screen with several deletion SPAD transaction code.
- With the periodic background job RSPO0041. Job RSPO0041 manages the TemSe database, with options for removing any spool data file that is corrupt or orphan.

When deleting a spool request, the system removes

- The spool request itself and associated table entries
- The print file
- All output requests that were generated for that spool request.

Connecting Printers to the Operating Systems Spool

Before you can define a new printing device in the SAP system, the printer must be physically installed and configured in the host operating system that is running the host spool system, and thus managing the spool request sent to that device.

Printers can be connected to several types of operating systems: UNIX systems, Microsoft Windows platforms, AS/400, and others, and can be connected either locally (physically attached to those servers) or remotely (through the network). SAP WAS supports all those types of connections, although the concept is slightly different.

From the point of view of the access methods, *local printing* means that the spool work process is running on the same server as the host operating system spool, and *remote printing* is when the servers are different and connected through the network.

A third way, known by SAP as *PC printing*, is when printers are configured on Windows PC systems through the print manager. There is also the option of *local PC printing* even when the printers are not defined at the SAP level.

At the same time, there are many vendors, models, flavors, print protocols, and so on for the printers. Not all understand the same printing language or support the same printing features and possibilities. Before you can define a new printer device within the SAP system, it's absolutely critical that you define, configure, and test the printer on the host system where the printer is connected. Only then can you be sure that the printer can be defined and will function properly within SAP.

For setting up printers on the operating system spool, every hardware vendor and operating system has its procedure. The SAP official online help documentation (*SAP Printing Guide*) includes instructions on how to set up printers in most of the supported operating systems. You can look in this documentation or the official administration manual of your server operating system for more information.

When printers are not directly connected to the host systems but are connected remotely to the network, commonly they use the TCP/IP protocol. In these cases, you must ensure that the printer is accessed by the network and test that it prints correctly. For instance, their IP address must be included in the *hosts* server file or in the domain name servers.

As requirements for proceeding with the definition of printers within SAP systems, the following information is needed:

- Printer or spool queue name at the host system
- Model and type of printing device
- Printing protocol supported: PCL, POSTSCRIPT, and so forth.

Defining SAP Printer Devices

For the SAP system, a printer is defined as an output device, just like a fax or optical archive equipment.

The SAP system includes an extensive spool administration transaction for defining and managing all aspects of printing configuration and output devices. To call this transaction, from the initial SAP menu, select Tools | CCMS | Spool | Spool Administration or, alternatively, enter transaction code SPAD in the command field. Figure 9-27 shows the initial Spool Administration screen.

You have many options to define how and what to see in the initial screen for spool administration: system managers accustomed to previous releases can use the old initial administration screen or can decide to switch to the new one. To select the initial Spool Administration screen that will be displayed when calling transaction SPAD, from the menu Settings | Selection Screen select the option required. By default the system shows the simple administration screen, and you can get additional options by clicking on the Extended Administration or Full Administration pushbuttons on the application toolbar.

The initial administration screen has several parts that will show more or fewer components depending on whether simple, extended, or full administration is selected. In the simple administration mode, you have a basic screen with two tabstrips: Devices/Servers and Admin.

Options for the Devices server simple administration screen include four items that are the only options for output devices:

- *Output devices.* This option is used for displaying, managing, and defining devices.
- *Spool servers.* This option shows all spool servers defined in your system and is also used for creating new spool servers or deleting existing ones.
- *Access methods.* This option shows all possible access methods, and can display devices or output requests for each existing method.
- *Destination host.* This option displays a list of destination hosts, associated devices, and possible errors.

When full administration is selected, the screen includes additional options for configuration of device types, output management systems, character sets, and text pools for title pages. You can find extensive information about extended options in the SAP online documentation *SAP Printing Guide.*

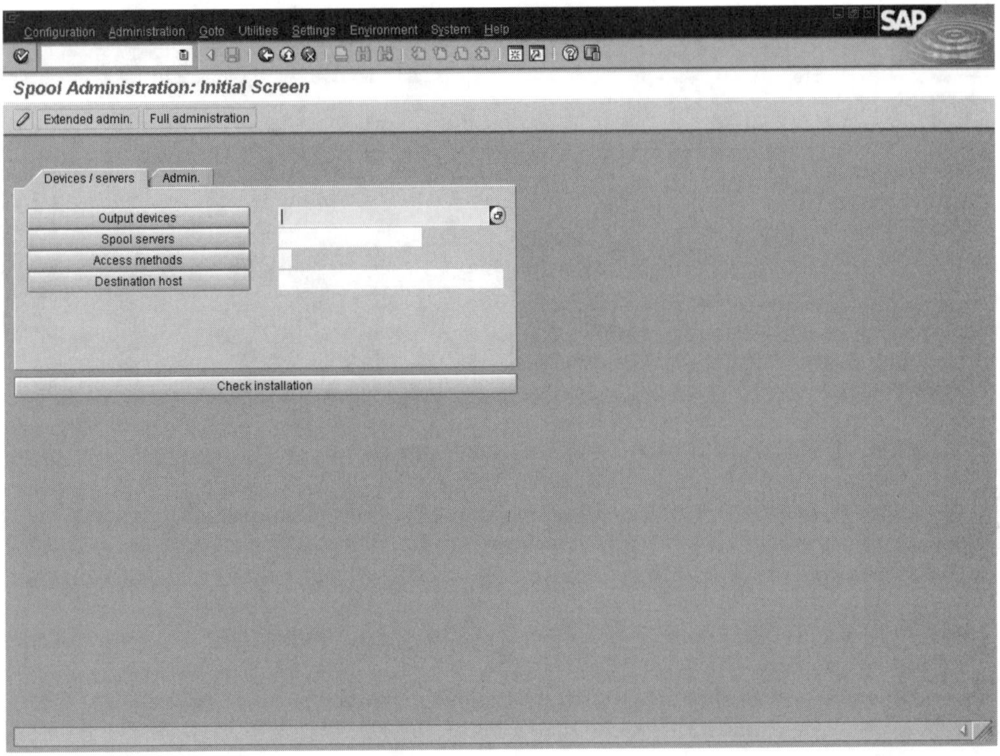

FIGURE 9-27 The Spool Administration initial screen (SPAD transaction) (Copyright by SAP AG)

The Administration tabstrip includes four pushbutton functions that are used for administrative purposes, including deleting old spool requests, performing checks and consistency checks of the spool system, and displaying a list of print requests.

In this section, only the process of creating a new printer—a new output device—is explained.

To change or create a new printer, from the Spool Administration initial screen, click on the Devices/Server tabstrip and then click on the Output Devices pushbutton, or select Configuration | Output Devices from the menu bar. On this screen, select the change mode by clicking on the Change icon on the application toolbar. The system will display the list of current output devices. On this screen, click on the Create icon for defining a new output device. Figure 9-28 shows the new display.

To define a new output device you must at least fill up the required entry fields. Notice that the system already has filled up some default values.

Fields on this screen are as follows:

- *Output device.* It's the name of the device as it will be known to SAP users.
- *Short name.* You can enter a four-character short name.
- *Device type.* Corresponds to the device model for the printer, fax, archive, or other output device. You can click on the possible entries arrow to show a list of available device types as included in the standard system. If the printer you want to connect

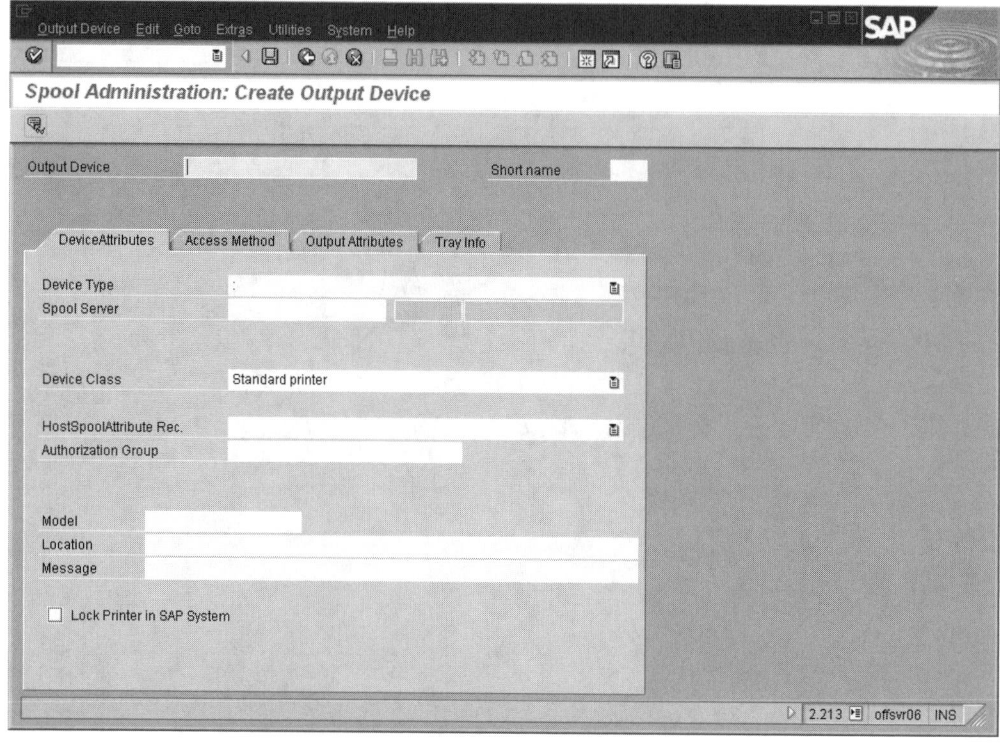

FIGURE 9-28 Screen for creating new output devices (Copyright by SAP AG)

does not exist and there is no compatible model, you might have to define your own device type.

- *Spool server.* It's the name of the SAP instance running a spool work process. If there is more than one SAP spool server, you can select it from the available list by clicking on the possible entries arrow.
- *Device class.* Shows the device type. Figure 9-29 shows the drop down list with the available device classes. For printers, which are the most common class, select Standard Printer.
- *Authorization group.* Can be used to specify an authorization group name to protect the device using the authorization system.
- *Model name.* This name is for documentation purposes only.
- *Location.* This field is intended for informative purposes only. You can enter a brief description here about the printer and where it's located. This is an optional field.
- *Message.* Together with the previous Location field, this is another field for informative purposes that can be used for administrators to display a special message when users select this printer as the output device. It's an optional field.

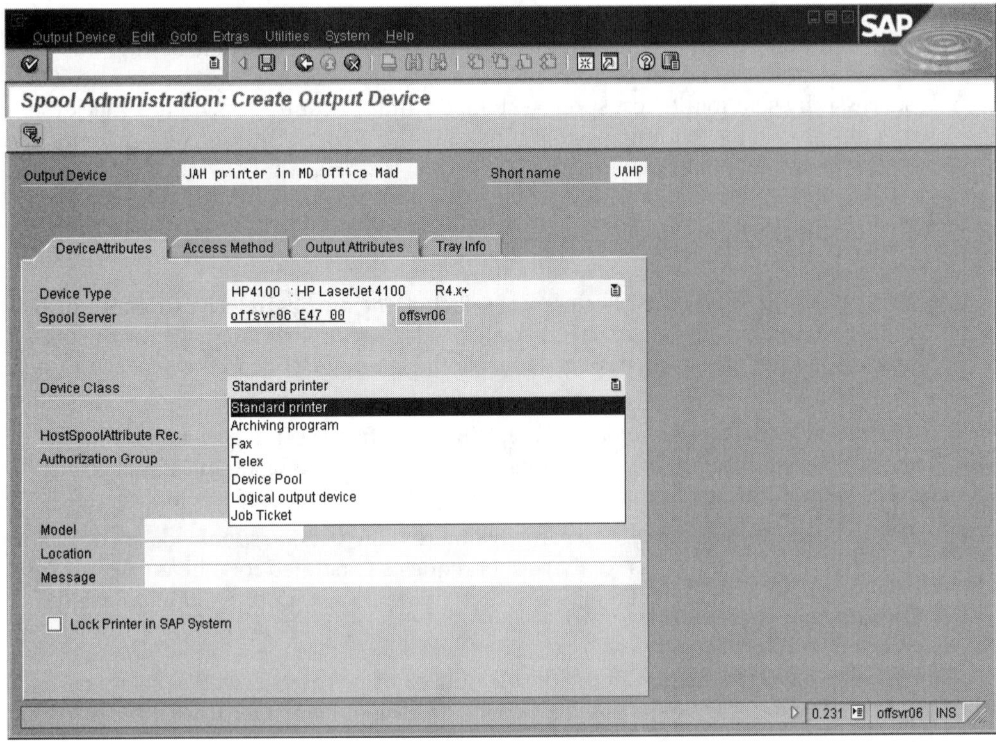

FIGURE 9-29 Dialog box with available device classes (Copyright by SAP AG)

When it is left blank, the system will show the informative text as entered in the Location field.

- *Lock printer in SAP system.* As an administrator, you can use this field to temporarily lock a printer from being used within SAP.
- *Access Method tabstrip.* The access method specifies the communication path between the SAP spool system and the host spool system: it's the method used by the SAP spool to transfer the data to be printed to the host spool system. Access methods specify how and when the print formatting is processed for the subsequent transfer and processing by the host spool system. You can display a list of the available access methods by clicking on the possible entries list arrow of the field Host Spool Access Method. Find on the following section an explanation of different access methods, which is of critical importance for configuring the right printing strategy and which also impacts heavily printing performance.
- *Host Printer.* It's the name of the printer exactly as it's defined at the operating system level. In Windows systems, it might be something like LPT1:, LPT2:, or even a UNC name such as \\myserver\myprinter.
- *Host Name.* This is a display field which shows on which host server the spool work process is running.

- *Do Not Query Host Spooler for Output Status.* When this option is set, the SAP spool system does not request the output status to the host spool system. Setting this option might be good for performance reasons; however, once the print request is successfully sent to the host spool system, the output controller will not check the actual status of the printing, so that if there is any error at the host system spool, the SAP system will not know.

Clicking on the Output Attributes tabstrip in the Spool Administration screen, you have some further options such as the following:

- *SAP cover page.* When this check box is selected, the output device by default prints out a SAP title page (a cover sheet). You can also specify the language for the text included in the title or cover page entering the language code in the *SAP cover page language.*
- *Monitor using monitoring infrastructure.* When this flag is set, the system monitors the spool requests. Some caution must be exercised when using this flag, because massive monitoring of output devices can affect the system's performance.
- *Process requests sequentially.* You can have more than just one spool work process for a server. If you want to assure that spool requests generated for a given device are processed sequentially, set this flag. Otherwise spool requests could be reordered during processing.

Other options include the possibility of selecting color printing as well as selecting advances printing modes (duplex, both sides, etc.) and even the printer trays.

Logical Output Devices and Device Pools

It is also possible to define logical printer devices. Logical printer devices are virtual devices that must be mapped against existing defined printer devices in the system.

When creating a logical printer device, what the system actually defines is a device of access type P or Pool Device, mapped against only one physical device. In this sense, a Logical Device can be considered as a Pool Device with one and only one physical device assigned.

About Pools

Device pools have the purpose of grouping devices of the same type (for example, PostScript printers) using a unique device name, thus permitting the spool requests directed to that pool to be printed by any of the devices assigned to the pool.

This type of device definition is completely equivalent to well-known logical printer queues of many operating systems, where a print job directed to the logical queue is output by any of the physical queues defined for the logical queue.

In SAP systems, what is assigned to the pool is not the physical printer itself but the output device, which can be either logical or physical. When the device is a logical device, it must be directly or indirectly mapped to a physical device.

A device pool covers two basic functions of the printing devices:

- Sending spool requests to all printing devices associated with a device pool
- Balancing the load of print requests among the devices that make up the device pool, avoiding possible spool bottlenecks

Defining a Logical Printer Device

To define a logical printer device, from the initial Spool Administration screen select the option Output Devices.

Then click on the Create icon from the application toolbar. The system displays the Spool Administration: Create Output Device screen as shown in Figure 9-28.

Proceed as usual, by filling in all required fields; then choose as device class Logical Output Device. This will change the screen layout by modifying the options in the Device Attributes tabstrip and removing others such as the Access Method tabstrip. Figure 9-30 shows the appearance of this screen. In the new field Map To, enter an existing device on your SAP system and save the new definition.

Defining a Device Pool

To define a device pool, select Output Devices from the Spool Administration initial screen. Then click on the Create icon from the menu bar. The system displays the Spool Administration: Create Output Device screen. Fill in the required fields and select P as access method and select Device Pool as Device class. The system will change the tabstrips by displaying a new one known as Device Pool, which must contain at least one device. See Figure 9-31.

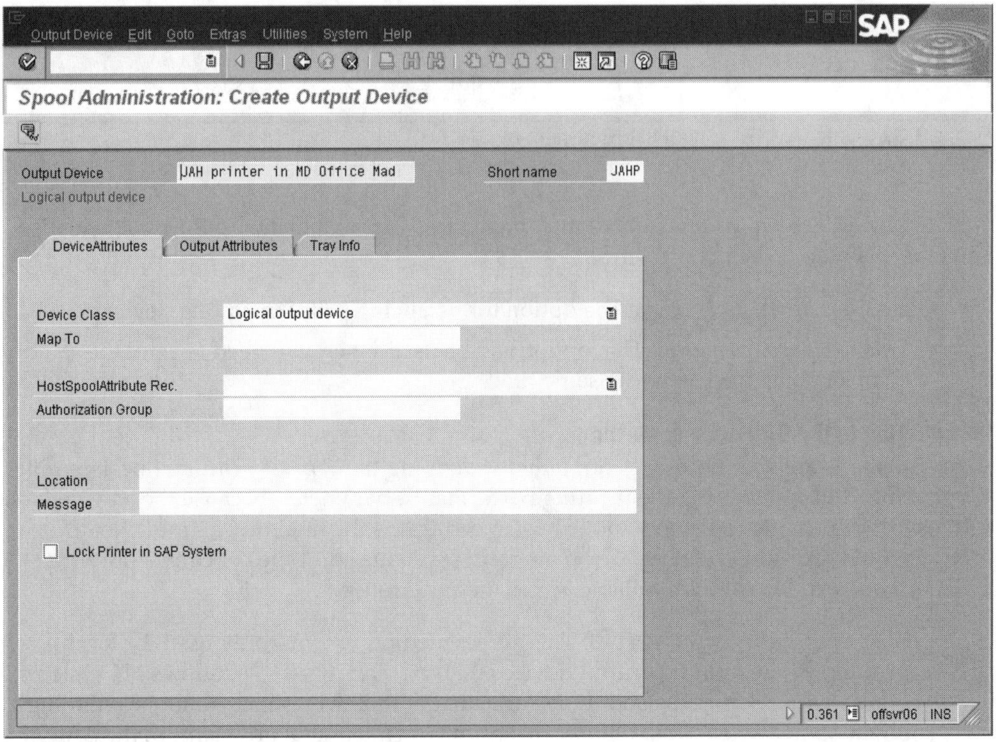

FIGURE 9-30 Defining logical output devices (Copyright by SAP AG)

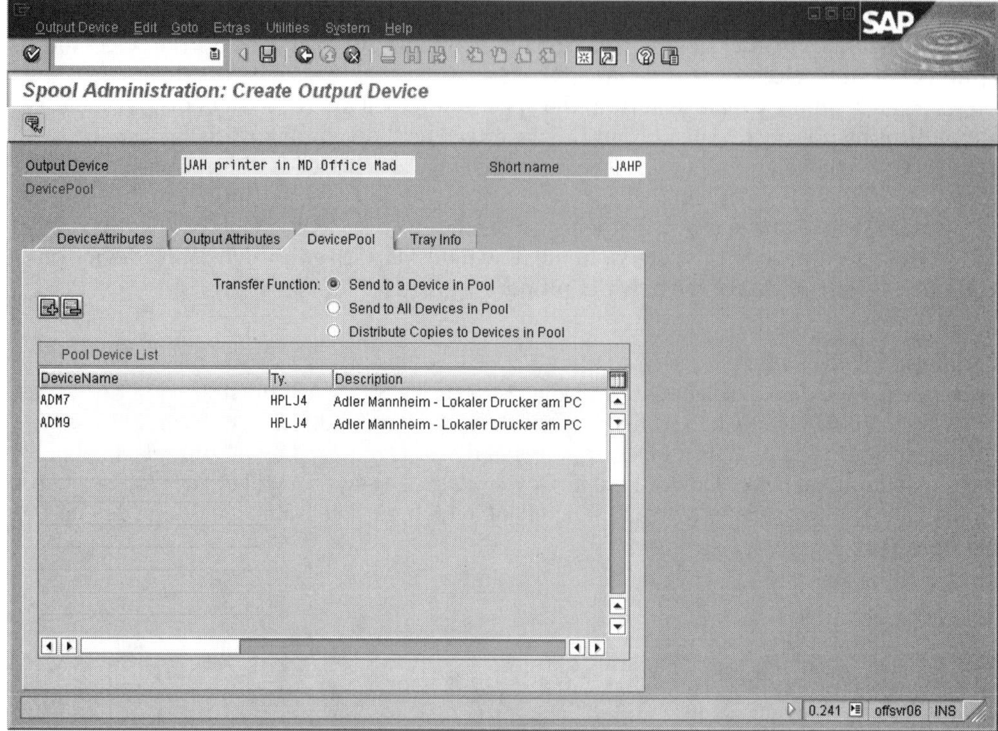

FIGURE 9-31 Entering device pool list (Copyright by SAP AG)

On the new screen, you have to define the devices that will make up the pool, and also you must also select the pool function:

- *Send to a device pool.* This is the option for balancing printing among devices.
- *Send to all devices in pool.* This option can be used when you need to send the same print job to all devices at the same time.

Introduction to the SAP Access Methods

Access methods are very necessary not only for defining the type of printing (local, remote, PC printing), but for defining the printing performance parameter, because the way the data is transferred from the SAP spool to the host spool affects the final throughput. Not all access methods are supported by all the operating systems and types of connections.

A brief description of the available access methods follows:

- *C—Direct operating system call.* This access method is commonly used for local printing when defining output devices that are managed by Windows NT systems. The spool work process and the print manager that drives the printer are running on the same server. This is applicable even to printers that are *shared* in the LAN. Behaves similarly to access method L in UNIX systems. Access method C does not allow for requesting status information from the SAP spool system to the Windows NT print manager.

- *I—Archive service.* This access method is for defining an output device to be used as an archiving system. You can define a printer as an archive service. When doing this, and users send documents to the spool system, these documents can be transferred directly both to the archive system as well as to the actual printer.
- *L—Print locally via LP/LPR with signal.* The SAP spool work process will use a command to transfer the spool requests to the host spooler. The actual commands, such as lp or lpr, are operating system dependent, and are set in the SAP instance profile parameter *rspo/host_spool/print.* Both the spool work process and the host spool are running on the same server.
- *P—Device pool.* This special access method is used for defining device pools. With device pools, output requests can be sent to more than one printer at a time, and they can be used for defining several printers to perform automatic print load balancing. Devices that compose a device pool must be *local*, which means that they must be accessible from the host spooler or print manager where the spool server resides.
- *U—Print on LPDHOST via Berkeley protocol.* This access method is used for implementing remote printing or even PC printing when the SAP spool work process is running on a different host than the server where the printer is connected. With access method U, the spool work process will transfer the formatted data to the target host spooler through the network link. Since there is the possibility of printing large volume jobs, this method is not recommended for slow WAN connections, because it might slow down the processing of other print requests. This method can be used for UNIX and Windows printers; however, it is not supported in some of the operating systems.
- *S—Print on LPDHOST via SAP protocol.* This access method is used both for remote printing and PC printing. It uses a special SAP communication protocol that includes data compression, transmission of the SAP title, and so forth. Access method S might be slower than method U and is mainly used for printers that are defined using the SAPWIN device type.
- *X—SAP comm.* This method is used for devices which are managed by the SAP spool system and handled by the SAP communication server, such as FAX, Telex, and EDI.
- *F—Print on front end (locally) via SAPLPD.* This is a variant for local or front-end printing. This access method is designed for those end users who require printing on their local (or default) assigned or attached printer, which has not been defined on the SAP system as an output device. In these cases the SAP dialog work process handling the user process sends the formatted request to the SAPLPD or lpd process, according to the type of workstation. If the SAPLPD process was not previously started, the system will start it automatically. More information about local PC printing can be found in a later section.
- *Z—Command interface spool exit.* This method exists for compatibility reasons but is being replaced by access method E from release 4.0 onward.

- *E—Command interface/RFC interface to OMS.* This access method is designed for output requests that will be sent to an output management system (OMS) that is compatible with R/3 printing commands.

Troubleshooting Printing Problems

The following is a list of possible steps to perform when you notice printing problems in the system. These problems can be very different: no printing at all, slow printing, printing garbage, and so forth.

In any case, you should

- Check and monitor the spool work process from the Process Overview transaction as well as from the operating system spool (print daemon or print manager). Also, check that the message server is working properly.
- Particularly, check that you can print normally from your operating system.
- Find which printer is causing the problems. Use transaction SP01 System | Services | Output Controller. Check the output request attributes, the log files, and the size of the print job.
- For remote printers, check the network connection.
- If a print job has been printed out but contains unreadable characters, check whether the device type is the most appropriate, whether the printer is working in emulation mode, and what the access method is for the device.
- When nothing is output at the printer and the output controller is in wait status, check the system developer traces and the system log and look for time-out messages. Check that all application servers running spool work processes are reachable.
- If the job has status Complete or Problem and nothing is output at the physical printer, it might be related to a wrong output device definition, a problem in the host spooler, the physical printer, or the SAPLPD transfer program. Carefully check the access method.
- If printing is very slow, possible causes might be lost indexes in the spool tables, too many spool table entries, slow WAN connections, or incorrectly defined access methods. Often you will need to review the printing strategy about distribution of output devices in several application servers according to their expected volume and size of print jobs. Refer to the SAP online documentation and the SAP Service Marketplace about some interesting planning strategies for the spool system.

As an additional analysis method, carefully check the spool profile parameters.

SAP Printing System Administration Tasks

The SAP printing system and associated tasks are a subset of those general administration tasks for the daily operation of the SAP system.

SAP system managers should be in charge of the following tasks:

- Periodically checking and monitoring the spool system, both at SAP and at the operating system level. Use the CCMS and workload monitor to check the spool work process performance.

- Deleting old spool requests or scheduling the background job which automatically deletes them.
- Defining new printers, device types, and other device elements.
- Using the statistical information of the system for fine-tuning the planning strategy.
- Troubleshooting the spool system.

From the initial Spool Administration screen, there is a pushbutton in the lower part of the screen, within the Administration box, which can be used to check the consistency of the spool system. Call this function by clicking on the Consistency Check of Spool Database pushbutton.

Spool System Instance Profile Parameters

To display the instance profile parameters directly related to the spool system, from the initial Spool Administration screen, select Utilities | Display SAPPARAM. Figure 9-32 shows an example. If you need to change any of these parameters, use the profile maintenance functions available within the CCMS.

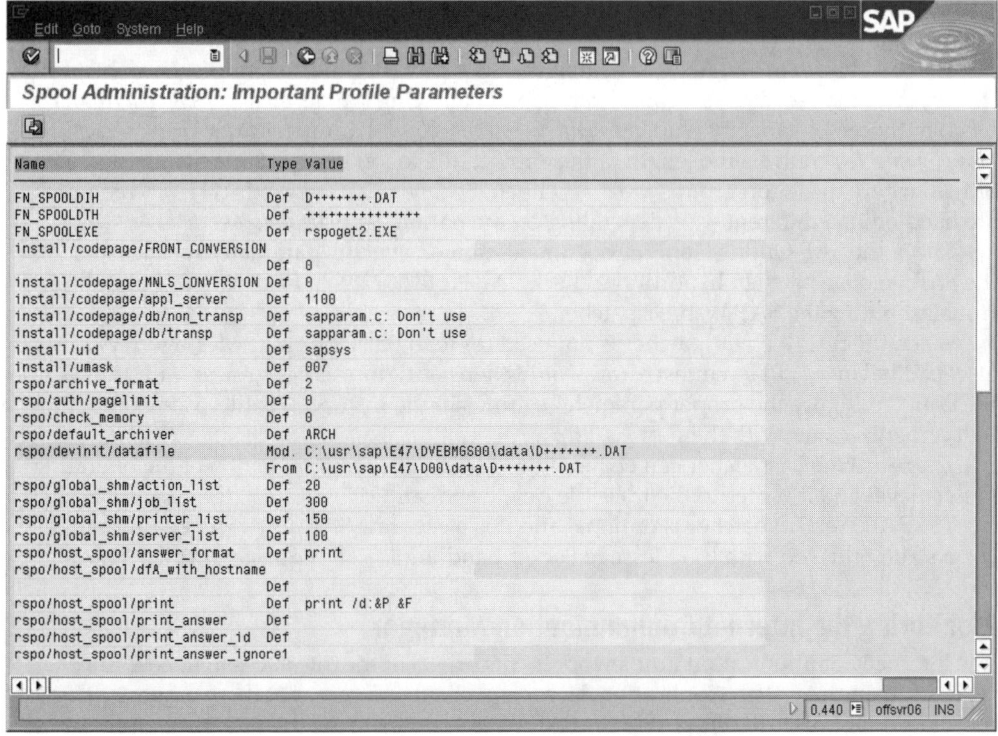

FIGURE 9-32 Display of the instance parameters for the spool system (Copyright by SAP AG)

The Web Components of the SAP Web Application Server

As it has been explained in Chapter 2, the basis layer of SAP R/3 Enterprise is SAP Web Application Server 6.20, which provides capabilities to communicate to the Internet via execution of Web applications with an additional set of processes. With SAP Web Application Server, several type of requests can be processed, such as ABAP applications, executed and managed by the ABAP runtime environment (classic client/server processing that we know), HTTP or HTTPS requests coming from the Internet handled by the Internet Communication Framework (and then communicated to the ABAP runtime environment via Business Server Pages, for example—see the description of BSPs later in this chapter), and Java applications processed by the SAP J2EE Engine.

The SAP Web Dispatcher

Load balancing capabilities are possible with the SAP Web Dispatcher program, which is similar to the Message Server in the traditional Basis architecture (*Warning:* the message server still exists, this is only a comparison).

The SAP Web Dispatcher routes HTTP requests to the SAP systems. This component is optional and normally runs in a demilitarized zone between the users' browser and the actual SAP system and can be the central access point for all Web requests.

The SAP Web Dispatcher can be configured with parameter setting in the Instance profile. You will recognize these parameter settings, because almost all of them start with the root *wdisp*.

The load balancing strategy to be followed is set by the parameter *wdisp/load_balancing_strategy*. You may set a classic round-robin load balancing (value: *simple_weighted_round_robin*) or by server capacity (value: *weighted_round_robin*). Parameter *wdisp/max_server_group_name_len* controls the length of the entry in the logon groups table maintained in SMLG, where the logon groups are maintained. Secure HTTP requests (HTTPS requests) are handled in a different way, depending on the parameter *wdisp/ssl_encrypt*.

Check the SAP Online Help for documentation on specific parameter settings for the SAP Web Dispatcher. In addition, check SAP Note 552286 to find out more about troubleshooting the SAP Web Dispatcher.

When the SAP Web Dispatcher is not used for load balancing, the Message Server can also load balance HTTP requests. You would then configure server groups with transaction SICF and configure the proper parameter settings in the Instance Profile. Many of them, you will recognize, start with the root *ms/http_*.

The SAP Web Dispatcher can be monitored using the program icmon at the operating system level and it writes to the trace file dev_webdisp.

The SAP Web Dispatcher is optional and it is a separate SAP software. Load balancing can also be achieved with the Message Server handling HTTP requests directly.

Monitoring the Internet Communication Manager

The Internet Communication Framework is comprised of the interfaces to handle Internet requests, using SAP Web Application Server as a client or a server of these requests. The most important piece of this part of the SAP WAS architecture is the Internet Communication Manager (ICM). The ICM provides direct communication between the Web browser and the work processes of a SAP Instance, but it does not provide with business logic.

Similarly to a work process, the ICM handles external user requests from the Internet in the form of an HTTP or HTTPS request using threads that communicate to work processes to handle those requests and determine what action is necessary to perform in the SAP system. And, similarly to the memory management concept of a SAP Instance, the ICM uses memory pipes to execute the application and manage the data to transfer between the threads and the work processes.

The ICM is also patched for bug fixes. Check SAP Note 508300 for the most up to date information on the released patches and bug fixes in the SAP ICM.

Execute transaction SMICM to check the ICM and its components. From here, you can troubleshoot the ICM.

The main screen of the ICM, shown in Figure 9-33, is very similar to the work process monitor that you are used to watching all the time and it displays the threads, with attributes, such as the number, the operating system thread PID (process identifier), the number of requests handled by every thread, the status (free or running–occupied), and finally what type of request is being processed. Many different possible type of requests can be seen here, such as read or write request or response, open, accept or close the connection, waiting for data or response, and so on.

Check that the peak number of threads and the connections used do not reach the "maximum" number configured.

The behavior of the ICM is controlled via parameter settings in the Instance Profile.

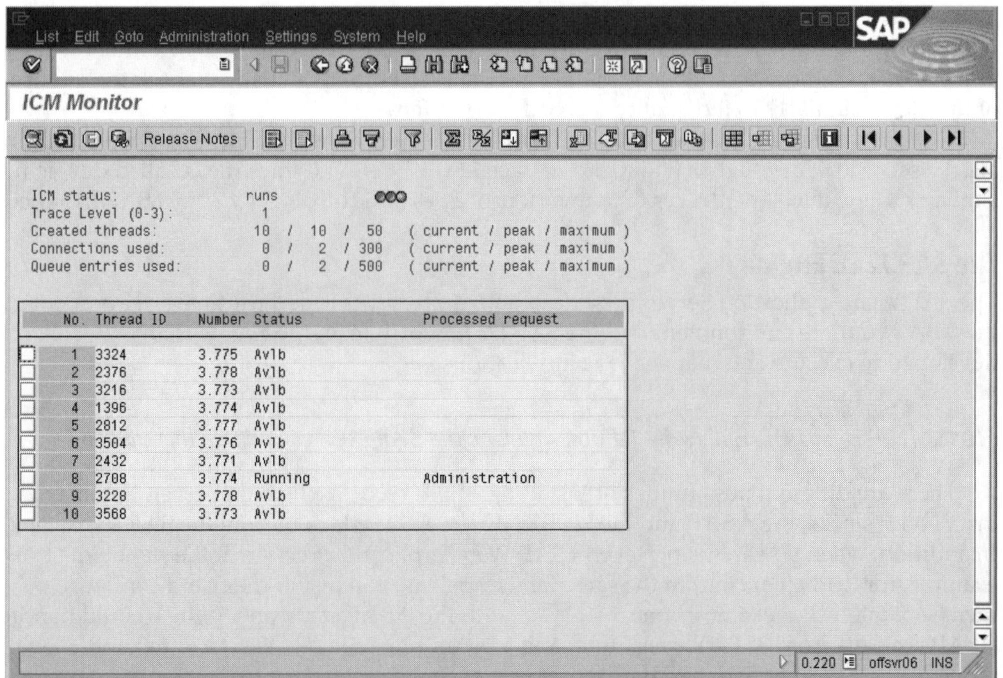

FIGURE 9-33 ICM Monitor screen (Copyright by SAP AG)

To start the ICM the parameter *rdisp/start_icman* must be set to true. Almost all of these parameters start with the root *icm*. You can see the parameter settings and change them from the ICM Monitor by choosing Goto | Parameters | Display.

Remember that the ICM communicates to the work processes and sends them requests. Therefore, proper parameterization of the work processes is essential for optimal performance and in order to make this configuration work well. If in addition to Web requests there are also dialog requests, the parameter *rdisp/min_wait_dia_wp* must be configured to allow dialog work processes to handle regular dialog requests. The same parameters that control RFCs are also important in the communication between the ICM and the work processes.

The parameter *icm/keep_alive_timeout* allows you to keep a network connection between the user and the ICM open for a period of time. Setting this to a very low number (if you set it to 1, it would never close the connection and 0 is not an allowed value) will incur in several opening and closing of sockets and that can overload the network. Setting it too high would be a waste of threads time.

TIP *To check the values of all the parameter settings in your SAP system, execute program RSPARAM and browse the resulting list.*

To monitor the memory usage of the ICM, browse to Goto | Memory Pipes | Display Data. The indicators to watch for here are #Mpi Buffers (number of memory pipe buffers) and Peak Buffer Usage. If Peak Buffer Usage reaches Maximum Buffer Usage, this is an indication of a bottleneck.

In addition, the ICM is capable to save parts of Web pages and images in a little cache that can be monitored by Goto | HTTP Server Cache | Display Statistics. Check the quality of this cache similarly to the quality of a SAP R/3 buffer.

You can display a trace file choosing Goto | Trace File | Display File. The trace level can also be set to lower or higher with Goto | Trace Level | Set. The trace file is called dev_icm, similarly to the developer traces of the work processes and the dispatcher in a SAP Instance.

The SAP J2EE Engine

The SAP Web Application Server provides you with two integrated runtime environments, the ABAP runtime environment and the SAP J2EE, which form the engine that SAP developed to execute and manage Java applications.

NOTE *J2EE is Java™ 2 Enterprise Edition standard and SAP J2EE complies to this standard.*

There are different possibilities of installing a SAP Web Application Server. You may install both stacks, the ABAP and the J2EE, only the ABAP stack or only the SAP J2EE stack. In addition, when you are using several SAP Web Application Servers at the same time (for example, for load balancing) in the same landscape, you can install them and configure them separately. For example, one SAP WAS with the ABAP stack only (which could handle ABAP requests from BSPs, for example) and another one with a JAVA stack (to handle Java requests) and another one with both.

Note that both stacks are completely integrated and reside in the same physical machine, offering openness to standards.

This is the way an HTTP request is processed by the SAP Web Application Server with an ABAP and a Java stack:

- The Internet Communication Manager receives HTTP/HTTPS requests from the Web and decides whether it is a BSP application to be processed by the ABAP runtime environment or a Java application to be executed by the SAP J2EE Engine. To determine this, you set the parameter *icm/HTTP/j2ee_##* (where ## is the entry number) with the appropriate values. The options to choose from are several and they include a prefix to redirect to the SAP J2EE Engine, a host to execute that request, the number of connections that can be open to that J2EE server, the port number of the J2EE server to which the ICM has to connect and encryption options.
- If the request is to be processed by the SAP J2EE Engine, the ICM sends it to the J2EE server.

Load balancing within the SAP J2EE is possible when using a cluster installation of the SAP J2EE. In this case, you will observe two different components, a dispatcher node and server nodes. The dispatcher node handles the distribution of requests among the available server nodes. In a single-node architecture, the request is handled directly by a server node in the SAP J2EE.

NOTE *However, an architecture with a dispatcher node and several server nodes still represents a single point of failure, because in case of a shutdown in the dispatcher, none of the server nodes are available. Therefore, note that load balancing does not prevent from single point of failure. In order to prevent this situation, several dispatcher nodes with their corresponding set of server nodes can be configured.*

The Java server that is in charge of processing the request handles such processing in local memory. Threads do not share memory. Therefore, this must be taken into consideration when sizing a SAP Web Application Server. A single thread, theoretically, could take up all the memory of a server. However, you can apply limits.

When the request involves the use of ABAP objects for business logic, the SAP J2EE Engine communicates to the ABAP runtime environment via the JCo (Java Connector), which comprises a set of RFCs and BAPIs that can actually access and manage SAP objects in the ABAP repository.

NOTE *You may also use Native JDBC, which is similar to Open SQL in ABAP, database-independent Java code. Other interfaces may also be used.*

In a cluster environment, you can use the Configuration tool (and you do not need to have a SAP J2EE Engine up and running, indeed!) to set up dispatchers and server nodes, as well as their properties for memory management, logging and tracing, locking, and so on.

Monitoring the SAP J2EE

The SAP Web Application Server offers several possibilities to manage the SAP J2EE Engine and monitor its performance. In addition, parameter settings that control the behavior of the SAP J2EE must be set appropriately. Most of these parameters start with the root *rdisp/j2ee*.

NOTE *For detailed documentation on all the parameters of the J2EE server, refer to the Online Documentation.*

In order to the SAP J2EE Engine to be started by the Dispatcher in the SAP Web Application Server, set the parameter *rdisp/j2ee_start* to 1.

To monitor the SAP J2EE, use the Visual Administrator, which is written entirely in Java, and it offers a user-friendly graphical user interface. It provides you with information about services, runtime, deployment, and logging and tracing.

The most important indicators to check in the Visual Administrator are the status of a thread, the memory allocated by such thread and the number of HTTP hits.

Additionally, log files of events are written into the directory <SAP J2EE engine installation directory>/cluster/server. You can also find system and application logs in the <J2EE>/cluster/server/log.

The CCMS Monitors (transaction RZ20) can also be used to monitor the SAP J2EE Engine. SAP CCMS agents running at the operating system level collect and send data to the CCMS monitors to be analyzed. CCMS agents and their patches are available in the SAP Service Marketplace. Follow the instructions in SAP Note 498179 to install and configure SAP CCMS agents.

10 CHAPTER

Performance and Troubleshooting with SAP Solutions

This chapter is intended to provide extensive information about performance and troubleshooting of SAP Solutions. It covers performance and workload analysis, SAP monitoring, and troubleshooting tools, and thus complements Chapters 2 and 9.

When dealing performance and monitoring of SAP systems, the objective is to introduce and explain ways to take preventive maintenance actions, or discover future bottlenecks, and therefore facilitate quicker troubleshooting of problems.

Performance Analysis

In SAP systems, there are performance monitors oriented to analyze the status of a system by observing statistics that are recorded. And there are other monitors that are more oriented to the resolution of a problem that has been detected. Such tools provide a detailed analysis of individual components of the system, such as the database, the operating system, and the work processes and instance configuration.

In this section we explain how to perform a performance analysis in a SAP system. To start, we define briefly each tool or monitor that is available, the meaning of the statistics that are recorded, and how to read such statistics to detect possible problems or to analyze the health of a system. Finally, we provide a possible solution to the performance issues that we have learned how to detect.

First, it is essential to differentiate the following two concepts: *availability* and *performance*.

Availability can be defined as simply as to have a resource or not to have it. A resource can be a work process, a CPU, disk space, memory, a server, the network, and so on. If a resource is available, then performance can be defined as how we can utilize that resource most efficiently.

Performance can be measured by response time. In order to evaluate the performance of a system, we will analyze the utilization of resources and how these perform to achieve a task in the lowest amount of time.

The next sections introduce how to check the current activities of SAP systems.

The Work Process Monitor

In order to have a view of our servers and instances from your own SAP system, execute transaction code SM51 or from the main menu select Tools | Administration | Monitor | System Monitoring | Servers.

In a central SAP system with only one instance, we will see only one line in this screen with one application server and the corresponding instance, as shown in Figure 10-1. In other cases, when your system consists on several application servers, all the servers with instances (one or more than one) will be displayed here.

As in previous releases, with SAP Basis, you can see which services or work processes are configured in each instance. These are Dialog, Background (also known as Batch), Spool, Update, Update 2 (Upd2), Enqueue (note that only the central instance, one and only in each system will have this service), and ICM. It is important to note that there is a new service in SAP R/3 Enterprise, the Internet Communication Manager (ICM). This new service is necessary to ensure proper communication between the SAP system and other Web services, systems or applications that use HTTP, HTTPS, or SMTP protocols. The ICM

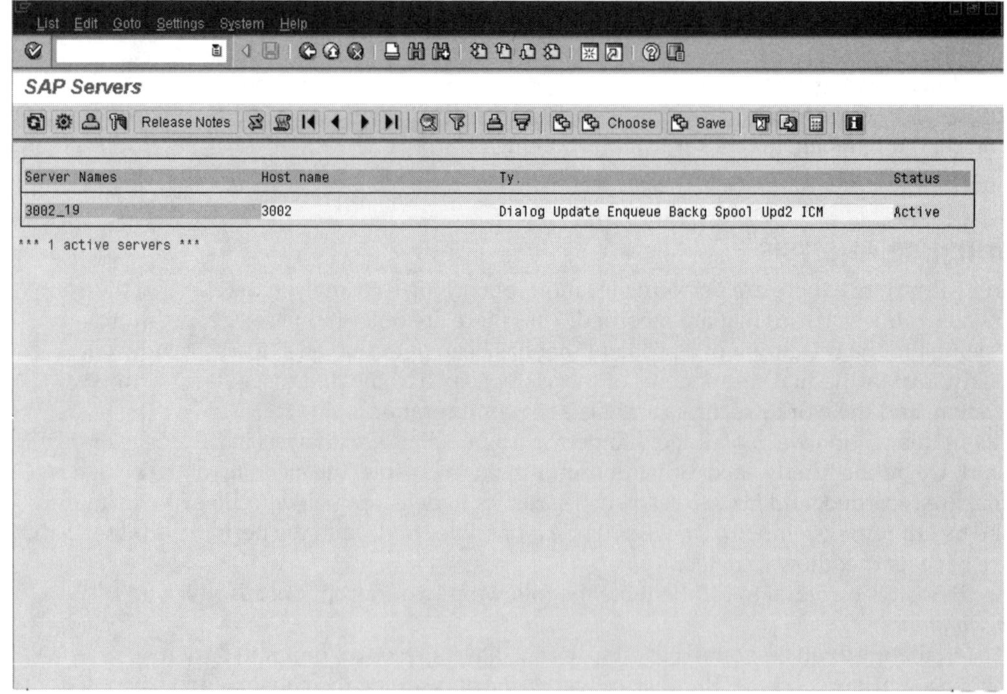

FIGURE 10-1 Displaying the application servers and instances in SAP (Copyright by SAP AG)

is part of the underlying SAP Web Application Server and it can be monitored separately with the ICM Monitor, although it is started by the dispatcher, as all the other services or work processes. Just as the other work processes, the ICM must be configured via parameter settings.

Double-click on any server from the list to go to the Work Process Monitor of that particular instance. You can also go to this monitor from the main menu following the path Tools | Administration | Monitor | System Monitoring | Processes or executing transaction code SM50. But in order to go to the Work Process Monitor of a specific instance, unless you are already logged on such instance, you may proceed as explained previously from the list of servers in SM51.

The Work Process Monitor (see Figure 10-2) provides with very useful information of the current status of an instance and a snapshot of what is going on in your system (again, separately by instance) right now.

Each instance is configured by its own Instance Profile with parameter settings that, among others, specify the amount of work processes of each type (dialog, batch, update, etc.). So you will be able to see several dialog work process (type DIA), several background work processes (type BGD), a few update and update 2 work processes (type UPD and UP2), spool work processes (type SPO), and one enqueue work process in the central instance only (type ENQ).

Individually, every work process has a number to be identified by the dispatcher (0 to *n*, where *n* is the last work process, no matter what type it is) and a Process Identifier (PID) that makes it differentiable at the operating system level.

This monitor displays a lot of information at a glance. The Status column indicates whether a work process is occupied (status *running*) or free (status *waiting*). If the work process is in status *running*, you may be able to see the action taken by it in the Action column. For example, you may see actions such as Sequential Read or Roll In in a dialog work process or actions like Delete or Insert in an update work process. In addition, the Table column will indicate which table is being manipulated or read.

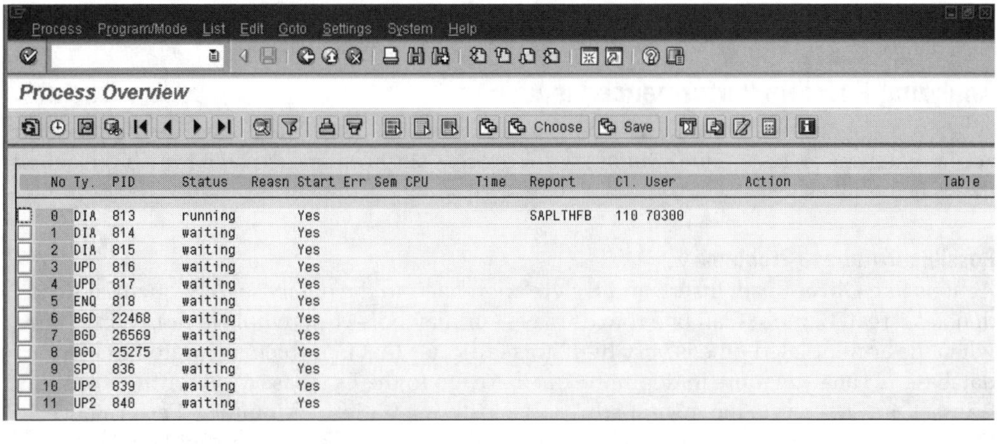

Process Overview

No	Ty.	PID	Status	Reasn	Start	Err	Sem	CPU	Time	Report	Cl.	User	Action	Table
0	DIA	813	running		Yes					SAPLTHFB	110	70300		
1	DIA	814	waiting		Yes									
2	DIA	815	waiting		Yes									
3	UPD	816	waiting		Yes									
4	UPD	817	waiting		Yes									
5	ENQ	818	waiting		Yes									
6	BGD	22468	waiting		Yes									
7	BGD	26569	waiting		Yes									
8	BGD	25275	waiting		Yes									
9	SPO	836	waiting		Yes									
10	UP2	839	waiting		Yes									
11	UP2	840	waiting		Yes									

FIGURE 10-2 The Work Process Monitor (Copyright by SAP AG)

Another possible status of a work process is *stopped*. Sometimes, a work process may be waiting for a communication from another instance or external system and you would see under the Reason column, the acronym CPIC. Other times, the work process is *stopped* in private mode (you will see PRIV under the Reason column).

None of the statuses is an indicator of a problem, unless the time accrued performing such action and in that status (see the Time column) starts to be excessive and your users experience higher response times. Otherwise, a performance issue is encountered and you must analyze the root cause. The Work Process Monitor gives you very useful clues on where to look and where to go. We explain this in much more detail shortly.

The Start column denotes whether a work process may be restarted by the dispatcher in case this aborts for any reason or not (so you will see "Yes" or "No" here). If a work process is terminated, the Err column will specify how many times.

The Semaphore column states which semaphore is being used by that work process and it is not normally an indicator of performance, but just information. Any concurrent programming language that users shared resources (such as work processes) must use some kind of "semaphores" to avoid interference and make good use of the shared resources.

In order to display values under the CPU column, you must click on the clocklike icon or go to the menu path List | CPU. This amount specifies the time that a work process has used the CPU in hours, minutes, and seconds.

Finally, under the Program column, you will see which program is being executed, by which user (column User) and from which client (column Client). All linked together, you are able to know individually which work processes are free or occupied, doing what, by whom and how long that action is taking.

The snapshot that you see in the Work Process Monitor can be refreshed by clicking on the Refresh icon or on the Check Mark icon to obtain a newer view of the activity in that instance.

There is also a way to display the activity occurring across all instances in a system. Execute transaction SM66 to obtain a snapshot of the work processes of all instances. This is somewhat of a cross view of SM51 and SM50, but looks like SM50 with the addition of a new column at the beginning denoting the instance name (application server) to which that work process belongs to. By default, you will only see the *running* work processes of every instance.

Analyzing Possible Performance Issues

When you are observing the activity of a system via SM50 or SM66 and notice that the time accumulated by an occupied (*running*) work process starts to be excessive, watch the action that is being taken.

Possible Database Problems

Actions like Direct Read, Insert, and Delete are related to the database. A Sequential Read denotes a read of more than one row (it may—or may not—be a whole table). Many times, when the accumulated time is very high, this indicates that a problem is located in the database. To analyze more in depth the database, go to the Database Monitor by executing transaction ST04 or via the menu path Tools | Administration | Monitor | Performance | Database | Activity. A good number of times, expensive SQL statements will be the root cause of these long times.

On other occasions, a Waiting for DB Lock action may indicate that a database lock is occurring and the way to analyze this is via transaction DB01 or following the menu path Tools | Administration | Monitor | Performance | Database | Exclusive Lock Waits.

Please refer to the discussion on database performance later on in this chapter for a better understanding of the statistics shown by ST04 and DB01 and how to analyze and solve problems in the database.

Possible Memory Configuration Problems

Actions like Roll In or Roll Out or Load Program taking a long time may indicate that certain memory areas are not configured properly. It is very likely that the SAP R/3 buffers are not large enough.

Also, when a dialog work process is in status *stopped* and the reason denoted is "PRIV," that indicates that this work process is in "private mode," locked until the transaction that it's executing is finished and an excessive amount of memory is being utilized. It is very likely that the memory areas configured for that instance are not large enough.

To analyze more in depth the memory configuration, execute transaction ST02 or follow the menu path Tools | Administration | Monitor | Performance | Setup/Buffers | Buffers.

Again, we will evaluate the statistics and how to detect and solve performance issues related to memory configuration later on in more detail.

Possible Communication Problems

When a work process is in status *stopped*, with the reason "CPIC," this may be due to a wrong or slow communication between servers or systems. Find out if there are network problems preventing a correct communication or if all the work processes in the other system are occupied and therefore the work processes in this instance are waiting for a communication from the other system.

Insufficient Work Processes

All work processes are used in a sequential mode. That means that when the dispatcher assigns requests to work processes, these will always be assigned in a sequential order. If the first work process of that type is occupied, the dispatcher will assign the request to the second one and like that subsequently.

For example, if there are 10 dialog work processes in an instance and they go from number 0 to number 9 (see Figure 10-2), the dispatcher will always assign a request to the first dialog work process, if this is free. If this is occupied, it will assign the request to dialog work process number 2, and like this.

This means that when you check the CPU time spent by each work process (as explained above), these times should be sequentially decreasing. If you observe that the last one or two work processes have high statistics, this means that all of the configured dialog work processes have been used at some point in time. Therefore, it is likely that users might have been waiting for a free resource (a free dialog work process in this case) and wait times (consequently, response times) might have been affected negatively.

You should configure your instances in a way that this does not occur and you have sufficient work processes to handle the workload. Be aware that the number of work processes that you can configure is not infinite and it depends on your hardware resources (mainly physical memory and CPU) of that server.

The Workload Analysis Monitor

The Workload Analysis Monitor helps you to analyze statistics in order to check the health of a SAP system via the observation of statistics that are collected and kept in the system. You can analyze general problems, as well as specific issues in business transactions.

Collecting Data in the Workload Analysis Monitor

Certain collectors must run on a regular basis to obtain these statistics and make them available. The ABAP program RSCOLL00 collects performance statistical data and stores these data in table MONI. In every SAP R/3 system the system administrator must submit a background job that executes the RSCOLL00 program hourly. This job is usually called SAP_COLLECTOR_FOR_PERFMONITOR and must be submitted by user DDIC in client 000 to run periodically every hour. This program uses the special table TCOLL (data collector configuration table), which includes the list of specific collector programs to be executed and the running dates and times for each of those programs. This is a standard SAP table and, although modifications are possible, make them only in accordance to SAP guidance. To access and maintain this table from the Workload Analysis Monitor (which can be accessed using transaction code ST03N), on the left-hand side of the screen go to section Collector | Performance Monitor Collector and choose Execution Times.

You can decide how much data and how many dates should be kept in table MONI. To define retention times (Figure 10-3), go to Collector | Performance Database | Reorganization. These settings might have some impact on the overall system performance, so you should proceed with caution when changing them.

Definition of Response Time and Statistics in the Workload Analysis Monitor

The response time of a particular transaction is divided into several components and the Workload Analysis Monitor keeps track of all these statistics at a very detailed level.

Response Time comprises the time from which a user clicks the Execute button in a transaction or enters data and presses ENTER until the system gets back to the user with the necessary data to display. Basically, the time that the user is seeing the hourglass on the screen while a request is being processed. This time is divided into the following components:

- *Wait time.* Time spent waiting for a free work process. A user needs a work process to execute a request. The user will wait until a work process is free to perform the task that needs to be done. For example, a dialog work process can be used to read data from a table and display a list. An update work process can be used to send an update request to the database and change a table. The dispatcher maintains a queue (the dispatcher queue) where all requests are put in place waiting for a free work process to perform that task. Obviously, this wait time should be minimal. Otherwise, this would indicate a performance problem.
- *Roll-in time and roll-out time.* When a work process is assigned to a user to perform a certain task, the work process must first roll in the user's user context. The user context comprises internal tables, variables, etc that are stored in the memory of the application server. When a work process has finished the task that it was supposed to do, it releases the user context (roll out). The amount of time that is spent rolling

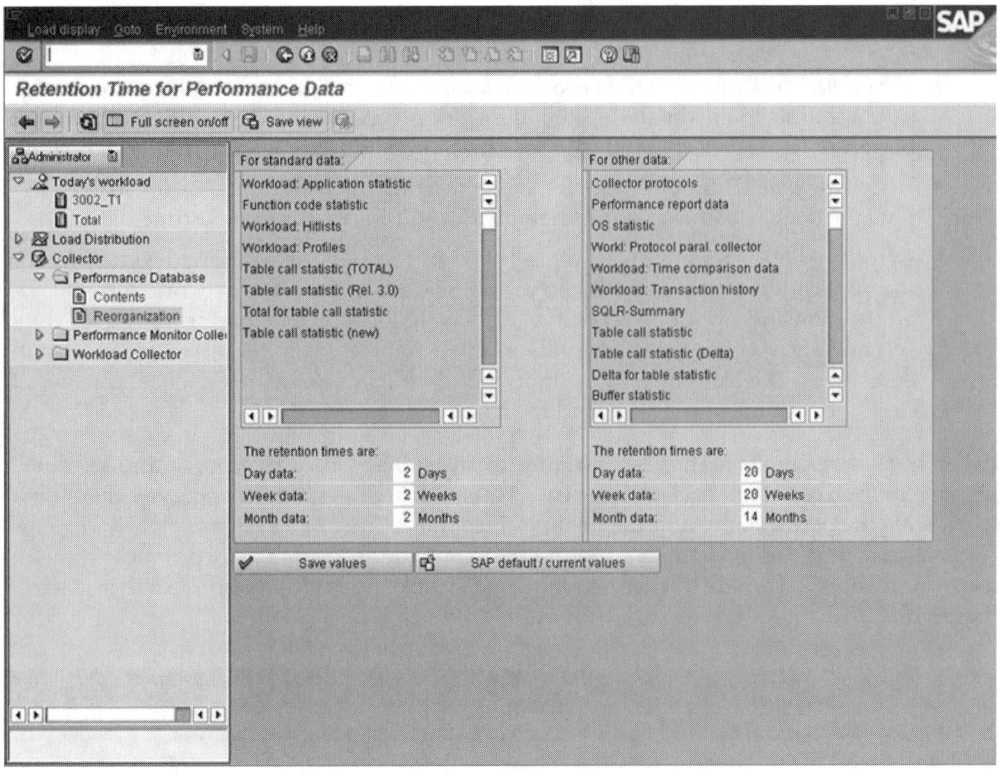

FIGURE 10-3 Retention times for collected data (Copyright by SAP AG)

in the user context is accrued as *roll-in time* and the amount of time spent rolling out the user context is *roll-out time*. Because the task is finished before the roll-out process and the data are sent to the user before that fact, the roll-out time is *not* part of the response time of that user. However, it could influence negatively the wait time of a following user that may be waiting for a free work process.

- *Load time.* Time spent loading all ABAP programs, screens, and so on that the user needs to execute in the SAP buffers, such as the Program Buffer and the Screen Buffer.
- *Database time.* Amount of time spent since a request is sent from the database interface of the work process to obtain the data that is requested by the user (display data) or to send an update request (change). In a three-tier architecture, where the database server is in a separate server, the time spent in the network (network time) is included in the database time. The requests sent to the database are sent first to the SAP buffers to try to obtain the requested data. Accesses to a buffer are on average 100 times faster than to the database. Since release 4.6C of SAP R/3 it is also possible to gather statistics on DB procedure calls, by means of the Workload Monitor in Expert Mode view.

- *Enqueue time.* This is the time spent during a work process sending an enqueue request.
- *CPU time.* To perform all the tasks indicated above (roll in, roll out, load programs, send requests to the database, etc.), the work process occupies the CPU for a certain period of time (cycles) and this time is measured and averaged with this statistic.
- *Processing time.* This is the time left of subtracting the wait time plus the load time plus the database time and the enqueue time off the total response time.
- *GUI time.* Time spent in the front-end server processing screens and results from the application server. It includes part of the time spent in the network between the application and front-end servers, since one dialog step may perform several "trips" sending and receiving packets of data between the application server and the front-end server. The Net Time is the amount of time spent in the first and last transfer of data between the application and the front-end servers.

All of these components of the response time of any transaction are recorded and kept in the system for a certain period of time. The Workload Analysis Monitor accesses these data to evaluate the performance and the history of response times of a system.

To access the Workload Analysis Monitor, execute transaction ST03N or follow the menu path Tools | Administration | Monitor | Performance | Workload | Analysis. See Figure 10-4.

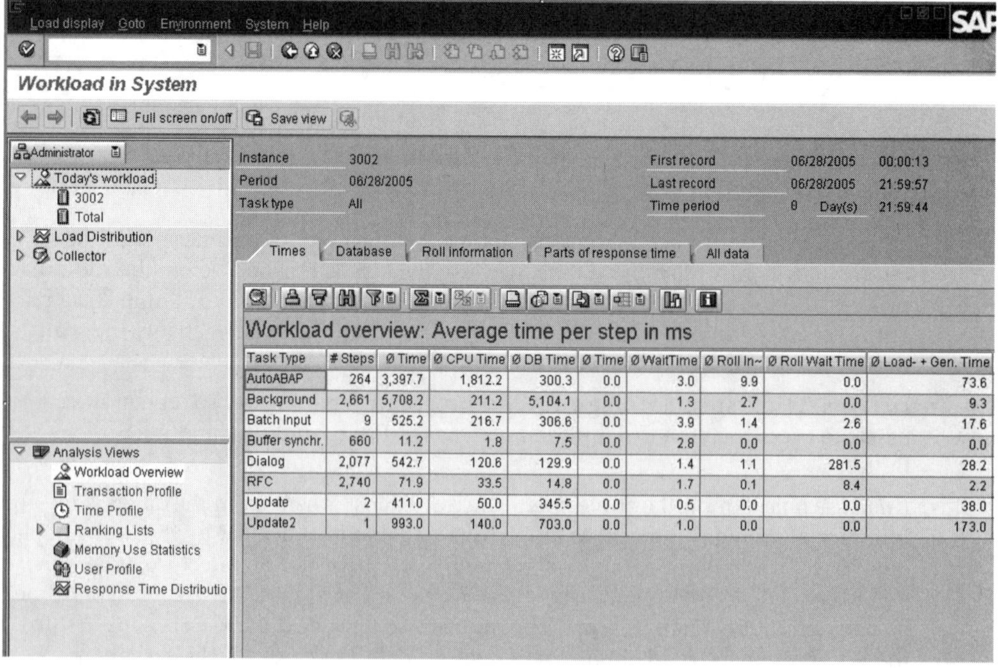

Task Type	# Steps	Ø Time	Ø CPU Time	Ø DB Time	Ø Time	Ø WaitTime	Ø Roll In~	Ø Roll Wait Time	Ø Load- + Gen. Time
AutoABAP	264	3,397.7	1,812.2	300.3	0.0	3.0	9.9	0.0	73.6
Background	2,661	5,708.2	211.2	5,104.1	0.0	1.3	2.7	0.0	9.3
Batch Input	9	525.2	216.7	306.6	0.0	3.9	1.4	2.6	17.6
Buffer synchr.	660	11.2	1.8	7.5	0.0	2.8	0.0	0.0	0.0
Dialog	2,077	542.7	120.6	129.9	0.0	1.4	1.1	281.5	28.2
RFC	2,740	71.9	33.5	14.8	0.0	1.7	0.1	8.4	2.2
Update	2	411.0	50.0	345.5	0.0	0.5	0.0	0.0	38.0
Update2	1	993.0	140.0	703.0	0.0	1.0	0.0	0.0	173.0

FIGURE 10-4 The Workload Analysis Monitor (Copyright by SAP AG)

If you want to see aggregated statistics records from a global point of view, you can also use transaction ST03G, which shows the Global System Workload Analysis.

Note that this is a new monitor replacing the old ST03 transaction. In fact, in any SAP system based on SAP Web Application Server, by default, if you execute transaction ST03, it will default into ST03N. The Workload Analysis Monitor is now divided in two sections. On the left hand side you choose the function you want to execute and the analysis view you may want to analyze. You are able to save the view that you last used by clicking on Save View and the next time you call this monitor, it will display the analysis view you chose, saving you time of navigating through screens.

There are three possible views: Expert Mode, Administrator or Service Engineer, which give you more or less detailed data.

You are able to analyze individual servers or a system in its whole by choosing Total or a particular server in the left hand side and the statistics will be displayed in the right-hand side.

As displayed in Figure 10-4, the workload overview shows the average response time by all task types (or work process type) and a breakdown of the components of the response time in which a particular transaction spends its time. The explanation of the meaning of all these components was provided in the previous section. The dialog response time is especially important to monitor, because it shows the performance experience of the user.

All the numbers are averaged by dialog steps and the statistical information that is displayed depends on the period of time that you choose. By default, from the start of the day until the moment you execute ST03N. It is possible to analyze a shorter or longer period of time by choosing a day, a week, or a month from the left side (note that this function is only available in the Expert Mode view). Or you can specify intervals of minutes or hours in the Last Minute Load in the Detailed Analysis from the left-hand side of the screen for a more specific analysis in time.

Analyzing the Data Provided by the Workload Analysis Monitor

This monitor provides you with several tabs with views of different breakdowns, as shown is Figure 10-5.

The tab named Database specifies statistics about the database accesses and the average response time. For example, you are able to see in average how long a dialog task took to perform a sequential read. High average times here indicate possible problems in the database.

The Roll Information tab corresponds to the number of roll-ins and roll-outs and the average time taken by a work process to perform this task. High average times here indicate possible problems with memory configuration.

The Parts of Response Time tab provides you with a breakdown in percentage of the components of the response time, making it very easy to identify where performance problems are located in a system.

There is not a set or specific "good" response time, because it depends on many factors, such as the resources, but also the type of applications executed in that system, the level of customization and modifications, and so on. However, there are guidelines and rules of thumbs to follow to determine whether these statistics reveal a performance problem or not. Not all work processes may be measured by the same thresholds, but the following are

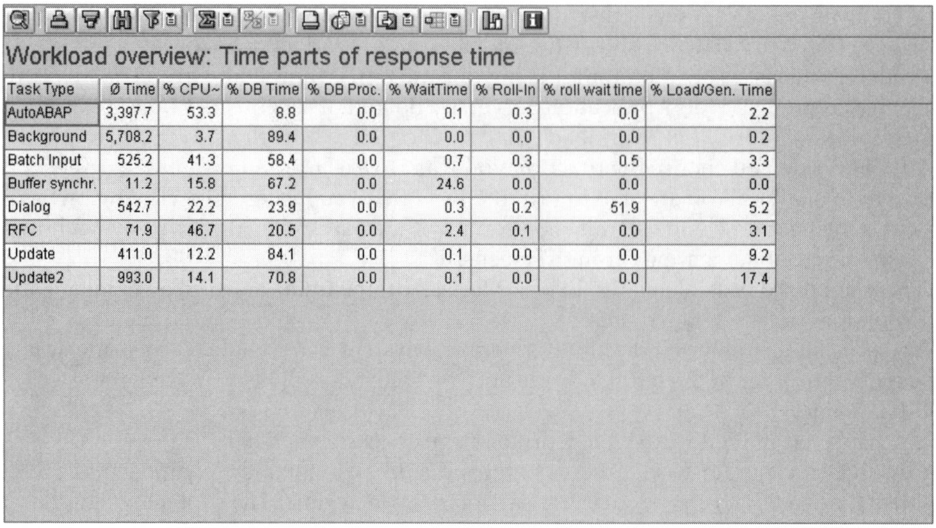

Workload overview: Time parts of response time

Task Type	Ø Time	% CPU~	% DB Time	% DB Proc.	% WaitTime	% Roll-In	% roll wait time	% Load/Gen. Time
AutoABAP	3,397.7	53.3	8.8	0.0	0.1	0.3	0.0	2.2
Background	5,708.2	3.7	89.4	0.0	0.0	0.0	0.0	0.2
Batch Input	525.2	41.3	58.4	0.0	0.7	0.3	0.5	3.3
Buffer synchr.	11.2	15.8	67.2	0.0	24.6	0.0	0.0	0.0
Dialog	542.7	22.2	23.9	0.0	0.3	0.2	51.9	5.2
RFC	71.9	46.7	20.5	0.0	2.4	0.1	0.0	3.1
Update	411.0	12.2	84.1	0.0	0.1	0.0	0.0	9.2
Update2	993.0	14.1	70.8	0.0	0.1	0.0	0.0	17.4

FIGURE 10-5 Breakdown of the components of the response time (Copyright by SAP AG)

guidelines to detect possible performance problems in dialog processing, therefore, observing the statistics of the dialog work process in the Workload Analysis Monitor:

- The wait time should fall under 10% of the total response time. Otherwise, it may represent a performance problem from several possible causes. One cause may be insufficient work processes.
- The load time should not be greater than 50 milliseconds and the roll times should not exceed 20 milliseconds. Otherwise, this may be due to problems with memory configuration, small buffer sizes, wrong parameter settings or a CPU bottleneck.
- The enqueue time should be smaller than 5 milliseconds. Normally, there are no performance problems related to this service, but if these statistics were high, it would represent an important problem that might affect system stability as well. The network may also affect negatively, if there is a problem there.
- Processing time should be below twice the CPU time. High processing time may indicate that the ABAP programs are very complex and the work process spends a large amount of time "interpreting" what is to be done.
- Database time should be under 40% of the total response time. Many areas can affect negatively this time, such as problems in the database, like expensive SQL statements, but also wrong parameter settings at the database level. In addition, the network may also affect negatively this time and if a contention problem is located in the physical disks (Input/Output problems), this time may also be affected and therefore it may increase considerably the total response time.
- The GUI time and the net time should not be greater than 100 milliseconds. The hardware configuration in the presentation server, as well as the network, influences

this time considerably. If these times are high, the perception of the user would be that the system is not performing well. However, the system may be responding well and there are problems in the network or in the presentation servers.

Response Time in External Communications

More and more communications with other systems, like a SAP CRM, a SAP BW, SAP APO, or other applications or external systems are taking a higher importance within your SAP Solution. That is why we are going to spend some time analyzing the performance of RFC communications and troubleshooting them in this topic.

Remote Function Calls are used to communicate to other systems and applications and that is why RFC Time is also measured in the Workload Analysis Monitor.

In order to analyze whether the response time of an external communication to another system is within your expectations, first observe the Roll Wait Time stored in transaction ST033N, as shown in Figure 10-6.

An RFC communication within two SAP systems is handled by two dialog work processes, one in each system. The dialog work process executing the RFC call has rolled in the user context of the user performing that request. Because the request involves an RFC call to another system, the dialog work process rolls out the user context and a dialog work process in the other system will roll it in again. This is necessary, among other criteria, for security purposes. You would not allow a nonauthorized user to log on another system to perform a task and the dialog work process can check the authorizations in the user context and verify that the user executing that call is authorized to perform such task in the target system.

The "wait" time between the time one dialog work process rolls out the user context of the user and the other one rolls it in is Roll Wait Time. The higher this is, the longer the response time that the original user will experience.

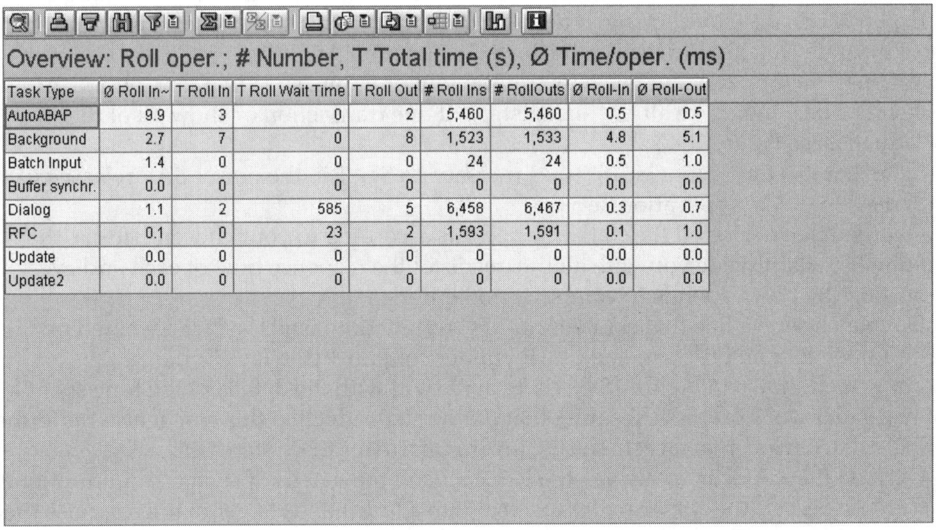

Overview: Roll oper.; # Number, T Total time (s), Ø Time/oper. (ms)

Task Type	Ø Roll In~	T Roll In	T Roll Wait Time	T Roll Out	# Roll Ins	# RollOuts	Ø Roll-In	Ø Roll-Out
AutoABAP	9.9	3	0	2	5,460	5,460	0.5	0.5
Background	2.7	7	0	8	1,523	1,533	4.8	5.1
Batch Input	1.4	0	0	0	24	24	0.5	1.0
Buffer synchr.	0.0	0	0	0	0	0	0.0	0.0
Dialog	1.1	2	585	5	6,458	6,467	0.3	0.7
RFC	0.1	0	23	2	1,593	1,591	0.1	1.0
Update	0.0	0	0	0	0	0	0.0	0.0
Update2	0.0	0	0	0	0	0	0.0	0.0

FIGURE 10-6 Roll Wait Time as indicator of response time for external communications (Copyright by SAP AG)

Possible causes of high Roll Wait Times may be due to having all work processes in the target system occupied. It is very important to configure the instances properly, especially when they must be designed to handle RFC communications.

Always ensure that you have sufficient work processes in each instance to handle both online and RFC workload, without forgetting that the number of dialog work processes that you can configure is not infinite and it depends on the hardware resources of the application server.

In addition, there are certain parameter settings that you can configure in order to obtain optimal response time and balance the RFC workload properly. The following are the most critical parameters to configure:

- *rdisp/rfc_max_comm_entries* specifies the maximum number of communications in an instance. No more dialog work processes will be given to the program calling the target system after this number is reached. It is a percentage and by default the value is 90 (%).
- *rdisp/rfc_min_wait_dia_wp* tells the number of dialog work processes to be always available for online users. By default it is 1.

Therefore, playing around with the above parameters and some others (parameter settings for high interface load are specified in SAP Note 74141), you can achieve optimal balancing of resources and avoid high response times in RFC communications.

Troubleshooting RFC Communications

Sometimes the RFC Times are high but the Roll Wait Times are not, and therefore you wonder where the time for that RFC communication is spent.

The best way to analyze a specific transaction is to use the statistical records stored in your SAP system. Execute transaction STAD or from the Workload Analysis Monitor, select the Expert Mode view by clicking in the list box at the top left side of the screen, and then follow the path Detailed Analysis | Business Transaction Analysis.

You may filter by user, by business transaction, program, specify a time period, group the results, and summarize all the dialog steps of one transaction or show all of them individually. See Figure 10-7.

Note that this transaction substitutes transaction STAT in the newer SAP releases with the underlying Web Application Server.

Once you have selected the statistical records according to your chosen criteria, the resulting list will provide you with all the details of the response time of each and every transaction (that corresponds to your selection criteria).

Double-click on a line that contains an RFC transaction, which will be denoted by "RFC" under column Program and by "R" under column T (for Task Type).

The screen shown in Figure 10-8 will provide you with the details of the time spent in that particular work process executing that dialog step, which in this case it also performed an RFC call to an external target. This is the granularity of these statistics!

Click on the RFC icon to display the RFC call and the details of such communication.

Click on Server (the cursor will transform into a little hand) to get to the response time details, as shown in Figure 10-8.

The remote execution time displayed is the actual time spent in the server that processed the RFC call. The calling time is the remote execution time in addition to the

Workload Edit Tools Goto Monitor System Help

Workload: Statistical Records

Download | Disp. mode | Sel. fields | Server ID

System: A   Number of RFCs which responded (without errors): 1 (1)
Analysed time: 06/28/2005 / 22:39:00 - 06/28/2005 / 22:49:00   Time frame: +/- 00:02:00
Display mode: All statistic records, sorted by time

Started	Server	Transaction	Program	T	Scr.	Wp	User	Response time (ms)	Time WPs
		*	*	*			*	0	
22:37:56	3002	ST03N	RFC	R	1000	0	SAPSYS	401	
22:38:32	3002	ST03N	RFC	R	1000	0	SAPSYS	3	
22:38:33	3002	ST03N	RFC	R	1000	0	SAPSYS	2	
22:38:34	3002	ST03N	RFC	R	1000	0	SAPSYS	2	
22:38:36	3002	ST03N	RFC	R	1000	0	SAPSYS	3	
22:39:13	3002		(B)OTHER	B		1	SAPSYS	39	
22:39:13	3002		RSPOWP00	S		9	SAPSYS	7	

FIGURE 10-7 Statistical records in a SAP system (Copyright by SAP AG)

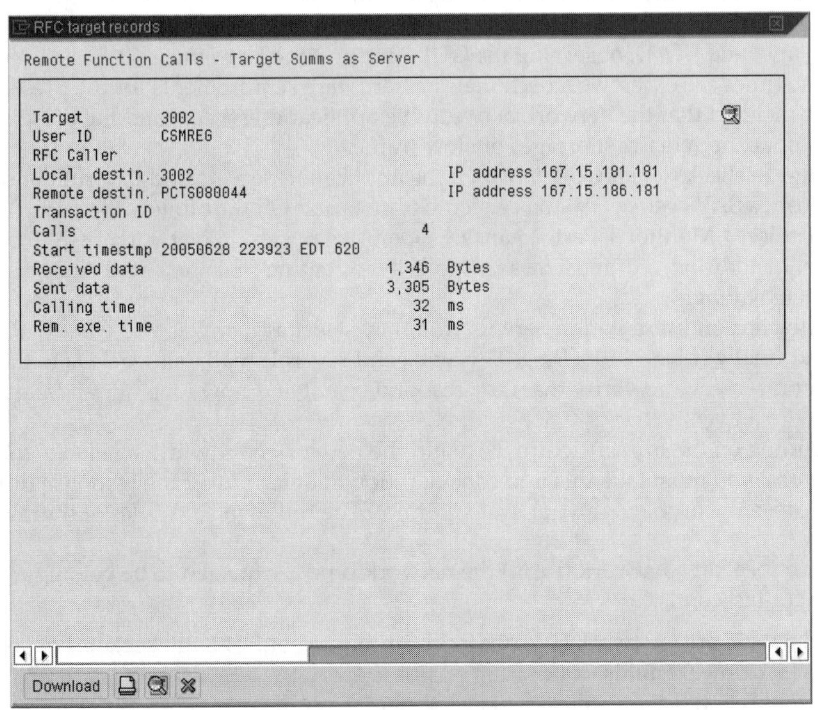

FIGURE 10-8 Details of the response time of an RFC communication (Copyright by SAP AG)

network time and the Roll Wait Time. Therefore, if you have eliminated the Roll Wait Time as a variable in your analysis for a possible performance problem, because you saw in the Workload Analysis Monitor that it was low and the remote execution time is also low compared to the total calling time, this means that the RFC call spends quite some time in the network. It is very likely that somewhere in the network (and that would include the complete infrastructure, network, routers, etc.), there is a problem that is affecting negatively the communication between servers and affecting the performance of processes that need external communication.

Troubleshooting the Presentation Server Response Time

In SAP R/3 Enterprise, but starting with a previous releases (4.6B and 4.6C), the SAP Graphical User Interface (SAP GUI) was redesigned for a more user-friendly appearance, which you can personalize, and it is able to incorporate more complex elements, such as Web applications. This represents advantages, such as scrolling through the screen and accessing full menus that are downloaded to the front-end server, instead of representing a dialog step, as in the old SAP GUI. However, the implications in performance are greater and the network traffic increases, as well as the hardware requirements for the presentation server.

In addition, with the new SAP NetWeaver components, such as Enterprise Portals, accessing the back-end systems requires more powerful network bandwidth and front-end servers.

You may analyze the GUI Time and the Net Time the same way you did before with the RFC Time, using the same tools, such as the Workload Analysis Monitor (ST03N, observing the GUI Time) and STAD, observing the GUI Time and the Net Time.

If these times are excessive, check that the hardware requirements for the presentation server are met and that the network between the application servers and the presentation servers is not experiencing shortages or slow traffic.

In order to check the network between the application servers and the front-end servers, from a SAP system you may execute transaction OS01 or follow the path Tools | Administration | Monitor | Performance | Operating System | Network | LAN Check with Ping. In addition, a different way to go is by executing ST06 or Detail Analysis Menu | LAN Check by Ping.

Double-click on Presentation Servers. You may select as many as you want with the Pick option and finally click on 10 x Ping. This will send several small data packets to the chosen presentation servers and verify that they respond or not and how long does it take for the packets to go and come back.

Depending on the infrastructure used and the network bandwidth available, these times may vary and you must take this into consideration to determine if the response times shown represent a problem in your system or not. The following are rules of thumb:

- In a local area network (LAN) the network time is expected to be below 20 milliseconds.
- In a wide area network (WAN) (for example, 256 or 384 KBit/sec), it is expected to be below 50 milliseconds.
- In a WAN (for example, 128 KBit/sec or less) it is expected to be below 250 milliseconds.
- Finally, losses of data packets should not occur at all.

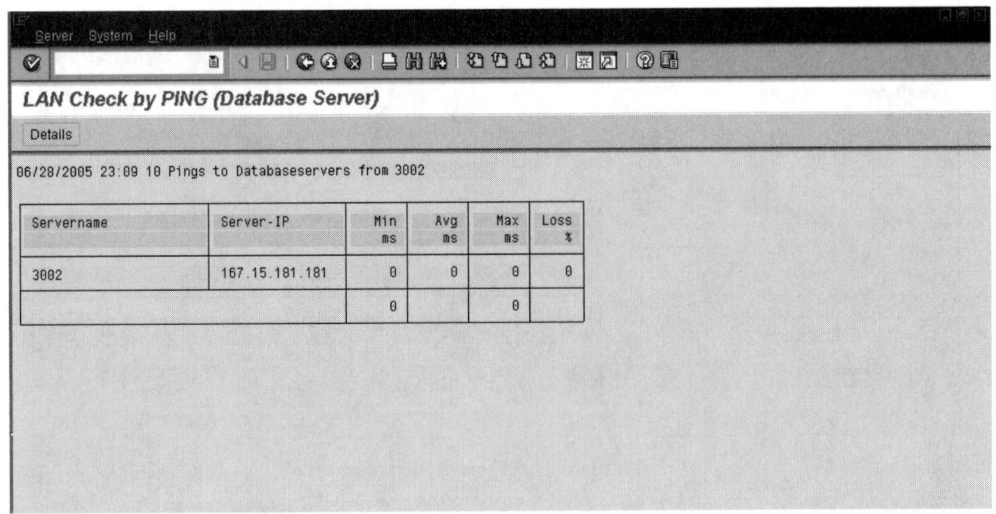

FIGURE 10-9 Checking the network between application and presentation servers (Copyright by SAP AG)

As you can observe in Figure 10-9, an example of each possible occurrence is shown. One presentation server experienced an "impossible link" or a loss of 100% of the packets sent. This means that something may be wrong with the network between the application server sending the data and that application server. All elements in a network, including routers, influence and should be checked by your network administrator with network monitoring tools.

Another presentation server is experiencing high response times and the same advise applies to verify possible causes of slow traffic between the servers.

It is important to note that these presentations servers may be located in two different geographical locations and not in the same LAN, which is why the results may be so despair from one to the other.

Analyzing Specific Business Transactions

There are several ways to check and analyze the statistics that are kept for specific business transactions from the Workload Analysis Monitor. As explained previously, you may execute STAD and check each individual business transaction. In addition, you may also choose a different view in the Workload Analysis Monitor. While in Administrator or Service Engineer view, in the left side of the screen within the Workload Analysis Monitor, choose Transaction Profile.

That view provides you with the top 15 business transactions (which can be customizable) that have been executed and the response times with a breakdown by component and that way you can analyze where most of the time is spent when executing that transaction. See Figure 10-10.

This way you can check if there are specific transactions that are experiencing performance. It is important to understand that the system may be performing well overall, but only a few users that execute certain transactions are affected and are not, therefore, a specific problem that you can isolate and analyze in particular.

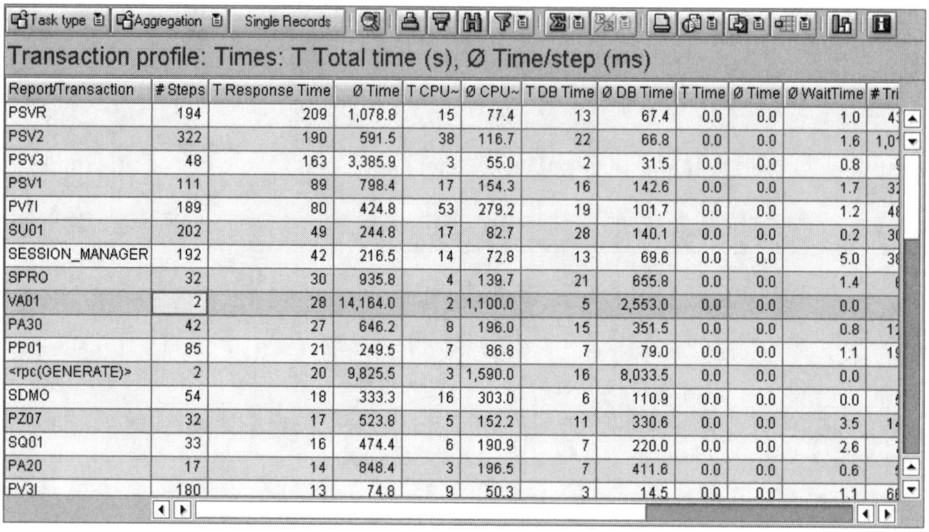

Task type | Aggregation | Single Records

Transaction profile: Times: T Total time (s), Ø Time/step (ms)

Report/Transaction	# Steps	T Response Time	Ø Time	T CPU~	Ø CPU~	T DB Time	Ø DB Time	T Time	Ø Time	Ø WaitTime	# Tri
PSVR	194	209	1,078.8	15	77.4	13	67.4	0.0	0.0	1.0	4
PSV2	322	190	591.5	38	116.7	22	66.8	0.0	0.0	1.6	1,0
PSV3	48	163	3,385.9	3	55.0	2	31.5	0.0	0.0	0.8	
PSV1	111	89	798.4	17	154.3	16	142.6	0.0	0.0	1.7	3
PV7I	189	80	424.8	53	279.2	19	101.7	0.0	0.0	1.2	4
SU01	202	49	244.8	17	82.7	28	140.1	0.0	0.0	0.2	3
SESSION_MANAGER	192	42	216.5	14	72.8	13	69.6	0.0	0.0	5.0	3
SPRO	32	30	935.8	4	139.7	21	655.8	0.0	0.0	1.4	
VA01	2	28	14,164.0	2	1,100.0	5	2,553.0	0.0	0.0	0.0	
PA30	42	27	646.2	8	196.0	15	351.5	0.0	0.0	0.8	1
PP01	85	21	249.5	7	86.8	7	79.0	0.0	0.0	1.1	1
<rpc(GENERATE)>	2	20	9,825.5	3	1,590.0	16	8,033.5	0.0	0.0	0.0	
SDMO	54	18	333.3	16	303.0	6	110.9	0.0	0.0	0.0	
PZ07	32	17	523.8	5	152.2	11	330.6	0.0	0.0	3.5	1
SQ01	33	16	474.4	6	190.9	7	220.0	0.0	0.0	2.6	
PA20	17	14	848.4	3	196.5	7	411.6	0.0	0.0	0.6	
PV3I	180	13	74.8	9	50.3	3	14.5	0.0	0.0	1.1	6

FIGURE 10-10 Checking the response time of specific transactions with the Transaction Profile (Copyright by SAP AG)

Sometimes it is not easy to identify the business area to which a transaction belongs to and there is a useful trick for system administrators to check what area a transaction or program belongs to. Execute program RSSTATUS in SE38 and enter the name of the program or transaction you want and press ENTER. The output will show you what area that program or transaction belongs to (for example, SD-Sales).

Troubleshooting Specific Performance Problems with the SQL Trace

There are certain tools that help you to analyze the performance of a particular program or transaction. One tool or another should be used, depending on what you observe in the Transaction Profile.

If the statistics for that particular transaction or program are showing high database times, a SQL Trace can be useful to check for expensive SQL Statements caused by that transaction.

A SQL Trace is started with transaction ST05 or Tools | Administration | Monitor | Traces | Performance Trace. Alternatively you can also use the new transaction code STKONTEXTTRACE.

Only one trace per Instance can be executed at a time. As a best practice, open two screens, one with the program or transaction that you have identified as performance impaired and another one with the SQL Trace ST05. If you are not tracing yourself, but another user, have the user work in only one screen executing that program or transaction and nothing else. Otherwise, the trace would not be useful, because everything that the user did would be traced.

Activate the trace (for yourself or using Activate with Filter selecting the user you want to trace). Run the program or transaction or have the user do it. When it is finished, deactivate the trace and click on Display Trace to observe the results. A filter can be used to display more or less data. For example, it is useful to display an Extended Trace list, which includes the program that passes the recorded SQL Statements to the database.

Observe in Figure 10-11 the results of an example of a SQL Trace. The records displayed are accesses to the database performed while executing the traced program. There are two important observations to make here. One is that if you run this program again and trace it, it is likely that several records will not show up in the trace results. Why? Because probably some tables will have been buffered into the R/3 buffers the first time you ran the program. Two is that only accesses to the database are recorded by this trace.

The Duration column specifies how long that particular SQL statement took to be read. If this time exceeds 150 milliseconds (note that the time is actually recorded in microseconds, therefore you would consider 150,000 microseconds as threshold!), such duration will be highlighted in red color, stating that that particular statement is considered expensive. You do not need to follow this threshold completely as written in stone, since many factors influence the access to the data in a database and therefore, depending on your hardware resources, the type of data that we are accessing, the disk devices, the network (if the database server is separate from the application server where you started the trace), and many other factors, this threshold may vary.

Once you have identified that a particular statement is expensive, your goal is to find out why, evaluating the access path that the database engine chose to access that data. Then

Transaction ST05	Work process no 1	Proc.type DIA	Client 110	User 70300	
Duration	**Obj. name**	**Op.**	**Recs.**	**RC**	**Statement**
79	TFDIR	REOPEN		0	SELECT WHERE "FUNCNAME" = 'SQLT_SYTIM_TO_LOTIM'
435	TFDIR	FETCH	1	0	
23	TADIR	REOPEN		0	SELECT WHERE "PGMID" = 'HEAD' AND "OBJECT" = 'SYST' AND "OBJ_NAME" = ' '
30,811	TADIR	FETCH	1	0	
17	T000	REOPEN		0	SELECT WHERE "MANDT" = '110'
29,284	T000	FETCH	1	0	
23	CVERS	REOPEN		0	SELECT FROM "CVERS" ORDER BY "COMPONENT"
1,320	CVERS	FETCH	16	1403	
863	PA0105	PREPARE		0	SELECT WHERE "MANDT" = :A0 AND "USRTY" = :A1 AND "USRID" = :A2
15	PA0105	OPEN		0	SELECT WHERE "MANDT" = '110' AND "USRTY" = '0001' AND "USRID" = '70300'
32,103	PA0105	FETCH	1	1403	
21	D347T	REOPEN		0	SELECT WHERE "PROGNAME" = 'SAPMP50A' AND "SPRSL" = 'E' AND "OBJ_CODE" = '001'
17,681	D347T	FETCH	1	0	

Transaction PA30	Work process no 1	Proc.type DIA	Client 110	User 70300	
Duration	**Obj. name**	**Op.**	**Recs.**	**RC**	**Statement**
1,020	LTDX	PREPARE		0	SELECT WHERE "MANDT" = :A0 AND "RELID" = :A1 AND "REPORT" = :A2 AND "HANDLE" = :A3 AN
49	LTDX	OPEN		0	SELECT WHERE "MANDT" = '110' AND "RELID" = 'RH' AND "REPORT" = 'EMPLOYEE' AND "HANDLE
14,014	LTDX	FETCH	1	1403	
28	LTDX	REOPEN		0	SELECT WHERE "MANDT" = '110' AND "RELID" = 'RH' AND "REPORT" = 'EMPLOYEE' AND "HANDLE
1,033	LTDX	FETCH	1	1403	

FIGURE 10-11 Example of a SQL Trace (Copyright by SAP AG)

eliminate the reason why that access path was not suitable and therefore eliminate what can be a very important performance problem. Sometimes, a secondary index in the table affected may help. Other times, buffer the table may help as well. Quite a few times, the selection criteria from the screen has not been very well defined by the user and this is requesting a lot of data unnecessarily. Finally, it may be necessary to change the code (especially in custom-developed programs) to provide with a more suitable way to access the data, avoiding overload onto the database.

Think that by identifying these performance issues in particular transactions or programs that are executed by the user community, you may be able to make the day of many people and ease their job quite a lot.

Troubleshooting Specific Performance Problems with an ABAP Trace

If the processing time of a transaction or program that you have identified in the Transaction Profile of the Workload Analysis Monitor is high, an ABAP Trace may be useful to identify exactly which function modules in that program or transaction are the cause of such lengthy times and therefore tune them.

An ABAP Trace is started with transaction SE30 or Tools | ABAP Workbench | Test | Runtime Analysis.

From this screen you can execute a program or transaction that you choose. Once you have typed the program or transaction name you have chosen to trace, click on Execute and you will be taken to the actual chosen program or transaction screen. The trace is activated automatically. Finish the task and go back with the green arrow until the main SE30 screen. Click on Analyze to display the file. A graphic showing where most of the time is spent, database, system or ABAP, is displayed. To obtain a list of all the function modules, click on Hit List and sort the list by Net Time in order to identify the most expensive function modules, as shown in Figure 10-12. The top ones' execution time differs greatly from that of the rest. The coding of such function modules are possible candidates for your developers to examine and determine potential improvement.

An important tip for developers can be found in the main screen of the ABAP Trace. Click on Tips and Tricks. You will be taken to a tool where you can measure the runtime of different ABAP commands that return the same data, yet when you compare the runtime results, they will probably differ greatly. Documentation is also included, so developers can learn to program efficiently.

In conclusion, the ABAP Trace and the SQL Trace are particularly useful tools while creating your own custom code and it is best practice for ABAP developers to be proficient at using them in order to achieve optimal performance in user exits and other in-house developed code.

Memory Management

As explained in the previous section, you are now able to identify performance issues that affect the system in general and specific problems in transactions or programs.

When examining the response time of your system and identifying that the load and generation time is excessive, it is likely that there may be problems related to memory

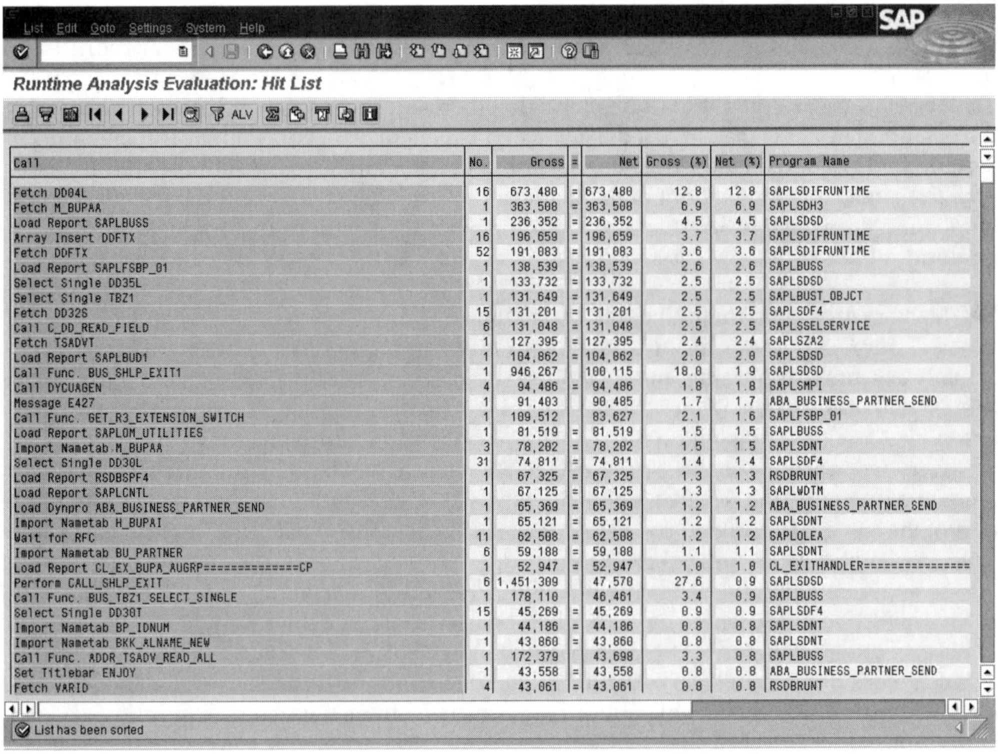

List Edit Goto Settings System Help

Runtime Analysis Evaluation: Hit List

Call	No.	Gross	=	Net	Gross (%)	Net (%)	Program Name
Fetch DD04L	16	673,480	=	673,480	12.8	12.8	SAPLSDIFRUNTIME
Fetch M_BUPAA	1	363,508	=	363,508	6.9	6.9	SAPLSDH3
Load Report SAPLBUSS	1	236,352	=	236,352	4.5	4.5	SAPLSDSD
Array Insert DDFTX	16	196,659	=	196,659	3.7	3.7	SAPLSDIFRUNTIME
Fetch DDFTX	52	191,083	=	191,083	3.6	3.6	SAPLSDIFRUNTIME
Load Report SAPLFSBP_01	1	138,539	=	138,539	2.6	2.6	SAPLBUSS
Select Single DD35L	1	133,732	=	133,732	2.5	2.5	SAPLSDSD
Select Single TBZ1	1	131,649	=	131,649	2.5	2.5	SAPLBUST_OBJCT
Fetch DD32S	15	131,201	=	131,201	2.5	2.5	SAPLSDF4
Call C_DD_READ_FIELD	6	131,048	=	131,048	2.5	2.5	SAPLSSELSERVICE
Fetch TSADVT	1	127,395	=	127,395	2.4	2.4	SAPLSZA2
Load Report SAPLBUD1	1	104,862	=	104,862	2.0	2.0	SAPLSDSD
Call Func. BUS_SHLP_EXIT1	1	946,267		100,115	18.0	1.9	SAPLSDSD
Call DYCUAGEN	4	94,486	=	94,486	1.8	1.8	SAPLSMPI
Message E427	1	91,403		90,485	1.7	1.7	ABA_BUSINESS_PARTNER_SEND
Call Func. GET_R3_EXTENSION_SWITCH	1	109,512		83,627	2.1	1.6	SAPLFSBP_01
Load Report SAPLOM_UTILITIES	1	81,519	=	81,519	1.5	1.5	SAPLBUSS
Import Nametab M_BUPAA	3	78,202	=	78,202	1.5	1.5	SAPLSDNT
Select Single DD30L	31	74,811	=	74,811	1.4	1.4	SAPLSDF4
Load Report RSDBSPF4	1	67,325	=	67,325	1.3	1.3	RSDBRUNT
Load Report SAPLCNTL	1	67,125	=	67,125	1.3	1.3	SAPLWDTM
Load Dynpro ABA_BUSINESS_PARTNER_SEND	1	65,369	=	65,369	1.2	1.2	ABA_BUSINESS_PARTNER_SEND
Import Nametab H_BUPAI	1	65,121	=	65,121	1.2	1.2	SAPLSDNT
Wait for RFC	11	62,508	=	62,508	1.2	1.2	SAPLOLEA
Import Nametab BU_PARTNER	6	59,188	=	59,188	1.1	1.1	SAPLSDNT
Load Report CL_EX_BUPA_AUGRP==============CP	1	52,947	=	52,947	1.0	1.0	CL_EXITHANDLER===============
Perform CALL_SHLP_EXIT	6	1,451,309		47,570	27.6	0.9	SAPLSDSD
Call Func. BUS_TBZ1_SELECT_SINGLE	1	178,110		46,461	3.4	0.9	SAPLBUSS
Select Single DD30T	15	45,269	=	45,269	0.9	0.9	SAPLSDF4
Import Nametab BP_IDNUM	1	44,186	=	44,186	0.8	0.8	SAPLSDNT
Import Nametab BKK_ALNAME_NEW	1	43,860	=	43,860	0.8	0.8	SAPLSDNT
Call Func. ADDR_TSADV_READ_ALL	1	172,379		43,698	3.3	0.8	SAPLBUSS
Set Titlebar ENJOY	1	43,558	=	43,558	0.8	0.8	ABA_BUSINESS_PARTNER_SEND
Fetch VARID	4	43,061	=	43,061	0.8	0.8	RSDBRUNT

List has been sorted

FIGURE 10-12 Results of an ABAP Trace (Runtime Analysis Evaluation) (Copyright by SAP AG)

management and buffer utilization. This may be caused by wrong parameter settings or a wrong configuration in an instance.

In this section, our goal is to identify those problems related to memory management and buffer configuration in a SAP system.

The Memory Areas in a SAP System

In a SAP system there are a series of buffers and memory areas that can be configured via parameter settings in the Instance Profile.

Buffers are areas of temporary storage that help to access more rapidly data and execute ABAP programs faster.

Likewise, there are memory areas used by ABAP programs during its execution that can be configured help to make the most out of the hardware resources of a server and achieve optimal performance. Let's define those areas and how to configure them.

It is important to understand that every server has a certain amount of physical memory or RAM and a certain amount of swap space that can be configured at the operating system level as a page file. This swap space or page file "enlarges" virtually the physical memory and the whole set can be seen as "virtual memory." The memory areas that can be configured in a SAP system will be addressed in the virtual memory of a server.

It is also very important to understand that there are several dependencies with the operating systems that are used. However, the general concepts apply to all operating systems and the parameter settings to configure the memory areas are almost all the time the same and independent of the platform. Ensure that you consult the installation guides and the available SAP Notes for specific parameter settings that apply to your platform.

SAP Memory Areas and Their Allocation Sequence

When a user needs to execute an ABAP program or any transaction, a work process will actually execute that program or those programs carrying out the task, extending the user context of a user and using the SAP memory areas that are defined via parameter settings, but indeed it will be consuming the physical resources, the virtual memory.

Every work process that is configured in an instance will be consuming a certain amount of memory, the *roll area*, defined by the parameter setting *zttz/roll_area*. A very little part of the roll area is defined by the parameter *ztta/roll_ first*. This is the very first area consumed by a dialog work process.

A very large memory area set by the parameter setting *em/initial_size_MB* defines the Extended Memory, where most or all of the user context of the user will reside while executing a program. After consuming the first roll area defined by *ztta/roll_ first*, a dialog work process will start allocating extended memory. It can consume as much extended memory as is available or until it reaches the quota defined by *ztta/roll _extension*.

Finally, part the heap memory defined by *abap/heap_area_total* is allocated by the dialog work process. It can allocate as much heap memory as is available or until reaching *abap/ heap_area_dia*. If the program is not finished after exhausting these limits, the program will abort with a dump that will comment about the memory exhaustion.

Otherwise, the program finishes successfully and the memory areas that were allocated get released.

However, there is an exception: if the dialog work process starts allocating heap memory, it enters into private mode (you will see status *stopped* in SM50 or SM66 and Reason "PRIV"), getting locked to that user until the transaction is finished, even if several dialog steps are necessary to complete it.

If this is the case, after a program finishes, the heap memory gets released, but not the swap space that was allocated before, creating a gap in memory and starting a snow ball sequence that can cause severe performance problems.

In order for the swap space to get released, the work process that allocated all that memory must be restarted. You can restart a work process manually, but in order to avoid administration efforts, the dispatcher can do it automatically. By setting the parameter *abap/ heaplimit* to a certain level, when a dialog work process reaches or passes that amount, it gets flagged. After finishing the program, the dispatcher detects it and restarts the work process. To avoid overhead, it is convenient not to set this parameter too high, so you ensure that work process that consume large amounts of memory are actually restarted so the swap space gets released; but not too low either, or the dialog work processes that reach heap memory will be constantly being restarted.

Monitoring the Memory Area Consumption

If, after examining the response time of your system, a lead takes you to monitor the memory consumption, you can do so executing transaction code ST02 or via the menu path Tools | Administration | Monitor | Performance | Setup/Buffers. See Figure 10-13.

You will be able to identify all the memory areas explained in the previous section and observe its level of consumption under Current Use. The Max Used indicator shows the largest amount of memory that has been consumed at some point.

Each instance in the system has its corresponding memory areas and therefore you will be able to monitor them separately.

When the use reaches or has reached at some point approximately 80% of the memory amount shown under In Memory, that is an indication of possible shortages and that area may be enlarged, if sufficient hardware resources are available.

Sometimes the workload is very high, which makes it difficult to isolate the cause of this excessive consumption. The root cause is simply that the workload is very high. If resources are sufficient, enlarging the memory areas would very likely solve the problem.

Otherwise, redistributing the workload among the available application servers, especially those that are not experiencing excessive resource consumption, would probably work to your advantage.

However, sometimes this excessive memory consumption may be due to a specific program or transaction that demands resources for its execution. You may be able to isolate the root cause by identifying certain programs that consume large amounts of memory from the Workload Analysis Monitor, in Administrator view, by choosing from the left-hand side of the screen Analysis Views | Memory Use Statistics.

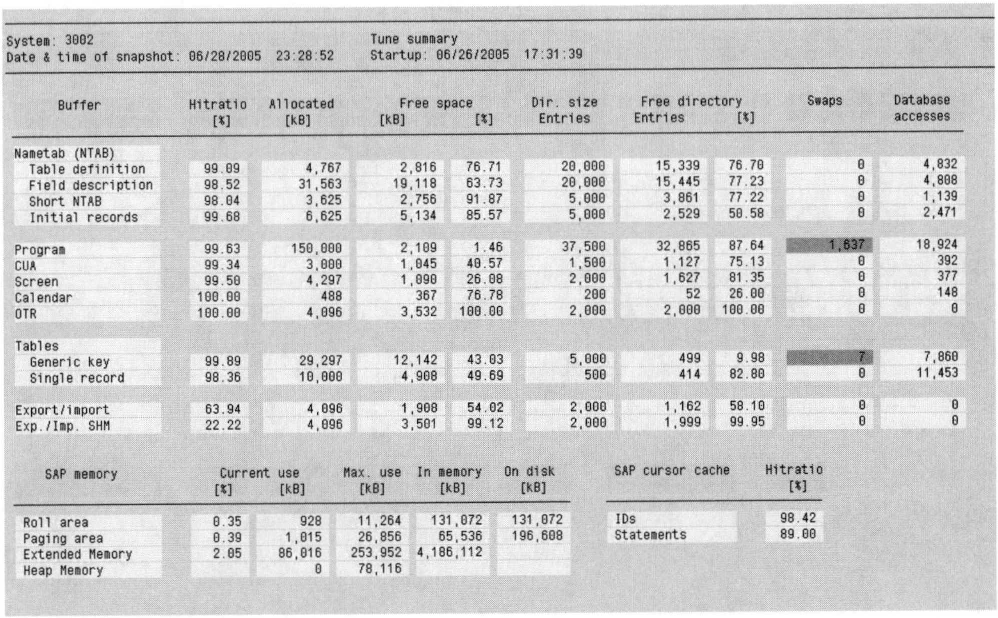

System: 3002 Tune summary
Date & time of snapshot: 06/28/2005 23:28:52 Startup: 06/26/2005 17:31:39

Buffer	Hitratio [%]	Allocated [kB]	Free space [kB]	Free space [%]	Dir. size Entries	Free directory Entries	Free directory [%]	Swaps	Database accesses
Nametab (NTAB)									
Table definition	99.09	4,767	2,816	76.71	20,000	15,339	76.70	0	4,832
Field description	98.52	31,563	19,118	63.73	20,000	15,445	77.23	0	4,808
Short NTAB	98.04	3,625	2,756	91.87	5,000	3,861	77.22	0	1,139
Initial records	99.68	6,625	5,134	85.57	5,000	2,529	50.58	0	2,471
Program	99.63	150,000	2,109	1.46	37,500	32,865	87.64	1,637	18,924
CUA	99.34	3,000	1,045	40.57	1,500	1,127	75.13	0	392
Screen	99.50	4,297	1,090	26.08	2,000	1,627	81.35	0	377
Calendar	100.00	488	367	76.78	200	52	26.00	0	148
OTR	100.00	4,096	3,532	100.00	2,000	2,000	100.00	0	0
Tables									
Generic key	99.89	29,297	12,142	43.03	5,000	499	9.98	7	7,860
Single record	98.36	10,000	4,908	49.69	500	414	82.80	0	11,453
Export/import	63.94	4,096	1,908	54.02	2,000	1,162	58.10	0	0
Exp./Imp. SHM	22.22	4,096	3,501	99.12	2,000	1,999	99.95	0	0

SAP memory	Current use [%]	Current use [kB]	Max. use [kB]	In memory [kB]	On disk [kB]
Roll area	0.35	928	11,264	131,072	131,072
Paging area	0.39	1,015	26,856	65,536	196,608
Extended Memory	2.05	86,016	253,952	4,186,112	
Heap Memory		0	78,116		

SAP cursor cache	Hitratio [%]
IDs	98.42
Statements	89.00

FIGURE 10-13 Monitoring memory areas and their consumption (Copyright by SAP AG)

This view shows a history of the top memory consuming programs and the breakdown of memory areas that the program needed to run, such as extended memory of heap memory (referred in this monitor as "private memory"). From here, once you know which programs consume a large amount of memory and may represent a performance "hog" for your users, it is best practice to find out the reasons of such resource consumption.

When you identify custom-developed programs, it is convenient to advise your developers to check these programs for tuning potential and a more efficient use of the resources, especially while creating and manipulating internal tables and so on.

There is another way to isolate the root cause of this problem. If you are monitoring the current usage of the system and workload, you may observe users in PRIV mode in SM50 or SM66. Your goal would be to find out why these users are in PRIV mode, is it because they are using excessive memory or because the available extended memory is exhausted and they need to reach heap? By using ST02 you can check the amount of extended memory being used. Double-click on Extended Memory line and you will be taken to a detailed analysis of the memory areas and its consumption. From there, click on Mode List. This view shows the memory consumed by user in that particular instance as shown in Figure 10-14. You will be able to identify which users are executing programs that consume a large amount of memory and obtain answers to the questions outlined above. Sometimes, certain programs that are very resource demanding consume so much extended memory that the rest of the users are left with a very small amount to use and they need to go to heap,

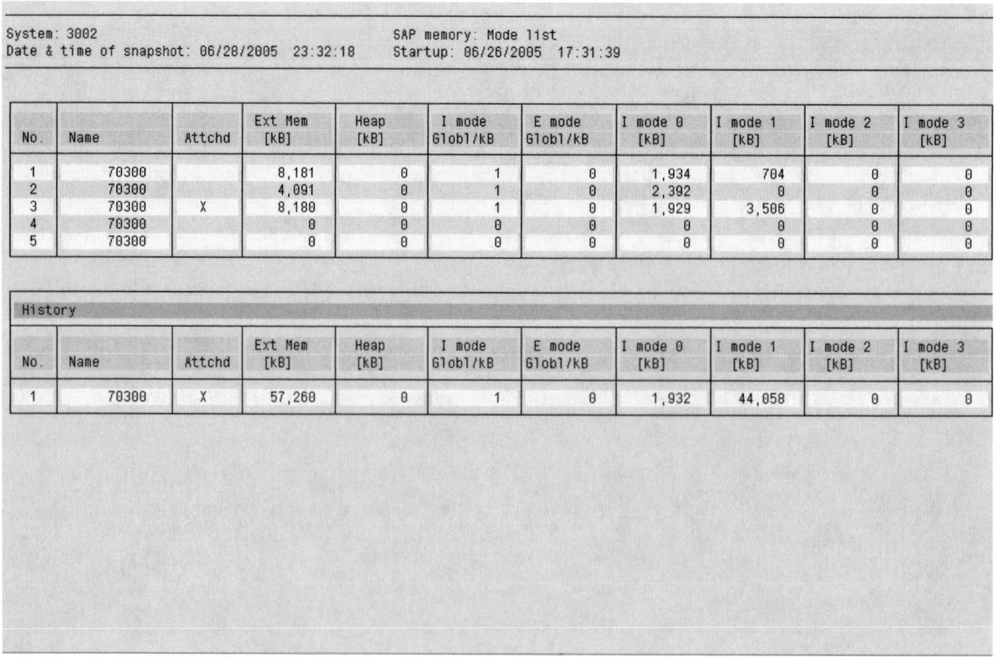

System: 3002 SAP memory: Mode list
Date & time of snapshot: 06/28/2005 23:32:18 Startup: 06/26/2005 17:31:39

No.	Name	Attchd	Ext Mem [kB]	Heap [kB]	I mode Globl/kB	E mode Globl/kB	I mode 0 [kB]	I mode 1 [kB]	I mode 2 [kB]	I mode 3 [kB]
1	70300		8,181	0	1	0	1,934	704	0	0
2	70300		4,091	0	1	0	2,392	0	0	0
3	70300	X	8,180	0	1	0	1,929	3,506	0	0
4	70300		0	0	0	0	0	0	0	0
5	70300		0	0	0	0	0	0	0	0

History

No.	Name	Attchd	Ext Mem [kB]	Heap [kB]	I mode Globl/kB	E mode Globl/kB	I mode 0 [kB]	I mode 1 [kB]	I mode 2 [kB]	I mode 3 [kB]
1	70300	X	57,260	0	1	0	1,932	44,058	0	0

FIGURE 10-14 Identifying the users that use excessive memory in an instance (Copyright by SAP AG)

entering in PRIV mode and leading to the consequences explained before in regards to not releasing the swap space and therefore contributing to further performance problems.

In order to make the best use of the available memory and configure the memory areas properly, you set up the relevant parameters in the instance profile.

Setting up the parameter settings for memory management depends very heavily on the amount of physical memory available and in the architecture. A 32-bit architecture has many limitations in the amount of memory that can actually be allocated, whereas a 64-bit architecture does not normally represent a problem and memory areas (as well as buffer sizes) can be generously defined.

Most of the parameters are operating system independent, although some of them are not or a few extra parameter settings must be set for optimal performance. It is best practice to check SAP Notes that contain the most up to date parameter settings for optimal performance. SAP Note 103747 is the central SAP Note to refer to.

There are not optimal parameters that magically work for all systems and all platforms and all sizes. Depending on those and other criteria, the optimal parameter settings for your system may differ from another. Testing in a quality system or a copy of production before implementing those settings in production is always a best practice.

The Buffers in a SAP Instance

Each instance that you define in every application server, even if there are more than instance defined in the same application server, has a set of buffers associated. The buffer sizes are defined by parameter settings in the Instance Profile.

There are several buffers and they help to access data more rapidly, as well as to execute ABAP programs faster.

The Program Buffer (also known as PXA buffer) is one of the most important ones. When ABAP programs are called to be executed, they will be buffered in this storage area. When this buffer is not large enough, buffer swaps (gaps) occur and this fragmentation in the buffer leads to performance problems, since the ABAP programs need to be reloaded over and over again.

Other buffers like the screen buffer, the calendar buffer, the CUA buffer help building the screens in each dialog step rapidly, because they store the "skeleton" of the screens, the calendars used, and the common pushbuttons and icons.

The table buffers store tables temporarily and follow certain important rules to be buffered and to be accessed by ABAP programs. It is best practice for developers to be familiar with these rules when creating custom objects and custom programs that access those objects for efficient access.

An access to a buffer can be one hundred times faster than an access to the database. Therefore, applying the rules with care can lead to optimal performance.

Table Buffering

There are three types of table buffering:

- *Partial buffering or single-record buffering.* When reading a single record (from the database) of a table that has been buffered as a "single record," that one record will be stored in the buffer. Then further accesses will be hits from the buffer.
- *Generic key buffering.* Accessing a record for the first time from a table that is buffered with "generic key buffering" with *n* number of fields will store in the

buffer the table region defined by those *n* key fields. All other accesses to a record that can be found in that region will be a hit in the buffer.

- *Full buffering.* When any record from a table with "full buffering" settings is read from the database, the whole table gets loaded in the buffer and further accesses will be found in the buffer. So other accesses to any record in that table can be found in the buffer.

Tables read from the buffer, then, improve performance. However, rules must be taken into consideration when accessing buffered tables. When a table is changed or updated, then the status in the buffer changes to invalid, meaning that the next access will be performed in the database. It must be that way to guarantee that you read the most up to date data. This leads to the following case: in a central system with only one instance, when a table is changed, there seems to be no problem to access the data again from the database and reload that data onto the buffer. However, what if we have several instances and application servers that have the same tables loaded into their respective buffers?

Imagine the following situation: a user logged on instance 1 updates table ABCD that is loaded into its buffer. That will invalidate the status of that table and the next access from a user logged on that instance will have to go to the database to read that data. Meanwhile, a user logged on instance 2 tries to read table ABCD that is also stored in its buffer. That user will read obsolete data.

In order to prevent this situation, these instances perform a mechanism called "buffer synchronization." When a user updates a buffered table, an entry is made in the database table DDLOG. Imagine DDLOG as a communication pipe between instances, like a message board. The instance that updates a buffered table will write a "message" in DDLOG, such that any other instance can read that "Table ABCD has been updated and therefore you may refresh your buffers now." All other instances, every certain tie, will read from this table and will update their buffered table status accordingly.

This buffer refreshing mechanism works by setting two parameters in the instance profile: *rdisp/bufreftime = sendon, exeauto* and *rdisp/bufreftime = xx*, where *xx* is the number of seconds (by default, 60) that makes every instance read from DDLOG.

So, basically, "sendon" means "write onto DDLOG" and "exeauto" means "read from DDLOG." You may set *rdisp/bufrefmode* to "sendoff" in a central system with only one instance, where no buffer synchronization is necessary.

Troubleshooting Table Buffering for Optimal Performance

Now that you know the different table buffering types, we will discuss what tables should be buffered or not, depending on a certain criteria and how developers in particular can take advantage of these settings for efficient and accurate programming techniques.

In the technical settings of a table you specify whether a table is allowed to be buffered or not and what buffering type. To do this, execute transaction SE11 and display a table that you want to change the settings of and click on Technical Settings. The menu path to get to this point is Tools | ABAP Workbench | Development | Dictionary. You may also choose to execute SE13 to display the technical settings of a table directly.

There you may choose if buffering is not allowed for that table or if it is and what type of buffering you choose.

In general, tables to be buffered are small and not frequently changed tables. By small, count up to a few megabytes in size. By not frequently changed, think rarely changed for best results. Customizing tables in a production environment do not change very often and are candidates to be buffered. Depending on your hardware resources (memory), you may be able to store more or larger tables in your buffers, if these are bigger.

On the other hand, tables that are large or frequently changed should not be buffered. These include normally master data tables and transactional data, for example.

The buffering type you choose for a table will also depend on the size and the type of accesses to that table. Developers know what their programs do and how they decide to access the tables that the use in their programs. Therefore, it is best practice to consider different table buffering types depending on the type of access to the data. For example, a program that accesses in a loop several single records of a table that is relatively big may have that table as a candidate to buffer that table as a single record instead of a full record.

You may also be troubleshooting a program or transaction with a SQL Trace and find similar statements in the trace and it would lead you to the same conclusion.

Another example would be to buffer a table choosing Generic Key buffering when using that table in a program that is going to use a certain company code or when you know that in a certain selection screen the user may choose from a very specific set of fields that are key in that table and having that region buffered would improve performance.

You may also skip the access to a table that is buffered in an ABAP program by choosing certain commands, such as SELECT (. . .) BYPASSING BUFFER. The clause BYPASSING BUFFER explicitly ignores the buffer contents and retrieves data from the database, no matter what type of buffering is chosen for that table.

A SELECT statement that does not include the clause SINGLE in its definition bypasses a "single record" buffered table. And in a "generic key" buffered table, if you do not specify all the keys, you bypass the access from the buffer as well.

A developer may choose to do this consciously, since in a program, at a certain point, the most up to date data may be needed and therefore, an access to the buffer must be bypassed.

Applying the simple rules from above when choosing to buffer or not to buffer a table and programming efficiently using the proper commands can help to improve performance.

You can monitor the access to the tables via transaction ST10 or by the menu path Tools | Administration | Monitor | Performance | Setup/Buffers | Table Calls | Calls. Choose the tables to be analyzed from the selection screen, all tables, certain tables buffered in a certain buffering type, and choose a period of time and a specific instance or all servers. See Figure 10-15.

The list displayed will show you in detail "table call statistics." So you will be able to see the number of calls passed from an ABAP program to the buffers and the database, the status of a table in the buffer, the size of the object buffered, the number of rows or records affected when a table is loaded onto the buffer, and the number of invalidations. The number of invalidations is especially important to check when a table is buffered and this number is high, because it is an indicator that such table may be a candidate to unbuffer or at least check what possibilities there are to avoid such overhead in the buffer.

On the other hand, when a table is very frequently accessed according to the number of "rows affected" from that monitor and it is not buffered, if it follows certain rules, like the small size and not frequently updated, it may be a possible candidate to buffer.

Again, it is important to check and test in quality systems or copies of production before changing these settings in a production environment.

System: 3002 Single record buffered tables
Time frame of analysis : 06/28/2005 19:15:15

Table	Buf key opt	Invali-dations	ABAP/IV Processor requests				DB act
			Total	Direct reads	Seq. reads	Changes	Calls
Total		20	697,062	601,860	89,916	5,286	96,578
/SOMO/MA_UPD_ERR	sng	0	0	0	0	0	0
AGR_DATEU	sng	10	227	211	0	16	45
AGR_DEFINE	sng	0	1,955	1,931	23	1	31
ALF1DEFLT	sng	0	1,045	1,045	0	0	0
ALGRPCUSGE	sng	0	103,052	101,920	0	1,132	1,134
ALGRPCUSMC	sng	0	42,632	42,632	0	0	0
ALGRPCUSMG	sng	0	4,608	4,608	0	0	0
ALGRPCUSPF	sng	0	33,408	33,408	0	0	0
ALGRPMCFIL	sng	0	0	0	0	0	0
ALMTCUSGEN	sng	0	21,888	21,888	0	0	0
ALMTCUSPER	sng	0	2,304	2,304	0	0	0
ALPFASSIGN	sng	0	116	0	116	0	123
ALPFCOLLTID	sng	0	232	0	232	0	246
ALTIDTOOL	sng	0	0	0	0	0	0
ALTRAMONI	sng	0	288	0	288	0	293
BDLSESS	sng	0	3	0	3	0	7
CSMBK_OB2	sng	0	2,088	0	2,088	0	2,106
CSMPRPINH2	sng	0	0	0	0	0	0
CSMTOOLASG	sng	0	24	0	24	0	28
CTSCURPRJ	sng	0	1	1	0	0	0
D347T	sng	0	2,620	2,620	0	0	0
DD30L	sng	0	723	723	0	0	0
DD30T	sng	0	24	24	0	0	0
DOKIL	sng	0	12,020	11,948	72	0	87

FIGURE 10-15 Displaying tables in the Table Call Statistics Monitor (Copyright by SAP AG)

Monitoring SAP Buffers

In order to control the size of the buffers in any SAP system, parameter settings in the instance profile can be set. When the buffers are sized too small for the workload and objects (programs and tables) start to be swapped out of the buffers, you can display "swaps" in these buffers in ST02 (the buffer and memory monitor). You can see the swaps as the number of objects displaced from a buffer. This indicator turns red in the buffer monitor (ST02) when the counter reaches even 1! You can see the free space in the buffer as well by double-clicking on a particular buffer in the buffer monitor to see the detailed statistics as shown in Figure 10-16. The statistics shown for table buffers differ slightly from the program buffer, but they have the same general meaning. When displaying the table buffers, the easiest indicator to see that the buffer is full and objects are being swapped is the free space, which could go down to 0.

The Program Buffer is one of the most important pieces in tuning an instance, because programs are constantly used and loaded to reuse. When objects are displaced from the buffer, gaps may occur. Gaps can be seen as fragmentation, space that is not usable (like "holes" in the buffer). Especially when the number of gaps reaches the "free space" in KB this means that the buffer is not utilized efficiently and that all free space is not usable. The hit ratio will likely decrease and more objects will be swapped. When this happens, it is time to enlarge the buffer to make more room for objects. There are other alternatives, if resources are limited, such as redistribute the workload among all application servers, especially when other servers are more free.

Parameter settings in the instance profile control the table and program buffers' size and can be changed to achieve optimal performance. After any change, the instance must be restarted to obtain the new value. Carefully change these parameter settings, if you are

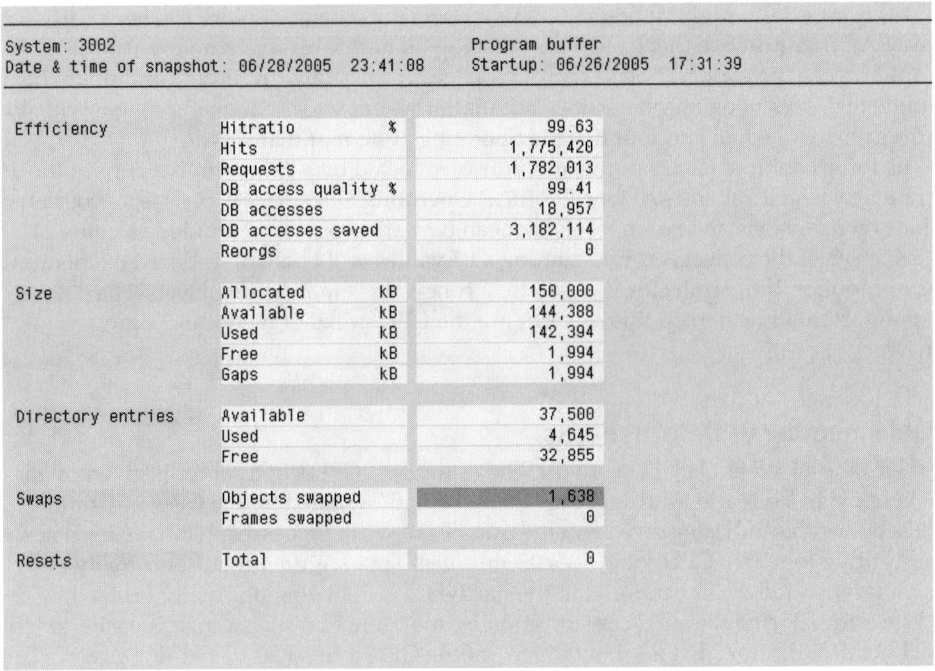

System: 3002 | Program buffer
Date & time of snapshot: 06/28/2005 23:41:08 | Startup: 06/26/2005 17:31:39

Efficiency	Hitratio	%	99.63
	Hits		1,775,420
	Requests		1,782,013
	DB access quality %		99.41
	DB accesses		18,957
	DB accesses saved		3,182,114
	Reorgs		0
Size	Allocated	kB	150,000
	Available	kB	144,388
	Used	kB	142,394
	Free	kB	1,994
	Gaps	kB	1,994
Directory entries	Available		37,500
	Used		4,645
	Free		32,855
Swaps	Objects swapped		1,638
	Frames swapped		0
Resets	Total		0

FIGURE 10-16 Detailed statistics of the Program Buffer showing the efficiency of the buffer utilization (Copyright by SAP AG)

experiencing poor performance and the root cause is the size of the buffers. Always follow SAP recommendations. The best documentation in parameter settings is located in the Online Help and typical values and recommendations are found in SAP Note 103747.

Hardware Capacity Analysis

As explained in Chapter 2, client/server architecture, such as the one SAP systems are based on, several servers might play the role of application servers, and only one is assigned the role of database server. A SAP system is scalable; therefore, you may add application servers, as needed, if the workload increases. It is essential to understand, though, that resources are limited, in particular, hardware resources.

In this topic, it is time now to check the capacity of your hardware in terms of physical memory and CPU. Monitoring the hardware consumption of your servers on a regular basis is a best practice that can prevent performance problems due to hardware bottlenecks, if these are detected on time and the proper actions are taken.

The Operating System Monitor

Execute transaction OS06 or choose the menu path Tools | Administration | Monitor | Performance | Operating System | Local | Activity. Transaction OS06 leads you to the same place and transaction OS07 leads you to the selection of remote servers, so you can choose one of them to monitor from where you are.

This is especially useful when you have a standalone database server where you do not have a SAP instance and, therefore, you must log on to that server remotely via RFC.

You can check the operating system of each server locally or remotely and if you have multiple instances in one server it does not matter where you are logged on, you will always see the same data when you monitor the operating system of that server.

The information obtained in this monitor is collected by a program that runs at the operating system level: the SAPOSCOL (SAP Operating System Collector) is a program with its own versions and patch levels that can be started or stopped independently of the instances. If the collector is not running, "0" values will be displayed in the Operating System Monitor. If the collector is obsolete, wrong values may be displayed. The most important indicators in this monitor are the CPU utilization and the paging activity.

Troubleshooting CPU Bottlenecks

First, we take a look at the CPU activity. The number of CPU's in a server is given by the number next to Count. In addition, the "load average" detailed by the CPU utilization figures below this indicator gives you the number of work processes that have been at some point waiting for a free CPU for 1, 5, or 15 minutes. These figures should normally be very low. Otherwise, it is an indication that the hardware is not being optimally utilized.

When monitoring the CPU consumption by the users in the system, it is easier to look at the CPU idle indicator (that is, "how much" of the CPU if this was something that we could count is free). As a rule of thumb, this should not go below 20% (that means a total CPU utilization for that server of 80%). Otherwise, you may risk a hardware bottleneck, if the CPU idle is very low for long periods of time through the day. During peaks of workload you may see the CPU idle go to very low numbers and this may be expected, if you sized your system accordingly.

A CPU bottleneck can come from a number of reasons. A simple program can cause a CPU bottleneck, if this is too resource demanding or if it is poorly written. Excessive workload in a server can easily cause a CPU bottleneck and nonoptimal workload distribution as well.

In addition, not only processes related to the SAP software are running in a server. External programs, such as monitoring tools, scripts at the operating system level, scripts on the database server, screen savers, virus scanners, backup tools, and so on may be running at the same time as your online users and occupying the available CPU's in your servers, which may lead your users competing for resources and experiencing performance problems.

In order to check all the processes that are running in a server, you may check so at the operating system level with the proper commands, or from the Operating System Monitor choose Detail Analysis Menu and then Top CPU. The list displayed shows all the processes running in that server and the CPU consumption related to each process. Programs that are named disp+work are the well-known work processes. In a database server, you may see database processes and in any given server you may see any kind of external processes as well. When external processes are the cause of a hardware bottleneck, the question you need to answer is, "Is that process necessary to run and, if so, must it run at this time, interfering with users?"

It is best practice to check whether the workload can be redistributed among all application servers and avoid overload, especially in the database server, because this

```
Tue Jun 28 23:46:47 2005  interval  10   sec.
CPU
Utilization  user     %            1   Count                       2
             system   %            1   Load average    1 min    0.13
             idle     %           97                   5 min    0.28
             io wait  %            1                  15 min    0.30
System calls/s                 1,384   Context switches/s        540
Interrupts/s                     607

Memory
Physical mem avail  Kb     6,291,456   Physical mem free   Kb    932,492
Pages in/s                         0   Kb paged in/s                   0
Pages out/s                        0   Kb paged out/s                  0

Swap
Configured swap     Kb    11,460,608   Maximum swap-space  Kb  16,255,220
Free in swap-space  Kb    15,309,648   Actual swap-space   Kb  16,255,220

Disk with highest response time
Name                          c2t2d0   Response time       ms         10
Utilization                        0   Queue                           0
Avg wait time       ms             5   Avg service time    ms          5
Kb transfered/s                    2   Operations/s                    0

Lan (sum)
Packets in/s                      13   Errors in/s                     0
Packets out/s                     13   Errors out/s                    0
Collisions                         0
```

FIGURE 10-17 Memory utilization figures in the Operating System Monitor (Copyright by SAP AG)

is a central resource and if this has a hardware bottleneck, all users in a system will be affected.

Troubleshooting Physical Memory

The paging indicators under Memory in ST06 show you the amount of pages going "in" or "out" of physical memory from or into hard disk and therefore it gives you an idea of how well the physical memory is utilized versus the hard disk. Figure 10-17 shows the indicators of memory utilization in the Operating System Monitor.

As a rule of thumb, consider 20% of RAM as the amount of paging that should not be exceeded on a regular basis. Again, excessive workload, nonoptimal distribution of it, resource demanding or poorly written ABAP programs or external processes may contribute to a memory bottleneck. Checking the memory utilization as explained in the section on memory management (in transaction ST03N, Memory Profile, or in ST02, Mode List) helps you to eliminate variables and find out if one of the causes of an excessive memory consumption comes from the users. It is a well important to train the users in an efficient use of the programs and transactions that are available, especially those with large reporting possibilities and selection screens that can make a difference when executed!

Database Analysis

The database is a central resource in any SAP system and for that reason it deserves special attention when it comes to performance and stability, since all users may be affected, if the database is not performing well.

SAP systems may use an Oracle, SQL Server, DB2 UDB, SAP DB or Informix database. Depending on this factor, the monitors and the indicators to look at when analyzing the database are different. With the exception of the individual indicators and characteristics of every database, analyzing a database follows the same general rules. You may check for hardware bottlenecks in CPU and memory in the database server, check for Input/Output contention in the hard disks, ensure that parameter settings are configured for optimal performance and stability and search for expensive SQL statements using the monitors in your SAP system. As an example, we will use a Database Monitor for an Oracle database in this chapter.

The Database Monitor (Oracle)

Execute transaction code ST04 or follow the path Tools | Administration | Monitor | Performance | Database | Activity. Figure 10-18 shows a view of the Database Monitor for Oracle. We will proceed to describe briefly the most important indicators of performance for the database next.

In an Oracle database it is important to pay attention to the following indicators:

- The data buffer, which should approach a value higher than 95% to indicate that when a call is passed to the database, most of the time the data are found in the buffer, instead of having to go to physical disk.

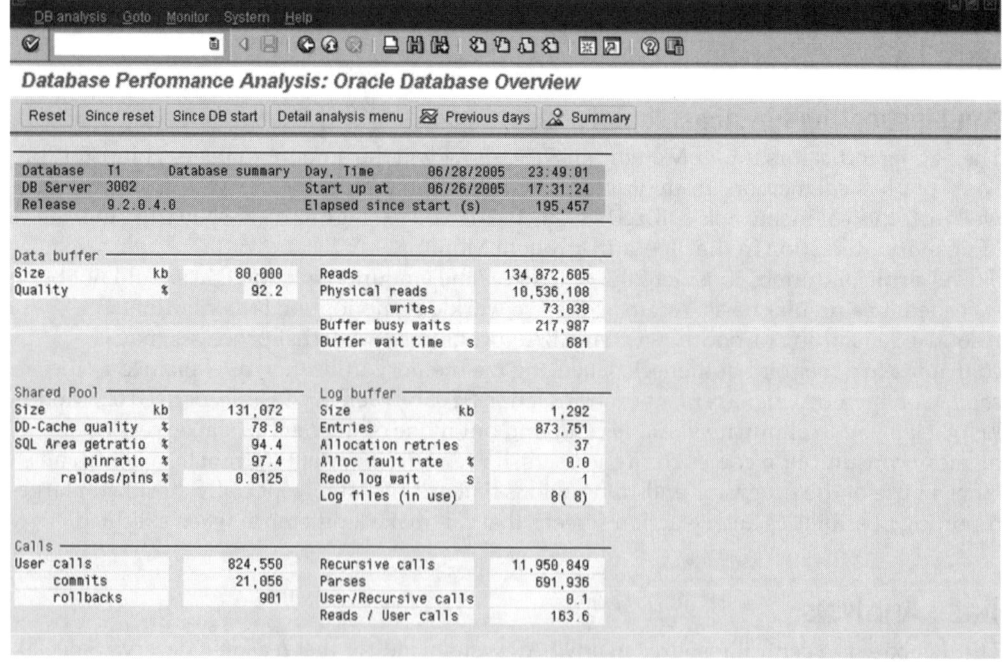

FIGURE 10-18 Displaying important indicators in the Database Monitor (Oracle) (Copyright by SAP AG)

- The Shared Pool SQL and Data Dictionary Pin ratio, which should approach 100%, as it indicates that most of the time the database engine is able to reuse to stored SQL statements from the Shared Global Area.
- The number of Reads/User Calls should be less than 20; otherwise, it may be a indicator of expensive SQL statements in the database. More information on detecting expensive SQL Statements will be found later on in this chapter.
- The Time/Users Call should be less than 20 milliseconds in order to achieve optimal performance.

Troubleshooting the Database: Expensive SQL Statements

When analyzing the response time of your system, you may encounter that the database request time in the Workload Analysis Monitor is excessive or that certain programs in the Work Process Monitor are taking long times performing actions in the database ("Sequential Read," etc.). This might be the time to look at the Database Performance Monitor and check for possible performance problems. Sometimes, an analysis in a particular transaction or program in the SQL Trace may lead you to perform a deeper analysis of SQL statements as well.

Note that many areas can affect negatively the database performance, such as the network communication with the application servers, the hardware capacity of the database server, wrong parameter settings, and so on. Therefore, in order to make this analysis the easiest, we will concentrate our efforts in checking the database for expensive SQL statements and try to give you some tips and tricks to detect possible performance problems related to expensive SQL statements and a few quick advises for tuning.

Expensive SQL statements may come from a variety of situations, but most of the time, it is the application layer, in the case of SAP systems, ABAP programming, that is the root cause.

It is important to detect expensive SQL statements before tables grow so large that they are difficult to manage and have your developers tune the custom code as much as possible in order to obtain optimal performance.

From the database performance monitor, click on Detail Analysis Menu and then on SQL Request. The pop-up selection screen that shows up allows you to filter and sort the output. The list displayed is the selected SQL statements in the Shared Pool of Oracle, accessible from the SAP Web Application Server. See Figure 10-19.

An easy way to analyze whether any of these statements is expensive and therefore causing overhead in the database and a rule of thumb to follow would be as follows: Sort the list by Buffer Gets, which is basically the number of blocks read from the database buffer. When this number exceeds 5% of the total number of reads from the database (Reads in the main screen of the database performance monitor), it is an indicator that such statement may be expensive, because it reads many blocks. Look at the number in the Buffer Gets row, which is how many blocks must have been read from the buffer per each record to satisfy the request. When this is greater than 5, this may mean that (of course, depending on other factors, such as parameter settings—let's assume they are set optimally) the statement is reading "too much" and therefore, the access path chosen by the database engine is not suitable. When this figure is small, it is likely that the access path chosen by the engine is suitable and it is just that the application requested (with the ABAP program that passed that statement to the database) a lot of data.

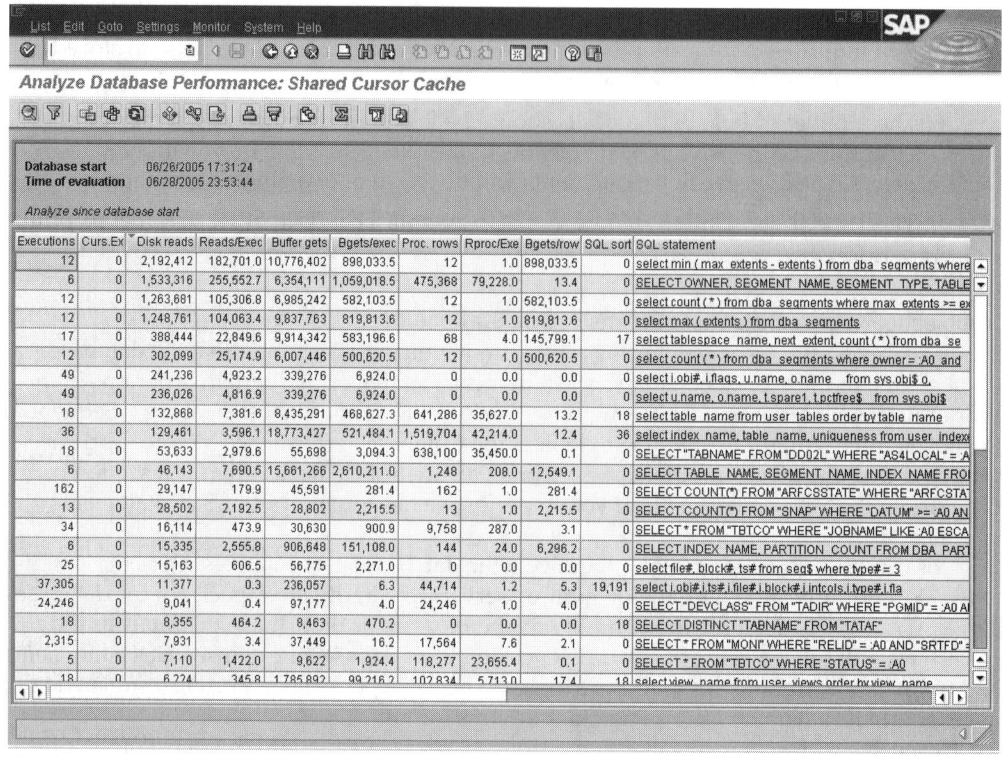

Executions	Curs.Ex	Disk reads	Reads/Exec	Buffer gets	Bgets/exec	Proc. rows	Rproc/Exe	Bgets/row	SQL sort	SQL statement
12	0	2,192,412	182,701.0	10,776,402	898,033.5	12	1.0	898,033.5	0	select min (max extents - extents) from dba segments where
6	0	1,533,316	255,552.7	6,354,111	1,059,018.5	475,368	79,228.0	13.4	0	SELECT OWNER, SEGMENT NAME, SEGMENT TYPE, TABLE
12	0	1,263,681	105,306.8	6,985,242	582,103.5	12	1.0	582,103.5	0	select count (*) from dba segments where max extents >= ex
12	0	1,248,761	104,063.4	9,837,763	819,813.6	12	1.0	819,813.6	0	select max (extents) from dba segments
17	0	388,444	22,849.6	9,914,342	583,196.6	68	4.0	145,799.1	17	select tablespace name, next extent, count (*) from dba se
12	0	302,099	25,174.9	6,007,446	500,620.5	12	1.0	500,620.5	0	select count (*) from dba segments where owner = :A0 and
49	0	241,236	4,923.2	339,276	6,924.0	0	0.0	0.0	0	select i.obj#, i.flags, u.name, o.name from sys.obj$ o,
49	0	236,026	4,816.9	339,276	6,924.0	0	0.0	0.0	0	select u.name, o.name, t.spare1, t.pctfree$ from sys.obj$
18	0	132,868	7,381.6	8,435,291	468,627.3	641,286	35,627.0	13.2	18	select table name from user tables order by table name
36	0	129,461	3,596.1	18,773,427	521,484.1	1,519,704	42,214.0	12.4	36	select index name, table name, uniqueness from user indexe
18	0	53,633	2,979.6	55,698	3,094.3	638,100	35,450.0	0.1	0	SELECT "TABNAME" FROM "DD02L" WHERE "AS4LOCAL" = :A
6	0	46,143	7,690.5	15,661,266	2,610,211.0	1,248	208.0	12,549.1	0	SELECT TABLE NAME, SEGMENT NAME, INDEX NAME FRO
162	0	29,147	179.9	45,591	281.4	162	1.0	281.4	0	SELECT COUNT(*) FROM "ARFCSSTATE" WHERE "ARFCSTA
13	0	28,502	2,192.5	28,802	2,215.5	13	1.0	2,215.5	0	SELECT COUNT(*) FROM "SNAP" WHERE "DATUM" >= :A0 AN
34	0	16,114	473.9	30,630	900.9	9,758	287.0	3.1	0	SELECT * FROM "TBTCO" WHERE "JOBNAME" LIKE :A0 ESCA
6	0	15,335	2,555.8	906,648	151,108.0	144	24.0	6,296.2	0	SELECT INDEX NAME, PARTITION COUNT FROM DBA PART
25	0	15,163	606.5	56,775	2,271.0	0	0.0	0.0	0	select file#, block#, ts# from seg$ where type# = 3
37,305	0	11,377	0.3	236,057	6.3	44,714	1.2	5.3	19,191	select i.obj#,i.ts#,i.file#,i.block#,i.intcols,i.type#,i.fla
24,246	0	9,041	0.4	97,177	4.0	24,246	1.0	4.0	0	SELECT "DEVCLASS" FROM "TADIR" WHERE "PGMID" = :A0 A
18	0	8,355	464.2	8,463	470.2	0	0.0	0.0	18	SELECT DISTINCT "TABNAME" FROM "TATAF"
2,315	0	7,931	3.4	37,449	16.2	17,564	7.6	2.1	0	SELECT * FROM "MONI" WHERE "RELID" = :A0 AND "SRTFD" =
5	0	7,110	1,422.0	9,622	1,924.4	118,277	23,655.4	0.1	0	SELECT * FROM "TBTCO" WHERE "STATUS" = :A0
18	0	6,224	345.8	1,785,892	99,216.2	102,834	5,713.0	17.4	18	select view name from user views order by view name

FIGURE 10-19 Analyzing SQL statements in the Database Performance Monitor for an Oracle database (Copyright by SAP AG)

In order to see the access path chosen by the database engine, select Goto | Explain SQL or click on the wrenchlike icon after highlighting the selected SQL statement. The Cost Based Optimizer is the way that the Oracle engine determines the best access path to data (using a secondary index, reading a full table, etc.) and the cost and estimated number of rows read will be displayed as well, which should be as low as possible.

When an index is used to retrieve the data, it is suitable when all or most of the fields from the WHERE clause of the statement are also included in the index. You can check important statistical data from that table and what indexes are created in that table by clicking on the table name in the Execution Plan showing the access path. The statistics date is important, because all tables in a SAP system, with exception of the some of them with special processing (please, check SAP Note 122718 and others), should have recent statistics. The Cost Based Optimizer engine needs to have current statistics in order to determine the most suitable access path.

The indexes in a table are also important to determine a good access path. Primary indexes have the name of the table followed by the tilde (˜) and the number 0. Secondary indexes may be followed by a different number or a letter. Check whether the fields on the indexes that are created in that table are selective or not by looking at how many "distinct" values the field have and if they are included in the WHERE clause of the statement passed to the database.

Another tip for optimal performance when using secondary indexes would be to avoid more than five indexes in a table and more than five fields in an index, because too many indexes may also be "confusing" for the database engine, and all of them need also to have recent statistics and be updated when the table has changed, causing overhead.

You can display the call point of the program that has passed that statement to the database by clicking on the icon with the glasses or via Goto | Display Call Point in ABAP Program. This way you save a lot of time and you can find out where exactly in which program that statement comes from. When you determine that the ABAP program is causing a poor selection and access path in the database, and this is a custom code, maybe it would be convenient, if possible, to change the code accordingly to obtain better performance accessing the data that you need.

Another criterion that defines an expensive SQL statement is the number of Disk Reads. When you observe this figure in a SQL statement and it exceeds 2% of the number of Reads, it may also be expensive, due to excessive reads in the data file and therefore excessive Input/Output.

Finally, it is also important to distinguish between the statements that are passed to the database by the different applications running in the database server. Those statements in upper case with the objects (tables and fields) that are accessed between double quotes belong to statements passed from ABAP programs. Statements in lower case without quotes may come from an external source, like a SQL script or a third-party monitoring tool, and so on.

Additional Troubleshooting in the Database

Let us provide you with a few more tricks to analyzer the performance and stability of your database.

It is best practice to verify that you are following SAP's recommendations in parameter settings for your database. In case of an Oracle database, SAP Note 124361 contains the parameter settings recommended for optimal performance to be set in the database profile initSID.ora, where SID is your system ID.

Ensure that there are no missing indexes in your database that are used or could be used in accessing tables. Execute transaction DB02 and click on Missing Indexes to verify.

Make sure that locks are not the root cause of high database response times. To monitor lock wait situations at the database level from a SAP system, check transaction DB01 or follow the menu path Tools | Administration | Monitor | Performance | Database | Exclusive Lock Waits. The list displayed shows the process that would be holding a lock in an object and the processes that would be waiting for that lock to be released. Locks are necessary for data consistency. However, programming efficiently and avoiding locks in loops is a best practice to avoid exclusive lock wait situations.

Check the data files' distribution for contention. From the database performance monitor ST04, go to Detail Analysis Menu and then File System Requests to check the time spent accessing blocks in each of your data files, which, depending on several factors, such as if you are using a cached storage subsystem or not, should not exceed 15 to 45 milliseconds optimally. Check the recommendations from the Installation Guides for advise in distributing the data files for performance and data security to avoid contention.

Also, check the order of the redolog files in an Oracle database by observing the V$ tables. These tables contain much historical and statistical data to analyze the database in a very deep detail. From the database performance monitor, choose Detail Analysis Menu and then Display V$ Values. Double-click on V$LOG and V$LOGFILE and check the order of the redologs and the sequence in which they are used to write log changes. If the sequence order in which they are written to is such that the same directory and physical disk is hit twice or more in a row, then contention may be affecting negatively the database performance.

Finally, do not forget to check the database alert log file under Database Message Log to check for possible errors that affect performance and stability in the database. For example, you may be able to observe messages like "Checkpoint not complete," which are caused by excessive load to the database and too small or too little number of redolog files.

There are other logs and traces available in the system that are output of the program BRCONNECT. This substitutes SAPDBA as database operation and monitoring tool at the operating system level. It is best practice to schedule BRCONNECT—check on a very regular basis (daily) to perform a complete check at the database level and display the output to check for any situation affecting negatively your database.

Workload Distribution

In a SAP system, such as SAP R/3 Enterprise, the client/server architecture is one of the biggest characteristics that allow a system to be scalable and therefore, to grow and adjust to new needs whenever necessary. We can observe three different layers in this architecture, the presentation layer, the application layer and the database layer.

This three-tier architecture can be a two-tier architecture or even a central system (one tier). Depending on the level of scalability and the resources that you require, you may choose one or another strategy.

The presentation layer would correspond to the user's PC, laptop, or presentation server. The database layer is where the database server can be found.

The application layer consists on one or several application servers in which one or more SAP Instances is (are) installed and available to run ABAP or Java programs and communicate with other instances and systems. We may also install an instance on the database server.

Instances are a very important resource in a SAP system and must be tuned for optimal response of a system and must be used and configured properly for optimal performance.

In this topic, we will learn how to configure the work processes in the SAP instances, maintain profile parameters and distribute the workload for an efficient use of resources via different options, such as operation modes.

The SAP Instance

An Instance is a set of programs that start of stop at the same time. In the case of SAP R/3, a SAP R/3 Instance consists on programs called Work Processes, which are started and stopped all at the same time by a process named Dispatcher, the process "parent" of all the work process in an instance.

There are several types of work processes and the number can be configured via parameter settings in the Instance Profile. Dialog work processes are used for interaction tasks with a user, while Background work processes can be used for batch processing "behind the scenes" without user interaction for longer processing programs to be executed at scheduled times. Any instance must have at least 2 dialog work processes. You can configure an instance with 0 to several background work processes.

Update work processes are dedicated to send update requests to the database in order to save changes in transactional data and spool work processes are in charge of output processing, such as printing or faxing from a SAP system. You may configure 0 to several update and spool work processes in any instance.

The Enqueue Work Process allows to lock logically at the SAP level (not at the database level) with lock objects to avoid inconsistency and it is unique, so there is only one in each system in one of the instances. That instance will be called the Central Instance, while the others will be called "dialog" instances. Few exceptions may allow more than one Enqueue work process, but only do so when SAP recommends it and follow SAP's instructions.

It is very common to see the central instance installed in the same server as the database when you do not have a standalone database server and distribute user workload across all the dialog instances, reserving the central instance for only a few administrative tasks without allowing end user access.

The maximum number of work process configured in an instance will depend on your resources. Since hardware resources are limited, so the number of work processes is. For advice on how many work process to configure, please check SAP Note 39412.

In addition to the aforementioned work processes, there are two more services that allow communication with other instances and systems: the Message Server (which allows a Dispatcher from one instance to communicate to other dispatchers) and the Gateway (which can be seen as a communication pipe to send requests and calls to other systems and applications).

In SAP R/3 Enterprise, with the underlying Web Application Server, there is a new process that allows communication with the Internet, the Internet Communication Manager (ICM). This new service is necessary to ensure proper communication between the SAP system and other Web services, systems, or applications that use HTTP, HTTPS, or SMTP protocols. It can be monitored separately with the ICM Monitor, although it is started by the dispatcher, as all the other services or work processes. And just as the other work processes, the ICM must be configured via parameter settings.

Transaction SM50, the work process monitor, helps you to monitor the work process of every instance separately (running SM50 separately in each instance), whereas SM66 allows you to have a system wide view of the work processes across all instances.

If your online users experience wait times or if you observe high average wait time in the Workload Analysis Monitor, it may be due to a lack of work processes. Similarly to the lack of work processes, if the workload for the ICM is too high, you may see that in SMICM the indicator for the threads "peak" is reaching maximum. In addition, statistics on processing times can be seen under Goto | Statistics | Display. For additional troubleshooting of the ICM, remember to review the Online Help documentation.

The parameter settings that control the number and behavior of the work processes and ICM are set in the instance profile. For the ICM you can display the parameters in the ICM Monitor via transaction SMICM and choosing Goto | Parameters | Change. Observe that some parameters can be changed dynamically right there, but the ones that are grayed out cannot be changed dynamically.

Finally, each instance has associated a set of R/3 buffers (tables, programs, calendar, screen, CUA objects, etc.) that allow temporary storage for faster data access and program execution. The size and configuration of the SAP buffers are also managed in the instance profile. The buffer configuration is important for optimal performance and distributing the workload efficiently helps to make an efficient use of the available resources.

The SAP Profiles for Parameter Settings

A SAP system needs three files to configure parameter settings related to the SAP Instances and to start them. These are files that can be edited at the operating system level or from the SAP system via transaction RZ10 (menu path Tools | CCMS | Configuration | Profile Maintenance) and you can display individually each parameter with documentation in RZ11. The convention naming is important, and so it is to maintain the values in the appropriate range to avoid problems starting up the instances, for example.

The three files (profiles) to maintain are as follows:

- The default profile named DEFAULT.PFL, which contains parameter settings that are common to all instances across the system.
- The start up profile, named START_<instance name>_<server name>, which contains scripts to start the instances and other programs, such as the system log collectors, that can be included as well.
- The instance profile, named <SID>_<instance name>_<server name>, where SID is the system ID. It contains specific parameter settings for each instance and therefore you will need to configure one for each instance in your system, as opposed to the other profiles. Such parameter settings include SAP buffer sizes, memory management parameter settings, number of work processes of each type, parameter settings for RFC communication, for the database interface, the online help and languages, login settings, traces, spool settings, and so on.

When you change these profiles from transaction RZ10, the system keeps track of all previous versions, so you could always go back to a previous version of the profile, if something went wrong changing a profile and you were unsure of what changes you made.

There are three levels of modification:

- *Administration data.* For any of the profile types, the administration data includes information such as the name and location of the operating system file, the date and time of modification and generation, username who changed it, and the reference server for parameter checking.
- *Basic maintenance.* This is very useful since it does not present parameters with technical names, so there is no need to memorize them. The available options depend on the type of profile but normally include the basic and most important profile parameters. The basic maintenance option presents the profile parameters in a very convenient modifiable form, with pushbuttons and so on.
- *Extended maintenance.* This presents the operating system profile file in R/3 list form without the comments. It allows you to maintain individual parameter settings in each profile. From the extended maintenance screen, it is possible to create

additional parameters that are not set in the profile and therefore assigned from the internal SAP code (kernel).

When modifying a profile, the system will automatically include a comment in the file indicating the date, time, user ID of who did the modification, and what the old value of the parameter was. When finished editing a profile, select Profile | Save or click the Save icon to store the profile in the database. When saving profiles, the system automatically performs a consistency check. If you want the profile parameters of an edited profile to be effective the next time an instance is restarted, you have to transfer the modified profile to the operating system level. You do this by selecting from the menu Profile | Activate, although commonly the system will automatically request you to activate the profile after it has been saved.

At any time, but especially after importing or modifying any of the system profiles, you should check the consistency of the profiles. This check includes from spell checking to verifying all the imposed conditions on parameters. When the SAP system checks a profile it also checks that all profiles are consistent among themselves; for example, it would not allow two different message servers in different profiles. To check the consistency of any profile, from the main screen, select the profile and version and click on the Check icon, or, from the menu, select Profile | Check.

When an application server is started, the system checks that the profile information stored in the database matches that of the operating system files. If there are differences, the alert monitor will display an alert message. You can always check and compare the profiles against the file on the operating system by entering the profile name in the input field and selecting from the menu Utilities | Check All Profiles | Of Active Server. Or you can compare against the profiles in the operation modes by selecting the menu option Utilities | Check All Profiles | In Operation Modes. Also, you can compare the selected profile in the profile name input field with the active profile by selecting Profile | Comparisons | Profile in Database | With Active Profile.

When a profile has been modified at the operating system level or a new dialog instance has been installed, you should import the new profiles, so that they are modifiable from the SAP system. To do so, enter the name of the profile and click on the Create icon, or select Profile | Create from the menu. The system presents the initial screen for entering the administration data, such as the description, the profile type, the filename (include the whole path), and the reference server. Enter the requested information and save your inputs. The system transfers the data to the database. Then proceed by selecting Profile | Import on the basic profile maintenance transaction screen. The system displays a dialog box where you have to specify the profile file at the operating system level. To display the available files, click on the possible entries list arrow. The values for the profile will be transferred and checked for errors. You can now edit the profile and save it into the database. You can also use the copy function to make a copy for another profile with similar values.

Finally, you have two options to delete profiles from the database:

- To delete a single profile, on the initial edit profile screen, enter the name and version in the corresponding input fields and then select Profile | Delete | Individual Profile.
- To delete all versions of a profile, select Profile | Delete | All Versions | Of a Profile.

The system will remove the entries from the database and will display a dialog box requesting whether you also want to delete the files at the operating system level.

TIP *To obtain a list of all parameters defined in the system and their values, execute program RSPARAM with transaction SE38.*

Working with Workload Distribution

Now that you know how to configure the SAP instances, we will give you some tips and suggestions on workload distribution. It is important to balance the workload in your system to achieve optimal response and system performance.

Workload in a system can be defined in many different ways and that is why there are also different tuning mechanisms to balance it. The number and the type of users influence and are part of the workload. The number and type of programs and transactions that are executed online, in background, via RFC, ALE, Web communication, and so on are also workload.

Resources are hardware (memory, CPU, number of servers, network, . . .) and software (number and type of work processes, memory configuration, system settings, . . .), and the better the workload is distributed among all the available resources, the better the system's response will be.

Workload Distribution among Application Servers

It is possible to analyze the distribution of the workload in a SAP system by choosing Load Distribution | Instance Comparison from the Workload Analysis Monitor. Moreover, you can also check the users that are logged in an instance with Load Distribution | Users per Instance.

That way you can observe if the response time of one application server is very different from another and if one instance is busier and more loaded of users than another.

In order to make the most out of your resources, try to balance the workload among all available application servers. To achieve this, you may use Logon Groups. You can configure Logon Groups with transaction SMLG.

However, it is important to consider that if resources are limited (memory, in particular), the way that users are distributed among application servers may influence R/3 buffer utilization. You may encounter many buffer swaps in some of all instances, due to an inefficient distribution of users. This may affect negatively performance is those servers, although the user workload is evenly distributed among all the available application servers. To avoid this situation, it is best practice to join users that use the same tables and programs in the same logon groups, making the most out of your resources that way. Just as an example, SD and MM users fit well together, because they access the same tables and programs (logistics), due to the integration between modules, and do not compete for resources, as well as FI and CO users (financials).There are other possible workload distribution criteria that could be taken into consideration, such as language, country, company, Internet users, and so on.

Working with Operation Modes

Operation modes are the way the R/3 system allows for flexible configuration of the available work processes across the system for optimal utilization of the system resources. With operation modes, you can define how many work processes of each type will be available in which mode of operation that you define and the system can automatically switch from one to another operation mode at your defined scheduled switch time.

When an operation mode switch takes place, there is no need to restart the instances (even though you will see that automatically certain work processes change from one type to another!).

In order to go to the main screen of Operation Modes maintenance, execute transaction RZ04 or follow the menu path Tools | CCMS | Configuration | Operation Modes/ Instances.

Operation modes are defined at the instance level, so an instance is assigned to one or several operation modes. To configure an operation mode, the instance profiles must be correctly set up, because the operation modes will use the instance and start profile information for performing their tasks. If you have not defined any operation mode yet, the system shows the <DUMMY> operation mode, which is a nonproductive operation mode.

To create an operation mode, click on the Create icon in the Operation Modes maintenance screen. Enter the name and a short description for the operation mode in the provided input fields. New in SAP R/3 Enterprise, by choosing a Monitoring Properties Variant, you may add this operation mode to the alert monitor. Now you are ready to assign the new operation mode to an instance.

If you click the Instances/Profiles button while in the initial screen CCMS: Maintain Operation Modes and Instances, the system shows the instances to which different operation modes are assigned (in the operation mode view). To create a new instance, select Profile | Create New Instance or click on the Create icon. Enter the server name of the instance, the START and Instance profile name. By selecting Administration User for Start/ Stop, you can additionally configure the user data for starting or stopping the instance. Next, click on the Save icon on the standard toolbar, or select Instance | Save. The system will save the instance data and check the configuration. Once the information is confirmed, and only when creating the instance for the first time, the system displays a dialog box CCMS: Maintain Work Process Distribution, where you select an operation mode (for example, Day) to assign the instance and maintain the work process distribution. Note that you can only use the + and – icons to add or subtract work processes of each type and that when you add a background work process, for example, one less dialog work process will be available and shown in the distribution. The total number of work processes in that instance or across the system cannot be modified, though! You must "play" with the available configure total number of work processes.

You can also choose another operation mode by clicking on Other Operation Mode (for example, Night) and repeat the same operation. The system now displays the list of operation modes for every active instance with information about the number and type of work processes assigned to them as shown in Figure 10-20.

Note that the total number, under the Sum column, should be the same for a single instance, regardless of the operation mode, because, as mentioned previously, the total number of work processes cannot be changed dynamically.

In addition, to assign a different operation mode at any time, click on one of the lines in the list of operation modes, and from the menu select Instance | Maintain Instance | WP Distribution. The system will display a new window to define the work process distribution for the instance, like before. Notice that the system includes the * to indicate operation mode independent.

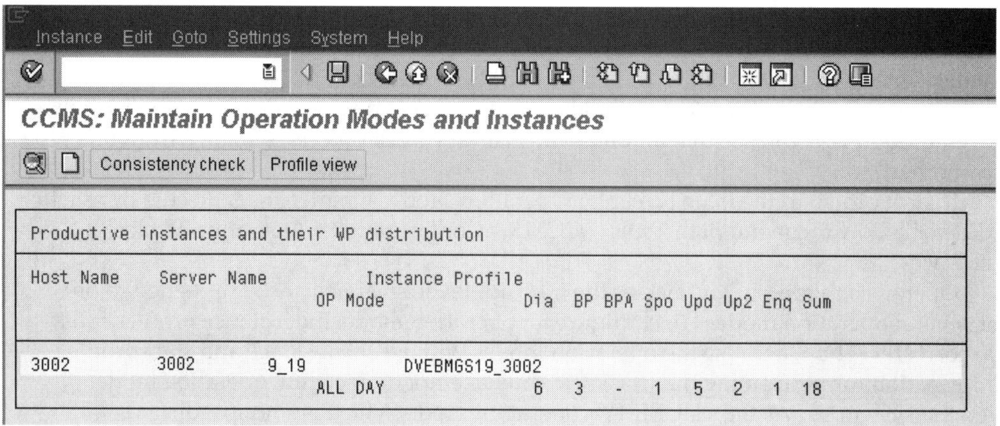

FIGURE 10-20 Operation modes and work process distribution in a SAP R/3 system (Copyright by SAP AG)

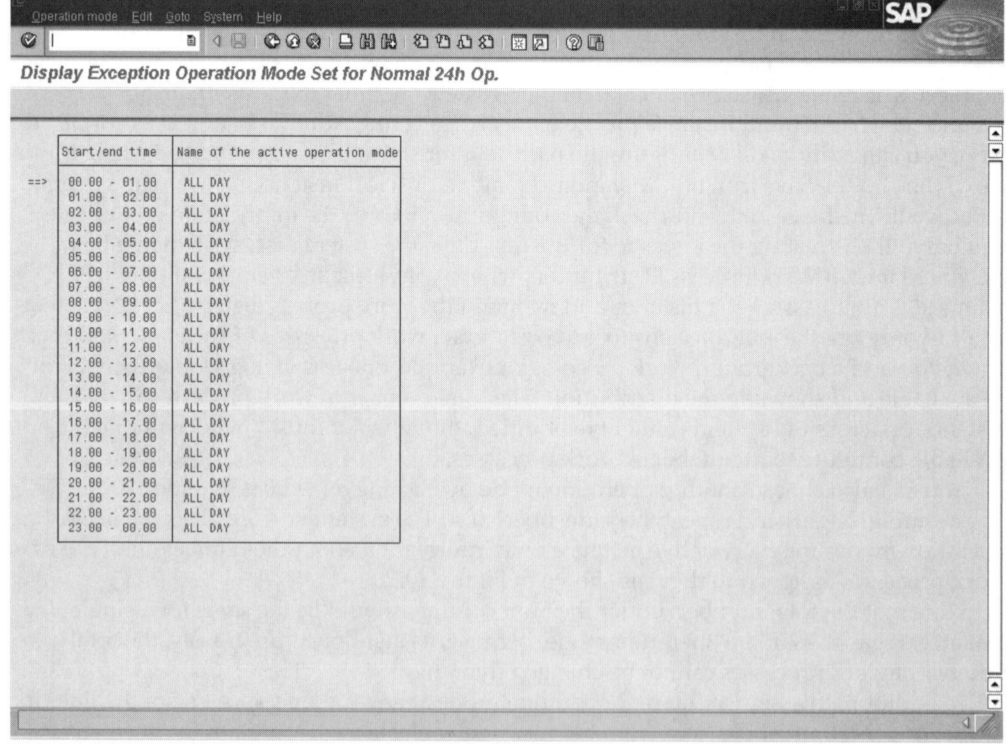

FIGURE 10-21 24-hour Normal operation schedule in a SAP R/3 system (Copyright by SAP AG)

Finally, notice that the number of spool processes cannot be changed and that the number of update work processes (both V1 and V2) can be increased or decreased as needed but cannot be set to 0. If an instance does have update processes configured, then you cannot make that number 0. It would first have to be defined on the instance profile that you do not wish update work processes in that instance by setting the corresponding parameter setting. Enqueue work processes should be left normally unchanged. Only one of the instances offers the enqueue service. If the instance has an enqueue process, it can be changed under certain limitations (1 to n or n to 1) but can never be set to 0. Only modify this value, if instructed by SAP.

The next step is to configure the timetable for operation mode switch. Execute transaction SM63 or follow the menu path Tools | CCMS | Configuration | Operation Mode Calendar.

Choose between Normal operation, which defines 24-hour cycles for the operation modes, and the Switches or Exception operation, which allows you to define an exceptional time period for the activation of an operation mode. This mode will only be executed once in the specified date and time interval. By default, the system displays 1-hour intervals, but you can change the intervals to smaller periods from the Edit | Time Period menu when in maintenance mode. You must define the whole 24-hour range and you cannot leave any time period unassigned for operation modes to work. Figure 10-21 shows an example of a 24-hour Normal operation schedule.

Troubleshooting in System Administration

When managing a SAP R/3 Enterprise system from a technical point of view, there are quite a few areas that need to be controlled and monitored on a regular basis in order to procure a healthy environment. Availability of resources, stability and performance of the available resources are aspects to look at.

In the following topics, we will touch base on troubleshooting techniques in general system administration of SAP systems.

Troubleshooting the Update Process

The update work processes are in charge of recording changes in transactional data and send requests to the database of such changes, as users work normally in the system.

The update work processes perform their functions when the ABAP applications are programmed with a statement IN UPDATE TASK. This type of updating is performed asynchronously in the system, meaning that the programs leave update records in a queue to be processed and then continue the execution. Even though the updating processes run without management intervention; nonetheless, SAP includes utilities to monitor, check, and perform management operations on the updating process, which can be very useful in case that problems arise.

To access the Update Monitor, follow the menu path Tools | Administration | Monitor | Update. Alternatively, enter transaction code SM13 in the command field. The system displays the initial Update Monitor screen, where you can select to display data according to your selection criteria. It is normal practice to check this monitor on a daily basis, though you can select a time period that includes data and time to filter. See Figure 10-22.

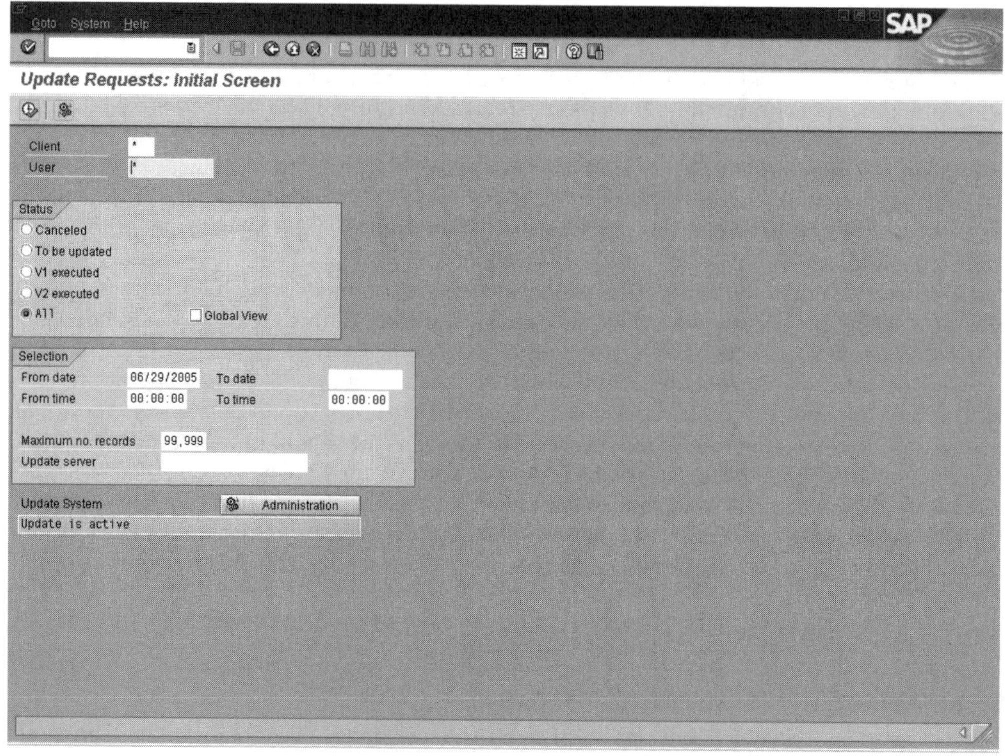

FIGURE 10-22 Initial selection screen in the Update Monitor (Copyright by SAP AG)

You can select to display the type of update records of your choice, by client and user, although you can enter a wildcard (*) to select all clients and all users as well. When you click on Execute, you will display a list with the records you selected and their status, as well as the user and transaction executed. From there, it is possible to retrieve user information and repeat updates, unless there is an error and the system will display so. In such case, the user needs to post the transaction from the beginning to avoid inconsistencies.

The Update Process Administration

You may access the Update Process Administration utility by executing transaction SM14 or from the Update Monitor clicking on Administration. This tool allows you to manage more complicated features in the Update process.

You can display all canceled update records, all update requests, reorganize incomplete update requests and deactivate the update process. Only when troubleshooting the update process and it rare cases you will need to deactivate the update process (if there is a stuck situation, for example). However, it is best practice to reorganize incomplete update records, because they take space in the database (you will see table VBDATA growing). There is another way to perform this reorganization automatically, which consists on setting the parameter *rdisp/vbreorg* to 1, which mandates the update server to reorganize incomplete update records when the instance is restarted. This also helps you to avoid inconsistencies, because you would not be reorganizing update requests during online hours.

The tabs Update Server and Server Groups in this tool help you to define update servers and server groups for load balancing. In addition, the Parameter tab allows you to define certain parameter settings dynamically and to display all parameter settings related to the update process to function properly.

Finally, click on Statistics to obtain very specific statistics on response time broken down by actions in the database by the update process, such as Delete, Insert, and Commit.

Be sure to understand clearly how the updating process can affect the system before performing any management options on update records. More information on update process management can also be found in the Online Help.

Troubleshooting Lock Entries

Lock entries are system objects in charge of protecting the integrity of the data by synchronizing the access, so users cannot modify the same data at the same time. The lock objects are defined in the ABAP dictionary as a mechanism to lock data and can consist on a table, a row, or even a whole transaction, so users cannot change the same data at the same time.

To display and perform some basic operations on lock entries, from the main menu, select Tools | Administration | Monitor | Lock Entries or execute transaction code SM12. You can select lock entries specifying client, user or objects that have been locked (lock entry arguments). By entering the wildcard (*) in the client and user, the system displays all current lock entries with the users holding locks and what table is affected by the lock.

Frequent monitoring of lock entries should be a common practice by either SAP R/3 administrators or operators, since unreleased locks can block other users from working in the same transactions for updating information.

Normally, locks are automatically released when transactions are committed or when users are finished working on the data. Special attention must be given to locks, which are held unreleased for several hours. Although this is not always a cause of alert, because in special circumstances, such as long-running background jobs which update the database, it can be a completely normal operation.

The lock monitoring functions offer the utility to manually delete unreleased locks. To manually delete a lock entry from the lock entry list, click on the line holding the lock you want to release and press DELETE from the application toolbar or select Lock Entry | Delete from the menu.

However, you should not delete locks directly before analyzing the reason for the lock. As much as possible try to avoid manually deleting lock entries, and do it only when you are sure that it will not affect an update process, a background job, or an active user. Otherwise, it might lead to data inconsistencies.

Some of the most frequent reasons for unreleased locks are as follows:

- *Abnormal termination of the SAP GUI.* If users shut down their PCs without logging off SAP, or if the SAP GUI terminates for other reasons, such as network or communication problems, the user session may remain active in the SAP system. If this happens while the user had lock entries, sometimes these locks remain unreleased since the user is no longer active in the system, and therefore they cannot be automatically released. In these cases you can manually release the lock either by deleting it from the lock entry list, or you can force log off the user from the User Overview Monitor executing transaction SM04 in the application server where the user was logged on. This information can be found in the lock entry details window.

- *Inactive SAP GUI.* Another common reason for holding a lock for a long period of time is when users currently working on the system leave their presentation services with unfinished transactions. Before manually deleting a lock entry that is preventing other users from working in the same tasks, try to locate and directly check with the user. Otherwise, you should either manually log off the user or delete the lock if this is seriously preventing other users' work. However, make sure the lock is not coming from an important background job.
- *Problems in update processing.* When there are update modules that are unprocessed by the system, these modules do not release the locks. The update process only releases the locks when either the update records have been completely processed or they have abnormally terminated with an error status. Only update modules with status INIT or AUTO (unprocessed updates) can hold locks. Normally, the lock entry list will highlight those entries that are held by update processes. If you press the Refresh button often on the lock entry list, you can sometimes see highlighted entries, which are released very quickly.

The System Log

SAP systems includes extensive log facilities to display and possibly correct the problems and errors occurred during system operation in the so-called system log.

Each application server registers a local system log. In a distributed environment, you can configure a central system log that collects the log records of all servers, but this is not available in all operating systems.

Physically, the individual application server log files (local system logs) are stored under the specific instance directory /usr/sap/<SID>/<INSTANCE_NAME>/log, with the name SLOG<INSTANCE_NUMBER>.

The log messages are written in a single circular file. When the file reaches the maximum allowable size, a log switch takes place and the system starts overwriting the file from the beginning. The maximum allowed size of a log file is specified in the system profile parameter *rslg/max_diskspace/local*. However, when the central system log is configured, it uses two files: an active file and an old file. The active file contains the current log. When the active file reaches the maximum length specified in the system profile parameter *rslg/max _diskspace/central*, the system performs a log switch. The system deletes the old log file, copies the active file as the old log file and creates a new active log file. This process is performed transparently to the administrator and does not offer any notification when it replaces the old log. The central system log is located under the SAP-shared global directory /usr/sap/<SID>/SYS/global with the default name SLOGJ.

To access the System Log from the main menu, select Tools | Administration | Monitor | System Log or execute transaction SM21.

The selection criteria to filter the display of the system log messages includes date and time, user ID, transaction code, type of work process and type of problems logged. It is important to remember that the system log records events, problems and warnings that are relevant to the kernel (work processes and such), therefore, not certain problems, such as database or operating system problems will be recorded (but if these affect the kernel, they may be recorded).

By entering DP in the SAP Process field, you will filter messages logged by the dispatcher processes. If you enter *D<n>* or *B<n>* or *S<n>* or *V<n>*, where *n* is the work process number, you will filter by dialog, background, spool or update work process number as displayed by the Work Process Overview screen; For example, D1, D2, and so forth. Choose MS to select messages from the message server.

By selecting from the menu System Log | Choose | Central Log, you can display the central log. Other options in the same menu allow you to select the remote and local system logs. The field Instance Name appears only when you select to display the central system log where it is located.

You may also choose a maximum number of pages you want to see in the log report. No. Pages for Individual Entries and select the check box With Statistics to show statistical information of the log analysis, such as message frequency by client, user, and transaction.

In order to dump the output somewhere, you can select Settings next to the Output To pushbutton. The default is the screen output and you can select other outputs, such as a printer with a certain number of pages to print.

Other settings allow you to change the layout of the output (selecting additional columns in the log, for example). Figure 10-23 shows the main screen of the system log.

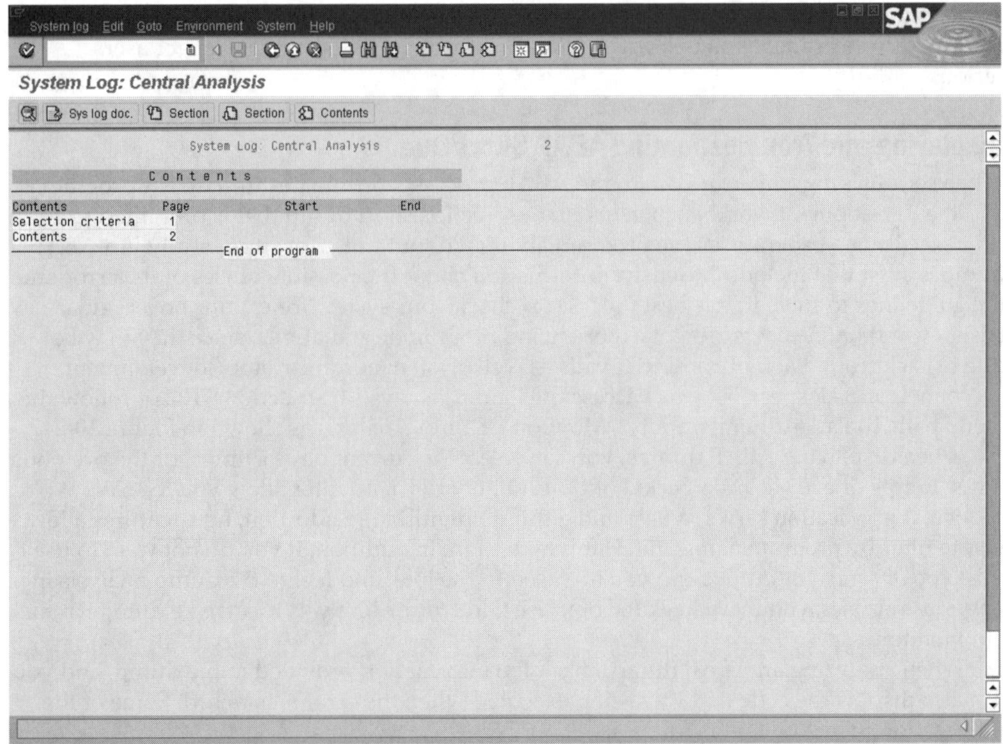

FIGURE 10-23 Main selection screen in the system log (Copyright by SAP AG)

Interpreting the System Log

The system log records all alerts sent to the kernel. Therefore, warnings and information and not only errors are also recorded. It is important to check the system log on a regular basis and to interpret the messages accurately.

The column named "MNo" in the log report shows the log message codes, which are associated with a type of log event. Most of these codes have associated documentation explaining the cause of the log and, in case of errors, the possible cause of the error.

To see this information, first double-click on a log entry to display the detail screen. In this screen, you can see the documentation for message codes. You can also display the short text documentation for the message code, by selecting See System Log Doc from the application toolbar. There is not always log documentation available.

You can also instruct the system to ignore certain codes by selecting Edit | Ignore Message from the menu. When you perform this function, the next time you request the log report, the system will not display messages with the ignored code.

Events when a work process switches from one type to another when switching operation modes are recorded as warnings and are purely informational, unless something went wrong, which would be recorded, if so.

The best documentation for system log messages is contained in SAP Notes and a simple search with the error code and a short text will very likely retrieve a solution that suits the symptoms recorded in the system log.

Pay special attention to system log messages related to operating system failures, database errors or inconsistencies, as well as printing problems that may affect users seriously.

Displaying and Troubleshooting ABAP Short Dumps

When serious program errors occur, the ABAP processor terminates the current program and the development workbench generates a so-called short dump that is presented to a user executing a program, as the program aborts without finishing successfully. An ABAP dump is a list that includes extensive information about the possible causes of the error and the guidelines to solve it. It is best practice to check your system for dumps on a regular basis, even if online users are not experiencing program terminations, since they may be due to background activity and RFC calls as well. System administrators, development personnel, or SAP specialists may access the Dump Analysis transaction ST22 or follow the menu path Tools | Administration | Monitor | Dump Analysis as shown in Figure 10-24.

When displaying ABAP dumps, you can select the current day's dumps, or the previous day's dumps or even select a period of time. Other criteria to filter allow you to select a particular application server, a user and a dump identifier. In addition, new features allow you to filter by program name and dump exception. In addition, if you do not wish to use this type of screen or output and you are used to the look and feel of the dump analysis in previous releases, you may check the box Use Old Dump Analysis to analyze dumps in the old monitor.

When analyzing an ABAP dump, check the information provided in the dump, and you can also display the code that was being executed when the error was raised. Some of the information to be found is as follows:

- What happened and why the program was aborted
- What program and what line in the code where the error occurred

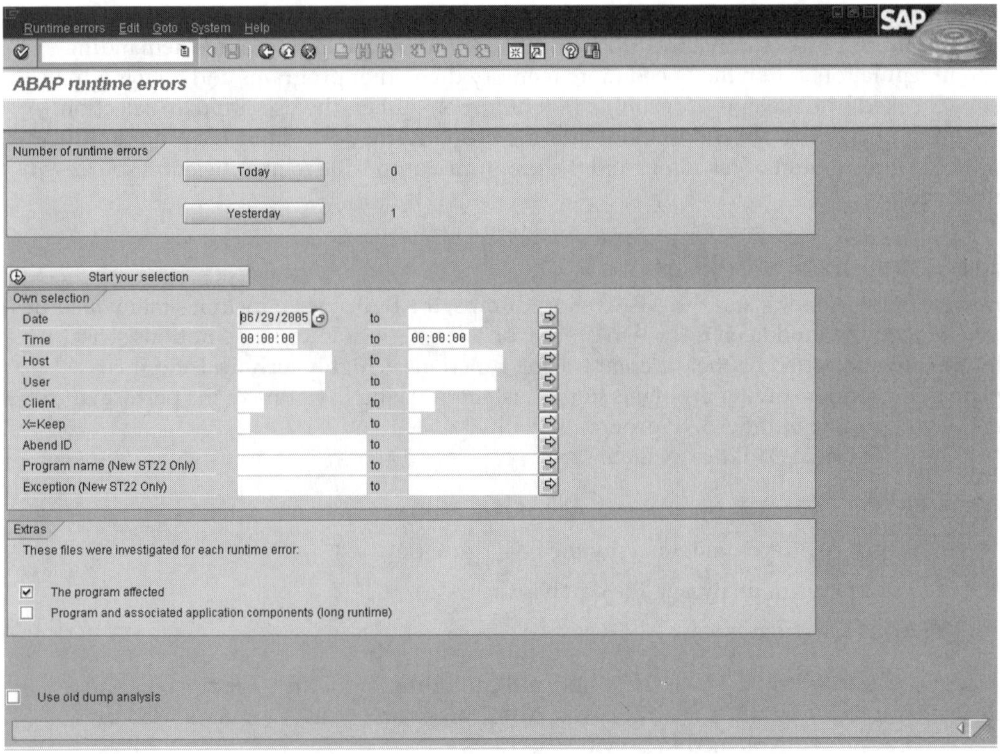

FIGURE 10-24 ABAP Dump Analysis in a SAP R/3 system (Copyright by SAP AG)

- What error message keywords are useful to search for possible solutions
- The values of the most relevant system variables are at the time of the error
- What tables were being used at the moment
- Management data such as user, transaction, application server, and so on
- Whether any other programs were affected

Old dumps occupy space in the database. It is best practice to delete these entries on a regular basis by scheduling a clean up job or manually by choosing Goto | Reorganize from the main dump analysis screen and selecting how old the dumps to be deleted must be.

However, you may keep dumps for further analysis. In the main selection screen you can choose to keep dumps by entering an X in the analysis list display, you can select whether there are any particular short dumps you want to keep for further analysis. Or, in the list of dumps that you selected, select the short dump to keep and click on the Keep/Release padlock-like icon or, from the menu, select Short Dump | Keep/Release.

Pay special attention to those dumps that are related to errors in the database (such as DBIF_RSQL_SQL_ERROR). Search for SAP Notes that explain the symptoms, because they will very likely contain a fix and an explanation for such dump.

In addition, watch dumps related to memory management, such as SYSTEM_NO_ROLL, SYSTEM_NO_MORE_PAGING, TSV_TNEW_PAGE_ALLOC, and others. These may be due to a couple of things, either wrong parameter settings in memory management, or insufficient resources, or that the programs that dumped were too resource demanding and in regular operation they need more memory than other programs and they might need to be checked by developers for tuning potential. Sometimes, the user input in selection screens is also important and without filtering properly, they may launch a program than needs a large amount of resources and the program dumps due to insufficient resources at that time.

The System Tracing Utilities

Besides the system log and the ABAP short dumps, the R/3 system includes many facilities to debug, follow, and keep track—in other words, trace—its internal operations. The information provided by the different tracing functions is highly technical and it is primarily used for solving problems in the system or trying to optimize the performance and/or the coding of the ABAP programs.

The basic tracing utilities available are

- System traces
- Developer traces generated by the SAP processes
- SQL traces for analyzing the database accesses
- ABAP program traces

This section covers the basic handling and configuration of the system traces and developer traces. Both the SQL traces and ABAP program traces are mainly used by developers and are explained in previous sections.

Using the System Trace

The system trace functions can be set up to include a very extensive group of technical information which can later be used by expert administrators, developers, or SAP specialists to solve or tune specific system problems. This section covers how to configure and set up system traces, which is not an obvious matter by navigating through the menus.

Each process in a SAP instance has its own trace buffer, where it writes the tracing information before being transferred to disk, if this option is selected.

Call the System trace function by selecting Tools | Administration | Monitor | Traces | System Trace from the main menu. Alternatively, enter transaction code ST01 in the command field. Figure 10-25 shows the initial screen for the system trace.

Select the trace records that you want to keep track of, such as authorization checks, kernel functions, database access, table buffer trace, RFC calls, and lock operations by checking the check box next to each option. Additionally, by clicking on General Filters, you may restrict the trace to a process only by entering the work process number, for a user, transaction or program. Otherwise, without specifying this data, when you activate the system trace, you will trace everything that happens in the system.

Therefore, it is important to understand that this tool is only to be used when errors occur and it is mainly used by kernel specialists.

The name of the trace file in a system is defined in the profile parameter *rstr/filename*. The default value of this profile parameter is */usr/sap/<SID>/<instance name>/log/TRACE00*. Its size can be configured with the parameter *rstr/max_filesize_MB*. When a file is full, it is

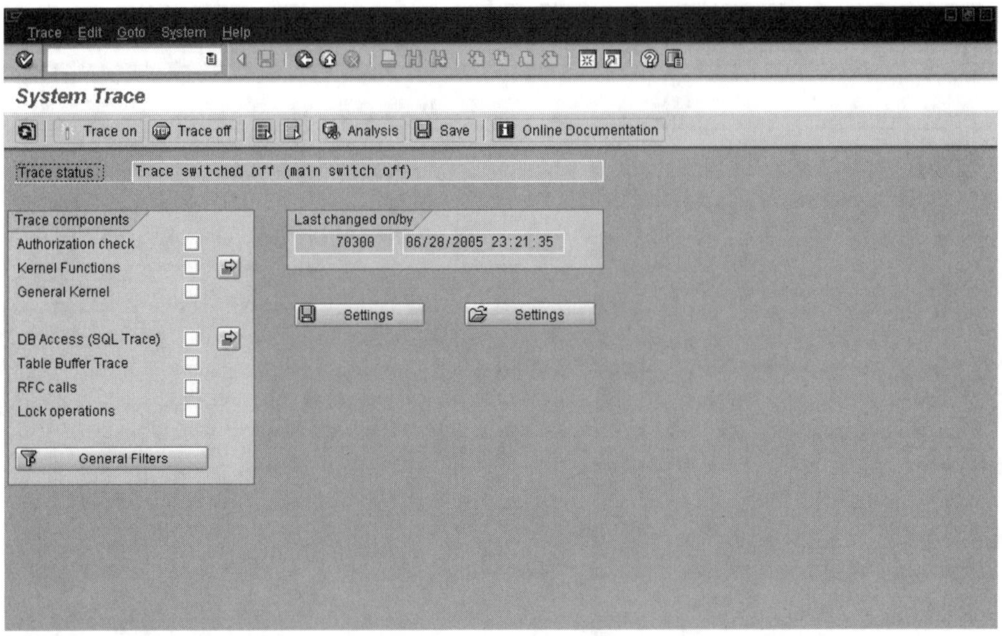

FIGURE 10-25 Starting the system trace and options for tracing (Copyright by SAP AG)

renamed with a different ending, a number from 00 to 99 and the maximum number of files is defined by rstr/max_files.

Using Developer Traces

The system developer traces are log files that contain technical information about the SAP work processes and other programs. They are normally used by specialized personnel, especially by SAP support, when looking for problems in the SAP kernel or the runtime programs. These traces can be useful also for administrators, since some of the files sometimes contain the explicit reason and explanation for system errors.

To display the list of developer traces, from the monitoring menu, select Tools | Administration | Monitor | Traces | Developer Trace from the main menu or execute transaction code ST11. The system will display a list with the title Error Log Files as shown in Figure 10-26. These files are actually operating system files located under the Work and Profile directories. To display the contents of any file, just double-click on them, or select Log File | Display from the menu.

When you display any of the files, look for lines beginning with the string *** ERROR => message, because they contain error information. The error lines can be useful for displaying what functions and what operations caused the error message.

If any of the entries are also writing system log entries, then the line begins with ***LOG <message ID>.

The names of all the developer trace files start with the character string dev_ followed by an identifier, such as the work process number, or rfc in case of an RFC call, icm for Internet Communication Manager, ms for the Message Server, and so on.

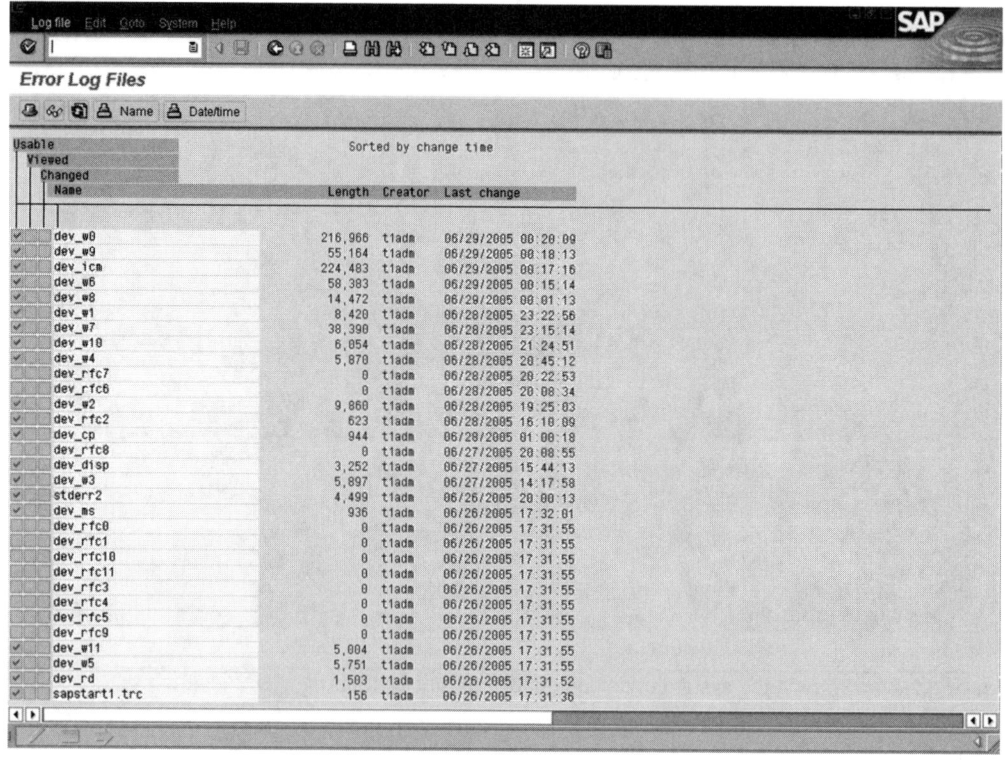

Usable	Viewed	Changed	Name	Length	Creator	Last change
✓			dev_w0	216,966	t1adm	06/29/2005 00:20:09
✓			dev_w9	55,164	t1adm	06/29/2005 00:18:13
✓			dev_icm	224,483	t1adm	06/29/2005 00:17:16
✓			dev_w6	58,383	t1adm	06/29/2005 00:15:14
✓			dev_w8	14,472	t1adm	06/29/2005 00:01:13
✓			dev_w1	8,420	t1adm	06/28/2005 23:22:56
✓			dev_w7	38,390	t1adm	06/28/2005 23:15:14
✓			dev_w10	6,054	t1adm	06/28/2005 21:24:51
✓			dev_w4	5,870	t1adm	06/28/2005 20:45:12
			dev_rfc7	0	t1adm	06/28/2005 20:22:53
			dev_rfc6	0	t1adm	06/28/2005 20:08:34
✓			dev_w2	9,860	t1adm	06/28/2005 19:25:03
✓			dev_rfc2	623	t1adm	06/28/2005 16:10:09
✓			dev_cp	944	t1adm	06/28/2005 01:00:18
			dev_rfc8	0	t1adm	06/27/2005 20:08:55
✓			dev_disp	3,252	t1adm	06/27/2005 15:44:13
✓			dev_w3	5,897	t1adm	06/27/2005 14:17:58
✓			stderr2	4,499	t1adm	06/26/2005 20:00:13
✓			dev_ms	936	t1adm	06/26/2005 17:32:01
			dev_rfc0	0	t1adm	06/26/2005 17:31:55
			dev_rfc1	0	t1adm	06/26/2005 17:31:55
			dev_rfc10	0	t1adm	06/26/2005 17:31:55
			dev_rfc11	0	t1adm	06/26/2005 17:31:55
			dev_rfc3	0	t1adm	06/26/2005 17:31:55
			dev_rfc4	0	t1adm	06/26/2005 17:31:55
			dev_rfc5	0	t1adm	06/26/2005 17:31:55
			dev_rfc9	0	t1adm	06/26/2005 17:31:55
✓			dev_w11	5,004	t1adm	06/26/2005 17:31:55
✓			dev_w5	5,751	t1adm	06/26/2005 17:31:55
✓			dev_rd	1,503	t1adm	06/26/2005 17:31:52
✓			sapstart1.trc	156	t1adm	06/26/2005 17:31:36

FIGURE 10-26 The developer traces (Copyright by SAP AG)

You can set the trace level by setting the parameter *rdisp/TRACE=<n>* in the instance profile file to any of these values:

- TRACE = 0. No trace is written to files.
- TRACE = 1. Write error messages in the trace file.
- TRACE = 2. Write the full trace.
- TRACE = 3. Write the full trace including data blocks.

Troubleshooting the Background Processing System

There are several options in the SAP system for monitoring and troubleshooting the background processing system. These options include utilities that can be used from the general administration monitoring utilities to extensive CCMS analysis tools. Where to look and what functions to use depends very much on the type of errors, which can range from configuration problems to authorizations or runtime problems.

In general, the order to look for background job problems can be

- Displaying the job log and analyzing the job status
- Analyzing the background work processes and the system log

- Using the CCMS general analysis tools
- Displaying the Job Log and Analyzing the Job Status

To display a job log and analyze its status, you must access the job overview list from a previous job selection screen. This screen may be accessed from many different places in the SAP system. For example, directly by entering the SM37 transaction code in the command field or by selecting Tools | CCMS | Jobs | Maintenance from the main menu. Enter the criteria for restricting the jobs to analyze and then display the job or list of jobs.

The first operation on a selected job will be to see its status and check it for possible errors by using the Job | Check Status function. If the job status is OK, the system displays a message in the status bar.

If you suspect an active job is running for a longer time than normal, you can debug it for analysis by selecting it while running and then choosing Job | Capture Active Job. The system will display a debugging window where you can analyze the code of the ABAP program running in background. The running program stops and you can debug it. Be extremely careful doing this and try to avoid as much as possible to debug in a production environment. Tests of this caliber should only be done in copies of production or test systems, where the code of the program is the same and the data that it works with is similar to that in production. From the debugging window, you can continue to execute the job at the point it was stopped.

Analyzing the Background Work Processes

Another step in the analysis of problems with the background processing system is to display the general process overview monitor. From the main menu, select Tools | Administration | Monitor | System Monitoring | Process Overview or just execute SM50 in the instance where the job is running or SM66 to see a global view.

The two types of work processes to look for are the background work processes and the dialog work processes. The Type column shows the type of work processes: BGD for background (batch) and DIA for dialog. And the Status column displays whether these processes are running, waiting, and so on. The first column of the process overview ("No.") shows the number of the work process. This number can be very useful if you later want to analyze the system log and want to restrict the search to problems with that particular work process. The process monitor shows other interesting information such as the program it is executing at the moment, the user under which the job is running, and so forth. Selecting one of those processes, you can get further detailed information by choosing Process | Details from the menu. You can also display the developer trace file by selecting Process | Trace | Display File. This will allow you to search for errors in the kernel, what happened while this background work process was executing the job, and so on.

With the system log, you can also analyze system errors, messages, or warnings regarding the background processing system. You can restrict your search just to the background work processes by entering the number in the SAP process input field.

The Job Analysis Tools

There is a set of utilities that can be used to analyze and monitor the background processing system.

The utility Check Environment is used for analyzing the configuration and the status of the background environment. To reach this function, select Tools | CCMS | Jobs | Check

Environment or execute transaction SM65. Figure 10-27 shows an example of the initial screen for performing simple tests on the background system.

These utilities check all the necessary conditions that must be met for the background processing system to work correctly. This analysis utility is helpful in determining if all the elements of the background system are configured and if there is any missing parameter. The analysis tools include two types of tests:

- *Simple tests.* These tests are used by the system to check if the profile parameters are correctly set and if the SAPCPIC user exists, because it is needed for starting external programs. These tests can be performed on a single background server or on all of them. To launch this test, from the initial screen click on the Execute button after selecting the background server of your choice or selecting of All Background Servers.
- *Additional tests.* These tests perform more extensive tests on the background processing system such as authorizations, consistency of the database tables and the TemSe database, status of background servers, and whether the dispatcher of a SAP instance has any entries in the queue for background processing. To reach these expert mode functions, from the initial screen select Goto | Additional Tests. Figure 10-28 shows this screen.

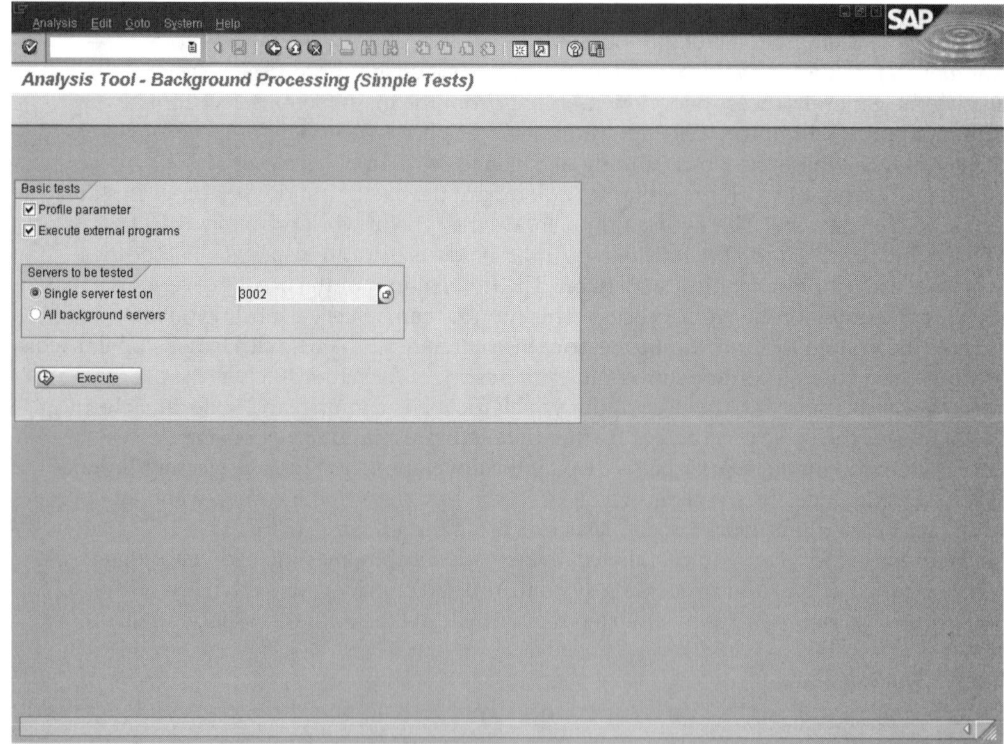

FIGURE 10-27 Checking the environment in background processing (Copyright by SAP AG)

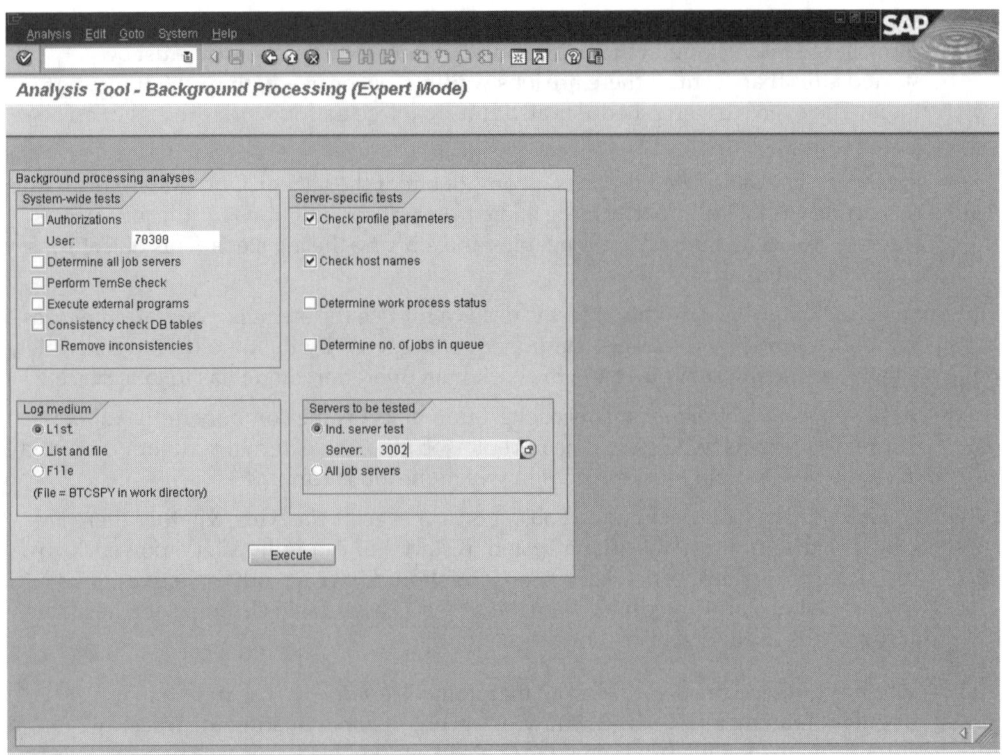

Figure 10-28 Additional expert tests in background processing (Copyright by SAP AG)

Job information is stored internally using several R/3 tables. With these additional tests, the system can find if there are any consistency problems in those tables, such as a missing index, duplicate entries, existence of all job data, and so forth. The results of the tests can either be displayed as a list or written to the file BTCSPY in the working directory of the application server to which you are logged on.

The utility Background Objects allows you to display and maintain the elements or control objects that make up the runtime environment for processing jobs. To reach this function, select Tools | CCMS | Jobs | Background Objects or execute transaction SM61.

These objects are as follows:

- *Time-driven scheduler.* This is the component of the background system responsible for starting jobs that have a start date and time specified. This scheduler is also responsible for starting jobs defined with a scheduled start option, such as After Event, After Job, and At Operation Mode, which could not be started at their scheduled time for some reason, for example, because there were no free background work processes. The scheduler is started by the SAP dispatcher in the period indicated by the rdisp/bdctime instance profile parameter. It is started in a dialog work process. For this reason, it is important that every instance configured for background processing must have at least one dialog work process for this task.

- *Event-driven scheduler.* When the R/3 system receives any events, this scheduler is in charge of checking in the background system for any jobs that must be started after that event. If there are jobs waiting for the event, this scheduler starts them. The event-driven scheduler also runs in a free dialog work process of any server.
- *Job starter.* The job started is another component of the background system in charge of starting the jobs and performing some preparatory functions for the job such as reading the needed data from the tables and starting the job steps. This object runs in a background work process.
- *Switch operation modes.* This object is used to initiate the switch of operation modes in a dialog work process. This component is triggered by the time-driven scheduler, which uses an internal timetable to check if an operation mode has to take place.
- *Starter for external programs.* This background object is the component that allows external programs to be started as part of a job step. An external program is started from the background work process in which the job is running.
- *Zombie cleanup.* This background object is in charge of checking whether there are jobs with the wrong status after a system restart. For example, after a power down and restart of an application server, no jobs should have a ready or active status with an initial start time previous to the restart. The zombie cleanup sets the status of those jobs to either finished or canceled.

Every background control object can be maintained separately. The maintenance consists of either defining and activating any of the objects or activating the trace information for them. On the initial screen for background objects, select Maintain Objects. The left column shows an entry for each host and the right column an entry for the object. From this screen, you can create an object by clicking on the Create icon, or you can modify the control information of the object. To modify an object, select the object and click on the Change icon. The system will display a dialog box where you can activate or deactivate the object itself or activate and deactivate tracing for analysis.

Finally, with the Activity Log button, you can display when the job was last run and when the trace was last activated.

Analyzing Job Performance

Select Tools | CCMS | Jobs | Performance Analysis or execute transaction SM39 (this transaction has been replaced by SM37 with SAP Enterprise) to reach the Performance analysis tools. Here system administrators can analyze the runtime of jobs that are active, finished, or canceled. To look for additional information about a particular job, just double-click on it.

It is important for everyone involved in the maintenance and care of a SAP system, as well as for everyone involved in an implementation, that jobs are analyzed for performance. It is best practice for developers that create background jobs to execute ABAP programs to fulfill a business requirement to look at the Duration column while testing the execution of such jobs, not only the Status column. Especially when tables grow and the system ages, or when additional workload hits the system, the designed jobs are likely to have a longer runtime than before. Think of jobs like Payroll or financial reporting transactions and programs.

Developers can use the trace utilities SQL Trace and ABAP Trace. However, tracing a background job can be more complicate and tedious than an online transaction, due to its forecasted longer duration. To trace a background job with the SQL trace utility (transaction ST05), try to start and stop the trace recording "chunks" of the job, save them to a local file and analyze them individually later on. This way, you can try to avoid the trace filling up and overwriting the records that were previously recorded.

To perform an ABAP trace in a background job that is currently running in the system, execute transaction SE30 and choose Enable/Disable under In Parallel Session. This will take you to a list of work processes similar to the one of the Work Process Overview monitor. In this screen, choose Start Measurement by clicking on the matchlike icon or choose Edit | Measurement | Switch On from the menu.

Under the On column you will be able to see a symbol, first as a yellow triangle that changes to a green circle to indicate that the trace is on and the background work process is active executing a job. You can refresh the display from this screen continuously and monitor the job from the job overview monitor in SM37. This will not affect the trace.

After the job is finished, simply deactivate the trace by selecting Edit | Measurement | Switch Off from the menu or by clicking in the extinguished matchlike icon. Afterward, go back once with the green arrow to the main SE30 screen and choose Analyze to check the file that was created. As explained in the section on workload analysis, you can proceed to analyze where most of the time was spent while this job was running, the SAP system or the database. Therefore, you can proceed to analyze further the most expensive programs and the database for possible tuning actions.

Common Background Job Problems

The following list summarizes some of the typical problems that can be found in the background processing system and the check actions to perform to solve the problem.

As a common practice for all of the typical problems, display the job log, the system log, and finally use the job analysis tool.

- *Job was not started.* First, check the job start time definition and ensure it has a start date and that the user who defined the job has authorization to release it. If the start date has been reached, check that there are free work processes in the background servers, especially if a target host was specified. If the job was to be started after an event, define a dummy job to test the event. If there are problems with the sapevt program, check the background objects and enable a trace for the event-driven scheduler.
- *Cannot display the job log.* This can indicate that the job log could not be created in the application server because of wrong permissions, the global directory is not correctly mounted on the application server where you tried to look at the job log, or there are inconsistencies in the TemSe database.
- *Job has been canceled.* Jobs can be canceled for many different reasons. The first step in analyzing canceled jobs is to display the job log to see if there are any error messages. Choose Job Log from the pushbuttons. If the message text is not enough, sometimes it helps to select from the menu, Goto | Long Text. Common problems are related to runtime errors of the ABAP processors (the program aborted in an ABAP dump that you can analyze separately), authorization permissions

(check the job utilities for permissions, check the authorizations of the user executing the job, etc), inaccessible operating system files when the programs read or write to external systems (check that the files and external programs are available!), and so forth.

- *An external program cannot be started or canceled.* Normally, the user <SID>adm is the operating system user with authorization to run external commands and programs. Ensure that the external command or program has been correctly defined and that and the user has the proper authorizations. You may also activate the SAPXPG trace utility to trace an external program. When creating the steps of a job and defining that this job will execute an external program, click on Control Flags. This will display a pop-up window where you can select, among other utilities, activate the SAPXPG trace. Or you may be able to start the SAPXPG trace when defining an external command or program in transaction SM69, as well as by setting the environment variable sapxpg_trace in the system where the external job will be executed. To check the log files for analysis, look into the developer traces dev_cp and dev_xpg.
- *Job remains in status active.* Sometimes you can find jobs with active status even after a system restart. It can also happen that there is an inconsistency between the real status of the job and the entry in the corresponding job table. In any case, you should verify the real status of the job by looking at the job overview and then selecting the Check status function. If it is an ABAP program, you can try to capture it to put it in debugging mode in case it is in an infinite loop status. In the case of an external program, you should log on at the operating system level and check whether the process is still running there; otherwise you might have a problem starting external programs. Look at the background object to see if the zombie cleanup is activated. If it is not, create or change the object so that it automatically deletes the zombie job.

Database Space Management

The database space in a SAP system is a central resource that must be monitored and taken care of continuously in a productive environment. A database standstill due to lack of space, for example, can lead to data loss. Therefore, it is best practice to monitor the data files and their growth constantly with monitors within the system or other utilities, if available. Such utilities and the indicators to look at depend heavily on the database platform. As an example, we will explain a few features of the utilities designed for an Oracle database.

The data in a SAP system using Oracle as its database are distributed over so called *tablespaces*, which are logical containers of one or more data files where the actual data are. Therefore, tables and their indexes are objects found in data files within tablespaces.

Objects, such as tables and indexes, occupy space allocated by the operating system in chunks denominated "blocks" that are normally 8 KB of size (although this depends on the operating system as well). Groups of consecutive blocks form *extents* and tables and indexes grow in extents whenever necessary.

There are several utilities within a SAP system to monitor tables, indexes, and tablespaces. At the operating system level, BRCONNECT is the utility (substituting

SAPDBA) to perform all kinds of monitoring, backups, reorganization and manipulation of objects in the database for a Database Administrator.

From a SAP system, several transactions and monitors are available to check the database.

The Tables and Indexes Monitor

From the main menu choose Tools | Administration | Monitor | Performance | Database | Tables/Indexes or execute transaction DB02.

The data from this monitor is refreshed once a day in a background job that executes a data collector program, but you can refresh the data from here (it may take a long time, so be careful when choosing this option!). See Figure 10-29.

In this monitor, you can check statistics available for tablespaces and tables or indexes. In order to check a brief display of the database history and growth, select Space Statistics from the main monitor under the Database System section. This list will give you an idea of how used the total available space is in the system. Pay special attention to the % Used column. It is possible to have a breakdown of tablespaces and tables or indexes by choosing so in the available pushbuttons. In addition, you can change the period of time to view this

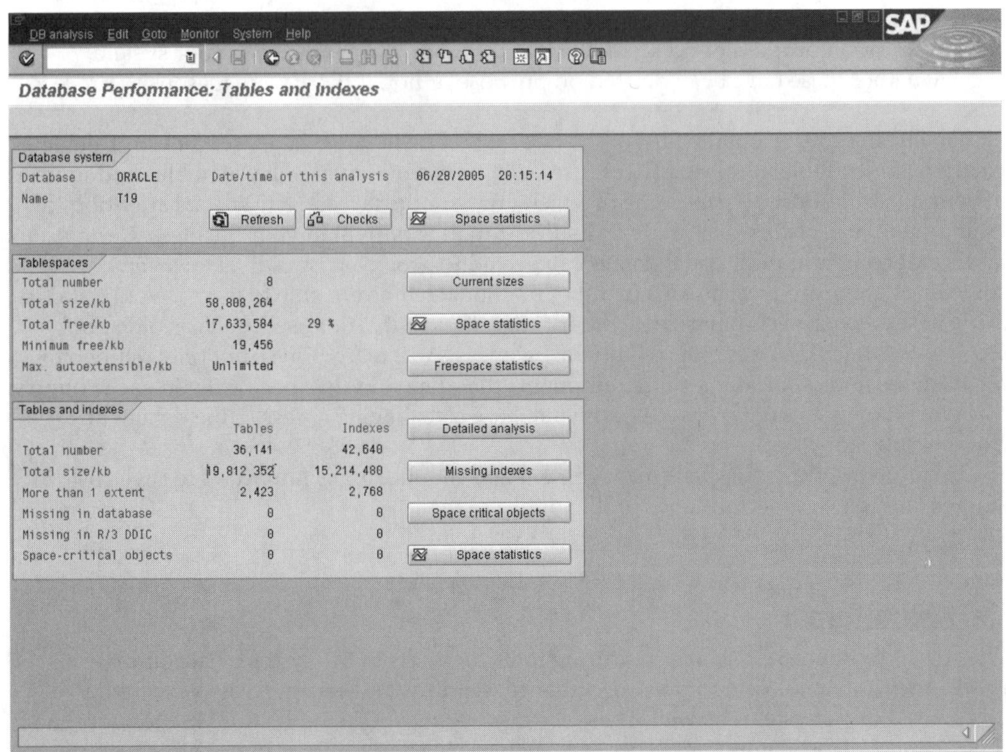

FIGURE 10-29 The Database Monitor for space management (Copyright by SAP AG)

history by month, week or daily basis. The same space statistics are available again for tablespaces and tables and indexes from the main screen under the corresponding sections.

It is best practice to check the utilization of the individual tablespaces. Check Space Statistics under Tablespaces. Pay special attention to the % Used column again, because this is an indicator on how used the space for that tablespace is and you would be able to estimate if it is going to overflow in the next few days or weeks by looking at how quickly it is growing by day, week or month once again. When the space used in a tablespace is reaching certain limits, it is important to extend it with BRCONNECT before it gets full to avoid a database standstill. It is up to you to define a comfortable level of space utilization.

To analyze particular tables or indexes, select Space Statistics under the section Tables/ Indexes. A filter will allow you to use wildcards (*) if you wish to display all tables and indexes in the database or to choose one object.

Tables that are reaching a very high number of extents are to be monitored. If a table reaches MAXEXTENTS (that you can define with BRCONNECT), the database will send an error and can stand still.

With Space Critical Objects, you are able to check what tables are particularly growing at a very fast pace and monitor it before anything wrong happens.

'Missing Indexes' will display a list of indexes that are created in the ABAP Dictionary and missing in the database or vice versa. Indexes are important for faster access to data. If they are missing, it can lead to performance problems. Sometimes, a reorganization of the database can make the database "lose" indexes or these can be deleted by the database administrator on purpose or accidentally. If you find missing indexes in your system, check whether these have been deleted on purpose or not, if there were reasons to proceed that way.

Finally, in order to obtain a list of the largest objects in your database, click on Detailed Analysis under Tables/Indexes. If you use wildcards, you will display all tables and indexes in your database. Sort by size to check which ones are the largest. Pay special attention to their growth and history and analyze if such growth is normal in your business. Certain tables that contain transactional data are expected to grow very rapidly. However, sometimes, there are mechanisms that the functional teams are able to use to avoid data that is not necessary or to summarize it. Other times, data that is not used, such as old spool logs, can be deleted, if not required by the business. And many times, but only defined by the business and especially legal requirements that depend very specifically in each country, archiving data is an option to reduce the database size, having access to the data in an external storage system.

In summary, database space management and monitoring is important to save costs in storage and to avoid performance problems.

The Alert Monitors

The Alert Monitors are a set of monitoring tools for alerts in the system that comprise a great variety of areas to check for performance, stability, and errors across your SAP R/3 system and other systems as well. These are also often called simply "CCMS monitors" and they are part of the Computer Center Management System utilities, under which are the jobs, spool and database administration and monitoring tools, as well as the configuration tools that you have learned to use in previous sections.

Architecture of the Alert Monitors

These Alert Monitors were introduced with a new architecture in release 4.0 and have grown exponentially in functionality and availability to be used as central monitoring tools for a SAP system. In fact, the monitoring capabilities of Solution Manager are based in the CCMS Alert Monitors. In order to understand how the alert monitors are built, let us define the elements that comprise the tools and how they are related.

- *Data suppliers.* Data suppliers are programs that collect information from different parts or components of the SAP systems, such as the operating system, the database, and so on. They keep information related to different Monitoring objects. The data collected are transferred to different Monitoring Objects visible from SAP.
- *Monitoring objects.* These objects represent different elements or system components that can be monitored within SAP and its environment. Monitoring objects are created by data suppliers, which are also in charge of collecting information about the monitoring objects. Each type of information that can be collected for a monitoring object is known as an attribute. For example, a monitoring object can be swap space and its attribute space used, with a value of 10 percent, which is the data collected by the data supplier. Monitoring objects are like branches in a tree, the monitoring tree elements. Another way of understanding monitoring objects is to consider them as instances of a particular monitoring template. This instance is fed with data provided by the data suppliers.
- *Data consumers.* These are programs that, depending on the monitoring object status, process the object information collected from data suppliers. This information is used for management, monitoring, and analysis. Like the data suppliers, the data consumer programs are linked to monitoring objects using BAPIs, so they can be either SAP or external programs.

Based on the information provided by the data supplier, you can work with the alert monitors to

- Trigger alerts in case of errors or warning, displaying them in different colors, Red, Yellow, or Green, depending on the severity. This can be defined by the delivered thresholds or you can customize them.
- Manage and display detailed information about the monitoring object, as well as permitting changes in its configuration, such as the definition of alert thresholds.
- Assign on-alert tools to the monitoring objects, so that automatic reaction to alerts can be configured.
- Assign analysis tools to the monitoring object for the analysis and determination of the causes for alerts.

You must assign the so-called methods to the configured monitoring attributes. A method can be a program, a function module, a SAP transaction, or a URL to be executed as a reaction to an alert. You can execute these methods within the Alert Monitor. If you double-click, for example, the monitoring tree element (MTE) for buffer swaps, you will be taken to the Buffers Monitor (transaction ST02), where you can start your analysis to correct

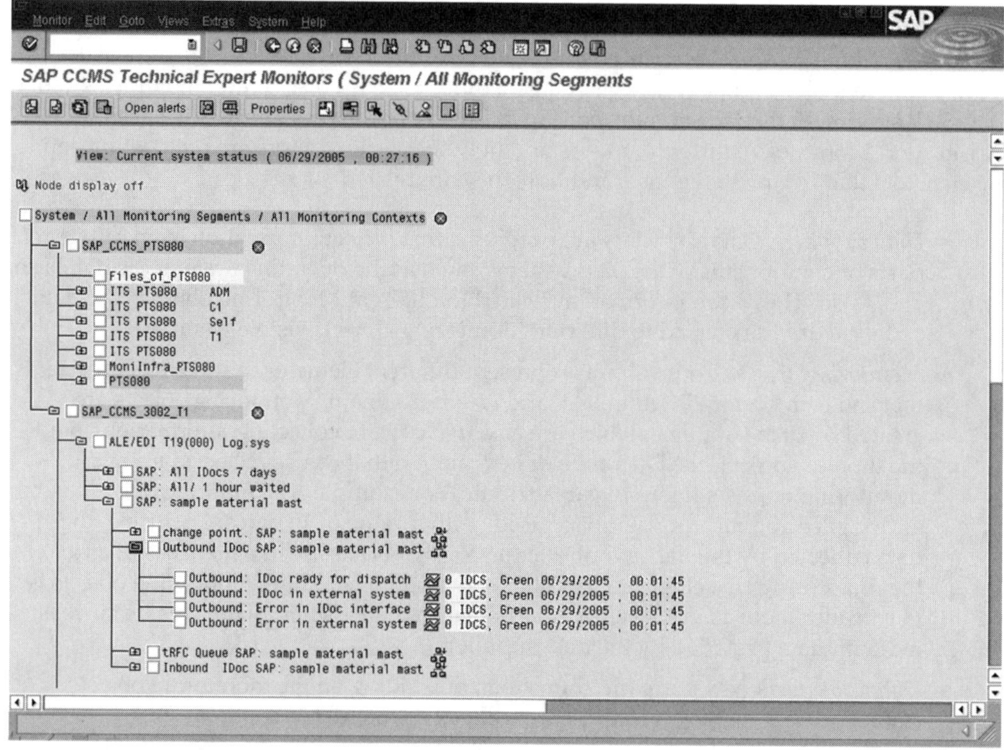

FIGURE 10-30 Displaying alerts in the Alert Monitor (Copyright by SAP AG)

the situation that triggered the alert. There are standard delivered methods that allow you to monitor the system. You can change the method assignments, if you wish for another one or a custom method. Also, you can transport method definitions to other SAP systems. Methods are different and have different properties. To define and assign methods, execute transaction RZ21.

There are Data Collection Methods, which basically accrue information and send it to the monitors at specified times. Also, there are Auto-Reaction Methods, which are launched automatically when an alert is triggered. With these methods, you can send e-mails to the system administrator or who you define as responsible for a certain area, call an operating system command or script. The Analysis Method leads you to detailed analysis of error situations from the Alert Monitor.

The Alert Monitors

Execute transaction RZ20 or follow the menu path Tools | CCMS | Control/Monitoring | Alert Monitor. You can choose between a list of monitor sets. The SAP CCMS Monitor Templates and the SAP CCMS Technical Expert Monitors contain the featured monitors in previous releases and more new utilities. The SAP Business Communication set is used to monitor SAPPhone and SAPConnect, and the SAP CCMS Monitors for Optional

Components can be used to monitor external systems or other components, such as a print server.

In order to check alerts in the system where you are logged on, expand the CCMS Technical Expert Monitors and double-click on the line named System/All Monitoring Segments/All Monitoring Contexts. The trees that you display will be colored according to the severity of the alert and you must go down the branches until the original root cause of the problem. See Figure 10-30. There you can start an analysis method, if it has been defined that way, or just display some statistics, if that is the method that you assigned. The view by default is the Current Status view, which gives you the actual status of the system. The Open Alerts view that you can choose by clicking on the pushbutton with that name gives you an overview of all the alerts recorded that happened at some point in time. Alerts will remain there until you "complete" them. To complete an alert, you must select it and choose Complete Alerts. There is a way to complete alerts automatically, but you must play with one of the methods and set its parameters accordingly. It is efficient to use the method CCMS_Segment_Space_Collect and change the parameter CMPL_ALERT_AFTER_DAY (number of days to keep the alert).

11 CHAPTER

SAP for IT Managers: Implementation, Planning, Operation, and Support of SAP Systems

This chapter is intended to provide an overview of the methodology, tools, resources, activities, and tasks involved in the implementation of SAP solutions and SAP projects, with focus on classical SAP R/3 Enterprise.

The following sections also describe and explain those aspects involving the planning, operation and support of SAP system landscapes or group of related SAP solutions. Based initially on the AcceleratedSAP, and now in the SAP Solution Manager, the guidelines provided in the next sections show some approaches for the implementation, maintenance, and support of the SAP systems, both before and after these SAP solutions go live in productive operation.

This chapter is based on many real experiences in SAP implementation projects since the middle of the 1990s, as well as new projects that are being now implemented on top of the SAP NetWeaver integration platform.

Initially most SAP projects were basically around SAP R/3, later in the Industry Solutions or New Dimension products, and the solution set or methodological framework used has been AcceleratedSAP. Recently, SAP released a new and powerful platform that aims to facilitate, help and streamline all the activities around the SAP solutions life cycle. This platform is the Solution Manager, and a broad overview of its possibilities is provided in this chapter.

SAP Projects

A SAP project might involve the design and implementation of one or more SAP solutions (whether mySAP ERP, mySAP Business Suite or any other individual component within SAP NetWeaver).

A SAP R/3 implementation within mySAP Business Suite makes sense if customers do not have an integrated ERP system and want to pursue the best possible integration among applications; however, in most cases a project implementing several mySAP Business Suite solutions is the natural evolution for existing and productive SAP R/3 customers.

Like traditional R/3 implementation projects, implementing mySAP solutions is fundamentally a business or e-business project, and so business managers should normally lead it.

But since the boom of Web enablement, eCommerce, collaboration, and integration needs, there is a fundamental difference in terms of implementation costs and efforts that companies should be aware of. In the case of mySAP projects, involving several components and a great deal of integration, technology issues have a much more important role and should be carefully considered. The reasons for this are discussed later in this chapter.

Even if the solutions within mySAP Business Suite are focused on strategic business processes, the mySAP implementation projects should be seen as part of the overall vision of the company. SAP solutions and even some of the components of the SAP NetWeaver integration platform still provide a horizontal and integrated view of the business processes, just as the ERP system, aka SAP R/3, used to do, even if now the integration can be both intra- and intercompany, cross-system, process oriented rather than component oriented, and not just at the database and data model levels.

Customizing is still the basic process for configuring most SAP solutions, but with additional possibilities, reuse of settings, automatic distribution of customizing, standard business content, Business Process Repository, global rollout functionalities, and new tools and facilities for making these tasks even easier.

Programming requirements are extremely reduced and left for those specific company processes not completely covered on standard systems. From experience in many real implementation projects, we learned that every company requires some level of programming to cope with changes in some specific business process, for data load or interfaces or for additional reporting needs.

It is very important when deciding to implement SAP Solutions and SAP NetWeaver projects that upper management is committed, understands the environment, and thinks that this type of project is not just another yet IT project.

The range of solutions within the mySAP Business Suite and the SAP NetWeaver integration platform incorporates not only state-of-the-art Web technology and Java Environment, but also (and as usual within SAP traditional history) efficient and collaborative e-business processes, which might lead to organizational or structural changes for dealing with new markets and new business partners.

Implementing SAP Solutions means to set up and configure one or more of the mySAP Business Suite or mySAP ERP, to handle the company's information needs and collaboration models enabled by the Web, and to support efficiently the current and future business processes.

According to the nature of the mySAP projects, a company might implement one or more of the mySAP solutions or the *migration* of the classical R/3 systems to a mySAP environment (other solutions within mySAP Business Suite).

However, implementing mySAP Business Suite solutions does not mean a migration from R/3, but an evolution and integration with it. A SAP R/3 upgrade might certainly be needed, depending on the current R/3 release and the degree of integration required with the rest of the mySAP solutions. This is specifically true if requiring the technology foundation of SAP NetWeaver. R/3 actually should be considered the ERP solution within the mySAP.com platform.

The activities to be performed by the project team must be supported by a corresponding solid implementation methodology. It was with R/3 that SAP developed the ASAP (*AcceleratedSAP*) implementation solution set as the set of tools, processes, and services to guarantee successful projects. In the more complex mySAP world, the set of implementation tools have evolved and improved for covering a full solution cycle and are supported by new tools and platforms to make it not only easier, but also more user-friendly.

SAP Implementation Tools

With the introduction of the extensive solution within mySAP Business Suite and SAP NetWeaver platform, SAP has evolved and included new implementation tools and aid for facilitation of the implementation of the mySAP solutions, including a new comprehensive umbrella covering the full solution life cycle management to preconfigured systems.

Following is an introduction of these SAP initiatives to streamline the implementation process and help customers in this type of projects. Some of these topics are covered with greater detail in the next sections of this chapter.

- *Solution life cycle management.* SAP calls solution life cycle management the full life cycle approach for the implementation and continuous improvement of enterprise software. Under this umbrella lies the collection of tools and methodologies to be used by SAP customers and consultants from the process of evaluation to the implementation and to continuous feedback and improvement. Among these tools, customer and consultants can find the ASAP methodology, ValueSAP, SAP Solutions Maps and Solution Composer, and the Solution Management strategy, which uses the SAP Solution Manager as the platform.
- *ASAP.* This is the well-known methodology for classical R/3 implementation projects, made later available for several of the SAP solutions. For most projects, ASAP, which encompasses the methodology, the project plan and several of the basic tools for implementation, will be the basic framework for the definition of the activities and tasks involved in SAP projects. ASAP is explained in detail in the following sections of this chapter. A variation of ASAP known as *GlobalASAP* is meant for supporting multisite and multiproduct implementations. These tools are shipped in specific CD Kits within the SAP solutions. ASAP methodology and tools are now replaced and included within SAP Solution Manager.
- *ValueSAP.* This was the first initiative in the form of a set of tools for supporting the entire customer cycle for the evaluation and implementation of a collaborative e-business platform, and so to help customers to transition to other SAP and mySAP Business Suite Solutions. ValueSAP consisted of supporting five phases in the solution cycle: identify, define, implement, manage, and improve. Figure 11-1 shows this cycle. Edition 2 of ValueSAP included ASAP, GlobalASAP, and the full solution life cycle for SAP R/3, SAP SCM (APO), SAP CRM, SAP BW, and mySAP SRM (e-procurement).
- *SAP Best Practices.* In short, the Best Practices for SAP are preconfigured and prepackaged mySAP Business Suite solutions available for different industries and cross-industry implementations, laying the foundation of the mySAP All-in-One

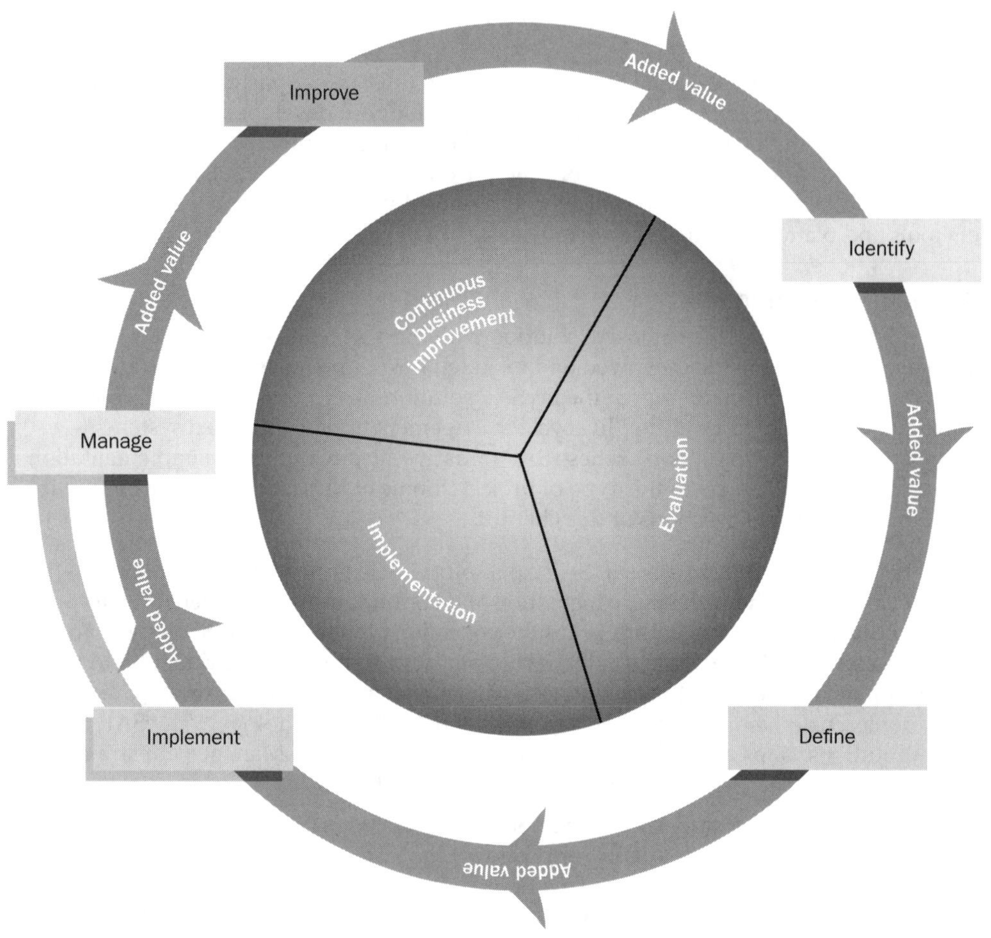

FIGURE 11-1 ValueSAP Solution life cycle

Solutions. With this type of prepackaged solutions, customers can quickly build prototypes and get systems up and running. It is obviously also a good solution for hosting or for ASP (*Application Service Provider*) solutions provided by SAP partners.

- *SAP Business Maps and Business Scenarios Maps.* These are SAP's approach for graphically describing and specifying integrated business scenarios or cross industry business blueprint supported by SAP solutions. They are particularly oriented to process integration and enterprise collaboration, and they can better show how the SAP solutions fit into this particular type of processes in search for efficiency among collaborating companies. The business maps are a collection of blueprints, including cross industry, specific industry and infrastructure. There are nearly hundreds of business maps and business scenarios. Figure 11-2 shows an example of a SAP Business Map for the mySAP ERP. You can find the most current collection at http://service.sap.com/bmet.

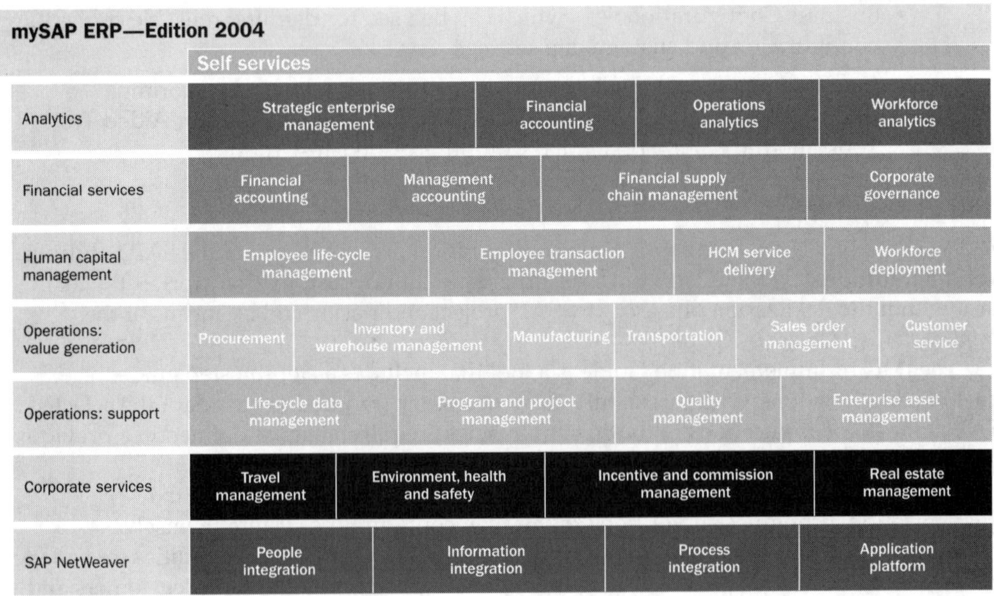

FIGURE 11-2 SAP business map for mySAP ERP

- *Solution Composer.* This is another tool, PC-based, that can be used by SAP customers to have a better view of the scope of the mySAP solutions. The Solution Composer includes access to the SAP Solution Maps and the SAP Business Scenarios Maps. With this view, companies can make a better definition of the functionality and their business processes, which are needed for the implementation of SAP and SAP partners' solutions. To download the Solution Composer and all the content, go to http://service.sap.com/bmet.
- *SAP Solution Architect and SAP Solution Manager.* This is best described as the SAP implementation and operation portal, and it is the latest implementation tool offered by SAP. The aim is to provide an online platform as a central point of access to all the other implementation tools, content, and methodology for supporting the full solution life cycle on SAP solutions: evaluation, implementation, quick adaptation, and continuous improvement. Besides customers, partners can also use this tool to create content for their own implementation products.
- *Implementation tools.* In addition to all the SAP initiatives to streamline implementation projects, all the SAP solutions include improved customizing and implementation tools coming from traditional SAP R/3 systems. These tools allow for easier and better-controlled adaptation of business processes within mySAP environments. Among these are the following:
    - IMG (Implementation Guide) as the electronic guide for doing a step-by-step configuration of the SAP applications, better known as SAP Customizing (see the next section)

- Business Configuration Sets, which can be used for defining reusable copies of configuration and customizing settings
- Test Workbench, which allows for setting test scenarios and performing integrated system and process checks with the CATT (Computer Aided Test Tool) and the eCATT (Extended Computer Aided Test Tool)

SAP Customizing

SAP customizing is referred as the main configuration process of any of the SAP Solutions. Within traditional SAP industry or cross industry solution, customizing work is the main task within the Realization phase of any SAP project and performed by means of the *Implementation Guide (IMG).*

The IMG or Implementation Guide is a tool that includes a step-by step guide to customizing functions, with direct links to all necessary transactions to adapt the selected SAP modules or applications to the current business requirements as defined in a previous Blueprint or Functional Analysis.

Using the IMG, it is possible to train end users (especially key users) in the customization techniques and options so they can configure the system themselves according to their business and organizational needs. The IMG includes utilities to manage the so-called *customizing projects.* Using these project management utilities, customers and consultants decide which parts of the system are to be customized, and institute projects for which the system automatically generates a hierarchical list of the necessary customization steps for the selected application modules. The IMG is accessed by opening the customizing main menu and then selecting the necessary functions or utilities under the Implementation Projects menu.

In traditional SAP R/3 system in latest releases, the IMG includes around 10,000 configuration objects. That number does not mean the need to customize all those settings, but only the ones relating to the business process modeling. Subsets of the IMG are set up using IMG projects, which can be generated by selecting and including those applications or components that are part of the project. The tool will also automatically select any previously required customizing object, even if the object was not selected. Figure 11-3 shows an example of the IMG.

The following sections explain in detail the ASAP methodology and SAP Solution Manager, which is meant to be the widely common framework for implementation and operation of SAP solutions.

Introduction to AcceleratedSAP (ASAP)

ASAP has been the traditional framework for SAP's implementation of R/3 projects and it was extended to cover not only R/3, but other SAP solutions, such as CRM (Customer Relationship Management), APO, e-procurement (SRM), and even a specific ASAP Roadmap for Upgrade projects, as introduced in Chapter 5.

ASAP was incorporated within the larger framework of ValueSAP, and it's now embedded within the SAP Solution Manager.

Within the context of the SAP solution life cycle management, ASAP was the basic and more important methodology for the implementation of complex projects. However, ASAP goes beyond just a methodology and provides a large number of its own tools and utilities

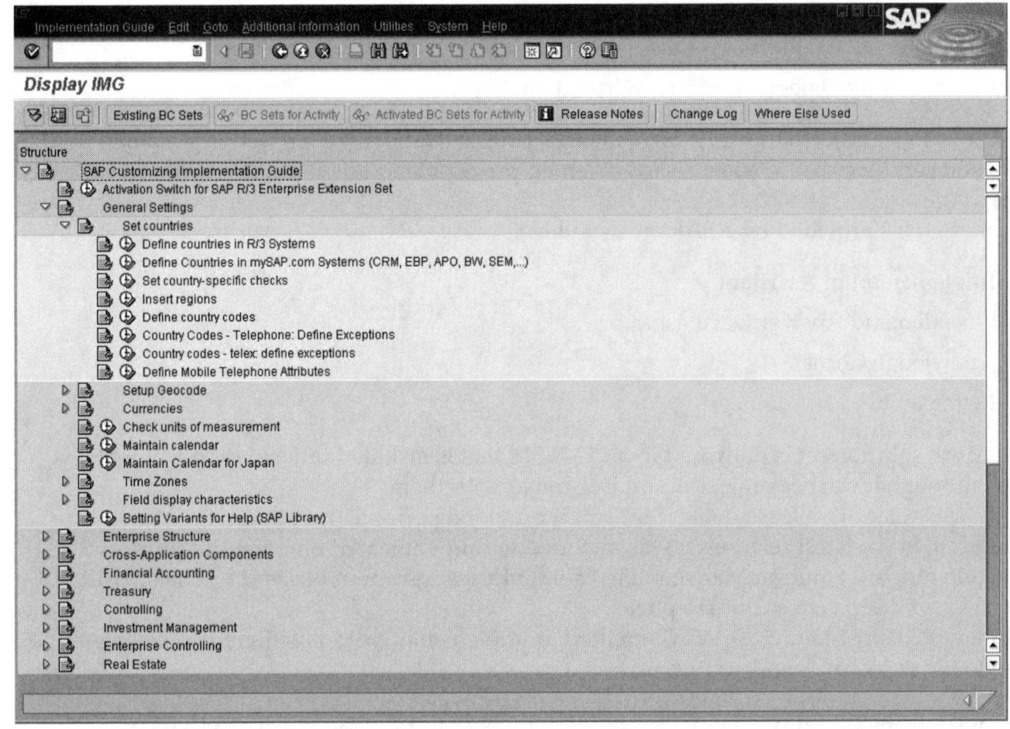

FIGURE 11-3 The IMG in SAP Enterprise (Copyright by SAP AG)

for simplifying the implementation process. ASAP can traditionally be complemented with SAP and SAP partners' implementation services, such as training, support, consulting, and so on.

Although there are different ASAPs for the mySAP solutions, the general phases are quite common to all of them, the main difference being the activities and tasks for building the business process maps and the configuration options. So in the following sections, the generic ASAP is largely introduced, with traditional SAP R/3 implementations as the core for the work packages and activities explained.

The path proposed by SAP to reach the goal of getting a fast return on investment—that is, accomplishing a fast and cost-effective implementation—is based on the idea of facilitating a quick implementation of SAP applications and guaranteeing the quality. To achieve a both fast and quality implementation, ASAP is based on the following issues:

- Clearly define the mission, objectives, and the scope of the project. A clearly defined project scope is key to adjust time planning and to approach project cost plans to real costs.
- Increase the feasibility of realizing a detailed planning at the beginning of the project.

- Standardize and establish a single project or implementation methodology, as defined by ASAP itself.
- Create a homogeneous project environment.

To realize those objectives, ASAP provides the project team with a methodology, tools, training, and services, as well as a process-oriented project plan known as the ASAP Roadmap.

The main tools provided by ASAP are as follows:

- Implementation Assistant
- Question and Answer Database
- Knowledge Corner
- Reverse Business Engineering

The ASAP solution set is delivered in a CD-ROM that is installed independently of SAP systems, although it can be connected and integrated with them.

ASAP was basically release dependent and it provided periodic updates in the SAP Service Portal. In the latest releases, it was included within ValueSAP, and now it's fully integrated in the SAP Solution Manager. For more information about kits and updates, visit the http://service.sap.com/valuesap page.

In line with SAP strategy, the ASAP method of implementation is positioned according to the following objectives and strategies:

- ASAP is the SAP implementation solution directly developed and supported by SAP and its partners.
- ASAP offers a preliminary planning of the resource needs—time, costs, people—based on the initial customer information and requirements.
- ASAP provides an optimal environment for many different SAP Solution projects, even upgrade projects.
- ASAP is aimed at and especially suited for those implementation projects where the number of changes to standard SAP applications is reduced to a minimum.

The *ASAP Roadmap* is the project plan of the methodology. It's a well-defined and clear process-oriented project plan, providing a step-by-step guide during the life of the implementation project. The Roadmap is made up of five major phases, each one describing the main work packages, activities, and tasks to achieve the expected results. Together with the activities and tasks, ASAP provides all the process descriptions, tools, training, services, and documentation that will be useful for carrying out these activities. The next sections briefly introduce the common Roadmap phases.

Phase 1: Project Preparation

At this first phase, project preparation, the project mission and scope are defined. Some key issues of this phase are as follows:

- Define clear project objectives.
- Reach total agreement on project issues among involved parties.

- Establish an efficient process for making decisions and resolving conflicts.
- Prepare the company for accepting cultural and process changes.

In this phase, ASAP provides tools, such as the Project Estimator, which helps and guides the project team using predefined questionnaires aimed at company upper management. Using the results of those questions, consultants can evaluate the answers and provide a high-level evaluation of the project scope, as well as an initial estimation of required resources and planning. This is the project starting point.

The outcome of this phase includes two essential documents in the implementation, the project charter and the detailed project plan. The management team or steering committee is responsible for evaluating such a plan and approving it if no objections are found. This will trigger the start for the next phase.

ASAP pays particular attention to ensure the quality in the whole project process and decisions taken throughout the execution of this phase. Any error or wrong decisions can negatively affect the subsequent flow of the project and might produce delays, which means longer project time and higher costs.

Phase 2: Business Blueprint

In the second phase of the Roadmap, the project team undertakes a complete and comprehensive analysis of requirements and business process, while documenting and defining the SAP applications implementation in the company. To achieve these results, ASAP provides a group of predefined questionnaires, customer input templates, group sessions, individual interviews, and so on. Information gathered is critical and extremely useful for the project team, which can analyze and help to document the business processes and the future business requirements for the company.

Classical SAP R/3 projects used the SAP Business Engineer, including the SAP Reference Model and the Question and Answer Database, which are used for generating the Business Blueprint documents and the Business Process Master List. ASAP includes a business application repository with the tools that allow users to interact with and test the business processes of some of the mySAP Business Suite applications.

In this phase of the project, ASAP provides a specific methodology for analyzing and documenting the business processes. The result is a complete blueprint of the business processes. Within an overall implementation project, this is probably the most challenging phase. In a typical nine-month implementation project, this phase could last five or six weeks.

This phase combines the analysis and documentation of the business processes with the first level of training of project teams in the different SAP solutions, applications, and technology.

Within this phase is typically the work package for starting the design of the systems environment, which includes the design of the system landscape, the technical infrastructure, and defining and testing the system administration procedures.

At this point, the development and test clients are set up, and the IMG is initialized for the starting of the customizing activities. Finally, an extremely important addition to this major phase is the inclusion of the Change Management program, in charge of dealing with all human and organizational factors that influence the implementation project.

Within the framework of the SAP Solution Manager platform, which is the actual framework for implementation of SAP solutions, the system includes great utilities to perform this phase using processes that can be automatically selected from a Business Process Repository. In a following section, this new utility and its features is explained.

Phase 3: Realization

With the Business Blueprint documentation generated as a result of the previous phase, the project team should be in good shape for starting the Realization phase, the main phase for translating business processes requirements into technical configuration settings, in other words, SAP customizing.

In this phase, ASAP includes a collection of work packages, activities, and tasks where actual implementation of business processes takes place.

From the Business Blueprint documentation generated as deliverable from the previous phase, consultants and project team members have enough information to make a valid proposal covering most business processes, reports, and daily business transactions, trying to match those of the SAP standard. If other processes are found that do not seem to cover perfectly the company's business procedures, reports, or transactions, requirements will be a matter of a fine configuration and tuning.

Most important work package activities within the Realization phase include the following:

- Review project management activities such as planning, activities, schedule, and scope.
- Provide advance training to project team.
- Establish the system management strategy and configure the technical infrastructure and system landscape.
- Sustain the change management program.
- Configure and test an initial prototype (baseline) for main functions and processes.
- Develop conversion, interface, and data transfer programs.
- Develop enhancements for scenarios not fully covered by standard SAP applications.
- Configure and verify final systems. This can be based on an iterative approach based on the prototypes.
- Create forms and reports.
- Establish the authorization concept and strategy.
- Plan and design the archiving strategy.
- Perform a final integration test.
- Prepare the end user documentation and training material.

As in every major phase, the last step will be a quality assurance realization process, where every element on the project phase is checked and verified. This phase will be the longest one in terms of time, efforts, and resources needed.

SAP Solution Manager includes specific utilities to facilitate the Realization phase, even in project involving several SAP Solutions and with the possibility of automatically linking configuration guides, IMG activities or test packages to the previously defined business processes.

Phase 4: Final Preparation

This phase, where all implementation elements and configurations are tested to finish the preparation for going live, requires a close collaboration between the full project team and the end users. Main objectives from this phase can be summarized as follows:

- *Verification of implementation.* The team and the users should test that all requirements defined in previous phases, as well as the correct behavior of the implemented business processes, are met. This phase is the appropriate time for doing stress tests, which are very important not only for verifying the sizing, but also for optimizing the system's performance. It is also very convenient to undertake simulations of real operation as the most important point of integration tests. This phase might be the convenient time to request for SAP help by means of the available services, such as a Going Live Check, which analyzes configuration and makes recommendations that can be evaluated and implemented.
- *End-user acceptance.* This is the main requirement for any project that is going to be deployed by a number of end users. Without a wide final user acceptance, the project's success is far from being guaranteed.
- *End-user training.* This is another key factor because the end users must receive the appropriate training according to their job profile and the needed application use. Training helps users to find themselves familiar and conformable with the new environment as soon as possible, which can provide an optimal user operation in less time.
- *Initial data loads and cutover.* At the moment that application and systems are ready for going live, all necessary data that is still resident in legacy or other systems must be transferred to SAP systems. All those load and interface programs should be prepared, tested, evaluated, and optimized, as should the quality of data that are going to be transferred and the time it takes for loading.
- *Help desk strategy.* When starting a productive operation, from the very first moment, every system user should know where to call and how to get help when there are problems or simply doubts. A support group, usually known as a help desk, should be created to answer end user questions efficiently and to solve or escalate both technical and application problems. Problems and doubts that might arise can be classified according to their nature. If using the SAP Solution Manager platform, you can set up your own help desk using the facilities provided by the CRM engine included in the system.

Phase 5: Go Live and Support

This phase starts the productive operation. The initial period after going live is the real evaluation period for everything done and designed in previous project phases. In most cases, it is recommended to have a progressive productive start, so that there is time to react to typical problems during this initial period, like the following:

- Not enough physical resources such as network, printers, and others
- Problems when printing reports, spool saturation, repetitive sending of the same output by the same users, and so on

- Wrongly configured end users' desktops, wrong server, deleted files, help files not reached, and so on
- Reports and transactions not completely meeting the full user needs
- Bugs in the standard systems requiring patches or repairs
- Database or run-time problems when running reports or transactions with real data
- Adding new users to the system
- Problems with authorizations
- Lack of proper knowledge, experience or end user training
- Help desk strategy not well defined or not defined at all

The degree of success or failure (unfavorable user reaction) in this initial period of productive operation will be a factor of the completeness and accuracy of the previous phases and how the possible problems were issued.

In this phase, a good procedure for communicating with SAP or partners to request their services might be important, for example, the realization of EarlyWatch (preventive maintenance) services. It is also the phase for testing the quality of operation and system administration procedures. Soon after, there will be a culture where the most frequent types of problems (around 80 to 90%) will already be classified and can be quickly solved.

From the technical and administration point of view, after the initial adaptation to the productive operation, there is a time for managing different activities of the productive SAP system, such as the following:

- Watching system access rights (authorizations) and security
- Managing the transports and change requests
- Applying and installing patches (collections of corrected programs and transactions)
- Planning EarlyWatch sessions
- Making changes and configurations as recommended by EarlyWatch reports
- Watching the systems performance and tuning most critical reports and transactions

SAP Solution Manager

The SAP Solution Manager is a customer platform that provides content, procedures and services to implement and operate SAP Solutions, including both simple and complex system and application landscapes. Figure 11-4 shows an overview diagram of the functions provided by the SAP Solution Manager.

The SAP Solution Manager is a SAP Solution (R/3 like) based in the SAP Web Application Server, unlike ASAP, which was a PC-based toolset. A major advantage of the SAP Solution Manager is its integration with other key SAP transactions, such as Project Administration, SAP Test Workbench, IMG, BC Sets, and CATTs, which support implementation activities.

With the wide range of current SAP product portfolio, solutions, and Integration platform (SAP NetWeaver), all the integration aspects that target both technical and

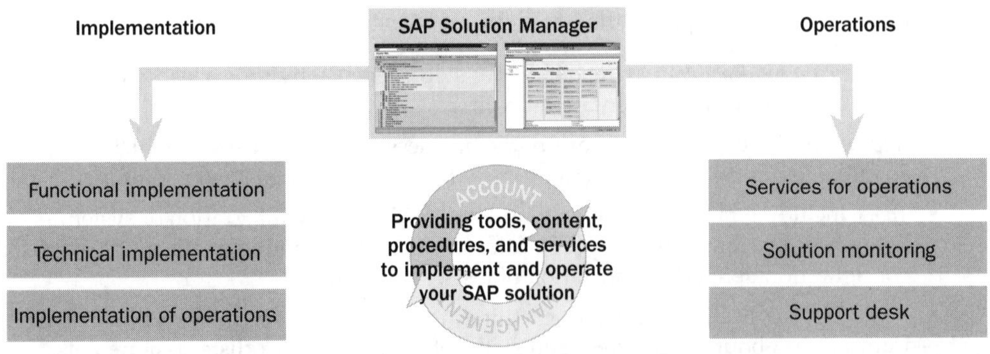

FIGURE 11-4 Solution Manager main functions

business requirements of heterogeneous environments are very important. SAP Solution Manager plays a key role in providing an infrastructure and a central unified platform to manage and implement these complex environments.

The SAP Solution Manager is also integrated with SAP Service Marketplace both for requesting service and support, or by automatically sending and collecting EarlyWatch report, and also the possibility of assigning traditional SAP notes to internal problems, or escalating problems to SAP.

In the following sections you will find a broad overview of the SAP Solution Manager and how this platform supports both the key implementation and operation activities, and how it can be used for service requests both internal, like a help desk, and external through SAP and its partners.

SAP Solution Manager for Functional Implementation

From a methodological point of view, that is, regarding the implementation objectives, Solution Manager is an evolution of ASAP, which is embedded, and it is based on the same phases and principles. In other words, the implementation methodology for the SAP Solution Manager is still based on ASAP concepts, but the toolset is different.

SAP Solution Manager supports the implementation of customer's solutions from a process-oriented view instead of the traditional component-oriented view.

The deployment of the SAP Solution Manager as the implementation platform, when designed and implemented correctly, can provide customers with many benefits, among which are the following:

- An organized project view, including the possibility for storing all the project documentation and issues
- A central point of access for all key implementation activities
- Tools to simplify the Blueprint, Configuration and Testing activities
- Standard scenarios provided through Business Process Repository
- The capacity of requesting the services aligned with the SAP implementation process

For implementation purposes, the SAP Solution Manager provides the following:

- *Implementation Roadmaps*, which includes step by step activities to lead the project team in the whole implementation process
- *Implementation Content*. By means of the business process repository, which servers as initial templates or input for a process-driven design of customer solutions
- *Tools*, including most of the tools found on ASAP, and the integration of system landscape definition, project preparation, blueprint generation, realization of the configuration defined, organization of tests, and so on
- *Reporting*, a collection of reporting utilities for project analysis, allowing to display information about the progress and status of the project, worklists, assignments, issues, and so on

Figure 11-5 shows the Implementation Roadmap within the SAP Solution Manager, which is meant to guide through the functional implementation process of customer process-oriented solutions.

Following sections discuss some of the available functionality and tools of the SAP Solution Manager for implementation.

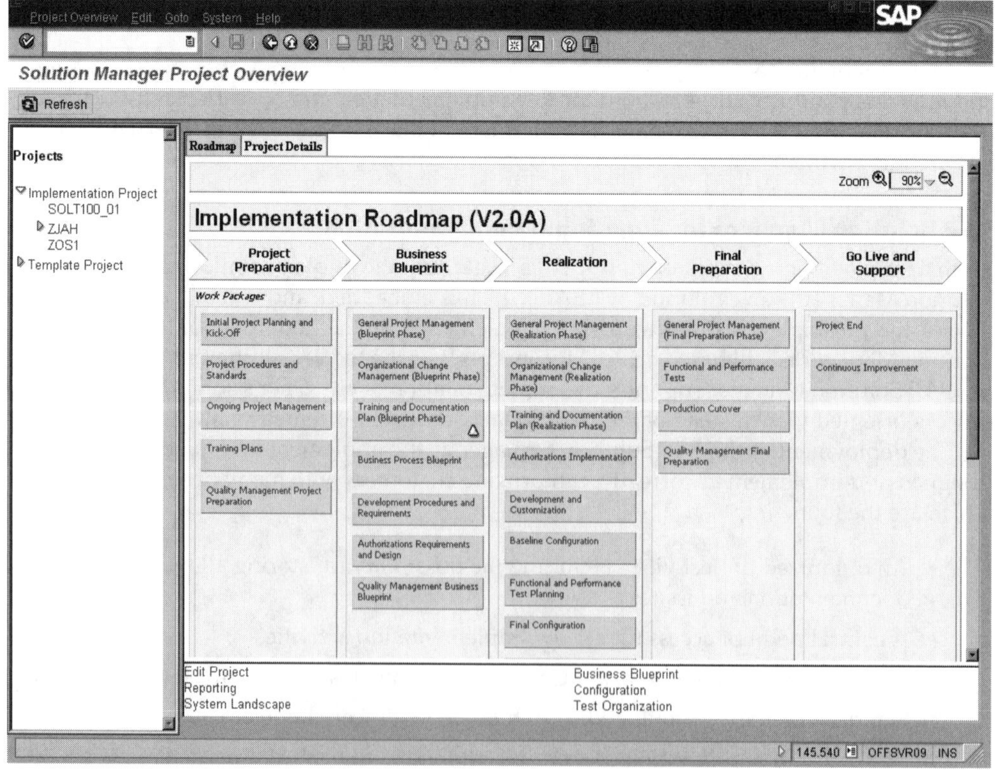

Figure 11-5 Functional Implementation Roadmap (Copyright by SAP AG)

Business Process Repository

As stated earlier, the SAP Solution Manager has been designed to support process-oriented rather than component oriented scoping of customer's solution.

The SAP Solution Manager provides the Business Process Repository with central access to the list of SAP-delivered business scenarios and supporting documentation that serves as a starting point to identify the project scope. The BPR is therefore a list of business scenarios that serve as a starting point to identify what is to be implemented. Customers can also create and document their business processes.

The Business Process Repository (BPR) is a package of reusable predefined business process content delivered by SAP. The BPR content varies for different scenarios but may contain the following:

- Business Scenario Documentation, including configuration guides
- Assignments to transactions
- IMG assignments in the Realization phase
- Predefined test cases

Besides the possibility of including these business scenarios from the BPR when in the Blueprint Phase and tool, within the Solution Manager, you can check the BPR in the Solution Manager section within the SAP Service Marketplace (service.sap.com/solutionmanager) and then choose *Functions in detail, Implementation, Implementation content.* You can see an example of a business scenario in Figure 11-6.

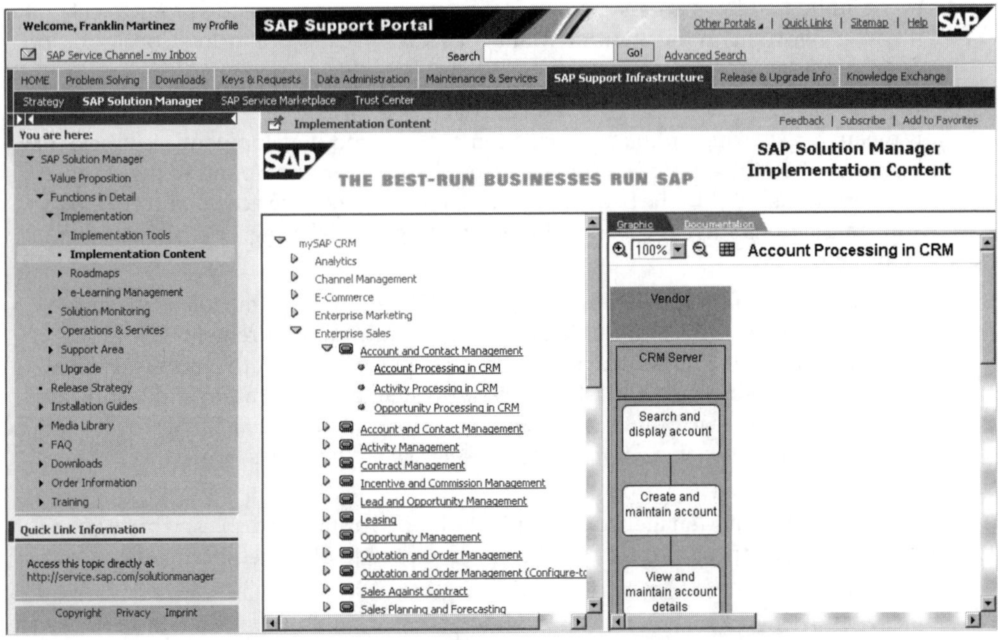

FIGURE 11-6 Example of business scenario within BPR (Copyright by SAP AG)

Implementation Roles within Solution Manager

The SAP Solution Manager platform includes some predefined user roles, which can be modified, copied, or adapted according to customer needs and which provides a user menu for each role, including the typical project implementation tasks that are associated with each role.

When logging on the Solution Manager using these roles, the members of the project team will be able to access implementation projects with the authorizations assigned to them within the roles and work their specific project activities. Remember that authorizations determine the degree of access to functions and transactions within the project. More information can be found in Chapter 7.

The authorization concept for the SAP Solution Manager is predefined for the following roles:

- *Project manager.* The predefined role is SAP_SOLAR_PM. Project managers are responsible for the supervision, control, and realization of the SAP implementation projects and to perform the daily project management tasks. They have access to Solution Manager functions Project Administration, Project Reporting, Business Blueprint, and so on.
- *Application consultant.* Predefined role is SAP_SOLAR_AC. The main task is to should ensure that the Business Blueprint and configuration defines correctly the target business processes, and all other requirements for a successful implementation, such as the analysis documentation, interfaces, reporting, and so on. Application consultants must have both business knowledge and SAP knowledge to configure and implement the customers' requirements. This role has more limited authorizations than project managers, and is intended for project members working in the Solution Manager with Business Blueprint, Configuration, Testing, Message Handling, and a few others.
- *Basis/development consultant.* Predefined role is SAP SAP_SOLAR_BC. This role is meant for working on the authorization concept and development activities, for instance when there is a need for customer development not found in the standard SAP Solutions. Within the SAP Solution Manager, they have access to functions and transactions such as Business Blueprint, Organize Testing, and Message Handling.
- *Technical consultant.* Predefined role is SAP_SOLAR_TC and this role is in charge of planning, designing, and implementing the technical requirements within the projects. Technical consultants are in charge of performing all the technical tasks in the systems, including all tasks typical to system administration and technical support, and access to Solution Manager functions such as *Defining System Landscapes, Synchronizing Customizing, Message Handling*, and so on.

Additionally, Solution Manager comes with another two standard roles, which can be also assigned to users or project team members, or adapted to other requirements:

- SAP_SOLAR_ ALL, corresponding to the role for all authorizations within the SAP Solution Manager implementation functions.

- SAP_SOLAR_RO, which is the Read Only role. Users assigned this role will only be able to display the functions in the system, without authorizations to do any modifications.

Solution Manager Roadmaps

Roadmaps provide the methodology to implement SAP projects and are delivered with the Solution Manager. They contain standard SAP implementation methodology and include the most important aspects and phases of a SAP implementation project. An example of Roadmap is shown in Figure 11-5.

You can access the Solution Manager Roadmaps from the user menu, by selecting Solution Manager | Roadmaps, or by running transaction RMMAIN from the command field.

A fundamental component of Roadmaps is links to accelerators and tools to perform project tasks. Accelerators are mainly documents, information, and document templates that are attached to structure items within the Roadmaps.

With roadmaps, you can do the following:

- Open and browse the roadmap structure to display all indications relevant to the project steps, whether the phases, work packages, activities, and tasks.
- Display accelerators, or documents linked to structure items within the Roadmap. You have also the option of assigning your own documents.
- Search for specific items within the Roadmap structure.
- Register and track the status for each structure item. You can assign your personal notes to these status settings.
- Create issues or messages within the system, to keep track of problems or open issues to be resolved.
- You can print any of the documents, or the information displayed in the structure items of the Roadmap.
- Filter structure items by role or subject area.

There are three types of standard Roadmaps within the SAP Solution Manager:

- *Implementation Roadmap.* This is the roadmap directing functional SAP implementations. It is meant mainly for Project Managers and Application Consultants. This functional roadmap synchronized with the technical one through the milestone concept.
- *Solution Management Roadmap.* The roadmap for the technical Implementation and Operations of SAP Solutions and aimed to the technical team and system managers. The Solution Management Roadmap synchronizes with the Implementation Roadmap using the milestone concept.
- *Global Template Roadmap* meant for multisite and multinational projects, providing a methodology for the implementation of a global customer solution. However, when a local implementation is to take place, you have to proceed with regular Implementation and Solution Management roadmaps. This type of roadmap is meant for Sponsors or Program Managers and Project Managers.

Other roadmaps that can be installed within the SAP Solution Manager are as follows:

- *SAP Enterprise Portal Implementation Roadmap*, which can be used for specific implementation work packages and tasks for the SAP Enterprise Portal, considering the large integration factor it represents.
- *Upgrade Roadmap*, which we briefly introduced in Chapter 5 and which is used to SAP solutions upgrade projects.

In their own specific project targets, each roadmap type contains the standard SAP implementation methodology and cover the most important aspects and phases of a SAP implementation.

Solution Manager Roadmap Structure View

You get the structure view when double-clicking the graphical view.

The structure on the left of the screen is the *project area* and contains the structure of the Roadmap with some of the attributes.

The text displayed in the right part of the screen is the *viewing area*, which contains the description according to the structure item selected in the project area.

The tabs and objects you find in the lower right hand of the screen is known as the *attachment area*. There you can find several tabstrips:

- The Accelerators tabstrips contains links to accelerators, when there are any available for the structure item.
- The Notes tabstrip is used to display or create notes about the particular structure elements.
- The Messages tab is used to create, send, display, and edit problem messages for the selected structure element. If needed, you have the option to attach documents to the message.
- Set Status. The status of a structure step is displayed as an icon in the structure and you can see it graphically in the Roadmap initial screen. To set the status of a structure item, just click the Status icon, which appears besides the structure item. Initially all status are set to Open. You must pay attention that status settings cannot be inherited along the structure in the Roadmap.

You can also assign new documents or accelerators to a Roadmap structure element. This include inserting or uploading new project documents, links to Web sites, or even execution of specific transactions. In order to do that you have to use the Project Documentation tab.

Implementation Roadmap

The Implementation Roadmap describes how to organize and run an implementation project from a functional perspective. It provides the methodological framework for the tasks involved in the implementation of a SAP solution. It includes, among other things, required project management, configuration of business processes, and technical aspects, test procedures, and training concepts.

Roadmaps provide a unified structure for all SAP components, and the component-specific content is found in the accelerator. It is to be noted as well that the roadmaps include several Milestones, typically after completion of a critical work package. Roadmaps also include some of the services provided by SAP and partners that can help in the corresponding activity within the implementation project.

Just exactly as ASAP does, and using most of the ASAP documents, the Implementation Roadmap divides the implementation process in five phases, with work packages, activities, and tasks assigned as sub items to each phase.

Based on the project scope, you can select different Roadmaps according to the SAP solutions or SAP application components being implemented. The lists of activities within the roadmap are not changed, but the Accelerators and tools linked to these activities will present specific information related to the SAP solution or application component selected in scope.

The Implementation Roadmap is intimately linked with the Solution Management Roadmap. They are aligned along the milestone concept with critical synchronization points.

The Implementation Roadmap consists of the following five phases, as we have previously seen within ASAP:

- *Phase 1: Project Preparation.* In this initial phase, you plan your implementation project and make all the preparatory steps, including setting the objectives for the project, determining the scope, defining the project plan, project team members and establishing the activities and sequence for the implementation activities. Within SAP Solution Manager, and alongside the roadmaps, this phase is also supported by the transaction SAP_SOLAR_ADMIN.
- *Phase 2: Business Blueprint.* The purpose of this phase is to determine the project scope and create the Business Blueprint. The Business Blueprint documents business process requirements and additional goals for your implementation. Within SAP Solution Manager, this is supported by transaction SOLAR01.
- *Phase 3: Realization.* The purpose of this phase is to configure and test the business processes defined in the Business Blueprint phase and create customer-specific end-user documentation and training materials. Within SAP Solution Manager, this is supported by transaction SOLAR02.
- *Phase 4: Final Preparation.* The purpose of this phase is to prepare and conduct end-user training and perform a final test of the SAP system before going live. You also prepare and execute data conversion from legacy systems to the production system. You should also resolve all open issues. Within SAP Solution Manager, a big deal of this phase can also be performed with transaction SOLAR02, specifically to run tests.
- *Phase 5: Go Live and Support.* The purpose of this phase is to move the SAP system to a live production environment, establish a help desk support organization for end users, and optimize the system performance and technical environment as far as possible. In this phase, you also plan follow-up training and define an upgrade strategy to continually improve the SAP system.

Solution Management Roadmap

The Solution Management Roadmap provides a methodology to implement and operate the technical infrastructure. The Solution Management Roadmap complements the Implementation Roadmap, and both are aligned along the milestone concept with critical sync points identified.

This technical Roadmap is targeted at Technical Leaders or project Managers, IT managers, Technical Consultant, Support Engineer, and System Administrators.

This Roadmap contains the methodological framework for implementation of the technical infrastructure and operations, providing the following facilities:

- A unified view of the technical implementation of a complete SAP solution landscape, which can consist of several components and systems
- Accelerators, providing many documents, tools, and links for helping to reach a successful implementation of the technical infrastructure and support
- Integration and handover procedures from the project team to the support organization

The phases include milestones and specific services aligned with them.

The phases within the Solution Management Roadmap, as stated, aligned with the Implementation Roadmap are as follows:

- Strategic Framework
- Technical and Integration Design
- Technical and Operations Implementation
- Cutover and Start of Production
- Operations and Continuous Improvement

In following sections we cover all the technical issues from a more general point of view, most of which are included within either the ASAP Roadmap or the Solution Management Roadmap.

Global Template Roadmap

The Global Template Roadmap provides a methodology for the implementation of global customer solutions. In global roll-out scenarios, you define a global template at headquarters, and place scenarios, Blueprint documents, and configuration in the template. You can specify the parts of the template that are relevant to the subsidiaries and if or to what extent they can change the template in their roll-out projects.

Main target groups are Program and Project Manager, Project Team in Global Template project. Overall structuring is as follows:

- Phase 1: Global Program Setup
- Phase 2: Global Business Blueprint
- Phase 3: Global Realization
- Phase 4: Global Maintenance and Support

The Global Template Roadmap does not sync with the Solution Management Roadmap.

Solution Manager Implementation Tools

Solution Manager includes several powerful tools for streamlining the implementation projects of SAP solutions. The following sections briefly introduce some of the capabilities of these tools. For more information, please refer to the online documentation, the documentation available in the SAP Solution Manager portal (service.sap.com/solutionmanager), or take the standard training course SMI310, which is very good.

System Landscape Definition

Although the project will start in the Project Preparation phase, you will need to define the system landscape for either a template or implementation project before you can access the component systems in subsequent project phases.

The SAP Solution Manager provides a tool for system landscape definition, allowing one to manage centrally all the component systems or logical systems you require for your project. This tool is the System Landscape Maintenance transaction, which can be accessed either from the Solution Manager user menu, or by running transaction SMSY.

This transaction allows you to define logical systems, products, and the related RFC destinations that are essential for being able to access component systems from the Solution Manager utilities.

A system landscape for the project contains the following information:

- Logical component
- Product version
- Logical systems for dedicated system roles

In the Business Blueprint, the system role Evaluation may be maintained to test-drive related transactions of process tasks. You can add the systems for other system roles during the course of the project. You cannot maintain the logical system information non-SAP products.

The following information is helpful for maintaining logical components:

- A logical component reflects a logical system set (instances) for a product. If you need to handle multiple instances of systems for a product, create additional logical components.
- The selection of the logical component influences the selection of scenarios/processes using the Business Process Repository in the Business Blueprint phase. Only those scenarios/processes that comply to the defined logical component and product version are released for selection.

The following functions are available based on the system landscape you define:

- Navigation to business content in component systems
- Generation of IMG projects in component systems and distribute central project data
- Comparison and distribution of customizing in the local systems

Project Preparation

When you are ready to proceed with the implementation project using the SAP Solution Manager, you begin by defining the system landscape and the project.

The purpose of the Project Preparation phase is to provide initial planning and preparation for the SAP project. Normally, each SAP project has its own specific objectives and scope, and the steps in Phase 1 help identify and plan the most important project areas.

To access the Project Administration utility, select Project Administration from the SAP Solution user menu, or run transaction SOLAR_PROJECT_ADMIN from the command field.

From this transaction you can perform all the central administrative tasks relevant for the project:

- Creating, deleting, and modifying projects
- Entering general project data and project language
- Assigning project team members
- Defining the system landscape for the project
- Defining project standards such as status values, keywords, or documentation types

Depending on the project type you select, you can also specifying transport request information. With Solution Manager you can create the following project types:

- *Implementation project.* The Implementation project type is considered for single-site implementations. If you create an implementation project, you can select predefined scenarios from template projects.
- *Template project.* The Template project type is considered for multisite implementations. It can also serve as an authoring environment to develop best practices, which customer can create for rollouts or those developed by SAP implementation partners.

If you create a template project, you can select predefined scenarios from template projects and you can transport template projects to other SAP Solution Manager systems.

The selected project type will influence the edit options available in the individual project phases (Business Blueprint and Realization) and must take into consideration that only one roadmap can be assigned for each project.

You define the structure of the project by specifying the project scope, which contains only elements that are part of the selected template(s). You can set the project scope in various ways, based on the selected project type.

- *Implementation project.* By selecting SAP and/or partner templates or user templates created in a template project.
- *Without selecting existing templates.* You should build the project structure using elements from the Business Process Repository or the Business Blueprint.
- *Template project.* By selecting one or more SAP and/or partner solutions as the basis for your project. Without selecting existing templates, you need to build the entire solution in the Business Blueprint.

This solution can be bundled centrally in transport requests and distributed across other systems.

All SAP scenarios that are transferred and saved to the project are copies. The original scenarios remain unchanged when the project structure is changed.

Let's review the main functionality of every tab within the Project Administration:

- The Scope tab also includes locking functions for the Business Blueprint. You can restrict the extent to which project members can work on the Business Blueprint in the Scope tab. For project documentation: All documents with flag Blueprint-relevant are protected in SOLAR01 as well as in SOLAR02.
- The Project Standards tab contains three tabs such as the following:
  - *Status values.* Provides information about the status of your project. A status value has a 10-character status ID and a description of the status. Status IDs should be meaningful. Note that status values used in roadmaps cannot be changed or adapted to project-specific needs.
  - *Keywords.* You can define keywords to flexibly categorize documents, for example, to facilitate search and reporting in the Project Analysis transaction. Keywords should be concise.
  - *Documentation types.* Various documentation types are available for all types of projects.

Standard values for status, keywords, and documentation types for your project are all set similarly in the Project Administration transaction. If values have not yet been assigned to a project, the project administrator can use the project template, which contains project-independent status values, keywords, and documentation types.

Each project type is assigned to a template that contains a number of values for statuses, priorities, and documentation types. You can adapt the project template to suit project requirements. The values set in the Project Standards tab are available as default values in the Business Blueprint and Configuration transactions.

Various documentation types are available for all types of projects. You can use the various documentation types delivered by SAP as templates to structure your project documentation or you can create your own documentation types.

Each documentation type has a unique ID. There are two types of project documentation, such as the following:

- *Project-specific documentation.* This documentation type is valid only for the project to which it is assigned.
- *Cross-project documentation.* You can identify this documentation type by the Global Doc. indicator.

You can create a template for project documentation in the Documentation Types tab. The template enables you to define the appearance and format of your documentation. You can use this template to create new documents during the Business Blueprint and Realization phases. Documentation templates are stored in the local Knowledge Warehouse of the Solution Manager and not in SAP Script tables. If needed, you can define further attributes for the documentation types: *Global Doc, Several Documents Allowed, File Extension,* or *CI Template (Customer input).*

The SAP Solution Manager contains a transport function for template projects. You can supervise change requests for your project in the Project Administration transaction.

If you selected logical components for the project and defined at least a development system, all customizing subprojects are displayed in this tab. You can generate the corresponding Project IMGs and distribute the central project data (general data, project members, project standards, country selection) for these Customizing projects.

When the Project IMGs are generated in component systems, everything is initially set in scope. The green and red traffic lights indicate if Project IMGs have already been generated and the corresponding data distributed. Project IMG in application component is assigned the same name as the project in the Solution Manager system.

Business Blueprint

The purpose of this phase is to create the Business Blueprint, which is detailed documentation of the business process requirements of the company, both functional and technical. Standard SAP business scenarios will be employed because they are delivered with predefined implementation content. At the end of this Phase 2, a Business Blueprint document should be generated and discussed for approval or modifications.

The Business Blueprint provides a general understanding of how an enterprise's business processes should be mapped in one or more SAP systems. The purpose of the Business Blueprint is to document in detail the scope of business scenarios, business processes, process steps, and the requirements of a SAP implementation.

The Business Blueprint functions within the SAP Solution Manager can be accessed from the user menu, selecting Business Blueprint, or alternatively using transaction code SOLAR01.

You will continue using the Business Blueprint in the Solution Manager during the Realization phase (configuration and testing) because it will use the same project structure you created in the Business Blueprint phase to configure and generate test plans.

Defining the Business Blueprint enables you to document the business processes that you want to use in your SAP system. You create a project structure in which relevant business scenarios, business Processes, and process tasks are organized in a hierarchical structure. You can also create project documentation to assign to individual scenarios, processes, or process steps. To define how business processes should run in SAP systems, you need to assign transactions to each process task.

Additionally, the transactions that you assign to process tasks in the Business Blueprint are placed in test plans during test plan generation. The transactions can be processed as function tests to test the transactions.

Tests are being carried to check if the transaction exists in the component systems. The SAP Solution Manager provides central access to the list of business processes as a starting point for the project scope.

When creating the Business Blueprint, customers select the preconfigured business processes they want to evaluate or implement or they can also create their own business processes. Based on the scenarios selected in the scope, the corresponding Business Process Repository (BPR) content is made available. Using the BPR, as introduced earlier, you get

- Scenario documentation
- Transaction assignments
- IMG assignments

- Configuration guides
- Predefined test cases

The Business Blueprint consists of the following structure items that are organized in a hierarchical structure:

- Organizational units
- Masterdata
- Business scenarios
- Business processes
- Process steps

You assign content, for example, project documentation, Business Configuration Sets, or transactions, to individual structure items in the SAP Solution Manager.

You can also create structure items for organizational units and master data below a business scenario. You use these structure items only if the organizational units and master data are relevant exclusively for the business process above them in the structure. All the levels of this structure can be modified to represent an entire specific solution.

You can use the Structure tab to create or change the project structure in which organizational units, master data, business scenarios, processes, and process steps are listed.

For organizational units, master data, and process tasks, you need to specify the component in the system landscape to which the structure item belongs. You cannot specify a component for business processes, because a few business processes run across components.

Assignment of components is performed at the process task level. If you chose a predefined structure item from the Business Process Repository, the system specifies the components for the system.

You can maintain new or changed structure items on the Project Documentation and Transactions tabs by assigning documents to scenarios, business processes, and process tasks.

There are many other functions within the Business Blueprint that you can use to facilitate the process of defining the specific scenarios or solution to be implemented, such as copying structure elements, pointing to existing documentation, display and modifying the graphic, and so on.

Realization

After the Business Blueprint is complete and signed-off, the next phase, Realization, proceeds with configuring the related system landscape and performing development work to meet the defined requirements.

Once configuration work is complete, the testing process should be defined, organized, executed, and documented to validate system performance.

The Realization phase uses the same structure previously defined in the Blueprint phase, and within the Solution Manager, the available tools for this phase are accessed using transaction code SOLAR02.

For the Realization phase, you can accomplish the following tasks with the SAP Solution Manager:

- Configure the specific solution defined in the scope and in the Business Blueprint using the IMG (Implementation Guide) and the Business Configuration Sets (BC Sets).
- Automatically distribute configuration options across components. This makes sense just for similar components or business processes.
- Organize and assign test cases (for example CATTs, eCATTS or manual test cases) to specific processes which can later be executed and reviewed using the Test Workbench.

Challenges of SAP Solution Projects: Technology Issues

Technical issues on classical SAP projects traditionally played a secondary role in favor of optimizing business processes and companies' efficiency. Technology was *just* the enabler. Technical implementation within a full a classical SAP R/3 project usually did not cost more than 10% of the total budget, excluding hardware costs.

In the new mySAP Business Suite and SAP NetWeaver world, the design, definition, and implementation of business processes are also the key. However, now technology plays an ever-increasing and more important role than it used to, in terms of its complexity, number of servers, and the integration within application and into the Web world. The lack of seeing the increasing needs for technology experts and the right tools can severely affect the success of these complex business projects that have a high degree of technology. In some of the mySAP solutions, such as mySAP CRM, or the SAP Enterprise Portal, the percentage of technical implementation compared to the global project can range into the 40 or 50% range, depending on the specific application.

As we could see in earlier sections, SAP is also aware of the importance of the technical implementation and provided the Solution Management Roadmap, in sync with the functional implementation. This roadmap is the methodology or guide for the technical implementation issues when dealing with SAP solutions.

As a reminder, the following is a list of some important technical issues that must be seriously taken into consideration when planning, designing, implementing, and supporting SAP systems and solutions.

SAP Technical Implementation

As was introduced in previous section, both AcceleratedSAP (ASAP for short) and Solution Manager are SAP's implementation solutions for SAP projects. Solution Manager and ASAP go beyond just methodology by providing a large number of tools and utilities that simplify the implementation process and cover extensive SAP and SAP partner implementation services such as training, support, consulting, and so on.

The path proposed by SAP to reach the goal of successful implementation projects is based on the idea of facilitating a quick implementation of SAP systems and guaranteeing the quality.

To realize these objectives, Solution Manager and ASAP provide the project team with a methodology and with tools, training, and services, as well as a process-oriented project plan known, whether the ASAP Roadmap, or the Solution Management Roadmap.

The ASAP solution set deals also with the technical aspects of the implementation and includes many papers, utilities, and templates for helping project managers to address the many technical issues involved.

Technical issues appear in every phase of the ASAP Implementation Roadmap, and it's a specific target of the Solution Management Roadmap. Within ASAP, these are the main work packages:

- Phase 1, Project Preparation, includes a work package consisting of the *Technical Requirements Planning*, mainly used to perform an initial sizing and procure the initial hardware.
- Phase 2, Business Blueprint, includes the work package *Develop System Environment*, which comprises the activities for installing and configuring the development system, including the definition of first system administration procedures.
- Phase 3, Realization, is the longest phase and includes many technical activities. Most importantly for technology- and infrastructure-related tasks, it contains the work package *System Management*, which is made up of a collection of activities such as the following:
    - Develop System Test Plans
    - Define Service Level Commitment
    - Establish System Administration Functions
    - Set up Quality Assurance Environment
    - Define Production System Design
    - Define Production System Management
    - Set up Production Environment
- Phase 4, Final Preparation, contains work packages for system management that target specific activities for the productive environment, especially for conducting system tests. It is also important to perform a quality check on technical issues in this phase.
- Phase 5, Go Live and Support, is an important overall phase for the full project team, providing extensive support and guarantees that the systems work as expected. This includes all infrastructure components and support of the basis system.

Systems Landscape

Designing a system landscape for mySAP means defining the strategy and layout of a group of servers where the SAP solutions will be installed, configured, and, finally, used productively. Normally for each of the solutions, a group of three types of systems is recommended:

- A development system, for configuration (customizing) and development
- A quality assurance system, where the previous work can be tested
- A productive system, where actual end users work with real transactions and operations

Some companies are installing an additional system called SANDBOX, where you can play with different technical configuration without affecting the development system.

Additionally, in the mySAP.com environment, we will find Web servers, ITS systems, and, in some cases, other additional systems, such as index servers, mobile devices, and others.

The issue of planning, defining, and configuring a systems landscape is very important, because it is not an isolated issue and will have a direct impact on other technical issues, mainly on systems sizing, how the customizing settings and developments are transported to other systems, and how the testing will be performed.

The design of the systems landscape will have a direct impact on the tasks involved for installing and configuring the mySAP systems, as well as for their management and monitoring.

Some considerations for this activity are as follows:

- A systems landscape configuration requires careful planning and systems sizing. Experienced technical consultants should perform this in the context of how it will affect other technical issues.
- The systems landscape design has to be clearly communicated and explained to the project team, even if the project team is not technical, and must be reflected in the project procedures. It is very common to associate project problems with just "machine" problems.
- Medium-term and long-term plans should be considered so there is a step-by-step approach to a full e-business systems scenario.

Sizing

Sizing is the process of analyzing and estimating the computing needs for the systems infrastructure, installation, and operation, in terms of computing power (CPU, memory), server's distribution, disk volume, and network bandwidth. This is a very complex and never-accurate process, which requires more involvement than it is commonly given, requiring the help of not only SAP and the hardware vendors, but also the IT department and end users so that a better estimation of real work can be performed. In terms of the difference from classical R/3 systems, for mySAP Business Suite solutions and SAP NetWeaver components, the sizing is a matter of both the specific solutions being implemented and the awareness of the possibility of thousands of connections through the Internet.

A failure to provide a good service level to users or business partners could be a disaster.

For these reasons, sizing on an overall multi solution SAP system landscape includes the following elements that must be considered:

- Several types of and possibilities for installations, which will be a factor of how many servers and the applications to be installed in each of them
- The hardware and network configuration, including Internet access
- Disk volume and the layout and size of the file systems for each solution
- The installation of the different databases

- Expected systems availability
- Distribution of servers and services

Finally, the objective of the sizing process is to calculate some important figures, such as how much CPU power will be needed (type of processors, memory, number of servers) for each system within the landscape, how big the databases will be (disk space necessary), and the minimum recommended network infrastructure.

The quality of the sizing will be just as good as the quality of the data supplied by the customer.

To ease the process, SAP provides the QuickSizer tool, which can be accessed through the SAP Service Marketplace (http://service.sap.com/quicksizer). With the QuickSizer service, mySAP customers can make an initial estimation of CPU, memory, and disk resources. The results in terms of SAP Application Benchmark Performance Standard (SAPS) and average disk volume requirements are immediately available, and customers can decide to pass on this information to the hardware partner directly from the QuickSizer form.

Security

The importance of security in the context of SAP projects has been largely dealt with in this book, specifically in Chapter 7. In the Web age, security, or the lack thereof, is the main concern of and the main barrier to e-business through the Web. Therefore, addressing security is key within SAP projects, with the objective of providing confidence to business partners as well as protecting valuable business data and ensuring continuous and stable systems operations. For more information, refer to Chapter 7.

SAP System Management

With the increasing complexity in the number, installation, and integration of several different systems within SAP Solutions landscapes, the issue of managing and monitoring these systems will be quite important and critical, both before and after the going live phases of the project. The need for performing systems management starts from the moment the first development systems are installed.

Administering the systems is the continuous process of monitoring, managing, supporting, optimizing, and securing the systems, with the objective of having a stable platform for smooth execution of business processes. The best practice for systems management is the one that is proactive, anticipating tasks and problems, rather than a reactive one. A proactive approach to system management can be achieved by having operating procedures and a daily and periodic checklist, either automated or by using third-party specialized tools, which takes into consideration the many different components within mySAP Business Suite and SAP NetWeaver solutions and systems landscapes.

The issue of managing the system while providing technical support is important before and after going live. It is import beforehand because systems management must be performed from the moment the development or integration system is installed and while customization is being performed.

In the SAP NetWeaver age, the skills and roles around systems management and monitoring are more demanding than were the classical tasks of SAP Basis system management, database administration, network monitoring, and configuration.

Now there are new tasks, such as Web administration, synchronized backups, increased security experts, and so on, in addition to the increased number of tasks regarding the integration among several systems.

This implies that there is an increased need for planning requirements on systems management, from the very beginning of the project. Some of the activities to be performed and taken into consideration are as follows:

- Provide adapted and advanced training for the technical team.
- Carefully plan technical infrastructure requirements, including sizing, and scalability.
- Test systems infrastructure and systems management procedures.
- Get acquainted with the SAP support lines and services.
- Design, write, and maintain technical documentation.
- Design a clear help desk and support strategy and communicate it efficiently.
- Focus on proactive systems management.
- Implement the SAP Solution Manager as the management, support and operation platform for the system landscape.

System management will be the lengthiest activity throughout the SAP life cycle, because it's a continuous task. As experience is gained through daily administration operations, new projects, and continuous change, a few challenges ensure and guarantee the smooth operation and stability of the SAP systems.

Topics and issues to consider for SAP system management include the following:

- *What are the roles involved in SAP system management?* Ideally, system managers of SAP systems should play several roles as defined in the operations manual. But this will be highly dependent on the size, complexity, landscape, and scope of SAP systems and applications being implemented. Very complex installations require a clear definition of administration roles, such as system manager, database administrator, network administrator, Web manager, SAP operator, transport system administrator, security manager, authorizations administrator, desktop infrastructure administrator, technical consultant, supervisor, and so on.

  As a starting point for defining the administration procedures, roles, and responsibilities, you can use the guidelines provided in the previous section or the operations manual template included within ASAP and Solution Manager.
- *How and when is training done, and what skill sets are necessary?* Technical training is a very time-consuming activity in SAP implementations due to the fact that there are large numbers of different and complex tasks to be performed—most of them continuously. The complexity of the training is closely related to the many components and layers of the technical infrastructure: operating system, database, SAP Basis or Web Application Server components, data dictionary, network, Web administration, client/server computing, security, authorizations, and perhaps development.

  SAP has an extensive education offering on technical training in the form of several knowledge products and self-training material. The availability of resources such as a test system helps a great deal in the technical learning process. Often, SAP and many SAP partners have SAP technical consulting services that can help in the initial phases of systems management while transferring their knowledge and experience to customers.

- *How many people are required for administering SAP systems?* In implementation projects there is always the question of how many resources are required. For instance, if an implementation project lasts for one year, how many basis/technical consultants are needed, and are they needed all the time or just during some phases? The answer is never accurate. The following estimation is based on experience and customer answers. Small and simple SAP installations, of a classical SAP R/3 system, for up to 50 users and 2-system landscapes might be adequately administered with two system managers doing most of the tasks and external resources for occasional help. More complex installations, and those customers in a continuous process of adding new technical components, will require a much larger staff. Experience has shown that installations that implement at least four application modules, with two other mySAP Business Suite or SAP NetWeaver components, with more than 200 users or more than 100 printers, that connect SAP systems with external services, such as a Web Interface, EDI, faxes, and external devices, and that are distributed over several geographical locations require a minimum of four people with the appropriate skill sets for systems management and support.
- *Who will support systems managers?* Systems managers can get support and take their problems or questions to SAP using SAP Service Marketplace or SAP customer support. Often, the support of the hardware or software partner will be required when there are problems with the servers or operating system components. Additionally, the best support for system managers is updated and accurate documentation of their tasks, roles, and responsibilities. An approach from SAP not only for advancing training but also for managing and searching documentation is to build your own Knowledge Management system, for instance using the SAP Enterprise Portal KM facilities and search engines.

Skill Sets for Systems Managers

Project managers and other responsible persons in the organization, such the IT manager, often ask what skill sets are necessary for the job positions of systems management within the project team. Following is an overview of the technical areas that need to be supported by systems managers or technical consultants:

- SAP administration:
  - Installations
  - User administration
  - Security and profile administration
  - Web administration
  - Configuration and management with CCMS: monitoring, operation modes
  - Client copies
  - Transport system administration

    - Management of batch
    - Front-end installation and distribution strategy
    - Administration of spool system and printing
    - Configuration of SAP systems for remote connection with SAP
    - Definition of SAP-related alerts within the CCMS monitors or using the SAP Solution Manager
    - Correction of bugs by applying SAP notes
    - Application of patches (support packages, legal change packages, kernel patches)
    - Workload analysis and performance tuning
    - Support of the functional team with data loads and interfaces
    - Assistance in the technical areas of cross applications such as ALE, archiving, or workflow
    - Assistance in the connection of external software or devices, such as fax, EDI, mail, GIS, CAD, and so on
    - Assistance in upgrading projects
- Database administration:
    - Design and maintenance of the database backup and recovery strategy
    - Assistance in tuning the database
    - Reorganization of the database
    - Management of database space allocation
    - Rebuilding of missing indexes or creation of new ones
    - Definition of database alerts
    - Definition of database administration and operation procedures
    - Planning for and design of database preventive maintenance
    - Securing of access to the database
    - Assistance for developers in tuning customer programs or reports
    - Performance of recovery tests
    - Design and documentation of database administration procedures
- Systems administration:
    - Installation and maintenance of the operating system
    - Setup and configuration of disk volumes and file systems
    - Assistance in operating-system-related tuning
    - Installation of operating system patches or corrections
    - Monitoring of usage and tuning of performance
    - Backup and recovery
    - Installation and configuration of additional software

    - Automation of periodic system tasks
    - Support for hardware maintenance or upgrades
    - Configuration of network protocols
    - Maintenance of shared file systems
    - Control of system security
- Network administration:
    - Design and configuration of the SAP server network and the SAP access network
    - Configuration and maintenance of the remote connection to SAP
    - Management of network security
    - Maintenance of the SAP router
    - Assistance in the configuration of remote connections with SAP
    - Provision of access for remote users
    - Support for the setup and connection of external services like Web browsers or the Internet Transaction Server (ITS)
    - Configuration and maintenance of routers and other network devices

Finally, with all the new development environment represented by the WAS including the J2EE engine, we will also probably need a SAP Web AS J2EE administrator.

SAP Basis and the SAP Web Application Server include many tools and utilities for managing and monitoring the SAP applications and systems. Most chapters in this book are intended for helping system administrators.

Having an administration and operations manual, and a process for incidence logging, can decrease the time needed for solving problems if similar situations have occurred previously and the resolution procedure is known. The easiest escalation procedure for system managers is to search the SAP Service Marketplace or request SAP's support.

Planning Systems Management

The process of managing SAP systems can be eased by careful planning during the implementation phase. Some of the activities to be performed during previous phases are as follows:

- Training the technical team
- Planning the technical infrastructure and scalability
- Designing, writing, and maintaining technical documentation
- Testing systems infrastructure and systems management procedures
- Carrying out advanced training for the technical team
- Getting acquainted with the SAP support lines and services
- Designing a clear help desk and support strategy and communicating efficiently
- Focusing on proactive systems management

One of the best ways of performing proactive systems management is to do a daily and periodic monitoring of the status of the main systems components. This is known as the operation daily checklist, usually carried out by SAP operators. The operation checklist is a list of transactions that should be executed and the result evaluated to assess whether the system is functioning well or presents errors that should be solved. This operation checklist is supported with the System Administration Assistant transaction (transaction code SSAA) and can also be integrated within the SAP Solution Manager.

Whereas most checks are performed using SAP standard transactions, some must be performed at the operating system level using operating system applications and tools.

Organizing Change Management and Transport Requests

As mentioned earlier, SAP includes several tools with the purpose of controlling and managing in an orderly form the development and transport of customizing and development objects between systems in a consistent way.

Either as an independent section within the procedures guide or as an appendix for the developing methodology used in SAP environments, it is important to define the rules that must apply for the transport system.

Chapter 6 is devoted to explaining the transport organizer and transport system concepts and management. Refer to that chapter and SAP official documentation for additional operative information.

The SAP transport system and organizer takes care of controlling automatically new developments and corrections; however, a misuse of available options can lead to unwanted results. To avoid such results, some type of procedure is needed. The following is a list with the topics that should be extended to define the customer-specific rules:

1. *Transport system setup rules.* The configuration is only done in the transport domain controller. When any changes are made to the configuration, this will be distributed using the available TMS options. There will be a *virtual system,* known as DUM, used for special transports. Transport routes will be defined as standard configuration for groups of three systems, such as development, QAS, and production.
2. *Packages (formerly development classes).* Are defined in the development procedures. Do not use local ($TMP) packages except for training purposes. Make sure that a new package is transported to or defined for all systems in the group Changes to object packages are not allowed and must be requested of the system administrator.
3. *Naming conventions.* Follow SAP standard naming conventions.
4. *System change options.* System change options for production systems, such as global settings, will be set to Not Modifiable so that no repository objects or customization can be performed in these systems. System change options for development and test systems are set to Modifiable. If consultants or SAP notes indicate that emergency repairs are required in the production system, the system manager will temporarily set the system change option to Modifiable. As soon as the repairs are released and confirmed, the system change option must be set back to its original value.
5. *Tasks and change requests.* Tasks are assigned by the development responsible for the users. These tasks will be released by their developers. Change requests will

be created by the development team responsible, which is also responsible for releasing them. For small developments and corrections, the developer can create his or her own tasks and change requests. It is forbidden to use another group's change requests.

6. *Repairs.* Are strictly forbidden except when coming from a SAP note? Apply only if strictly necessary for applications. Repairs must be performed in development systems, tested, and, if accepted, transported to other systems. They are not to be left unconfirmed.
7. *Performing imports.* Imports can be used to test a system at any time, except when receiving other indications. Imports are always performed by the system or transport administrator after receiving the import request form. Imports to productive environments must be preceded by imports to test environments, when possible. For performance reasons, importing to a production environment is restricted to once a day at 2:00 A.M., right after backup. For security reasons, only imports that are in the buffer before 8:00 P.M. will be performed. In urgent or exceptional situations, partial or special imports to a productive system can be performed after receiving management authorization. Developers are responsible for checking both export and import logs.
8. *Special management options.* Transporting between different clients in the same system is restricted to the system administrator. Bear in mind that a wrong transport or an out-of-sequence import can cause a lot of damage to your system, so be sure to establish some organization and rules to avoid such situations. In the preceding example procedures, it is significant that the import to production system is performed right after backing up the system, so that at least you could recover the state of the system as it was before the transport in case some critical errors occurred.

You can surely come out with additional rules for managing and controlling your transport system.

Installations and Upgrades

Another challenge that has special impact, especially during the first phases of the project, is the increased number of installations and interconnection between SAP systems and external non-SAP systems, which often are different installation or upgrade processes with different requirements, patches, newer releases, kernels, and many SAP notes and installation manuals.

There is additional work in mySAP Business Suite landscapes because postinstallation steps or technical customization requires the integration of several systems. Thus, depending on the solution being installed, the installations of plug-ins, the definition of RFC destinations, and so on are required.

For these tasks, a high level of technical expertise with operating systems, management of database systems, and Web servers will ease the way into fast and successful installations. Other possible challenges occur when deploying highly available or clustered systems, which normally require some additional technical efforts.

In the case of upgrade projects, SAP landscapes should not offer more difficulty than traditional SAP R/3 systems. However, some attention should be paid to what happens with the connected systems during the periods when some systems are down for taking them to the next release, especially in those cases where there is a transfer of data and information back and forth.

Information Integrity Issues

Information integrity refers to those issues concerning both the quality and consistency of the data managed by the system (*logical integrity*) as well as those issues having to do with the hardware elements and system availability (*physical integrity*).

When there are errors in the system that affect the logical integrity such as wrong user inputs and unintentional deletes, these issues are either resolved using the system's own application facilities or by having a comprehensive backup and restore strategy. It must be pointed out that logical integrity can be a more difficult issue than physical integrity. However, the physical integrity and therefore the system availability (for unplanned downtime) can only be achieved by means of redundant hardware components, thereby avoiding *single points of failure.*

In SAP installations and any other business-critical applications, some advisable hardware and software elements can be used to avoid system downtime by reducing the single points of failure. These include the following:

- Use RAID technology for mirroring or shadowing disks, which can avoid system downtime caused by a single disk failure.
- Set up high availability or clustered systems (see next section), which can take over the other's functions in case of a system crash.
- To protect against power failures, attach your system to a UPS (uninterrupted power supply). Also consider having double power supplies for all hardware elements: disks, servers, network hubs, and so on.
- Set up double network links and even two network providers for remote locations, to protect against network failures.
- Store your backup tapes or other backup media in a safe and fire-resistant cabinets.
- Further security can be achieved by defining a disaster recovery plan or Business Continuity plan, within the framework of a global Enterprise Risk Management initiative.

This type of protection service can be provided by many hardware vendors as well as big service and consulting firms.

High Availability and Cluster Systems

Availability in a general computing sense is the period of time in which the system can be used to perform the functions for which it was designed and implemented. The opposite of availability is *downtime.*

Downtime can be of two types:

- *Planned downtime.* Performing offline backups, database reorganizations, and hardware upgrades.
- *Unplanned downtime.* System crash, disk failure, electrical power failure, software system error, network failure; and so on. Availability is not defined as an isolated

hardware or software element but as a property of the group of the system elements. For instance, even when neither the software or the server hardware presents errors but when in fact the network lines are broken, prohibiting users from performing their usual work, you have what is defined as a downtime situation. SAP project managers should clearly understand that the key measure of system availability is not the time the servers are up and running (the system manager's point of view) but rather the perception by the end users. A few years ago, SAP started a high-availability project known as the *zero downtime project*, and its goal was to reduce to a minimum both planned and unplanned downtime. To reach that goal, SAP invested in developing new solutions, together with its main partners, software and hardware solutions.

When thinking of availability in the SAP system environment, the following factors should be considered:

- What are the availability needs of the business? Is it 24 hours, 7 days a week (24/7)?
- Reasons for a planned downtime: software upgrades (SAP systems, patches, operating system, database, third party).
- Reasons for unplanned downtime: hardware and software unexpected failures.

One of the first components that has been developed by SAP hardware partners to maximize availability and minimize the unplanned downtime is the switch-over systems (fail-over systems) or cluster systems. These types of systems consist of a group of hardware and software elements that basically consists of the following:

- At least two servers (normally database server and application server) sharing a common group of disks.
- Reacting to servers, disks, or network failures: when a system crashes, the SAP services are automatically passed onto the standby server, and vice versa.

The switch-over system mostly works by dynamic assignment of SAP services to TCP/IP addresses using TCP/IP alias addressing facilities. A nice advantage of the switch-over system is that when there is the need for hardware upgrade or service maintenance, services can be manually switched over to the other system without interrupting normal system work.

You must remember that having switch-over systems will require an additional SAP license, because this is attached to the network controller card of the server. SAP usually has provided this additional license free of charge when registering the switch-over software and systems. Normally, each hardware vendor provides its own switch-over or cluster solution.

Extensive information about high availability can be found on the SAP Service Marketplace under the SAP NetWeaver portal or under the link service.sap.com/ha.

Backup and Recovery

In classical SAP R/3 projects, the backup and recovery strategy has been a critical issue for both the technical implementation and operation of the SAP systems and because it was the only way to protect business-critical information and to guarantee the system's operation in the event of failure. Again, in mySAP Business Suite and SAP NetWeaver system landscapes, it can be a bit more complicated. For instance, consider the scenarios of Mobile Sales within

SAP CRM implementation, which is also connected to a back-end ERP (SAP R/3) system, or the several components of the SAP Enterprise Portal that could be installed in several different servers. The failure of any of the components must be taken into consideration to be able to recover a synchronization status among systems.

Backup and restore strategies are meant for the following tasks:

- Avoiding the loss of critical system data in case of failures (either hardware or software)
- Recovering from a logical integrity error (this is the *only* way to do so)
- Protecting the business
- Allowing full-system copies
- Safeguarding critical management operations

For the analysis and definition of options in SAP backup and recovery strategies to fit the landscape and business requirements, the following factors must be considered:

- *System availability.* The first issue to consider is the amount of downtime for backup your systems can accept. It can range from no downtime, or a 24/7 systems operation (24 hours a day, 7 days a week), to other possibilities, such as 24/6, 15/5, and so on. For instance, if you decide on any of the 24-hour operations, then your only choice at the moment is to perform the available types of *online backups*.
- *What to back up.* You must consider whether you are going to back up the full system, including the operating system files, SAP runtime files, and the database, local drives, interface files, and so on. Critical to SAP backup strategy is to back up the full database, because it's the piece of the application that changes most frequently. Other system files can be backed up only at periodic times (such as once a week) or on those occasions where changes took place. You can define a consistent backup strategy by having different backup periods for different types of file systems. In SAP installations, you also have to consider the backup of the archive or journal log files.
- *Size of files to back up and backup performance.* Together with the previous factor, the size of the files to back up will affect the time it takes the backup to complete. Consider also the estimate growth of the system and database files. These factors will determine the devices required and the time available.
- *Synchronization of backups.* Analyze interdependencies of all SAP components within the mySAP Business Suite or other SAP NetWeaver components.
- *Type of backup.* This will be a function of the other factors. You can decide whether to perform either full or incremental backups, although for the database, an incremental is not recommended since the tablespace organization makes most of the database files change just by starting the database. Based on the system-availability factor , you can also decide whether to perform online or offline backups. Additionally, you can decide to verify the backup procedure. A mix and match of available types is also possible.
- *From where to back up/restore.* You must also decide if you are going to perform backups with the same system where the data is located or if you are going to use a

different server for doing backups and restores. Currently, there are many client/server backup solutions. In any case, you have to consider also the CPU, input/output, and network capacity, both from the server to back up and the server from which to back up.

- *When to back up.* You have to decide the dates, times, and frequency for performing backups. This decision will be affected by other factors such as the system availability, the expected backup performance, and the size of the files to be backed up. You must consider what is the right period between two full backups, especially for large backup volumes.
- *Backup devices.* There are many options for backup devices, from simple tape drives to automated robots, which can perform backups using several tapes in parallel. There are also other alternative media to tapes, such as magnetic disks, optical devices, DVDs, and, most recently, virtual disks on the network. For volume, performance, and growth-estimate reasons, you must consider what are the most convenient backup devices.
- *Backup management tools.* It will be very important to find the most suitable and reliable tools for managing backup and recovery processes. You should try to find the software that offers the most extensive features but that should be at the same time easy to use and, above all, reliable. Another consideration is to decide whether you want to use the SAP standard tools, such as *brbackup* for the Oracle databases, or any other third-party tool or software that can be integrated with it using the *backint* interface.
- *Backup tapes management.* In the backup strategy, you must also decide how the tapes or other backup media are going to be managed: how to label them, what their retention and recycling periods will be, where to store them, and so on.
- *Recovery procedures.* Often you find a clear backup strategy, but when there is a need to restore and recover what was previously backed up, lots of problems can be found. Defining a recovery procedure is not easy because there are so many possible situations: from simple copy procedure (backup and restore) to a single file missing. The point is to define the possible situations where a restore might be needed and *test it*.

When checking your requirements against the previous factors, you might come up with the solution that might best fit your company needs. The main message must be to test and monitor your backup and recovery strategy before going into productive operation.

The next sections show some possibilities of backup strategies mainly concerning how the backup is performed.

Performing Backups with brbackup

As it was introduced previously in Chapter 9, brbackup is the utility provided by SAP to perform backups in the SAP systems for Oracle databases. The brbackup tools have been largely improved in later versions. Currently, they support online and offline backups as well as backing up other system files besides the database. The tool also supports two level backup (first to disk and then to tape), performing brbackup and brarchive in one run, backup of data tablespaces only, partial backups also useful for completing backups with errors, standby database server, and other features.

Using the backint interface, you can use brbackup together with other third-party software and hardware, allowing for greater performance and different management interfaces.

The brbackup advantages are as follows:

- Full support from SAP.
- Comprehensive tape management.
- Integration with *sapdba* and the restore and recovery procedures.
- You can schedule backups from within SAP.

The main disadvantage of brbackup is that it might be slow, and it must be run from the same database server, which can affect the system performance.

Operating System Backup Utilities

Every hardware vendor and some third-party software companies offer many backup hardware and software solutions. Using this type of utilities usually offers the advantage of being faster and more flexible than brbackup, and many of them can run in a client/server mode, therefore avoiding the need to run the backup in the same database server.

Some of the operating system backup utilities can make a backup of several servers using the same devices. For example, backups can be made of several SAP systems or even the application servers.

The disadvantages of these solutions are that they are not supported directly by SAP, and you normally cannot perform online backups, since the system must be stopped to shut down the database in a consistent state.

Several database and software vendors are developing methods to allow for online backup in a client/server fashion also.

Backup Using the Triple-Mirror Approach

This type of solution is based on both software and hardware elements and can be best applied in systems with a high-availability configuration. And more recently storage software vendors are offering many solutions in this area.

This approach consists of having every disk or volume with two additional mirrored disks or volumes: actually there is a lot of redundancy since the same information is copied in three different volumes.

The backup will be performed in the standby switch-over system that has the tape devices, or other tertiary storage device connected.

At a certain point, the system is stopped to have the database in a consistent state. At that moment, the third mirror is detached from its volume so that the two mirrored disks continue their normal operation. This third mirrored disk is then passed to the switch-over system that mounts the file systems contained on the disks, then it starts the backup.

At this moment, SAP can be started again in the original system. With convenient hardware and software tools for stopping SAP, detaching the third disk, and starting again, the application might take less than ten minutes. When using only one server, the third disk must be mounted in a different location, the backup devices must be connected to the database server, and the backup must be performed by the same server, which can degrade system performance.

When the backup is finished in the standby server, the third mirror is put back online to synchronize for the next backup. You don't need to stop the application again. This synchronization process might slightly affect system performance, especially input/output. The trick is to measure carefully the input/output bandwidth of the disk controllers. The advantages of this approach are minimal downtime for offline backups and extra safety with the three mirrored copies. In case of failure, before starting to synchronize the disks back, make sure a full backup copy resides on the disks of the third mirror.

The disadvantages of this solution are that it is costly and it requires many disks and disk controllers. It only allows for offline backup, so the system is stopped, however minimally. Synchronizing back the disks online can be costly to I/O and CPU.

Standby Database Server and the Roll-Forward Approach

This solution consists of having an additional server based on a complete offline copy from the database server. The standby database server can be located in a different building, even many miles apart, but be connected with reliable network lines.

Once both servers are in the same initial state, the original database server will be constantly sending the archive redo log files, journals, or transaction logs to the standby server, which can then by applied (rolled forward) either synchronously or asynchronously so that both servers are almost in the same database situation. The only difference will be in the time it takes for the archive redo logs to be sent and then applied.

With this solution, you can perform the backups in the standby server. While the backup is going on, archive redo logs cannot be applied; but once it's finished, they are all sequentially recovered.

This solution presents the drawback that recovery procedures can be more difficult. Another disadvantage is that it can be costly to maintain an additional server that cannot be used for anything else. However, with this approach, you don't need to stop the original database system for backups. Additionally, this backup solution can serve the purpose of covering part of a disaster recovery situation.

SAP Procedures Guide

The goal of a procedures guide, also known as *operating procedures*, is to define the rules of the game when working and operating the SAP systems. It should include clear norms, answering questions such as what, when, why, and who.

This manual should identify roles and responsibilities in the implementation and operation of the systems. It should not be confused with an administration and operation manual, which goes into more specific details about the system architecture operation and administration, providing clear "how to" steps to daily operation.

The rules in the procedures guide might range from a clear definition of the SAP system implementation goal to who is allowed to enter the computer room (data processing center).

The following list provides an approach to the contents that can be included in a procedures guide:

- Introduction to the procedures guide
    - Goal of the implementation and operation of the system
    - Project scope

    - Team roles and organization
    - Systems and application architecture description
        - System landscape definition
        - Business applications definition
- User management procedures
    - Authorization and profile security measures
    - Management of users leaving the company
- Functional implementation procedures
    - Enhancements and change requests management
    - Developing methodology
    - Guide for implementing new modules
    - Functional test procedures
- Technical implementation procedures
    - System administration and operation rules
    - Backup strategy
    - Front-end installation and distribution strategy
    - Printing strategy
    - Networking procedures
    - Systems fail-over procedures
    - Periodical (daily, weekly, monthly, etc.) operation tasks
    - Rules for implementation of new technical projects
    - Technical test procedures
- Cross-functional application procedures
    - Change management and transport system rules
    - Use of Business Workplace and business workflow
- Upgrade strategy
    - Hardware upgrade procedures
    - Software upgrade procedures
    - SAP system upgrade procedures
- User support management and organization
    - Support guidelines
    - Help desk organization
    - Keeping records of problems and incidences
    - Escalation of problems

- Personnel issues
  - Training procedures
  - People backup and holidays permissions
- Contingency procedures
  - System crash procedures
  - Emergency situations guidelines
  - Disaster recovery plan or procedures
- Security issues
  - Remote connection procedures
  - Access to SAP net
  - Web access
  - Access to the computer room
- Procedure for making changes to this guide

You can extend or compress the contents of this list as the scope of your installation requires. You can, for example, add some of the guidelines available in ASAP or SAP Solution Manager Roadmaps, or you can also include the meetings and approval procedures.

Now, to answer the question, who is in charge of preparing such a document? it should be a collective work of the project team with the consent and approval of the company managers. Also, many of the consulting and partner companies may offer the service of preparing this kind of document.

The Administration and Operation Manual

The goal of this manual is to provide systems information easily and quickly to technical support personnel and step-by-step instructions on how to perform the most usual administration and operation tasks. This way, not only can this guide help to have the system functioning properly, but it can also be very useful for a backup person in case someone from the technical team must be absent from work for any reason. This manual must comply with the rules and procedures established in the procedures guide. To what extent there should be only one manual or a set of two (administration and operation) is a matter of the specific company organization.

The administration and operation manual will include two types of information: detailed descriptions of the systems and step-by-step instructions. You can either decide to put them all together or enter an instruction code within the descriptions, leaving the instructions ordered by code at the end of the manual.

If you intend to describe *all* the administration and operation tasks, the manual can become very large, so a little effort must be made to include only those descriptions and instructions that are most important for the system, whereas others can be referenced, either in other manuals or in the official documentation. Diagrams and pictures can be very useful for this type of guide. Just as in the procedures guide, the following is an approach to the possible contents that should be included in this manual:

- Systems information
  - Hardware and software inventory
  - Physical layout of disks and file systems configuration for every system
  - Support hotline numbers
  - Hardware maintenance
  - Software maintenance
  - Instructions for computer and operating system startup and shutdown
  - Instructions for handling storage: adding disks or space, removing, and so forth
- Error situations
  - Logging and escalating problems
  - Instructions for notifying users with system messages
- SAP systems and related components startup and shutdown
  - Normal procedures
  - Error situations
- Backup procedures
  - Tape management: labeling, schedules, types
  - Starting backups
  - Checking backups
  - Recovery procedures
  - Archiving or journals backup procedures
  - Backup error conditions
  - Backup problems and incidence log
- System monitoring
  - Alerts definition
  - Systems
  - Web servers and Internet connections
  - Network
  - Processes
  - System logs
  - Backups
  - Batch input
  - System performance quality (buffers, workload, etc.)
  - Storage and freespace

- SAP system general maintenance and administration tasks
  - Cleaning procedures
  - Background processing management
  - Handling priority jobs
  - Changing system parameters; profile maintenance
  - Printers and spool management
  - Archiving management
  - Definition of operation modes
  - Role and Authorization management
  - General accounting control
  - System and process auditing
  - Service level reporting
- SAP system database maintenance
  - Checking database state
  - Adding space to database files
  - Reorganization procedures
- Administration of the transport system
  - Performing imports
  - Checking imports
- User Interface and SAP logon
  - Installation instructions
  - Upgrade and distribution policies and instructions
- Users management
  - Users at operating system level
  - User master records: add, change, delete
  - Changing passwords
  - Locking user access to the system
  - Unlocking users
- Security management
  - Security at the presentation: virus protection and access restrictions
  - Security at the server level
  - User password control
  - Network and Web security
- Accessing SAP net (SAP Servers at SAP)
  - SAP router configurations

  - Registering new users
  - Enabling remote access to the systems
- Guide changes management
  - Guide availability
  - Quality controls
- Appendix A: Instruction index
- Appendix B: Instructions

Roles When Implementing and Supporting SAP Solutions

The number of people and the actual management organization to which they belong will heavily depend on the size and budget of the company and the size and importance of SAP systems and applications. Of course, several of the roles that are presented in the following discussion can fall upon a single person. Many companies decide to have their help desk or even their entire IT department outsourced to external and competent organizations.

The first and most important entity that every person or role in the organization must consider is the *business* itself and the mission. SAP solutions might be implemented because corporate management made a strategic decision to support a new business model, maybe as the result of a reengineering process for supporting the changing business needs to compete in a global market. What is for sure and obvious is that no company should invest in a new system like this without expecting to get some benefit from it. It must be taken into consideration that one of the most important aspects for successful productive operation and organization among all the entities is a fast and efficient communication path among them.

The following is an overview of the various roles.

End Users

Users of the business applications that do the work of feeding the system information and obtaining results to help in the decision-making process. End users usually have a partial but very important vision of the business, and sometimes they are the ones who know the very specific details of some business processes. For this reason, the end users also feed information to the business superusers. End users will probably be the largest group in terms of people, and they will be the main requesters of functional and technical support. Normally, in a good organization, end users should not directly call the application experts but instead call a form of help desk that can be a first line of support which redirects the call to the appropriate person or organization.

Business Superusers

This is a group of expert users with a comprehensive knowledge of the business. This group is usually the driver of the whole SAP project and should be made up of people who can make fast decisions.

Normally, they belong to the *steering committee* for the project and assign a project manager or project leader for each of the business areas on which the implementation is based. For example, one leader may be appointed to the FI treasury module, another one to the materials management, another to sales, and so on.

Business Consultants

In medium-size to large companies, management often requests an impartial view of the business and help in the implementation techniques, the know-how of the SAP applications software, and the ability for knowledge transfer. Because of the business nature of these projects, it is common to find *external business consultants* in most SAP projects. These consultants may also have the responsibilities of project managers or project management assistants. SAP has a large number of consulting partners, including the biggest consulting firms plus hundreds of smaller local consulting companies.

SAP Functional Support

Some of the participants in the group of business superusers make up the next group in the figure, *SAP functional support*. The function of this group is to help in the customizing of the system as well as solving user problems that directly relate to business processes and applications. It is also the function of this group to lead the corrections, enhancements, or new developments in the system according to user requests. Usually, this group is in charge of training the end users in their specific modules as well as receiving support calls that might relate more to functional system aspects than technical problems.

This team is called in when a user gets an error after posting a financial document, or when a user needs a higher customized report of the inventory, and so on. The SAP functional support might rely on an internal or external development team as well as the overall support of the technical group.

The Development Team

This team is only necessary when new developments are needed. When only the development of simple reports is needed, the technical support group could assume some of the development functions. However, in preproductive stages of the SAP implementation, some help might be needed for tasks such as massive data loads from legacy applications and development of batch input programs, business-customized menus, screens, and so on. Developers need to stay in very close contact with the functional group, since this group is supposed to know the business and user requirements. At the same time, a developer will often need the help of the technical group for things such as system requirements, database resources, and transport requests.

The SAP Technical Support Group

This team is in charge of all the technical aspects of the SAP system installations. This group gives continuous support to the development and functional teams participating actively in the technical parts of SAP projects. It is usually also the second-level line for solving users' technical problems. This group can be subdivided into SAP technical specialists, Web administrators, SAP system administrators, and operation personnel. In small SAP installations, all functions can be assumed by a single person as long as the procedures to maintain the system are well documented and mostly automated.

The technical group must have a wide range of skills, including client/server computing, operating systems, Web technology, database and SAP solution-specific expertise, and good knowledge about PC technology and even networking. These technologies can be totally or partially supported by existing technical group, such as the network support or PC support groups, besides having maintenance contracts and support with the corresponding hardware vendors. Some of the functions of this group could be handed over to existing IT resources. For example, if there are operating system managers, they could well assume the management of new servers once the architecture of R/3 is introduced to them. Just as a brief summary, here is a list of functions that are normally assumed by the SAP technical and administration group:

- *Administration of the operating system, database, and sometimes even the network.* This includes such things as doing all typical functions of DBAs, such as reorganizing the database, monitoring storage, backups, and the like.
- *Administration and monitoring of SAP systems.* This includes management of background jobs, users, the authorization system, the printing system, interfaces, the transport system, remote communications, profile and instance maintenance, tuning, and so forth.
- Defining and implementing the system backup and recovery strategy.
- Solving and reporting technical problems as they are being logged in the system.
- Support for new modules going into production by allowing sufficient space, checking technical settings of tables, doing previous exports/imports, and so on.
- Support for all kind of maintenance upgrades, including the installation and configuration of corrections to the system such as support packages, kernel patches, and so on.
- Support and implementation of new technical or cross-functional projects in the R/3 environments such as the implementation of the SAP Business Workflow, ALE, archive link, Internet server, and e-mail.
- Implementing the EarlyWatch suggested recommendations and corrections into the system.
- Always observing the highest system availability.

The SAP Operation Staff

These people can be responsible for checking system critical log files such as backup logs and the system log and reporting the observed problems. This staff can also be responsible for the system and database backups as well as doing daily backups of the archived redo log files. Even when this process is automated without manual intervention, someone has to check the log and change the tapes sometimes. This staff can also periodically check some of the system monitors and the states of spool and background systems.

In any case, the administration and operation group should design a comprehensive guide such as an administration and operation manual that can be easily followed by anyone who could eventually substitute for or help this group.

The Help Desk

This is the central support group in charge of receiving user calls and doing first-line support. This group must be actively in touch with the rest of the support groups, so, for example, if network lines are not available for whatever reason, or the SAP system has been shut down for maintenance reasons, the help desk can quickly assess the situation and react to and answer user queries. This group might use one of the many available help desk software applications, including features such as automatic call transfer, problem logs, and incidence recorders.

The Role of SAP Itself in the Big Picture

The demand for SAP services such as the installation and implementation of the SAP solutions should be understood as the project goes along. SAP offers an extensive range of services, especially within SAP net and those aligned within the SAP Solution Manager, and should actively assist in overall support, both functional and technical. You might consider SAP for the following activities (and maybe some others):

- On-site and remote consulting (both functional and technical)
- Main source for project team training
- Help in stress testing definitions
- Collaboration in a quality check before going productive

Finally there is the central figure of the *project manager*, who has overall responsibility for the success of the implementation project after going live, supporting the project , optimization, and continuous change management. The project management itself constitutes a very important implementation issue.

Introduction to the Help Desk

The support of SAP systems and applications consists of solving all types of problems and questions that arise during the operation of the SAP systems. Supporting SAP users and SAP systems is one of the main activities during and after going live.

If support is not provided in an efficient and timely manner, users will not be able to perform their jobs as expected, systems will not be stable, many questions will remain unanswered, and many application and technical issues will remain unresolved. This can severely affect business operations. There are many reasons why problems exist or can arise:

- System bugs
- Human error
- Lack of knowledge
- Problems with continuous data migration, conversion, and interfaces
- Technical infrastructure problems: PCs, printing, batch, network connections

Problems are better solved when postimplementation support is planned in the first phases of implementation. There are, however, several typical mistakes and problems encountered when establishing the support staff or help desk procedures after implementation. Some of these are as follows:

- Lack of proactive support and communication
- Lack of training
- Poorly documented support requests
- Unclear help desk processes

A good support strategy is based on proactive systems management and application management, as well as on a well-established, trained, and organized help desk.

Besides documentation and other sources of information, end users typically have two lines of support:

- Key users or department superusers, who are normally close to the business operations and who have helped during the implementation phase. These persons can sometimes help end users with basic operations questions, doubts, or problems related to the applications.
- The help desk, as the central source of support. On many occasions, the help desk should be able to provide an immediate solution or answer to end users—for instance, the existence of a network problem on one of the lines, instructions for changing a password, SAP logon connection parameters, and so on.

On the other hand, the help desk will most typically log and prioritize the users' calls and dispatch calls to appropriate expert support. Expert support is normally provided by the SAP project team, including functional and technical personnel and even developers. These people are knowledgeable about business processes and systems functioning. Often they are responsible for calling users back with answers and documenting problems for later occasions.

Finally, when the project team is not able to solve those problems, it can use SAP support services such as SAP Service Marketplace or SAP customer support services. There are other sources of support, such as hardware partners, database vendors, or other software or service companies.

Besides having a defined help desk process, there are several other requirements for establishing the help desk. Most important are as follows:

- Defining what will be supported.
- Establishing levels of priorities.
- Implementing hours of operation and methods for contacting support and logging calls.
- Establishing standards and procedures for support.
- Establishing service levels and response times for callback.
- Assigning help desk roles and responsibilities.
- Establishing communication channels.
- Developing help desk logistics: equipment, phones, faxes, facilities.
- Implementing the help desk application. In this sense it must be noted that one of the latest facilities of the SAP Solution Manager is the inclusion of a powerful Support Desk, based on the underlying SAP CRM. You might consider this platform as it integrates seamlessly with the whole SAP service catalog, and the connection with the technical and the functional implementation documentation, as well as with the central point for SAP landscape monitoring and operations.
- Providing needed skills and resources.
- Developing an escalation process.
- Providing initial and continuing training. The number and skills of the support staff personnel will largely depend on the size of the user base, as well as the scope

(modules, applications or components) and status (continuous change and open projects) of the SAP solutions or components implemented. For instance, only a small number of support staff personnel will be necessary for small and closed implementations, whereas large and open implementations may require many support staff people, both technical and functional, including developers.

For medium to large and complex implementations, a larger support and help desk staff will be required. This is closely related to the issue of the resources needed after implementation (after going live).

Common recommendations for resources after going live are as follows:

- At least two consultants or business superusers for each of the SAP components or application modules being deployed.
- A strong technical team, with at least two basis experts plus a systems manager and a good database administrator. At least two of these people must have thorough knowledge of how to monitor performance and tune the systems.
- One or two ABAP programmers, or Java if using the J2EE (for instance, for Enterprise Portal iViews, XI, etc.) when there is the need for additional reporting or development, and also for upgrade projects.

Large companies and value contract SAP customers with several SAP installations including various mySAP Business Suite applications and SAP NetWeaver components, and intensive support needs are advised to create a Customer Competence Center (CCC).

The task of beginning the planning process for defining the postimplementation support is included in the Project Preparation phase within the ASAP Roadmap and the SAP Solution Manager Roadmaps.

Index

Page numbers for figures and tables are in italics.

A

ABAP Debugger, 316, 317–319
 activating, 317–318
ABAP development environment
 DCOM Connector and, 324
 new system features, 324–339
 workbench elements, 27–28
ABAP Dictionary, 63–64, 274–303
 data elements, 284–285
 DDIC user and, 384–385
 defined, 274
 dictionary objects, 212, 278–296
 domains, 279–284
 field definitions, 284–285
 functions, 274–277
 lock objects, 303, 515
 object activation, 277
 Repository Information System, 277–278
 services, 296–303
 structures, 285
 tables, 285–286
 "Where-Used List," 277
 See also dictionaries
ABAP Dump Analysis, 518–520
ABAP Editor, 230
ABAP interpreter, 52
ABAP language editor, 314–315
ABAP load generation, 210
ABAP object repository, 63–64
ABAP objects, 16
ABAP open SQL, 63
ABAP Program Directory
 directory selection screen, *180*
 searching for report names with, 179
ABAP programming language, 21, 24, 27, 303–315
 comments in, 310–311
 conventions in, 311
 data objects, 305
 data types, 306
 executable programs, 64
 features of, 106–107, 304
 floating comma numeric type, 309
 floating number numeric type, 309
 "Hello World" program, 314–315
 including with directives, 344
 integer types, 306–308
 internal tables, 333–334
 new elements of, 333–339
 new system fields, 338
 as object-oriented language, 304–305
 operating interface and, 49–50
 operators, 311–314
 packed number types, 308–309
 predefined data types, 306
 relational operators, 311–314
 for server side scripts, 340
 source, 64
 SQL features, 336–337
 SQL sentences, 336–338
 string character type, 309
 string data type, 334–335
 syntax basics, 305–314
 testing and debugging, 315–321
 Transport Organizer and, 221
 type groups, 306
 unit testing, 320
ABAP/4 programming language, 16, 21, 27. *See also* ABAP programming language
ABAP programs
 buffering, 495
 as steps in background jobs, 433–435
ABAP Trace
 for background processing, 527
 results of Runtime Analysis Evaluation, *491*
 troubleshooting performance problems with, 490
ABAP transactions, 48
ABAP Workbench, 271–274
 features of, 272
 transactions, 273–274
ABAP Workbench program editor
 defining background jobs with, 183–184
AcceleratedSAP (ASAP). *See* ASAP (Accelerated SAP)
access methods, 450, 461, 464–466
access path evaluation, 489–490
access privileges, 385
accounting, 356
accounting number field, in user master records, 376
action logs, 252
actions, creating, 127–128
activate sapgui trace level field, in SAP Logon utility, 94
activation
 administrators, 399
 defined, 277
 in profiles and authorizations, 390
 of updating, 414
ActiveX controls, 323
activity fields, for authorization objects, 389
activity groups (user roles), 165, 371
actlog directory, 261
Adapter Environment, 118
additional command line argument field, in SAP Logon utility, 94
additional data hexdump in trace field, in SAP Logon utility, 94
additional tests, 524, *525*
add-ons, 20
adjustment methods, in modification adjustment, 213
ADJUSTPRP phase, of upgrade, 212
ADK (Archive Development Kit), 37
administration and operation manual, 577–580
administration data, profile modification and, 508
Administrator Workbench, 113, 114
Advanced Business Application Programming Language. *See* ABAP programming language
advanced corrections, 211
advanced program-to-program communication (APPC) server, 51
After Event scheduling option, 185
After Event start option, 438–439
After Job scheduling option, 185
After Job start option, 438
AGate program, 75
ALE (Application Link Enabled) technology, 13, 26, 69, 72–74
 functions of, 76
 sample scenario, 72–73, *73*
Alert Monitors, 530–533
 architecture of, 531–532
 elements of, 531
 functions of, 531
 options, 532–533
allocation sequences, for memory areas, 492
ALLOG parameter, 262
all or nothing operations, 47–48
alternate spool servers, 451–452
ANSI-SQL language, 25
APIs (application program interfaces), 45
 ALE model and, 14
 remote function calls and, 66
APPC (advanced program-to-program communication) server, 51
append structures, 292
Application administrators, security responsibilities, 364
application consultants, 550
application data, *223*
 defined, 221
 gateway server and, 62
application help, 177
application integration, 28

Application Integration Technology, 20
application level, 69
SAP features, 361
security, 352, 363–364
workload distribution and, 506
Application Link Enabled (ALE) technology. *See* ALE (Application Link Enabled) technology
application platform, for SAP NetWeaver, 104
application program interfaces. *See* APIs (application program interfaces)
application server field, SAP Logon, 93
application servers, 69
defined, 24, 53
displaying and monitoring, 402–404
message server and, 61
new file handling features, 334–335
Application Service Provider (ASP), 538
application services, workload distribution among, 510
applications menus, navigation of, 169–171
application toolbar, 157, *157*
architecture, basic concepts, 46–48
Archive Development Kit (ADK), 37
ASAP (Accelerated SAP), 15, 16, 29, 537
implementation, 542
introduction to, 540–546
Global ASAP, 537
Team ASAP, 15
objectives of, 541–542
technical issues, 560–561
tools, 542
ASAP Roadmap, 541–542, 543, 549
phases, 542–546
asynchronous processes, 60
At operation mode scheduling option, 185
attributes
direct, for data elements, 284–285
for domains, 279
for dynpros, 297, *298*
memory, 52
for objects, 253–255, 305
for packages, 254
page, 349
print, for spool requests, 187–188
spool requests, 456, 457
Attributes tabstrip, 327
auditing, security and, 369
authentication, 354. *See also* user authentication
author ID, 254
AUTHORITY-CHECK function, 389
authorization administrators, 399
authorization fields, 389
authorization objects, 371, 387–389
authorization lists for, *388*
defined, 387
grouping in object classes, 388
technical names for, 387
authorization profiles, 370, 385, 386–389
authorizations, 352
activation concept in, 390
for background jobs, 431
defined, 355, 387
management of, 370–371
process, 355–356
in SAP Solution Manager, 550–551
specifying for spool request, 187
technical names for, 387
tracing, 397–398
authorization system, 385–390
authorization profiles, 385, 386–389
check transactions, 397, 398
composite profiles, 387
error analysis, 397
features of, 385–390
hierarchy of, *386*
organizing maintenance of, 398–399
roles, 389–390
automatic modification, 213
Automatic TAB feature, 162
AUTO status, in update records, 414
availability
defined, 473
high availability systems, 570, 571
product availability matrix, 206
system, backup and restore strategies, 572

B

back action, 128
background control objects, 525–526
background jobs, 55–57, *56*
ABAP programs as steps in, 433–435
active status and, 528
authorizations for, 431
common problems, 527–528
components of, 429
control flags for, 436
defined, 183, 429
defining, 431–441
deleting, 442
deleting automatically, 445
deleting manually, 445
displaying details about, 445
external commands as steps in, 433, 435
external programs as steps in, 433, 435–436
graphical job monitoring tool for, 445–447
information storage, 525
job definition fields, 432
job logs, 442, 445
for job status, 443
management operations, 441–445
modifying scheduled jobs, 444–445
periodic, 441
priority of, 432
releasing, 431
repeat intervals for, 440–441
scheduling, 184–185, 431
selection criteria for, 434
sending output to a spool, 441
start conditions for, 436–441
troubleshooting, 522–528
working with, 183–186
background luminosity, 161
Background Objects utility, 525–526
Background Print Parameter screen, 441
background processing, 183, 427–447, 507
additional test, 524, *525*
analyzing, 523
configuring, 429
defining programs for, 183
event-driven scheduler, 526
external program starter, 526
introduction, 428–429
job analysis tools, 523
job starter, 526
job steps, 433
management operations, 441–445
performance analysis, 475
problems, 522–523
purpose of, 428–429
scheduling jobs, 184–186
simple tests, 524, *524*
specifying external programs, 185–186
specifying print parameters for, 441
specifying spool list recipients for, 441
specifying start time, 185
starting, 430–431
steps in, 185–186
switch operation modes, 526
system load and, 183
time-driven scheduler, 525
troubleshooting, 522–528
zombie cleanup, 526
backup and recovery, 571–575
backup devices, 573
backup management tools, 573
backup tape management, 573
brbackup tools, 573–574
database, 210
file size, 572
files to back up, 572
operating system utilities, 573
strategies, 572–573
tasks, 572
triple-mirror approach, 573–574
type of backup, 572
backup directory, 261
BAPIs (Business APIs), 71–72, 304
ALE model and, 74
SAP Business Information Warehouse (SAP BW) and, 114

basic maintenance, profile modification and, 508
Basis administrators, security responsibilities, 367
basis/development consultants, 550
basis system, 21
batch jobs, 55–57
batch scheduler, 56
BEx Analyzer, 116
BEx Broadcasters, 116
BEx Portfolio, 116
BEx Query Designer, 116
BEx Web Application Designer, 116
BI. *See* Business Intelligence (BI) *entries*
bin directory, 260
bit masks, relational operators for, 313
BOR. *See* Business Object Repository (BOR)
BPR. *See* Business Process Repository (BPR)
brbackup tools, 573–574
BRCONNECT program, 506, 528–530
BREAK macro keyword, 318
breakpoints
  conditional (watchpoints), 318
  setting in ABAP Debugger, 318
BREAK-POINT statement, 317–319
BSP applications
  activating, 345
  creating, 342–345
  elements of, 345–349
  "Hello World" program, 341–375
  pages vs., 342
  running, 345
BSP pages
  BSP applications vs., 342
  creating, 342–343
  elements of, 347–349
BSP properties, 347
BSPs. *See* Business Server Pages (BSPs)
buffer directory, 260
buffered tables
  access considerations, 496
  functions of, 495–496
  improving performance of, 496–497
  types of, 495–496
Buffer Gets, 503
buffering, 287–289, 495–499
  accessing buffered table data, 287–288
  defined, 287
  performance and, 290
  synchronization and, 288, 289
  types of, 288
Buffer Program (PXA buffer), 495
buffers, 495–499
  configuring, 491
  defined, 491
  gaps in, 498
  monitoring, 498–499
buffer synchronization, 496
Business Application Program Interfaces (BAPIs). *See* BAPIs (Business APIs)
Business Blueprint, 558–559
  ASAP Roadmap, 543, 549
  Solution Management Roadmap, 553, 561
  system landscape definition and, 555
Business Configuration Sets, 559
business consultants, 581
Business Explorer, 113
Business Framework, 304
Business Intelligence (BI) Information Broadcasting, 115
  features of, 116–117
  scenarios replaced by, 116–117
Business Intelligence (BI) Information Portfolio, 115
business logic level, 106
Business Object Repository (BOR), 71–72, 304
business packages, 145. *See also* packages
business partners, 14
business processes, 3
Business Process Repository (BPR), 549, *549*, 558–559
business process teams, 201
Business Server Pages (BSPs), 105, 340–349
  applications vs. pages, 342
  BSP properties, 347
  concept overview, 345–349
  creating applications, 341–345
  developing, 340–341
business superusers, 580
business transactions, performance analysis, 487–488
Business Workplace function, for sending messages between SAP users, 189
byte type data, relational operators for, 312

C

CA (Composite Application Framework), 105
CA (cross-application) modules, 21, 30, 37–38
calendar start option, for background jobs, 440
Call Center, 6
call interfaces, 275
call points, displaying, 505
candidate keys, 281
cardinality, 281–282
CCMS. *See* Computer Center Management System (CCMS)
CCO (Customer Competence Center), 585
central instances, 67, 507
Central User Administration, ALE model and, 74
Certification Authority (CA), for protecting public keys, 368
Change and Transport Organizer (CTO)
  defined, 216
  functions of, 222–224
  initializing, 237–238
  transport system concepts, 220–235
Change and Transport System (CTS), 215–268
  components, 216–217
  configuration steps, 218–220
  CTS tools, 215–216, 217
  new features, 217–220
change management activities
  in SAP upgrade projects, 195
  technology and, 568–569
Change Management program, 543
change requests
  automatic creation of, 219, 247
  for client-dependent objects, 419–420
  creating, 225–226, 246–248
  for cross-client objects, 419–420
  customizing, 227
  defined, 225
  displaying, 249–250
  documentation for, 229
  forwarding, 258
  functions of, 220–221
  local, 227
  manual creation of, 247, 248
  numbers, 226
  releasing, 219, 223, 226, 248
  tasks, 219
  team leaders and, 222–223
  transportable, 226, 227
  transport system, 568–569
  types of, 220–221, 227, 246
Change Screen Assignment dialog box, 182
check variants, 327–328, *329*
CIC (Customer Interaction Center), 6
Class A priority, 432
Class B priority, 432
Class C priority, 432
Client Administration menu, 417, *418*
client certificates, user authentication and, 76
client codes, 221
Client Copier and Comparison Tool, 420
client copies, 416–427
  authorizations for, 421
  client copy tools, 417–421
  creating new clients, 418–420
  deleting, 423–424
  executing in test mode, 420–421
  logs, 425
  requirements for, 421–425
  restarting process, 425
  in same system, 423
  system number ranges, 422
  transporting between SAP systems, 425–427
Client Copy tools, 417–421
client-dependent data, 416

client-dependent objects, 419–420
Client field, in Logon screen, 150
client-independent data, 416
client-independent objects
  changes, 420–421
  copying, 422
clients
  in Change and Transport System, 221
  copying, 417–423
  copying table entries between clients, 426
  copying table entries between different systems, 426–427
  creating, 417, 418–419
  defined, 48, 69
  deleting, 417, 423–424
  deleting with R3trans, 424
  hardware-oriented view, 44
  management functions, 417–418
  restrictions, 420
  in SAP Mobile Infrastructure (SAP MI), 112
  software-oriented view, 44
  status after deletion, 424
  storage requirements, 420–421
  transporting between two SAP systems, 425–426
client/server systems
  advantages of, 23
  building, 67–74
  configurations, *23*, 70
  Internet layer, 23, *25*
  multitier solutions, 22–24
  SAP definition of, 21
  scalability, 71
  as software concept, 69
  three-tiered (multilevel) architecture, 23–24, *24*, 67, 70–71
  two-tier configuration, 67
  workload distribution, 70
client settings, 239
client-specific data, 221
client transport, 417
clipboard, 163
clustered systems, 570
cluster tables, 64
CO (Controlling) module, 31
code completion feature, 121
code formatting tools, 122
Code Inspector, 327–330
  check variants, 327–328, *329*
  creating user checks with, 330–332
  data sets, 328–330
  initial screen, *328*
  performing inspections with, 330–332
  purpose of, 327
code templates, 121
code wizard, 136
cofiles, 226
cofiles directory, 260
collaboration, 107, 110
Collaboration Rooms, 110
Collaborative Service Architecture, 20
collective search helps
  defined, 298
  example, *299*
  information entered in, 299
Color Picker window, 161
color schemes, SAP GUI window, 161
COM4ABAP, 323
comments, in ABAP, 310
COMMIT WORK statement, 47
Common Gateway Interface, 75
Common Programming Interface Communication. *See* CPIC (Common Programming Interface Communication)
communication
  defined, 64
  interfaces, 48, 64–65
  operating systems level, 64–65
  performance analysis, 477
  programming level, 65
  protocol, 26
  technology, 26–27
compilation, 122
Component Controller, 132–133
Component Installation Guides, 141
Composite Application Framework (CAP), 105
Composite Applications, 11
composite profiles, 387
compound contexts, 132–133
COMPUTE clause, 308
Computer Center Management System (CCMS)
  Alert Monitors, 530–533
  profile maintenance tool, 84, 88, *89*
confirmation of listbox entry delete field, SAP Logon, 93
connection info, 79
connectivity, for SAP NetWeaver, 105
connectors, 320–324
consistency checks, 509
consolidation routes
  defined, 224–225, 244
  for packages, 228
  rules for, 250
constants, 338–339
consulting services, 38
Content Management, 110
contexts, 122
  assigning UI elements to, 135
Context tabstrip, 133, 134
control data, 64
control flags, 436, 528
Controlling (CO) module, 31
conventions, in ABAP, 311
copy function, 163
copy of transports, 247
corporate portals, 9
corrections, 229
correction tasks, 230
Cost Based Optimizer engine, 504
CPIC (Common Programming Interface Communication), 65–66
  defined, 24, 65
  protocol, 61, 65
  remote function calls, 65–66
  starter set, 65
CPU idle indicator, 500
CPU time analysis, 479
CPU troubleshooting, 500–501
Create Application option, 136
Create Request dialog box, 247
Create Sessions function, 168
Create Support Message, 177
creating a system message dialog box, *409*
creation wizard, creating Web Dynpro components with, 125–126
cross-application modules, 21, 30, 37–38
cross-client customizing data, 221, 222, *223*
cross-client object changes, 420–421
cross-project documentation, 557
cryptography
  defined, 356–359
  public key, 357
  in SAP systems, 358–359
CTO. *See* Change and Transport Organizer (CTO)
CTS. *See* Change and Transport System (CTS)
CTS tools
  functions of, 215–216
  at operating system level, 217
cursor
  caching methods, 63
  position, when clicking on a field, 163
  setting behavior, 163–164
CUST change requests, 220–221, 246
  table keys in, 221
custom-developed objects, 399
custom-developed transactions, 399
Customer Competence Center (CCO), 585
Customer Interaction Center (CIC), 6
customer objects, package naming conventions, 235, 236
customer service, 38–39
customer service team, 38–39
customer support, 39–40
customizing
  process, 211
  projects, 540
  requests, 227, 247
  screen, *29*
  tables, 221
  tasks, 28–29
  transactions, 220
customizing data, *223*
  defined, 221
  transport of, 222
custom-specific rules, 568–569

D

data
  client-specific, 221
  repetitive, entering, 174–175
  transportable, 222
  types of, 64, 221–222, *223*
data archiving, 37

database
- administrators, 365
- alert log files, 506
- analysis, 501–506
- backup and recovery, 210
- cursors, 63
- locks, performance analysis, 477
- performance analysis, 476–477
- relational, 63
- selections, 181
- sizing, 146
- space management, 528–530
- time, analysis of, 479, 482
- transactions (LUWs), 47–48
- upgrades, 206
- views, 294

database-dependent parameters, 261, 262
database interface, 48, 50, 63–64
database layer, 506
database level, 69
- SAP security features, 361, 364–365

Database Message Log, 506
Database Monitor (Oracle), 502–503, 528–529, *529*
- indicators displayed in, *502*

database servers, 69
- with central instance, 67
- defined, 24
- for SAP Web Application Server, 67

database table DDLOG, 496
data binding
- dynamic generation of text lines with, 135–136
- with UI elements, 132

data browser (transaction SE16), 253
data buffers, 502
- data class parameters, 287

data collection methods, 532
data consumers, Alert Monitors, 531
data dictionaries, 28, 63–64, 274
- defined, 275
- metadata in, 275
- objects, 276
- using, 275
- *See also* ABAP Dictionary; dictionaries

data directory, 260
data elements
- defined, 284
- direct attributes for, 284–285

data encryption, 356–357
data mining techniques, 113
Data Modeler, 28
data objects, 305
data pipes, 79
data sets, 328–330
data suppliers, 531
Data Type Definition (DTD), 77–78
data types
- ABAP predefined types, 306
- enhancements to, 338–339
- relational operators for, 311–314

data warehouses, 113, 115
Date/Time start option, 438
DBHOST parameter, 262
DBNAME parameter, 262
DDIC users, 383, 384–385
- password for, 384–385

DDLOG database table, 496
deactivating updating, 414
debugging applications, Eclipse IDE, 122
Debugging Perspective, 122
debugging utilities, ABAP, 315–321
DECIMALS keyword, 308
default language, 151
default profiles, 85, 87–88, *88*, 508
- parameters, 87–88

defaults
- input fields values, 175–176
- setting for user master records, 377–379
- for user master record, 377–379
- user parameters input field values, 175–176
- window size, SAP GUI, 163

DefaultTextView, 129, 131
Define Steps button, 185
Delete Immediately After Printing option, 188
deleting
- background jobs, 442
- client copies, 423–424
- clients, 417, 423–424
- Delete Immediately After Printing option, 188
- external users, 408
- external user sessions, 414
- lock entries, 416
- lock objects, 515
- profiles, 509–510
- with R3trans utility, 424
- spool requests, 457
- update records, 414
- user groups, 379
- user master records, 379
- users, 379
- user sessions, 408, 414

delivery class, 422–423
delivery routes, 224–225, 244
delta sets, 229
dependencies, creating, 133–134
dequeue function, 59
description field, SAP Logon, 93
Designer view, 127, *127*
desktop workstation, downloading files to, 190
developer traces, 521–522
- low-level, 407

development classes, 326. *See also* packages
development consultants, 550
development environment, ABAP
- concepts of, 272–274
- new system features, 324–339

development objects
- defined, 220, 272
- grouping in transport layer, 224
- in repository, 220
- version management, 228–229
- working with, 124

development projects
- grouping tasks in, 228
- packages, 228

development request service, 39
development systems, 233
development teams
- grouping tasks by, 228
- roles, 581

device pools, 462–464
DIAG protocol, 62
dialog instances, 67
dialog servers, 53
dialog steps, 46–47, 54
- data flow, 54, *55*
- defined, 46
- dynpro control of, 46
- in work processes, 51–52

dialog work processes, 405, 406, 506–507
- defined, 54
- per instance, 54
- update work process and, 59
- user support, 54

dictionaries, 211
- SAP-declared tables, 64
- *See also* ABAP Dictionary; data dictionaries

digital envelopes, 358–359
digital signatures, 357–358, 358–359, 362
- security of, 358

directives, including ABAP with, 344
directory access protocol, 360
disable editing functionality entry field, SAP Logon, 93
disk reads, number of, 505
disk space, for SAP upgrades, 206
dispatcher nodes, 471
dispatcher process, 50–51, 53
- dialog step data flow, 54

display fields, 172
display-only fields, 164, 172
documentation
- online, 177
- for requests, 229
- types, Project Administration utility, 557
- *See also* project documentation

documentation help, field helps, 302
document transfer–level security, 367
DOMAIN.CFG, 240, 241
domains
- defined, 279
- displaying definition, *282*
- finding, in Repository Information System, 278, *280*
- technical attributes defined within, 279
- uses of, 279–284

downloading files, to desktop workstation, 190
downtime, 570–571
- planned, 570–571
- unplanned, 570–571
- upgrade projects and, 202

downtime minimized upgrade strategy, 205, 207
drag-and-drop techniques, 325
DTD (Data Type Definition), 77–78
Dump Analysis, 518–520
dumps, ABAP, 518–520

DUM virtual system, 568
dynamic spool server assignment, 451, 452
dynamic SQL, 336
dynpros (dynamic programs), 27, 49
  attributes of, 297, *298*
  control of dialog steps by, 46
  creating, 124
  defined, 46
  interpreter, 52

E

EarlyWatch, 38–39, 41–42, 546–547
EarlyWatch Alert, 39, 41–42
  sample report page, *41*
EC-CS management consolidation system, 32
EC (Enterprise Controlling) module, 31–32
Eclipse IDE
  code completion feature, 121
  code formatting tools, 122
  code templates, 121
  compilation, 122
  debugging applications, 122
  editors, 120–121
  IDE overview, 120–121
  Java development in, 119
  plug-in architecture, 119, 120
  programming with, 121–122
  refactoring tools, 122
  Run menu, 122
  SAP version, *120*
  toolbars, 121
  views, 121
eCommerce, 4
  encryption and, 356
  external communication and, 26
  mySAP.com for, 8–10
  SAP R/3 support for, 15
EDI (electronic data interchange), 26
editors, in Eclipse IDE, 120–121
EIS (executive information system), 32
elementary search helps, 300–301
  defined, 299
  dialog behavior, 300–301
  hot key for, 301–302
  information entered for, 300–301
Employee Self Service (ESS), 145
end users
  roles, 580
  training, 545
enhancements, 211
EnjoySAP, 17, 155
  graphical user interface (GUI), *19*
enqueue function, 59
enqueue time, analysis of, 479, 482
enqueue work process, 58–59, 507
Enterprise Controlling (EC) module, 31–32
Enterprise Portal, 8–10
Enterprise Resource Planner (ERP) software
  development of, 5
Enterprise Services Architecture (ESA), 101–102
  evolution of, *102*
Enterprise Software Vendors, 15
entry flags (SRCDEP), 255
ERP. *See* Enterprise Resource Planner (ERP) software
error lines, developer trace files, 521
Error Log Files, 521
ESA. *See* Enterprise Services Architecture (ESA)
ESS (Employee Self Service), 145
event-driven scheduler, 526
event handlers
  in BSP applications, 348–349
  implementing, 127–128, 135–136
events
  After Event scheduling option, 185
  After Event start option, 438–439
  defined, 305, 438
  starting background jobs after, 438–439
exclusive but not cumulative (type X) locks, 58, 59
exclusive (type E) locks, 58
exec. target field, for background jobs, 432–433
Execute button, 180
executive information system (EIS), 32
expensive SQL statements, 488–489, 503–505
expiration fields, for system messages, 409
expiration parameters, 80
export phase, of transports
  execution of, 246
  team leaders and, 223
exports
  performed by SAP subsystems, 260
  performed by tp program, 258
extended maintenance, profile modification and, 508
Extended Memory, 492
extended program check, 319–320
extended transport control, 225
external attacks, 352
external commands, as steps in background jobs, 433, 435
external programs
  problems with, 528
  specifying, for background jobs, 185–186
  starter, 526
  as steps in background jobs, 433, 435–436
  troubleshooting, 500
external systems, in Transport Management System, 242
external users, deleting, 408
external user sessions, deleting, 414

F

Favorites list, 164, *165*
FCS (first customer shipment), 39
F1 help, 176, 177
field data, 172
field definitions
  advantages of, 285
  data elements and, 284–285
  direct type, 285
field helps
  creating, 296–297
  documentation, 302
  F1 help, 176, 177
  field search helps (F4), 296–297
  See also help system
field length, 172
field names, 172
fields
  automatic tabbing between, 162
  defined, 172
  determining cursor position when clicking on, 163
  display-only, 164
  required input, 172
  types of, 172
field values
  permitted, 283–284
  restriction on, 279–281
FI (Financial Accounting) modules, 31
file access handler, 80
file handling
  new ABAP features, 334–335
files, downloading to desktop workstation, 190
Final Preparation phase
  SAP Roadmap, 545
  Solution Management Roadmap, 553, 561
financial applications, 30–32
firewalls, 352
first customer shipment (FCS), 39
floating comma numeric type, 309
fonts, changing, 160
Fonts scrollbar, 160
foreground luminosity, 161
foreign domains, transporting among, 258
foreign key fields, 281
foreign keys
  cardinality and, 282–283
  defining, 297
  displaying, *284*
  field values permitted, 2 83–284
  relations, 297, *298*
  types of, 281–282
foreign key tables, 281
format, for report printing, 188
forms, 450
fourth-generation languages, 303
fragmentation, buffers and, 498
"free space," buffering and, 498
full buffering, 288, 496
functional layer, 21
functional teams. *See* business process teams
function field, 251
function library, 71
function module trint_tp_interface, 219–220
functions, navigation with, 171

G

gap analysis, 200
gaps, in buffers, 498

Gartner Group, 15
Gateway, 507
gateway server, 61–62
general table maintenance function (transaction SM30), 253
generic area buff, 288
generic key buffering, 495–496, 497
generic types, 338–339
Get Variant . . . button, 182
Global ASAP, 537
global classes, creating, 331–332
Global Information box, 249
global parameters, 261
Global System Workload Analysis, 481
Global Template Roadmap, 554
Glossary, 177
Go action, 128
Go Live and Support phase
 SAP Roadmap, 545–546
 Solution Management Roadmap, 553, 561
graphical editor, 244
graphical job monitoring tool, for background jobs, 445–447
graphical user interface (GUI)
 EnjoySAP, *19*
 features of, 27
 GUI time analysis, 479, 482–483
 SAP R/3 release 3.0, 13, *18*
graphic elements, creating, 130
groups
 activity groups (user roles), 165, 371
 defining in SAP Logon application, 92
 logon, 89–92
 transport, 224, 258
 type, 306
 user, 379, 380, 384
GUI. *See* graphical user interface (GUI)
GUI time analysis, 479, 482–483

H

handlers
 ICM, 80
 See also event handlers
hardware
 capacity analysis, 498–501
 platforms, 142
 requirements, 141, 203–204
heap memory
 allocation of, 492
 limits on, 492
"Hello World" program, 38, 305, 314–315
 creating with Business Server Pages (BSPs), 341–345
 results, *315*
help desk, 38–39
 introduction to, 583–585
 roles, 582
 strategy, 545, 583–585
Help menu, 156
 options, *176*
help system, 176–178, *176*
 F4 field search helps, 296–297
 F1 help on fields, 176–178
 online, 176–178
 See also field helps
help views, 294
hierarchical list editor, 244
hierarchies
 defined, 451
 in spool work process, 451, 452
high availability systems, 570, 571
history list, finding transaction codes on, 171
HoldData function, 174–175
horizontal views, 121
hostname
 for message server, 61
 remote, 87
host printers, 461
host spool system, 449
 output status queries, 462
hot keys, for search helps, 301–302, *302*
hotline, 38–39
HR (human resources) module, 32–33, 74
HTML pages, 76–77
HTTP, 76–77
HTTP plug-in, 79–80
HTTP protocol, 360–361
HTTPS protocol, 360–361

I

IACs (Internet Application Components), 14, 75
IBUs (industry business units), 5, 6
ICM. *See* Internet Communication Manager (ICM)
ICNV transaction (Incremental Conversion), 204
 functions of, 209
ICOEs (industry centers of expertise), 5
IDE (Integrated Development Environment), 119
IDOCs (intermediate documents), 72
 ALE model and, 74
IM (Capital Investment Management) module, 32
IMG (Implementation Guide). *See* Implementation Guide (IMG)
immediate start jobs, 437–438
immediate value display, for elementary search helps, 300
Implementation Guide (IMG), 29, 220, 251, 539, 540, *541*
implementation projects, 556
Implementation Roadmap, 548, *548*, 552–553
implementation tools, 539–540
import phase, of transports
 execution of, 246
import queues, 219
 accessing, 255
 adding requests to, 257
 closing, 257
 example, *256*
 opening, 257
 security of, 255
 transferring transport requests to, 256–257
imports
 with function module, 219–220
 performed by SAP subsystems, 260
 performing, 569
 performing with tp program, 219, 265–267
 single, 257–258
 with system import queues, 219
"impossible link," 487
inbound points, for views, 126
Incremental Conversion (ICNV), 209
 ICNV transactions, 204
indexes, 295–296
 creating, 290
 defining, 295
 identification of, 295
 missing, 505, 530
 nonunique, 295
 primary, 295, 504
 secondary, 504–505
 unique, 295
 WHERE clause and, 296, 504
index monitor, 529–530
industry business units (IBUs), 5, 6
industry centers of expertise (ICOEs), 5
information, working with, 171–176
Information Integration layer, 103
information integrity, 570
information technology systems, 4
initialization (INI) files, 95
Initial Job Definition screen, *184*
initial password field, in user master records, 376
INIT status, in update records, 414
inner joins, 293
input fields
 default values, 175–176
 defined, 172
 displaying list of entries for, 174
 possible entries for, 172–174, *173*
 value ranges for, 181
insert input method, 172
inspections, performing with Code Inspector, 330–332
installation planning process
 documentation requirements, 142
 hardware requirements, 141
 installation and planning concepts, 140–141
 installation elements, 141
 installation notes, 147
 platforms, 143
 SAP NetWeaver, 139–147
 SAP NetWeaver Rapid Installer and, 144–145
 sizing process, 145–147
 software requirements, 141
 system landscapes, 143–144
installations, technology and, 569–570
INSTANCE_NAME variable, 86
instance profiles, 84, 85, 475, 491, 498, 508
 configuring work processes with, 506–507

function of, 88
parameters for, 88
instances
creating, 511
defined, 67, 305, 506
performance analysis, 474–476
SAP instance profiles, 67–68
workload distribution and, 506
integer data type
arithmetic used by, 307
features of, 306–308
Integrated Development Environment (IDE), 119
Integration Builder, 118
integration layer, 106
Integration Server, 118
integration technology, 20
SAP Business Framework architecture, 69
integrity
defined, 356
technology and, 570
interactive phase, of transactions, 46
interactive processing, 427
interenterprise collaboration, 3–4
Interface layer, 20
interfaces
defined, 305
SAP Business Framework architecture, 69
intermediate documents (IDOCs), 72, 74
internal attacks, 352
internal data highway, 3
internal information highway, 28
internal tables, 333–334
international applicability, 3
Internet Application Components (IACs), 14, 75
Internet applications, SAP R/3 support for, 14–15
Internet Business Framework, 10, 43–44, 76–78
Internet Communication Manager (ICM), 471
components, 79
controlling, 469–470
functions of, 78–79
handlers, 80
monitoring, 468–470
parameters, 80, 81
plug-ins, 79–80
role of, 507
server cache, 80
web dispatcher, 81, *82*
Internet-level security
SAP security features, 362
security failures, 369
Internet server, ICM, 80
Internet standards, 76–77
Internet Transaction Server (ITS), 15, 74–76, 107
architecture, 75
communication tasks, 75
components used by, 74
function of, 74–75
processes, 75
security, 76
Internet user authentication, 76
IN UPDATE TASK statement, 410, 513
inventory management module, 34
invoice verification module, 34
IS-Media, 7
ITS. *See* Internet Transaction Server (ITS)
iViews
assignment of, 109
defined, 109
properties of, 109
sources for, 109
technology, 110

J

Java
applications, development environments, 119
SAP Web AS components, 107
Java-BAPI, 323
Java engine, Enterprise Edition (J2EE), 106. *See also* SAP J2EE Engine
JavaScript, 340
JDR plug-in, 122
J2EE. *See* SAP J2EE Engine
job analysis tools, 523–526
job class field, for background jobs, 432
job definitions, for background jobs, 184–185
Job Log function, 444
job logs
for background jobs, 442, 445
common problems, 527–528
job name field, for background jobs, 432
Job Overview screen, 442
job print parameters, specifying, 441
job starter, 526
job status, for background jobs, 443
job steps, for background jobs, 433
Job wizards, scheduling background jobs with, 185
join of tables, in views, 293
Junit, 320

K

key combinations, 169
key users
implementation and, 540
support strategies and, 584
upgrade process and, 201
keywords, Project Administration utility, 557
kill command, 82
kill.sap script, 98, 99
Knowledge Management Platform, 103, 107, 108
functional areas, 110

L

language
default, 151
selecting, 151
language field, 251
in Logon screen, 151
SAP Logon, 93
Layout menu, 159–164
options, 159
layout sets, 450
Layout tabstrip, 130, 131
LDAP (Lightweight Directory Access Protocol), 77, 360
Lifecycle Management, 104
utilities, *104*
LIKE keyword, 305
line comments, 310–311
lists
defined, 178
hierarchical list editor, 244
objects l, 212
output, 450
variants, 181
"Where-Used List," 277
load balancing, 89–96
CPU bottlenecks and, 500–501
device pools and, 462
logon, 83–84, 89–92
with SAP J2EE, 471
with SAP Web Dispatcher, 468
spool server selection and, 453
load factors, 146
load generation, 210
load time analysis, 479, 482
local change requests, 227, 248
Local Client Copy, 417
local customer developments, 211
local files, saving data to, 190
local packages, package naming conventions, 235
local parameters, 261
local printing, 448, 457
local programs, execution of, 87
local substitute variables, 85
local system logs, 516–518
local variables, 85
LOCKEDALL status, 252
LOCKED status, 252
lock entries
automatic release of, 515
defined, 415
deleting, 416
managing, 415–416
selecting for displaying, 415
troubleshooting, 515–516
unreleased, 515–516
lock/import status field, 251
locking users, 379–380
lock monitoring functions, 515
lock objects, 58–59
deleting, 515
functions of, 303
troubleshooting, 505
types of, 58–59
lock tables, 58
lock work process, 58–59
log directory, 260
LO (general logistics) modules, 34
log files
checking, in troubleshooting, 214
spool requests, 456
system developer traces, 521–522
logging
security and, 369

table logs, 288–289
logging handler, 80
logging off, 150
automatic, 150
procedures, 154–155
logging on. *See* logon
logical components, 555, 558
logical expressions, 339
logical integrity, 570
logical printer devices, 462–463
logical units of work (LUWs), 47–48
logistics applications, 33–37
Logoff dialog box, 154–155
logon, 149–150
first time, 151
multiple, using same username and password, 151
passwords, 354–355
process, 150–151
Logon button, 92
logon groups, 510
configuring, 89–92
creating, 90–91, *91*
editing, 90–91
load balancing options, 91–92
response time options, 91
user limit options, 91
logon load balancing, 83–84, 89–92
configuring logon groups, 89–92
installing and configuring SAP Logon Windows application, 89, 92–96
Logon screen fields, 150
log records, update work process and, 60
low-level developer trace files, 407
luminosity, foreground and background, 161
LUWs (logical units of work), 47–48

M

main package, 326
maintenance services, 38
Maintenance Status tabstrip, 295
maintenance views, 294
main toolbar, Eclipse IDE, 121
MAM (Media Advertising Management), 7
management consolidation (EC-CS) system, 32
management organization roles, 580–583
mandatory fields, in user master records, 374
MAND T field, 48
manual adjustment, 213
MAPI (Messaging Application Program Interface) technology, 26
massive updates, of print parameters, 332
master data, *223*
ALE model and, 73
defined, 64, 221
Master Data Management, 103–104
Master Guides, 141
matchcodes, 172
MaxDB database, 143
MAXEXTENTS, 530
Max Used indicator, 493–495
Media Advertising Management (MAM), 7
media industry, SAP solution map for, *8*
Media Sales and Distribution (MSD), 7
memory
configuration, performance analysis, 477
display, 414
mapping, 66
paging area attributes, 52
physical, 501
pipes, 79
roll area attributes, 52
web dispatcher requirements, 81
memory areas
allocation sequences, 492
configuring, 491–492
consumption monitoring, 493–494
memory consumption by, 493–495
monitoring specific users, 494
statistics, 493–495
memory management, 490–499
buffers, 494–499
configuring, 66–67
consumption monitoring, 493–495
dumps and, 519–520
functions, 66–67
memory areas, 491–494
monitoring specific users, 494
menu bar, in SAP GUI, 155
messages
short, sending, 189, *190*
support, 177
system, 409
MESSAGE sentence, 338
message server, 61, *61*, 507
host location, 61
hostname, 61
message server time-out field, SAP Logon, 93
Messaging Application Program Interface (MAPI) technology, 26
metadata, 275
metadata repository, 28, 113, 115
methods
defined, 305
new features, 339
Microsoft Management Console, 100
Microsoft Office Suite, 13
Microsoft Server Cluster Services (MSCS), 100
Microsoft SQL, 143
Microsoft Transaction Server (MTS), 324
middleware, 45, 101
middleware layer, 21
migration, 536
MIME objects, 325
mirrored disks backup approach, 573–574
Missing Indexes, 505, 530
MM (materials management) modules, 34
mobile applications
development of, 111–112
Web Dynpro, 106
mobile devices, 111
Mobile Sales, 6
Modifiable option, 232
modification adjustment
adjustment methods, 213
after SAP upgrades, 210–214
types of modifications, 211
modifications
to SAP standard, 211
types of, 233
modified objects, 211
monitoring objects, 531
Monitoring Properties Variant, 511
MSCS (Microsoft Server Cluster Services), 100
MSD (Media Sales and Distribution), 7
MTS (Microsoft Transaction Server), 324
multiconditional testing, of system access privileges, 385
mySAP All-in-One, 12
mySAP Application Hosting, 9
mySAP Business Scenarios, 9
mySAP Business Suite, 3, 105, 537
applications, 7
components, 7
implementations, 536
security features, 362
solutions within, 10–11
mySAP.com, 2, 4, 7, 8–10
mySAP.com Technology, 9
mySAP CRM, 6, 7, 145
mySAP ERP, 11, *11*
mySAP Marketplace, 9
mySAP Workplace, 8–10
mySQL database, 143

N

name, specifying for spool request, 187
named users, authenticating, 76
naming conventions, 568
in ABAP, 311
Native JDBC, 471
native statements (Native SQL), 293
navigation, 169–171
among views, 126–128
functions for, 170
implementing, 127–128
schemes, 127
transaction codes for, 171
Navigation modeler, 345
/NEND transaction code, 155
Network administrators, 367
network-level security
SAP security features, 361–362
security failures, 365–366
network traffic, sizing and, 146
new authorization checks, 399
New Dimension, 16
New Password dialog box, *152*, 154
New Visual Design
menu, 160, 161
screen, *161*
/NEX transaction code, 155

nonexclusive spool servers, 451–452
noninteractive processing, 427–428
nonrepudiation, 356
nonunique indexes, 295
Normal operation, *512*, 513
Not Modifiable option, 232

O

object activation, 277
object classes
  authorization objects grouped in, 388
  purpose of, 305
Object Directory Entry screen, *230*
Object list maintenance screen, *251*
object name field, 251
Object Navigator, *325*
  new features, 325
  transaction, 228, 229, 230
object-oriented languages, 304
object repository, 27, 272
objects
  ABAP, 16
  attributes of, 253–255, 305
  authorization, 371, 387–389
  background control, 525–526
  client-dependent, 419–420
  client-independent, 420–421, 422
  corrections to, 229–230
  creating, 219
  custom-developed, 399
  data, 305
  development, 124, 220, 224, 228–229, 272
  identity of, 304–305
  lock, 58–59, 303, 505, 515
  making to appear as originals, 230
  MIME, 325
  modified, 211
  modifying, 219
  original, 229, 230
  repairs to, 230
  repository, 212, 222, 229, 246
  shadow, 207
  specifying for transport, 250–251
  system owners of, 229, 230
  test, 235
  transporting from source to target system, 217–220
  version management, 228–229
  visibility of, 327
objects list, 212, *251*
object type field, 251
obligation, proof of, 356
/O command, 171
OLAP processor (server), 113
olddata directory, 261
Old Dump Analysis, 518–520
old dumps, 518–520
onActionBack() event handler
  source code, 128
onActionGo() event handler, 128
OnCreate event handler, 348
OnDestroy event handler, 349
OnInitialization event handler, 349
OnInputProcessing event handler, 349
Online Analytical Processing (OLAP), 113
online documentation, 177
online help, 176–178
online help documentation, 507
Online Service System (OSS), 38, 39, 40
Only Display in Catalog option, 183
Only for Background Processing option, 182
OnManipulation event handler, 349
onPlugFromStartView() event handler, 135–136
OnRequest event handler, 348
OOP (out-of-band) pipes, 79
Open SQL, accessing table data with, 293
open systems software
  development of, 4–5
open technology, 24–27
  application level, 26
  communication protocol level, 26
  database level, 25
  desktop level, 26
  external communication level, 26–27
  system level, 25
operating procedures, 575
operating system-dependent parameters, 261
operating system–level security
  SAP security features, 362
  security failures, 365
Operating System Monitor, 499–500
operating systems
  backup utilities, 574
  files, 521
  keywords, 261
  processes, 404–405
  spool, connecting printers to, 457–458
  upgrades, 206
operation modes, *512*
  starting background jobs after change in, 439–440
  workload distribution and, 510–513
optimistic locks, 58–59
options, for user master record, 377–379
ORACLE, 143
Oracle databases, 502
  database space management, 528–530
  redolog files, 506
Oracle parameters, 262
Organizational Management, 390
original objects
  defined, 229
  system owner of, 229, 230
original system (SRCSYSTEM), 255
OR logic, for authorization objects, 388
OSS (Online Service System), 38, 39, 40
outbound points, for views, 126
outer joins, 293–294
Outline view, 128, 131
out-of-band (OOP) pipes, 79
output device (printer name)
  creating, 459–462
  specifying, 186
output requests, 450
  defined, 449–450
  displaying log files, 456
  log files, 456
output status options, 189
output status queries, for host spool system, 462
overtaker mode, 267
Overview of Variants button, 181
overwrite (replace) input method, 172

P

Package Included, 327
Package Interface, 327
packages, 326–327
  administrating, 327
  attributes, 254
  creating, 219, 235, 327
  defined, 227, 228, 235, 273
  definitions, *230*, 327
  functions of, 326–327
  local, 235
  main, 326
  managing, 235–236
  naming conventions, 235–236
  nesting, 228, 326
  private test classes, 235
  rights of use, 327
  structure, 326
  technology and, 568
  visibility of objects within, 327
packed types, 308–309
  arithmetic used by, 309
page attributes
  in BSP applications, 349
  creating, 349
page fragments, in BSP applications, 348
page properties, in BSP applications, 347–348
page types, in BSP applications, 348
page with flow logic, in BSP applications, 348
paging area, 52
paging out, 52
PA (personnel management and personnel administration) module, 33
parameter ID
  field, 175–176, *175*
  in user master records, 379
parameter names (PIDs), 175
parameters
  checking values of, 470
  database-dependent, 261, 262
  data class, 287
  local, 261
  operating system-dependent, 261
  Oracle, 262

precedence of, 261
print, 332
setting for user master records, 378–379
setting profiles, 508–510
setting values, 85–86
transport system, 261–263
user, 175–176, 378–379
user printing, 187–188
See also profile parameters
partial buffering, 495
partial line comments, 310–311
password field
in Logon screen, 151
in user master records, 374
passwords
automatic generation of, 154
changing, 153–154, 380–381
changing for other users, 154
expiration of, 154
forbidden, 153
logon, 354–355
management, 380–382
minimum length, 381
restricting strings, 382
restrictions and requirements, 381–382
rules for, 151–153
security and, 353
valid and invalid, 153
paste function, 163
PC files, downloading and uploading, 190
PC printing, 448
People Integration layer, 103
performance analysis, 473–490
ABAP Trace, 490
business transactions, 487–488
communication, 477
databases, 476–477
hardware capacity analysis, 498–501
memory configuration, 477
presentation server response time, 486–487
RFC Communications, 484–486
SQL Trace, 488–490
tools, 526–527
Work Analysis Monitor, 478–484
Work Process Monitor, 474–477
performance monitors, 473
periodic jobs, 441
peripheral security, 353
perspectives bar, 121
physical integrity, 570
physical memory, troubleshooting, 501
PKI (public key infrastructure), 359
Planning Guides, 141
planning systems management, 567–568
plug-in architecture, 119
plug-ins, Internet Communication Manager
HTTP plug-in, 79–80
tasks performed by, 79
PM (plant maintenance) modules, 35
pooled tables, 64
portability layer, 49
Portable Operating System Interface (POSIX), 49
Portal Infrastructure, 107
portal pages, iViews assignment to, 109
Portal Platform, 108, 110
Portal Server, 370
power failures, 570
PP (production planning) modules, 35
PRD (production system), 211
precedence, of parameters, 261
predefined roles, for users, 377
PREPARE program
execution levels, 206
phases of, 207
preparing to run, 202–205
running, 205–209
presentation interface, 48
function of, 62–63
SAP GUI as, 149
presentation layer, 69, 105
workload distribution and, 506
presentation-level security, SAP features, 361, 363–364
presentation servers, 54, 69
defined, 24
response time analysis, 486–487
preventive services, 38–39
preview, in BSP applications, 349
primary indexes, 295, 504
primary update components (U1 or V1), 60, 411, 413–414
Print Dialog screen, 332, *332*
printers/printer devices
connecting to operating system spool, 457–458
creating, 459
defining, 458–462
logical, 462–463
Print Immediately option, 187, 188
printing, 186–189
local, 448, 457
parameters, massive updates of, 332
PC, 448
remote, 448, 457
user, 186–189
See also printing system; user printing
printing system, 447–467
access methods and, 464–466
administration tasks, 466–467
defining printer devices, 458–462
logical output devices and device pools, 462–464
operating system spool connections, 457–458
spool requests and, 453–457
spool servers and, 451–453
spool system architecture and, 448–450
spool work processes and, 450–451
troubleshooting, 466
print requests, 450
handling, 448
modifying status of, 189
Print Screen List dialog box, 186, *187*
priority, of background jobs, 432
privacy, 356
private keys, protecting, 368
private memory, 494
private test classes, package naming conventions, 235
PRIV mode, 494
procedures guide, 575–577
Process After Output (PAI), 47
Process Before Output (PBO), 47
process identification number (PID), 405
processing time analysis, 479, 482
Process Integration layer, 104
Process Overview (transaction code SM50), 404, 406
product availability matrix, 206
production systems, 233–234
Profile Generator, 165, 355, 371, 391
configuring, 392–393
working with, 392–397
profile modification, 508–510
profile parameters, 508–510
customizing, 84
functions of, 84
for handlers, 80
for instance profiles, 88
for memory management, 67
in SAP instance, 86
setting values, 85–86
for start profile, 86–87
tuning, 54
values of, 85–86
profiles, 84–88
activation concept in, 390
default profile, 85, 87–88
deleting, 509–510
editing, 84, 88
instance profile, 85, 87–88
local substitute variables, 85
maintenance of, 88, *89*
modifying for groups of users, 380
for parameter settings, 508–510
saving, 509
start profile, 85, 86–87
structuring, 84
system checks on, 509
types of, 84–85
in user master records, 377
for users, 377
variable substitution in, 85
Program Buffer, 498–499
program ID field, 250
programming
with Eclipse IDE, 121–122
languages, 121
technology and, 536
program selections, 181
program-to-program communication, 65
Project Administration utility, 556, 557
project charter, 543

project documentation
 cross-project, 557
 project-specific, 557
 See also documentation
Project Estimator, 543
Project IMGs, 558
projection views, 293, 294
project management utilities, 540
project managers
 authorization of, 228
 change requests and, 223
 SAP Solution Manager role, 550
project planning, 543
project preparation phase
 ASAP Roadmap, 542–543
 Solution Management Roadmap, 553–554
project system (PS) application, 35–36
proof of obligation, 356
properties view, selecting values, 129, *129*
protection
 certificates, for public keys, 368
 from hardware, software, and environmental failures, 352
 private keys, 368
 SAP* users, 384
 Security Policy, 353–354
 of transport requests, 252
 from unauthorized access, 352
Protect Variant option, 183
PS (project system) application, 35–36
public key cryptography, 357
public key infrastructure (PKI), 359
public keys, protecting, 368
purchasing module, 34
PXA buffer, 495

Q

QAS (quality assurance system), 211, 234–235
QM (quality management) modules, 36
qRFC (queued remote function calls), 71
quality assurance systems, 211, 234–235
QuickSizer tool, 146, 563

R

RAID technology, 570
ramp up program, 39
reactivating updating, 414
Reads/User Calls, 503
Realization phase
 SAP Roadmap, 544
 Solution Management Roadmap, 559–560
real-time collaboration, 110
real-time software integration, 3, 28
reason code, for work processes, 406
Rebuild Project option, 138
recovery procedures, 573
redirect handler, 80
redolog files, 506
refactoring tools, 122
reference master records, creating user master records from, 375
reference profiles, 387
regression testing, for SAP upgrade projects, 195
relational databases, 63
relational operators, 311–314
 for any data types, 311
 for bit masks, 313
 for byte type data, 312
 for string character types, 311–312
relative start option, 440
Release Notes, 177–178
relocations, creating, 247
Remote Client Copy, 417
remote communications
 SAP security, 362
 security failures, 367
Remote Compare, 229
remote execution time, 484–486
remote function calls (RFCs), 65
 defined, 65, 71
 functions of, 65–66
 performance analysis and, 483–486
 queued (qRFCs), 71
 SAP Web Application Server architecture and, 71
 transactional (tRFCs), 71
remote hostname, 87
remote hosts, running programs on, 87
remote printing, 448, 457
repairs, 230, 233, 569
repair tasks
 defined, 230
 transporting, 244
repeat intervals, for background jobs, 440–441
Repeat Update option, 414
repetitive data, entering, 174–175
report classes, 179
report names, looking for, 179
reports, 178–183
 background jobs, 183–186
 defined, 178
 executing, 180
 looking for, 179
 printing, 186–189
 scheduling, 431
 selection criteria, 178–179
 starting, 178
 working with variants, 181–182
Report Selection screen, *179*
repository
 ABAP object repository, 63–64
 accessing MIME objects, 325
 Business Object Repository (BOR), 71–72, 304
 Business Process Repository (BPR), 549, *549*, 558–559
 defined, 220
 development objects in, 220
 metadata repository, 28, 113, 115
 object repository, 27, 272
repository data, *223*
Repository Information System, 277–278
 finding domains on, 278, *280*
 screens, *280*
repository object directory, 253–254
repository objects, 212
 source systems for, 229
 transport of, 222
 Transport Organizer and, 246
Repository Switch procedure, 205
Request Queue information display, *404*
request queues, 54
required input fields, 172
reset to original, 213
resource minimized upgrade strategy, 205
response time, 54
 analysis of, 478–481, 481–483, 487
 in external communications, 483–484
Restricting Search Values dialog box, *174*
Restriction dialog box, for field search helps, 296
ResultView, 126, 127
 assigning UI elements, 135
 layout, 131–132
RFC. *See* remote function calls (RFCs)
RFC communications
 analysis of, 484–486
 connections, 256
 maximum number of communications per instance, 484
 troubleshooting, 484–486
RFC Library, 324
rights of use, packages, 327
risk analysis, 353
rlogin service, 366
Roadmaps
 ASAP Roadmap, 541–542, 543, 549
 Global Template Roadmap, 554
 Implementation Roadmap, 548, *548*, 552–553
 SAP Roadmap, 545
 Solution Management Roadmap, 551, 553–554
 Upgrade Roadmap, 196–197, *197*
role administrators, 390
role-based scenarios, 164–166, 352
Role Maintenance, 371
 operation of, 392
 screens, *394*
 views, 393–394
Role Maintenance tool, 389, 391–397
roles, 389–390
 assigning user master records to, 390
 concepts for working with, 393–394
 creating, 394–397
 defined, 164, 371, 389
 management of, 370–371

modifying for groups of users, 380
roles field, in user master records, 376
roll areas, 52, 492
rollback, of transactions, 60
roll-forward approach, 574
roll-ins, 481–483
defined, 66
number of, 481
time analysis, 478–479
roll-outs, 52, 66, 481
time analysis, 478–479
Roll Wait Time, *483*
analysis of, 483–484, 486
root elements, selecting, 129, 130
RootUIElementContainer, 129, 131–132
R3TRANSPATH parameter, 262
R3trans utility, 258
copying table entries with, 426–427
deleting clients with, 424
run configurations, 122
Run menu, Eclipse IDE, 122
Run . . . , 122
Run As, 122
Runtime Analysis, 316
results, *491*
runtime minimized strategy, 207
R3UP.exe, 209–210
monitor, 208
preparing to run, 202
RZ10 (Edit Profiles) transaction, 84

S

Sales Force Automation (SFA), 6
SANDBOX, 562
SAP Advanced Planner and Optimizer (APO), 6
SAP AG
history of, 1–2
research and development, 2–4
strategic vision, 4–5
SAP Application Benchmark Performance Standards (SAPS), 146, 563
SAP ArchiveLink, 37
SAP Automation, 15, 323
SAP Basis Middleware (R/3), 362
SAP Basis system, 43
SAP Basis Technology, 9
SAP Best Practices, 537–538
SAP Business Connector, 322
SAP Business Engineer, 543
SAP Business Framework
ALE model and, 74
architecture, 7, 69
SAP Business Information Warehouse (SAP BW), 7, 103, 112–117
architecture of, 113–115, *114*
BW kernel, 115
defined, 112
functions of, 113
implementation costs, 115
new features, 115–116
reporting scenarios, 114
within SAP NetWeaver, 115
staging scenarios, 114
uses of, 114–115
SAP Business Intelligence (BI), 7
SAP Business Maps, 538, *539*
SAP Business Objects, 71
SAP Business One, 12
SAP Business Partners, 12
SAP Business Scenario Maps, 538
SAP Business to Business (B2B), 6
SAP Business Workflow, 37
SAP Business Workplace, 37
SAP connectors, 320–324
SAP cover sheets, printing, 188
SAP Customer Relationship Management (CRM), 6, 7, 145
SAP Customizing, 539, 540
SAP DB, 143
SAP DCOM Connector, 323–324
SAP-declared dictionary tables, 64
SAP dispatcher, 46
defined, 50
role of, 50–51
SAP Easy Access
accessing user maintenance functions from, 372
window, 151, *152*
SAP Enterprise Portal (SAP EP), 107–111
architecture of, *108*
components of, 107–108
predefined content and content tools, 111
purpose of, 107
SAPEVTPATH parameter, 263
SAP Exchange Infrastructure, 117–119, 144
communication system parameters, 119
components, 118, *118*
defined, 117
messaging concepts, 119
options, 119
SAP for Industries, 3, 5–6, 10
SAP for Media, 7
SAP gateways, 61–62
SAP graphix utility, 63
SAP GUI, 27
abnormal termination of, 515–516
application toolbar, 157, *157*
automatic tabbing feature, 162
clipboard, 163
cursor behavior, 163–164
customizing layout, 164
Favorites list, 164, *165*
help system, 176–178, *176*
installation of, 149
Layout menu, 159–164
main screen elements, 155–157
menu bar, 155–156
performance analysis, 486–487
as presentation interface, 149
presentation server response time, 486–487
security, 363–364
shortcuts, 166
standard toolbar, 156–157, *156*, 158–159
status bar, 157, *157*
system status information, 166–167, *168*
toolbar, 156
user printing, 186–189
user utilities, 189–190
window, 155–157, *156*
window layout options, 159–164
window size, 163
working with information, 171–176
SAP GUI for HTML, 27, 74–75
Sapgui Start Options, 94
SAP implementation tools, 537–540
SAP Industry Solutions, 6, 10
SAP instance profiles, 67–68
buffers in, 495
profile parameter list, 86
SAP instances, displaying and monitoring, 402–404
SAP Java Connector (JCO), 323
SAP J2EE Engine, 20, 43, 50, 80, 106, 470–472
installation options, 470–471
monitoring, 471–472
technology issues, 567
web dispatcher and, 83
SAP kernel, 22, 43, 49
SAP Knowledge Warehouse (SAP KW), 7, 110
SAP Library, 177
saplogon.ini file, 95, 96
SAP Logon utility, 89–92, 92, 149–150
administering, 94–96
configuration dialog box, *94*
configuring, 92–94
INI files, 95
Logon options, 93–94
main menu, *92*
New Entry input fields, 93
Sapgui Start Options, 94
starting, 92
SAP Marketing, 7
SAP Marketplace Connector, 322
SAP Master Data Management (SAP MDM), 117
SAP Mobile Infrastructure (SAP MI), 111–112
client elements, 112
connection types, 111
defined, 111
server elements, 112
SAP Mobile Solutions, 112
sapmsg.ini file, 95, 96
sapnames directory, 260
SAP .NET Connector, 323
SAPnet-R/3 front end, 38, 40, 41
SAP NetWeaver, 1, 7, 9, 10, 11, 12, *12*
application platform, 104
components installed by SAP NetWeaver Rapid Installer, 144–145
connectivity, 105
defined, 2, 102–103, 105

documentation requirements, 142
elements of, 103–105
hardware requirements, 141
implementations, 536, 537
installation planning process, 139–147
integration layers, 102–103
overview, 101–147
security features, 362
software requirements, 141
vertical or cross layers components, 104–105
SAP NetWeaver Application Platform, 105–107
SAP NetWeaver Developer Environment, 119
SAP NetWeaver Developer Studio, 119–139
creating Web Dynpro with, 124–139
defined, 105
new project wizard, 125
SAP NetWeaver Rapid Installer 2.0, 144–145
limitations of, 145
NetWeaver components installed by, 144
software installed by, 145
SAP NetWeaver Security Infrastructure, 351–352
SAP Notes
for SAP R/3 Enterprise upgrade project, 203, 204
searching, 203
sapntkill command, 82
SAP Online Library, 142
SAP operation staff roles, 581–582
sappad editor, 84
SAP Partner Connectivity Kit (PCK), 117
SAP Passports, 370
SAP Portal, 106
SAP Printing Guide, 457, 458
SAP procedures guide, 575–577
SAP Product Data Management (PDM), 6
SAP product portfolio, 10–12
SAP project types, 535–537
SAP R/2, 2, 4–5
SAP R/3
business processes, 3
complexity of, 13
components, 21–22, *22*
customer installations of, 5
development of, 2–3, 5
EnjoySAP release 4.6, 17
evolution of, 1–2, *11*, 13
features, 3, 21–30
graphical user interface (GUI), 13, *18*, 27
handler, 80
implementations, 536, 543
international applicability of, 3
kernel system, 22
Logon screen, 150, *150*
plug-ins, 203
readying for productive business work, 100
real time software integration, 3
release 3.0, 13–14
release 3.1, 14–15
release 4.0, 15–16
release 4.5, 16–17
releases, 3
setup utility, 88
starting and stopping, 99–100
SAP R/3 Basis, 10
features, 45
interfaces, 45
SAP Web Application Server, 20
SAP R/3 buffers, 508, 510
SAP R/3 Business Engineer, 28
SAP R/3 Enterprise
extensions (or add-ons), 18–19, 20
installation planning process, 140
integration technology, 20
modules, 7
new features in release 4.7, 193–194
release 4.7, 43
release 4.7 features, 17–19
release information, 194
upgrading to, 191–214
SAP R/3 Enterprise Core
applications overview, 30–38
development of, 18–19
features of, 20–21
financial modules, 30–32
human resources applications, 32–33
integration technology, 20
logistics applications, 33–37
SAP R/3 Enterprise upgrade project, 191–214
ABAP load generation, 209
considerations for, 191–194
hardware requirements, 203–204
modification adjustment, 210–214
preparation for, 202–205
running PREPARE program, 205–209
R3UP.exe, 209–210
SAP Notes for, 203, 204
SAP Support Packages for, 207
SAP upgrade process, 195–200
technical issues, 201–205
time required for, 201–205
troubleshooting, 214
upgrade strategies, 205, 207, 209
upgrade team for, 200–201
See also SAP upgrade projects
SAP router string field, SAP Logon, 93
saprout.ini file, 95, 96
SAP runtime directory, 405
SAP Sales, 7
SAP Script, 450
SAP security, 361–370
application layer, 361
database level, 361, 364–365
improving, 363
Internet, 362
layers of, 361–370
network level, 361–362
objectives of, 352
operating system level, 362
presentation layer, 361, 363–364
remote communications, 362
security concepts, 352–361
standard features, 362
See also security
SAP Security Library (SAPSECULIB), 359, 368
SAP Self Service (XSS), 145
SAP Service, 7
SAP Service Manager, 99–100
SAP Service Marketplace, 38, 39–42, 177, 178, 546–547
"Release Info" section, 194
SAP-supported systems, 25
Upgrade Center, 196
SAP services, 38–42
consulting services, 38
maintenance services, 38
preventive services, 38–39
SAP Smart Business Solutions, 12
SAP_SOLAR_AC role, 550
SAP_SOLAR_ALL role, 550
SAP_SOLAR_BC role, 550
SAP_SOLAR_PM role, 550
SAP_SOLAR_RO role, 550
SAP_SOLAR_TC role, 550
SAP Solution Architect, 539
SAP Solution Manager, 30, 39, 535, 539, 542, 546–560, 584
authorization in, 550–551
Business Blueprint, 558–559
Business Process Repository (BPR), 549, 558–559
defined, 546
functions, 547–548, *547*, *548*
implementation and, 543–544
implementation features, 548
Implementation Roadmap, 552–553
implementation roles, 550–551
implementation tools, 554–558
integration of, 546–547
Solution Management Roadmap, 551–554
system landscape definition, 555
technology issues, 560–575
SAP Solutions, 11
documentation requirements, 142
hardware requirements, 141
installation planning process, 139, 140
maps, 7, *8*
software requirements, 141
SAP Solutions for Industry, 30
SAP Supply Chain Management (SCM), 6
SAP Support Packages, 207
SAP system administrator
log off options, 150
upgrade projects and, 203
SAP system group, 224
SAP system landscape, 224
SAP System Landscape Directory (SLD), 143–144, 145

multiple server installation, 143
single server installation, 143
SAPSYSTEMNAME variable, 86
SAP systems
adding to transport domains, 241–242
customizing, 28–29
SAP tables, 64
SAP technical support group roles, 581–582
SAP transactions (ABAP transactions), 48
SAP Trust Center Services, 370
SAP Upgrade Guide, 202
SAP upgrade projects, 191–214
change management activities, 195
considerations in upgrading, 192–193
disk space for, 206
gap analysis, 200
process, 195–200
project planning for, 195
reasons for upgrading, 192
regression testing for, 195
success factors in, 196
team for, 195
time needed for, 195, 197–198
training for, 195
Unicode conversion for, 214
upgrade project plan, 197–199
Upgrade Roadmap, 196–197
upgrade script, 199–200
See also SAP R/3 Enterprise upgrade project
SAP* users, 383–384
password for, 384
protecting, 384
turning off special status of, 384
See also superusers
SAP user sessions, 168–169
SAP Web Application Server (SAP Web AS), 20, 43–100
ABAP installation, 50
ABAP + Java system installation, 50
as application platform for SAP NetWeaver, 104, 105–107
architecture of, 78–83
authorization system, 385–390
Business Server Pages (BSPs), 340
Change and Transport System (CTS) and, 217
client/server system, 67–74, 68–71, *70*
components, 106–107
features of, 20, 44, 340
history of, 1–2
installation options, 49
integration technology and, 20
introduction of, 2
Java system installation, 50
layers, 105–106
release 6.20, 204
release 6.40, 106–107
standards, 46, 50
starting and stopping, 97
starting from SAP Service Manager, 99–100
system management, 401–472
upgrade to SAP R/3 Enterprise and, 191
variants, 142–143
as web client, 83
web components of, 468–472
SAP Web Application Server (SAP Web AS) ABAP + Java system, 142
SAP Web Application Server (SAP Web AS) ABAP system, 142
SAP Web Application Server (SAP Web AS) ABAP system + SAP Web AS Java system, 142
SAP Web Application Server (SAP Web AS) Java system, 142
SAP Web Dispatcher, 468
SAP xAPPs, 11
SAP-XML, 78
SAPXPG trace utility, 528
SBUs. *See* Strategic Business Units (SBUs)
scheduled jobs, 431
modifying, 444–445
releasing, 444
scheduling
After Event scheduling option, 185
After Job scheduling option, 185
At operation mode scheduling option, 185
background jobs, 184–185, 431
background processing, 525, 526
batch scheduler, 56
event-driven, 526
with Job wizards, 185
reports, 431
Start on Work Day Mode Scheduling option, 185
time-driven, 525
24-hour Normal operation schedule, *512*, 513
SD (sales and distribution) modules, 36–37
Search and Classification (TREX), 110
search helps, 172, 298–301
example, *299*
exits, 301
field search helps (F4), 296–297
hot key for, 301–302, *302*
types of, 298
uses of, 298
secondary indexes, 504–505
secondary update components (U2 or V2), 60, 411, 413–414
Secure Network Communications (SNC), 352, 356, 362, 365, 366
Secure Sockets Layer (SSL), 356, 360–361
Secure Store and Forward (SSF), 352, 356, 358–359, 362, 367
security, 351–399
application layer, 363–364
application level, 352
basic processes, 354–356
client copies, 420
database level, 364–365
external attacks, 352
importance of, 351
import queue and, 255
internal attacks, 352
peripheral, 353
as protection from hardware, software, and environmental failures, 352
as protection from unauthorized access, 352
user authentication, 76
web systems, 563
See also SAP security
Security Guides, 141
security policy
basics, 353–354
defined, 353
efficiency in, 354
protection measures, 353–354
threat identification, 353–354
selection, of views, 293
Selection Conditions tabstrip, 295
selection criteria
defined, 180–181
entering with variants, 178–179
for reports, 178–179
types of, 181
using, 180–181
Selection Options button, 181
semaphores
number, for work processes, 406
performance analysis, 476
semiautomatic adjustment, 213
"separated" environments, 221
sequential mode, 477
Sequential Read, 476
serial directory, 261
server cache handler, 80
server monitoring, 402–404
display, *403*
servers
adding in SAP Logon application, 92
defined, 53, 67, 69
hardware-oriented view, 44
performance analysis, 474–476
in SAP Mobile Infrastructure (SAP MI), 112
SLD, 143–144
software-oriented view, 44
server-side scripts, 340
server system hardware, 67
service providers (servers), 69
service requesters (clients), 69
services, defined, 53, 67
session number, 168
sessions
closing, 168
creating, 168–169
defined, 168
ending, 169
key combinations in, 169
limiting number of, 168
moving among, 169
working with, 168–169
SetData function, 174–175

Set System Change Options screen, *232*
settings, 177
SGEN, 210
SGML (Standard Generalized Markup Language), 77
shadow objects, 207
shadow systems, 204, 207
shared memory, 66
Shared Pool SQL and Data Dictionary Pin ratio, 503
shared (type S) locks, 58
shortcuts, creating, 165, *167*
short dumps, 518–520
Short Message function, 409
short messages, sending, 189, *190*, 409
shutdown processing, 99
signal handlers, 79
simple tests, 524, *524*
single imports, 257–258
single points of failure, 570
single-record buffering, 288, 495
Single Sign-On (SSO), 359–360
size category, for tables, 287
sizing process, 145–147, 562–563
skill sets, for systems managers, 564–567
SLIN, overview, 319, *322*
smart-card authorization, 355
SMTP protocols, 26
SNC. *See* Secure Network Communications (SNC)
SOAP processor, 324
software requirements, 141
Solution Composer, 539
solution life cycle management, 537, *538*
Solution Management Roadmap, 551, 553–554
source systems
  for repository objects, 229
  transporting clients from, 426–427
  transporting objects from, 217–220
Space Critical Objects, 530
SPACKAGE transaction, 235
SPAD transactions, 459
SPAU transactions, 211, 212
  defined, 212
  using, 212–213
SPDD transaction, 211
  defined, 212
  using, 212–213
special management options, 569
Spool Administration screen, 458, *459*
spool assignment, dynamic, 451, 452
spool list recipient, specifying, 441
Spool Request List screen, 456
spool requests, 57
  attributes, 456, 457
  defined, 449
  deleting, 457
  displaying and modifying, 456
  generating, 448
  log files, 456
  managing, 453–455
  print attributes for, 187–188
  printing and displaying, 455–457
Spool Request screen, *188*, 189
spool servers
  alternate, 451–452
  defined, 447
  defining, 452–453
  dynamic assignment of, 451, 452
  load balancing and, 453
  nonexclusive, 451–452
  relationships among, 452
  selection criteria, 454
spool system, 447–464, *449*
  access methods, 464–466
  architecture, 448–450
  features of, 447–448
  instance profile parameters, 467
  spool work process, 450–451
spool work processes, 57–58, *57*
  data storage, 57
  hierarchies in, 451, 452
  number of, 513
  process, 450–451
  spools per instance, 58
SQL requests, database interface and, 63
SQL statements
  expensive, 488–489, 503–505
  new features, 336–337
SQL Trace
  for background processing, 527
  troubleshooting with, 488–490, *489*
SSF. *See* Secure Store and Forward (SSF)
SSL. *See* Secure Sockets Layer (SSL)
SSL/HTTPS, 360–361
SSO. *See* Single Sign-On (SSO)
stable methods, 71
staging engine, SAP BW, 114
standard application software
  development of, 4–5, 5
  evolution of, 1–2
Standard Generalized Markup Language (SGML), 77
standard toolbar, 156–157, *156*
  icons, 158–159
standby database servers, 574, 575
STARSAP parameter, 263
start conditions, for background jobs, 436–441
STARTDB parameter, 263
start field, for work processes, 406
Start Import function, 256
Start on work day mode scheduling option, 185
start profile, 85, 86–87
  defined, 86
  location of, 86
  permitted parameters, 86–87
  system variables, 86
startsap program, 86, 96–99
start up profiles, 508
StartView, 126, 127, 128
  dependencies for, 133–134
  layout, 128
status
  performance analysis and, 475
  of work processes, 405
status bar, 157, *157*
status screen, 167
status values, Project Administration utility, 557
status window, 167, *168*
steps
  in background jobs, 185–186
  defined, 55
STMS transaction, 240
STOPDB parameter, 263
stopped work processes, 476, 477
STOPSAP parameter, 263
stopsap program, 96–99
Strategic Business Units (SBUs), 6–7
string character type
  features of, 309–310
  relational operators for, 311–312
string data type, 334–335
structures, 285
structure types, 338
subhandlers, 80
superusers
  defining administrator roles, 399
  designating new, 384
  managing, 383–384
  profiles, 228
  support strategies and, 584
  See also SAP* users
support messages, 177
support strategies, 583–585
swap space, releasing, 492
switch operation modes, 526
switch-over systems, 571
synchronization
  backup and restore strategies, 572
  buffering and, 288, 289
SYSLOG parameter, 262
SYST change requests, 220–221, 246
system access privileges, multiconditional testing of, 385
system administration
  ABAP short dumps, 518–520
  authorization of background jobs by, 431
  lock entries, 515–516
  system log, 516–518
  troubleshooting in, 513–528
  update process administration, 514–515
System Administrator
  changing passwords for other users, 154
  tools, 83–96
system availability, backup and restore strategies, 572
system central interfaces, 48–51
  communication interface, 48
  database interface, 48, 50
  operating system interface, 48, 49–50
  presentation interface, 48
system change options, 239, 568
system fields, 338

system import buffer, 255
system landscape
    definition, 555
    design and configuration, 561–562
System Landscape Maintenance transaction, 555
system load, background processing and, 183
system logs, 516–518
    dumping output of, 517
    interpreting, 518
    maximum size of, 516
    selection criteria for, 516
system management
    application servers, 402–404
    background processing, 427–447
    client copies, 416–427
    general, 401–416
    installation monitoring, 402
    Internet Communication Manager (ICM), 468–470
    posting system messages, 409
    roles in, 564
    SAP instances, 402–404
    SAP J2EE Engine, 470–472
    SAP printing system, 447–467
    SAP utilities, 401
    skill sets and, 564–567
    staff requirements, 565
    support for, 565
    system work processes, 404–408
    technology and, 563–565
    update records, 410–414
    user sessions, 408–409
    Web Dispatcher, 468
System menu, 156
system messages
    creating, 409
    expiration of, 409
    posting, 409
system number field, SAP Logon, 93
system owners, for original objects, 229, 230
system profile, 87, 509
systems
    development, 233
    functions of, 232–233
    production, 233–234
system status information, 166–167, *168*
system switch, 205
system switch upgrade, 206–207
System trace, 397–398, 520–521
system types, 231
system work processes, monitoring, 404–408

T

tabbing between fields, 162
table buffers
    functions of, 495–496
    improving performance of, 496–497
    troubleshooting, 496–497
    types of, 495–496
table call statistics, 497
table definitions, modifying, 290–292
Table/Join Conditions tabstrip, 294–295, *295*
table logs, 289–290
    displaying, 290
tables
    in ABAP dictionary, 285–286
    append structures, 292
    buffering, 287–289
    data class parameters, 287
    determining when to buffer, 497
    logging, 289–290
    size categories, 287
    technical parameters for, 286–290
    transportable, 222
    types of, 293–295
    views, 293–295
X TABLES keyword, 276
tables monitor, 529–530
tablespaces, 528, 529
table TADIR, 253–254
table TDVC, 235
table types, 285
Tag Browser, 325, *326*
target field, for background jobs, 433
target hosts, 433
    for background jobs, 185
    instances, 433
target systems
    change requests and, 226
    importing objects into, 219
    transporting clients to, 426–427
    transporting objects to, 217–220
task handler, 52, 54
task numbers, 227
task profiles, 376. *See also* roles
tasks
    creating, 223
    defined, 227
    grouping, 228
    releasing, 219, 248
    searching for, 227
    in Transport Organizer, 227–228
    transport system, 568–569
TCP/IP network protocol, 61, 64, 95, 458
TeamASAP, 15
team leaders, change requests and, 222–223
teams, upgrade. *See* upgrade teams
technical consultants, 550
technology issues
    backup and recovery, 571–575
    change management, 568–569
    cluster systems, 570
    high availability, 570–571
    increasing role of, 560
    information integrity issues, 570
    installation and updates, 569–570
    planning systems management, 567–568
    SAP technology implementation, 560–561
    security, 563
    sizing, 562–563
    system manager skill sets, 565–567
    systems landscape, 561–562
    systems management, 563–565
    transport requests, 568–569
template projects, 556, 557
TemSe (temporal sequential objects), 57, 450
terminal processes, 62
test objects, package naming conventions, 235
test systems, 234–235
thread control, 79
threads, 79
threats
    identifying, 353
    types of, 354
time-driven scheduler, 525
time field, for work processes, 406
Time of Printing, specifying for spool request, 187
TIME_OUT errors, 54, 56
time setting option, 162
Time/User Calls, 503
Title, specifying for spool request, 187
tmp directory, 260
TMS. *See* Transport Management System (TMS)
toolbars, in Eclipse IDE, 121
    main toolbar, 121
    perspectives bar, 121
toolbars, in SAP GUI, 156
tp import command
    options, 265–266
    syntax, 265
TPPARAM (transport parameter file), 238, 261–263
    location of, 261
    parameters, 261–263
    predefined variables, 262
tp program, 223, 258–268
    ABAP interface, 268
    displaying options for, 263
    importing objects with, 219, 256–257
    managing special transports, 267–268
    operating system level, 260–261
    options, 263–265
    performing exports with, 258
    performing imports with, 265–267
    programs used by, 258
    requirements for, 259
    setting up, 238, 259
    starting, 256
    TPPARAM global parameter file, 261–263
    unconditional modes in, 267
trace level, 522
traces
    authorizations, 397–398
    developer, 407, 521–522
    displaying files, 470
    options, 407

system, 397–398, 520–521
tracing utilities, 520–522
developer trace, 521–522
system trace, 520–521
training, 540
implementation and, 545
systems, 233
upgrading to SAP R/3 Enterprise and, 193
transactional environments
remote function calls for, 71
transaction codes, 46
for creating new sessions, 168–169
defined, 171
entering, 171
finding, 171
memorizing, 171
navigation with, 171
transaction data, 64
Transaction Profile, *488*
performance analysis, 487–*488*
transactions
defined, 46–48
interactive phase, 46
rollback of, 60
types of, 47–48
update phase, 46
TRANSDIR parameter, 262
transparent tables, 64, 292, 293
transportable change requests, 226
packages and, 227
transport control program (tp). *See* tp program
transport directory
configuring, 218
SAP systems and, 241
setting up, 238
standard, 259, 260
subdirectories, 260
system authorization for accessing, 260
tp program and, 259, 260
transport domain
adding SAP systems to, 241–242
configuring, 240
transport domain controller
creating, 218
setting, 238
transport groups
defined, 224
transporting among, 258
transport layer, grouping development objects in, 224
transport logs, 252–253
displaying, 252
example, *254*
files, 220
information provided in, 252–253
levels of detail in, 252
overview screen, *253*
return codes, 252
types of, 252
unconditional modes and, 267
Transport Management System (TMS), 239–246
configuring, 238–239
configuring systems and domains in, 240
defined, 216, 239
distributing and verifying configuration, 245–246
editors, 244
functions of, 239
importing objects with, 219
overview screen, *242*
performing transports with, 255–258
transport system security and, 366
Transport Organizer, 28, 246–255
ABAP development workbench and, 221
activating, 246–255
checking transport results, 252–253
creating change requests, 246–248
defined, 220
initializing, 218
integration system, 233
main screen, *226*
monitoring transports and repairs, 249–252
object attributes, 253–255
releasing tasks and requests, 248
tools, 227, 255
transport process, 217–220
roles in, 222–224
transport requests
changing order of, 264
protecting, 252
rules for, 250
specifying objects, 250–251
transferring to import queue, 256
transport routes
configuring, 218, 243–245
defined, 224–225
system groups, 243–244
types of, 244
transports
beginning transport process, 256
copy of, 247
execution of, 246
export phase, 223
import phase, 246
monitoring, 249–252
at operating system level, 217
performing with TMS, 255–258
transport system, 28, 29
components transported by, 246
concepts, 220–235
configuring, 218, 236–239
functions of, 232–233, 246
new features, 217–220
purpose of, 217–218
set up rules, 568
system change options, 231–232
system types, 231
technology and, 568–569
transporting objects from source to target systems, 217–220
transport system–level security, 366
transport tools, 216
tRFC (transactional RFC), 71
triple-mirror backup approach, 573–574
troubleshooting
background processing, 522–528
presentation server response time, 486–487
printing problems, 466
RFC communications, 484–486
SAP R/3 Enterprise upgrade project, 214
with SQL Trace, 488–490
system administration, 513–528
table buffers, 496–497
TR (Treasury) module, 32
Trust Center Service Certification Authority (CA), 370
24-hour Normal operation schedule, *512*, 513
type definitions, in BSP applications, 349
type groups, *307*
ABAP predefined types, 306
features of, 306
TYPE keyword, 305

U

UI elements, 122, 128–129
assigning to contexts, 135
data binding definition in, 132
unauthorized users, 364
unclassified requests, 248
unconditional modes, in tp program, 267
underscore (_) sign, in local variables, 85
Unicode, 20
conversion, for SAP upgrade projects, 206, 214
modification adjustment, 210
Unicode-enabled programs, 214
unification server, 107
unification technology, 110
unique indexes, 295
unique primary key, 281
unit testing, 320–321
UNIX environment, starting and stopping programs in, 97–98
Unix-flavors file system types, 218
unknown adjustment mode, 213
unlocking users, 379–380
unplanned downtime, 570–571
update components, 60
Update Monitor, 513, 514
update phase, of transactions, 46
Update Process Administration, 514–515
Update process monitoring screen, *410*
update requests, 60

update transactions (SAP LUWs), 47–48
update work process, 59–60, *59*, 410–414, 507
- activating updating, 414
- concepts, 411
- deactivating updating, 414
- deleting update records, 414
- distribution of, 412
- monitoring update records, 412–413
- reactivating updating, 414
- repeating update records, 413–414
- selection criteria, 412–413
- update statistics, 414
- for U1 update components, 405
- for U2 update components, 405

Upgrade Assistant, 208
upgrade directory, 203
Upgrade Manual, 199–200
Upgrade Monitor, 208–209
Upgrade Roadmap, 196–197, *197*
- accessing, 196
- phases, 196–197
- upgrade project plan, 197

upgrades
- creating scripts, 199–200
- project plan, 197–199, *198*
- strategies, for SAP R/3 Enterprise upgrade project, 205, 207, 209–210
- version management and, 229

upgrade teams
- functions of, 200–201
- members of, 200–201
- for SAP upgrade projects, 195

upgrade tools
- Incremental Conversion (ICNV), 209
- PREPARE, 205–207
- Upgrade Assistant, 208
- Upgrade Monitor, 208–209

Use Access, 327
user addresses, specifying for user master records, 377
user administration
- creating users, 372–375
- decentralization of, 399
- dividing administration responsibilities, 399
- initial screen, *372*
- maintaining user master record fields, 376–377
- managing superusers, 383–385
- managing user master records, 371–372
- modifying user master records, 379–380
- overview of, 371–385
- password management, 380–382
- setting defaults and options for user master records, 377–379
- user information system functions, 380

user administrators, 398–399
user authentication, 76, 352
- administrator responsibility for, 364
- purpose of, 354–355
- security failures, 364

user authorization data, *223*
user buffers, 390
- controlling number of entries in, 390
- defined, 390

user checks, creating with Code Inspector, 330–332
user context, 66
user context area, size of, 66
user default values, for user master records, 377–378
User field, in Logon screen, 150
user group field, in user master records, 376
user groups
- creating, 379
- deleting, 379
- modifications to, 380
- modifying profiles or roles for, 380
- SUPER, 384

user identification (user master record), 150
user information system, 380
user interface, 27
User Interface (UI) Elements. *See* UI elements
user master data, 221, *223*
user master records
- assigning to roles, 390
- client dependency of, 373
- contents of, 371–372
- copying, *375*
- creating, 373–375
- creating from reference master records, 375
- creating from scratch, 373–374
- defaults and options, 377–379
- defined, 371
- deleting users, 379
- fields, 376–377
- locking and unlocking users, 379–380
- managing, 371–372
- mandatory fields, 374
- modifying, 379–380
- password field, 374
- for superusers, 383–384
- types of users, 376

usernames, user authentication and, 76
User Overview screen, 408
user parameters
- input field default values with, 175–176
- parameter IDs, 175–176

user passwords, 151
user printing, 186–189
- common problems, 189
- monitoring status of print requests, 189
- parameters for, 187–188
- print attributes for spool requests, 187–188
- specifying output device, 186

user requests, logical flow of execution, 51
User Role Management, 110
user roles, 165
- iViews assignment to, 109

users
- business superusers, 580
- creating, 373–375
- end users, 545, 580
- external, 408, 414
- Internet user authentication, 76
- locking, 379–380
- management of, 370–371
- named, 76
- SAP*, 383–384
- sending short messages between, 189–190
- unauthorized, 364
- *See also* key users; superusers

user sessions, 168–169
- deleting, 408, 414
- displaying memory for, 408
- displaying user information, 408
- monitoring and managing, 408–409

user type field, in user master records, 376
user utilities, 189–190
U1 update components, 405
U2 update components, 405

V

validity period field, in user master records, 376
value ranges, for input fields, 181
values, restrictions on, 279–281
ValueSAP, 537, *538*, 542
value tables, specifying name of, 281
Variant Directory, 182, *182*
variants
- background jobs and, 433
- creating, 183
- defined, 178, 181
- displaying list of, 181
- entering, 178–179, 181–182
- specifying environments for, 182
- uses of, 181

verification tables, 281
version management, 213
- for development objects, 228–229

vertical views, 121
view composition
- creating, 123
- defined, 123

view contexts, 122, 134–135
view layout, designing, 128–132
view page type, in BSP applications, 348
views, 121, 293–295, *294*
- creating, 125–126
- defined, 123

defining, 293
horizontal, 121
inbound points, 126
layout, 123
navigation among, 126–127
outbound points, 126
purpose of, 293
technical characteristics of, 293
vertical, 121
view sets, 123
virtual memory, 492
virtual systems, 242, 568
visibility, of objects within a package, 327
V$ Values, 506

W

wait time analysis, 478, 482, 483, 507
warehouse module, 34
watchdog, 79
watchpoints, 318
Web Application Builder, creating BSP applications in, 341
Web browser support, 14
web dispatcher, 81–83, *81*
command line options for starting, *82*
requirements, *81*
SAP J2EE Engine and, 83
starting, 82
stopping, 82
Web Dynpro, 27
for mobile clients, 106
Web Dynpro applications
basic application, 123–124
building, 138
creating, 136–138
creating components, 124, 125
creating views, 124–125
deploying, 138
designing view layout, 123
development of, 122–139
modeling, 123
requirements for, 124
running, 139
steps in creating, 123, 124
visual elements, 123
Web Dynpro window, 123
WebReporting, 74
WebRFC, 74, 75
Web services, 101
Web Services Description Language (WSDL), 101
Web Transactions, 74, 75
Welcome Application object, 138
WGate program, 75
WHERE clause, 296, 504
"Where-Used List," 277
wildcards
for background jobs, 442
in report searches, 179
specifying nonpermitted password strings with, 382
window, SAP GUI
changing colors of, 160
color options, 161
default size, 163
layout configuration, 159–164
navigation, 169–171
standard elements, 155–157
Windows initialization (INI) files, 95
Windows NT, using sapntkill command in, 82
work areas, database interface and, 64
Workbench Organizer, 28
tools, 255
workbench requests, 227, 247
Workbench tabstrip, 326, *326*
workday start option, starting background jobs with, 440
worker threads, 79
workflow
ALE model and, 74
automation systems, 37
Workload Analysis Monitor, 478–484
analyzing data in, 481–483
analyzing specific business data in, 487–488
collecting data in, 478
remote function call analysis in, 483–486
response time, 478–481
screen, *480*
workload distribution, 506–513, 510–513
among application services, 510
defined, 510
operation modes and, 510–513
work processes, 51–53, 53
aborted, 476
actions, 406
configuring number of, 511
configuring with Instance Profile, 506–507
defined, 50, 506
dialog steps in, 51–52
distribution of, *512*
insufficient, 477
layout design, 405
maximum number of, 507
monitoring, 404–408
per application, 52
performance analysis, 474–476
per instance, 57
reasons for, 406
for SAP Web Application Server, 67
semaphore number, 406
as servers, 53
start value, 406
status of, 405
stopped, 476, 477
terminating, 407
types of, 52–62, 405
See also specific work processes
Work Process Monitor, 474–477, 507
work process multiplexing, 54
Work Process Overview screen, 405
worksets, iViews assignment to, 109
WSDL (Web Services Description Language), 101

X

XML (eXtendable markup language), 77–78, 101

Z

zero downtime project, 571
zombie cleanup, 526